12/12/13
$39.99

David Ben-Gurion and the Jewish Renaissance

This book offers a reappraisal of David Ben-Gurion's role in Jewish-Israeli history from the perspective of the twenty-first century, in the larger context of the Zionist "renaissance," of which he was a major and unique exponent. Some have described Ben-Gurion's Zionism as a dream that has gone sour, or a utopia doomed to be unfulfilled. Now – after the dust surrounding Israel's founding father has settled, archives have been opened, and perspective has been gained since Ben-Gurion's downfall – this book presents a fresh look at this statesman-intellectual and his success and tragic failures during a unique period of time that he and his peers described as the "Jewish renaissance." The resulting reappraisal offers a new analysis of Ben-Gurion's actual role as a major player in Israeli, Middle Eastern, and global politics.

Shlomo Aronson is Visiting Professor at Tel Aviv University and Tel Aviv–Yaffo Academic College, as well as professor emeritus at the Hebrew University of Jerusalem. His scholarship has focused on Nazi Germany during the Holocaust, Israeli domestic and foreign policy, nuclear proliferation in the Middle East, "post-Zionism," and current anti-Zionism. He is the author of a number of books, including *Conflict and Bargaining in the Middle East*; *The Politics and Strategy of Nuclear Weapons in the Middle East*; and *Hitler, the Allies, and the Jews*.

David Ben-Gurion and the Jewish Renaissance

SHLOMO ARONSON
Hebrew University

Translated by Naftali Greenwood

CAMBRIDGE
UNIVERSITY PRESS

CAMBRIDGE UNIVERSITY PRESS
Cambridge, New York, Melbourne, Madrid, Cape Town, Singapore,
São Paulo, Delhi, Dubai, Tokyo, Mexico City

Cambridge University Press
32 Avenue of the Americas, New York, NY 10013-2473, USA

www.cambridge.org
Information on this title: www.cambridge.org/9780521197489

First published in Hebrew as *David Ben-Gurion and the Waning of an Age* by Ben-Gurion
University Press 1999
First English edition published 2011

Printed in the United States of America

A catalog record for this publication is available from the British Library.

Library of Congress Cataloging in Publication Data

Aronson, Shlomo, 1936–
[David Ben-Guryon. English]
David Ben-Gurion and the Jewish renaissance / Shlomo Aronson.
    p.   cm.
Includes bibliographical references and index.
ISBN 978-0-521-19748-9 (hardback)
1. Ben-Gurion, David, 1886–1973.   2. Labor Zionism – Israel – History – 20th century.
3. Israel – Politics and government – 1948–1967.   4. Israel – History – 20th century.   I. Title.
DS125.3.B37A7613   2010
956.9405'2092 – dc22   [B]   2010024412

ISBN 978-0-521-19748-9   Hardback

This book is dedicated to the memory of Tony Halle, Principal of the New High School in Tel Aviv: An exemplary educator, and my model scholar of history.

Contents

Preface and Acknowledgments

The purpose of this book is to sketch the persona of David Ben-Gurion and interpret some of his feats in a way that departs from the conventional wisdom. This is because the conventional wisdom, for better or worse, is strongly evident in the descriptions of his actions, from the beginning of his career until its apex in the 1930s through the 1960s. My intention, in contrast, is to offer a historical explanation for these actions and probe the man's inner world both before and after this period and, by so doing, to portray a man who combined intellectualism and leadership in a singular way. These two terms require clarification: Even though no one disputes that Ben-Gurion was a leader, the hybrid coinage of "leader-intellectual" is a concept that contemporary readers might dismiss with hardly a thought on the grounds that such trappings do not suit Ben-Gurion, that their depth does not fit his coarse demeanor. If anyone deserves this sobriquet, they would say, it is Ben-Gurion's colleague Berl Katznelson, regarded as the spiritual leader of the mainstream Zionist Labor Movement.

One is tempted to compare and contrast these two figures, yet my aim is to analyze and explain – rather than merely describe – Ben-Gurion's practical pursuits and intellectual interests, particularly those that in my opinion have not been interpreted in the correct light; to set him in his proper place within the Israeli and Jewish history in which he acted; and to define these periods of time and the man who tried to shape them, foiled though he was by historical changes that took place because of his own deeds, as well as the historical processes that transcended any individual's capacity to mold, such as the Holocaust. Yet in spite of many obstacles, Ben-Gurion emerges from this discussion as indeed the founding father of Israel, whose reputation requires a sort of rehabilitation next to his failures. Perhaps his most important failed endeavor was his campaign to reshape the Israeli government system in due course, on the basis of the British constitutional model.

The discussion of the British constitutional model in this book was derived from the basic rules of the British polity in Ben-Gurion's times, notwithstanding

its well-known political complications, for example, the role of third parties
(such as today's Liberal Democrats) that may dictate the results of the general
elections. In the case of the post–World War II Labor Party, Roy Jenkins, one of
Labor's outstanding figures, tells us[1] that "the relationship of the Labor party
machine to the party leadership was both confused and endowed with potential constitutional danger [by machine politicians and leftist members of the
Parliamentary Party trying to impose their views on the majority in this body].
It caused considerable difficulty both to Hugh Gaitskell when he was leader
of the opposition and to Harold Wilson when he was leader in government."
In Ben-Gurion's case, with the proportional ballot and the multiparty system
of Israel, much more serious schisms between him as the leader in government
and members of the secondary leadership of his party, and later the party's
machine, would tear the party apart formally – a result that the British system
would hardly have made possible.

The use by Ben-Gurion of the relationship between the political level and
the British Army was selective. He avoided the complexities of World War I
and the role played by Field Marshal Lord Kitchener as secretary of war during
the saga of Gallipoli, among others; the role played by John Fisher, the First
Sea Lord, in imposing Winston Churchill's departure from the Admiralty, but
also Fisher's own demotion by the political level when Fisher, the sailor, tried
to impose himself on a civilian prime minister; and other frictions between
generals and elected politicians. He did invoke his own experience as a British
Jewish soldier at the time, as we shall see. Churchill, the civilian victor of World
War II, remained his hero.

The leader-intellectual is a rare species in our milieu and, in fact, in any circle.
Jewish society, it is true, has never been lacking for thinkers, scholars, and men
and women of culture. In the Jewish society of Eastern Europe, however, most
people were religious – either traditionalists who never doubted their religious
values or men who immersed themselves in practicing Jewish rituals. Some
fashioned a severe world of moral concepts that views the Chosen People as
the people of the Torah, so that anyone who breaches its bounds must be
an enemy of the people and the direct cause of the catastrophes that have
visited it. Others developed religious moral systems that were almost modern
in complexion, for example, Rabbi Yisrael Salanter's Mussar movement. Still
others bruited less stringent interpretations of the tragedies that have befallen
the Jews, foremost the Holocaust. All, however, subscribed to a value system of
religious morality that shaped their world and obliged them, at the very least,
to act according to its principles in many different ways.

The era of the Haskala – the Jewish Enlightenment – saw its own varied views
of Judaism adopted, including, possibly, its renunciation of tradition to a larger
or lesser degree. The Jewish intellectual, however, had many reasons to vacillate
over issues of society, state, and ethics, as these themes developed in Czarist
Russia and in the West. Thus, our perception of a late nineteenth-century Jewish
intellectual such as Ben-Gurion would be one who had broken away from
traditional Judaism, who knew the Jews of his era and milieu, who had studied

in his youth the writings of Spinoza, and who as an adolescent considered himself a philosopher with a future. He would be a practical intellectual beyond his activities as a wheeler and dealer for the Jewish proletariat, the embodiment of the organizational man, and a more (or less) seasoned politician than he is usually perceived as being, as well as a statesman much occupied with tactics and strategy.

Even if we demonstrate that Ben-Gurion was a thinking statesman and a practical intellectual, we still have to explain what he and the self-proclaimed Zionist renaissance have to do with each other. Further, this book deals with the Holocaust and the lessons he drew from it; a variety of internal matters including the debate over an Israeli constitution; the discussion of the moral foundations of a secular Jewish state; and the bitter controversy surrounding the "Lavon Affair," a political scandal that brought about his decline and fall. The treatment of important aspects of foreign affairs and defense departs from the conventional wisdom, especially in respect to the decision to embark on Operation Kadesh (the Suez-Sinai Campaign of 1956), the creation of Israel's nuclear infrastructure, the relations between Israel and Germany, the buildup to the 1967 Six Day War, and the debate over its outcomes.

The tie that binds all these issues is Ben-Gurion as a leader-intellectual. In his prime, he could be considered a Renaissance man because he dealt in all types of fields, some cultural and humanistic, others scientific and ethical. However, it is not my intention to use the term in this simplistic, aphoristic sense. Instead, I intend to show that the man was the product of a period in Jewish history in Eastern Europe and later in Palestine that somewhat resembled the European Renaissance in its intellectual and practical essence.

Many people of Ben-Gurion's time were modern in terms of the complexity of their personalities, their needs, and the issues that occupied them. Ben-Gurion was a complex person, too, but he was not troubled by the quandaries, issues, and difficulties that disturbed the peace of mind of, for example, his friend Berl Katznelson. As his biographers show, Katznelson was a modern man whose Zionism was only one part of his anguished personality, though it was the main component of his public life and an important element in a heart ridden with doubt, guilt, loyalty to Jewish religious life, emptiness, and alienation, as well as criticism of self and of others.

In contrast, Ben-Gurion lived with the social problems of his time, knew well its grand ideologies, took interest in the scientific achievements of his era, and, to the best of his ability, learned from others about systems of government and political and military matters. He was less provincial than Katznelson, who made Herbert Samuel, the British Jew who served as High Commissioner of Palestine, into a sort of Pontius Pilate and conflated villainous ancient Greece and Hadrian's empire with contemporaneous reality. Ben-Gurion was also less literary, living less than his friend in the idiomatic world of Hebrew poetry and European verse as the vernacular of realities in Palestine/Israel, though he was much occupied with that world and drew a great deal from it. He sought to learn from ancient Greece, to delve as much as he could into the writings of

Plato, to study the Bible and the scientific Jewish historiosophy of his time, and to resort again to Spinoza. Ben-Gurion, however, also tried to be a creative, active person, one whose heart, unlike Katznelson's, was not terribly torn. Both men were very critical and very positive people, but Ben-Gurion was free of Katznelson's inner struggles, and in their absence it is hard for us to see Ben-Gurion as a full-fledged modern man.

Truth to tell, modernity can be a creative, active, optimistic, intellectual, and scholastic quality that draws ideas from the Greek and Roman classicists, as we know from the eighteenth century. Furthermore, the European Enlightenment, which ostensibly originated in that century, undoubtedly had much influence on the Maskilim – Jews who were exposed to and adopted the traits of the European Enlightenment – and their Eastern European Zionist successors. However, perplexities, doubts, and ethical and intellectual difficulties that can be traced to the crisis of Western civilization had already eroded the "modernity" of the late nineteenth century, in consequence of complex social and economic processes and in the face of persistent attacks by science on all religious truth and tradition at large. The secularization of religious values that modern thinkers distractedly launched in the eighteenth century – as if it were obvious for many that Man is a rational and good creature from birth, from which premise his social and political way of life should follow as a paradise on earth – had become, by the end of the nineteenth century, simplistic and outmoded in the eyes of many. Therefore, many people of that era were particularly envious and fond of the Renaissance, for it neither simplified matters, as the scholars of the eighteenth century did, nor devised social theories, all-embracing pretensions, or political doctrines, that is, precise guidelines for statecraft and governance. The Renaissance was known for its creative, optimistic, externalized character, which did not intrude on people's inner lives but, rather, saw life as an "act of art" – and not only the oeuvre of a Leonardo or a Machiavelli. For many, the Renaissance was the worldview of a unique era that saw beauty, ability, creativity, and modern depth in life and in man, freed from the challenges posed by human impulse and its murky aspects. This view of the world was not only spurned during the periods preceding the Renaissance but was also resisted with full fury, locking man's mind and senses behind bars of faith, fear, and inevitable sin.

A hallmark element in the Renaissance is the liberation of man and the reconciliation of man with nature. Its function is to restore classical Man to his former glory – without harming the tenets of religious faith by which people lived, even though, in fact, they departed from them in many directions. Two such directions were the rediscovered sciences and the newly discovered continents that were being settled, resulting in the development of an enormous interest in other cultures and in consolidating national entities that had been conceived in the Middle Ages. The offspring of the Renaissance swerved from the principles of religious faith without a modern theoretical understanding of what they were doing, without inner vacillations of the modern sort, and without concern about the outrageousness of conflating ideas from the distant and recent past with those newly propounded. Since such a conflation is found in the Zionist theories of Ben-Gurion's era, it is easy today to condemn them in the name of modern and postmodern approaches and in the name of religion. Just the same, this mix of issues remains a historical fact that no criticism can gainsay.

The European Renaissance was no easy time. In Italy, for example, the centuries of transition between the Middle Ages and the new era were filled with wars, plagues, and moments of social and personal insecurity. People's lives remained short and often strewn with troubles and pitfalls. Meanwhile, people's attitudes toward the intrinsic worth of their own lives and toward nature underwent substantial change. Renaissance people lifted their heads and freed their spirit, and that spirit burst forth – for better or worse – at the expense of previously accepted patterns and methods of thought and behavior. They turned to earlier eras and their cultures – Classicism, ancient languages, philosophy, and rhetoric – and inserted them into the history of their time without causing this history to shatter.

There is no doubt that late nineteenth-century secular Zionists sought to shatter traditions, modes of conduct, and beliefs and opinions that they viewed as constraints, prejudices, and genuine menaces to their people and themselves. However, they wrapped this undoing in classical sources – that is, the Hebrew language, the Bible, Eretz Israel (the Land of Israel), and nature – producing a revolution in worldview that, in my opinion, was not complete because it pretended to be a "renewal" rather than a revolution. Similarly, the "negation of exile" that Ben-Gurion's Zionist contemporaries stressed became a psychological and political necessity for its exponents, even though their attachment to the European Diaspora and its significances remained firm until the European Diaspora was destroyed.

This shattering of old ways of thinking, in the eyes of Ben-Gurion and his contemporaries, had a decidedly socialist character that was totally absent in the European Renaissance. Yet even this emphasis on egalitarianism and manual labor was tied to classic sources: the prophetic writings and the Jewish ethical requirements, though without religious faith. These Zionists sought to fulfill religious commandments and sustain a unique, historic nation, but at a remove from the nation's erstwhile way of life, on the grounds that this way of life doomed the nation to a living death. Viewing the products of Judaism with a concurrent blend of condescending pity, esteem, and deep affection, they played the role of trailblazers with the self-confidence of a generation freed from the previous generations' shackles. This is particularly true of Ben-Gurion himself.

In this book, I propose that the totality of Ben-Gurion's life-work flowed from trends of thought, historical ideas, and his realization that their survival was not assured. He and his peers blended them into a variegated Zionist theory. Some developed them into structured philosophies, such as the Marxist version of Zionism, each according to his own approach, while others, including Ben-Gurion and Katznelson, refrained from proposing overly set theories, instead striking a consensus on several basic universalistic and Zionist-Socialist-Jewish principles. Ben-Gurion continued to develop his thinking (though some in our generation maintain that he progressively narrowed his thinking) as an outgrowth of the momentously changing reality of his times, the setting in which one should seek the common thread that binds his actions. Some would say that he regressed from revolutionary to conservative or from a successful revolutionary to an incorrigible establishmentarian.

The common thread that I propose tackles the task of defining what was revolutionary in Ben-Gurion's Zionism. He and his peers invoked the concept of a "Zionist renaissance." The European Renaissance, after all, was not a revolution but rather a conflation of the old, which had been held illegitimate for centuries, with the extant and the new. The Zionist renaissance, too, as formulated by Katznelson and Ben-Gurion, was not a revolution of culture and values in the full sense of the expression. Both men sought neither to reject Judaism nor to jettison most of its values but to revive it and give it a secular meaning. They did not begin history anew, from the point at which they stood, as did the exponents of the French Revolution. They saw in history an objective reality on behalf of which they wished to speak; they sought to preserve some of its values in their own way. They acknowledged various and different interpretations among Jews and, by so doing, refrained from committing history to a deterministic Zionist posture while fighting to make their version the "winning" one. What they did not see in history was a source of "scientific" duty that they were bound to fulfill. But if their aim was the revival of Judaism and some of its values, then let us bear in mind that the term *renaissance* denotes rebirth, not revolution. Indeed, the term *Renaissance* was applied to that era only later in history; its contemporaries were not consciously concerned about what was happening to them at the time. Therefore, all historical comparisons with the Renaissance – or with any other period, for that matter – entail strict limits.

Ben-Gurion was well aware of the meaning of his actions, the ethical and cultural foundation for which was established in his character, by his upbringing and education acquired through years of great intellectual effort. This foundation was derived from the world of a Jewish society standing at the crossroads of many options: to desist, disappear, and assimilate into the nations of the world; to persist as a minority in worlds belonging to others, maintaining a religious or historical-cultural identity within these worlds; or to engineer a rebirth in Eretz Israel. For Berl Katznelson, the spiritual leader of Labor Zionism, for Chaim Nachman Bialik, the poet of Zionism, and for others, "rebirth" was a linguistic, cultural, and sociopolitical matter. In Katznelson's thinking, for example, the political aspect related to the Labor Movement. For Ben-Gurion, it was much, much more. His approach toward the question of rebirth was political ab initio. Ultimately, the tidings that Theodor Herzl – the founding father of political Zionism – brought to Zionists everywhere concerned not just the revival of the Hebrew language, culture, and literature but also the rebirth of Jewish sovereignty in the Jewish homeland, so that Jewry could govern itself as a viable national entity and would be worthy of so doing. This cause, "auto-emancipation," was a question of political culture. Consequently, the survival of Judaism in its struggle against massive historical-cultural forces and the justification for its survival; the recruitment of messages from its religious culture in the service of a secular Jewish society; the use of statehood to assure Jewish survival in a world of unrecognizable changes; the moral justification of acts of state; the criticism and proper supervision of these actions during war and prolonged conflict; the securing of support from a public unused to sovereign rule, a collective whose ethno-cultural makeup was in constant flux – all these were concrete issues that occupied Ben-Gurion until the end.

To resolve them, one should follow two common threads. One originates in a thinking leader, a student and a scholar, that is, a leader-intellectual. The second flows from the era of which Ben-Gurion was a product. Although a man of his times, Ben-Gurion stood on his own merit, "one of a kind in his generation," as his admirers and flatterers called him in his prime. For he allowed himself, consciously and as deeply as possible, to stamp the Jewish rebirth with his own individualistic, autonomous interpretation, one that assuredly included ideas borrowed from the thinking of others and the approaches and experiences of other peoples, alongside those that stemmed from his initial thinking and the changes in the reality of his times. Katznelson, in contrast, though greatly influenced by non-Jews, remained locked in the timeless Jewish culture, forever seeking cultural meaning for a Jewish synthesis that would fit the "New Jew" that he hoped to create in Eretz Israel. Ben-Gurion also spoke abundantly about the New Jew but wove into it the influences of non-Jews in the political realm in the broadest sense of the term – including the concept and form of the system of government for a sovereign Jewish society. For this purpose, he waged rhetorical war and made political compromises when necessary, though at his height and a fortiori at the end of his days, he always retained the last word. An intellectual, independent, autonomous, free man owes nothing to anyone – not to popes, not to plutocrats or tyrants, not to thinkers or intellectuals he disagreed with, not to media moguls, and not even to world leaders. Politically, Ben-Gurion owed a great deal to others and even pursued compromises on more than one occasion, as far as his fiery, explosive, disputatious personality allowed. Intellectually, however, he was truly a free man in a way that only extraordinary historical periods allow a man to be. He had an excellent facility for studying the world as it is – not only as it is supposed to be or as it should be.

This unusual freedom is recognizable in many great Renaissance figures, the most important of whom was the political philosopher Niccolò Machiavelli. But in proclaiming themselves to be the sons and daughters of a Jewish renaissance, Ben-Gurion and his peers tried at least to see reality as it was in order to change it, as this was preached by many during the Renaissance. This is in contrast to the Enlightenment century, which sought to fashion a revolutionary reality through the power of beliefs and opinions – some of them very inflexible – about human nature, and to lead man to a universalistic paradise by this trait alone. The Renaissance did not delve much into the question of human nature; thus, it was spared many doctrines that seek to fashion the future direction of society and political life by whatever means, including force.

The Jewish renaissance was definitely influenced by beliefs and doctrines that originated in the Enlightenment and its successor century, the nineteenth. Ben-Gurion himself was influenced by them. The Renaissance man in him, however, could not wear any particular doctrinaire robe for long. His Socialism was a combination of classical Jewish and universalistic values coupled with the needs of the Jewish and Israeli society of his time. Yet even here, the man was free of dogmatic shackles and acted in view of the empirical reality of his era and of Israeli society. Since he was a product of his time, Socialist Zionism remained at the foundation of his philosophy and in his thinking, even as he tried to ignore and excuse the inescapable contradiction between freedom and equality. Equally, however, he was able to acknowledge the power of profit as a tool for economic development and to allow it, too, to build Israeli society and provide a livelihood for its members. This aside, Ben-Gurion was a very critical leader of his people in the Diaspora and in Israel, even when he presumed to lead them to the last secure stop in their wanderings, lauding various achievements though he himself was unsure of their ultimate success and the Jews' ability to sustain them in the long term. These favorable and critical dimensions troubled him all his life – the former arising from faith and determination, the latter from observation and doubt; the former flowing from the positive imperatives of leadership, the latter from leadership's need to deter, warn, and educate. Here, then, is the leader of a unique democratic society in the twentieth century, whose actions we must not try to wedge into a simplistic "Renaissance" framework.

Instead, let us try to redefine *renaissance* as an extraordinary historical trend of thought, of psychology, and of behavior that allowed its adherents intellectual freedom of a kind not experienced before or after, a freedom that doctrinarians – both religious and secular – later presented as heresy. The content of the Renaissance was a wonderful blend of values from diverse worlds that had been hitherto disparate until they erupted from the catacombs of the Middle Ages. They were the values of the Greek rationalists, the Roman classicists and statesmen, and Christianity, including values culled from Judaism – foremost the freedom to pick and choose among them and combine them. This act of mingling is not modern because it lacks a reflexive and introspective basis, an aspect of rummaging through the human psyche and confronting its darker depths. It does comprise a wondrous illumination of the psyche, splendid manifestations of the physical, and the beginning of an investigation into the secrets of nature. But that era lacked all manifestation of the modern "angst" and offered no established "scientific" method with which "reason" would discover social laws. Modern thought along this line would have to wait until the seventeenth century. At the beginning of the twentieth century there was no such wondrous integration in the realms of form and content. Nevertheless, Ben-Gurion's refusal to heed the "angst mongerers" among Israeli intellectuals due to their vacuity – from the very outset of statehood – and his battle with exponents of various scientific "isms"– both dogmatic Marxists and those on the Right who began to slide into Fascism – had an element of the charm and intricate simplicity of the Renaissance.

Ben-Gurion's particular interest in ancient Greece and the theories of state that it had fathered was markedly unusual and eventually served as political ammunition against him. Just as Greece had been a source of inspiration for the European Renaissance, so the Bible became a renewed source of inspiration for the Zionists of Ben-Gurion's generation. The integration of Greece and the Bible, however, was characteristic of Ben-Gurion alone. He did, on occasion, see the British as the heirs to the evil Roman Empire, especially when they wavered between the Arabs and the Jews during the 1920s and 1930s; this is why he and Katznelson leveled such a rich variety of accusations against them. Ben-Gurion, however, also contemplated the British men of state at the Saint James's Conference – which led to the British decision to jettison the Jews in favor of the Arabs in May 1939 – from the inquisitive perspective of a political thinker and not just that of a Zionist propagandist. Katznelson, in contrast, saw that select elite as the rulers of an incorrigibly heinous, antagonistic nation of *goyim*. Ben-Gurion could shower them with invective, do what he could to reverse their decrees, and concurrently learn what he needed to learn from them by constantly studying the changes that they and the British political constellation had undergone during World War II, and by trying to change or adapt his policies to the demands of the changing situation. Katznelson's attitude toward the Arabs – whom he initially viewed as other than the source of the conflict, which he blamed solely on the British Mandatory government – evolved into simple enmity. Ben-Gurion understood the reasons for the Arabs' animosity and developed various tactics with which to deal with them, directly and indirectly. Yet he always insisted that at the end of the day – a very long day – a "Jewish–Arab alliance" would arise.

All of this is to say that Ben-Gurion was a statesman in a world of forces that had to be learned, researched, and struggled with for the purpose of creating a new order. The order at issue was not an irreconcilable war between nations, the sort that developed in Europe in the eighteenth century as a consequence of the Enlightenment and the French Revolution, but a sui generis historical act: the repatriation of a nation/non-nation in a land that it had left thousands of years previously. Ben-Gurion's way of thinking was to acknowledge the singularity of this history, the changes that had transpired, and the opportunities squandered hitherto, which the Jewish people would now have to exploit to the utmost in order to change that history to the greatest possible extent.

Ben-Gurion did not deal in prophecy and did not believe in deterministic fortune-telling. His world was much more open than it seemed during those times when his position required him to speak in the name of the past and to commit the future to its vows. That is why it is very important to distinguish between Ben-Gurion's rhetoric and his methodology as a statesman, between things he said publicly and things he said privately.

He was undoubtedly a staunch believer in the values of the past, but he did not busy himself at first, as did Katznelson, with the question of whether the new Jewish society in Eretz Israel, and particularly its youth, would remain lacking in Jewish culture and traditional Jewish values that had to be preserved, if secularized. Katznelson was troubled about such issues because for most of his life, these areas were the concern of the intellectual leader of the Zionist Labor Movement. At that time, Ben-Gurion's aims lay elsewhere. His Zionism, while striving to make Jews into workers returning to productive labor in their land, aspired above all to make them free citizens, a people capable of sovereign rule. Therefore, the essence of the Jewish national identity seemed self-evident, whereas the moral-political problem that Ben-Gurion increasingly perceived after the Holocaust and the establishment of statehood was the nature of the secular values that a Jewish state should have – an issue of content and modes of conduct that now had to be changed. How interesting it is that he of all men – who more than anyone else seems to have created the *Yishuv* system with its leaders, faults, and modi operandi – sought to tackle this problem above all others.

From the historical standpoint, one must stress that Ben-Gurion was only one of the leaders of the Yishuv, certainly not the only one, and often not even the one with the most authority. Only time made him the leader of the pack. He was graced with a quality unusual among politicians: the ability to learn, infer, and draw operative conclusions from the changes that he and those of his era experienced. This ability contributes to the depiction of Ben-Gurion as a leader-intellectual. Hence, at a later stage, he invoked "justice" as the main trait of Judaism and messianic hopes and inspiration as the dimensions of Jewish civilization that should be acknowledged and blended together with the proper reform of Israel's government system.

Ben-Gurion sought to meld the old with the new and animate the most incessant changes possible. Others – those of other times and from other backgrounds – found it hard to understand his motives, his ideas, and his energy, as well as their expression in practical affairs. They considered his unceasing innovation an act of coercion, an unwarranted if not ludicrous intellectual hubris, and reactionism rather than progress – his refusal to understand modern life and a retreat into an old world deficient of meaning. Some of this criticism – the problem of the moral and cultural content of Israeli society – remains problematic to this day.

Ben-Gurion pledged himself to the study of this question through his own intellectual prism while being embroiled in an enormous number of existential, legislative and governmental issues – including the Lavon Affair – to an extent that leaves one astonished at the thought of one man's dealing with them all, one after the other and at once. This book reflects the multifarious nature of his dealings, especially in the second half of the twentieth century.

Nevertheless, the account that follows has not necessarily lauded Ben-Gurion's successes in matters of internal governance, internal politics, and security and diplomacy. He was emphatically unique. His demarches were unconventional for his time. Some succeeded, such as the preparations for statehood and the decision to declare it; some have been controversial since Israel's War of Independence; some, such as Ben-Gurion's acts of commission and omission during the Holocaust, are described today as practical and moral failures; and some went up in the smoke of the Lavon Affair and its aftermath in the 1960s until the Six Day War, a war that he opposed. However, it was Ben-Gurion himself who established with his own hands the political instrument – the Rafi Party – that allowed his followers, such as General Moshe Dayan, to gradually make radical changes in approach from the one that he himself pursued until 1967. Over time, objections to the "Bolshevik" character of the state he established, of his old party Mapai, and of Ben-Gurion himself were added to his fading laurels, as if he had been some sort of Jewish Lenin. Unlike the founding fathers of "healthier and quieter peoples than ourselves," as he himself once declared in a discussion with the commanders of the left-nationalist Palmach units in the Israel Defense Forces (IDF), Israel's founding father became a kind of pariah, the root of all the incurable evils of contemporaneous Israeli society. He has been criticized for his "tyranny" for refusing to adopt an American-style constitution for Israel, exempting the ultra-Orthodox from military service, imposing military government on the Israeli Arabs, treating the 1948 Palestinian refugees as he did, deciding to launch the Suez Campaign in 1956, and so on. In his day, these criticisms were heard from his political opponents; today they emanate from their spiritual heirs and the offspring of newer ages, who blame the difficulties of the present and its concepts on the past.

Yet what is needed is an attempt to connect the various dimensions of Ben-Gurion's feats with the ways in which he conducted himself – that same independence of decision making and relentless striving toward changing goals that is often simply called "leadership," "personal charisma," and the like but is viewed by others as tyranny and authoritarianism.

As we have said, this is a historical explanation, not just a historical description within the broadest possible historical context. Some today consider historical explanations misguided or impossible. The writer of these lines believes it possible to bring history alive even after it has become history. There is great value in history's being written by its contemporaries or by those who knocked on its doors before they slammed shut, provided that they have access not only to historical imagination but also to primary sources and the necessary critical faculties to study them. "Historical imagination," however, implies taking the liberty of comparing historical periods, that is, contemplating history through a comparative prism. Indeed, some of the explanation for Ben-Gurion's leadership, it seems to me, was his sense of history as reflected in his activities, based on the knowledge of history and the comparative study of history that taught him similarities and differences. To get to know such a personality (Churchill and de Gaulle were leaders of this type, notwithstanding their differences), a historian must make historical comparisons that seem artificial on the surface or simply metaphoric. Yet since Ben-Gurion and his peers perceived themselves to be Renaissance people, some comparisons between this self-perception and the European Renaissance may be justified. Moreover, in my opinion, such periods truly have uniqueness, a flavor, and accomplishments whose particularity cannot be grasped by their immediate successors, especially if they took place at a time that was already quite modern and has now become "postmodern."

The aim of this book, therefore, is to give posterity a bit of the flavor of this period in Jewish history and to describe its limitations and difficulties, assuming that this generation is willing to accept them. It is a job that no artist can do, no matter how great an author he is. It is a truly daunting task that entails multiple talents such as those of the great painters in history, even though few of them were capable of both painting and historical analysis. Nevertheless, there are historians whose style and fluidity of prose and diction lighten the reader's burden and make his or her study an esthetic pleasure. Since Ben-Gurion was a man of diverse interests, the task of integrating them into an artistic, fluent, readable biography, as is expected these days for works on even the most complex personalities, is beyond me.

Thus, instead of unveiling one more biography of Ben-Gurion, I have written a monograph that deals with various practical aspects of his leadership and attempts to explain them. The question is whether the Zionist renaissance was nothing more than a common manifestation of nineteenth-century European nationalism; whether it was not a return to roots of the sort that other peoples underwent at that time, reviving ancient languages or reinventing them almost from scratch in order to create a personal identity for themselves in the nationalist era; or whether it was nothing but an ordinary ethnic-cultural-nationalistic phenomenon that mobilized ancient terms and tools for modern necessities. My answer will be that Judaism is indeed a unique phenomenon; it has been a national culture since its inception in classical times, and it maintained its national singularity during the Middle Ages in its own characteristic way. This is why the "renaissance" of Judaism as a nationality has been sown with historical meaning from the outset. The rekindling of this development was fated to wait for the proper circumstances but is not mainly a modern invention.

As a historical, cultural, and behavioral entity riddled with contrasting components, Judaism was an aberration well before the period of European nationalism; for this reason, it became the target of criticism by universalistic opponents of nationalism before and during the European Enlightenment. Its great struggle with other outlooks and cultures was not just a religious conflict but, rather, a clash with modern approaches toward the question of nationalism itself, both to its right and to its left. Consequently, Ben-Gurion's contemporaries had to struggle for the soul of Judaism as he viewed it, in a world that had many opponents and few friends. Ben-Gurion had to do battle outwardly and act inwardly to give real meaning to the aspirations that pounded in the hearts of impassioned young people who wrestled among various choices for the future of Judaism, of which Zionism was only one and sometimes the least fitting of them all.

While the Renaissance swept whole generations and imbued them with a dominant spirit, the enthusiasm of Ben-Gurion and his peers for it was not shared by many of his contemporaries. This, however, is the key to understanding terms such as "man of authority" and "sword-wielding prophet." Our subject was a self-proclaimed Renaissance man in an unstable modern world that seemingly confronted innumerable ideals, challenges, and risks; a minority leader at a time when the majority was mired in its various fates and worlds, amid a dispersed, fragmented people whose very definition as a people demands inquiry.

Part of this puzzle is the Holocaust, an event that silenced many Zionists of its generation, either crippling them emotionally – perhaps another explanation for Katznelson's decline at so young an age – or infusing them, as commonly found in the Zionist Right, with a spirit of mobilization and action whether they understood their reality or not, to the detriment of Zionist interests in the eyes of Jews and non-Jews at the time. Ben-Gurion's ability to act while methodically and diligently studying current reality, even during this cataclysm, recalls the actions of other figures of his type, whose Renaissance spark continued to flicker within them during plagues, devastations, and innumerable wars, and who continued to strive without losing their faith in mankind. A skeptical, nondoctrinaire faith of this kind was a facet of Ben-Gurion's personality despite all the disappointments and failures of Judaism, including Zionism, not only in respect to the dictates of his leadership. For this reason, he had not only the constitution of a political organizer and manipulator but also that of a propagandist, an apologist, and a debater of public issues in countless and diverse circles. He had the strength to advance step by step toward his goals as he prioritized them, not only to accumulate organizational power but also aggressively to persuade, explain, and preach, powered by his skeptical belief in the ability of mankind to understand the reality in which it lives.

"Skeptical faith" is unquestionably the right term for Ben-Gurion's way of thinking during most of his life, since his contemplation of people convinced him that man is more than merely a rational being. Because he found this eighteenth-century claim simplistic, he cannot be viewed as a doctrinaire leftist. However, he was definitely a moderate leftist – a social democrat in a world in which Zionist social democracy had become a militant alternative to the grand ideologies of the Right and the far Left. None of these existed during the European Renaissance, but Ben-Gurion inherited from the Jewish renaissance, as he preached it, that special spirit and inherent justification for his actions that had been blurred in the hearts of others, or forgotten altogether, or had changed too quickly from an approach striving for change, improvement, and constant learning of lessons to a style of action suited for settled times and the routines of ordinary daily life. This was Moshe Sharett's approach when he temporarily succeeded Ben-Gurion, and it was also that of Levi Eshkol, another successor. Thus, the discord between these two men and Ben-Gurion was a true rift between the spirit of leadership and the content issues of government – between ferment, learning, and pursuit of change and continuation that cannot rest on laurels, on the one hand, and routine, on the other.

His Zionism was a Zeitgeist or one of several that visited the Jewish street in Ben-Gurion's time. If we ignore it, we cannot properly understand what the man accomplished. All we can do is analyze this spirit to the best of our ability and portray its manifestations in several intellectual and political acts. We can memorialize it since, after all, it did become a monument even as an object of scorn and disregard, loathing, and anger that the very same spirit combated most of its days with some degree of success.

This book, originally published in Hebrew by the Ben-Gurion Institute of the Ben-Gurion University of the Negev, was adopted and nursed by Dr. Tuvia Friling, then-Director of the Ben-Gurion Archives at the Institute and subsequently Archivist of the State of Israel, from a series of articles that I published in the Israeli newspaper *Ha'aretz*. By "nursed," I refer to constant help and moral and practical support without which the research and the writing would have been impossible. It was also thanks to Dr. Friling that I was able to recruit Mr. Razi Yahel of Sede Boqer to do the archival research on the early history of the IDF. Some of it is being published here in English for the first time, among other primary sources translated from the Hebrew. The readers of the original Hebrew manuscript, Professor Moshe Lissak of Hebrew University and Professor Yosef Gorny of Tel Aviv University, augmented my initial efforts with their good advice and profound knowledge. However, I alone am responsible for the final results. Dr. Michael Greenberger of the Hebrew Section and Dr. Lester I. Vogel of the Visiting Scholars Program of the Library of Congress made my research at the library both enjoyable and useful.

Much of the translation into English and the updating work of the original Hebrew version were done during my three-year visiting Professorship at the Judaic Studies Center, University of Arizona, Tucson. I am very much indebted to Professor W. Edward Wright, the Director, and to his colleagues, for their continued support, help, and generosity during my stay. Professor David Graizbord was very helpful in discussing the European Renaissance, but I alone am responsible for the outcome. The Hebrew University of Jerusalem contributed its share to the funding of my research, also making it possible for me to hire the services of Mr. Naftali Greenwood, my devoted translator. I am also grateful for the good services of my outstanding copy editor, Mrs. Phyllis L. Berk. The Littauer Foundation, New York, was extremely kind in granting me the necessary funding for the production of the book. I am also indebted to Ms. Jacqueline Goldstein, New York, and the American Friends of the Hebrew University for their support. Mr. Lewis Bateman, my editor at Cambridge, was and remains a careful, solid, vigilant, and critical friend.

The Hebrew University of Jerusalem, August 2009

Introduction

> The ultimate aim of the Zionist renaissance – the national rising of the Jewish people in its homeland – will ascend from the process of building the future Land of Israel. The Land of Israel will be a Jewish land insofar as the will and ability of the Jewish people will make it so. A Jewish state, a labor society, and Jewish–Arab cooperation are the three goals that conflate in the actions and aspirations of the Jewish worker in his land.[1]

The "renaissance generation," as the poet Chaim Nachman Bialik termed it, produced a colorful pantheon of personalities – including authors, poets, teachers, pioneers, and activists who were products of reading and who produced books as trees produce leaves. The Second Aliyah (wave of immigration of Zionists), which after many incarnations and augmentations would beget the State of Israel and was a manifestation, as it were, of Bialik's poetry, used the term *renaissance* a great deal and saw itself as a practical revival movement. Secular Zionism at large grew accustomed to using the term *Jewish renaissance* to describe its endeavors.

One who speaks of Ben-Gurion has to note that his long life included different periods with different emphases and priorities. I cannot discuss all of them in this monograph. I will try to examine some of the issues that occupied him and mention several sobriquets that he adopted or that others proposed in order to define his motives and deeds. The first is the "man of the Jewish renaissance," or "rebirth." What does it mean? What were its characteristics? How is it understood today? The second is the "man of the Jewish state," even as the father of an exaggerated role assumed by the state known at the time as "statism on account of voluntary efforts." What is this "state," and what role did the party occupy in Ben-Gurion's theory and practice, in light of the history of his public life, including his resignation from the party that he founded and the bitter criticism that he leveled against it in his last years? How does this relate to his attitudes toward Jewish revival and renaissance? Third, some credit Ben-Gurion with special historical intuition, a "sense of history" that characterized his leadership and explains his various demarches. If so, how does this sense of history blend with his own description of his generation as a "generation of rebirth" that ostensibly arose from history, as the necessary outcome of history, and that mobilized him as a servant and mouthpiece?

Ostensibly, a facile comparison of the Jewish revival movement with the European Renaissance is wholly out of place. The latter period was considered an era of cultural revolution, a psychological revolution in man's relation to himself, and its best-known expression was in the arts, which flourished gloriously. The towns and cities of Eastern Europe – from which grassroots Zionism emerged by dint of the *Maskilim* (intellectuals influenced by the non-Jewish Enlightenment) and numerous strata of what is customarily called "the Jewish people" – did not reach outcomes similar to those produced in abundance by the cities of Italy, France, and Germany, each in its own manner, or by English cities during Shakespeare's time. In the cities of Eastern Europe, a cultural and political upswelling did occur amid other areas of endeavor, but only by overstatement can one liken it to the movement that had swept Europe five centuries earlier. Despite the differences, however, there was a similarity in circumstances that requires analysis. An example is the return to classic Jewish sources – particularly the Hebrew language and the Bible – without the religious faith formerly attached to them. The exponents of the Renaissance discovered their own pre-Christian classicism, and the European continent rediscovered Roman law (England was an intriguing exception in this respect). However, they continued to inhabit a largely religious culture, even as some ventured into outright heresy, if not cynicism and corruption.

The Renaissance at its finest is recognized for its eruption of creativity, innovation, and seemingly unlimited resort to the values of the classical past. It is recognized for its appreciation of human beauty and the supremacy of the human spirit and potential, as befits a period that combined a variety of influences in an exceptional way unachieved by other ages. We shall therefore make do, at this stage, with defining the Renaissance, for our purposes, as a historical period inhabited by people who were capable of synthesizing values from the distant and recent past; acting unceasingly according to these values in the present, due to newly acquired strengths; and acting in a self-assured manner, free of self-examination and self-doubt, even though their successors neither wholly accepted nor even understood their feats.

When speaking of Zionism, however, a product conceived and born in the nineteenth century, one must immediately ask why it is of particular value to ponder what occurred in Europe during the Renaissance – the era that ended the Middle Ages – as an explanatory framework for the birth of a Jewish national movement hundreds of years later. Judaism succeeded in extending its own middle ages right into the modern age, with certain adjustments and variations (that in the eyes of important scholars were themselves deviations from traditional Jewish society in the Middle Ages), such as the rise of Lurianic mysticism, Sabbateanism and its collapse, and the rise of Hasidism.[2] In Ya'akov

Katz's opinion, too, what was occurring was the adaptation of a traditional society to the needs of a changing present mediated by traditional terms and ideas. This, he concludes, explains the divided, polemical character of traditional Judaism ever since. Be that as it may, the changes that took place in Europe from the end of the Christian Middle Ages engaged Judaism much later – at the beginning of and during the nineteenth century – at the pace and under the unique conditions of the modern era.

Nineteenth-century European nationalism exhibited manifestations of rebirth and creativity but operated in another world, partly industrialized, influenced by scientific achievements that originated in the Renaissance, and possessed of political ideas and social experiments that had been accumulating since then. In the nineteenth century, there was no shortage of thinkers and exponents of culture who longed for the simplicity, charm, spontaneity, and creativity of the Renaissance. However, these characteristics, many of them believed, could no longer be revived. To their regret, the European Renaissance itself had already shown distinct nationalist tendencies alongside the universalistic and individualistic, and these coexisted, with a typically odd measure of harmony, with the rediscovery of Greece and Rome and the traditional religious framework. Thus, the European Renaissance marked the beginning of modern nationalism and the modern outlook on government and politics. These tendencies were not accepted by everyone of that period and ultimately, the reactions against them were incorporated into the Counter-Renaissance and Counter-Reformation – the Reformation that was, among other things, a product of the Renaissance itself.

Ironically, it seems, at least on the face of it, many participants in the East European Jewish renaissance adopted a trend of thought that was essentially naive, a blend of many cognitive inputs that were commonly espoused at the time, without really thinking them through beforehand. Not only had they not experienced the tribulations undergone by the Western nations from the Renaissance onward, but they had also not learned any lessons from these tribulations or from subsequent developments. Even so, it bears examination as to whether the Jewish renaissance shared other characteristics with the nineteenth-century-style European nationalism that developed in the wake of immense changes in Western and Central Europe, changes that affected the Jewish street in many ways. Yet Ben-Gurion was an exception in this regard. He took a keen interest in Western European, mainly British, models of governance and the role of the military in a democracy. At the same time, however, he tried his best to combine the old and new in Jewish history in a way that blended Renaissance-like intellectual liberty with a characteristic Renaissance-like interest in the "past before the past" for the purpose of achieving a better future. Anchored in a distinct Eastern European Jewish environment, this Zionist renaissance differed widely from the German-Jewish variety, which emerged as a result of the failure of the Jewish-German "symbiosis" and the cult of the European Renaissance by the end of the nineteenth century in Germany.[3] There were some German inputs, mostly indirect ones, on Eastern European Zionism and also some grounds for criticism of Ben-Gurion's Zionism by German-Jewish thinkers seeking to combine the concepts of certain German philosophers with their own visions of a Jewish renaissance, but this goes beyond the scope of the present book, except for some specific cases, to be discussed later.

One may say confidently that Ben-Gurion's Jewish renaissance acquired distinct classic characteristics of its own, foremost the revival of Hebrew, the rebirth of national poetry and literature, and the firm connection of these with Eretz Israel. The inception of this renaissance is a matter for further discussion. One may see its provenance in the *Haskala*, the Jewish enlightenment movement, which focused on the revitalization of Hebrew and scornfully rejected traditional Jewish *shtetl* life. One may claim that the rebirth of Hebrew as a spoken language far surpassed anything done in the European Renaissance. The proponents of Hebrew battled Yiddish and the many other spoken and written languages of the Jewish Diaspora, such as German, Ladino, and Arabic, and purposely dissociated themselves from those who spoke them and from their world. The consciousness of these acts renders them distinct from the accomplishments of the European Renaissance. One may view the Jewish renaissance as a singular phenomenon born in the 1860s, closely linked to the neo-Romantic, nationalist, and socialist thinking that developed in Eastern and Central Europe. This seemingly makes it difficult to liken the Jewish renaissance to the world of the European Renaissance.[4]

At issue are purveyors of culture such as Ahad Ha'am (Asher Ginsberg, 1856–1927), a major Zionist thinker, and artists such as Bialik, who began their work in the late nineteenth and early twentieth centuries. Bialik, for one, though considered a classicist of the Zionist renaissance, was not free of doubts about the capacity of Jewish roots to be regenerated and also entertained modern-style angst. The pace and substance of life was different in Bialik's time and place. In Europe of the late Middle Ages and the dawn of the modern age, people's ways of thinking changed slowly. Eras were smooth and bounded, if only in the eyes of historians. They were governed by dominant states of mind and perceptibly affected by specific individuals. By the early twentiety century, however, the poet Avraham Shlonsky was applying modernist criticism to Zionist classics even during Bialik's lifetime, and the poet Uri Zvi Greenberg was producing a mixture of Walt Whitman's, European-modernist, and quasi-Fascist nationalist poetry of fantastical bent.

Both Shlonsky and Greenberg, though their paths diverged to opposite extremes, were political Zionists and activists in their own ways. They and their predecessors, such as Bialik, were almost of the same generation, which became mainstream not as a slow and direct outgrowth of historical processes and previous generations' ideas but by sprouting alongside other possible responses to the severe crisis that buffeted traditional Jewish society. This crisis included a retreat to ultra-Orthodox Diaspora traditions and a search for escape in Jewish territorial solutions outside of the Land of Israel, Jewish revolutionary Socialism in the existing East European Diaspora (Bundism), and assimilation. As a result, Zionism from its outset until the mid-1930s was a militant and ostensibly cohesive movement that struggled for its future and was maligned by its rivals. "Ostensibly" cohesive, I say, because Zionism did not lack for internecine tension that escalated into overt schism. The later victory of Zionism papered over the difficulties of the movement and underscored its status versus the alternatives that had presented themselves to Jewry at the turn of the twentieth century. It did this so effectively that we think of the Zionist leaders today as seasoned politicians who had been successful from the start by dint of their zeal and the political prowess that was intrinsic to people of their like. It is for this reason that any comparison between the Zionist leaders and Renaissance men seems artificial and vain.

Many of these leaders, however, defined themselves in Renaissance terms and displayed a vigor and vitality that powered their careers for a variety of reasons, including what they considered the Renaissance character of Zionism – a matter whose definition we will develop. Since Zionism was embroiled in controversy from the start and diverged into sometimes contradictory factions and customs, its leaders did become political creatures early on.

Indeed, what began as a political-cultural movement with an anti-Socialist bent in the early days of Theodore Herzl[5] eventually – during the Second Aliyah – the second wave of Zionist immigration to Ottoman Palestine at the beginning of the twentieth century – metamorphosed into a multichrome Socialist settlement movement that emerged from small beginnings to place its decisive stamp upon events in Eretz Israel. It was anything but a monolithic movement; many of its leaders had been literati, thinkers, and writers in their youth. Thus, in order to determine to what extent they presumed to be Renaissance men, we must delve into and analyze their cultural and behavioral world. After all, the members of the Second Aliyah expressed, in their personalities and their actions, not only the dynamism and the supreme vitality of the Jewish renaissance in whose name they spoke but also the Jewish sociocultural crisis from which they had come and that they attempted to reconcile in their activities in Eretz Israel.

Their most prominent intellectual leader, Berl Katznelson, dealt with everything – social action, political activity, settlement, literary endeavor, and publicistic journalism – but for good reason was considered first and foremost a writer, according to one of his greatest admirers, Professor Dov Sadan.[6] Another visible stalwart of the movement, Shlomo Tzemach, was one of the founders of Israeli agriculture. However, he engaged extensively in literature, literary criticism, and political criticism – which often abounded with overt doubts about the leadership of his townsman, David Ben-Gurion – and filled his diaries (which were concealed during his lifetime) with writing that reflected the jealousy and hatred that disturbed his peace of mind in his grim loneliness.[7] Ben-Gurion himself engaged in the "sin" of literary and philosophical writing, to which we shall return. However, he became a pioneer and a farm worker, a Socialist leader and a statesman. For most of his life, he combined optimism and faith – in what we shall call "vision" – and for this purpose repeatedly used the term *Jewish renaissance*. His vision, however, was accompanied by doubts and actions that aimed to surmount these doubts, which only worsened with time.[8]

Ben-Gurion's doubts arose due to the existential crisis of Judaism and the fears expressed by others and by him in his own way. That is, he offered a mainly optimistic vision while addressing the general public but expressed doubt and tough criticism of Jewish-Israeli realities mostly in closed meetings: specifically, that the Jews had no hope of standing on their own feet as a nation after the great calamity that had destroyed most of the Zionist hinterland in Europe. In what sense does this resemble the European Renaissance? The intention is not to find similarities at all costs; one must also take note of the dissimilarities and the historical uniqueness of different periods. One must also be mindful of the terms that this generation itself used and distinguish between them and the accepted scholarly terminology.

Ben-Gurion's generation made much use of the concept of *tehiya* – revival, rebirth, or renewal – in reference to the rebirth of the "people" and the "nation," the "Jewish nation." We must probe the essential character traits, the condition, the difficulties, and the risks of this revival, and decide what revival it was that certain members of the Second Aliyah had in mind and what Ben-Gurion was aiming for when he spoke of this renaissance at particular times. We should examine what the Holocaust wrought and study the concept of "state" – a "Jewish state" – that served as a political goal for the rehabilitation of the nation and its components or, as Ben-Gurion's critics claimed, that served him as a goal unto itself.

It is crucial to present these concepts at this early juncture and to widen the list to include others such as "citizenship" and "citizen" in a Jewish state, "voluntary groups" and other social networks, the "governance" of this entity and the form that said governance should take. These concepts are important if we wish to examine the way Ben-Gurion developed his "renaissance" terminology – as he himself called it – into systematic thought and action in these respects, and to elucidate the basis of his thinking at a very early stage. For the time being, it behooves us to show the points at which Ben-Gurion's Zionism was most critical and where it comprised a mixture of vision and doubt that only the work of a statesman and active public elements could enhance and reconcile with the complex world of the European Renaissance, if such reconciliation is at all possible:

Woe upon us, upon Jewish history, if after the external obstacles are removed [and we have a state] our inability is revealed.... A state is a framework; I shall explain.... It shall be revealed in all its emptiness, in all its weakness and haplessness, unless a pioneering spirit arises that has so far not arisen.... We will need to bring half a million Jews to Israel in a short time ... and this mass of people will not be a reserve force. With the establishment of the Jewish state, Jews in the Diaspora will stop being a private reserve force for [various competing pre-state political groupings and rural-settlement movements]. They will be their own raison d'être and if the youth then do see themselves as their pioneering servants, they and we will fail.... These Jews, like all Jews in the Diaspora, have not been citizens in the past eighteen hundred years, for a person is a citizen only in his own state, in his own land. These Jews have no sense of citizenship, particularly the Jews who know what their countries did to them in Poland, Germany, Lithuania, and the other lands that became cemeteries.

The anarchist instincts that live within Jews are strong. Citizenship is a deep psychological characteristic. If the English have any greatness ... it is their sense of citizenship, perhaps unmatched by any other nation in the world, and the sense of citizenship is not measured by whether people are willing to give their lives to protect their land.... Citizenship is when people pay taxes.... European Jews have no such sense. I am afraid that it does not exist in this room either.... In Europe, Jews only make demands, and rightly so. Who can ask anything of a person whose wife has been killed, whose children, whose parents have been exterminated? If they come here and view us as people who owe them something that they are demanding, we will have to bear it and get used to them, to understand them.... Unless we arm ourselves with love, we will not be able to work with them and will have to serve them. Imparting this sense of citizenship means that [the individual] should know first of all that something is being demanded of him, that the public has nothing but what the individual gives it.⁹

Some circles in pre-independence Israel did regard Jews in general, and Diaspora Jewry in particular, as a sort of reserve or human resource that various groups could use in the pursuit of their own affairs. Ben-Gurion considered this a serious problem from the outset of his activity in Eretz Israel:

I have seen this in all sorts of shapes and forms, throughout my forty-six years in this country. It started with the workers' kitchen in Petah Tiqva [one of the first Zionist settlements in Palestine] – did it belong to [some Labor Movement outfit] or to all the workers? Was it for the public or was it someone's private reserve? A youth movement is someone's private reserve, but there is something more important, and that is the public.¹⁰

Ben-Gurion made this situation in Eretz Israel part of his criticism of the Diaspora and blamed it on the importation of the Diaspora mentality. In one of his critiques of Israeli society not long after victory in the War of Independence (described by him as one of the greatest of all times), he spoke of

the worthless, malignant legacy that the Diaspora has bequeathed us – the legacy of divisiveness, clannishness, and strife that left its marks on the Yishuv [the pre-independence Jewish community in Palestine] as well. The inferior habits of thought and action that have clung to us over that long time [when we had] neither independence nor autonomous responsibility for our fate. We have not yet managed to wean ourselves of them even in these great times ... of the renewal of our sovereignty. The curse of our submissiveness before world tyrants [referring to Stalin], our emotional and intellectual servitude ... to foreign lights, imitations ... are lethally poisonous to the State of Israel and to Diaspora Jewry.¹¹

Plainly, the "New Jew" – the creation of whom was Ben-Gurion's declared aim years before the establishment of the state – was supposed to be, among other things, a "citizen" in the British sense and not a Soviet-style "subject," a devoted neo-Marxist, a neo-Kantian German-Jewish intellectual idealist, a

French-inspired existentialist, or a disciple of other uncritically imported foreign ideas, although Ben-Gurion himself strongly doubted the Jews' ability to
become true citizens in the short time history had provided them. Hence, we
should study the actions he took to surmount these doubts.

The Zionist personalities mentioned here adhered strictly – outwardly, in the
main – to the idea of their being "mobilized" or "regimented" for the cause
of change and revolution in the Jewish way of life. The great tension in their
interrelations, which sometimes spilled into the public domain and required
"rules of the game" – the public virtues of politics as a game played by rules –
eroded this mobilization until it collapsed into overt accusations and rifts from
the founding of the state onward.[12] Shlomo Tzemach continued to write lethal
criticism (mostly for his desk drawer) of local and world events to the best of
his understanding. Personal ardent interest in, and practical involvement with,
literature and writers was an inseparable part of Tzemach's Zionist renaissance.
Ben-Gurion criticized the Jews' ways of life on the basis of philosophical and
practical reasoning drawn from Jewish virtues and values, secularized as they
were, and the thought of other peoples. He strove primarily for the revision of
these ways of life at the level of society in Eretz Israel, a revision that eventually
led to internal political reform. Tzemach and those of like mind viewed all this
with much skepticism and disapproval. From their standpoint, Ben-Gurion was
a "tanner" (a term culled from Jewish sources that denotes the practitioner of
an unpleasant but essential task), a man of action who found within himself
the strength to do what others only spoke of, that is, to establish a state and
an army and to win a war.

    In Ben-Gurion's own eyes, however, his main accomplishment – establish-
ing a Jewish state despite all the difficulties – was not enough. At this stage,
he viewed the founding of the state as an arena for reforming the customs of a
nation needing rebirth. When the Yishuv method of governance overshadowed
the state without effecting the change that he felt essential, he resigned his public offices as prime minister and minister of defense and retreated to Kibbutz
Sede Boqer for the first time, an act that will require study in due course. During
his retreat, Ben-Gurion slowly formulated the principles of a comprehensive
British-style governmental reform that we shall discuss later. However, the
requirements of Israeli security, which always competed with his other priorities, induced him to return in stages to his two erstwhile portfolios one by one
and to attempt to change the system of government on the basis of selected
Jewish values that he culled from the spiritual corpus studied years before.[13]
Yet his attempt to implement that reform failed, ultimately furnishing one of
the reasons for the brutal political struggle among the Israeli social-democratic
elite – a struggle moral and ideological in nature, at least on the surface – that
ended with his downfall.

    Yet the very fact of that initial mobilization by the Second Aliyah generation
had Renaissance-like fundamentals. That is, some of its conflated contents and
values were taken for granted by that generation, which is why they could not

be passed in the same form to subsequent generations. Among those contents and values were some that could only clash with the modern, modernist, and postmodern fundamentals that moved the founding generation and subsequent ones, as well as collide with the religious and traditional legacy. These issues require examination in depth.

Ben-Gurion began his career in Eretz Israel not as a statesman but as a "class-man," a young man of the Jewish working class, which hardly existed in the territory to which he emigrated of his own volition and conviction. In time, he worked to deepen his Zionist ethos and rest it on two foundations. Since he had come from a traditional society in which the Orthodox studied only the Pentateuch and the Talmud and used Yiddish as their vernacular, he based his ethos, first of all, on those parts of the Bible that appealed to him. Toward the Talmud he developed a distaste that he maintained all his life, viewing it as a work of rabbinical legal discourse largely divorced, since sealed off, from an unceasingly changing reality. From the Bible, however, Ben-Gurion not only learned to love Eretz Israel but also developed a faith in the conceptual and behavioral autonomy of the Jewish people and its independence of political culture, which had protected the Jews in their homeland and in the Diaspora as well as possible.

This "autonomy of thought" was a significant matter to Ben-Gurion; apparently it even dictated extra caution against attempting to replicate the world of the Bible in our time. By studying the Jews' autonomy of thought in political cultures, he learned that it had withstood the greatest powers of their periods – Egypt and Babylonia – immense cultures with vast accomplishments of their own. Throughout his life, such autonomy – which, while engaging with the great cultures of the day refuses to assimilate into them culturally, politically, or ethically – was the second central foundation of Ben-Gurionic Zionism.[14] However, it was necessary to choose ideas from religious values that would maintain this autonomy for the future. He made this choice in stages throughout his life, as our discussion will show.

Under the inspiration of the mentors of his generation, such as the philosopher Ahad Ha'am, the historian Simon Dubnow, and the philosopher-writer Micha Josef Berdyczewski, the adult Ben-Gurion declared that he had invested much soul-searching and thought to giving the clearest possible meaning to the concept of "Jewish cultural autonomy." After all, following its stand against Babylonia and Egypt, Judea had to deal with the Hellenist culture, a universalistic *haute culture* that had a greater influence on humankind than its predecessors. Ben-Gurion tried to understand this struggle in its own right and also the Greek influence on Judea. "The ancient Jewish worldview," he said, expressing his own worldview, "was intuitive and theocratic. During medieval times, Jewish sages made attempts ... to meld theocratic Jewish thought with the philosophical Greek worldview that was prevalent among enlightened people in those times."[15] In other words, he drew a distinction here between "philosophy" – rooted in Greek intellectual inquiry based on empirical observation of reality, for the purpose of doing good and attaining beauty – and "intuition," which he further distinguished from theocracy. These three, especially the Platonic and Aristotelian philosophy, blended in traditional Judaism but did so when few intellectuals such as the Rambam bothered to try to incorporate Greek philosophy into Judaism. Still, Ben-Gurion claimed, Jews gave humankind "the universal vision of redemption, the vision of peace, freedom and justice for all mankind."

From Judaism's dispute with Christianity and from his desire to defend its singularity in secular terms, Ben-Gurion suggested that the greatness of this vision was in its directionality, pointing to both past and future, creating constant hope and striving for what ought to be. Judaism offered a constant, active moral obligation, rather than the passivity in the Christian claim that mankind had already been saved and need do nothing but believe in salvation through Jesus – that is, to persist in a direction that leads to the past and dictates the present. The attempt to distinguish Judaism from its greatest historical enemy drew the adult Ben-Gurion toward Judaism's other two great historical enemies in the classical era, Greece and Rome, which had given mankind the tools for contemplation and examination of reality in order to improve and beautify it, and had also given mankind "laws of state and rules of war."

Ben-Gurion's approach is evident both in his contemplation of and learning from other cultures and in his recognition of the "singularity" (*yihud*) and "destiny" (*yi'ud*) of the Jewish people – ideas that require clarification precisely because these terms sound pretentious, vacuous, and even ludicrous today. In the following chapters, we shall see that from the outset, secular Zionism aroused criticism that strongly resembles the current variety for its arrogance in regard to "destiny" and "singularity." This may explain his valorous and indefatigable attempts to instill these concepts broadly.

Ben-Gurion's third minister of education, B. Z. Dinur, Dinur's successor, Zalman Aranne, and Ben-Gurion himself tried mightily to instill "Jewish consciousness" and a Zionist interpretation of Jewish history in Israeli students. This was easy enough in the early years of statehood, since many Israeli-born students were still familiar with the full range of Jewish literature, including accounts of Jewish life free of Zionist indoctrination – from Bialik's autobiographical sketch *Safiah* (Appendix) to the stories of Yitzhak Leibush Peretz and Zalman Shneor and the warm, touching humor of Sholom Aleichem. They respected some fundamental Diaspora values and rejected others, for the Zionist syndrome that many of them had studied and mastered was equivocal, sending many different messages. Two of these accepted values were the veneration of martyred parents or ancestors – a core belief in Jewish Orthodoxy of all stripes – and the conviction that in the future Jews would no longer die this way.

Respect for tradition and its demands originated in the literature that they had read, including descriptions of the Spanish Inquisition in *Memoirs of the House of David*, *The Heroes of the Tower of York*, and similar works published by Am Oved, the Labor Zionist publishing house – depictions that fit well with the poetry of Shaul Tchernichovsky. The Zionist message conveyed by these accounts of life in exile seemed natural and unforced. The basic consensus values were recognition of the singularity, the principled morality, and the suffering of the Jewish people. These inspired feelings of affection, identification, pride, superiority, and rejection of assimilation. After the Holocaust and the victimization that those snared in it had experienced, they understood better than others could, and had a deeper understanding of, the human condition, one supposedly unknown by people of other cultures. Here lies the reason for the scorn that many Israelis of the author's generation heaped on teachers and parents who tried to teach them "Zionism," even though they accepted those teachings with love and a fair measure of agreement.

When the earlier books lost favor and young people moved on to the deep, sophisticated, and sometimes spiteful writings of Samuel Yosef Agnon, later a Nobel Prize laureate, and lesser writers and poets, they naturally found the education in Jewish consciousness, and later the official mourning rites for the Holocaust, to be an "establishment narrative" of Zionist ideology. Such a narrative dictated an almost natural antagonism on the part of maturing youth, in view of the rapidly changing face of reality from the 1950s onward. Even so, many did find ways to internalize this narrative, reconciling it as well as they could with other influences, including the open, progressive, creative educational approach of John Dewey. In Israel, teachers such as Professor Akiva E. Simon implemented this approach even as teachers from the blatantly atheistic kibbutz streams of the leftist movements taught children their own singular values. The results of this amalgam may explain the criticism leveled today against Ben-Gurion himself and against his period – but that would be putting the cart before the horse.

Like many other products of the nineteenth century, Ben-Gurion saw science as a definitive dimension of modern reality. That is why he thought it important to become acquainted with the sources of Western scientific thinking, a rival (in a sense) of "political science" – the attempt to formulate secular theories of government, a cornerstone of Western political thought and a subject foreign to Judaism. Ben-Gurion learned the wisdom of Socrates from the mouth of Plato, the very wisdom according to which one must seek truth by rational means that have moral content. He must have been enchanted by Socrates' refusal to embrace conventional wisdom and his ability to smash and undermine them. Plato's claim that Socrates had linked the Good and its necessity in political life with probing rational thought, on the basis of his belief in their essential and innate harmony and beauty, greatly interested a statesman who had crossed the bounds of religion in search of a secular basis for the pursuit of the Good and the Beautiful as identified with the side that is Right. However, Ben-Gurion also compared the Greek foundation of Western moral theory with the Jewish one and sometimes found Judaism to have an advantage over Greek culture. What he found in the Jewish foundation was a nexus of the moral, the historical, and the emotional – unlike the nexus of the rational and the Socratic – that could be culled from the Bible and Jewish history if it were to be revived in its native soil.

Ben-Gurion took no interest in the tiny Platonic "state" in its concrete sense, with its class structure and its awarding kings the credentials of philosophers, since he regarded this side of Plato's thinking as completely irrelevant to modern life. However, Ben-Gurion did contemplate Athenian democracy as actually practiced: "Why were the Greek people [intellectually the greatest people in human history because they had invented the world's first democracy] destroyed? When the entire people had to come [to the Athenian Assembly] to make decisions together, and they were widely dispersed, of course only a few professional politicians came, so the idea just withered."[16] Thus, Greece was an intellectual school from which one could study basic principles in those matters that Judaism had not known how to develop. Still, Ben-Gurion's aversion to "professional politicians," of all things, is strange, considering his involvement in politics himself for almost his whole life. Indeed, we will have to define this concept further on. For now, we may say that he viewed himself not as a professional politician but as a statesman. He had learned that the Western culture of governance, stemming from Greece and Republican Rome – and particularly the specific case of England – rested, among other things, on the development of the premise that people can use their intelligence to seek the truth in rational ways that incorporate moral content. The statesman's task is to stimulate this ability and induce people to make the right decisions. This culture had led to the development of democratic rule, in which the relationship between elected and electors rests on the aforementioned premise, among others.

Ben-Gurion was well aware that this was a conflation of fundamentals and tried to bring it about by reconciling this essentially liberal premise, which will be developed later, with elements of Judaism. Similarly, he sought, in his typical way, to interpret Judaism as a "religion of justice" and, thereby, to liberate and absolve it from traditional rituals and matters of faith that cannot lend meaning to the life of a secular society. The characterization of Judaism as a religion of justice – this being Judaism's contribution to Western culture as a whole, an intrinsic outcome of the Jewish people's self-identification as a "chosen people and a light unto the nations." It would become critical for Ben-Gurion and would be one of the reasons for his stance in the so-called Lavon Affair, a major crisis among Israel's elite and the beginning of their decline in the early 1960s. This crisis, too, will preoccupy us later to a considerable degree.

This matter of chosenness and its concomitant, moral arrogance, had identified the Jewish religion in previous historical eras. A secular Jewish state needed a moral foundation that would bear up to investigation and perfection. In order to determine the political regime of such a state – including its citizens' conduct, the position of the individual vis-à-vis the collective, and individuals' willingness to come together to bear the burden and responsibilities of Jewish sovereignty – governmental systems had to be studied and the question of government had to be viewed as a central, independent issue (alongside the social, economic, and cultural issues that occupied Ben-Gurion and his contemporaries).

This is why Ben-Gurion thought it insufficient to study the Bible and the writings of the Greek philosophers. As soon as statehood was attained, he tried to adopt principles that were culled from a modern theory of government that, in turn, was drawn from Greece and Rome, from the Jewish sources of Christianity, and from the rich historical experience of a specific method: British parliamentarism, with all its important elements, including "British justice" and its special manifestations in the English system of government:

The English people invented the great science of representation. They did not invent something that was ideal but they invented the most efficient method in the world.... This educates the opposition in responsibility, for every opposition can become a government.... If we want to strengthen [our] state ... to make representation real, not on paper ... we must do it right, something that has been tested and that peoples in the greatest political sense in history have maintained for centuries.... It is England that has political genius. True, it was not always so; England was once a corporate state. But it is a great political genius of a people. We have none of their character. We must fashion it. At this time, a corrupt system will corrupt it; a healthy system will heal it.[17]

This belief in social engineering was widely held in Britain at the time, and among Ben-Gurion's peers. Only in time – in our time – are its costs and damages being discussed, particularly in the context of the ethnic "melting pot" and under the influence of contemporary American and British concepts and values:

The foundation of democracy in our times, when direct government by the entire citizen body is no longer possible, is the election of representatives who derive their power from the general [electorate] and are answerable to it. Among us, with the Balkan electoral system [which causes divisiveness and dog-eat-dog war] that we either chose or inherited from the Zionist Organization, the citizen does not actually have the right to choose his representative and those elected have no connection with their voters.... The elected are actually chosen not by the voter but by those who draw up the party lists, by a "Mr. Anonymous" [a Labor Party "boss" in charge of a regional party "machine," or the bosses of the Labor Party's national machine] who never appears before the voters. It is this Mr. Anonymous, usually the party's central committee, who actually decides who will sit in the *Knesset* [the Israeli Parliament] and who will not.... This electoral system is nothing but a caricature and falsification of democracy.... The Israeli ship is being borne on malicious waves in a stormy sea. To bring it to shore safely, we have to fix our democratic regime.[18]

Of course, it was not possible to transfer to Israel the unique historical roots of the British system. Furthermore, Ben-Gurion surely did not wish to adopt the manifestations of British class society and its array of institutions, including the crown and the House of Lords. He did wish as far as possible, however, to adopt essential British governmental tools and principles and tailor them to

maximize an egalitarian workers' society, which, he believed, needed them for
its long-term survival.

These tools and principles (simply and briefly, as warranted at this stage of
our discussion) were the following:[19]

1. Parliamentary sovereignty: Parliament may pass or repeal any law with-
    out the executive authority, the judicial authority, or any other body,
    such as the crown, being able to prevent it. Only parliament can amend
    parliamentary legislation. The House and its laws are not liable to judicial
    review. The judicial system, in turn, is not dependent on political insti-
    tutions. Its rules of jurisprudence are anchored in common law, the law
    that applies to every citizen great or small, which is basically an intricate
    set of precedents, changes necessitated by the Zeitgeist – the so-called
    laws of equity – and the main legislation by Parliament that supersedes
    everything else. Britain is unique among European countries in that it
    was not influenced by the rediscovery of Imperial Roman law during the
    Renaissance, including the pronounced tendency of Roman law to give
    Caesar far-reaching powers and recognize his personal sovereignty.
2. A unitary state: Great Britain, unlike the United States, Canada, and
    Germany, was not a federal state. Therefore, governmental power is not
    divided between central authorities and those of the member states of the
    federation, nor any other bodies. The United Kingdom is constituted of
    three different peoples: the English, the majority people in the kingdom,
    and the Scots and the Welsh, who maintain their singularity. (Northern
    Ireland notwithstanding. The question of the individuality of the Scots
    and Welsh, which was not an issue in Ben-Gurion's time, has resurfaced
    recently and has begun to change the character of the unitary British
    state.) In Ben-Gurion's time, supranational partnerships such as the one
    formed when Britain joined the European Community were not an issue,
    though even within this framework Britain has been protective of its
    sovereignty as far as possible, nor did the ideas and praxis of today's
    multiculturalism exist.
3. Government under the principle of a fusion of power, unlike the Amer-
    ican principle of separation of powers. Parliament is the legislator, the
    executive, and the highest court of law (just as the crown and the House
    of Lords, which is the supreme court of appeals, are subject to the ulti-
    mate authority of the House of Commons). The fusion of legislative and
    executive authority is expressed mainly in a government that is made up
    of almost a third of the House of Commons or its equivalent (includ-
    ing cabinet members, ministers who are not cabinet members, junior
    ministers, and ministers' parliamentary aides) and is answerable to said
    House. After the fact, the government translates the laws, under the con-
    stant review of the opposition, into accepted practices and agreed rules
    of the game.

4. The special status of the prime minister in the cabinet system of government and the principle of shared responsibility: In the cabinet, the collective decision-making mechanism, the prime minister has a special status but not a separate and independent one, except for his prerogative to dissolve Parliament and call new elections. Many scholars call this system "prime-ministerial government," but all agree that the cabinet – as a collegial unit – runs the government and is collectively answerable to Parliament and the public. After the fact, the legislative and executive powers are fused within it.

5. A house of representatives is chosen in general elections by a district or constituency-majority system that usually ensures stable two-party rule. The British parties were always large entities that historically maintained ideological distinctiveness and multifaceted organization. In general elections, the public handed a mandate to the parties and not their district representatives, even though the latter expressed various and sundry interests on their behalf. Once elected, the representatives and the government whom they appoint may use their discretion, due to changing circumstances, to deviate from the mandate given them by the electorate. Hence, the British democracy is a representative, not a direct, democracy.

6. The elected government, which may be replaced every five years, operates via an apolitical, incorruptible, and professional civil service that remains in place irrespective of the election results. The public services that earn the greatest public esteem are the British army and police.

All these, of course, are classic manifestations of the British system of government as they were expressed during Ben-Gurion's time and are no longer equally valid. Yoel Krieger (see note 19) stresses the importance of the perceptible transfer of power from the House of Commons during its golden age to the government, as legitimized by the House of Commons. Ben-Gurion himself undoubtedly recognized the importance of this transfer of power and knew of any number of difficulties and distortions relative to the ideal picture of the British system of government, but he found this system preferable to the alternatives. At the time, at the dawn of Israeli statehood, he was troubled by other weighty matters, foremost the very survivability of the nation, that is, the current and long-term security problems. These matters often overshadowed all his attempts at fundamental reform of the Yishuv method of governance, which, in his opinion, had not undergone enough change since the establishment of the state.

After all, the very decision to declare statehood had been by the Yishuv institutions, without consulting those of the World Zionist Movement. This itself was a constitutional revolution of sorts, which seemingly could be expanded into other areas of Yishuv life. At that juncture, Ben-Gurion went through an initial burst of enthusiasm – very typical of him – believing that with the establishment of the state, it would be possible to animate revolutionary behavior among the various parties and the public at large. Quickly, however, he discovered that this was not the case – concerning the existing political system, the absorption of mass immigration, and the other immense responsibilities that Israel faced in its first years. Even Mapai – Ben-Gurion's own party, as it were – defied its founder's will in many respects, contrary to what people think today.

From the outset, Ben-Gurion tried, in the best British style, to shift the center of gravity in Israel's sovereign governance to the parliamentary faction of his Labor Party, Mapai. However, he failed due to Mapai's pluralistic nature – an amalgam of trade unions, rural-settlement movements, and many other groups that sought to maintain, if not enhance, their status as much as possible.[20] Concurrently, Ben-Gurion tried to establish a civil service along British lines and to fashion the IDF in the image of the British army, with a few original additions of his own, most notably the requirement that every soldier perform farm labor during his or her first year of service. He studied other armies, too, including the model of the American citizen-soldier, and eventually adopted the model of reserve duty employed by the Swiss.

The issue at hand, however, transcended the creation of an army. An attempt was being made to formulate a regime suited to a Jewish state, with the understanding that the citizens of this state were not accustomed to sovereignty and might ruin it. Although considered one of its founders, Ben-Gurion had long deemed the pre-state regime flawed and – because it underwent no real change in the transition to statehood – dangerous. Indeed, he had been one of the strongest critics of this regime as far back as the 1930s, but he saw no way to reform a voluntary Yishuv whose institutions were both autonomous and coalitional and subordinate to the World Zionist Organization, with a plenum that had been paralyzed since the beginning of World War II. Now the task was to move from pre-state forms to those of statehood. If Ben-Gurion saw no way to accomplish this via comprehensive political reform of the various coalition bodies during the transition from Yishuv to statehood immediately after the War of Independence, he now viewed the establishment of the national army and the determination of its special complexion and duties as an instrument for public action that could not be accomplished by conventional means.

The first pressing problem was the depolitization of the army, after which came the initial decisions about the power structure of the regular forces, the consolidation of the reserve system, and preparations for a possible "second round" should the Arabs attack again. After designing the army, Ben-Gurion put it to extensive use in absorbing the immigrants and blending them and the existing population into a single community. He could do this because he wielded decisive control of the army as minister of defense. In other areas, including the delicate area of labor relations, the head of Mapai and the ostensibly all-powerful master of the *Histadrut* (the General Federation of Labor) encountered major difficulties from the very first. In civilian life, the changes he considered necessary immediately after the War of Independence – such as linking wages to a rise in productivity – suffered from inertia and from the vested interests and internal politics of powerful unions. An atypical issue – one that has been investigated in recent years and is pursued in this study as well – is the partitioning of the Yishuv education system into "streams" – general, labor, and national-religious – and the metamorphoses of this system in the early statehood years until the passage of the National Education Law did away with the nonreligious streams. Ben-Gurion opposed this division from the outset but was unable to prevent it.[21]

These difficulties, however, were not all. The Zionist Labor Movement, of which Ben-Gurion was one of the leaders, had various social theories and sociopolitical action plans. But it did not have a developed theory of self-rule, that is, of politics as the autonomous dimension of life in society. This dimension would require study and revision for the eventuation of Jewish sovereignty. For in Ben-Gurion's time, a variegated Jewish settlement was taking shape, which he and others kneaded and fashioned to the best of their limited abilities.

The waves of immigration were of different origins and brought many indigenous ideas, including some that Ben-Gurion found foreign to his knowledge and upbringing. Nevertheless, he became the leader of this multichromatic population and led it to political sovereignty amid a reality of tragic strife immeasurably greater than that in which he had begun his work. At the pinnacle of his career, then, he tried to give this sovereignty new forms and ideas that he thought superior to those that had characterized it in its infancy – but he was unable to carry them far enough.

Another explanation for his decline is the historical period in which he functioned. This period, which he and his contemporaries called the Jewish renaissance, fashioned him and gave him some freedom of action due to the drive and vigor of his generation. But the period was brief and it coincided with troubles, tragedies, and changes that succeeded one another at a pace unknown in former generations. The Jewish renaissance era, according to those who propagated it, was problematic from the start. It combined with other historical forces and world upheavals until it gave way to a "counter-renaissance" in many respects. All of this explains Ben-Gurion's decline and the rise – and fall – of most of his successors.

In sum, Ben-Gurion was a product of an era and the crafter of special conditions that held sway in the Jewish world of his time. Therefore, anyone who wishes to learn from his actions must recognize their uniqueness in their own time and beware of judging them with the tools of our own era. Ben-Gurion himself recognized this uniqueness and tried to take advantage of the Zeitgeist and its potential as an instrument for permanent change. In this, he succeeded partly – and also failed.

I

The Intellectual Origins of Ben-Gurion's Zionism

The European Renaissance and Its Interpretations

The partitioning of Italian and northwestern European history into radically different periods, as they are sometimes proclaimed to be, originates in the writings of two great nineteenth-century historians, Jules Michelet and Jacob Burckhardt. The two scholars had distinctly different backgrounds and views of history. Burckhardt was a well-rounded and occasionally somber Swiss who harbored conservative leanings. He was captivated by the Middle Ages and saw in the Renaissance much light but also the kind of shadows that a historian of his time would find due to the changes in the traditional religious social order and the release of man to follow his own talents, capabilities, loss of conscience, and vile cravings – and be subject to the authority of the cruel and powerful who would arise, as it were, from the masses of freed humanity.[1] Michelet, by contrast, was a personable, modern, ebullient, secular Frenchman who regarded the Renaissance as an era that had broken off from the benighted Middle Ages (which he considered as having been strangled by the shackles of the church and the hairsplitting rhetoric of Scholasticism), opening the way for humankind in the modern age. Both of them saw the Renaissance not only as an era of artistic efflorescence but also as a unitary whole, during which the pinnacle of the arts, the exploration of new continents, and scientific innovations came together to create a general "discovery of the world and discovery of Man," for better or worse.

Others, however, starting with Petrarch, gave the Renaissance a distinct self-consciousness, a clear-cut sense of departure from the medieval past and a return to the past before the past, and stressed its forerunners as the pioneers who paved the way to a new era.[2]

If so, given that Zionism was a national liberation movement, what connection could it have to the Renaissance? The roots of the Zionism of Ben-Gurion and his contemporaries should be sought in Russian literature; Polish poetry; the European heroism of Byron, Adam Mickiewicz, and Victor Hugo;[3] the nationalistic romanticism of Italy and Central Europe; the Czarist Russian literature, poetry, and struggle for liberation; and the Hebrew-language *Haskala* [Jewish Enlightenment] texts of Peretz Smolenskin, Ahad Ha'am, and others. Furthermore, since Ben-Gurion was seen as a fundamentally political figure, a "monist" with a one-track mind – the pursuit of Jewish statehood at all costs – it seems completely ludicrous to liken him, in his own eyes, to a Renaissance man, given the special sensitivity of that era to beauty, art, and the nonpolitical esthetic and creative endeavors of the individual.[4]

Humanism

The modern concept of humanism was coined by nineteenth-century German intellectuals to highlight the strong emphasis that Renaissance humanists had placed on classical studies, which they saw as both an educational tool and a social compass. Such studies were the occupation of educators and teachers who became known at the end of the fifteenth century as *umanisti*, and of professors and students of classical literature. The key word, the Latin term *humanitas*, denotes striving for an intellectual and political ideal that all members of the movement accepted. This key word means bringing the development of latent human capacities to fruition by any and all means. Thus, *humanitas* embraces not only the modern concept of "humaneness," that is, understanding, goodwill, concern for others, and compassion, but also more active and almost aggressive components of human nature that originated in the five cardinal classical virtues of prudence, courage, temperance, fortitude, justice, and even the pursuit of honor – a characteristic that we will explore later.

The conclusion, however, was that a person graced with all of these characteristics could not be an ivory-tower philosopher or just a simple writer. Rather, he had to be active in society. Just as action without profound understanding of its significance was considered unacceptable, so was profound thinking without action deemed sterile. Humanistic theory demanded a delicate balance between action and thought, with action arising not from compromise but from an acquiescence that worked both ways. The theoretical goal of this approach was political in the broadest sense of the word, that is, not only to educate youth but also to guide adults, including the leaders of the time, by means of philosophical poetry and rhetoric of political import. Thus, humanism entailed not only criticism of the behavior of contemporary society but also utopian dreams, not only analysis of the past but also designs for the future. Humanism preached reform (albeit not the overthrow) of the past as a step toward the creation of a new order that would allow the entirety of humankind's creative and constructive potential to find expression. However, humanism called for more than reform; it also had a messianic dimension that would extend from the realm of the individual to the life of the state.

The wellsprings of humanism were derived from classical literature and Greek and Roman thought, which were all reopened for study during the Renaissance. So far as the exponents of the Renaissance were concerned, there was nothing wrong with the ideas of thinkers who had lived thousands of years before, foremost Plato and the Romans Cicero and Livy. The classical works had a fructifying dimension lacking in those of medieval Christian thinkers, and their students felt newly in touch with reality. Ancient philosophy seemed unencumbered and objective in comparison with medieval thought and the praxis that had typified Christianity in the preceding era, that is, a dualism in the imperatives of religion and real life. Classical thinkers dealt with morality and politics separately and on their own merits, without mingling them with the flesh and blood of Jesus. The humanists continued to regard themselves as believing Christians even if after the fact they became unconfessed atheists. Amid all this, classical literature became a model for public discourse and behavior. Regarding affairs of state and the behavior of the rulers of states, allowing the free analysis of international relations and the use of power in their actions, the humanists placed much emphasis on the arts of rhetoric and persuasion, which, in their decline during the sixteenth century, slowly evolved into the arts of debate and dialectic.

Soon enough, as new versions of old forces rose to the fore, the entire Renaissance seemed to become a thing of the past. The humanists' grand pretensions were viewed by later generations not only as brazenness toward God but also as a vain liberation of humankind, a foolhardy act that gave human talents a field of action that turned into a mere arena of power struggle. All the same, the Renaissance opened the way for the Christian Reformation, for the forms and institutions that had arisen in medieval times could not continue unchanged after such a burst of creativity and freedom of thought.

Nation-states, too, such as France and England, owed their origins to the Renaissance, even though their roots had been planted in medieval soil.[5] The Renaissance and its successor, the Reformation, contained a fair measure of nationalism that was influenced, among other things, by the Jewish vision of "chosenness" and the Biblical conception of a "chosen land," that is, the national spirit that has infused Judaism since time immemorial – and has been its curse more than once – alongside the Renaissance-inspired revival of the Jewish Bible and other classical sources. Contemporary critics of nationalism, including those who became anti-Zionists, such as Hans Cohn, argued that Judaism, or to be more exact the Jewish Bible, invented this dangerous notion, which links a certain people or ethnic group with a territory that it considers holy and God-given.[6] Some would even link the American Puritans' sense of Biblical chosenness to racist ideas that they held after reaching their American "Canaan."

Be that as it may, Judaism itself has undoubtedly been a national culture since its inception and views itself as tied to a specific territory. These ties proliferated and acquired various interpretations over the centuries, including the traditional exposition that the nation in exile is not permitted to leave its exile – that is, its long-established condition – absent Divine intervention, which is not in its own hands. The renaissance of such a culture, in the words of those involved in it, was at least a manifestation of the challenge to this and other traditions, a challenge described by some contemporaries, and by historians, not as a Renaissance but as a revolution, a complete break – and a serious one, in view of its long-term consequences – from the entire Jewish Diasporic tradition.[7] In this book, we will try to clarify the extent to which this was a continuation or a break, or both.

The triumph of the Hebrew language – a necessity without which there could have been no dialogue among the members of this multilingual people – was unquestionably a revolution. Yet some would say that the uprooting of Yiddish, with its homespun wisdom, its skepticism, and its sophisticated human humor, caused severe long-term psychological and cultural harm, as others would say about the displacement of Arabic from its speakers in Israel. Furthermore, secular Hebrew culture was not rich enough to create an identity such as that of other powerful cultures (and today, even these cultures are struggling for survival against television and other technological innovations that have brought profound changes to their educational systems). Moreover, it may be that the assets of secular Zionist culture are only "religious assets that have been 'reworked' by expelling God and wrapping them in a romantic Zionist mantle that is now being torn to shreds under the influence of disasters like the Yom Kippur War and the assassination of Yitzhak Rabin."[8] Indeed, there is something to that argument, but we will try to set it in a much broader historical context and we will ask whether the fork in the road was neither the Yom Kippur War nor the assassination of Yitzhak Rabin, but rather the Holocaust.

Michelet's and Burckhardt's definitions establish at least two specific frameworks that may help us to understand the Zionist renaissance and the actions of some of its participants. According to these two historians, medieval man knew himself only as a member of a group who was not permitted to use his own intellect and judgment in deciding whether to affiliate with that group and help to determine its character. Rather, he was required by force of tradition to affiliate and to accept the group's beliefs or reject them entirely and leave – that is, if he were allowed to leave and after having paid the price of secession from traditional society in the sense of its reaction to him. The Renaissance, in contrast, gave him the scope to become intellectually independent, free to base his conduct on his own intellect, including the choice of affiliation with a group in which he could contribute to its character, behavior, and definition to the best of his cognizance.

In Burckhardt's eyes, the Renaissance man's "cognizance" of himself and of humankind was a characteristically pretentious insolence. With it came the aggrandizement of the nature of man and faith in his innate basic goodness – even though no theory was developed in support of any of these claims, and even though these claims carried immense destructive potential for existing social frameworks and threatened to reduce them to isolated elements and defenseless subjects of "hobnailed gangs." In due course, ironically enough, Ben-Gurion himself and his aides, Moshe Dayan and Shimon Peres, were accused of similar qualities by a number of intellectual moralists, several of whom belonged to religious schools of various roots.

First, however, we should say a few words about the exponents of the Renaissance themselves. There is no question that during this period, a material change took place, or came to fruition, in people's attitude toward their historical horizons and their very essence. This is because people began to pay heed to time that preceded that of traditional history, the one beginning with the crucifixion of Jesus. By so doing, they renewed the dialogue – both within and outside the context of Christianity – with the giants of the traditional past. Once again mankind was recognized in its natural, human, and sensory aspects, and its artistic endeavors were revived. Consequently, people reshaped their relationship not only with the past but also with the present, viewing it as something that to be lived to the fullest, not just as a link in an endless chain of generations that observed immutable ancestral customs. The future also took a new shape, evolving from a vision of religious apocalypse to a time when shrouded secrets would yield to man's decoding in many different respects.

One of these respects was the discovery of new continents, which began during the Renaissance and took on a double meaning: the delimiting of the Old World and the expansion of the boundaries of Christian Europe into the New World. This, however, also meant an encounter with new cultures, some of them powerful and ancient – such as the Chinese, which obviously shrank the centrality of the Christian world, in its own eyes, and strengthened its division into national cultures – and others that were, from the Renaissance perspective, primitive and barbaric. Indeed, for Ben-Gurion, the Arab ocean surrounding Israel proved to be primitive and barbaric once he tried to find common ground between the Arabs of Palestine and the Jews and tried to talk to, and even negotiate with, their leaders after World War I and in the 1930s. His efforts to do so entailed the use of prudent political and military measures, which were always based on the progressive assumption that Arabs possessed the necessary qualities for improvement and peacemaking, in due course, thanks to Israeli understanding of the challenges involved in the state of affairs in the Arab world. In China he could already see the upcoming superpower.

We may say, then, that the Renaissance had a significant element of synthesis and renewal – a blend of things that had not been soluble before – and a spirit of innovation and a contemplation of reality that were open to things that prior generations' eyes had not considered worthy of seeing. The resulting Zeitgeist would later be criticized on the grounds of pretension, of constructing a hodgepodge that lacked a theoretical and analytical foundation, yet this explains that generation's special strength and the inability to understand it properly afterwards.[9]

The Future of Individual, Society, and State

There is a "revisionist" view of the Renaissance: the onset of the creation of the "individual" as a freely standing being who independently chooses how to relate to the collective – a process that culminated in the formation of Western political frameworks, insofar as this process can be described so simplistically. However, the pitched battle between church and state that began in the Middle Ages established precedents and traditions for the separation of these institutions that Judaism never experienced. Some schools of English historiography claimed that personal liberties and their maintenance under the common law of those parts of the kingdom that would eventually be united also began in the Middle Ages – or were accepted as if they had been an ancient heritage.[10] One may argue that the process that led to the Protestant Reformation began during the Renaissance, and that due to this process and other factors that we cannot pursue here, the emphasis in certain societies shifted to the individual and his or her social conduct.

As the autonomous Western person slowly surfaced, the question arose about his or her rights versus coercion and demands that regimes once could have made of their subjects with the backing of religion, tradition, and force of arms. In seventeenth-century England, a new political theory was devised, on the basis of the philosophy of the father of liberalism, John Locke, that upheld the "natural rights" of the individual – following Thomas Hobbes and his *Leviathan* – in purely secular terms. Locke greatly expanded the premise of Socrates, as attributed to him by Plato, that man is capable of using his intellect as a foundation for the establishment of governance, by extending it beyond the realm of the few who, according to Plato, were alone capable of doing so. This marked the beginning of the dichotomy between secular theory, which stressed the supremacy of the individual and the sanctity of his property as his natural right by virtue of his being a rational creature (from which would later flow the justification for the rule of individuals within the ever-improving framework of parliamentary democracy) and conservative theory. In other words, as a counterweight to liberal theory, another doctrine was devised that justified political freedom, property, autonomous groupings in society, traditional institutions, and equality before the law in terms of a historical development, as Edmond Burke, the patriarch of modern British conservatism, construed them.[11]

The conservatives based their stance on their own country's political history, the product of an amalgam of accumulated human experience and institutions that had developed from medieval times onward and had endured upheavals, crises, and adaptations since the Renaissance. Even so, we maintain that despite the ideological differences between conservatives and liberals of all stripes, a system of government – "rules of the political game" and governing institutions – did arise that ultimately combined elements of both approaches. It was this combination that interested Ben-Gurion, who viewed it as a model worth learning from. We also propose that the very ability and readiness to contemplate these matters of government, its legitimacy, its institutions, and their modes of operation was atypical in the milieu of Israel's founding generation, the members of the Second Aliyah. Indeed, many of them dealt instead with culture, society, art, and labor, leaving Ben-Gurion to study the rules of state and apply them the best he could as instruments without which it would be impossible to maintain culture, society, and art.

On the heels of Locke and other British intellectuals, an even more ambitious secular theory took shape in France – that of Jean-Jacques Rousseau, which derived the freedom and ceaseless drive for wholeness of the individual from his or her membership in the human collective, living a life of liberty and equality in communion with nature. Rousseau himself, in his own way, was a philosopher who sought to return to ancient Greece and who viewed modern life as inevitably corrosive. In this respect, he had a powerful influence on many of his contemporaries and their successors, including members of the Second Aliyah. Such a collective could be the nation – as Rousseau wrote to the Poles[12] – or a group of individuals living collectively on a kibbutz in Eretz Israel, who were influenced by Rousseau's ideas directly or indirectly via Tolstoy and other intermediaries. The classic dichotomy that the liberal school of Locke's time established between individual and society – or, to be more precise, between individual and state, with a decisive preference for the individual – yielded to a trilateral relationship among the individual, the group or the voluntary social network (from which and of whose like civil life is built), and the state. This triangle became the topic of theoretical debates and practical decisions in the Western world in the aftermath of nineteenth-century urbanization and industrialization.

Rousseau's own philosophy allowed for various ways of governing society and dealing with personal rights vis-à-vis the collective. One possibility was to force individuals to do good in the name of an abstract majority, one that expresses a "general will" that strives intrinsically to do good, as opposed to serving the "common will," even if some members of the "common" are evil or blind. This issue occupied the Socialist Zionist avant-garde in Eretz Israel in various ways. Ben-Gurion himself, however, shrank from abstract, doctrinaire arguments such as these. Although he acknowledged their power, he was inherently averse to abstract, "scientific," formulaic thinking in matters of government and state. One reason for Ben-Gurion's admiration of Lenin was the quality of flexibility that he saw in him and in Lenin's readiness, as he perceived it, to adopt different, contradictory stances at different times in his maneuverings, which dictated "a powerful sense of right and justice, though wrapped in a veil of theory," that transformed "aspiration into triumphant fact."[13] In other words, Ben-Gurion attributed motives or "aspirations" to Lenin that were essentially ethical and fundamentally historical but donned a "veil of theory" that, while pretending to strict consistency, was bound up with an ostensibly surprising flexibility in practice.

In the early 1920s, Ben-Gurion took an ardent interest in Lenin and what was happening in the Soviet Union; he even traveled there. However, he reached the general conclusion that the Soviet experiment was mortally dangerous to Zionism, banned and persecuted by the regime. In time, he also concluded that the Soviet Union – as it developed under Lenin and Stalin – would not be long-lived due to its doctrinaire underpinnings, its inhumanity, and its internal contradictions, which prevented Marxist-Leninism from being a "triumphant fact." In this respect, Ben-Gurion was an empiricist, not a dogmatist, that is, the kind of person who contemplates the world, society, and the individual through the investigative eyes of one who studies them as they are, not as they should be. This was a characteristic of the Renaissance, during which reality as it is was studied from the posture of critical faith in man and an undeclared readiness to free him from the original sin that tradition had imposed on him, without forfeiting all of tradition's elements. This faith in man did not lead to the conclusion during the Renaissance that decisions must be those of the majority, that is, to democracy, but it had roots that would lead to democracy.

It goes without saying that the contributions of the seventeenth, eighteenth, and nineteenth centuries were necessary for the ascendancy of modern democracy, and Ben-Gurion recognized them and interpreted them in his own way. At this stage of our discussion, we may determine that he constantly strove toward majority decisions, that is, to impose the "will of all." The question was how to accomplish this, and to answer it Ben-Gurion began a demarche that proposed to culminate in the complete reformation of the Israeli political system. However, the very interpretation of this issue – after the reform gambit not only failed but also threatened the existing system – was, at the end of his life, a source of terrible divisiveness, in which he was accused of tyranny and of ignoring the will of the majority in the manner of Robespierre, Rousseau's late eighteenth-century disciple.[14]

That century, the eighteenth, had had a substantial element of analysis – not synthesis. It gave the world what Isaiah Berlin calls a pretentious "scientific" foundation.[15] Yet even though Ben-Gurion took much interest in sciences, the only true science in his eyes was natural science. In society and politics, he refused, sometimes bluntly, to recognize the existence of "sciences," that is, universally immutable and inviolable laws that should govern human conduct, as argued by radical eighteenth-century Enlightenment philosophers such as Condorcet, Helvetius, Adam Smith in his way (abhorring any economic theory that seemed to allow the free market alone to control society), and Locke's successor David Hume in his.[16] Even Montesquieu, with his theory of separation of powers, would have seemed to Ben-Gurion too theoretical, compared with the empirical British development of fusion of power within the construct of a parliamentary democracy and an independent judiciary. Rousseau was a complex, unique case, but he also had all-encompassing pretensions of knowing the human soul. Only thus could he offer his own approach toward the education and governance of human beings, as if they stood no chance whatsoever absent the system of government that he proposed.

To be sure, that mostly lovely, radiant century brought the world the declaration of human rights and it also, in its own way, was in love with the Greco-Roman classics, with their heroes and values. When we speak of Ben-Gurion himself, however, it seems to us that comparing the Zionist revival to aspects of the Renaissance is problematic but more germane than comparing it to aspects of the eighteenth-century Enlightenment, particularly because of the tendency of many French philosophers of that century toward abstract, deterministic thinking, the kind that originated in the scientific revolution of the seventeenth century, and the general European tendency at the time toward "scientific" generalization. Much of the European thinking was guided by an approach that saw man and society as subjects for scientific inquiry that sought to reveal natural laws and believed that the discovery of such laws was but a question of time.[17]

This rationalist approach could profess to be observing reality – that is, having an empirical foundation – but the claim about the existence of natural regularity in human and social affairs countered the English empirical tradition that rejected scientific regularity in such matters specifically. The political system that reigned in the British Isles was linked – for various historical reasons – to religious concepts, the lessons of religious wars, and social and institutional developments that no one had designed in advance but that had created a unique political culture over the centuries. This mixture of traditional values, precedents, and liberal lessons and ideas had even produced a unique imperial ethos in which Ben-Gurion had no interest, of course. However, "scientific management" of society could have been instituted as a consequence of repressive dogmatism and disregard for the richness and complexity of human nature and the demands of people's changing circumstances, to the extent of nullifying personal rights and conflicting with human rights by invoking human rights as was the case during the last phase of the French Revolution, when terror reigned in the name of the highest values, of which the Jacobin state would be the sole interpreter.

Today, Ben-Gurion is considered in certain circles, and in his time was even publicly accused of being, a Jacobin or Bolshevik revolutionary of sorts, who not only allowed himself to act with great arbitrariness and ignore others' opinions but also did so on the pretense of speaking in the name of some unlegislated, unfounded natural law, perceiving himself a kind of Platonic philosopher-king but in fact following the Jacobin model,[18] that is, the British model of government as discussed in the Introduction, far as it was from any kind of Jacobinism. The presumed source of this alleged natural law was the Jacobin world of thought and action and its doctrinaire extensions in the twentieth century. The supremacy of the state in Ben-Gurion's eyes made him a sort of Israeli Robespierre in the eyes of his critics. Thus, a contrast was created between those who invoked this imagery to describe the "Western tradition" of a "civil society" that above all defends individual rights and those who undertook to speak in the name of the socialist tradition, seeking to protect the class associations that interested them and the "Jacobin-Bolshevik" tradition that subjugates individual and socialist groupings to the "state"; and Ben-Gurion was considered, as it were, the prophet and almighty ruler of the state.

Those who made this claim, however, were not sufficiently familiar with the two main examples of European "civil society" and the European nation-state as they actually existed in their time, as against their existence in the writings of assorted philosophers. In fact, in France of the nineteenth and twentieth centuries, there arose what one of the leading scholars of our times calls "the French perception of singularity," which resembles, to some extent, the Jewish-Israeli perception of singularity and the Ben-Gurionic perception of the state that would evolve in the 1950s:[19]

The French tend to attribute universal value to their language, culture and history, with a particular regard for their propensity for rational argument.

The French consider the republican state to be the arbiter and protector of the commonweal; an entity above and removed from private interests.[20] *The nation is understood to be fashioned by the state and its institutions, as the French conflate citizenship and nationalism* [emphasis added].

Ultimately, the French ambition is greatness on the world stage.[21]

This description of the French national ethos does not differ significantly from the British national ethos of those times. There were, of course, substantial historical differences between France and Britain, as well as France's extra emphasis on Gallic rationalism and Britain's upholding of common law and independent courts free of allegiance to the tradition of Roman law, and the abiding ethos of individual liberty in the English political tradition, to name only a few. Still, both countries used to have a strong tradition of nation-statehood that entailed an ethos of "the common good" and institutions that were supposed to define and seek it. However, whereas in the British system, which defined this concept via constant compromise, a degree of historical continuity – without revolutions and bloodshed – was achieved, in France the essence of the "common good" and how to define it have been topics of heavy controversy, manifested in endless revision of electoral methods and governing institutions based on widely different constitutions. In another difference, the British tradition maintains the old English skepticism about "clear rational argument." After all, neither people nor reality is fully rational, as the French analytic approach that flourished in the eighteenth century, fathered by Descartes, would have it. Tradition and traditional values, customs, and accumulated experience transcend the importance of rational argument.

Furthermore, several champions of the eighteenth-century French Enlightenment disallowed erstwhile ways of life and began history from scratch – that is, from themselves – relating to historical ideas, except those preceding the history of religion, as if they were a collection of vanities and frauds. This sounds like Ben-Gurion's attitude toward the Diaspora: as if it had never existed or as if it were unimportant. However, if the exponents of the Zionist renaissance wished to imitate those of the European Renaissance, they were ultimately different in this respect, for most representatives of the European Renaissance surely did not reject the past and its ideas as sweepingly and blatantly as the Zionist renaissance did.

Ben-Gurion and his associates were, of course, products of a different world, whose common denominator with the European Renaissance that emerged from the Middle Ages expressed itself historically in the success of traditional Judaism in extending its own medieval period well into the modern age. Traditional Judaism accomplished this by using various tools to tailor tradition to changes that were needed in Jewish society and its milieu from the time of the rise of Kabbalistic mysticism to the advent of Hasidism. Then, however, it was struck as if by lightning by the innovations of the eighteenth and nineteenth centuries, which toppled traditional Jewish societies into a severe crisis that requires separate discussion.

Notably, however, many leaders of the Second Aliyah did not wish to jettison the national past – including the period of exile – as if it were utterly worthless. In the eyes of their contemporaries, the power that had sustained the Jewish people under oppression was of great value, and the centrality of Eretz Israel in the nation's dreams and religious worship crossed over to them in secular form. The Jews' refusal to assimilate into Gentile culture – in order to preserve their peoplehood against the challenges of the environment – their suffering for their faith, the tribulations of their erosive poverty, and the mystery of their survival under conditions of ghetto and shtetl were a source of pride and criticism that coexisted in the entire Zionist syndrome. Ben-Gurion lodged serious charges against the Diaspora mentality and lifestyle, and since he could not learn the "rules of government and war" from these exilic characteristics, he had to learn them from others – starting with the Greeks and ending with the British. The declared approach of the Zionists of Ben-Gurion's generation toward the Diaspora stemmed from the political need to dissociate from it and its mentality, and not only from the need to negate it as such. The result was a mixture of "rebellion" against Diasporism and a need for the Diasporic past and present, leading to selective use of both with characteristic innocence and innovativeness, in a manner somewhat similar to European Renaissance trends of thought that had no "scientific" pretensions of discovering valid universal laws for social life and human behavior.[22]

The Renaissance created a synthesis among the recent past, the ancient past, and the present, a synthesis that at the time aroused no surprise among most people, who found it self-evident due to the special mode of thought in such historical eras: a trend toward cultural rebirth and human creativity with no particular theoretical basis or infrastructure. In fact, as Isaiah Berlin says, the theoretical experiments performed by later generations, especially the radical thinkers of the eighteenth-century Enlightenment, those sages of ostensibly unchallengeable analysis, carried great danger. For anyone who repudiated the seemingly political and societal truths that these analytical sages uncovered was judged by them most severely. The Renaissance, the era of synthesis, gave its members an advantage, for one doubts that they were able to contemplate themselves – to peer into the human soul and social conduct – by means of devices that were created centuries later. Nevertheless, the Renaissance did take much interest in external manifestations of cultural behavior, including its political manifestations.

A Zionist Utopia or a Unique Historical Approach?

The Zionism of Ben-Gurion and his contemporaries was typically an uncoerced choice to affiliate with the group and shape it according to the cognizance and judgment of the individual, who seemingly picked and chose from history and culture. Not only had this choice been available in the past, but it could also be challenged on the grounds that, on the one hand, it was a form of heresy and, on the other, that it was somehow superficial and frivolous; that it had dangerous traits culled from the world of the Bible, for example, the conquest of Eretz Israel in Joshua's time, which threatened the wealth of humanistic values in the Book of Books itself, the analytic-humanistic values of the Enlightenment, or liberal values that originated in seventeenth-century Britain and subsequently in the United States. Ben-Gurion and his peers in the Labor Movement indeed faced such accusations from time to time. These accusations, however, express a lack of understanding of the historical factors behind these Zionists' behavior, the free choice afforded to their generation, and the ideologies that it assimilated from sources as diverse as the Bible, the Jewish *mussar* (ethicist) tradition, elements of Jewish mysticism and Hasidism, the Enlightenment, German philosophy, and socialist theory – if we enumerate, for the time being, only a few of the ideas that individuals of that generation mixed into their philosophy with Renaissance insolence, without giving developed theoretical expression to these ideas, some of which, naturally, were typical of the late nineteenth century.

According to these approaches, the individual should assume the weight of responsibility for Jewry at large and for the collective that was then gathering in Eretz Israel – the practical translation of which was a subject of dispute within the Zionist Labor Movement itself. In other words, the relationship between individual and group – the individual's pioneering initiative and voluntary participation in the pioneer community, the attitude of these communities toward the many who did not follow their path, the creation of broader settings for joint action, and the formation of mechanisms for the attainment of consensus – were all subjects for a variety of experiments and arguments within the Yishuv. By the time the state was founded, they were resolved through compromises within the Labor Movement, which saw itself as the vanguard of the Jewish masses in exile, particularly with respect to its relations with other Yishuv bodies.[23]

One of the underlying principles shared by many leaders of this vanguard was the view of Diaspora history as a set of shackles from which they wished to be liberated, along with the scholasticism and Talmudic sophistry of that past, which sapped the creativity of its sons. In the spirit of Jules Michelet's interpretation of the basic worldview of the European Renaissance, the members of the Zionist renaissance saw this past as a period of severe intellectual fossilization and falsification of the basic ethical values professed by that culture itself. The opportunity to renew these values could be found in the ancestral land, where Jews would lead independent, decent, productive lives in the spirit of socialism, the messages of the prophets, the Jewish ethical teachings, and the Hasidic love of fellow Jew, as conflated by the vanguard itself.[24]

Thus, this aversion to the Diaspora, called today *shelilat ha-gola*, "rejection/ negation of the exile," was not a matter of surrendering the assets of the Jewish past; in fact, people at that time even sought to revive them, albeit selectively and in their own secular way. Furthermore, as we have said, they did not renounce the accomplishments of the Diaspora. Indeed, they admired the Jews' cultural steadfastness and adopted several of these cultural values as their own, saying, for example, that Jews had a humanistic ethical purpose in the world, valuing their scholarship, and respecting their commitment to their ethics during the exile, all of which were associated with their attachment to Eretz Israel. Also, however, they argued that the lengthy exile had largely turned these values into rote mannerisms, a refuge from the challenges of changing reality, a source of the kind of passivity that is intrinsic to exiles, and the root of existential danger to themselves and their children. Personalities like Ben-Gurion tended to emphasize, in particular, the need for physical revival and the capacity to act, including self-defense – an approach that they had brought with them to Eretz Israel, the product of the lessons of the Jewish self-defense brigades in Eastern Europe. Naturally, they doubted the viability of their colleagues' Tolstoyan idealism. All members of the "Jewish renaissance," however, saw Judaism as a patient who had the potential to recover and be reborn.

Indeed, these Zionists were animated by the spirit of renewal. The European Renaissance had created its own spirit of renewal without requiring analytic theories of behavior (it simply looked at reality, like the observations of Galileo and Machiavelli) and without an awareness of its psychological origins. By contrast, in the Jewish renaissance, in addition to these drives, there were typical concerns that Judaism was headed for a greater political, social, and cultural catastrophe than that which threatened Machiavelli's Italy. There was also great hope, but it was mixed with fear that Judaism had missed its opportunity, that it was a walking corpse of the sort reported in Ezekiel's prophecy or one of Bialik's last fatalities in the desert – the sort that needs resuscitation, that needs to be saved from itself and from others by being in its homeland, to which it had kept faith in a unique way, unparalleled in the history of other nations.

How such a thing might be done, how to resolve the expected conflict between Jews and Arabs, and what should be done if it became necessary to use force and shed blood to attain the salutary goals of Zionism – in these matters, the Zionist Labor Movement in Eretz Israel was characterized from the outset by various currents, from Tolstoyan pacifism to anarchism. Eventually, this issue awakened the spirit of the Tolstoyan, anarchist, socialist-Marxist tradition, which would join other ideas and motives to challenge the concepts of state and army that Ben-Gurion would develop in time. To understand this perspective, however, we must first fashion an appropriate framework for historical analysis.

A classic Renaissance belief that Ben-Gurionic Zionists adopted was the triumph of the spirit over the hardships of the body. During the Jewish renaissance, it was possible to link the idea of the supremacy of the spirit and its embodiment in flesh and blood with the Jewish heritage itself, couple it with the wish to recognize the body and nature imbued in it, and combine it with the redemption of the ancestral land. The result was a unique blend of Jewish idealism and decidedly Jewish-style socialist theories, which viewed the supremacy of the spirit as the essence and dearly valued the active human will that rested on it – but also acknowledged the additional importance of the material.[25]

This combination was sure to arouse the opposition of the ultra-Orthodox, devout Marxists such as Lenin in his way and Rosa Luxemburg in hers, Zionist fascists such as Yonatan Ratosh,[26] and German-speaking Jewish intellectuals, such as Martin Buber, who were greatly influenced by Protestant Christianity and by its great enemy, Friedrich Nietzsche. In their youth, these personalities had absorbed Nietzsche's influence in different ways: They were impressed by his positive outlook on the Jews as a creative spiritual community and his well-demonstrated antinationalist attitude toward his German nationalist compatriots. Numerous German-Jewish intellectuals of stature incorporated elements of this influence into their Zionist philosophies – some leaning toward German Neo-Romanticism mixed with an interpretation of Judaism, and others leaning toward neo-Kantianism under the influence of Johann Gottlieb Fichte, the prophet of German nationalism. They also took up Hegel himself and ultimately fell prey to the influence of the most modern philosopher of all, Nietzsche.[27] The Hegelians and Kantians among them viewed the spirit as the essence; others construed the spirit as a mere product of the material, according to Marx's militantly materialistic, universalistic class definitions; and yet others saw individual will as their essential interest – the ethics that an individual derives from the attachment to his and her people and to humankind at large and from moral esthetics. The latter thinkers sought moral beauty and spiritual vitality in Judaism and wished to derive from it the spiritual strength that Nietzsche himself claimed that Jews possess, which they would adapt to their time and to the religious instinct that pulsed within them; they did not seek concrete political salvation in the conflicted reality of Palestine.[28]

The Holocaust further complicated the world of such people, the disciples and intellectual offspring of Hermann Cohen and Franz Rosenzweig, who "lived and worked within the world of Christian intellectual thought."[29] They and their spiritual successor, Emmanuel Levinas of France, learned from the Holocaust to attribute to Judaism "a dialogue character... an outlook and way of life entirely based on love, compassion, disinterested concern for the other, as an essentially ethical [and not political] philosophy... stressing the closeness of this philosophy to Christian goals and the difficulty in associating it with the Jewish ethos."[30]

Although they became decidedly practical people who were keenly aware of the need to establish economic and political entities, Ben-Gurion and those of like mind nevertheless developed ethical and intellectual expectations of the Jewish person and hoped that he could surpass himself and his daily needs for his own sake and that of the public, both Jewish and general. They conflated all of these expectations in their original, East European way, and coupled them with critical skepticism of the ability of the *jüdischer Mensch* to accomplish this unless he should think and be made to act in the Zionist revivalist spirit. After the fact, the leaders of the Zionist Labor Movement adopted a dual approach: as the generation's vanguard and as protagonists who had already won the struggle of their generation, actively translating their pretensions and values into the language of deeds. Hence, their right to challenge others to adopt their ways and glorify their actions. Thus, we need to distinguish between the self-confident canon ideology that the leaders of the movement adopted at a very early stage, claiming that the act of Zionist renaissance in Eretz Israel had already succeeded, and their criticism of their people and their incessant demands that it get up and follow the trail that they had blazed for it. Ben-Gurion gave this combination of tendencies a decisively political expression in his actions, both during the Yishuv period, when compliance was voluntary, and after the founding of the state – *mutatis mutandis* in view of the differences between the periods and the Holocaust that arose as a buffer between them.

One may argue that that this critique of the nation expressed a sort of Jew-hatred, as Yeshayahu Leibowitz claimed, or that it caused Ben-Gurion to neglect European Jewry during the Holocaust, as some post-Zionists claim in our times. This, however, is indicative of a historical misunderstanding on the part of Ben-Gurion's critics, or conscious refusal to understand Judaism and the criticism of it along a continuum that was not disrupted by the "rejection of exile" that Zionists of his type maintained. The recent past, that is, the Jews' exilic past, ceased to exist, but not because the Zionists rejected it. As Ben-Gurion wrote to Professor Nathan Rotenstreich, one of his intellectual rivals, "The recent past, unfortunately, does not exist, because the Judaism of the recent past has been destroyed. I fear that you do not fathom the full significance of this terrible fact in our history."[31]

This conflation of faith and criticism convinced Ben-Gurion that the Yishuv could indeed strive for sovereignty and survive its war for independence if the minimal preparations were made in time and despite the heavy risks involved. It prompted him to warn against its dangers and severity in surprising language for a person who seemed duty-bound to demonstrate confidence and instill it in everyone around him then and later.[32] However, this conflation could not view the establishment of statehood as the ultimate aim; rather, it strove mightily to fortify the state both without and within, not only as a political-military entity but also as a productive society, that is, one that dwells in its land and derives its livelihood from it while sharing a common past, language, and cultural treasures, foremost the Bible.[33]

This happened at a time when the task of instilling other cultural treasures – including Bialik and Ravnitzki's *Sefer ha-aggada*, a collection of legends, historical lessons derived from previous histories, and moral and political ideas culled from the Talmud, newly made available to readers such as those who populated the world of the secular Zionists – had just begun and was expected to continue in Eretz Israel and the Diaspora. The effort was cut short due to the detachment of Soviet Jewry from the rest of the world and the physical destruction of the centers of Jewish culture in the European Diaspora.[34] The revival of Jewish cultural treasures in Eretz Israel and the linkage of these treasures to egalitarian and productive life there bore no resemblance to the mystical, organic nature of a revival in which the individual sprouts from the landscape of his or her country, in the sense that nineteenth-century German nationalism was a product of the Nordic nature, taking no interest whatsoever in the social problem or the wish to make Germans self-governing citizens. Many of the German philosophers who did not subscribe to the extreme nationalism that thrust its roots among their people busied themselves with the spirit in its most abstract, most apolitical, personal, and internalized sense – a spirit that struggled for and sought a grand fundamental truth and a solution to the problems of the individual and society. However, they took no particular interest – in fact, no interest whatsoever – in the social problem, just government, and an egalitarian society. An exception in this sense, of course, was Karl Marx with his vision of violent class struggle and the utopian, postnational rule of the proletariat, and German Social Democracy with its typical hope for gradual reform. Although Marxism sank roots in the left wing of the Zionist Labor Movement as well, Ben-Gurion and his peers considered it not only historically wrong but also politically and morally unacceptable.

The quest for the most egalitarian society possible was, in contrast, a fundamental component of the Second Aliyah, which also opposed the brand of Jewish nationalism that was influenced by the decidedly nonegalitarian mystical and organic visions that had also taken root in the soil of Zionism. The leadership of the Zionist renaissance, by its own definition, recognized many political dangers – from both the Right and Left – amid Ben-Gurion's supreme effort to transform the Jews into citizens capable of establishing and maintaining a sovereign, egalitarian, productive nation.[35]

One might construe the political-ideological struggles that developed in this reality as evidence of an aspiration to power and rule for their own sake, group favoritism, jealousy, hatred, and rivalry between the exponents of the renaissance and their contemporaries and successors. In the absence of proper criteria for understanding the motives of Renaissance men like Ben-Gurion, we may regard these struggles as simple nationalism or as nationalism disguised as socialism, especially if we compare them with the exponents of the "real" Renaissance, who never put the brakes to their divisiveness and conflicts, especially during the decline of the Renaissance in the sixteenth century.

If the previous argument is correct, where did the state – the public order and the values that are important for its sustenance and destruction – figure in the philosophy of the Renaissance men themselves? Many of them dealt in the arts; the question did not occupy them. However, the Renaissance is noted for a desire to study and a quest for knowledge that far surpassed limits of study and inquiry that had been accepted as unchallengeable and inviolable. Some exponents of the Renaissance – such as da Vinci and Galileo – were already occupied with the revival of the natural sciences and showed how to research and debate physical and physiological reality. Others, including philosophers and activists who influenced posterity, such as Niccolò Machiavelli, saw the state and its regime as topics for investigation and analysis free of old religious content.

Consequently, Michelet and Burckhardt proposed another framework for analysis that will further our effort: the state as conceived during the Renaissance. This state is the fruit of human thought and deed, an "artistic creation" as opposed to an organic and ostensibly "natural" entity that existed from time immemorial, with a government dictated by tradition. It is certainly not a divine legacy. The attitude toward politics – the art of governing the state, as Machiavelli termed it – evolved in Renaissance times, according to Burckhardt and Michelet, into that of a willed decision of statesmen, subject to human reason, requiring study and inquiry so that they could rule properly. "Properly" for whom? For rulers themselves? For their subjects? What obligations and rights do rulers have? What may they do to further the interests of the "state" and the good of its subjects, and what may they not? Who determines this? The essential *problematique* of such a regime and the question of its moral foundation, absent a religious foundation, opened a chasm between Michelet and Burckhardt, who saw the shattering of this foundation as a threat to culture, order, and tradition. Even though the world that arose after this shattering was rich, wonderful, and shining in many respects, it also lacked a moral foundation and system that would guide it for the long term.

Machiavelli, in his time, could no longer accept as a historical given a religious world inhabited by ethics that had crumbled, grown moldy, and become corrupt. He first maintained that rulers must free themselves of the obsolete baggage of beliefs and opinions that have nothing to do with the creation and maintenance of a state, for these are products of a traditional society not organized as a self-aware political unit, which no longer exists as it used to. It follows that administering the affairs of a state – the action ostensibly termed "politics" or "statecraft" – is the *art of government*: the combination of force and prudence, a dimension of autonomous, central importance in the life of a political society, even when – we may add – its main occupation is social change and cultural revival.

Machiavelli himself was a conflation of contrasts: a decided republican when it came to his hometown of Florence, who called for strong, central, effective government in Italy as a whole, under the leadership of a worthy "prince." The provocative, amoral character of his prince, however, was a direct outcome of his time – a time of general insecurity in Europe, of the collapse of the international sanctions that had previously been accepted for the sake of maintaining the medieval international order, and of direct dangers that threatened the city that Machiavelli served as a diplomat, that is, dangers from within a fragmented Italy and those looming over it from the surrounding powers, especially mighty France and Spain. Experience had taught Machiavelli that the representative of a small city-state has no standing, that the power of a state is measured in force, and that force means arms.[36] Neutrality employed weakly and in halfway measures only brings ruin upon their practitioners. Pondering the dismissive attitude of France toward Florence, as if it were a *ser nihilo*, a "Mr. Nothing," he concluded, "In the modern world in which only money and arms carry weight, the small man must sometimes hit below the belt, if he wishes to survive the battle of life and death."[37] Machiavelli learned that the old readiness to negotiate, bribe, or maneuver without worthy allies, instead of fighting within the required strategic framework, was a sure recipe for disaster when it was necessary to stand against an uninhibited "prince" like Alexander VI, Cesare Borgia, or the king of France or the Holy Roman Emperor. When he left on his mission to Paris, he learned what multitalented and potent princes did with the lazy, foolish Frenchmen who seemed incorrigibly divided. Since he regarded Italy – with no idealization or self-delusion – as a single cultural-historical unit, Machiavelli believed that with proper government, it could be saved and made into a flourishing national unit without waiting futilely for divine aid and abandoning its cities to the tragedies that befell them in succession and would surely continue to befall them in the future.

Ben-Gurion, too, was a product of his time, which was divided into several subperiods. Some were times of belief in the international powers and the world order that they had created until, during, and after World War I up to the early 1930s. Then this belief was progressively undermined due to the lessons of the 1930s and the events that occurred at their end, as well as the Holocaust, as we shall see. The lesson was not one of Machiavellian theory, that is, of relationships in which arms and money were the only tools that counted in a cruel world. It did, however, have Machiavellian elements in the sense that absent power and its proper employment – that is, absent its being detached from moral content and moral hope – a Jewish state had little if any chance of surviving under the special regional and global circumstances that prevailed when it arose. Therefore, it would have to fortify itself and strike sufficiently deep roots before its enemies could recover and obliterate it, which they would do for their own good reasons. Thus, preparing the forces – including the military forces – was an inseparable part of the view of revivalist Judaism as a historical force that could not actualize its independent selfhood in any location but its own land.[38]

In principle, Judaism would have to return as a historical entity with physical might, since it had once been a doctrine of life and life cannot exist without might. However, under the circumstances of its return to history and given the baggage carried upon its return, the Jewish state would indeed have to adopt "Machiavellian" behavior on occasion, as other states do without the justification that Israel has. In Israel's case, however, a mix of actions would be needed: creating, as far as possible, an infrastructure and model for a working, law-abiding society that would serve as a model to others, serving not only itself but also people in the entire region. Concurrently, the country would need keen intellect and "artistic" judgment to know what to do and how to do it in very sensitive areas that demand suitable discipline and secrecy on the part of executive entities, including the army, and appropriate support by the administrative echelons at times of crisis. By and large, such discipline had been lacking in the Zionist past, and a model was needed that would make it possible, at least, to establish a political society that could endure in the long run.

On the topic of "art," the regime of the state is not a mere mechanical or normative thing that can be managed by laws and judges who act "in the spirit of the law" and according to abstract principles, such as "separation of powers," that had taken hold in eighteenth-century France (hundreds of years after the latter country had become a great power in the heart of Europe, had degenerated, and needed repair) – at least according to the great thinkers. Several abstract French principles influenced some of the founding fathers of the newly established United States. So what is that "spirit"? And what did Baron Montesquieu mean when he brought this concept to the world of an existing, self-perpetuating sovereign state? What was the difference between mighty France and the Jewish state that arose anew in part of its ancient land, in an even stormier, more unstable environment than that of Renaissance-era Florence?

It was a drama to fire the imagination. Governing the Jewish state, however, was not a matter for "drama" but, rather, something that demanded answers and deep thinking. Other concepts that had been developed for other needs and other specific histories, that is, that tended toward French logical abstraction and that did not necessarily have any connection with multifaceted reality, had to be rejected. In reality, one has to recognize the art of timing political decisions, the need to make changes incrementally when necessary and to act decisively when necessary. One must unceasingly study the demarches of enemies, rivals, and neutrals and understand their motives in representing their peoples and rulers. One has to understand their political reasoning and the policies forced upon them by their internal needs, public pressure, and relations between their states and others and the superpowers. From all these considerations, one must formulate Israeli responses to the external challenges at various times, which require a state to act as a state – that is, to pursue its own interests and, sometimes, to apply the controlled force that allows a government to deal with its opponents as one does in war or to prevent war from breaking out. The necessity of ruling and not allowing rule to be fragmented, to strengthen it and not to weaken it, and to protect its legitimacy carefully – the essence of the art of government as practiced by its elected officers – would be one of Israel's challenges.

When the United States was founded, these issues were central in the debate between the Federalists and the advocates of decentralized government, a debate that ended in a compromise that finally led to civil war. President Lincoln's slogan that democracy is "government of the people, for the people, and by the people" was not accepted so simply by others. The American separation of powers, which Lincoln himself ignored in many cases during the crisis of the Civil War, endangered his position and the just cause for which he fought in that crisis. This separation was not properly maintained at all during the term of the great president's successors, even though – and perhaps because – its principles were enshrined in a rigid, written constitution. In particular, this separation has not held firm in foreign affairs and defense, sometimes forcing presidents to act covertly and in contravention of constitutional principles or to engage in drawn-out battles over their authority – a debate that has led to a pendulum that forever swings between the power of "imperial presidents" and those who do nothing.

Britain applies democratic governance but has never accepted the American idea of separation of powers, as discussed previously. The essence of British democracy, as L. S. Amery put it, is government of the people, for the people, and *mediated* by the people, that is, via the people's representatives and not by the people themselves, within a framework of powers that are integrated, not separated. Ben-Gurion introduced this system to his own people as though it were a natural outgrowth of the English people. By so doing, he tried to give it full-fledged democratic legitimacy.[39]

Britain never accepted an American-style formal constitution, which would have forced its executive branch and a large portion of the other branches to hold general elections in the midst of world wars. Parliament had sufficient authority to declare war via its government, to create wall-to-wall emergency coalitions at the height of the crisis, and to extend its term until the crisis passed. The dual-authority concept in the British system indeed gave elected representatives two levels of authority: one as a mandate from the people, given to one party in its contest with the other in general elections, and one in the form of the representatives' autonomous discretion during their terms in Parliament, related to, but not depending on, constant connection with the public mood, the fashioning of which entails unending effort by the representatives themselves.

Hence, the need to be acquainted with more suitable models in order to perfect the system of government and adapt it to the needs of a society whose members freely and not so freely choose the heavy responsibility that state sovereignty imposed on the Jews, who had not borne it for millennia.[40] The resulting political system would give maximum expression to the diverse wishes of its heterogeneous society at a time when this society was becoming a true "people," but without infringing on majority rule. Still, we must distinguish between positivist, enthusiastic, flowery (by current standards) rhetoric, which was one aspect of Ben-Gurion's policy and the one regularly used in public to describe the Zionist renaissance as if it had already succeeded, and the opposite, manifested in his polemics in the Knesset, his appearances in smaller settings, and in his diary – which in demanding, challenging tones expressed misgiving about this success. An example is his recitation of Bialik's poignant poem, "I Saw You Again in Your Inadequacy," during one of his debates in the Knesset, which was fragmented and mired in its factions' short-term interests.[41]

The method at issue would allow the majority to internalize the conduct of a proper political elite. It would be flexible enough to meet the requisites of life in a complex society whose security was not assured; it would be just enough to meet the requisites of Jewish and Western principles of law and justice. However, law would not be allowed to defeat justice and the political wisdom needed to maintain the State of Israel against its sea of enemies from without and a possible ocean of differences of opinion from within.

Ben-Gurion would express this virtue of flexibility by rejecting an American-style written constitution for Israel – though this was not the only reason, as we shall learn from a separate discussion on the constitutional debate in Israel's early days. Likewise, this virtue would come into play in Ben-Gurion's public stances, in contrast to what he said in internal, closed circles. He did not hesitate to keep the truth to himself in critical matters of foreign affairs and defense when he believed that speaking out would damage public interests, even though he did not always go about this with the alacrity of a seasoned liar. He turned a blind eye to Moshe Dayan's sex life and even justified it by referring to King David's affairs, refusing to forgo the man and his talents because of his personal failings and marital misconduct.

This attitude would eventually find expression, on the one hand, in the prosecution of the Kafr Kassem massacre – when Israeli police guards murdered Arab civilians in cold blood during the 1956 campaign – and his acknowledgment of the court's right to give existing laws a normative interpretation that would become accepted principle for the future, a method of statutory interpretation that was widely accepted in British courts due to the general and quite broad character of British lawmaking, in contrast to that of the United States Congress. On the other hand, as was necessary, he displayed a famous measure of mercy in exercising his power of clemency, which had been returned to the executive branch, toward those who were sentenced for acting as they did in the absence of clear procedures and the existence of a gray area between different military organizations at the time of the 1956 War. Ben-Gurion also exhibited mercy toward the murderers of Dr. Reszö (Yisrael) Kasztner, a Labor Party executive in Nazi-occupied Hungary, who was blamed for collaboration with the Gestapo in a famous libel case initiated by the attorney general of Israel against Kasztner's political enemy, since the murder had been masterminded by political agitators who could not be indicted due to missing evidence. In contrast, he went out of his way to dismiss senior army officers for seemingly minor transgressions. In Ben-Gurion's opinion, this quality of flexibility, allowing the elected executive elite to act as it sees fit under political and historical conditions in pursuit of long-term goals, was commensurate with the British system to a reasonable degree, if an attorney general could open, or close, a case such as Kasztner's that occurred abroad years before, under the impossible conditions of the "Final Solution of the Jewish Question" in Hungary, and leave the matter to historians.

Ben-Gurion was enchanted by the status of the British Parliament, that of a supreme legislative body that can overrule all precedents and adapt sacred traditions to the needs of changing life, that does not yield to abstract principles that may infringe on the latitude of a government that stems from it and is answerable to it – and that can be replaced by a democratic process, whose replacement can be replaced, meaning that mistakes can be corrected and lessons learned from accumulated experience. It was different from the abstract – in the sense of the French – Lockean theory that took root in the American Constitution – and institutionally divided the nature of American mass democracy with its unique conditions and its decidedly individualist and capitalist tradition in due course. The far-reaching nationalization legislation of Clement Attlee and Ernest Bevin's Labour government, of all things, was the model that Ben-Gurion considered the right one to adopt. Such a thing was inconceivable in the American system. No Congress could pass laws that breached the fundamental constitutional principles that sanctify private property, especially in light of the United States Supreme Court's staunch protection of these principles.

Nevertheless, a British-style Parliament cannot act properly without a stable party structure or an election system that can ensure its creation. Absent these, it would ultimately land in the kind of morasses that the French parliaments of the Third and Fourth Republics encountered irrevocably. The basic problem concerned not only the governing institutions themselves but also the citizens' political habits, their readiness to contribute to the public good, their culture of ideological and political debate, the social networks to which they belonged and gave their main attention, and their ability to stand united in an emergency. Obviously, no reform of governmental institutions could turn Jews into Englishmen and Englishwomen. However, the existing political-party system – the profusion of parties (which Ben-Gurion considered artificial), their narrow horizons, and their activists' tendency to concern themselves with the marginal, the trivial, the incidental, and the personal – made it necessary to limit their numbers and assure the pluralization of political bodies that would be forced to work together if united through a comprehensive reform of the governmental system. To explain this whole complex more deeply, we must probe for the stages of experience and intense thinking at which Ben-Gurion came to this realization, and the extent to which he was influenced by the model of governance and the behavior of the British elite and the British public, which he knew due to his years of familiarity with this elite and his observation of the English people during Hitler's blitz.

We can only show how the British model was slowly adopted in certain respects from the War of Independence period onward. However, we may say that Ben-Gurion long understood "to what extent Jews lack the habits of political life and do not understand the content of political life." He said these words at a meeting with representatives of the Maccabi (a moderate right-wing association) Central Committee, who approached him in May 1939 at the height of the British White Paper crisis, when the British abandoned the Zionists in favor of the Arabs, with a suggestion that a "tripartite dictatorship" headed by Ben-Gurion be established to seize the reins of the voluntary Yishuv, in order to fight the British decision.[42] "It's not their fault," he continued, "since they never led political lives. On the one hand, they will demand, 'Give orders!' And on the other hand, they'll say, 'We won't obey the orders [unless the orders satisfy our wishes.' What is more,] the Jews are asking for... a drama of sorts. War [the struggle against the British, in this case] isn't waged for the sake of drama [to give vent to urges and frustrations]. War is waged for victory." This, in Ben-Gurion's opinion, was the important difference between his own approach and the habituated ways of exile. He included in this category the typical approaches of the Zionist Revisionist Right, which he considered theatrical and rhetorical – characteristic of the disconnect of the Jew who had become a nationalist – and a melodrama that imposed itself upon proper politics.

Addressing the Mapai Council in April 1939, Ben-Gurion engaged the leaders of the left flank of the Zionist Labor Movement in a debate about relations with the Arabs. He saw in the stance of the Left – no less than in that of the Right – evidence of political shallowness in studying the forces at work among the Arabs of Palestine and in the Arab world, which he attributed to dogmatism and refusal to look reality in the eye.

One of the necessary means for the advancement of Zionist interests was a dose of power – "Macht," as it is called in the jargon of political science, that is, a combination of moral and physical strength. Therefore, "[p]ower is not power if no one knows that it exists, if we lack the talent, the knowledge, the will, and the ability to use it wisely and for a cause, and not out of rage or hatred. Even toward the Mufti [the pro-Nazi Palestinian leader Hajj Amin al Husseini, former Mufti of Jerusalem], I calculate... how to act against him but my calculus does not include hatred. When I wish to consider a political matter, I am a calculating machine."[43]

The Marxist Left, in contrast, was anything but a "calculating machine" that coldly contemplated reality. Instead, in Ben-Gurion's eyes, it was a victim of "analytic" doctrines, of beliefs, opinions, and hopes that it developed without sufficiently independent thought, free of prejudice and "scientific" approaches. These matters took on a political complexion and were debated by political parties such as Ha-Shomer ha-Tsa'ir and Po'alei Zion Left, and even in "Faction B" (*Si'a Bet*) of Mapai itself.

The Humanists

Several submodels in Burckhardt's model may help us to understand the Zionist renaissance. One of them is his treatment of the humanists. This phenomenon – the ascent in status of intellectuals, scholars, and teachers, who began to appear in the courts of Renaissance leaders and became fashioners of the Zeitgeist – seems entirely salutary at first glace; it lends the height of the Renaissance its depth, content, and flavor. Burckhardt, however, also discusses the decline of the humanists in the sixteenth century, sketching a framework that helps us to understand the processes that influenced the Jewish people, the reality in which Ben-Gurion and his contemporaries worked, their difficulties and the great stresses among them, and the pointed criticism that they faced in their time and in ours.

According to Burckhardt, criticism of the humanists was first voiced by the humanists themselves: "There was never before a type of person of status who knew so little as they of the cooperative feeling toward their class... and as soon as they began to supersede each other, all means became legitimate in their eyes. At lightening speed, they moved from scientific arguments to provocations and the basest abuse; their desire was not to disprove their opponents' ideas, but utterly to crush them."[44] Many Zionist personalities and Jewish leaders in general were graced with this trait, although during the initial pioneering period they tried to mask it, accepting the leadership of Berl Katznelson, David Ben-Gurion, and Yitzhak Tabenkin, each in his field, and challenging it only on ideological and party grounds and not for personal reasons.

If we contemplate this group – which Katznelson left in 1944 (when he died in his midfifties) and to which secondary leaders were annexed, such as Moshe Shertok (Sharett), Pinchas Lavon, Golda Meir, and Levi Eshkol – and other members of the lesser branches of the Labor Movement, intellectuals and men of letters close to it, and independents, political opponents notwithstanding, then in fact many of them struggled, fought with, and sought to crush one another when the other got the better of them. They created coalitions among themselves and under various circumstances cooperated with one another; however, they harbored many mutual enmities that seriously overshadowed the political process. And if they did not literally crush each other, even within the many streams of the Labor Movement they got along only during the intermittent periods. Sometimes they made temporary compromises that were unsustainable over time due to the severity of the decisions that had to bc made; sometimes they immobilized each other.

Thus, one of the keys to understanding Ben-Gurion's actions as a statesman is his awareness of this Jewish trait and his ways of surmounting it – ways that during the voluntary Yishuv period were often tactical and entailed immense patience. When immediate strategic decisions were needed, he made them to the best of his understanding and brought them about by using the democratic mechanisms that were customary in the Yishuv. Such were the key elections in 1944, which Ben-Gurion imposed on his divided party by rallying unaffiliated voters and entities like Ha-Oved ha-Dati and Ha-Oved ha-Tsiyyoni (Labor-affiliated national-religious and liberal parties) in elections for the Histadrut (General Federation of Labor) convention and the Asefat ha-Nivharim (the Assembly of Electees, the Yishuv's "parliament").[45]

In the Asefat ha-Nivharim elections, the representative body of the Yishuv, Mapai, Ben-Gurion's party, came away with the key prize, the status of the largest party. Although its plurality was no greater than 37 percent, it held a pivotal position, since without Mapai, the other parties, divided among themselves, could not build a ruling coalition. Ben-Gurion made the most of this by arguing topically and appealing to his listeners' capacity for reason in order to undermine the ideas of the pro-Soviet leftist leaders who wished to keep Palestine undivided and hand it over to an "international" (Soviet–American) mandate. One of his arguments was that the millions of Jews for whom the struggle for control of all of Palestine should have been prosecuted no longer existed. However, he learned repeatedly that others were unlikely to accept these arguments at face value. Instead, they would surely demand "scientific" justifications from this or that "scholarly" school about which they had read, such as the Marxist one, or would make do with vituperation and crude verbal abuse from other sources.[46] Ben-Gurion discovered this when he expressly sought a senior position in the decision-making apparatus of the Zionist Movement and the Yishuv, convinced that his abilities and talents were superior to those of others, for the purpose of constantly studying the factual situation and making decisions accordingly.[47] This senior post was not attained easily, and its achievement – the policy that was eventually established – was greatly assisted by maneuvers among the various factions at the Zionist Congress: Ben-Gurion the activist, fighting for immediate Jewish statehood, was aided by the dovish Ha-Shomer ha-Tsa'ir movement, which backed the idea of a binational Jewish–Arab state at the time – by virtue of this faction's dispute with his rival, Chaim Weizmann.[48]

Criticism of Ben-Gurion, on the Left as much as on the Right, however, was much more common then than it seems to us today.[49] The subsequent transition period, which paved the way to the War of Independence and statehood, was ostensibly a grace period, a time when one elected leader dominated and defined a generation. Ben-Gurion earned this grace period by the success of his earlier controversial assessments and demarches, including his decision to favor mass immigration. At the time, however, Ben-Gurion had very bitter enemies, including several leaders of the War of Independence generation and erstwhile members of the nationalist-leftist Faction B of his own Mapai Party and the Marxist Ha-Shomer ha-Tsa'ir, who formed their own political party, Mapam, in January 1948. At the end of the war, many members of Mapam – particularly army men – viewed him as the man who had deprived them of the fruits of their victory and had positioned Mapai and its activists as their overlords. Moreover, much of the intelligentsia of the time – writers, poets, potential and active intellectuals, educators, youth-movement counselors – were alumni of Mapam's parties or aligned themselves closely with Mapam and subjected Ben-Gurion to genuine hatred and severe criticism. Manifestations of this criticism were evident in public and artistic endeavors and current-affairs publications and studies by members of that generation and those raised in their midst. Among the public at large, however, Ben-Gurion had become an object of adulation. He tried to take maximum advantage of this to effect change, improve the functioning of government institutions, and transfer power from Yishuv bodies to institutions of the egalitarian, pioneering, fledgling state. It has been argued that the decline of these values as early as the beginning of the 1950s led Ben-Gurion to attempt to revive them by setting the personal example of retiring to Kibbutz Sede Boqer in the Negev desert in 1953.

I would say that Ben-Gurion's retirement was precipitated not only by the difficulties in putting socialism into practice but also by his refusal to accept as a constant the predisposition among the country's political bodies to regress to the Yishuv era, when things were accomplished via elaborate compromising and negotiations. Not only did Ben-Gurion dismiss the principled need for this method after the establishment of the state – that is, from the moment the burden of Jewish self-rule and sovereignty was accepted as a basic tenet of the Zionist renaissance – but he also saw it as an obstacle to Israel's progress in doubling and tripling its population and sustaining itself against an Arab siege.[50] Later on – during his retirement in Sede Boqer, thanks to his prestige and the special status of critic attained by his no longer heading a serving government – Ben-Gurion launched a campaign for comprehensive political reform and the adoption of the main facets of the British governmental system. This move, however, was cut short when he returned from Sede Boqer amid a security crisis to act within the existing political system.

Afterwards, the launching of the Suez-Sinai Campaign known as Operation Kadesh in 1956 gave Ben-Gurion another grace period, or so it seemed. At this time, he worked to justify and consolidate a conflation of Jewish cultural and traditional values and non-Jewish principles of philosophy and government, to be integrated as a "spirit of Israel" that would underlie Israel's independence and its challenge to Diaspora Jewry. This combination, which had a secular messianic element and defined Judaism as a "religion of justice," requires broader discussion, which we will provide. Here, we only note that it aroused the opposition of many intellectuals, including those who wrestled with fundamental questions of ideology and government at the time – after Operation Kadesh, after Ben-Gurion's subsequent decision to base Israel's security on nuclear weapons, and after the Eichmann trial, a major event in Israeli history pertaining to the Holocaust, when the opportunity arose to contemplate retrospectively the great totalitarian regimes of the twentieth century. Hannah Arendt and other intellectuals defined these regimes as disseminators of various forms of "secular religion" or "secular messianism," and some, following Sir Karl Popper, identified Plato as the father of this defilement.

This period ended with the volcanic eruption of the Lavon Affair, which even Ben-Gurion could not dodge. Others' struggles with "the Affair" were clearly related to practical matters, the advancement and defense of party and personal interests, and exploration of methods of government – all of which were subsumed into, and conflated with, intellectual-cultural criticism of Ben-Gurion, which crescendoed into a storm of public protest against him and became part and parcel of overt and covert debate about other issues. One such issue was Israel–German relations, which became the topic of an unvarnished dispute between Ben-Gurion and rivals to his left and right. Indeed, on this issue and in regard to the construction of the nuclear reactor in Dimona, not far from Beersheba in the Negev desert, which became a matter of debate and secret controversies, his rivals of all stripes finally found a common language. This combination of internal adversaries (led by former allies, such as Pinchas

Lavon and Moshe Sharett) and rivals from the Left and the Right created a political morass that disrupted, and perhaps even permanently paralyzed, Ben-Gurion's ability to act.

Burckhardt attempted to explain the "guilt" of such former partners and, perhaps, to soften the severity of the judgment against them. First of all, he said, their education was at fault. That is, they had received the education of young people in whom unusual talent had been found, leading them to think that they were above ordinary mundane matters, "graced from birth with noble character of thought." In Berl Katznelson's Hebrew, one may translate this as "a shining mind in a dark soul,"[51] an expression that Katznelson used to characterize Pinchas Lavon's problematic character. It is very likely that such an education gave its possessors – particularly if they held an appropriate traditional "pedigree" – an enormous ego that blemished their character with "indifference to all accepted ethical traits. . . . Such types cannot be found without a measure of arrogance" that originates in a combination of talent and education.

This matter of education in traditional East European Jewish societies even after the decline of tradition – its influence on the gifted among them and its damage to the less gifted – was no simple matter and has not been sufficiently studied. The influences of the Jewish family, relations between parents and between parents and children in the shaping of the latter – including the severe physical and emotional punishment that was accepted in those days – have not been examined properly. The influence of educational institutions – the family, the traditional *cheder*, that is the traditional Torah school of learning, the "improved" cheder, and so forth – on youngsters at the times of crisis and change discussed here is not clear. In this field, stereotypes and important and grotesque literary works, from Bialik's autobiography *Safiah* to the writings of Philip Roth and the Israeli playwright Hanoch Levin, are known to Hebrew and not a few English readers. They constitute a primer, as it were, on the study of the Jewish father and mother who, for better or worse, were the prime movers behind a child's inflated yet insecure and aggressive ego.

Obviously, it is necessary to probe all of these influences during the period in which the traditional communities began to disintegrate or were in advanced stages of disintegration. Traditional virtues that might have restrained these characteristics or channeled them in traditional directions were confounded by the human stress that typified these traditional communities, influenced by the non-Jewish literature and philosophy that followed. We see this in the literature and in the behavior of those gifted youth who rebelled against the age-old ways and became active Zionists in typical Jewish social settings.[52] The social networks at issue were created by the breakup of traditional societies, replacing them; these networks explain the public discourse in which their members were engaged. It must be said here that Ben-Gurion was not a member of any "social network" for long; indeed, he sought to surpass them.

Ben-Gurion may have had a rather "brilliant mind" in the eyes of the more gifted members of the successor generation of *Maskilim*, that is, Jews who had been exposed to non-Jewish literary and scholarly inputs. Those who still attended *yeshivot*, the traditional institutions of higher learning, and alumni who remained loyal to the yeshivot and to at least some of their traditions, however, had a different view. Traditional education and the rules of behavior that stemmed from it apparently remained the true test. Thus, such a traditional Jew once virulently reproved Sholom Aleichem when he saw the great author playing cards and smoking on the Sabbath. Perhaps the combination of this traditional education and systematic general schooling was at issue. As Shlomo Tzemach, the son of a prominent family and writer of some distinction, and one of the Zionist pioneers who emigrated to Palestine ahead of Ben-Gurion from the same Polish town, mockingly said of him: He, the son of Avigdor Green, the half-educated upstart from Goat Street in Plonsk, lacked both.

We shall return to this matter as well, for Ben-Gurion collected and devoured history and philosophy books in huge numbers and was sensitive to his lack of formal schooling, not only because he felt its absence but also because he considered it a trap and a source of dogmatic thinking of both the leftist and the rightist kinds. He respected erudite persons who escaped the trap of dogmatism, such as Tzemach, but also saw in Tzemach's words a hatred and jealousy dressed in moralistic language, for which reason he distanced himself from him. As the poet Uri Zvi Greenberg said at the outset of the Lavon Affair, "Jews love to destroy each other with moral arguments." Tzemach often behaved like a sixteenth-century Italian humanist in his attitudes not only toward Ben-Gurion but also toward the Nobel laureate S. Y. Agnon, the Hebrew poet Avraham Shlonsky, and others who had surpassed him in accomplishments and, a fortiori, in fame.

One of the great difficulties in studying this behavior originates in the differences among Jewish communities and the conditions that they exhibited, even though they shared a certain family structure and the customary educational principles of the late nineteenth and early twentieth centuries. The generation gap and its influence on nineteenth-century Jewry is expressed in the memoirs of Abba Achimeir (Abba Shaul Geisinovich – a unique figure on the Zionist Right, who, alongside Uri Tzvi Greenberg, led the radical wing of the Zionist Revisionist Movement, a wing that Ben-Gurion and Berl Katznelson fought with all their might).[53] Achimeir came from Bobruisk, Belarus, a tranquil Jewish community, firmly positioned in the Russian empire and free of Ukrainian and "Greater Russian" antisemitism. His literary schooling was both Jewish and secular, and his writing exudes a mixture of the Bible, Maimonides, the rabbinical authority known as the Malbim (Meir Leibush b. Jehiel Michel Weiser), the early modern Hebrew writers Judah Leib Gordon and Peretz Smolenskin, Micha Yosef Berdyczewski, the poet Bialik, the writers Uri Nisan Gnessin and Yosef Chaim Brenner, the language of the Talmud, and the influence of "the splendid Russian culture" from Pushkin and Lermontov to Alexander Blok, as well as echoes of classic Greek literature, Mickiewicz's letters, Ibsen, and the ultra-conservative French thinker Joseph de Maistre. Achimeir's writings evince the quality that Israeli historian Pinchas Ginosar called "acute contemplation" of the Jewish reality whence he came, for example, his characterization of the Jewish "philanthropists" of Bobruisk, who were divided into anti-Hasidic "Patricks" and Hasidic "Plebs." Very important is Achimeir's essay "Shelosha dorot [Three generations]," in which he contrasts the grandparents' generations, whose ideal in life is honor or, rather, traditional status as the learned elite (cf. the guests in Bialik's "Aryeh ba'al guf [Big-Bodied Aryeh]"; the parents' generation, which aspires only to riches (Arye himself); and those of the third generation (Achimeir's), who dream of a "Napoleonic career," which is egoistic and also "walks hand in hand in our fantasies with a career that is global in scale yet humanistic."

Where did this Napoleonism come from? The young Ben-Gurion also entertained this kind of self-image; it reflects the heroic way of thinking that typifies a period of historic revival that young people view as a personal, national, and global platform spread out at their feet, waiting, as it were, for them to conquer it by storm. In Achimeir's case, however, it seemed that a strict upbringing and personal talents sought an outlet in dreams of personal grandeur and frenetic national and nationalist political activity. Indeed, after having been involved but failing to find his place in the Zionist Labor Movement, this "Napoleon" lurched to a position that verged on Fascism. Eventually, through various periods, Achimeir became a sharp, coarse, and combative "literatus" who spent his life on the edge, half-persecuted and half-tolerated in Israel.

Burckhardt's other explanations for the decline of the humanists relate to our issues only incidentally, due to the different reality with which he dealt: the extreme self-indulgence that they displayed when success shone upon them; the existential insecurity of their external lives, in which abundance and poverty so easily alternated in accordance with the fickle desires of their masters and the villainy of their opponents; and lastly – more topical for us – the misleading influence of the ancient world. "This world damaged their morals – without granting them any measure of its own ethics," Burckhardt commented. For our purposes, the problem at hand involved the transfer of traditional Jewish ethics to the needs of a Jewish state, with recourse to classic cultural models and nontraditional ones that arguably failed to equip several among their owners with a new and sufficiently valid ethic.[54]

In other words, secular Zionism aroused debate in any case, both internally and within Jewry in general, as to its moral foundation and the ethical-political development of secular Jewish society in Eretz Israel, even though many Zionists in those days saw this as no issue at all. Renaissance, after all, is a state of mind that allows people to use history and cultural values of assorted provenances more or less as they please. However, a consensus on underlying principles, including the basis and authority of secular morality and its application in the life of a Jewish state, with its changing boundaries and its internal and external challenges, would not hold sway among them and their successors for long. Ben-Gurion was particularly sensitive to this issue, despite the image generally held of him today as a man interested only in rule for its own sake and in sustaining the power of the party that he and others had created.

To seek a basis for secular morality for a democratic state whose members are loyal to religious principles or to a mixture of influences from different directions, Ben-Gurion turned to the study of Greek culture.[55] This was not study for its own sake; instead, it was an attempt to understand how the Greeks turned the problems of governing society into a subject for intellectual inquiry that was completely detached from their religion and how they learned practical lessons from their ultimately unsuccessful attempts at self-rule. Ben-Gurion needed to make this rational inquiry in order to become an authority in this area, the mentor of his generation, no longer a "tanner," that is, one immersed in "dirty work," a practical man among his contemporaries. In his debates and polemics in the Knesset, he made use, with varying success, of the knowledge that he acquired in this field and his readings and observations in regard to government and systems of government – until the early 1960s, when his involvement with Plato itself became a stumbling block, for reasons that we will explain.

Still, Ben-Gurion refused to leave the bounds of Judaism, as if this limitation were self-evident. In fact, he saw material in Judaism that could be interpreted and adapted to the lifestyle of a secular Jewish society that was returning, as far as possible, to its Biblical origins and its land. Obviously, it would not be a return in the simplistic sense, that is, to the past of thousands of years before. Equally, it would not involve integration into the expanse that predated the Arab conquest and would not demand dissociation from the Jewish people, for cultural-political reasons of mystical-Fascist complexion, such as Canaanism, that is, Zionist nativism seeking to terminate all ties between Israelis and Jews abroad, and contemptuous dismissal of the lessons of other cultures. Jewish philosophers had also acknowledged Plato and Aristotle, in their time. Plato, they believed, had learned from Judaism to connect the striving for good with the striving for *imitatio Dei*. Ben-Gurion recognized this element in medieval Jewish religious thinking but postulated that this idea had remained essentially theocratic.

Later, he studied the "great revolutions of our times," the French and the Bolshevik, both of which demanded that the Jews "eradicate their national identity" and almost managed to accomplish this until "this most ancient of peoples ... could not withstand the tide of the nineteenth century, instead submitting and committing heresy against its essence and lowering itself to the level of a religious sect whose parts tried to fit into the body of other peoples." Still, the Jews' "historic will" overcame all this as well: "Jewry largely shed its theocratic form and donned a secular form, but its attachment to its ancient historical roots and homeland grew, its ancient national language awakened itself and created a secular Hebrew literature, and the Hibbat Zion movement [early Zionist activities] and Zionism arose."[56]

Ben-Gurion knew, of course, that secular Zionism was rooted in religion and religious culture, but he saw as insufficient the "historic will" of a people that had been so badly depleted by other options, such as Communism, Bundism, and other outlets, and then by the Holocaust. The necessity of lending religious and cultural values nontraditional interpretations, he believed, was many times greater: The essence of Judaism lies in the ethical content that it had earned and conferred to others. In the absence of political-moral content to guide Jewish internal life, the damage to the nation would be irreparable, both due to its moral pretensions of the past and because morality necessitates a just society and a worthy system of governance. Therefore, Ben-Gurion's secular interpretation of religious and traditional values took on a socialist-nationalist-universalistic slant. He insisted that Judaism was broad enough to sustain such an interpretation and that no one held a monopoly on any particular interpretation. Still, his sense of reality and his desire to prevent an irreparable rift within the diverse society that did not agree on these issues dictated a compromise with all religious bodies in Israel.[57]

Still, the image of a ruthless, power-thirsty politician, devoid of public ethics, became attached to Ben-Gurion during his State of Israel period. It was regularly expressed by members of radical circles, leftists, German-born or German-educated intellectuals such as Martin Buber, and Orthodox politicians and thinkers such as Yeshayahu Leibowitz.[58] Eventually, this image justified the revival of traditional morality in its various forms and its attack on the exponents of the Zionist renaissance for being amoral and vacuous, as had happened to the humanists, who had been called heretics in their time. Likewise, Zionism came under renewed attack for having harmed universal values, humanism, and the individual Jew, who is entitled to develop him- or herself anywhere and not only within the confines of a narrow national-state that had arisen at the expense of the Arabs in Palestine and would not last long against the rage of the region's dominant majority.[59]

Ben-Gurion gave thought to this issue in his own fashion: the establishment and physical securing of the state and struggle over its form of government. He prosecuted this struggle in the following stages: a campaign to change the system from the ground up, then an attempt to change it partly, and finally an attempt to fill the state with secular Jewish content beyond his occupation with what he called "tanning," that is, sheer politicking. These issues conflated uniquely with the question of where the Israel Defense Forces figured in all these realms, a matter that entails study and expansion. First, however, we must study a large number of background issues. Only then can we flesh out the picture.

The Influence of Berdyczewski and Heinrich Heine – Reality and Allegory

Ben-Gurion's contemporaries were raised under various cultural influences. Some were educated in traditional *chadarim* and yeshivot with all their stringencies, and only at a later stage – with no small indecision among the alternatives – made their way to Zionism and sought with all their might to anchor it permanently in culture and history.[60] Others, striving to fashion a Zionist socialism, combined influences that originated in developments within Judaism in their own time and somewhat earlier, for example, Yisrael Salanter's Mussar movement, which itself had been fed from different streams, including Benjamin Franklin ("What did I do on the day that I was allowed to live properly?" in Salanter's words)[61] and the surrounding Russian culture. This Russian culture was itself influenced by other cultures, including the contribution of German idealistic philosophy to the revolutionary movement in Czarist Russia.[62] Others pursued their inquiries with the help of Marx.

One of the key figures that influenced Ben-Gurion and his contemporaries was Micha Josef Berdyczewski. In his critique of Judaism, Berdyczewski was torn between negation of the "Judaism of the Book," the Judaism of "submission and humility," and his dependence on and love for it, a seemingly unsolvable dilemma. But like Friedrich Nietzsche, his master and teacher, and Nietzsche's predecessor Arthur Schopenhauer, Berdyczewski, more than any other intellectual, viewed himself above all as a "poet and a human being," as he called himself in his diary when explaining his complex relationship with Nietzsche. These ties caused him to speak of a "total transformation of values," an *Umwertung aller Werte*, a basic concept in Nietzschean philosophy, which he regarded as a problem of political culture that demanded the use of feelings and urges and not only of Reason, that sole mainstay of the eighteenth century:[63]

Together with the new form that we intend to give the Jewish People, it must also be given a new meaning. There is a need for a secular culture and general human values in lieu of religious values. When the Jews return to Canaan to live the life of a people on their land, they must again grasp the ancient historic strand that the prophets cut off with their moralism. We need a political and spiritual revival: a revival as a people, but as a Hellenistic people. Religious and purely intellectual Judaism stripped the people of its political strength and rendered it helpless by depriving it of the necessary qualities for its existence. . . . I have reached the realization that you can build this structure only on purely secular foundations, pagan, as it were.

Thus, the Greece of Berdyczewski, who borrowed it from his predecessors Nietzsche and Heine, was a culture that connected man with nature and immediately reinvigorated him as a being of feeling and reason. Berdyczewski's emphasis at this stage, as noted, focused on the demand for a change in values en route to the revival of the Jewish people's "political strength." Still, he did not dissociate himself from the people and its values; he continued to study them intensively and wrestle with them all his life. His points of reference in doing so, however, were the great thinkers whom he had encountered on his way and the Zeitgeist, from which Freud and his psychological pessimism stemmed and that caused an awareness, in great fright, of what Nietzsche had already marked and what Freud named the subconscious. These were the key points in Berdyczewski's later development, when he lost his connection to his Zionist disciples in Eretz Israel due to World War I and its European ramifications. His later development also had its ups and downs in his attitude toward Diaspora Jewry, prophecy, and Hasidism.[64]

However, as we have argued, the attitude of the Second Aliyah leadership toward its people, notwithstanding Berdyczewski's great influence, was not as unequivocally negative as it seems today. Manifestations of affinity for the ideas that he preached to them in their young years (which were connected with Nietzsche's ideas, of which they knew little) were such that these people, who had donned a cloak of intellectuality thanks to Berdyczewski and others, were driven to take actions that were rooted in the individual will – actions that rejected tradition and were seemingly detached from history, for the purpose of reviving the Jewish people of history as an active agent driven by both emotion and reason. Berdyczewski himself merely observed reality and analyzed it. He constantly wrestled with the import of the Jewish past and the philosophical currents of his time, occasionally returning to Schopenhauer's pessimism, which he linked with Freud's.

Still, Nietzsche's philosophy, which projected a willful activism on its young readers during its early formative period, and to which Berdyczewski remained bound, was a necessary adjunct, so to speak, for anyone who at that time sought a tool for the critiquing of tradition and a means to be liberated from it, other than the means devised by the eighteenth century or the Romanticism of the first half of the nineteenth. Eighteenth-century thinking, after all, was largely universalistic, rationalist, mechanistic, and simplistic. The Romanticism of the first half of the nineteenth century was a reaction to the eighteenth century and, to a great extent, a desperate nostalgia for the medieval past. In many instances, it culminated in a return to the embrace of the Catholic Church, to the great fury of Heinrich Heine, one of Nietzsche's spiritual fathers (to whom we shall return). Under Nietzsche's influence, important criticism of both schools – simplistic rationalism and simplistic Romanticism – was expressed. His influence also included criticism of the integration of radical materialism with the philosophy of Georg Wilhelm Friedrich Hegel, Heine's teacher – the idealistic quest for Zeitgeist that emerges from history by way of dialectics, which surely enchanted those who combed history for the forces that determine reality. Such materialism evolved in far-left thinking from the eighteenth century onward and would eventually be annexed to a new sort of collectivism, that of the international proletariat.

In the second half of the nineteenth century, nationalism in all its permutations was making waves in every part of Central and Eastern Europe, and secular nationalism, which was considered a revival movement in political culture, began to raise its head among the Jews as well. Under the specific circumstances of Central and Eastern Europe, the Enlightenment movement among European Jews, known as the Haskala, took root among them but could not offer a unified solution to their special problems. The Jews at issue here – after all, many others had assimilated, spoken of local Jewish autonomy, or sought a solution away from Europe in Britain and America – are those whose cultural, intellectual, socioeconomic, or political problems remained unsolved despite the Haskala and even the formal political emancipation that Germany, for example, gave them. They were Jews who identified with the anticipated social revolution, which would stress the proletariat, that is, the international proletariat and that of the peoples amid whom they lived. Those who refused to accept this option, for example, the leaders of the Second Aliyah, adopted a synthesis of values and arguments that were historically and contextually different from each other and could be combined at the existential-intellectual level into a package widely understood only in a "renaissance era" of this unique kind – as Berdyczewski himself, and as Bialik and his associates, called it – that Eastern European Jewry was experiencing at this time.

Thinkers such as Katznelson and Ben-Gurion, who did not view history as a literal Hegelian system and did not identify with Marx's vision – which left no room for nations generally and for Jewry particularly – considered human will (the individual will and their own) a major tool of sorts for the engendering of change in their society, which, they thought, was mired in a grave historical-cultural-political crisis. In their eyes, history, the vessel of tradition and the medium of Marxist dialectics, had to be given an atraditional interpretation. Moreover, they had to free themselves of dependency on history (without forfeiting history altogether) and move from history to will: the will of individuals acting in the present, individuals motivated by passion, obligation, and a sense of emergency, forward-looking individuals who simultaneously sought to be free of history, to act within it, and to bend it to their needs. At the same time, the use of the Nietzschean term *transformation of all values*, which Berdyczewski had adopted, was not purely Nietzschean to the minds of the Second Aliyah thinkers. After all, even the most forgiving interpretation that one could apply to Nietzsche's own "change of values" aroused great skepticism in regard to his concept of justice – an aristocratic, haughty, antidemocratic justice that delights in experiments that verge on the criminal.[65]

Ben-Gurion perceived the justice of the prophets, against which Berdyczewski sometimes virulently railed, as Judaism's special quality and contribution to humanity. The Zionist leaders at issue in our discussion did not adopt Nietzsche's morality wholesale; they frowned in particular on his distinction between supreme *Übermenschen* and various inferior types and on his loathing of democracy. Certain later thinkers on the Zionist Right, such as Dr. Yisrael Eldad (Scheib), gave these and other components of Nietzsche's philosophy – especially the creative will that holds the key to true power, combined with Russian *narodnik* Romanticism – an extreme right-wing interpretation. This, however, should not be taken to mean that Berdyczewski's influence, with its Nietzschean connection, did not play an important role in the stages of building the personalities and identities of social-democratic leaders such as Ben-Gurion.

Berdyczewski claimed the right to challenge Jewish life on a grand scale and to treat Jewish history with unswerving ruthlessness. In so doing, he embodied the special character of the few and their private, unique world, which was closed to the masses. Berdyczewski's work justified the predisposition of someone who read his works and heard his speeches to individuality and to the following of a path that tended ab initio to chart its own course as against

Jewish collectivism or, as Berdyczewski put it, "Diaspora collectivism." This begins to explain why people such as Katznelson and Ben-Gurion built grand structures, sought a connection to the masses, and spoke in their name, yet remained above the people and behaved in ways that appear through today's lenses as condescending, introverted, and authoritarian.[66]

Until then, the individual had been a derivative, or an enemy, of the traditional Jewish collectivity. Absent a connection to the collectivity and its source of authority and vitality – tradition – the individual seemingly had no place within it; his only option was to divorce himself from the collective altogether. The new relationship between the individual, who stands on his own authority and chooses his future via his own free will, and the Jewish community, whose traditional way of life the revolutionary individual wished to change, needed an intellectual as well as an emotional foundation that would allow the two to commingle legitimately. In his debates with extreme Marxists, Ben-Gurion never denied – indeed, he stressed – the emotional foundation of his Zionism[67] and saw no contradiction between this foundation and the intellectual one. After all, the intellectual foundation, which he appropriated from Berdyczewski, contained emotional elements related to the autonomy of the will.

The will played a role for the young Ben-Gurion – his later actions attest to this at length – that found picturesque metaphorical expression in youthful writings about Herzl that bear the stamp of the Renaissance spirit, a spirit of emancipation and primacy of man in the universe. They may even bear a German philosophical influence of the provocative, optimistic, Nietzschean kind, which speaks of Übermenschen with hope and faith, in contrast to the Nirvana-seeking and art-worshipping pessimism that verges on Buddhism and other Indian philosophies, á la Schopenhauer. Nietzsche was rooted in Western philosophy with its Greek origins and its revival in the Renaissance, a philosophy centered on Man, not on his dissolution into a Nirvana that denies – if only he is privileged to attain it – his selfhood. However, he studied exceptional individuals who were able to rise from the abyss of the conventional, the common, the historical, the comfortable, and the easy thanks to their true "will for power" – the will to bring about the full development of their potential. It is the strength of these people's wills that makes them Übermenschen, superior to simple mortals (Nietzsche's ideal was Goethe, who combined sensuality and spirituality into a perfect whole) and akin to demigods, who alone have the capacity to make such an ascent.

This image of the emancipated man who rules himself and the world around him, striving to do good and seek beauty while rejecting the exaggerated spirituality of the Jew, was common in the nineteenth-century literature that Jews read. It also appeared – along with its antipode – in the prose and poetry of Heinrich Heine, who influenced both Nietzsche and Berdyczewski. In Nietzsche's eyes, however, the will for power was the human being's most important motivating force, one that exceptional individuals could refine and invest with exalted moral meaning. On these grounds he challenged existing morality and religion, which he considered tools for weaklings who inhabit a reality that has no objective meaning. These exceptional individuals, who fight the power of the collective, the masses, and those who use conventional morality to dominate them – that is, to rule them by means of the accepted interpretation of the past, aided by tradition – indeed suffer, but do so from a position of true strength, powered by noble solitude and the reversal of conventional values. This terminology would help the individual to break the shackles of convention and tradition and acquire a "noble" character, a moral character true to his solitude and his distinction from the traditional or assimilating environment of his time. Alternately, it would challenge him to do what others profess but never carry out.

Contrary to Romanticism, the outcome at issue is not one of inescapable suffering and nostalgia for a futureless past. Neither is it a Schopenhauerian pessimism sweetened by the ability of the few to reach Nirvana or to be liberated from selfish wish by the artistic abilities that they possess. Nietzsche's philosophy contains an assurance of the future and a political potential – which did not interest him personally but which, by nature, could be combined with other elements to provide philosophical inspiration for political action in the "National Era" – not only for the Right alone, a potential that better fit the spirit of his ideas, but also for the moderate Left. In the young Ben-Gurion, who had not yet become a Socialist, we can discern a language of the politically heroic that may be attributed to a Neo-Romantic nationalist trend of thought that lacks any kind of deep philosophical understructure, a language centered on the self and its free will combined with a nonreligious, anti-Diasporic mind-set.[68]

All the same, the teenage Ben-Gurion's rhetoric could not help but have been influenced by Berdyczewski's polemics against traditional Judaism, the assimilating masses, and the *fin de siècle* "drifters," after he had acquired a reputation as a critic and publicist back in the 1890s, when the leaders of the Second Aliyah were still children. This rhetoric of Ben-Gurion's expresses what Yosef Chaim Brenner – Berdyczewski's friend and great disciple – called Berdyczewski: "a trailblazer for the individual who is emancipated from the yoke of the Jewish collective."[69]

Katznelson appreciated Ben-Gurion from this standpoint, for he said and did what it took to leave the old collective and create a new one that, he believed, could be grafted atop Jewish traditional and cultural roots that are "deep, transcendental elements that pass from generation to generation" in the Jewish people.[70] The two leaders were mutually complementary in their time. Katznelson was undoubtedly more "traditional" than Ben-Gurion and more sensitive to religious matters – at least in terms of their symbolic place and their cultural significance. Ben-Gurion was more sensitive to matters of statecraft, policy, governance, and the public-ethical justification for acts of governance. Both were equally sensitive to the creation of public authority and its preservation within the confines of their party. Katznelson's sensitivity to matters of the spirit also induced him to fight ideological enemies so furiously as to censor and gag them insofar as his control of the Labor Movement daily *Davar* allowed.

Katznelson died in 1944. Some view the Holocaust as the end of his world, for it destroyed all the vessels that could contain those "transcendental elements that pass from generation to generation" in Judaism. One doubts that Ben-Gurion, who by then had become a statesman who thought in cultural and historical terms, could have believed in such "transcendental foundations." Surely he viewed the "nation" and the people as a real, concrete given, divided into countries of origin and streams, raised under different systems, and bearing different values, which had to cope with the consequences of the Holocaust without breaking down or succumbing. For this reason, the Holocaust forces us to undertake a specific and separate analysis of its development and consequences.

Ben-Gurion, the quintessential statesman, did not believe in gagging people; he preferred to debate his opponents – and in the present context, he continued even after the founding of the state to rail against "Zionists" who spoke about, donated to, or prayed for Israel but did not immigrate, a polemic somewhat reminiscent of Berdyczewski's tirade against Zionism at large. In Berdyczewski and his influence one may definitely seek the roots of Ben-Gurion's eventual interest in Greece.[71]

The leaders of the Second Aliyah set themselves to the very act of which Berdyczewski himself, like his colleague and disciple Brenner, doubted the Jews capable. Berdyczewski may have clung to his conviction due to philosophical-psychological doubts over the nature of the will, his renewed realization of the importance of religion, and various other matters that influenced him at the time, which also led him to identify completely with imperial Germany in World War I.[72]

In his earlier incarnations, Berdyczewski blamed the Jews themselves for their destruction, and in his youth he certainly urged them to stanch the downslide by thoroughly changing their way of life and escaping the Diaspora. He influenced young people who sought a goal without God by way of his disputations with Ahad Ha'am (Asher Ginzberg, a major Zionist thinker [1856–1927]) and others, who, with characteristic simplicity, construed the prophetic message of the Bible as Judaism's contribution to world culture and tried to build atop it a positivist, nationalist structure of national culture in which Eretz Israel would appear essentially as a "cultural center." This influence affected members of the Second Aliyah such as Katznelson and Ben-Gurion. A cultural center that projects "Biblical values" on Jews and the world at large, however, was too simple an exercise and was doomed to fail from the start. The Zionists had to revive the nation in its land, no less, and the revival had to be more than the establishment of a cultural center.[73] By implication, the youthful Ben-Gurion was drawn more to Berdyczewski than to Ahad Ha'am.[74] After all, a young person like Ben-Gurion had to free himself of the bonds of tradition despite being unable to submit totally to the spirit and assumptions of the prior century, the eighteenth. Ben-Gurion could accept neither Diasporistic religious historicism nor the existing religious ethic, and he had yet to encounter Marxist historicism. He needed a pluralistic interpretation of history that would include pre-Diaspora history for three contrasting purposes: to deprive the various religious vehicles of their monopoly over it, to combat the complete rejection of Judaism as was rampant among the assimilationists, and to make Judaism attractive to the masses of young people like himself.

In his later incarnation as a statesman, Ben-Gurion expanded this pluralistic interpretation with the help of the Bible and Spinoza, as we learn from the arguments that he left behind after his debates with rabbis and from his Spinoza polemic,[75] when he attempted to interpret Judaism so pluralistically as to include the great pantheist rebel. Truth to tell, here Ben-Gurion did not stray far from a plausible interpretation of Spinoza's philosophy as an integral limb of the body of Judaism.[76] To propose such an interpretation, one needs the license to treat the past as one wishes. The prerequisites are the freedom of will, a nontraditional attitude toward historical values, and a revival of even earlier values – which the inhabitants of this world called the Jewish renaissance.

The expressions "freedom of will" and "moral and intellectual independence" run like a thread through the remarks of Ben-Gurion the statesman (even when he imbues all of Jewish history with the maintenance of these values) in his debates with secular political opponents, whom he viewed as sectarian and cultic leaders who negated their disciples' freedom of will and choice in favor of this or that "credic collectivism."[77]

It was a great contradiction indeed: the Jews' refusal to accept spiritual coercion and their internal fragmentation into diverse sects holding worldviews that could not easily be changed, on the one hand, and on the other hand, the integration of these people into a single community. The only apparent way to resolve it, in Ben-Gurion's opinion during the statehood years, was to induce the Jews to work in joint institutions according to agreed rules. This is why the solution had to come by way of far-reaching reform at the level of political ethics.

Thus, the all-powerful party leader, Israel's Lenin as it were, was concurrently a staunch individualist and an anticollectivist, two traits that were deep and integral to his identity. This leader explained the new Jewish emancipation in terms of inner freedom and negation of the decrees of fate by the application of independent sovereign power that nevertheless entails the striving for a socialist society. He viewed his political opponents as imitators of foreign cultures and values. This explains his struggles with the factions of the far Left to his dying day, even though he could not adopt a rightist interpretation of will and self-rule and reviled incarnations of rightist thinking that veered to Canaanism, that is, a total rejection of any ties to Diaspora Jewry and the quest to create a new identity in Eretz Israel, divorced from Judaism and entailing conscious Fascist traits. In a nutshell, he was a moderate leftist. Even though in his youth he had attained a sort of extremism in this respect, he would not find it difficult to free himself of it when the time came to focus on the community at large, rather than on the working class alone. Equally, he could profess in his lifetime to English-style constitutionalism from the perspective of an affinity for the British political Left, coupled with admiration for Churchill, and could display a flexibility that seemed to be nothing but a thirst for power.

Ben-Gurion's terms of reference, however – the Jewish people, Eretz Israel, the emancipation of the individual Jew within the framework of a Jewish society that strove for, and would eventually attain, self-rule in its land, or at least in part of it, which he was to serve with the force and full autonomy of his will – had been determined long before. Power, which was necessary to attain these goals, was sometimes a sociopolitical matter that many would understand through their feelings and reason, and sometimes a matter of the conscience of the few, that is, those who possessed a will to power and the rare ability to put it to good use by understanding the facts and the Zeitgeist. The awareness of the need for power, for force, for the strength that would allow the individual to live by his or her own counsel, primarily by way of the Zionist act, served Second Aliyah leaders by allowing a flexibility that tradition did not. Other messages of the time, primarily the Marxism of the Soviet-inspired far Left and the Fascism that succeeded it, were their main enemies on the secular front. Thus, a Zionist leader of the sort who initially spoke on behalf of the few against opponents of all types among the Jewish populace, saw great importance in his own will and in the will of the few like him to battle tradition and assimilation, the far Right and the far Left, at the same time.

Berdyczewski's dreadful polemics in his early periods against the exilic reality, unlike those of writer Mendele Mocher Seforim, were aided by a philosophical foundation. These polemics expressed the free individual Jew's intellectual capacity to tell the truth, to condemn falsehood and fraud, and to expose the ills of his people, not only with the aid of this philosophical foundation but also through its connection to a deep critical knowledge of the Jews' own sources down the generations. All his life Ben-Gurion repeatedly claimed that Jews had not created anything truly new since the ninth century, that is, the Talmud and its progeny. Even though he dissociated himself from this creation, his claim is not far from Berdyczewski's claims about the loss of Jewish creative power in exile due to the nation's detachment from the land, nature, and reality. To Berdyczewski's thinking, the Jews had become a nation of sealed books and their commentaries. At least members of that generation argued this way outwardly, although they knew that post-ninth-century Judaism had also created contents, symbols, and traditions that abounded with meaning – which did not interest them, just as Thomas Aquinas and the giants of medieval Christian Scholasticism had ceased to interest the exponents of the Renaissance.

The quest for creativity and its renewal was a sociocultural goal of central importance in Nietzsche's aims, though his aristocratic and condescending attitude toward it neither appealed to nor served the needs of leftists, Berdyczewski's disciples, who drew whatever suited them from his arguments.

Nietzsche's "will for power" theory is recognizable in the personae of the heroes that Berdyczewski borrowed from him and attributed to a primitive pagan Israel that was neither bound to the tradition of the Book nor divorced from the nature of a land that Berdyczewski had never seen. The heroization of the Zionist – its elevation from the childish act, if you will, of genteel youths who rebelled against their parents and went off to a land of dreams that they had conjured themselves, which they believed was empty and desolate – was undoubtedly assisted by Berdyczewski's attempt to interpret Jewish history in a heroic, Nietzschean, morally unconventional way and to grant the legitimacy of uniqueness and self-sovereignty to youth who were capable of it. Thus, Ben-Gurion wrote to his wife in 1918, speaking of his uniqueness and of his having prepared for the two of them "a world of supreme happiness, a wonderful universe, a world that only a few are privileged to enter, for only rich souls and deep hearts may enter it."[78] One might construe this as the poetic license of a young man aspiring to greatness, but the very fact of such an aspiration, the consciousness of the uniqueness of the few who can penetrate realms that are barred to others, is indeed wholly in the spirit of the nineteenth century, a century in which heroism had an authentic, widely accepted meaning throughout Europe, a meaning embraced by various circles that rejected the pessimistic aestheticism of the Romantics from a posture of total disregard of society and the world of the here and now.

Heroism may be linked to disdain for the current regime and in this manner invested with political significance, as in Byron's thinking, or be tied to the progressive, rational ideas of the eighteenth century and the Jewish heroics of the Bible. Nietzsche hitched it to the individual's will to replace the current falsehood with a new ethic and to deep psychological inquiry that left no further room for the rationality or the mechanistic concepts of the eighteenth century, just as it was not related to Schopenhauer's pessimistic aestheticism. What is more, this heroism, as adopted by left-leaning circles, took no interest in the depths of man's soul. Even Katznelson, while sensitive to the matter, did not delve into it much because he feared the limitations that such an inquiry might impose on the will. Instead, he turned his interest to society, the nation, and the special individual. It was an externalized heroism, although it did not entirely ignore the inner person. Nietzsche's influence on it was by necessity partial, since it drew on other sources as well and since his people were not philosophers but, rather, leaned – insofar as they had to and via mediators – on German philosophy. Berdyczewski was keenly interested in politics; his journals reveal a sharp eye and sometimes a brilliant sense of political analysis. However, he was gnawed by doubt and was too pessimistic during the later period of his life. Sometimes, too, his journals reveal rightist leanings that the Zionist Left of Katznelson and Ben-Gurion could not accept.[79]

For Ben-Gurion and his associates, in contrast, the main purpose in self-liberation was to reach out to the Jewish masses, because they saw themselves simultaneously as their peers and their guides. Well aware that they were living in the era of the masses, they sought both to conquer the majority and to rule on its behalf. No other system seemed relevant to them, and since they lacked the wherewithal to delve into the theory that views government as an autonomous dimension in the life of a new society, they still placed their emphasis on the individual and on society.

Berdyczewski suffered from a syndrome with the tendency to loathe these new times and their rules so passionately as to leave no room for action. Even from an analytical, philosophical perspective, he could not in his lifetime have accepted the implications of Nietzsche's philosophy regarding the change in all values resulting from the free will of the few, since will itself – in the light of Freud's and Schopenhauer's pessimism – often seemed a function of uncontrollable forces. During his Nietzschean period, Berdyczewski made the latest philosophies of his time known to his Jewish disciples, who shared his critique of Jewish life in exile; these served as a bridge that carried his ideas to people who became political and then used them in their careers.

Ben-Gurion integrated them into a leftist-Zionist synthesis. Eldad (Scheib) integrated Nietzschean ideas and Jewish ultranationalism, which leaned on the distant past, into a pseudo-Fascist right-wing synthesis. One must admit, however, that Ben-Gurion was free enough of leftist dogmatism, or at least had no difficulty in shedding it, that when the time came – apparently under Berdyczewski's inspiration – he turned to Athens in order to study Greek philosophy and delve into Plato (whom Western thinkers in the 1950s regarded as the sire of antidemocratic thinking throughout the ages). Ben-Gurion truly felt – possibly again under Berdyczewski's inspiration – that Judaism was devoid of a theory of government, originating in Greece, that had given Western civilization a political dimension that Judaism lacked in this form. In fact, Ben-Gurion's interest in the Greeks and their philosophies, which prompted him to study classical Greek long before his interest in Plato's Republic had been awakened,[80] was concentrated on the Platonic idea of the Good and his idea of Justice, since both were major features of Judaism as well, but anchored in the Jewish faith. Hence, the study of Greek philosophy was essential for allowing secularized Jews to use a different tool to pursue justice and seek for the truth, as both were also parts of their own Jewish heritage. The Socratic battle for the truth and the refusal to flee or run away from those who manipulated the truth may have motivated Ben-Gurion during the hopeless struggle in which he would find himself much later during his public life.

Ben-Gurion's ability to be so motivated, which earned him enemies among Israeli intellectuals, of all people, originates in freedom of the will and observation and in the examination of tools for the purpose of creating a nontraditional ethic for a Jewish state, an ethic that would mobilize tradition, too, for its needs.

Berdyczewski – an East European Jew – embraced German patriotism during World War I and ultimately received German citizenship.[81] By that stage of his life, he had practical successors in Palestine itself, including Ben-Gurion and Katznelson, who seemingly wished to cull whatever they found expedient from the great teacher's philosophy and art and actualize them in Eretz Israel in concrete ways, leaving the rest aside. They adopted the emancipation of the individual's will from the bonds of tradition, of which Berdyczewski spoke greatly, and the ability to remain Jewish without faith, which Berdyczewski borrowed from Nietzsche's doctrine of the will. It is the individual's will that determines his or her being and affiliation. This is permissible and possible in light of the "death of God." However, Ben-Gurion did not ascribe importance to the Nietzschean principle of the haughty, aristocratic individual who busies himself with ethical aesthetics for its own sake. The ethics of the prophets – the pinnacle of the special Jewish contribution to humanism, as Ahad Ha'am termed it – in combination with socialism, could continue to exist even without God in the Jews' land.

Berdyczewski's dispute with Ahad Ha'am over this issue caused their young readers, members of the Second Aliyah, to view the latter as an old-fashioned liberal. The urges, sensuality, and savagery that Berdyczewski revealed in his literary works under the spiritual-idealistic mantle that ostensibly cloaked the Jewish shtetl taught his readers that despite his terrible criticism of that mantle, Judaism had vital force. What is more, Judaism had a future – in its land – and one had only to marshal these forces by setting an example and issuing a challenge that would appeal to the first recipients to mobilize for it.

Berdyczewski's students were already free of the bonds of their tradition; now they became secular Zionists who claimed the right to be Jews and to feel and act as Jews who, though lacking faith, embraced the erstwhile religious culture as they defined it. It was also their right, they said, to return both to nature and to the historical homeland as an outgrowth of the forces that pulsed in the veins of Diaspora Jewry, applying these forces to future needs in Eretz Israel in various collective settings.

Nietzsche, Berdyczewski's predecessor by a generation, was much more optimistic than Berdyczewski about Judaism and viewed it as an enduring, self-revitalizing force. The Jews, as Nietzsche described them, were undoubtedly the strongest race in Europe: They knew how to sustain themselves and endure even under the worst conditions by means of specific positive virtues, foremost the strength of vigorous faith. Nietzsche's remarks clearly echo Heine's claims about the merits of traditional Judaism and his own words about the merits of great creative figures, such as Baruch Benedict Spinoza and Heine himself, two scions of Judaism who, in their own ways, expressed Jewish values and their rejection by dint of their spiritual independence and their originality. From Spinoza's *Tractacus Politicus*, Ben-Gurion would adopt the definition of the law, as he would use it during the debate on the Israeli constitution. He viewed Spinoza as a product of Judaism in its Israeli secular form that could reclaim his much broader philosophy as a secular option at the very stage in which, as stated, he sought to expand Judaism in all directions and lend it an expansively pluralistic interpretation.

It is Heine, however, who deserves brief attention here, both due to his influence on the Zionists of the generation that followed his and due to the damage that he caused, which are important for understanding two things: the criticism of Judaism and Zionism that has persisted in our own day, and

the difference between Heine and those similar to him in contrast to the founding Zionists of the Second Aliyah. With his keen political sense – a dimension in
which Nietzsche never excelled and about which Berdyczewski demonstrated
a chasmal, prophetic fear and often an amazing lack of discernment – Heine
foresaw the terrible tragedy that would befall Judaism due to the ascendancy
of modern mass society and its forces, such as the demise of Christianity,
the emergence of new secular ideologies, quests for radical social change, and
the old elites' responses in opposition to them. As these forces struggled with
one another, he said, the Jews would find themselves in the very midst of the
cauldron and be ground to bits.[82]

Heine predicted that Germany, his country of birth, would play a key role
in these processes, in which he foresaw the shattering of the cross – that Judeo-
Christian amulet that restrained the pagan, martial, savage, coarse tradition
that, in his opinion, pulsed in Germany underneath its Judeo-Christian mantle,
which had not completely mastered it. This made the Jewish problem both a
serious psychocultural matter and an immensely powerful sociopolitical issue.
The ascent of the masses and their demand for equality and power would
awaken counterforces that would fight this ascent and its claims and probably
enlist the masses for their purposes. The Jews would find themselves in the
breach, unaffiliated with one side and unacceptable to the others in a world that
had dropped the reins of tradition on all sides. Heine also severely criticized the
high and mighty Jews of his time – the Rothschilds and their ilk – who had taken
the helm of the capitalist world without becoming an organic, accepted part of
the non-Jewish capitalist leadership that had enslaved the people and was due
to reap their vengeance. Many Zionists were influenced by this "catastrophic"
analysis, which preceded Herzl's revelation at the Dreyfus trial.

Heine, however, did more than merely predict this sort of pre-Zionist catastrophic vision for Judaism. He also argued, in debate with the antisemitic
Enlightenment that preceded and was contemporaneous with him, that Judaism
was free of a desert tribe's cynical, condescending separatism from the rest of
humanity on the pretenses of "chosenness," a covenantal arrangement between
this tribe and its god, as Voltaire put it – a contemptible kind of relationship
in the age of reason and equality. On the contrary: Judaism, he wrote to his
French readers, was an expression of unsullied spirituality; for in its eyes, man
became a son of God because he reviled his body and viewed his soul and mind,
the divine spark that had metamorphosed inside him, as the essence.[83] This is
why Jesus the Nazarene was but a concrete expression, a human pinnacle of
sorts, of Jewish spirituality and its revulsion for flesh, nature, and desire, in
favor of a spiritual, moral existence.

By putting it this way, Heine made Judaism once more the foundation of
Christianity but did so now in secular terms, even though he found this foundation unnatural and problematic. He accepted the ghastly German distinction
between Hebraism and Hellenism, between the Judeo-Christian "spiritual"
and the Greek-Dionysian "natural," and exported it to all of Western Europe
and, particularly, to England of the second half of the nineteenth century.[84]

In Germany itself, Heine paved the way for philosophers such as Nietzsche, who viewed the Christian incarnation of the strict Jewish ethic, as presented by Heine, as "an ethic of slaves" that had taken on only a portion of Judaism's obligations, seriousness, and depth of relationship with God. This relationship in itself was but the human invention of a morally dubious and philosophically absurd nexus of punishment and forgiveness. Nietzsche, however, recognized in the Judaism of his time a psychological fortitude and a capacity for independent thinking that few Christians displayed; that is, he lauded the spirituality and the intellectual stubbornness that Jews had demonstrated in recent generations, in contrast to Christians who lived by rote – meaning, in his opinion, incapable of grasping true morality as leaves driven by the wind.

In the next generation, Berdycewski and his colleague and disciple Yosef Chaim Brenner assessed Judaism similarly. They considered its spirituality dying, if not already dead, pretentious, or dangerous to its possessors in a hostile environment that would not suffer this pretension for long.[85]

This distinction between Hellenism and Judaism, however, became one of the roots of Zionism without developing into a severe, all-out attack on Judaism at large. It found expression in the poetry of Shaul Tchernichovsky and may explain his craving for nature and Eretz Israel before he went to live there. Ben-Gurion, in contrast, sought in Greek culture an explanation for the history of Western science and the Western art of government – an explanation that was both an indication and an expression of liberation from the traditional Jewish past, which in many sectors saw only evil in Greece.

In Heine himself, alongside the aforementioned far-reaching defense of Judaism and his lovely poetry of nostalgia for Zion, we find more than a little contempt for and recoil from Judaism, as are typical of secular Zionists' attitudes in our day. Thus, some view him as a prototype of the "third Jew,"[86] one who leaves traditional Judaism but not Judaism itself, who secedes from the Jewish religion but not from the Jewish people and what we may call Jewish civilization, that is, the moral contents of Judaism, without faith. I do not know if this description is valid for a person who was so complex, convoluted, multifaceted, and possessed of such decisively liberal-universalistic interests before it became possible to reject tradition and religion completely – a person who, to his dying day, expressed all these contradictions of his time with varying emphases, while languishing in what he called his "mattress-grave," a confinement to bed that reawakened in him Jewish pangs of vacillation.

The leaders of the Second Aliyah took a similar attitude toward Judaism but with a fundamental difference: They did not content themselves with rejecting elements of Judaism that they could not relate to, criticizing its condition in the Diaspora, prophesying the impending destruction of the Diaspora, and the like. Instead and additionally, they explicitly nominated themselves as leaders of a Jewish national revival movement with universalistic aspirations. The Jewish renaissance generation was one of emancipation but not of total rejection, a stance that people of the eighteenth century took toward Christianity (and, in the cases of Voltaire and Thomas Paine, toward Judaism). Rather, it was a generation of selective revival, which many of its members set out to actualize by emigrating to Eretz Israel, working its soil, and reforming those who came there. They sought to combine the will of individual Jews with the rejection of elements of their past without completely dissociating from it, and to establish the nature of this will through both conscious and natural choices, although they often refrained from turning this into a systematic philosophy.[87]

One may explore this selective revival in greater depth by comparing these Zionists and their behavior with the colorful figure and actions of Heine himself. He was truly a late and sometimes disillusioned humanist. At the end of the day, Heine – the enlightened, liberal intellectual who often laced his thinking with a dose of skepticism and cynicism – transcended Judaism and Christianity. He praised both, castigated both in the name of humanistic and universal values, and expressed serious doubts about the practical validity of these very values without religion and tradition, to the immense harm and subversion of both.

Heine fought battles against real and imaginary opponents, including some who were close to him ideologically but had piqued his dark wrath. He decried their private lives, external appearance, and sexual habits without justice or mercy, earning terrible ire in return.[88] His scientific biographer, Jeffrey Sammons, reports this in an attempt to destroy Heine's image as a "cultural hero," in whose colorful writings everyone finds arguments – however contradictory – in his defense. Heine was a man of great, creative, progressive soul, his biographer writes, who fell victim to the reactionary repression and vile narrowmindedness of his time and was eventually victimized by racist, oppressive, antidemocratic and antiliberal forces. In this sense, Heine was a cultural hero of human freedom. The truth, however, is that the opposition was of his own making, partly intentionally, with a high sense of historic mission, and partly from poor judgment and moral inattention. He had an uncompromising side: He never allowed himself the capacity of introspection. The tragedy of his acceptance by the public is rooted not in the fury of his natural enemies but in the tension created with his allies and friends. His story reminds his biographer of Norman Mailer. People stood agape at his immense talent and his passionate, rich, individualistic imagination. Some saw themselves as his partners in the struggle of reason and imagination against petty, cruel human evil. At the same time, his narcissistic primitivism makes it very hard for serious people to take him seriously.

What was this "narcissistic primitivism"? Sammons could only have meant Jewish traits and forms of behavior that condescend, that do not live up to their own requirements, do not delve into the meaning of their words and motives, and do not distinguish among them as they should.

Therefore, it comes as no surprise that conservatives like Thomas Carlyle saw Heine as a model of the rootless, liberal, Jewish intellectual who savagely vilified every value, while English liberals such as Matthew Arnold viewed him as a cultural hero who offered a modern interpretation of the damage that Judaism had inflicted on Christianity due to its excess spirituality and its detachment from nature.

It seems to me that the Zionists of the Second Aliyah knew – or, if they did not know well, then sensed or at least noticed – the validity of some of the objections that Judaism and its exponents as seen by non-Jews aroused against them in the West, specifically in the modern era. Their point in emigrating to Eretz Israel was to absolve the Jews of this criticism and its inevitable political consequences and to invest Judaism's historic pretensions with a character at once reliable, true, national, and universalistic.[89]

Still, we may exempt few of them, if we return to Shlomo Tzemach and his kind, from the applicability of such probing definitions with respect to the untamed Jewish intellectual, and there is no telling what arouses such a person or when he might muzzle himself. The concept of "normalcy" of which Zionism spoke in order to deal with these definitions could not reframe them in one generation; it could only make them popular slogans during the Yishuv period, necessitating further examination after the attainment of statehood – at least in the case of Ben-Gurion himself.

Zionists of Ben-Gurion's type, however, also adopted from Heine what was convenient for them: the dream of returning to nature in the land of the patriarchs, Judaism's moral-cultural pretension of being a religion of justice and empathy and a "light unto the nations," by merit of the past and also by their actions in Eretz Israel in the present, without the traditional belief in God. This issue could not but arouse a debate over the various components of this past, particularly the question of messianism and its place in Judaism as a longing for redemption and an expression of the Jews' unbroken tie with Eretz Israel, which was therefore a highly important source of legitimacy for secular Zionism.[90]

In the late 1950s, Ben-Gurion himself bent this messianic aspiration to a secular interpretation and viewed it as a historic given. It seemed, however, as though he was beginning to walk down an irrational and mystical, though secular, path of "political messianism" – as if he were trying to turn a religious value into a secular-religious value and to station it at the center of civil society's world. His transformation seemed to resemble those of the great secular religions that were born in the Age of Enlightenment, which ultimately metamorphosed into Leninism and Fascist theories that linked the flesh-and-blood state to quasi-religious mysticism. Such a mysticism, which allows heads of state to speak and act politically without the requisite public debate and review, appears to have been at work in the Lavon Affair.[91]

To discuss the mental world of the members of the Second Aliyah, especially Ben-Gurion, however, we must set it in its proper historical perspective. Their attitude toward "politics" and statecraft was not simple, partly because they felt victimized by it most of their lives, especially when it came to foreign rulers and world leaders. Even when they dealt with Judaism and its treasures, they still

had to concern themselves with current events and the forces whose ascendancy
Heine had indicated. Heine had even contributed to the ascendancy of these
forces by having aroused great wrath and creating, as it were, an archetype of
the modern Jewish humanist. The Zionists also had to wrestle with non-Zionist
or anti-Zionist "humanists" who deliberately imitated that great poet and with
prominent intellectuals who attempted to become "cultural heroes" in, and
under the patronage of, non-Jewish courts. They went about this by criticizing
Judaism, their culture of origin about which they did not know much, as
assimilated German Jews, or as non-Zionist Jews, as if Zionism had violated the
universalistic and humanistic ideals of Heine and his like and had transformed
Judaism from a challenge and a worldwide problem of humanistic significance
into a wretched, hopeless province-state in Arab Palestine. Prominent among
such critics were those with German backgrounds, such as Hannah Arendt,
who imitated Heine a great deal all her life.[92]

Even Zionists like Martin Buber, and others who were influenced by the
Kantian, Heinean German-Jewish universalistic tradition, and later by Nietzsche's individualistic-elitist moral credo while maintaining a quest for religious
meanings in their Jewish identity, entertained a hard kernel of criticism toward
the heads of the Zionist Labor Movement and its doings in Eretz Israel after
the Yishuv became a state and engaged in acts of state. A complex mixture
of diverse influences blended in these people's minds. Buber himself was a
complex, convoluted man. He went through periods of German-influenced
Jewish nationalism and, in the early days of the state, unstinting support of
Ben-Gurion's "melting pot." Nevertheless, his eyes were always turned to the
West and to Germany, and to international recognition.[93] Despite his Eastern
European origins, he was at one with German Zionists and was their guide,
albeit via a roundabout route paved with contradictions.

The young Buber, who, as Gershom Scholem said, "grew up with the Zionist movement itself and became one of its leading disciples," seemed to be
living proof from that era of the conscious use that Zionists made of the term
renaissance:

In his youth [Scholem says], the word "renaissance," Jewish revival, was very common
in his writings and its connotations in its original sixteenth-century meaning were not
absent in his usage: opening up sources of inspiration that had been sealed, ampli-
fying the sense of effervescent life, a cult of "creativity," modernity. But the simple
fact of his efforts to establish something "modern" – a word that had a very positive ring that has become almost unfathomable to us today, who see only the ludicrous, the nonsensical in it – to inspire hearts to a renaissance of Jewish creative
power, is what ultimately led Buber to his great discoveries. He sought the sources
of "modernism" [release from tradition and its fetters in order to face the future and
uncover its hidden contents] and revealed the most ancient, the novelty of which won his
heart. [His revelation,] the light in Hasidism . . . was not scientific, historical, or critical;
instead, it was mixed with esthetic urgency [originating in the influence of Schopenhauer and Nietzsche] and religiosity, a highly characteristic mixture for the young
Buber.[94]

This mixture, however, also made Buber an "oppositionist" within the Zionist movement as far back as Herzl's time and, in fact, an oppositionist who subsequently entertained doubts about political Zionism. Buber told Scholem that while serving as editor of the Zionist journal *Die Welt* in Vienna, he approached Dr. Herzl "and told him that he wished to resign as editor of the movement's organ. Herzl asked him why. 'To establish an opposition.' The intrigues of statecraft left Buber ill at ease."[95] At that time, the young Buber delivered "three speeches about Judaism" – surely heavily influenced by Johann Gottlieb Fichte and his nationalist speeches to the German people. He

promised the frozen Jewish world a revolutionary arousal from within, promised the revelation of hidden life under the frozen official forms. [However,] talk about a hidden Judaism being in struggle with official Judaism and such did not conform with reality, since reality is much more complicated than these simplifications – and it did not take long for Buber himself to repudiate and totally abandon them. . . .[96] The more cohesive his knowledge and the greater his despair, the fainter were the sounds of promise and the magic in his words. However, the fundamental recognition that he shared with Ahad Ha'am [but which was much sharper in Buber's case; note in Scholem's text] runs like a common thread through all of his writings about the Jewish people and the Land of Israel: that the decision of each individual among us, that which he decides in the privacy of his heart, decides the fate of the Israelite nation long before all the slogans and the political and social facts do, and more than they do.[97]

Fundamentally, there was little difference between this claim of Scholem's and Ben-Gurion's views on this matter: that the nation's fate would be determined by the decision of the individual, particularly the leader-individual and the many individuals who would follow him, as per Ben-Gurion's remark that we quoted at the outset of this chapter. Buber, however, sought "spiritual depth" and spoke of "personal actualization" – which he did not actualize in his own case until he emigrated to Palestine in the late 1930s – in a Nietzschean, individualistic, aristocratic sense that put him at an ever-increasing distance from what was happening in Israel itself. As Scholem put it:

It is to Buber's credit that he did not peddle his concept of the paths to true fulfillment, which has unfathomable spiritual depth [Nietzsche's demand of the few who are able to be deep, moral Übermenschen by virtue of their personal superiority] and responsibility for the best of our heritage, and he did not acquiesce in a reality based on victories that in all probability he would not consider victories at all. Fulfillment as he spoke of it is a reality of our inner spirit and its cloaking in corporeality, and a reality that does not place its responsibility before the spirit that speaks through the mouths of the Jewish prophets is no longer a state of Israel – particularly if its name is the State of Israel! Buber, an old Polish Jew who had witnessed the villainy of tyrants and the Holocaust of the Diaspora, during which he worked toward the renewal of his nation from within – who can blame him for loving the vanquished more than the victors? Sometimes one feels in reading his words the pernicious fear that we may lose in our victory the entire world that we earned by being vanquished, the image of God that our sufferings taught us to maintain within ourselves and to respect in our fellows.[98]

Indeed, this criticism – comprised of many elements, including typical Christian and universalistic fundamentals that we discuss later – gave way to Ben-Gurion's authority and unforeseeable successes and even mobilized to help him at the dawn of statehood, until it came back to haunt him afterwards.[99]

At issue, then, are various reflections on the crisis of traditional Jewish society – a society that Jews simultaneously clung to and protested against – and the criticism of this society and its values as was widely expressed in the West at the time. This crisis demands the most profound contemplation possible, both of it and of the responses to it in non-Jewish society, with which Ben-Gurion and his peers had to contend.

The Crisis of Traditional Jewish Society

As the European Renaissance waned, many of its exponents wound up adhering with greater vigor – and in various forms – to the Christian past, while others paved the way to the Reformation. It was then that the process of transferring religious ethics to the secular foundations of the modern state began. From that point, it would take hundreds of years, and in England many stages, for the formation of what Ralph Daherndorf calls "a society of public virtues,"[100] that is, the transition in a society's life from the ideological stage to its consolidation on the basis of sovereign rules of behavior that guide the practices of its governing organizations and public at large.

The key word here is "virtue," the Greco-Roman *virtus*, which makes one a moral person. In Western culture, personal virtues are matters of consensus, although there are differences of opinion about how to apply them and whether they are truly applicable at all. One of the expressions of this disagreement is that some of these virtues, such as the pursuit of justice, courage, good judgment, faith, temperance, and even charity, are both behaviors and values – that is, they carry different kinds of religious content.

Disagreements over the application of these virtues, flowing from varying ways of interpreting them, used to breed religious wars and power struggles. Thanks to society's efforts and the thought invested in proper social management, these disputes slowly lost their relevance in English history and were supplanted by the art of avoidance via a system of structural compromises within institutions led by a powerful Parliament that generates strong government relying on consensual "citizenship."

Thus, the English political philosophy is based on the planting of "public virtues," which Dahrendorf likens to the behavior of members of a sports team. Members accept inviolable rules of fair play that demand mutual cooperation, voluntary submission to their captain (who is chosen via a specific process anchored in tradition and history), consideration of the community, and collective development of their talents. Citizenship, too, involves not only personal rights but also the individual's answerability to the group. Individuals obey the "rules of the game" not because the rules are forced upon them but because they are guided by self-respect, rather than by rote, to respect their teachers, peers, and social conventions. Still, the picture that Daherndorf draws is something of an idealization of Britain and its leaders, a picture in which Ben-Gurion found different facets at different times.[101]

Here we have a case of typical disregard by the liberal school, of which Dahrendorf was a leader, of the traditional roots of "the society of public virtues." These virtues exist neither on their own account nor for strictly utilitarian reasons. In the second half of the nineteenth century, this issue evoked weighty philosophical and practical debates in England itself, centering on the basis for, and essence of, the British political system from both the liberal and conservative standpoints. In the eyes of modern conservatives, public virtues are associated with tradition, common law and its changes, and religious values in their refined versions, that is, versions that lost their former innate aggressiveness and underwent partial or full secularization, without the entire tradition disappearing in favor of abstract "rules of behavior."

One may discern various levels in the English "tradition," including the contribution of Greece and, in part, of Rome; of the Bible and of great personalities from the past; the values that should be acquired from them; the lessons that should be learned from their struggles with their opponents and rivals; and the customs and rules of the game that are sanctified by a tradition that no government would ever have the right or the ability to breach.

Even the strongest government does not violate this tradition, thus obviating the "direct democracy" that destroyed Athens, so long as it enjoys the support of a competent representative institution. Such a government also possesses freedom of judgment once it earns the requisite public support. The public obeys it not due to coercion but from its sense of citizenship and participation in the rules of the game, expressed not only in general elections but also in government – opposition relations and the behavior of members of the government, who are not allowed to swerve from these rules – which, after the religious and civil wars that preceded them, were collected, engraved in the minds of successive generations, and cemented into customs, laws, and their amendments.

These rules, however, give the elected representative a great deal of maneuvering room with which to further the state's interests, particularly in regard to its external enemies. In states of emergency, then, the British "state," through its elected institutions, abrogates the rights of voluntary groups that do not accept the authority of these institutions and their decisions, or it tries its best to find a way to incorporate their representatives into an emergency government that takes their interests into consideration, provided they are ready to accept the agreed "rules of the game."

This approach imparts a recognized institutional status to a prime minister who is chosen by his or her parliamentary faction and not by an amorphous clutch of party conventions or primaries that have no long-term responsibility for their selection. From the moment the party makes its choice, the prime minister serves as its leader and cannot be called a dictator when standing firm

against one of his or her ministers. It is inconceivable that a foreign minister –
even one as meretricious as Moshe Sharett – should disagree with the premier
and form a coalition against him or her and still retain that government post.
But we precede ourselves. At this stage, it is very important to stress that this
political system no longer rests on a religious foundation but derives its ethics,
justice, and freedom of action in its state and defense affairs from an eclectic
mixture of experience and the moral and practical ideas of generations who
had founded the specific British system of public virtues. Therefore, when the
time came and Ben-Gurion strove to impose on Israel the institutions and some
of the ideas of this system, such as parts of the Bible, parts of Plato's philosophy
as he interpreted it for his needs, and his own interpretation of Judaism as a
religion of justice, he seemed to be straying excessively from his Socialist roots
and becoming a Machiavellian "statesman," one who was moving toward a
system whose spirit drew on tradition and conservative institutions, which,
unlike Daherndorf, he did not disregard.

Worse still, the adoption of secular-messianic ideas by Ben-Gurion – who
recognized the process that Israeli society was undergoing, one of shedding
traditional values, of secularization, of vacuity and lack of a substitute for
the challenges posed by American civilization – marked the beginning of what
German-born liberal and liberal-religious intellectuals, veteran Socialists, and
Neo-Socialist intellectuals viewed as a serious and, later, an intolerable shift
to the right. All of which happened in due course, if we completely disregard
the personal, factional, party, and group interests that were intertwined with
issues of ethics and justice, in the unique manner of Jews of Eastern and Central
European origin.

However, as Professor Yisrael Kolatt said in his characteristic way:

The messianic authority that Berl Katznelson denied the Soviet Union in the 1940s was
adopted in the 1950s by David Ben-Gurion on the State of Israel. The need to cement
the legitimacy of the state and the change in the composition of its population [by immigration that was largely traditional minded] impelled Ben-Gurion to depart from the
character of Zionist ideology. Zionism ceased to be presented as a Jewish emancipation
movement and became an expression of a "messianic vision." Ben-Gurion's "messianic
vision" invoked traditional idioms and traditional Jews' devotion to them. However, he
revised the contents of the messianic idea and used it as a sort of social-cultural-ethical
guiding principle – freedom, empathy, revelation of the secrets of existence, and other
such messianic ideals, which were intended to give the State of Israel its uniqueness and
justification.[102]

In my opinion, all of these were inherent in Katznelson and Ben-Gurion's
"Renaissance-style" eclecticism. Kolatt, however, continues, on the same page,
to explain the resistance that this mixture aroused during the statehood period:

Ben-Gurion's opponents resisted the identification of a flesh-and-blood state and government, entangled in specific circumstances and participating in power struggles, with
the redemption process and the fulfillment of absolute, ultimate values. It must be said,
however, that Ben-Gurion too did not invoke the messianic idea to justify any particular

political step. The conflation of the Sinai revelation with the Sinai Campaign [Operation Kadesh – the Suez-Sinai Campaign of 1956] was not a factor in political reasoning in regard to relations with Egypt and the great powers, [the principal aim of which was to acquire a nuclear infrastructure from France].

Thus, Kolatt grasped a bit of Ben-Gurion's singular use of values and ideas, in contrast to his politics. Indeed, in Ben-Gurion's eyes, politics – or statecraft – had to rest on an ethical-cultural foundation without its becoming the essence of practical statecraft in matters of state and defense. Others, however, did accuse him of degrading values that he had professed for the sake of "politics" or of exploiting them for the gratuitous benefit of a "flesh-and-blood state."

One doubts that the critics knew the British system well, be it in its internal actions or in its conduct in state and defense affairs. For in these, too, a mixture of values and cold, calculated interests was employed, and Ben-Gurion was certainly capable of striving toward them with the same degree of cool judgment. The British system, which was a fusion of beliefs and opinions – including some culled directly or indirectly from the Bible – and of institutions that furthered values and interests according to rules of the game, allowed for decisive actions and compromises, legitimized in the eyes of public opinion, and attempted to apply these values and interests via acts of state. The resulting state carried global responsibilities throughout the nineteenth century and a good part of the twentieth, thanks to an accumulation of particular circumstances. International order and peace were maintained largely by the guns of the Royal Navy. The state furthered its interests, sometimes mercilessly, with the cool calculation and haughtiness that were typical of the Roman Empire, on account of its imperial ethos. Yet not only was Britain ruled neither by Roman Caesars nor by their laws, but even after becoming a world empire, it also rid itself of the authority of its royal house once and for all, terminating its active role in British political life. It treated its colonies with a measure of equality before the law and with "British justice" wherever local conditions permitted, sometimes with great success and sometimes amid constant compromise between local actualities and its concepts of responsibility toward its subjects and its own interests. Put here in the most simplistic fashion, Britain demanded that foreigners be considerate of its values and interests on a "live and let live" basis, displayed much flexibility in not imposing itself on others, and sought common ground with them if they had the power to make trouble and upset the existing order. However, it did not hesitate to mobilize military forces and, ultimately, the entire nation against those who threatened it in the name of their own "private virtues," transformed as they were in support of German hypernationalism and militarism.

Once democracy had been imposed on Germany after World War I, a "private virtue," according to Daherndorf, became any absolute idea in which a person believes for any reason, in which others do not believe, and which by its very nature – in that it is a supreme value to its possessor – inspires its possessor to impose it or to cause others to adopt it or accept its authority by other means. Such an idea may be religious, "scientific," or other – any belief that an individual embraces privately or shares with his or her peers or church and that should not be imposed on a heterogeneous public that does not agree with it. Those who would turn society into a battlefield among such beliefs transform their societies into arenas of conflict among principles whose adherents are obviously unwilling to relinquish them. By so doing, they make public life unbearable. The ethical basis of "a society of public virtues," in contrast, is "fair play," which allows coexistence to occur. This definition, as we have said, has much to offer but is not enough. After all, the contents of fair play were moral-religious-traditional, and even though parts of them endured, most of them turned secular. In this "game," of course, reality dictates compromises, and the elected institutions that are charged with interpreting it are built on the basis of the game's tradition and on a methodological basis of empirical study and examination of reality as it is and not as it is supposed to be – and in this respect, the English were very different from the French and the Germans. Thus, such a game is never simply fair; instead, it is anchored in tenets of culture and tradition, specific institutions, and demands of its players, including training for the holding of public office.

Therefore, once it passes the public test that empowers and enables it to rule. a political elite is allowed to exercise its reasoned, informed judgment on the basis of experience and thorough consideration of the forces acting upon and against it. This judgment leads to decisions that Ben-Gurion would surely term the products of the "art of government" – intelligent products of a mixture of values, interests, and reactions to steps taken by others amid a constantly changing reality that the statesperson must learn and constantly follow, based as they are on an "inner strength" without which statecraft is utterly valueless.

This inner strength rests on an appropriate elite and an appropriate citizenry. To carry out its policies, the political elite depends on an honest, efficient civil service. Admittedly, it is not a council of angels and is not free of power struggles among its own and, at times, with its superiors. Quite often, its membership includes some who err and mislead themselves, their subordinates, and their superordinates. Still, absent this administration, a modern society is hard to sustain. Proper training of its members, their loyalty to the "common good," and their professional pride in being "public servants" are assets that explain much of the success of the United Kingdom in its prime and also during its inevitable decline. In Ben-Gurion's view, one of the roles of the Israel Defense Forces would be to create such a cadre of public servants, and his own role was to provide it with support and protection from without. Ben-Gurion considered this a central principle when he created the IDF, and it would resurface in the debate over "the Affair." It must be interpreted properly in its proper place.

The secularization of traditional ethical values that modern government performs without relinquishing any of their substance was a process that in England bore no similarity to that which took place on the European continent, including the way it influenced the Jews there. The Zionist renaissance was preceded by great changes, including the exchange by Europeans of tradition for secular nationalism. These changes, originating in the scientific revolution of the seventeenth century, the Age of Enlightenment of the eighteenth century, Romanticism and Central European Neo-Romanticism, and the second scientific revolution in the nineteenth and early twentieth centuries, combined to effect economic and political changes in the status of Judaism until they precipitated a severe crisis in that ancient yet living civilization.

In Eastern Europe, following the Age of Enlightenment and the Napoleonic wars that ensued, the Haskala movement – the Jewish Enlightenment – stirred growing doubts among Jews as to the validity and moral significance of their culture. The result was a rift between *Maskilim* (exponents of Haskala) and those loyal to tradition. The latter, too, were not cut of one cloth; they were divided – roughly, for our purposes – between various groups of *Hasidim* and *Mitnagdim* ("opponents," i.e., anti-Hasidim), resulting in enormous tension, which still exists, between the streams of traditional Judaism. The metamorphoses of this stress may be found among the products of these schools, including those who became Zionists and carried on with the labors of this division in their own way. One may, for example, regard Mitnagdism as the basis for Yeshayahu Leibowitz's battle against Ben-Gurion, to which we shall return.

The significance of the Haskala, however, was that Jews began to see aspects of their culture and past as things to toss aside, in whole or in part, from the belief that other cultures were greater than theirs. This very grave process often prompted Jews to abandon Judaism (in stages that are not our concern here) and criticize it using the sharp, grating tools that it had given them, in content and a fortiori in form. Others maintained their ties with Judaism but in a secular, enlightened way, as we find among the forerunners of Zionism and the Zionists themselves. It follows that many traditionalists viewed Zionism and an attack on traditional Judaism as one and the same, even though the first flowerings of Zionism actually emerged from the camp of rabbis, such as Zvi Kalischer, and ultra-Orthodox lovers of Zion strove to establish cooperation with Maskilim, who realized that conflict between the Orthodox and freethinkers in the Zionist camp was imminent.[103]

Ultimately, both groups organized within camps, institutions, and parties. Many among the Orthodox in the Diaspora declared all-out war on both Haskala and Zionism, and so it remained until Religious Zionist shoots first took root after World War I and the non-Zionist Orthodox began to view aliyah as a practical possibility. Consequently, the New Yishuv quickly diversified and absorbed immigrants of multiple hues of religious faith, whom the Zionist "Renaissance people" either treated with consideration – as Ben-Gurion and Berl Katznelson did – or shunned and even resisted, as the left flank of the Labor Movement did.

Katznelson and Ben-Gurion, who in their respective ways and at different stages in their public lives operated within the context of the severe crisis that had befallen traditional Jewish society – partly as a result of the penetration of the Haskala into their centers in Central Europe – sought to revive the concept of Jewish chosenness and to give it real meaning in the combined spirit of Judaism, Haskala, and nineteenth-century socialism. Since these Zionists considered themselves integral members of Jewish society and the revivers of Jewish concepts, they did not disavow the Jewish pretense to chosenness as such. However, they shared the maskilic, social, historical-empirical, intellectual, and topical criticism of the pretense to chosenness of the Jewish Diaspora. Something about it seemed hollow to them, and in their estimation, Judaism had no future in twentieth-century Europe in any case.

Still, all Zionists were aware of the social and economic changes that had caused the Eastern European Jewish elite to prefer for its youth a general, secular education and business and scientific experience, rather than a traditional education in the Jewish religion and its texts, whence identity and prestige had once sprung. The rise in the status of the Jewish wealthy class, which in this respect deviated from the traditional relationship between the "well-heeled caste and the traditional maskilic stratum" (i.e., from the basic literature of the Jewish people); the development of a Jewish proletariat, whose relations with the wealthy steadily worsened; and the creation of the Jewish *talush* (the "rootless," next to the revolutionary socialist and the reckless capitalist), who had left tradition without finding satisfactory meaning in the secular Enlightenment – combined to create Socialist Zionism and its exceptional, hostile attitude toward the high-and-mighty among the Jews.

Unique in this constellation were the courts of the Hasidic *tsadiqim* (i.e., the courts of Hasidic rebbes), whose power was hereditary and charismatic as well, who considered themselves above the common people and their lay leaders. Their many followers accepted the status of "ignoramus" relative to their saintly leaders. But Zionism also created "courts" around leaders who could enjoy preferential status in their adherents' eyes, thanks to this tradition. These courts, however, were secular, and even if their leaders enjoyed no small measure of traditional grassroots support, much as Hasidic and rabbinic leaders did, their followers were divided among themselves and often struggled mercilessly with one another. This is why the search for new organizational settings, such as the Histadrut (General Federation of Labor in Palestine) and the modern democratic way of solving political problems – general elections and award of victory at the ballot box to several of the contestant parties – seems today a more natural solution than that accepted by traditional societies when they lost their preeminence. Among all possibilities, the proportional, multiparty electoral system seemed at first the most natural and obvious.

When we speak of the destruction of the traditional Jewish societies, however, we must consider the economic and political changes that non-Jewish governments forced on them and ponder their result, the growing devastation of the Jewish collectivities in Russia and Poland. Due to the partitioning of Poland, the ensuing havoc in the communities there was different from that inflicted on those under Austrian imperial rule. Jewish life in Hungary and independent Romania also developed differently. The result was the colorful, multifaceted creature that we call "the Jewish people." This people emigrated en masse from czarist Russia to Britain and the United States until those countries slammed their gates shut – Britain (with some exceptions) in 1905 and 1919 and the United States in a series of acts of Congress from 1921 to 1924. At that time, the various Western countries envisaged Eastern European Jewry as a many-headed hydra that was crawling toward them, with their focus on masses of Jews, as they appeared to be in London's East End and New York's East Side. Not only were they numerous; they were also seemingly problematic. After rapid politicization, they, or many of them, seemed to exhibit styles of political behavior and strong-arm interests that threatened the existing order. This may be one of the reasons for the perception of Zionism among European and Western statesmen, such as Balfour and Churchill, as a solution to the latent threat that the Jews posed to the existing order in their country, and as a blessing to Britain's imperial interests.[104]

As World War I neared, several specific types of Jewish people emerged and were memorialized in the critical literature of the time. Foremost among them was the aforementioned *talush*. As portrayed by the deep thinkers in Hebrew literature, Uri N. Gnessin and Y. H. Brenner, the talush is someone who, though having left tradition and tasted the Haskala, cannot find his place anywhere; a person who verbally protests the wretched state of affairs and finds refuge on the wings of his imagination, which provides no real shelter; a *luftmentsch*, a dreamer, who feels that he and his world have lost their substance and direction irretrievably. This crisis in Judaism, in my opinion, preoccupied the Zionists more than anything else. The destruction of the spirit and the sense of ruin and loss particularly afflicted the Maskilim and occupied the best writers. Thus, many of those who grew up on this literature hardly realized that among the Jews of Czarist Russia and Poland, powerful communities and economic and political activities that sought to invest Jews with status and power in their places of residence had also arisen. Some wished to be part of this accomplishment via assimilation; others preferred the Socialist, anti-Zionist Bund, and yet others operated via Zionist parties that served as mechanisms for the nurturing of vibrant Jewish bodies in the Diaspora – all of which until World War I came into being and changed everything.[105]

Even so, we find that a great energy had accumulated among the residents of the crumbling shtetls and of the many urban Jewish quarters, such as that of Warsaw, that had remained intact and even grown in strength. Sometimes this energy failed to find an outlet and destroyed them, but sometimes it became a razor-sharp practical skill, a keen genius and ability to survive under changing conditions. Such prowess may have been nurtured by traditional Jewish education and its mental honing that was conducive to practical issues, by their family structure, and by the community's great pressure on, and often its harsh social criticism of, its members. Here, in all likelihood, lie the origins of the energy that pulsed within the Jewish sectors in Europe, an energy that accumulated due to all of these factors, together with a business acumen – engendered by the terrible poverty and existential struggle that preceded this emancipation – and a craving for recognition and prestige, which were bound to get them, and other Jews, in trouble.

Zionism recognized such trouble early on because many of its leaders were empowered by this very energy. Socialist Zionism sought ab initio to forestall this trouble not only by leaving the dangerous European "valley of fantasy" but also by improving the energetic but pushy and unvirtuous Jew who had left the bosom of tradition. This improvement, however, entailed not only social change and a linguistic and cultural renaissance but also the modification of habits of political behavior and the adoption of suitable tools of government – at such time as a Jewish state would arise. Not everyone understood this.

Now consider the cynical capitalist who does not flinch from any exploitation or defrauding of those less shrewd than he is, who treats the entire world as his personal arena. We encounter him in the works of Sholom Aleichem, such as "The Train." This story deals, among other things, with the character of the Jewish panderer who settles in a distant country and then revisits his native shtetl in Bessarabia or Belarus in order to display his accomplishments and, as it were, to return to his roots. Such people often maintained Jewish solidarity despite the kinds of work they did and, of course, were object lessons of contempt to German and veteran Western Jews. These Jews, such as Walther Rathenau, Walter Lippmann, and Edwin Montague, became such patriots in their countries of residence and identified so thoroughly with those countries' particular values that one may speak of "German Jews," "English Jews," and "American Jews" who regarded *Ostjuden* as a plague and sought to dissociate from them or at least to "educate" them whenever they appeared in the West. These high-minded Jews, however, whose patriotism would in the German case exact a ghastly price, had already moved so far from Judaism that it was only a secondary, marginal, and sometimes annoying aspect of their German, English, or American essence.[106]

The famous "Jewish solidarity" that had existed for half a century in the late nineteenth and early twentieth centuries – by dint of international and national relief and charity organizations – was almost lost in the great storm created by World War I and the Bolshevik Revolution, on the one hand, and the subsequent rise of Europe's nation-states, on the other. Jews were involved in all of these events in various ways. The tumult of the war brought about the destruction of many communities in czarist territory and, soon after, the eclipse of all of Soviet Jewry by the shadow of Lenin and Stalin's rule. In independent Poland, the Baltic states, the newly independent countries of Central Europe, and the Balkans, Jewish life of all complexions flourished, but it was threatened by the specter of local nationalism and postwar economic crises. As the world war wound down, the Zionists won their Balfour Declaration, about twelve years after Britain suspended Jewish immigration and several years before the United States would do the same. From then until the Nazi accession and the outbreak of World War II, Ben-Gurion and his contemporaries were given only a few years to act in Palestine with a reasonable modicum of freedom.

The Nazis and the war transformed the Jewish crisis into a blatantly political matter and, practically speaking, an inescapable trap amid the forces that took hold during the 1930s.

Any discussion of Zionism that is not based on this complex picture of the Jewish condition and the societies and cultures in which Jews lived, in the shadow of a crisis that had begun in the first half of the nineteenth century, is not a historical discussion. After all, nineteenth-century England, no less, was jolted by the process that shifted traditional values onto a modern secular, ethical foundation, even though the British elite managed to defend its basic values and accepted form of government while reforming it against severe assaults. The West was vulnerable to modern science's attacks on all conventions, starting with permissible commentary on Darwin's theory as regards the contemporary understanding of man's origin and the rules that determine his life and future. Freud's theory, with its pessimistic, deterministic foundation, exposed the West to a deeper understanding of the human psyche even though this revelation had already surfaced from various directions. Accepted moral rules were being reviled as if guilty of perpetuating uncondonable social injustice and suffering. By the end of the nineteenth century, the West and parts of Central and Eastern Europe faced the artistic revolution of modernism; at the beginning of the twentieth century, they confronted the technological revolution and awaited the new age with bated breath. The so-called *fin de siècle* state of mind was conflicted and riddled with contradictions. Many considered it optimistic, positive, and hopeful; to others it was threatening, exposed to harsh truths theretofore unknown, and in need of drastic change. This approach was translated not into political action but, rather, into novel developments in philosophy, the natural sciences, the arts, and, to an increasing measure, literature. Then, a short time later, the West was embroiled in the slaughter of World War I and the Bolshevik Revolution, from which it emerged with its skeptical, innovative, and traditional states of mind having been turned into political trends and forces.

Amid this reality, the simple Zionism of the Eastern European shtetl, an expression of awareness of the crisis of Jewish civilization that had been building for several generations and the conviction that it had a clearer solution to offer, had to contend with forces whose depth it did not really know, or used them selectively for its own purposes, as was shown by our earlier discussion of the indirect influence upon it of German philosophy. Zionism had to change from being a movement of cultural revival and practical social criticism that had a clear and simple political aspect, as expressed in Herzl's *The Jewish State* and *Altneuland*, into a political movement in the world of the 1920s and 1930s, in which cultural, moral, economic, and social issues evolved into a massive political struggle. Ultimately, this struggle exploded into a second world war that plunged European Jewry into utter devastation. During this buildup to World War II, many Zionists developed their own views of these matters, and Jews who had emigrated to Eretz Israel, for whatever reason, expressed either these views or a blend of values and expectations that they had brought from their countries of origin. Zionism's ideological surge was cantilevered on the expectation of a revolution in the ways of life of a living nation;[107] the death of this nation immobilized some exponents of the abstract revolutionary theory of Zionism that had struck root among semiassimilated Zionists in Germany.[108]

The leaders of the Zionist Labor Movement stuck to their guns even though the world of their youth had evolved into the changing world of the 1920s, 1930s, 1940s, and 1950s. Thus, it is not surprising that their path ended in the 1960s, and not only because of their age. Ben-Gurion, perhaps the only one of them who had started out as a shtetl boy who sought a cultural and social renewal in Eretz Israel for the Jewry of his time, understood the need to control this motley nation as much as possible, recognized its fragility and internal difficulties, and sought to consolidate it enough to allow it to survive in its environment and in a world that was changing beyond recognition. Ultimately, however, he was overcome by both past and future forces (i.e., a combination of Jewish nationalism rooted in the crisis of the West on the eve and as a result of World War I; modernist, Marxist, neo-socialist, and liberal "humanist" criticism; neo-Orthodox and shtetl habits). In retrospect, Ben-Gurion became the victim of the postmodern and neo-neo-Marxist criticism of our day.

His attempt to turn politics into statecraft failed to gain traction and sank in the morass of politics. That is, Ben-Gurion believed that once statehood was attained, he should be able to change its approach, as well as possible, from the politics of a voluntary society to the statecraft of "public virtues" and create the requisite tools for this transformation with a celerity entailed by the internal social changes and external challenges. Things that were necessary in a voluntary society such as the Yishuv, which was subordinate to the world Zionist movement in basic issues like the problem of borders, demanded rethinking and change in a state.

Since this state was a tool not only for the expression of Jewish independence but also for the correction of Jewish behavior, the challenge was all the greater. During the Yishuv period, it was tackled mainly via the tools of rural settlement and the cooperative umbrellas of the General Federation of Labor and of the Zionist Labor Movement. These tools remained valuable because even after the establishment of the state, Ben-Gurion and his like wished to improve the Diaspora Jew, that is, to make him or her into a tiller of the soil of Israel. Thus, immigrants were steered to rural settlement and given land not only to make the wilderness bloom but also to bring about a welcome (or "blessed," as the Hebrew term had it) change in the lifestyle of Diaspora Jews. Equally, however, the emphasis now had to shift to the betterment of Jews, and their transformation into ordinary citizens of a sovereign Jewish state, under a strong democratic regime that had the ability to decide big issues. A soundly functioning state that faced existential problems even after having been born in the cauldron of war could not continue to use the tools of the Yishuv period and make do with low-level compromise dictated by the pre-state realities that often had to be respected.[109]

This compromise persisted in various forms even after the founding of the state, as we shall see later, though not in all areas. One of the main areas was the IDF and the symbolism of its status: an army of the people totally subordinate to an elected civil authority, an army whose commanders should behave as "public servants," in the British sense of the term. Yet today, many call Ben-Gurion a dictator and his reign a time of suffocating benightedness. The man who twice quit the government voluntarily – after all, on both occasions he could have continued to cling to the horns of the altar – became a figure whose personality and era were viewed by both friends and rivals as driven by lust for power and rule. One explanation for this characterization was the decline of the "renaissance Zeitgeist" in which he operated.

Even if the similarity between the European Renaissance and the Jewish renaissance was less than material in many respects, in others the resemblance remained visible for some time: the sense of renewal and rebirth among members of a generation that did not tumble into complete despair or cynicism; faith in man and faith in the potential betterment of the Jewish person; refusal to accept the inertia, cynicism, and corruption of prior generations as self-evident; willingness to mobilize in order to translate this state of mind into novel "acts of creation" in diverse cooperative settings that arose, thanks to others' experience and theories (the kibbutz, the moshav), in military operations and foreign and defense policy; and the consent, albeit with reservations, to the partitioning of the country when the cause demanded a creative solution of this sort – an issue that in the eyes of many today, as then, concerned high principle that lent itself to no "creative" solution. The territorial integrity of Eretz Israel, to which Ben-Gurion had been committed since the days of the Biltmore Program of 1942 – to be discussed – and that seemed attainable during the War of Independence, was abandoned for weighty political and strategic reasons. Thus, Ben-Gurion did not strive to attain it during the war, partly due to concern that the British would interfere in order to prevent Jordan's ouster from the West Bank territories that it had occupied, and also because he did not want to impose Jewish rule on an Arab population in these sensitive areas. Instead, he began to turn his attention to the unpopulated and less sensitive Negev Desert, seeing in it a solution for the expansion of Jewish settlement.[110]

A Renaissance spirit pulsed through all of these discussions, for Zionist Renaissance people of the Ben-Gurionic type were permitted to act in ways that tradition and dry principles forbade in other times. This trend of thought encompassed classical concepts that seemed to contradict the "art" of Renaissance politics. The contradiction, however, was ostensible only. Incorporated into the return to the ancestral land was the freedom to act "creatively" within it. Such action would become necessary once the Zionists studied and familiarized themselves with the realities of their surroundings, including the Jews' limitations and the dictates of their history – foremost the Holocaust, which had destroyed the original Zionist living areas and greatly reduced the number of Jews who would come to live amid an ocean of Arabs. The millions of Jews who had been annihilated could have taken over all of western Palestine and neutralized the hostile, rebellious, and dangerous significance of the Arab minority of the area, which marched decisively to the tune of pipers like the Mufti of Jerusalem, who became Hitler's ally. The Holocaust ultimately necessitated the partitioning of the country and disengagement from the Arabs because of the mistakes of their leaders, who spurned all forms of compromise at the time. Rational thinking, which contemplates reality without preconceived notions – the process that Ben-Gurion called a "calculating machine" – furnished an analytical tool for this purpose.

These components merged with Neo-Romantic and Socialist ways of thinking to form an eclectic mix that masked grave doubts and is easily criticized today for being theoretically invalid. Ben-Gurion understood better than others that one dared not rely on the fleeting existence of this mix despite its accomplishments in its time, for it probably sufficed to create a state but not to consolidate one.[111]

It is the Jews' way, as Ben-Gurion learned from their past, to establish sovereignty and then to lose it. Here lay the critical difference between Burckhardtian "humanists," such as Martin Buber or Shlomo Tzemach, and the stern, austere statesman.

On "Politics," Politicization, and Statecraft

Politics concerns itself with governing, that is, the ability to rule over people. In practical terms, it means the acquisition and maintenance of power (or *Macht* in the jargon of political science) via the conscious use of instruments of power that are typical of the age of the masses. It refers to a great number of tools apart from those specific to the use of governmental power in the legislative and socioeconomic realms. It refers to both mobilizing the masses and heeding their wishes, via images, symbols, and rational discussion, in order to induce them to choose among alternatives that politicians establish within a given sociolegal order or aimed at changing it and even changing an international order. That is, we view politics as a struggle among people, groups, or organizations for power or influence for their own sake or for the articulation of drives, egos, and sundry beliefs. The tools used for these purposes may be any that serve the power-mongering goals of the actors in the political "jungle": behind-the-scenes intrigues; enlistment of support in exchange for a quid pro quo from some side, including an ideological enemy; or all-holds-barred defamation by double-dealing, media manipulation, and leaking. Here, we argue that Ben-Gurion – who used this definition regularly – always distinguished between politics and statecraft. "Political science" – the science of statecraft – distinguishes among such different kinds of "politics," but ultimately views them all as the use of power, that is, the pursuit of power by any means that can be attained and its sources and instruments of legitimization, including its loss or transfer to other contenders on a national and international level, entailing the use of military force.

Some scholars argue that the political process is but one expression of the activity of a "civil society" and is often not the most important of them. Viewed from the perspective of the present time and the standards of other modern civil societies, life in Yishuv and Israeli society seems to have been highly, if not excessively, political. Some express this by saying that society in the Yishuv and early Israel was very "ideological," that is, clearly and typically mirroring differences of opinion in matters of worldview and values. I would say, following the historical methodology to which I adhere, that Yishuv and early Israeli society was a fragile thing, a scaffold-like structure of diverse outlooks, opinions, and traditions that, for lack of time, the absence of a suitable educational and cultural background, and the Holocaust, could not be fashioned ab initio into a Western civil society. Thus, we cannot know what such a society in Israel would have looked like or whether it would have evolved naturally in a Western style of the sort that emerged after World War II. Such societies sprout elites, middle classes, working classes, values, and rules of the game that are typically Western. The "state" is an overarching framework that these civil societies accept by consensus in the best case (the British one) and/or embrace amid controversy and adjustments in the worst case (as in France and, for some time, the United States during the Civil War).

Now we must understand Ben-Gurion's politics – which, of course, originated in his world of concepts and values, discussed in the context of the development of the Yishuv from a collection of small communities into what it became on the eve of, in the course of, and in the aftermath of World War II. In the discussion that follows, Zionism at large, and Ben-Gurion himself as one of its leaders, are tested in light of various states' interests vis-à-vis voluntary groups in crisis on the eve of and during global war, the enduring criticism of the performance of civil society in the West, and the view, conventional today, of the singular nature of "Western culture."

For Ben-Gurion, "politics" was always a tool in the service of a classic Zionist goal: the revival of a people that, though not even a people in many senses, had its own history and culture, and the concentration of large numbers of them in Eretz Israel for their own betterment as they returned to nature amid difficulties within and without. Ben-Gurion's premise was that only in its land, and certainly in its own sovereign state, could the Jewish people become sovereign and self-sufficient. In this sense, Zionism had a clear-cut political goal that could not be fulfilled in the Diaspora for two reasons: the nature and content of the Jews' lives there and the multitude of interests and considerations that Gentile societies and values dictated, including rampant antisemitism and dual-allegiance problems that did not allow Diaspora Jews to pursue Jewish interests fully.

The difficulties that Ben-Gurion encountered at home and abroad, as I will show, were two: the inability of Yishuv circles to think in fully Jewish sovereign terms and ultranationalist exaggeration that spoke in terms of sovereignty and a "grandeur" culled from the world of others, absent the socialist and personal change that Ben-Gurion's pioneering Socialist theory entailed. These difficulties required the self-styled "calculating machine" in order to become a "disputatious and contentious person," in his own words. Still, from the time statehood was declared, the main goal of the "dispute and contention" became the rebirth of Jews in their own land as a chosen people, that is, a people with values and a political way of life that would allow it not only to survive by virtue of the power that it displayed under the particular conditions of the War of Independence but also to develop in the future in order to preempt new circumstances by means of its culture, social accomplishments, system of government, and rules. The last two should resemble, to the extent possible, the tools of governance and "rules of the game" of the British state, even though they would not be organic products of Jewish history and even though an English-style civil society, the sort that generally assumes the burden of statehood via its elected institutions, did not exist in Israel.

This belief, which made it possible to fashion a society, or at least give it an indelible stamp, was characteristic of the renaissance generation and certainly of Ben-Gurion himself, who demonstrated this faith and applied his personal and moral power (and his charisma, the product of years of difficult and so far successful efforts) to its actualization and spent most of his life mobilized on its behalf to the limits of his ability. In other words, Ben-Gurion himself distinguished between the institutions and rules of governance and what might take place in society. Different forces act within a society, and he sought to shape them the best he could and enlist them in his cause. The institutions of governance, he believed, should be fashioned along British lines so that they might influence the fashioning of a democratic society.

Just the same, his approach carried several contradictions, some structural and others ostensibly related to political ethics. One of them concerned the status of the General Federation of Labor – the Histadrut – its interests, and its ability to function under changing economic conditions as a central institution in the life of a society that was meant to be socialist but free. Non-Jews of the Anglo-American liberal and conservative persuasion paid much critical attention to the Yishuv society for its dual pretension in this matter, as we shall see.

Another contradiction, of both style and performance, may be discerned from steps that Ben-Gurion tended to take that aroused controversy and confrontation and were painful to the point of cruelty, stemming from motives that ostensibly aimed to bring consensus between the peoples of Palestine and even a "Jewish–Arab alliance" at a very early stage. Never, however, did Ben-Gurion undertake to create either consensus or an alliance at any price. Instead, he dealt in building a nation – or, when the time came, the vestiges of a nation – and in planting it in a hostile environment.[112] The nation-building act had several aspects: social, economic, moral/ethical, institutional, and cultural, each receiving different emphases during Ben-Gurion's long life.

Due to the special status to which he aspired, Ben-Gurion was considered the fashioner of modes of living and their underlying ideas in the early statehood years. Yet though his influence was great, it was limited by, and subject to, his order of priorities. Like it or not, the man became in the eyes of his generation, his critics at the time, and their contemporaneous heirs a symbol of the despotic, domineering "establishment," even though from his standpoint no establishment worthy of the name had yet been formed. As time passed, he acquired the widely held image of a hard, ascetic, puritan, inflexible, intolerant, and old-fashioned man, even though most of his critics in those days – from the radical journalist Helmuth Ostermann (Uri Avneri) to the religious anarchist Professor Yeshayahu Leibowitz – were, in respect to the contents of their arguments, immeasurably less tolerant than he was, power and influence seekers at any price, and inconsistent in that the topics and substance of their criticism changed abruptly. Just the same, these two extremes and others managed to slowly erode Ben-Gurion's public image and help the rapidly changing Zeitgeist to make him, in the eyes of many, a figure of the past, uninvolved in real life, indifferent to personal freedoms and freedom of expression, and interested only in the security of the Jewish state in an authoritarian fashion and imposing it on all its citizens, as he understood it.

This last phase in Ben-Gurion's career would eventually diminish his public standing among the youth, who would find his language hard to understand and strive to climb out from under his moral warnings and political threats. For them, the self-styled Renaissance man had become the high priest of an outdated church.

Another contradiction was between the attitudes and "ruses" that Ben-Gurion adopted for outsiders – the British, the Arabs, and the Americans at different stages of his activity – and the demandingly moralistic character of his behavior vis-à-vis the domestic scene. It is often hard-core politics to take stances that obscure true motives and to maneuver among forces in the field. Such maneuvering creates the impression of political cunning, if not of guile, dishonesty, and lack of integrity. So, too, for domestic consumption and for people who lost his trust due to thinking that was shallow, doctrinaire, narrowly "political," or all three at once.

Here, the reader should note my distinction between the "politics" of the voluntary Yishuv, within which Ben-Gurion operated before the attainment of the various phases of statehood, and "statecraft," which he sought to fashion after the state's founding. From the perspective of political science, obviously both of these are politics. Once statehood was attained, however, Ben-Gurion drew a necessary and growing distinction between unavoidable acts vis-à-vis outside players and things that must not be done for domestic consumption. For outsiders, certain things had to be done, and to do them one needed not only to study reality but also to have an instrument for domestic use. This instrument, however, was limited in its latitude due to the democratic nature of the governmental system and, a fortiori, the nature and stances of people who did not fully understand the significance of having attained statehood and did not realize that their institutions, systems, and power needed change, limitation, and adaptation to new needs, those of a state. The change they would have to adopt in due course would be the transformation of the entire political system.

Here lies another difference between the Yishuv period and its successor, the statehood era. When we contemplate the capacities of a democratic politician, such as the American President Abraham Lincoln within a specific political system such as the American one, we know that his strength derived not only from his outstanding political skills. Lincoln's status was anchored in two additional pillars: the Constitution and also the mythological figure of the "father of the nation," George Washington. Washington's image empowered the presidency in matters of war and peace, and his successors benefited from this power and could use it to restrain rivals, occasionally including vicious and unbridled ones such as Lincoln's, who presented truly severe challenges to his status in the supreme state of emergency of the Civil War. Lincoln himself was a highly seasoned politician. To keep his adversaries from becoming personal enemies, he co-opted them into his government, and when he had no choice but to dismiss them because they undermined him overtly, he compensated them with extragovernmental positions that surprised even them. Of course, Americans had learned the lessons of the War of Independence and the demands of its commander and father of the nation, which, when the time came, installed President Washington as commander in chief and gave him, to a reasonable degree as he saw it, the capacity to act within the framework of "separation of powers." Even there, however, in a country where the future mass of democracy rested on a rigid written Constitution, separation of powers, and a Supreme Court that gradually became supreme as the interpreter of the constitution, there was no escaping a civil war when the president had been disfavored by a large, powerful minority. Lincoln enlisted the prestige of the presidency the best he could, but the path before him was strewn with obstacles and almost ended with his downfall in the election of 1864 on account of difficulties both within and without.

Ben-Gurion was not given the chance to finish the work of a "founding president." One reason was the divided, aggressive, polemic nature of Jewish politics in Israel. Unlike America – where the birth pangs and problems of the Declaration of Independence were learned and discussed in a search for compromises suited to the United States and its particular federal structure – Jewish politics in independent Israel lacked the tools, personalities, interests, and ideas that the formula used by the framers of the United States Constitution could resolve, albeit not without a civil war. When we compare the birth of the American nation with that of Israel, we must distinguish between different periods in these birth processes (to which we will return briefly). One of them was the transition from Yishuv to state and from the Hagana to the IDF in 1946–1949. After that time, it appears as if Ben-Gurion tried to behave in a Lincolnesque manner toward many of those who, due to their pride, their past, and the erstwhile settings in which they developed and that they represented, threatened the policy to which he aspired as an elected statesman-in-chief and menaced a system that did not resemble the American one and that was adjusting to the British cabinet form of government and to his senior status as the prime minister of his cabinet.

According to the British system, the prime minister is not allowed to overrule the majority in the cabinet but can steer the majority and influence it to the best of his ability on the basis of his prerogative to dissolve Parliament and call general elections. Also, the British ballot law created a two-party system, which – in most cases – allows one party to win an absolute majority in the House. In Israel, thanks to the proportional electoral system, Ben-Gurion's Mapai never won an absolute majority, leading to coalitions dominated by Mapai so long as the other parties were divided among themselves and unable to unite against it. Thus, Ben-Gurion was careful neither to destroy nor to sever his connections with the leaders of left-wing Mapam and, particularly, Meir Ya'ari, the head of Marxist-Zionist Ha-Shomer ha-Tsa'ir. Accordingly, he included Ya'ari in important Knesset committees despite – or perhaps because of – Mapam's Soviet orientation, which he publicly opposed and castigated. Members of Mapam's right wing – Mapai's former Faction B – who had been commanders in the disbanded commando unit, and later, regular units of the Palmach, left the IDF and became senior reserve officers if they wished, while those who chose to remain in the apolitical army that had been founded, such as Yitzhak Rabin, were appointed to key positions commensurate with their talents. (Veterans of other persuasions were excluded outright: former members of Menachem Begin's IZL – the Irgun – after the succesionists' rebellion against the authority of the majority in the past and during the War of Independence, and some former agitators in Lehi – the so-called Stern group that had adopted a mystical, Nietzschean view of Israel's spirit and aspirations, including Dr. Yisrael Scheib-Eldad, for whom the small, poor State of Israel established in only part of Eretz Israel did not suit their mystical, majestic vision.)

Ben-Gurion also avoided hopeless battles with Religious Zionists and the ultra-Orthodox and maneuvered the best he could – thanks to Mapai's key position as a plurality centrist party – among the many Knesset factions in his quest for partners who would be well suited to his priorities. Mapai's "pivotal position," however, was founded on a lack of commonality among all the other parties. Therefore, it was an evanescent status that would be doomed the moment the political dynamics of the minorities would induce them to reach out to one another and form a majority. This was another reason to demand the redrawing of the party map in order to render the Knesset a two-party parliament, in the hope that the moderate Right – the General Zionists – would be subsumed into Menachem Begin's ultra-rightist Herut (Liberty) Party as a decisive, moderating factor, there being no chance at that time for the latter to fulfill its territorial dreams.

Politics can be seen as a tool for the attainment and, in greater or smaller measure, the preservation of power in national or international public spheres. However, it can also be the striving for and preservation of power for purposes found worthy by a statesperson who constantly studies changes in the world, the region, and his or her own society. Amid this effort, the statesperson maintains and furthers interests that relate to what he or she considers worthy goals by means of institutions that represent the public and ongoing dialogue with the public. Alternately, if divisiveness and paralysis of power make unattainable the changes that are deemed necessary in a new historical situation, the statesperson may seek to enact an institutional reform and, for this purpose, try to marshal the consent of the majority of the public and its representatives. This, according to our definition, is statecraft – something that can be accomplished within the framework of a state and that requires a suitable governmental structure.

Ben-Gurion strove to practice such statecraft while attempting to sustain for the future the spirit of voluntarism that he called "pioneerism" in an omnibus way, including immigrant absorption and rural settlement. He also tried to wed pioneerism with politics, that is, to integrate the fragmented interests of the kibbutz settlement movements into the political entities that had both amassed power and found reasons for contentiousness with him and his party. In other words, from the earliest days of the state, the left-wing parties were in opposition to this majority. After having accepted its authority during the War of Independence, they become a bitter and militant opposition, especially in their organs of expression: daily newspapers, literary supplements, and sundry periodicals that gained much influence at the expense of the sclerotic, establishmentarian daily *Davar*. This exhaustion was probably rooted in the lengthy mobilization – from the Arab revolt of 1936–1939 through service in the British Army during World War II to the Hagana and the long, bloody War of Independence – at which point the Holocaust caused the spearhead of the Zionist renaissance in Palestine to come uncoupled from its Diaspora "reserve."[113] The fount of Zionism's rejuvenation with people, ideas, and concepts could no longer flow from that source, as Avi Bareli said, because of the Holocaust.

This, however, is not the only explanation for Mapai's conceptual wilting and its loss of sense of destiny and conceptual energy. They are, of course, connected to the party's successes in the early statehood years – its penetration of realms in which it had once had to submit to minority views (e.g., separate party-affiliated school systems), its success in becoming the key player in socioeconomic affairs, its organizational strength in elections and in mobilizing support among recent immigrants, and the special status that its leader had acquired. However, it came at a price: The "iron law of the oligarchy," on the one hand – that pretended to be grass roots and egalitarian and that maintained a few symbols of this pretension even after it had become an oligarchy – and an ideological aridity that can be traced to social-democratic ideology itself, on the other hand, implemented as it was by invoking rampant bureaucracy and economic control.

In both realms – the ostensibly foreseeable attack on the Yishuv leadership during the Holocaust and the argument that even then it had suffered from aggressive "Palestinocentrism" and ideological vagueness – the Holocaust would exert a severe retroactive effect. It happened because many activists

among the surviving ghetto fighters and partisans identified specifically with
the Zionist Left. Moreover, in the first statehood years, the Holocaust became
a battering ram for use against the Mapai elite by the leftist parties, which
declared themselves spokesmen for the fighting survivors – the partisans, who
had not gone "like lambs to the slaughter" and, for this reason, represented
the spirit of the accepted Israeli ethos.

Menachem Begin and his Herut movement, in contrast, anointed themselves the mouthpieces of decimated European Jewry and blamed the Zionist
mainstream, and particularly Mapai, for blunders in rescue work both before
and during the Holocaust. These allegations escalated in the early 1950s as
Herut spokesmen accused its mainstream political rivals of betraying the Jewish people and selling the victims of the Holocaust for German reparations.[114]
The Herut leaders did not limit their arguments to attacks on Mapai and its
chairman. On account of the Mapai leadership, they claimed, the Knesset was
"stained with the blood" of Holocaust victims, and they made great use of the
Knesset podium, more than any other public realm, to delegitimize the elected
government and its decisions. Unsurprisingly, Ben-Gurion answered them personally and with no less pungency, arguing in reverse that Herut's use of the
Knesset for its own purposes had devalued its status and ability – including
the ability of its committees – to discuss weighty problems in Israel's foreign
and defense affairs, such as its ties with West Germany. Later on, after the sen-
sational Kasztner trial – to be discussed – and in reference to Israeli–German
relations in the early 1960s, Mapai was accused by the parties on its left *and*
its right – despite their differences – of consorting with a neo-Nazi regime.
What was the truth quotient of all this rhetoric, and what has "politics" got
to do with it? Can one speak of the politicization of the Holocaust, and what
does this term mean? We take up this term again, in the specific context of the
Holocaust and its background.

The Mapai elite was composed of various apparatuses that provided the
nascent State of Israel with most of the personnel that its operative entities
needed. This is because one could rely on the positions of the party's central
committee, unlike those of the pro-Soviet leftist parties and those of Begin's
Herut, which originally repudiated the Knesset's authority in the matter of
German reparations and did not recognize the 1949 partition lines. Within
Mapai itself, however, apparatuses that marched to their own drummers took
shape. In education, they took control of immigrant youth and enrolled them
in Labor Movement schools. In matters related to economics, industry, and
essentially every area of life in which they could seize control and influence,
they did so, often clashing with the wishes of the Mapai chairman himself. The
lack of proper public supervision over these apparatuses and their members'
relations with government bodies, tracing to the lack of a direct connection
between them and their voters, led to rampant corruption. The whole turgid
scene energized Ben-Gurion and prompted him to propose a trial of his comprehensive reform after his first retirement to Kibbutz Sede Boqer in 1953. The
reform, however, could not win the necessary majority in the Knesset, partly

because the larger parties spurned it in order to retain the smaller parties' cooperation in the future.

Under these circumstances and given the requirements and challenges of Israel's security, Ben-Gurion returned to the government within the framework of the existing system. At the supposed height of his power, however – after his great victory in the 1959 elections – the seemingly cohesive package of the Mapai elite came untied. One reason for this was the Lavon Affair, an embodiment of all the unsolved problems of the governmental system and the rules of the game. Another reason was the end of a period of external pressure – the "mobilization" period that had begun in the 1930s – when tension along the frontiers eased considerably as a result of the 1956 Sinai-Suez Campaign. A third reason, which must be examined in depth, was the public contradiction between the Eichmann trial of 1961–1962 and the belated impact of the Holocaust, as I call it, and Ben-Gurion's German policy, a nexus that bridged Left and Right and salvaged Menachem Begin's Herut movement from the political wasteland into which Ben-Gurion had misled it.

We must, therefore, discuss the phenomenon called politicization. This discussion is needed in order to understand the plight of the Jews from the 1920s until after World War II and to appreciate Ben-Gurion's politics and statecraft then and later.

What is politicization? It is the creation of a state of violence in society and an understanding of societal developments in terms of acute force: intrigue (or what passes for intrigue) and verbal and physical violence that seek to change the existing order by means of force, threat of force, terror, mass demagoguery, and external war. It is a radical revision of the understanding of reality in terms of rival forces that seemingly have concrete, though by nature masked and subversive, manifestations that have to be fought in various ways, including their own. Antisemitism, from the standpoint of those who thought this way, is the consequence of a real 2,000-year-old Jewish plot to destroy the values, offspring, economy, and future of Germany. Everything that happened since World War I was translated into such terms as a matter of principle, and in the eyes of its alleged German victims this "conspiracy" supposedly required a forceful response. Such "politics," then, first became widespread in Europe after World War I. One of its expressions was Fascism in its different forms. On the far left and among the political radicals at large, however, a clear tendency could be seen to understand the world in terms of power and intrigue that must be countered with force, and to seek the politicization of society in order to rescue it from its enemies by any and all means. This politicization was assisted by propaganda, intrigue, mobilizations of the masses under a "leader" or sundry "leaders," the creation of submissive hierarchies, the blocking of information that contradicts official doctrines, and the physical persecution of real and imaginary internal and external enemies.

This also explains why members of the elite and many public strata in Anglo-American Western circles feared that the mobilization and activation of the masses by means of intrigue, propaganda, and force on behalf of some private virtue would menace both their civil society and its governing institutions. Ultimately, Western conservatives and liberals alike saw this as an intolerable challenge to public virtues, the Western ideal of freedom, individual rights, and the functioning of a state that took to heart its market economy, the interests of its elite, and the welfare of its masses (without including them greatly in the political process), its international status, and its future in a world whose order would now be captive to such foreign ideas and forces.

Unfortunately, however, the sprouting of ideas and modi operandi of this type was imputable, at least in part, to the contributions of Jews to societies that actually had been founded on private virtues that were now being implemented by physical force. We are referring to the Bolshevik Revolution and the Communist parties that arose outside the Soviet Union. This, however, was preceded by the widely held opinion that Jews were not the originators of accepted morality, since they did not adhere to it but, rather, cared only for their own crowd – a grave allegation that deserves separate interpretative attention here. Moreover, civilized people did not find antisemitism repugnant. Indeed, many Western "civilized people" subscribed to it in various forms and even saw it as an explanation for the rise of Nazism in Germany. They viewed the Jews as the fomenters and creators of antisemitism, whether by their own fault or by the fault of the Germans' foolishness and immaturity, which had combined to elevate Hitler to power, thus creating a severe problem for the West. Jews and the unwanted politicization of Western societies were, in the eyes of many, two phenomena that marched in tandem, hand in hand. Socialist Zionism ostensibly sought to mobilize the masses by dint of comprehensive nationalist-socialist "ideas" without asking their opinion. The Zionist Labor Movement, in turn, seemed to be recruiting them by using Bolshevik tactics and dismissing their value as individuals.[115]

Western Culture versus "Uniqueness and Destiny"

"What makes the West 'Western'?" the late Samuel Huntington, one of the most important conservative thinkers in the United States, asked in our times.[116] Huntington's answer, given in a list of definitions that are, of course, succinct and simple, is valuable for the continuation of our discussion. First, he said, it refers to the Western classical tradition, that is, the "third generation" culture that draws extensively from its predecessors, foremost Greek philosophy and rationalism, Roman law, and Latin culture and Christianity, as distinct from the Islamic and Greek Orthodox cultures (Greek Orthodox referring to the culture that influenced the Russian heritage). Western Christianity, Huntington continued – first the Catholic and then the Protestant – is the most important single characteristic of Western culture. This determination, which we consider essentially correct, divides Judaism and Zionism from "Western culture" and creates an ineluctable tension between them, which Ben-Gurion recognized and deemed to be self-evident. Huntington omits all mention of

Judaism among the civilizations that contributed to this culture, whereas Ben-Gurion and other Zionists claimed, like Heine in his time, that Judaism made a weighty contribution to Western culture and humanity at large, without forfeiting its uniqueness as a national religion that does not aspire to subjugate humanity to its beliefs and even has internal disagreements about several of its main tenets.

To make his case, Huntington argues that when Westerners set out to conquer the world in the sixteenth century, they did so for the sake of God and gold alike. Later, the Reformation and the Counter-Reformation divided the West, creating a dichotomy of central political and intellectual importance in Western history that is completely absent from the history of Eastern Orthodoxy and Latin America. Huntington then listed the national languages of the West, which took on lives of their own from the sixteenth century to our day. The next characteristic of Western culture, in his opinion, is the bifurcation of spiritual and secular authority. God and Caesar, church and state, form a duality that is dominant in the West. In Islam, in contrast, God is Caesar; in China and Japan, Caesar is god; and in Greek Orthodoxy, God is Caesar's junior partner. The separation of church and state that is characteristic of Western culture is unmatched among other cultures and has made a major contribution to the development of freedom in the West. If so, those who regard Judaism as a theocratic culture that cannot properly separate church and state and that entertains the pretension of giving its members dominion over the whole world will see Judaism as an enemy of the fundamental values of the West.

The Jews, however, abandoned their missionary pretensions generations ago. Their uniqueness is manifested in their desire to remain unique and separate and to sustain the conceptual contents of their singularity in a world that finds it increasingly difficult to accept this stance for various reasons – classic-universalistic-Christian, liberal-socialist, and modern-nationalist. Secular Zionists inherited the Jewish consciousness of a special destiny; from this perspective, the Jewish religion should not have raised any problem for them. After all, religion was the cultural wellspring of their selective, historical, and secular being. Admittedly, they regarded it not as a source of authority for their political lives but only as an inspiration, a highly valuable historic memory, and one of the foundations of their identity. This perspective, however, could be adopted only in a historical period that allowed for it, that is, that of the Zionist renaissance. Some of those who held this outlook and were more sensitive to its difficulties, such as Ben-Gurion himself, would do their utmost to invest it with stable content. Such content formed the basis of Ben-Gurion's slogan, *yihud ve-yi'ud* ("uniqueness and destiny") for the Jewish people in its land. This slogan captured the intermingling of several things: the Bible, with special emphasis on the ethics of the prophets; Jewish sovereignty; repairing the psyches and behavior of Jews in their land – even if this meant only a part of it; and demonstrating their past contribution to humanity at large, obligating them in the present to act as a people that is valuable to itself and others.

Huntington listed the other components of Western culture as he viewed them: rule of law, social pluralism, civil society, representative institutions, and individualism. The important thing, he said, is not each of these components in isolation, since they exist in various forms in other cultures (with some exceptions), but their existence in combination, which gives the West its special merit. Indeed, the civil rule of law in its Roman sense, the English common law, and, particularly, the concept of "natural law" that ensures individual rights and crimps the authority of the king are principal contributions of Western culture to world civilization, even though rulers of all types often violate them. Judaism, in this portrayal, seems to stand apart from all these developments or perhaps beneath them. Arguably, however, Judaism's concepts of universal justice – foremost the creation of man, that is, every human being, in the image of God, the Ten Commandments, the rebukes of the prophets, and the Jewish moral demand that people treat each other lovingly, mercifully, and charitably – were central in creating the essence of the Western rule of law until said rule came uncoupled from all religious justifications. Even today, however, Huntington depicted this uncoupling as less than absolute due to the centrality of the Christian heritage in Western culture. Nevertheless, the development of social pluralism and civil society in England, America, and France – each country in its own way – did engender, as Karl Deutsch put it, "the rise of various autonomous groups irrespective of kinship or marriage ties." Thus, one of the classic Western arguments against Judaism would concern the blood tie among Jews, which ostensibly denies recognition of any autonomous groups as of equal value to Jews yet sets the relationship among Jews on a foundation of blood.

The problem for secular Zionists was to base the connection among Jews on something other than kinship, even though acknowledging this tie as such. What they sought was a connection of historical experience, culture, *and* religion that would be adapted and tailored to the needs of a secular national society. Obviously, then, Ben-Gurion and his colleagues would not view the religious heritage of Oriental Jewry as the only or main basis for their settling in Israel; instead, they chose the idea – reviled today by leftists, of all people – of the "melting pot," based on the combination of biblical and, especially, prophetic moralism and secular social democracy derived from progressive European ideas. Paradoxically and ironically, Huntington himself concluded, after listing the reasons for the "decline of the West" and its internal fragmentation in our time, that immigrants to Western countries from other cultures should be placed under restrictions and that the unique Western culture should be protected by means that strongly recall those used by secular Zionism in its attempt to protect and preserve chosen elements of Jewish culture and history.

Diaspora Jewry did have representative institutions, but they fell far short of institutionalized representation as it had developed in England and the United States, the great differences between which Huntington blurred for his own purposes. Individualism in England and in America also differed in character and historical development. In fact, England was the cradle of various forms of individualism, for religious, economic, and political reasons that are unique to the inhabitants of that island. This, however, was not enough to prevent the lower classes from imitating the behavior of the upper classes out of deference, an imitation that was often scorned and did not suffice to prevent tension between classes that lived alongside each other, not with each other, and the ghastly condescension of the higher classes toward the others. It was sufficient that class mobility, according to the profound political wisdom that strove for long-term treatment of the injustices wrought against the disadvantaged classes, prevented a violent breakdown in class relations – all of which was abetted by a strong state and sophisticated institutions that served it on the basis of ever-improving rules of the game.[117]

Huntington's account may help to explain why many in Western culture found Socialist Zionism so hard to fathom. After all, the Zionist Labor Movement was originally a collection of individuals who demanded the overturning of their way of life and, as a consequence, tried to fashion a new society almost ex nihilo. Afterwards, that is, after Hitler's rise to power, they had to deal with a drastic change in the status of Diaspora Jewry. Jews and their principles – especially Jewish particularism, alleged Jewish egoism, and Jewish shrewdness and aggressiveness – were tarred in Germany and the West with the accusation of "politicizing" the world. Some in the West supported Zionism and considered it the right solution for the Jews themselves and for those around them. Others nodded favorably at Jewish ethics and morality and noted its contribution to Christianity but did not see the Jews of their times as ethical people and saw in Zionism a "private virtue" of nationalists and Socialists who had disowned their own Jewish tradition.[118]

The Socialist Zionists knew well that given Europe's upheavals and the Jews' role in them, the world after World War I had become a dangerous place for Jews. The confused, strange 1920s began with a difficult transition in Europe and with isolationism in America but continued with stabilization in Europe and economic growth in America. It seemed as though things had returned to normal after the Great War. Under the surface, however, views, processes, and decisions regarding the Jews were churning, couched in political terms and geared to prevent any such form of politicization that they might allegedly instigate. Hence, the decisions to close off the British Isles and the United States to Jewish immigration.

Before we return to the Yishuv and its leadership in the 1930s and 1940s, we need to bear this in mind as a necessary background for understanding Ben-Gurion's conclusions and measures from this time onward. We must also discuss the tragic pinnacle of this drama – the Holocaust – in order to understand not only its effects on the Zionist avant garde in Palestine but also its demarches during that time, which also underwent politicization. In other words, the debate over the Holocaust, the rescue issue, and the analysis of the Yishuv leadership's moves at this time became a matter of politics, that is, of power mongering or power struggle, an instrument for the advancement of disputants' political aims irrespective of historical truth. The debate ostensibly revealed despicable intrigues by Mapai and its leaders, which bordered on the criminal in the worst case or on selfishness and villainy in the best. This debate was taken up by Ben-Gurion in spite of his doubts as to whether it was too early to be pursued, for he knew how hard it would be to progress toward this goal among the Jews, that is, to prompt them to debate difficult historical and other issues in their own right. We must remember, however, that this picture of the Jews, one of a people capable of concocting unfounded and dangerous conspiracy theories about others, was widely held in Western circles and led to disapproval of the politicization that their behavior seemed to have disseminated in their own surroundings.[119]

The Labor Zionist spearhead in Palestine considered itself a vanguard that would precede the arrival of most members of this problematic people in Eretz Israel in various stages. This characterization remained attached to this people, although they criticized it and demanded that habits and modes of behavior that had made it the object of hatred be abandoned, as one would expect in the age of the masses – and that they turn to antisemitic action. In this sense, Socialist Zionism aspired to more than social change; it entertained the ambition, as Ben-Gurion called it, of "building souls," a grand pretension that its exponents translated in the social and behavioral realms into manual labor. In the cultural realm, it was not given a real opportunity to acquire meaning beyond the massive exertion of teachers, translators, and authors in Israel and abroad in the fourteen years between 1919 and 1933, followed by the pre–World War I cultural efforts, and between 1933 and 1939 (after which European Jewry ceased to exist). These efforts must not be taken lightly: Along with the Hebrew-speaking *Tarbut* (Hebrew culture) school system in Poland and the Baltic states and the Hebrew-speaking schools and journals in Europe and America, they made Hebrew not only a living language spoken by more and more people but also a language of technology and works of art, some poor and some very good.

It must be remembered that the great Hebrew authors and poets – Bialik himself, Shaul Tchernichovsky, and S. Y. Agnon – labored in the 1920s in Germany specifically and hoped to establish themselves by riding the wave of opportunities that Hebrew enjoyed there due to various publishers and a Hebrew-reading hinterland in Europe. The hyperinflation that struck Germany, that is, the foreign-currency sources that were available to them, helped them for a while until the recession in Germany, the economic crisis that battered Polish Jewry, and the final severance of contact with Soviet Jewry prompted them to make aliyah and become the leading speakers of the small Yishuv society. At work in this society, however, were people of culture and literature who, despite being quite anonymous, had already written literary treasures of all sorts and of the highest caliber in the Hebrew language.

In our home, my parents spoke Russian, Polish, and Yiddish to each other and Hebrew with us, despite the fact that my mother had no real command of the language. I remember two examples of this triumph of Hebrew: my father's journal *Techniqa u-mada'* (Technology and science), which delivered the contents of foreign-language books in science and engineering, and *Entsiqlopedia ne'urim* (Encyclopedia for youth). These two publications were not provincial and limited to issues of concern to the Yishuv and the Jewish world; they carried a range of information about biology, astronomy, world geography, general and Jewish history, and discussion of global events during World War II. They were intellectually stimulating, too, and even gave off a scent of the Hebrew culture of the Diaspora, making a connection with it as if it still existed. The children's magazine *Itonenu* (Our magazine), published in Warsaw until no longer possible, did the same.

Ben-Gurion's mission from then on was to view the survivors as "the people," understand what had happened to this people in the Holocaust and what had to be done as a result of these events, and to establish a state for this people that would prevent not only a holocaust from without but also destruction from within. This, too, involved the use of force, the sort of thing that one may scorn and call politicization. That is, one may give Ben-Gurion's moves during and after the Holocaust a negative, aggressive, unbridled, amoral, and conspiratorial interpretation.[120]

By the same token, it was undoubtedly an attempt to invest the Jewish people in its land with a sense of uniqueness and destiny. The main idea was historical, not religious-cultural. From the Jewish religion, values of justice and modes of behavior were selected and linked to far-reaching social change in national life. Thus, the "uniqueness and destiny" in Ben-Gurion's teachings represented an attempt to predicate the Jewish national ethos on Jewish history and ethical values of religious origin that the Jews would accept on a "live and let live" basis, rather than in accordance with an obligatory and dependency-promoting code of religious law. However, since the history at issue involved communities that were religious and largely based their existence on religion, Ben-Gurion's Zionism coupled the refusal to accept religion's rule with a degree of appreciation for the erstwhile religious culture. It marked an attempt to extract from the Jewish religion those values and modes of behavior that would suit the needs of a secular society that makes its own decisions on how to treat its religious legacy – all of which without the historical secularization process that Western culture had undergone and amid censure of some of this culture's main ideas.

The censure was expressed in Socialist Zionist criticism of the excessive materialism that accompanied Western individualism and sometimes acquired a predatory complexion in the age of capitalism, as well as criticism of the excessive rights that "autonomous groups" arrogated to themselves in society in the exercise of their "natural rights," including the innate right to retain their inherited property and their special privileges (which Huntington did not treat at length). Still, the topics worthy of the name and rule of law, combined with a strong state and a sophisticated political system such as, in particular, the British one – the same Britain that maintained its uniqueness and destiny in the divisive, confused Western world, at a time when the entire West was wallowing in a crisis of faith about its values, in which some were drawn to Fascism, on the one hand, and to American isolationism, on the other, that same West that had volunteered so little, at first, in the war against Nazism – represented a field for thought and action that developed in the mind of David Ben-Gurion during that terrible war itself.

2

The Holocaust and Its Lessons

The Trap Is Set

To research the sources that are available today, it is not enough to acquaint oneself with, collect, and consolidate sources that may be accessed in various countries or those recently declassified and opened for research.[1] One must also use the related languages – especially German – and be acquainted with the political culture and history of the relevant nations and the diverse segments of Jewry. All these elicit a very complicated picture of the state of Judaism and Zionism from 1919 onward. At the simplistic level, the Zionists of the Labor Movement – including Ben-Gurion, Mapai members, and the Yishuv leadership in general – seem to have concentrated in the 1920s, 1930s, and 1940s on their small experimental projects in Palestine and on governing the Yishuv. Essentially, according to this view, they neglected Diaspora Jewry and did not do enough to save Jews in 1939–1945 due to this ironic notion of "Palestinocentrism." Further, they are seen as having developed a posture of condescension and contempt toward the Diaspora, taken a hypocritical interest in the tragedy that befell Diaspora Jewry, and used the survivors to further their own narrow nationalistic and sectarian goals.[2]

Among those who so argue are the offspring of German-born parents, whose progenitors often experienced this patronizing, belittling attitude by the Eastern European-born Zionist Socialist elite. The basis for their attitude was the role that this elite assumed as the advocates of the "Jewish masses" – that is, those of Eastern Europe descent, as opposed to the withered German branch of Jewry, which generated a mere trickle of immigrants to Eretz Israel and even this only after the Nazis rose to power.[3] These Eastern European Jews were free of the uncertainties that German Jewry had entertained since the onset of the emancipation and that community's tragic attempts to become the Jewish limb of the German nation. These attempts went up in the smoke of the Holocaust and left German Jewry with an array of complex and simplistic doubts, repressions, and rationalizations about what had happened to it and the German people during that time. The Eastern European Zionists knew antisemitism very well and were not overly surprised by its violent, unbridled expression – though none had predicted the Holocaust in all its horrors. Consequently, they took a somewhat belittling attitude toward German Jewry's dilemmas and philosophical and practical solutions before and after the war. After all, they approached the matter as members of a people, albeit one in serious crisis as they saw it, that had its own culture and history and was ostensibly absolved of the peculiar world of German Jewry.

One doubts, however, whether most members of that generation, regardless of their various backgrounds, as well as their offspring, realize today that the trap had been set for European Jewry even before Hitler's rise to power. It is a certainty that after he took the reins of power in 1933, European Jewry was maneuvered into an ever-tightening snare. To be aware of what they were up against, Jews needed more than a political understanding of their status among the nations, which few of them had. They also needed the ability to read Hitler's mind and foresee that their destruction was not only an outcome of the inhumane character of his regime but also due to the particular relations that existed between Nazi Germany and other peoples and regimes under which Jews lived and were menaced. The violent nature of the man and his party were plainly visible from the outset. This person, however, saw himself as a "politician," who gradually began to make violent threats against all and sundry. Thus, the issue was the Jews' ability, or inability, to grasp the "politicization" of the profound cultural, social, psychological, and political crisis that had befallen Germany at the end of World War I and was steadily worsening as time passed. This crisis caused bewilderment in the West, which responded by construing the reasons for it in typical fashion until it threatened vital Western interests.

In Germany, the crisis brought "sewer rats" to power, functionaries who considered themselves politicians of the future in a mass society and conquerors who had revived the glory of the Teutonic order, which now rested on a modern, ostensibly "scientific" theory – the theory of race. In the resulting situation, the Zionists had to comprehend two sets of responses to this crisis, the West's and Stalin's, and the considerations and politics of both. The Jews were caught between the Nazi hammer and three anvils – the Western, the Soviet, and the Arab – and slowly their fate became totally dependent on relations among them all.

Ben-Gurion's Zionism represented at least an attempt to make Jews contemplate reality as it was and draw personal conclusions from it: to make the impending catastrophe a source of Zionist effort for large-scale immigration to Palestine – the absorption of which would be orchestrated as much as possible with the help of the Yishuv's Socialist organs and their extensions in the World Zionist Organization – and for the settlement of the country with the requisite momentum. "Absorption" meant, in the main, training prospective immigrants and creating diverse sources of livelihood for them. Their age, numbers, and occupations were determined by the Mandatory government at

different points in time. Consequently, the immigrants were either young people who had been trained for occupations in demand – mostly various kinds
of manual labor – or the "wealthy," that is, persons who had at least 1,000
British pounds. The transition to the Hebrew language and the need for a new,
youthful, self-confident Palestinian-Jewish ethos – as it came to be expressed in
advertisements, popular songs, and mobilizing literature of the time – would
help the immigrants make their mental and cultural adjustment. This kind of
absorption evidently appealed to young immigrants and children born to immigrants, who were divided among a variety of youth movements, including, from
the 1930s onward, some with an increasingly Soviet orientation; others, such
as Mapai, with moderately leftist leanings; and movements based on the philosophy of Jabotinsky and his disciple, Avraham "Ya'ir" Stern, who split with
him and turned in a radical direction that verged on Fascism.

Even before the Holocaust, several of these groups accused Mapai of kow-
towing to the British in regard to illegal immigration, collaborating with them,
indulging in "disgraceful" restraint in dealing with the Arab revolt of the
1930s, caring for their own people only, and other severe charges of the same
ilk that fell only slightly short of outright treason. Thus, the political and
ideological struggle over the fate of European Jewry before and after the Holocaust followed a continuum.[4] The story of young immigrants from Germany
and elsewhere who turned to Fascist "Canaanism" shortly before the outbreak of World War II deserves its own discussion. Likewise, the world of
older immigrants and those who failed to uncouple from their roots – those
"Yekkes" and "Polacks" who established entire neighborhoods in Tel Aviv,
Haifa, and Jerusalem from the Fourth Aliyah of the mid-1920s onward – has
not been properly researched. Many of them lived in the Tel Aviv of my youth
as if in a bubble of Polish, Yiddish, or German speakers. Those who accli-
mated more successfully felt that their full absorption and integration into the
existing Yishuv and its elite ranks were being thwarted by other preferences
and existing political entities, causing resentment and leaving thick residues of
mistrust.[5]

To Ben-Gurion and his colleagues, however, the Jews' distress in Europe
was a platform from which moral and political support might be sought from
others – the leaders and masses of the West. In view of this distress, a distinction
had to be made between the enemy and those who, while not the enemy, were
unable or unwilling to assist for their own reasons, which had to be challenged,
influenced, ameliorated, and negated. To accomplish this, further distinctions
were needed between certain kinds of British and the Nazis and between the
Americans and the Soviets, even though some of the public, concurrently influenced by the cruelty of the situation and mired in their own affairs, were not
up to the task.[6] Until the Holocaust, these distinctions were not necessarily
correct, but during and after the Holocaust Ben-Gurion did a formidable job
of removing their impurities, clarifying them to himself and to the public as
well as he could.

One of these distinctions, widely embraced in the Yishuv during the "appeasement" period under Neville Chamberlain and its aftermath, the Holocaust, was the popular criticism of the "democracies" for their refusal to mobilize in time for that struggle against Nazism; the short-term considerations of their citizenry, which cast a poor light on their values and their long-term utility; their lack of true empathy for others who were suffering; their concern for their own benefit only; and the attitude of their Protestant-Christian elites toward Jews and Judaism. This latter attitude was complex at best and often forced Jews in their midst to humble themselves, limit themselves to particular corners of non-Jewish society, take on Gentile names, and so forth. It was from truths and perceptions such as these regarding the Western democracies that Socialist Zionism derived its sense of moral superiority.[7]

Thus, the mind-set that people today call Zionist "Bolshevism" created a sense of mobilization and sacrifice for the cause of settling the country and ensuring immigration, while accruing the strength to ward off intensifying Arab opposition to both. Although this ambition was not fully embraced by all sectors of the Yishuv reality, it had important ramifications during the struggle for statehood in the 1940s and in Israel's fledgling period, reflected in Israelis' sense of superiority and belief in their moral advantage over others. The authenticity of this feeling explains Israeli behavior after the Holocaust, both toward non-Jews and toward immigrants who ostensibly represented the Jewish world that had not moved to Eretz Israel before the Holocaust as the Zionists had counseled.

Ben-Gurion himself shared this style of thinking; it figured in all his behavior and actions. Still, he did not adopt it entirely and was sometimes very critical of its pretense, as if a real nation, not to mention a supposedly "chosen people," had already come into being in Israel. Thus, when the time came, he wrestled with the question of the system of government that should be desired. Surely, it would not be American-style mass democracy. His ruminations led him to British representative democracy, to which he brought the typical Socialist disapproval of the failings and some of the typical markers of Britain's class society. The lessons of the 1930s and World War II did much to influence his choice of the system, since in those years there was a need for a strong government capable of occasional far-reaching actions and decisions that even the British had quite a hard time making. Ultimately, however, the British passed the grand test in Ben-Gurion's eyes, for after they had unseated Chamberlain's government and replaced it with an emergency government without an internal coup, they mobilized as one in defense of their freedom.

"How innocent we were," Ben-Gurion said afterwards. Indeed, in the early phases of the war, he regarded Britain's courageous stand in defense of its freedom, which he had personally witnessed in London during the Blitz, as being associated with Jewish interests in general and Zionist interests in particular. At various stages, he distinguished between the English and their government and the British bureaucracy, believing that the latter could be fought by marshaling public support that would influence Parliament and the government and, thereby, the professional civil service. To understand what he meant by remarking, "How innocent we were," it is worth quoting some of his arguments in this vein:

> The English are a people who, in the throes of war, knew how to defend their political freedom and democratic fundamentals, and though of their free will they gave their government unlimited authority to confiscate property . . . and impose heavy taxes, they still reserved the freedom to criticize, the freedom of speech, so that every Englishman may criticize his government and object to any error or injustice that he perceives in its actions.[8]

Evidently, Ben-Gurion had not yet realized that the British government itself was highly aware of this state of affairs and that, for that very reason, it and the British bureaucracy had taken great care not to entangle themselves in Jewish interests and, by so doing, give to their people the impression of fighting for the sake of the Jews.

Ben-Gurion made further remarks at the time:

> Perhaps it was precisely due to this freedom and democracy, which was maintained during the war, that England was saved. After all, it was only due to the existence of democracy in wartime England that a new government could be formed. The government of Churchill and the workers . . . organized the English people's valorous defense, first in their psyche, consciousness, and will and then in their bodies, in the nation's physical and military might. . . . [Britain] has a people that under no circumstances will subject itself to slavery and submission; a people prepared to see its home, its town, and its land destroyed and laid waste without surrendering. . . . In view of the destruction of millions of Jews [this was before the Final Solution], we must adopt a grand Zionism . . . rapid transfer [of Jews] once the war ends . . . to the only territory in which the territorialist experiment has been successful.[9]

He then listed three contributory factors that would work in concert with Jewish independence to abet immigration and settlement on a vast scale. First:

> The regime – with England's victory – "the victory of democracy and freedom," victory . . . of the regime in the Anglo-Saxon world. . . . In these countries the people are not subordinate to the government but rather the reverse. The government is subordinate to the people, and the people's opinion and consent are won – then the opinion and consent of the government is also won. . . . The second factor: the Jews of the Anglo-Saxon world as a force and an independent factor. Three: The moral factor plays an important role, since more than in any war until now, there is a clash of values [between the Western world and the Fascist Axis] no less than of interests. . . . The moral factor plays an enormous role in these countries. This is perhaps the secret of the great courage that the English people has displayed in this war. It is also, to a great extent, the guarantor of its victory. Wherever moral forces arise and become powerful the prospects of Zionism also rise and become powerful, for Zionism is only the demand for justice for the Jewish people. And in England and in America there is now – in broad popular circles – an ear that is attentive to a moral demand, the demand for justice.[10]

In political language, Ben-Gurion was speaking of mobilizing British and American public opinion to put pressure on their respective governments for two purposes: the Zionist cause and the neutralization, to the extent possible, of the antagonistic British bureaucracy in Palestine and Cairo. This is why Ben-Gurion set out on lengthy trips from Palestine in late 1940 and late 1941. His contemporaneous critics held this against him, of course; from their perspective, he should have stayed in Palestine and dealt with rescuing people from the terrors of the Holocaust, even though Hitler himself had not yet decided on it at the time. At that stage, however, Ben-Gurion had not yet managed to mobilize real support for the Zionist idea, for reasons that we shall delve into later. Only during the Holocaust and when the Allies declared that Germany must surrender unconditionally did he himself begin to realize how weighty these reasons were.

The power of moral superiority backed by indispensable force was a value that Ben-Gurion subscribed to even after the Holocaust, both externally and internally. His awareness of it, however, was much more refined than that. It was without illusions that Ben-Gurion, when speaking to IDF commanders and civilian leaders, sometimes used the word "cruel" to describe the Jews' situation in the Middle East and the world during the Holocaust and its immediate aftermath.

The cruelty was this: The more Britain widened its struggle against the Nazis, with growing American support – ascribed by Hitler to Jewish control of both countries, which was of course completely nonexistent, with both powers shunning everything Jewish in order to avoid the impression that they were fighting for the Jews – the tighter the trap around European Jewry became, almost to the point of no escape. On every side, including the British one, the steps that Zionists like Ben-Gurion took and the conclusions that they adduced from the situation were those that will occupy us as we progress through this narrative.

During the Holocaust, 460,000 Jews were dwelling in Palestine, inhabiting a part of the world that was controlled by the British and populated mostly by Arabs. At the height of the Holocaust, the Nazis threatened to conquer this region and murder its Jews as well. The lessons learned from this trap contributed to the establishment of a state for the Yishuv, the survivors from Europe, and the Jews of the Arab world. By the time statehood was attained, however, the Zionist elites found themselves bereft of that segment of Jewry of which it figured to be the avant-garde. Since the thing that had happened was an act of genocide – the murder of a people that had been comprised of sectors, communities, diverse groups, individuals who no longer saw themselves as members of the people, and others who considered themselves only partly affiliated with it – the Holocaust provided ex post justification for the original Zionist arguments and warnings. However, the catastrophe also left what remained of Jewry badly ruptured, and it is no wonder that the Zionists saw the State of Israel, once established, as a sort of remedy and answer to this rupture. For until then, the Zionists, in their own eyes, had only been the nation's vanguard. They acted in its name and on its behalf, even though few responded to them in the short time in which they had begun to establish a toehold and an infrastructure in Palestine. This infrastructure now carried on without the large superstructure that the Zionists had aspired to build atop it, waiting with open arms to welcome the "Jewish masses" under the conditions and with the opportunities for action that the Yishuv possessed.

Therefore, those who would study this period of time must ask, on the basis of documentation now available, how the tragedy happened and what dilemmas the Zionists faced after Hitler rose to power and during his reign. How did the Jews view themselves? How were they viewed by others, including key figures in the West? And what did Hitler and his cohorts intend to do within the global political-power context that evolved after World War I? It was a complex situation, which first began to develop not so much upon Hitler's rise to power as upon the conclusion of World War I. It was a genuine "Jewish problem," for which only the Zionists tried to find a practical and behavioral solution that stood any real chance of succeeding ab initio – until the trap closed on all sides.

The Glass House

The findings of historical research in recent years provide explanations not only for the Zionists' actions and the futile rescue attempts of activists such as Yisrael Kasztner at the height of the Holocaust in Hungary, to which we shall return. They also explain the enmity and animosity of non-Jews toward Jews from the key year, 1919, onward. These explanations add depth to the accepted picture. Western intelligence documents, many of which were barred to research until 1985, if not until the late 1990s, paint a portrait of the glass house that the Jews, gathered in groups that were considered one people, inhabited starting in the 1920s. What did others think of them? How did non-Jews judge the Jews' talents, their "national character," their self-designated leaders, their ability to destroy and build, to love and hate, to cause damage and pursue justice?

We begin the inquiry by discussing an top-secret internal American intelligence evaluation from 1919, when the Jewish problem suddenly leaped, as it were, to the top of the Western agenda. One reason for the West's growing interest in the Jews was their leading role in the Bolshevik Revolution. Other reasons had to do with the crisis that engulfed the Western elites in the complexity of their relations with the masses, in a world whose compass had been destroyed by the world war. This compass, now flitting in different directions, had been quite unstable since the late nineteenth century, when modern science presented its challenge to the truths, traditions, conventions, and values of the time – including accepted morality, the belief in progress, and the Judeo-Christian tradition itself.

Since different Western countries experienced the process in very different ways, it is difficult to generalize. In the United States, the period preceding

World War I was a time of reforms, including those attempted by Theodore Roosevelt and those implemented by Woodrow Wilson and his Progressive supporters. Reforms in America generally elicit conservative counterreactions. Thus, once the Great War was over, the country embarked on an era of reversion to the past, its values, and old-fashioned Protestant nationalism. This apparently explains why the American nationalist Right felt threatened by the unrestricted immigration of the late nineteenth century, which included millions of Jews from Eastern Europe. In Europe, the challenges and protests that surfaced in the wake of the world war against Western culture, its systems of government, and its past and future were a political matter. All of existence seemed dubious in the eyes of much of the Western middle classes and even the elites. The redoubled crisis that struck the United States bore no resemblance to what was happening in continental Europe and Britain. Everywhere in the West, however, people were exposed to attacks by vulgar Darwinism on the traditional value system. Then, after the war, came Bolshevism, other forms of Socialism, long-lasting economic crises, Franklin Roosevelt's sweeping socioeconomic reforms, and the rise of modern arts and communication media that abetted the development of feelings of alienation, threat, and destruction of accepted values.

It was most evident among various social sectors in the United States, such as the white Protestant majority and the Catholic minority.[11] Educated people of all types, having been exposed to "scientific" theories about racial enhancement or other sociogenetic ideas and the scientific revolution in the *fin de siècle* years, now looked with revulsion and great concern at developments in Soviet Russia, the grave crisis that their country underwent in the late 1920s and early 1930s, and the agonies of Weimar Germany. Thus, some ceased to believe in the existing order and its eighteenth-century underpinnings. A few even began to cast doubts on democracy and the whole Western governmental system. A number of people, in turn, were drawn to increasingly extreme antisemitism, which served them as an explanation for the upheavals that were battering their own countries.[12] In Britain and the United States, mammoth forces were devoted to the preservation of the existing order as far as possible, that is, Western establishments, particularly in their security and foreign affairs segments in the 1930s, and highly influential political personages such as Lord Beaverbrook.[13]

These were the years of worldwide economic crisis, the rise of Fascism, and the sanctification of Bolshevism in the eyes of a growing minority in the West as the only alternative to parliamentary democracy, on the one hand, and Fascism, on the other. What role did the Jews play in this cauldron, as viewed by a West that was reeling under an existential crisis that the British and American elites were managing to control only with great effort? Some saw the Jews both as symbols of, and threats to, the old parliamentary-capitalistic establishment in their countries, particularly when it came to foreign Jews who operated within this establishment as communists and radicals. Some Westerners accused the Jews of having abetted the rise of racist Nazism; after all, in Germany they had served as fertile ground for the growth of Hitler, who would become a severe threat to the West. A few among them even depicted Nazism as an "understandable" response to the challenge presented by "racist" Judaism.

The process of internalizing the Nazi threat as one that was aimed at the West – not just at the Jews – was anything but simple. Not everyone thought it necessary to respond to the threat vigorously and fight it for various reasons, including important internal ones, until far-reaching attempts were made to accommodate Nazi Germany and recognize some of its demands.[14]

In the case of Britain, the moment the brutal Nazi dictatorship and the coarse, grotesque character of Nazi racism became apparent – as manifested, among other things, in pogroms against the Jews – the domestic antidemocratic and pro-Fascist leanings died down because they had evolved into the slogans and crude demands of a foreign enemy power. Nevertheless, the decision to go to war against Nazism shoved the Jews off the British agenda, at least in the sense that their cause was dwarfed by the main issue: stopping the Nazis' vandalism and political-strategic demands on the continent and averting the domestic political menace that Nazism presented. What mattered now was to maintain the holy flames of public wrath against Hitler and not to dilute this rage with Jewish issues, insofar as the pogroms being unleashed against them brought such issues to the fore.

This may be an overly extreme presentation of the matter. After all, Britain admitted several tens of thousands of Jews whom the Nazis had expelled. That, however, was only the beginning. Hitler intended to get rid of all Jews one way or another, meaning that the West was supposed to accept them, and the West saw no practical or political way of accomplishing this. The Jews themselves would have to resist Hitler with all the might that they did not have. Yet they did seem to have a separate interest in the matter: Even if they were to fall victim to Fascism in various European countries, why should the West concern itself with their troubles except for their international connections and alleged unity? They were liable to drag the West into a war not its own against antisemitic Fascism.[15] And if the West were to fight this ugly phenomenon, which had sunk roots in the soil of a hostile foreign power that entertained unacceptable aspirations to European hegemony and world domination, it would be doing so for its own interests and values, and not for those of the Jews.

As for "the Jews," the issue went beyond the traditional image of financial magnates, usurers, and Shylocks. It also transcended the cause of citizens of their own countries, in whose "internal affairs" the English legalistic tradition generally refrained from meddling. The image that had been current since the beginning of the century – the reason for the legislation that had partly halted Jewish immigration to Britain after 1905 – was of a many-headed hydra, an enormous mass of people, a horde of millions of migrants who, by the late nineteenth century, had already burst out of Eastern Europe and moved west; a mass headed by individuals whose fame in the West did not fall short of Karl Marx's in his time or of the Rothschilds' in theirs. Indeed, the 1905 legislation was aimed at preventing Arthur James Balfour's government from admitting

Jews to Britain due to the Conservatives' distaste for their tribal customs, their foreignness, and their tendency to radicalize additional Jews. The Jews were also shut out due to lethal criticism from contemporary British liberal and leftist circles, led by members of Sidney and Beatrice Webb's Fabian Society, of leaders of the Jewish masses for their ostensible total lack of "basic human traits," that is, social conscience.

From then on, the Jewish problem never ceased to occupy both radical and conservative personalities, although to lesser degrees of intensity. However, if it seemed that the anti-immigration act of 1905, the Balfour Declaration, and the supplemental anti-immigration act of 1919 had contained the problem, it merely resurfaced in the form of an acute political quandary to the dictates of which, as handed down by Hitler, Britain in the 1930s knew it must not succumb. From the British perspective, Palestine remained a refuge for Jews due to the reality that the Zionists had created there, Britain's own prior undertakings and official commitments, the images of Jewish power in Britain and the United States, and the resourcefulness of the moderate Zionists who were active in London. At a crucial moment, however, because of preparations for war with Nazi Germany and because of Arab pressure, Palestine itself was made off-limits to large-scale rescue immigration.

To expand the purview and discuss the dilemmas that the Zionists themselves faced at this crucial juncture, we must again contemplate how Jews – and Zionists – were pictured by others, and not by the Zionists themselves, from the moment the "Jewish Question" became a political quandary that forced Western governments into taking political steps and investing decidedly political attention. At the end of World War I, the intelligence service of the U.S. Department of War began to build dossiers on Jews, Judaism, and Palestine.[16] The resulting folders were quickly mothballed and left in that condition for almost seventy years, until 1985. There was good reason: The first document that appears in them is *The Protocols of the Elders of Zion*.[17]

One of the chiefs of U.S. military intelligence (MID, Military Intelligence Division, War Department), a Colonel Dunn, was asked to tender his opinion about the veracity of the *Protocols* pursuant to inquiries by American citizens and, perhaps, public figures of the highest order such as Henry Ford, the antisemitic automobile tycoon. Ford also published the *Protocols* in his own newspaper, a rather popular antisemitic organ in the 1920s. By standing out amid a sea of supposed Jewish influence in America, Ford kindled hopes in Hitler – who eventually presented him with a decoration.[18] The inquirers even transformed Lenin into a full-blooded Jew. They impugned the creator of the concept of "global revolution" and the patriarch of the weapon of the general strike, the Jewish social-democratic theoretician Israel Helphand ("Parvus"), a highly influential personality in his time, and the international scoundrel Ignácz Trebitsch-Lincoln. Parvus was more than a left-wing theoretician of the highest importance who was active in Imperial Germany; he was also a practical economist who had become a successful businessman and amassed wealth in the service of the "Young Turks." It was Parvus who, in common counsel with the Kaiser's government, arranged Lenin's transfer in a sealed railroad car from exile into Russia in order to bring down the detested czarist regime at any price. Later on, however, Lenin contemptuously spurned his advice to install a socialist market economy in Soviet Russia. One may say that Parvus foresaw the economic destruction of the Soviet Union and the price that the Bolshevik venture would claim.[19]

Trebitsch was a different case: a lapsed Hungarian Jew from a rabbinical home who had converted, emigrated to Canada as a missionary, and made his way to England, where he was elected to Parliament as a member of the Liberal faction under the name of Lincoln. He was quickly exposed as a charlatan. Afterwards, he hired himself out to the Kaiser and labored in America to thwart the latter's entry into World War I in support of the British, thereby causing the British a great deal of harm. In due course, Britain had him extradited and placed in prison for several years. In the 1920s, he acted on behalf of the White International (an organization of unseated European nobility). He died in Shanghai in the early 1940s while serving as a German intelligence agent in the guise of a Buddhist monk. The archives of the Western security services are packed with material about Trebitsch. Several leading officials in these services, at the time and in the future, were excessively suspicion about Jews and developed the idea that they had had a lot to do with the ascendancy of Bolshevism.[20]

A Smaller Than Average Brain

Even though the head of American military intelligence, Colonel Dunn, dismissed the *Protocols of the Elders of Zion* as a forgery that probably originated in Germany, at the same time he said that a similar Jewish world conspiracy was true in principle. Thus, the allegations that the *Protocols* had inspired refused to die. Inquirers who turned to American intelligence, as stated, compared excerpts of the *Protocols* with excerpts of the writings of Theodor Herzl, the founding father of Zionism, and concluded that Zionism exuded an antidemocratic and an anti-Christian spirit. They attributed enormous political power to Zionism, blaming it for having brought on the surrender of Lord Balfour, the British aristocrat who had sealed his own country's borders to the Jews but had given them the Balfour Declaration, that is, permission to steal the Holy Land from Christendom.

Although the ostensible theft of Palestine from the Arabs had not become the main problem – not yet, at any rate – the U.S. Departments of State and War quickly began to speak in a conflated anti-Zionist and antisemitic tone of voice, viewing the Arab problem and the Muslim response to Zionism as an issue that was only growing worse and worse. On November 17, 1920, pursuant to the anti-Jewish Arab violence in Palestine that year, the American consul in Jerusalem warned of the menace of Bolshevism in Palestine. The gods, he said, had blindsided the British Foreign Office (whose minister had given the Jews the Balfour Declaration), which was willing to bring on a war of two million Jews against a hundred million Muslims. American Jews, the consul opined, were not about to go to Palestine; they were living well in America. Palestine would be settled by Russian, Polish, and Romanian Jews, the "scum," as he put it, of the Jewish race. Consequently, the Jewish Bolsheviks were creating a Bolshevik state with England's unwitting complicity. Russian Jews were accustomed to revolution, and their willingness to endure any hardship made them good soldiers, the consul averred. The only way to keep them from transforming their Jewish state into a Bolshevik one, he counseled, was to destroy Bolshevism from the root. Otherwise, Jewish Bolshevism would join forces with local national movements and spread to Egypt, India, and so forth.[21]

These remarks contained quite a few points of prophecy. Indeed, the left flank of the radical Zionist faction known as the Stern Gang, Lehi in Hebrew, which included Jews of Polish origin such as Nathan Friedman-Yellin, would eventually dream of linking Zionism and radical liberation movements in the Arab world into an anti-Western nationalist endeavor.

The Department of War also turned its attention to a cable from Switzerland, dated December 6, 1920, which mentioned indications of blatantly hostile Jewish activity against non-Jewish economic systems around the world and a Jewish intention of destroying Christian property everywhere. Three organizations were specifically accused of this: (1) the Zionists, that is, the general Zionists or the non-Socialist majority in the Zionist Movement at the time, led by Dr. Chaim Weizmann among others; (2) Po'alei Zion, the variegated Socialist-Zionist organization to which Ben-Gurion belonged, a few of whose members had embraced Marxist ideology; and (3) the Bund, a Jewish Socialist mass movement that urged the Jewish proletariat to join the various local Socialist movements, take their interests into account, and integrate with them wherever they lived while maintaining their separate, Jewish identity. The Zionists, the author of the cable reported, had a pronouncedly national and anti-Bolshevik outlook. The British government had recently forced Weizmann, the head of the "Jewish government" (i.e., president of the World Zionist Organization) in London, to reveal publicly where the Zionists stood on the question of Bolshevism. Po'alei Zion and the Bund confined most of their activities to Eastern Europe. Their political organizations, the cable continued, were much less important than their numerous economic organizations, which pursued financial interests in the main. The Jews' political interests and their economic interests were one and the same. The Jewish idea, the cable advised, was to establish worldwide Jewish economic hegemony; hence the Jews' economic institutions should be considered political, which would spell the destruction of Christian property. The result was a confluence of interests between the Bolsheviks and the Jews, thereby explaining why the Jewish organizations threw their support behind the Bolshevik movement. Collectively speaking, the Jews neither were nor ever had been Bolsheviks; they simply used this movement to attain their goals.[22]

Another MID document, dated April 14, 1923, described the "intense anti-Zionist feeling" among the Arabs of Palestine due to political, economic, and cultural reasons, including the "Jewish attitude to women," which would unify the Arabs of the whole area to create a "United Arab State." The Zionists would be massacred or expelled in due course, with all possible foreign support. Thus, "Americans are frequently asked if it is true that Henry Ford will probably be the next President of the United States."

The U.S. intelligence files from the early 1920s reveal a substantive-looking research study on "Jewry from psychologic, environmental, physical, and racial points of view."[23] Whoever it was that commissioned this report was probably influenced, among other things, by the copious popular literature of the time, as described by Leonard Dinnerstein, which concerned itself with the Jews' special capabilities and traits. Many also seem to have been influenced by a thesis published in 1919 (sometime before the study at issue) by Thorstein Veblen, one of the founders of modern American social science, claiming that the Jews actually were intellectually superior to others. Some in the American defense establishment deemed this thesis worthy of systematic examination.[24] We do not know who instigated this "study," which spanned some eighty pages and was based in part on Jewish sources, and how it found its way into the files of American military intelligence. One may surmise, however, that MID itself took an interest in the matter, since no other federal authority undertook to debate these issues at the time. MID also appeared to be a convenient and safe place to probe so delicate a topic, given the slick and sensitive nature of the object being investigated. It is very likely that the results of the investigation served the aims of the American nativists and politicians who had long wanted to shut the gates of the United States to "undesirable aliens," including Jews. Indeed, in 1921, shortly after the study was completed, Congress initiated a legislative process that, once concluded in 1924, banned Jewish, Asian, and Eastern European immigration altogether. The seal became virtually hermetic in 1929, four years before Hitler's rise to power, when a very rigid quota of immigration visas was introduced. By then, however, the de facto injunction against Jewish immigration had been in place for nearly a decade.

Once this legislation was enacted, the United States had seemingly washed its hands of the Jewish problem. However, Hitler's rise brought it back in full fury and made its victims into a political issue of the highest order. In due course, Congress threatened to reduce the immigration quotas that it itself had approved, which were stingy to begin with, if Roosevelt were to allow the entrance of Jews in such numbers as would exhaust the quotas.[25]

The aforementioned study accounts for some of the background of this behavior. First, its official nature made it a representative document. Second, it reflected the ideological thinking of the time and, by so doing, reveals the boundaries of what official circles considered acceptable. Finally, it was highly confidential and therefore was written with unusual candor.

The study begins by expressing truths that any Socialist Zionist from the Second Aliyah – raised on criticism of Diaspora Jewry as voiced by the writer Mendele Mocher Seforim, Berdyczewski, and Bialik – could agree with in some parts and dispute angrily in others. It takes only a superficial observation, the author of the study said, to show that the Jew seems to have superior and, in any event, above-average intellectual capabilities. However, he continued, painstaking study and examination has elicited the interesting fact that, when all is said and done, this exceptional capacity might not originate in hereditary intellectual development, racial singularity, or uncommon talent, but rather in the experience of oppression and discrimination, which forced Jews to live by their wits for generations.[26] Ghetto life in the Middle Ages and the special restrictions that had been imposed on Jewish education, coupled with the hostile environment, had fostered among Jews an ineradicable predisposition to commerce, financial legerdemain, speculation, and so on. Since "the Jew" had been forced to concentrate on these domains, he was assured of developing for his race the intellectual ability, cleverness, and enterprise that they required. However, physiological examination of his brain revealed no exceptional properties, in contrast to the legend of his exceptional brain size. In fact, the Jewish brain was found to be slightly lighter in weight than the average European brain.[27]

The authors of the study were loath to endorse biological antisemitism. However, their contention about the Jews led them in a very grave direction. As they put it, Jews were oblivious to the limits and dangers of power; they lacked the basic tools to understand Anglo-American civilization and its overarching concepts – the rules of fair play and the need to apply self-restraint and caution in the use of social and economic power. The Jews, the authors said, are a singular group with very high pretensions that always revolve around their own utility – a radical element that stirs ferment, a revolutionary collective that demands of others what it never honors itself.

"Not Truly a Nation" and the Question of Chosenness

From the national standpoint, according to the authors of the American study, the Jews' efforts to maintain racial unity have met with immense difficulties due to the lack of a national language. For this reason, they do not have a national mind. By implication, the Jews are not a nation in the positive modern sense of the word. They are not a state that lives by dint of its hard work and a natural division of labor among its members. They amount to a race, a religion, a historical culture that has multilingual manifestations, a culture whose language is the ancient dead language of the Bible in which prayers are interpreted and understood in Yiddish and other cultures' national vernaculars. This, however, captured the very revolution that Berdyczewski, Ahad Ha'am, Bialik, and the other spiritual patriarchs of Zionism had long wished to bring about, each in his own way. It also pointed to the process that their

disciples – Katznelson, Ben-Gurion, and the other leaders of the Labor Movement – had begun to bring about in the decade preceding the American study,
which placed such strong emphasis on the bizarre, threatening, and menacing
situation of the stateless Jews for the very reason of their statelessness. Indeed,
Jews knew nothing about the essence and meaning of a statehood of their own.

Even though its researchers were basing their evaluation on Mendele Mocher
Seforim and Berdyczewski, the American MID at the time knew nothing about
Bialik, Weizmann and his modus operandi, and Jabotinsky, not to mention Ben-
Gurion and Katznelson. However, Socialist Zionism was indeed an attempt
to return the Jews to their place in history as a sovereign people. Instead of
surrendering the singularity and pretensions of Jewishness, it sought to fill them
with real content as reflected in the outlook of its various factions – content
that had a connection with universal values. The envisioned unity was no
longer a matter of "race," religion, or historical culture, but rather a product
of the latter two and of contributions from the non-Jewish surroundings that
combined with the crisis that had struck nineteenth-century traditional East
European Jewish society like a bolt of lightning.

Since Gentiles continued to view Jews monolithically, the authors of the
American study described the Jew's characteristics in a specific way after concluding their discussion of the volume of the Jewish brain. Physiologically, they
said, Jews display horrific concern and anxiety over trifling illnesses and indulge
in hysterical sobbing and excessive grief when death occurs. These, however,
are acquired traits that can be modified by adjusting the surroundings. In that
case, Jews will take on characteristics of the local race. In other words, Jews
can be changed and "fixed." Once they learn the customs of "fair play" that
American culture ostensibly practices, as well as other American values such
as the ability to suffer and sacrifice a son for the homeland and the maturity to
assume the burdens that originate in membership in a real nation (and, within
this generality, to endure wartime losses in a manner worthy of a society that
had lost 2 percent of its population in a civil war), they will be accepted. The
problem of the Jews, however, was not only a matter of behavioral psychology
that could be ameliorated by enrolling them in the host culture's "school." It
was a problem of "behavioral philosophy," anchored in the idea of chosenness
and a covenant with God.

The authors continued: Since the Jews had created a theocratic state at
the dawn of history, and since they had been forcibly dislodged from their
place of origin and hurled into the wide world, rejecting any other affiliation
and seeking only a place to lay their heads, they continued to believe that
they would proliferate like the proverbial sand on the shore and rise to world
domination. This argument against Jewish chosenness was widely held among
Western liberal circles, of all places, and had been a fundamental tenet of secular
antisemitism since Voltaire's time. Voltaire was the first among liberals to
have expressed this claim against chosenness and against the covenant between
the "chosen people" and its exclusive God in secular liberal terms. After all,
the deity promised his children special benefits and made them, in Voltaire's

grotesque expression, haters of all the rest of humanity. This is not a classic Christian allegation but rather a modern liberal one, and it passed from the French liberals to their British and American disciples and weighty segments of the entire European Left of the time.

Although dispersed in all directions – the study continued – the Jews stayed connected. Their "Oriental" and "fatalistic" patience and their unchallengeable confidence in their ultimate triumph played an important role in holding them to their prophets' promises. Thus, in the authors' eyes, the Hebrew prophets were not prophets of universal justice and peace and portenders of Jesus, as Christianity claimed. It was on the grounds of this reasoning that the church had furiously decried the Jews' repudiation of the Gospel and that church leaders and grassroots exponents alike, justified the punishment that had been brought against the Jews from on high. From the standpoint of the authors of the American report, Jews are prophets of an inhuman tribe that cultivates the soul and the spirit by instilling fear of punishment and love of reward. Such traits, the report asserted, are typical of those who conceive of God as a deity exclusive to the Jews. The idea shared by Jews is that only their souls originate with God and that others' souls come from somewhere else. To be more precise, the authors counseled, only a Jew is a full-fledged human being; *goyim* – the word was used in the original Hebrew – qualify merely as animals.

Indeed, the world of Orthodox Jewry is a Jewish world. The People of Israel is indeed the crux of the Creation. The Jews' acts of commission and omission – as God judges them – spin the world on its axis and explain why no messiah has come and when he will come ("when all the Jews become saints – or when all become sinners," as the Gaon of Vilna pronounced). Yet in the days when religion reigned supreme, this ethnocentric view of the world entailed the acceptance of a yoke of unendurably difficult obligations. It offered little by way of rights and virtually no hope of "ruling the world." Traditional Jewry had opted out of history, positioned itself over history, and attempted to live within history by its own lights.

Radical key personalities in Britain saw the matter differently. The roots of Nazism, they claimed, lay in Judaism and its pretense to chosenness, singularity, and exclusive relationship with a sanctified territory at a time to come. On these grounds, noted radicals such as George Bernard Shaw and H. G. Wells portrayed Nazism as an understandable response to the Jewish conceit to chosenness. This is why, as the Holocaust roared to its climax, the Jews' dire fate would be treated with notable estrangement and disregard and blamed disapprovingly on outlooks, forms of behavior, and specific histories that people in liberal and radical Western circles, of all places, lumped together in these inclusive categories.

The Zionist Labor Movement did wish to give Jewish chosenness and the prophets' message a social, national, and universal complexion, but it was accused – at the very peak of the Holocaust and by American and British personalities, intellectuals, and laypeople alike – of promoting something akin to National Socialism, that is, a "fanatic nationalism" that was attributed to

Ben-Gurion specifically and that contradicted the West's moral goals in the war, not to mention its interests in the Arab-Iranian world.[28]

"Chauvinists, Capitalists, Conservatives"

The authors of the American intelligence study in the early 1920s had more to say. The Jews, they admitted, could be viewed as "optimists." They resist troubles with uncommon strength and adamancy to carry on, no matter what. They have a passionate craving to know "why," and when concrete and visible matters are at issue their curiosity is truly ardent. The assumption was that this propensity originated in ordinary ignorance and that the Jews lack the ability to think abstractly and to fathom matters pertaining to deeper wisdom, especially since they are but go-betweens – buyers and sellers.

This premise stood at the center of the Zionist revolution of the Labor Movement and its goal of rendering the Jews a nation "like all others." However, the Zionist revolution was not about striving for drab "normality," à la the writer A. B. Yehoshua; instead, it wished to secularize the Jewish chosenness and give it real meaning in its kibbutzim and in other rural cooperative efforts known as *moshavim*, in making the wilderness bloom, and in urban cooperative enterprises – the process that today is defined as Mapai's "Bolshevism," a one-plank doctrine ostensibly centering on one-party and one-man rule.[29] Obviously, the historical reality was different. The Labor Movement mainstream, headed by Katznelson and Ben-Gurion, followed parallel paths in the Yishuv era and did so without undue exaggeration, adopting the phrasing of the European Far Left but eschewing its methods and fanaticism. Thus, it acted with the pragmatism of what was once called Zionist "constructivism."[30]

The authors of this American study, however, were altogether unfamiliar with Zionist Socialism and perceived all Jews as an uninhibited, power-hungry Right. The Jew, they said, has immense power with which he resists any challenge and seeks a position of leadership for himself wherever he can. The acquisition of wealth, the prerequisite of freedom and power, is one of the tenets that Jews imbibe with their mothers' milk. The Jew discharges his racial duty by making money. He has been so successful in this endeavor that Jewish power is indeed felt in politics and other areas of public life. By implication, America by the early 1920s, and more so when World War II broke out in view of its main goals and pressing needs, regarded the Jews as possessors of power – a largely illegitimate power that should be limited, but also something that should be taken into account and, when necessary, manipulated and neutralized.

In this regard, the authors of the study rejected the Communist nexus that was regularly attributed to the Jews. Communism, they said, does not fit the Jewish character. Having accustomed themselves to a life of fierce competition for advantages, the Jews have evolved into a race of individualists whose supreme aim is the attainment of a personal edge. Generally speaking, they are conservatives, chauvinists, capitalists, and individualists. Such was the authors' judgment. However, the Jews' story is not so simple because they have clashing pretensions. In fact, the authors alleged, Jewish teachings have long been socialistic. From the era of the prophets to our times, they explained, the Jews have inveighed loudly against heresy, materialism, exploitation, and wealth. They themselves, however, have always fallen into the snare of the last two. They always protest these injustices as affronts to the fraternity of man, while positioning themselves above the fray with the typical contempt of the chosen people of a tribal God.

Here, the study initially surmounted a liberal assortment of antisemitic allegations and acknowledged Judaism's contribution to human ethics. It claimed, however, that this people is unworthy of its contribution and, by speaking in its name, has become a dual-edged political and social problem. This hypocrisy, the authors state, makes the Jews – past, present, and future – enemies of the existing order and fomenters of a new order. One always finds Jews wherever extremists congregate in theory and in practice. Jews always have one leg planted in this sphere of theoretical idealism and the other leg in the very materialistic and practical sphere of the economic world, where they have influence.

This last sentence sounds like something Professor Ze'ev Sternhell of the Hebrew University could have written about Mapai without realizing that the authors of this study surely would have termed him an "extremist in theory and practice," an "enemy of the existing order," and a "fomenter of a new order."[31]

The preceding is one explanation for the Americans' reluctance to admit more Jews to their "club" when Hitler began to deport them en masse, that is, before he decided to close the gates and exterminate them. However, they were loath to admit masses of Jews many years before the problem became a political question of "importing antisemitism," one that would weigh severely on the attitudes of the Western elites toward their own masses and eventually would interfere with the enlistment of them for war against Hitler – the man who had deported the Jews.

Among the Western security elites themselves, World War I augured severe changes that, while not directly related to the "Jewish problem," would have implications for the treatment of the Jews in the next global crisis. The change that mattered, according to Bernard Porter, was first evinced among the British upper middle class after World War I (which by then was already viewed as a "total war"). It gave men and women who had served in the British and American defense forces the feeling that they were fighting enemies who were not "gentlemanly" and who inhabited a dirty world that had no further room for gentlemanly customs.[32] As the West began to make serious preparations for a stand against Hitler, his collaborators, and his possible allies, including Arabs and Muslims, the Jews could not change these dominant trends of thought and could not force foreign political and defense elites to admit them or concern themselves with their woes.

What lessons did Ben-Gurion learn from all this? He did his utmost to change the situation, or at least to understand it. The purpose of his learning endeavor was neither to hate the non-Jewish world nor to thirst for revenge against it. Ben-Gurion's Zionist renaissance positioned criticism of Diaspora Jewry side by side with the goal of rescuing it; therefore, the lessons of the Holocaust included both. First, there was an assault on Diaspora Jewish customs and a wish to rescue the Jews from the experience of exile by establishing Jewish sovereignty. Second, when the Holocaust was at its peak, the Jews should take their fate into their own hands but should not give up on the world and reject what was beautiful and good in it, despite the world's hatred of, estrangement from, and crimes against them. These, after all, can be traced to the world's interpretation of its values, its politics in a given historical situation, and its image of Diaspora Jewry through its own lenses. This historical situation was indeed a given, but the Zionists had the power to change it and, therefore, were duty bound to try to change it, even at the climax of an unparalleled catastrophe, in areas where they could pursue such change.

This point needs elaboration; we provide it later on. At this juncture, however, it is arguable that, under certain conditions, Ben-Gurion may have viewed Jewish efforts in Eretz Israel, and it alone, as the key to Jewish continuity and survival, albeit in only part of its homeland, without forfeiting the possibility of support from the "world." The Holocaust taught him an exceedingly tragic lesson about the limits of this support and forced him to probe the depths of the perversity of the entangled, contradictory, and continually changing world that we inhabit – and, within this generality, to stare into the mirror through which others viewed the Jews.

A Non-Nation Nation in a Trap

The slamming of the U.S. gates to Jewish immigration, definitely abetted by the aforementioned "intelligence study," did promote a different cause: aliyah. Many of the *olim* (Jewish immigrants to Palestine) were neither Zionists nor idealists but refugees from Poland and Germany who settled in towns, developed Tel Aviv along the lines of a late 1920s and early 1930s city, and established the *Hadar Hacarmel* and *Ahuza* quarters of Haifa. Some had been given or exposed to a Zionist upbringing but did not view Zionism as their main driving force at the time.[33]

Now they found themselves in the Orient, living within a framework that had been created slowly and steadily in the decades preceding their arrival by the Zionist Labor Movement, even though the movement's institutions – foremost the Histadrut (General Federation of Labor) – were voluntary and did not embrace the entire Yishuv. Contrary to the "Bolshevik" image of the Labor Movement, in the 1940s only about one-fourth of the Yishuv population carried Histadrut cards, and the Histadrut itself often failed to mobilize its members for operations that it considered extremely important, for example, hard manual labor in harvesting fruit or staffing the Dead Sea Works. An internal schism opened up within the Histadrut in the 1930s and worsened steadily in the 1940s, for reasons including a dispute that broke out between the mainstream and Mapai and the party's left-wing faction and the Marxist Ha-Shomer ha-Tsa'ir over the question of enlisting in the British Army during World War II. (The mainstream's stance was that joining the war effort was a supreme necessity.) The contretemps were put to rest by means of difficult compromises, including the Left's consent to join the Jewish Brigade Group in the ranks of the British Army in 1944, once the British finally yielded to Zionist demands to create a distinct "Jewish army" of the kind that would serve outside the boundaries of Palestine.[34]

The Labor Movement had to operate under the prevailing economic conditions in Palestine, which were dictated by the Mandatory government, a heavyweight employer that engineered booms and busts for reasons of its own and in response to factors determined by externalities.[35]

By the time of Hitler's rise to power, the roots of the Labor Movement in Palestine were ten to thirty years old. The movement had gone through several phases and metamorphoses until Hitler took over and turned the world upside down in steadily accelerating stages. It was anything but monolithic; it was composed of various historical layers, including a flank that contemporaneous observers would call "dovish," a pacifistic and Tolstoyan-inspired party known as Po'alei Zion (Workers of Zion). Eventually it was also joined by Gordonia, an entity with quasi-anarchistic leanings. Gordonia was led by a cohesive bunch that wished to safeguard their leading position but found it difficult to impose their will on their constituents.[36] The supreme leader of Gordonia, Pinchas Lavon, was an important Socialist theoretician but also an aggressive, narrow-minded politician who had no grasp of regional and world politics. Fearful of the outbreak of war after the proclamation of statehood, he opposed this proclamation and subsequently clashed with Ben-Gurion on the question of mass immigration in the early 1950s, fearing the impact of less idealistic masses coming from the Arab countries. After a period of passionate support of Ben-Gurion's methods of fighting both the Right and the Left and a truncated term as an extreme, strident minister of defense, Lavon would dispute him in matters of state and of Israel's functioning in a neo-Socialist spirit. Eventually, he set up an oppositionist group of his own called Min ha-Yesod (From the Ground Up), which would accuse the Ben-Gurionistic "state" of wishing to take over the Histadrut and its affiliates, which were "voluntary organizations," as he tried to portrait these huge bureaucracies, and of depriving them of their due status.[37]

Ha-Shomer ha-Tsa'ir was another story: a separate collectivist pioneering movement that had sustained itself and its membership in various parts of Poland. Over the years, this movement adopted such an overtly Marxist and pro-Soviet stance that only the subsequent persecution of its members by Stalin and the discovery of his crimes freed it of this ethos, and even then not totally.[38]

What everyone in the Labor Movement shared at this time was the vision of transforming the Jews into a nation of pioneers in their land. Once Hitler came to power, however, the movement split into parties and factions. Some continued to uphold the movement's agrarian idealism, which focused on the cream of the Jewish crop, those who had been trained and educated in the Zionist youth movements and on their training farms in Europe. Others spoke of the debt that Zionism owed to the Jewish people at large and acknowledged the historical reality of a fractured and fractious people, susceptible to different influences and interests, and the movement's obligation to receive such fragments that would be tossed ashore in Eretz Israel.

Indeed, Mapai, formed in the early 1930s shortly before Hitler's rise to power, exhibited the combination of traits that the authors of the aforementioned American study termed a mixture of idealism and pragmatism. It was a compromise between the wish to enlist the *olim* in transforming the ways of life that they had brought to Palestine and the need to recognize the paucity of means available to the voluntary Yishuv leadership, that is, capital raised by the Zionist Movement in the Diaspora. The resource constraint carried much weight in the thinking of the delegates to the Jewish Agency Executive, both from the Zionist Movement and from non-Zionist bodies. It vied for their attention with the immigrants' habits, the Mandatory government's immigration rules, and the intense and steadily worsening friction with the Arabs who surrounded them. Under these conditions, many Jewish collectives in the West, specifically, found the Zionism of the Labor Movement unacceptable. Ben-Gurion did make personal efforts from the early 1930s onward to recruit American Jews, men and women alike – especially the large and ramified Hadassah organization – for Zionist activity, and his exertions did have some payoff in financial and political terms. However, American Jewry had just begun to emerge from the great economic crisis of the late 1920s and early 1930s, and many of its members were more committed to immersing themselves in the American melting pot than in Zionism.[39]

These considerations show, of course, that American intelligence's premise about the unity and full cooperation among Jews was but a myth. Even the practical Zionists who emerged at this time disagreed with one another in many respects. Therefore, the "Bolshevism" of Mapai and other constituents of the Zionist Labor Movement sought to seize the economic and political levers of the Yishuv by establishing entities of their own for this purpose, or by strengthening their influence over existing entities in the Yishuv and the world Zionist movement, channeling their resources to the settlement of Palestine and the advancement of the goals of Socialist Zionism, a dynamic and active minority among a dispersed and fragmented people. They attained this control by reinforcing rural settlement in various ways within the collective Yishuv and by providing the public at large with services, including jobs, health care, and a source of identity. They also furnished assistance in election campaigns, even if the main political battle was taking place among Zionists abroad in general elections for the movement's supreme institutions (until the world war thwarted such elections and suspended the highest institution, the Zionist Congress). However, the Bolshevism that all segments of the Labor Movement shared was a state of mind – a call for mobilization, personal fulfillment, and acceptance of authority and obligations – that focused more and more on the security issue, from the Arab uprising in the 1930s onward.[40]

Not everyone accepted this burden of obligation, and disagreements among parties within the Yishuv proliferated. Jews who tended to the hedonistic, competitive, and egoistic states of mind that the aforementioned American study attributed to the entire Jewish people – as we recall, it portrayed the Jews as a "race" with a singular degree of internal cohesion – despised the mobilized mind-set that the Labor Movement adopted during the inferno of the Holocaust. The late Yosef Almogi, who was a German prisoner of war during World War II, also recounts in his memoirs the difference between prisoners from the "organized Yishuv" in Palestine and others from the same location.[41]

Here lay the uniqueness of the Labor Movement's Zionism: It sought to reclaim these Jews, even as many of them complained that the "organized Yishuv" was looking out for its own well-being and did not always trouble itself properly with the newly arrived.

In the meantime, the Mapai stalwart Israel (Rezsö) Kasztner stood within the jaws of the Holocaust, facing an immeasurably ghastly reality in his relations both with the Nazis and with Hungarian Jewry. Even before Hitler occupied Hungary, Kasztner had tried to operate as a political Zionist and impose a burden of obligations, authority, and rescue mobilization on rival Zionist bodies that were busy with their own affairs,[42] and afterwards on a scattered and fragmented community that in great part did not recognize him since he represented the small Labor Zionist minority among the otherwise non-Zionist or anti-Zionist Hungarian Jews.

The activities of the Zionist Rescue Committee in Hungary, of which Kasztner was a leading member, combined independent initiatives and guidance from the Yishuv's rescue mission in Istanbul.[43] However, these entities themselves were conflicted and factionalized – mirroring the Yishuv at the time – until they mastered the rudiments of the art of cooperation. Observing them at the peak of the Holocaust, Ben-Gurion exclaimed, "We can't act as one people anymore. Look, we're not dealing here with controversial political matters but rather the question of rescue."[44] Moreover, these Zionist rescue entities were not operating in a vacuum; most of their activities were known to the Allies and the Germans alike. The Nazis monitored their actions with interest and did whatever they could to sabotage them, terminate them, or exploit them for their needs. The Western Allies' security services regarded Jewish emigration from occupied Europe as an activity that would cause them trouble and embroil them in entanglements with the Arabs.

A report from the American military attaché in Egypt in the middle of April 1943 deserves a brief reference here. This document, circulated by the intelligence division of the American forces in the Middle East half a year after the Allies were finally convinced that Nazi Germany was physically annihilating all European Jews who fell into their clutches, identified the traffic of Jewish refugees, primarily between Europe and the Americas, as being supported by three agencies that were orchestrated by the American Jewish Joint Distribution Committee. The document then expressed alarm, citing counterintelligence reports based on British intelligence sources, about the possibility that the enemy would use these refugees as spies and saboteurs. The conclusion to adduce from the evidence, the report advised, was that the Jewish organizations, though in no way officially related to German planning, should be carefully monitored anyway for two reasons: the dubious nature of certain individuals associated with them and the opportunity they created to infiltrate foreign agents into America.[45]

The U.S. Department of State did its utmost to impede Jewish immigration to the United States, not only for these reasons but also because key officials in the Roosevelt administration refused to accept American responsibility for the fate of the persecuted Jews and the outcome – that is, the antisemitic implications – of receiving them in the Western Hemisphere (even though they did not admit this outright), and were loath to allocate the resources needed to accomplish it. Later on, they also began to fear Jewish pressure that would try to water down the imperative of leading Germany to unconditional surrender.[46]

As mentioned previously, Foreign Secretary Eden's statement in the House of Commons late in 1942 calling the Holocaust by name "was regarded as a mistake by the Foreign Office, for it raised public expectations of government action in aiding the Jews of Europe, when no such policy was intended."[47] British officials of that kind, reflecting the "establishment's" opinion, had now become doubly afraid of their own people and of Arabs in respect to rescuing Jews: They were conscious both of domestic antisemitism and of domestic sympathy toward Jews, which arose later in the war, and had to maneuver between these concerns and the Zionists. They decided not to help any Jews in order to avoid domestic repercussions, to forestall trouble with Arabs, and to preclude possible problems with Stalin, who was known to be worried that the Western Allies might negotiate separately with the Germans, possibly under Jewish pressure. Yet at the same time, they had to display humane concern in order to avoid domestic repercussions of the opposite kind. Playing the game both ways required skill, which various British officials and agencies succeeded at almost till the end, sometimes against Churchill's own efforts, at least in regard to Palestine, and they carried their American counterparts with them most of the time.

To officials such as Eden, giving too much attention to the Jewish issue spelled every conceivable sort of risk, from the greatest – making real concessions to Hitler – to the least – giving the impression that the war was "Jewish," which in fact it was, because Jews were its main victims. Several British politicians made their own calculations clear in this regard, describing, in mid-1942 "growing domestic anti-Semitism" in their discussions with their American colleagues, whose basic support they gained or rather reinforced. A letter from the Franklin Delano Roosevelt Memorial Library provides a good example: On July 1, 1942, Myron Taylor, the American ambassador to the Vatican, forwarded to the president a letter by Sir John Hope-Simpson, in which the latter, a colonial officer and refugee expert of sorts, argued that "anti-Semitism is not confined to Central Europe and Arab countries as there is a great danger of it in Great Britain and probably in the U.S."[48]

Such arguments, plus public Jewish pleas for some kind of Allied negotiations with the Germans to stop the carnage, led to the almost zero outcome of the aforementioned 1943 Bermuda Refugee Conference. British policy was made clear enough to Zionist leaders as follows: In a letter to Dr. Chaim Weizmann, president of the World Zionist Organization,[49] the British minister in Washington, Ronald I. Campbell, responded in the name of the ambassador, Lord Halifax, and Foreign Secretary Eden to Weizmann's bid to allow 70,000 Romanian Jews to emigrate to Palestine immediately, an idea that seemed, in Zionist eyes, to have been endorsed by the Romanian government. Hence, it seemed to be at least a possible open rescue route from a German-allied nation such as Slovakia or Hungary. Campbell wrote, that

His Majesty's Government has no evidence to show whether or not the Rumanian proposal is meant to be taken seriously. *But if it is, it would still be a piece of blackmail which, if successful, would open up the endless prospect, on the part of Germany and her satellites in Southeastern Europe, of unloading at a given price all their unwanted nationals on overseas countries* [italics added].

Campbell went on to say that his government, in conjunction with the governments of the United Nations, would continue to give earnest study to all "practical means" of alleviating the refugee position, which, however – and this was his main point – "were consistent with the fullest war effort. *But to accede to blackmail and slave purchase would be a serious prejudice to the successful prosecution of the war*" [italics added]. He further stated that, as his political superiors saw it, the whole complex of humanitarian problems raised by the German domination of Europe, of which the Jewish question was an important but by no means the only aspect, could only be dealt with completely by an Allied victory.

The trap was clear: In one camp, the Jews were viewed as a potential obstacle to destroying the Nazi war machine, at the very time that the Nazi machine was in fact destroying them more than all others, while in the Nazi camp, they were being blamed as the engineers of that anti-Nazi war machine that emerged as a result of Hitler's war against the Allies. At the same time, the British officials often repeated the cunning argument that any step calculated to prejudice the war effort would not be in the real interest of the Jews of Europe – if any of them were to survive to have any "interests" at all.

To assess the attempts by Zionists in occupied Europe to take action during the war, we need to study a report by Reuven Zaslany-Shiloah, head of the Yishuv's embryonic security service, which operated with the Jewish Agency Political Department. Zaslany-Shiloah summarized succinctly the agency's efforts to work out cooperative arrangements with the Allies from 1940 onward,[50] most of which were torpedoed by the British for political reasons

and concern about spies and an alleged commonality of interests between the
Zionists and the Nazis in regard to Jewish emigration to Palestine.[51] Matters
came to a political and public head at the conference in Bermuda on Jewish
refugee affairs in the middle of 1943, when the Western Allies announced that
they would not negotiate with the Germans for the rescue of Jews. The reasons
for this policy will continue to occupy us in this chapter.

As for what the Germans knew about the Zionist rescue activities, one
of the examples recently discovered in the U.S. National Archives is a cable
from Frank Wiesner, head of the Office of Strategic Services (OSS) mission in
Bucharest after that city was liberated in the summer of 1944. When Wiesner
took up his post, he received documents from the German legation, including
the files of the local "Jewish affairs adviser," Adolf Eichmann's emissary in
Romania, Gustav Richter.[52] In his cable to Washington (October 27, 1944),
Wiesner reported on three individuals whose names appeared in the Gestapo
files: Hans Welti, a Swiss journalist whom the Zionists trusted and who served
them as a courier; one Hensley (also a Swiss journalist and a courier for the
rescue emissaries); and one Willman, president of the "Jewish center" (the
Romanian equivalent of the Judenrat). These documents identified all three
as wholesale denouncers of Jews. The Gestapo documents also indicated that
American Jewry had transferred some $500,000 to Switzerland and recorded
the money as personal donations. It had been sent for the purpose of transfer
to Palestine, but most made its way to Romania.

At the time the money was transferred, Palestine was a legal destination
for donations collected by American organizations, but Romania, as Nazi
Germany's ally, was not. Thus, the transfer ostensibly violated the rules of
war. The transfer of rescue funds to Zionist and non-Zionist players in occupied Europe concerned the British and the Americans greatly and touched off
a vigorous dispute between them, which was ultimately resolved in favor of
forwarding the money.[53]

Another tragic irony deserves mention here: Richter's files document three
years of activity on the part of Eichmann's agent in Romania, including his
public attempts to see to the extermination of this Jewish collectivity – most of
which survived due to a change in policy on the part of the Romanian dictator,
Jon Antonescu. The files were forwarded to the OSS in Washington in real
time, that is, before the end of 1944, and were transferred about a year after
Wiesner's cable to Dr. Charles Irving Dwork, a young Jewish historian who
had been put in charge of the "Jewish desk" of the Central Intelligence Agency
(CIA). Dwork studied the material that Richter had spent almost three years
posting to his direct supervisor in Berlin – none other than Eichmann himself –
and regarded it as grist for the preparation of the Nuremberg trial. However,
preparations for the trial were already under way and did not treat the Jewish
issue as a matter of priority.[54]

Thus, the Zionists' attempts to establish secret ties with entities such as the
OSS for purposes of intelligence cooperation and rescue were doomed to many
hardships from the outset and yielded scanty fruit during the Holocaust, as the

Gestapo infiltrated the rescue activists' ranks not only with Swiss traitors but also in a way that was many times worse, as we will see when we take up the Joel Brand affair.

The Jews of Hungary viewed the Zionist rescue activity not as a challenge but as a source of trouble and danger to themselves. At the onset of the Nazi occupation, they considered Kasztner a usurper whose rescue policy, which he imposed on them, would force them to make financial sacrifices and negotiate an agreement of some kind with Eichmann and his men – an agreement that would depend on the West's willingness to accede to the Nazis' demands. Failing to secure such willingness, Kasztner attempted in 1944 to drive a wedge between Eichmann and other Nazi officials who were aware of the impending demise of the Third Reich.[55]

An action of this kind was reflective of the typical Zionist, who wished to act in order to save Jewish brethren in Poland by helping them to find refuge in unoccupied – as yet – Hungary, instead of doing nothing. The various Hungarian Jewish community leaders, however, looked out for their own members in traditional ways and disregarded demands for funds as voiced by members of Zionist youth movements – whom Kasztner financed with money from the Yishuv, some of which had been forwarded to him in Budapest from the United States in the manner noted earlier – even though these movements had used the money successfully to rescue thousands of individuals and smuggle them to Romania.[56]

In all, the chances that the Zionists and the Western Jewish leadership would fail during the Holocaust were many times greater than their chances of success, because it was the Nazis, and not some third party with whom the Zionists could try to speak, who controlled the Jews' fate. The tragic paradox that must be understood is that the Zionists, and other Jewish entities, could rescue Jews here and there, provided that only a few were at issue. The moment the flow of survivors became a torrent, the Nazis mobilized to stanch it with all the formidable means that they possessed. The aforementioned Gestapo document in Bucharest shows us that even in Romania – a Nazi ally that the Germans had not occupied physically – Germany needed only to intervene in order to prevent Jewish departure on any real scale, even though the Romanian authorities weighed the possibility of allowing such departure and the Zionists labored prodigiously to bring it about. Hence, from the onset of the Holocaust to its expansion throughout occupied Europe, the problem of rescue became a hopeless war against the Third Reich itself, which had absolute control over the lives of Jews within its confines, and not just another struggle against Western governments that refused to accommodate refugee Jews then and afterwards.

After all, even as the Holocaust advanced apace, some Western officials continued to view Jews and Nazis as two sides of the same coin – racists and nationalists whose only concern was their own supremacy and power – and considered the Zionism of Ben-Gurion and his associates a form of "national socialism" that defied all sense and clashed with the Western Allies' universalistic, antinationalist, and antiracist goals of the war.[57] The British high commissioner in Palestine, Sir Harold MacMichael, spoke in this vein. The same sentiment was reported to Washington at the peak of the Holocaust in the name of the American consul general in Jerusalem, Lowell Pinkerton, even though Pinkerton maintained correct relations with the Jewish Agency leadership and sometimes helped it by offering his services in forwarding information.[58]

Ordinary Americans who served in Palestine at the time complained, in recently revealed letters, about the Jews' "whining." The Jews, they said, thought in the midst of the war only about their brethren who were being killed in Europe and blamed America for it, even as the whole world was suffering no less than they were and as their wailing caused complications in U.S.–Arab relations.[59] Various circles accused both Labor Zionists and American Jews immediately after the Holocaust, and continue to do so today, of not having raised enough of an outcry. Had they done this, they claim, more Jews could have been spared from the horrors of the Holocaust.[60]

Others, while not actually arguing that this was so, still say that the Yishuv did not mobilize for a large rescue enterprise of a type "neither pragmatic nor calculated, even if fundamentally hopeless," because its leadership, blinded by its goal of creating a Diaspora-repudiating "new Jew" in Palestine, had estranged itself from the "exile-Jew." This estrangement persisted after the Holocaust as well: The Yishuv used the survivors for its Zionist needs but refused to appreciate their distress, cope with their suffering, and deal with the entire Holocaust, which for this reason became a site platform for nationalist rituals.[61]

We judge these arguments to be fundamentally groundless because, among other reasons, they are rooted in the imaginary and nonexistent term "exile-Jew," a stereotype invented by a contemporaneous historian who resorted to the literary-poetic reality of the Holocaust and post-Holocaust eras.[62] There were various "exiles," and their attitude toward the Zionists themselves, and the dangers that they faced, stemmed from the very nature of the Diaspora, a multifaceted entity that had coped with multiple challenges in numerous ways before the Holocaust. Most Diaspora Jews were being murdered for motives and in ways over which the Yishuv leadership had no influence whatsoever as it strove to build a home in Palestine for those who wished to come before the Holocaust and to save as many of them as possible during it. Under these conditions, it was impossible to break out of the trap that had snared all Diaspora Jews indiscriminately and in ways that will be addressed briefly.

The foregoing argument, then, is deficient in deep political understanding of the Holocaust-era trap that better explains the Yishuv leadership's inability to effect a rescue than the "Palestinocentric," anti-Zionist explanations of our post-Zionist era.

The trap developed in stages. At the stage when Hitler was deporting Jews (1933–1940) and even after the British–French declaration of war against Nazi Germany, key officials in British governing institutions, who had become increasingly antisemitic since the time of Parvus and Lenin, accused the Jews of having helped Hitler ascend to power as a result of their nefarious and harmful contribution to German politics, which had played into the Nazis' hands. Quite a few leading British intellectuals even saw a resemblance between Judaism and Nazism in terms of narrow-mindedness, parochialism, misuse of power, and racism. The political establishment had a calculus of its own with respect to the deported Jews, one that definitely kept in mind this form of antisemitism and the grassroots variety as well. Eventually, important British officials began to think that a Zionist–Nazi interest had evolved – or, to be more precise, a common Zionist–Gestapo interest in removing Jews from Europe to the Arab Middle East in order to sabotage the interests of the entire West.[63]

The Nazi deportation policy, implemented by the Gestapo, had two goals: eliminating the presence of Jews in areas of German hegemony and flooding the West with Jewish refugees, since Stalin would not admit them. This "flooding," in the eyes of those who feared it, carried the following danger: If the Western countries indeed allowed masses of Jews to find refuge within their borders or in their spheres of influence, this would aggravate antisemitism and thereby play into Hitler's hands. The West kept its gates shut – having sealed them long before – for reasons including a reluctance to create fertile domestic soil for antisemitism, which would serve those who were deporting the Jews. The concern was that the absorption of large numbers of Jews would weigh heavily on the Western elites at a time of economic downturn and serious domestic social strain. Eventually, it would impede the West's ability to fight the self-same Hitler, who in the meantime was advancing apace, in a war that would require all-out mobilization. The victims of racism would therefore become its disseminators in the eyes of Western leaders, whereas the West's war against Nazism – if and when it were prosecuted – would have to be protected from the slightest hint of concern as being a "Jewish war." The emigration of Jews to Palestine was a separate issue in itself; the British increasingly considered it an obstacle in their struggle against the Axis in the Middle East, North Africa, and Indo-Burma.

An exceedingly important question to ask is whether the Yishuv leadership was aware of this trend of thought and, if so, when. After all, on the one hand, as Yehuda Bauer says, the Yishuv leaders considered the White Paper policy, which closed the gate of Palestine to mass Jewish immigration when Hitler was still deporting thousands of Jews, the second step in Britain's "appeasement" policy toward Hitler himself. The first step, Britain's policy of appeasing the Arabs, marked the continuation of the march to moral bankruptcy of the Chamberlain-MacDonald administration.[64]

The closing of Palestine's gates to aliyah, however, was actually a consequence of Britain's *abandonment* of its appeasement policy toward the Nazis, a corollary of their willingness to go to war with Germany if the latter were to attack Poland. It was for this reason that the Arabs had to be appeased. The Yishuv leadership may have been aware of the true considerations and argued as they did in order to bring Chamberlain and his associates under pressure.

The Hagana historian Yehuda Slutsky acknowledged this argument, at least after the fact:

The prime rationale in the refusal [to permit large-scale aliyah after May 1939] was fear of Hitler's anti-Jewish propaganda. Antisemitism was the Achilles' heel of the nations that were fighting the Nazis. It was widespread among their masses and also, to a greater or lesser extent, among their ruling and managerial strata. It nested in the subconscious of many liberals and democrats among them, the product of generations of education and legacy. The Nazis were well aware of this and in their psychological warfare they invoked with great success the slogan "This war is the Jews' war," with which they poisoned countless minds in their enemies' camp. The Allies did not dare to counter this propaganda in full force. They chose to ignore it, to blur the Jewish problem as much as possible, not to mention it, and not to underscore the Jews' role in the general war effort. "If there is anything that frightens all the Allies, without exception," Ben-Gurion said, "it is that, heaven forbid, [the Nazis] would say that this is the war of the Jews, who declared war on Hitler in order to avenge the insult that [he] dealt them."[65]

I was unable to trace the source of this key sentence, which demonstrates Ben-Gurion's superior insight into the Allies' demarches as they occurred and afterwards. The expression "insult" may provide weak evidence of the existence of a prior intuition about the trap before it evolved into the Holocaust. Slutsky's ex post writing, however, reflects the Zionists' typical resentment of their brethren in the Diaspora:

A rabbinical legend has it that when the final Day of Judgment arrives, the Holy One will cause the evil inclination to cross in front of the righteous and in front of the evildoers. To the righteous, it will look like a towering mountain, and to the evildoers – like a slender thread.... The righteous will wonder – how had we surmounted this towering mountain? The evildoers will agonize – how could we have failed to snap this slender thread? Something like this may be said about the Jews of the interwar generation. They were handed a uniquely fine opportunity – the privilege of having their own homeland. But most of them remained complacent and indifferent and did not wake up until it was too late. Many were swept away by the misleading enticements of Communist, Bundist, and Autonomist redemption. Some of them were Zionist organizers and believers, who exhausted themselves in vain efforts to establish national institutions on the shaky soil of exile. Immeasurable national energy was wasted on these actions... and only two or three institutions were established in Palestine. The historical opportunity was squandered.

As the Nazis' forced-emigration policy persisted into World War II, however, it seemed as though this "historical opportunity" was still at hand, but the British were closing it off. So things remained until the Final Solution decision in 1941, the reasons for which included the heroic war being waged by the very same British, the aid given them by the Americans, and Hitler's decision to blitz the Soviet Union. The last-mentioned decision was made for a number of reasons, including Britain's ongoing struggle, which was taking an increasing toll on the German economy, and the wish to deny the West a dangerous ally in the future.

Under these conditions of global drama, the Jews' interest was more than dwarfed. Many in the West considered it a "narrow" and "particularistic" interest: The Jews wished to rescue their brethren from the Nazis due to a complex tracing to the special nature of the Jews in their scattered condition. In earlier stages, not a few Gentiles suspected that the state of dispersion explained the wish of the dispersed Jews, who had neither a state nor might of their own, to drag the surrounding peoples into fighting their wars. However, the Zionists' demand for aliyah – as a practical step toward the elimination of the state of dispersion – was repeatedly rejected before World War II began all the way to the "White Paper" on Palestine of May 1939, which closed the gates of Palestine to Jewish refugees under Arab pressure.

Even if Winston Churchill himself was not complicit in this policy and opposed it furiously in public as long as he did not have governing responsibility, he upheld it for practical motives of his own. Churchill's most important motive for opposing this policy was his hope of mobilizing the neutral United States – with the support of that country's Jews – on Britain's side in its war. He soon realized, however, that American support of the British, albeit limited, would be forthcoming in any case, that American Jewry wielded no influence in the matter and had no separate reckoning of its own, and that the president's senior advisers, such as OSS chief Col. William Donovan, actually viewed the Arabs, along with British control of the Middle East without an Arab uprising, as an asset that should not be risked by helping the Zionists get their way. These rationales aside, Churchill's grasp did not suffice to amend the White Paper policy completely, but to suspend its political clause, which promised independence to the Arabs in due course. There were additional reasons for the limits imposed on the pro-Zionist Churchill: resistance on the part of British authorities in the region itself, opposition from senior ministers in his government, and his own refusal to settle scores with the heads of the "appeasers" in his party, including the antisemites and anti-Zionists among them, so that he could assure political and national unity in the supreme crisis of the war.[66]

The White Paper itself was hatched during the Chamberlain-MacDonald tenure. The British authorities, who initially allowed most Jewish deportees from Germany to enter Palestine provided they met the Mandatory immigration rules, began to rethink this policy in view of London's preparations for war and the lessons of the 1937–1939 Arab uprising. The uprising subsided in the summer of 1939 under the pressure of prodigious British efforts, but the concern remained that if large-scale Jewish immigration were allowed, Arab violence would reerupt in a much more intensive form and would spread throughout the region and the Muslim world. The process went through several interim phases.

In January 1939, Hitler first publicly proclaimed that "[i]f the international Jewish financiers in and outside Europe should succeed in plunging the nations once more into a world war, then the result will [be] the annihilation of the

Jewish race in Europe." In view of this proclamation, the Jews were presumably expected to make every effort to avert war and, a fortiori, to prevent it from becoming a worldwide conflagration. Naturally, then, they did their utmost to decry and fight Nazism, or they sank into their own community affairs. Most Zionists, apart from Avraham "Ya'ir" Stern and those of his ilk, viewed Nazis as a threat not only to their brethren and themselves but also to every value that they held dear, irrespective of their factions and splinters. Thus, they occupied themselves, each in his or her own way, with aliyah. After the Nazis stiffened their deportation policy in 1938, aliyah, including the clandestine form, was "nationalized" by the Jewish Agency and became a facet of the agency's political war against the White Paper policy.[67]

Now let us return to our description of the trap. By now, Hitler had publicly threatened to annihilate the Jews if a second world war were to erupt. What is more, he undertook to carry out the threat as his limited war in Poland and in Western Europe expanded. He had several reasons for acting this way. First, the British spurned his hegemony and continued to fight even after the fall of France. Second, the Americans stepped up their assistance but stopped short of direct intervention in the war, giving Hitler the idea that America should be neutralized by using the Jews under his control as hostages for the time being. Third, the Soviet Union seemed to be concurrently weak and demanding. Stalin pressed various claims on German *Lebensraum* in the Balkan countries and the vicinity of the Bosporus; furthermore, his economic accords with the Third Reich made the Nazi war economy, which in several critical respects was also being hard-pressed by the British blockade and the requisites of the war in the West, dependent on him. The USSR seemed to be juicy prey for two reasons: An attack on the USSR would absolve Germany of this burden and would keep Stalin from eventually breaking out of his alleged military weakness and joining the Western powers.

These were matters of global magnitude; to this day, scholars have not fully fathomed some of them. As they unfolded, no one could predict how they would develop, let alone their immediate implications for the industrial-style extermination of European Jewry.[68] The leaders of the "Jewish people," too, could not have foreseen them, and even had there been a "Jewish people" whose leaders would try to keep the war from spreading in order to save their brethren – even as Hitler himself widened it in response to his rivals' actions – they would have subjected themselves to ridicule and calumny. More importantly, they would have been ignored for once again having pursued their particularistic interests.

At the outset of this immense drama (May 1939), the British proclaimed the White Paper for Palestine and closed the gates of the only country on earth that they themselves had until recently recognized as the "Jewish national home." Some key officials at the British Foreign Office and the defense and counterespionage bureaucracies, and afterwards at the American foreign and defense services, ceaselessly suspected Hitler, his deportees, and his refugees as working in tandem to sabotage the West's war efforts.[69]

From their standpoint, the war was being fought to eradicate the Nazi threat to Western freedom, culture, and interests. After all, Hitler was demanding hegemony in Central and Eastern Europe and sought to render these areas a continental empire for hundreds of millions of Germans raised on his teachings. The West had no choice but to resist this demand and disregard its antisemitic postulate. Although the postulate was being translated into the forced emigration of Jews for the time being, it incorporated the intent to make the Hitlerian Europe of the future *judenrein*, with Western consent or otherwise. Since Hitler linked these two demands, the refusal to bow to his will in regard to the former led to refusal to accept it in the latter.[70]

In the next stage, Hitler invaded France and drove the British forces off the continent. Again he proposed that the British recognize and accept his hegemony. Now he destined the Jews to Nazi-supervised exile on Madagascar, to make sure that their brethren in America would behave well.[71] The British brushed off the message and clipped the Luftwaffe's wings in the Battle of Britain. Just the same, isolated and pining for allies, they spared no effort to maintain their position in the oil-rich and Arab-populated Middle East, and part of this effort involved making the region off-limits to Jewish refugees. By so doing, they helped to worsen the Jews' entrapment even without dealing much with this trap themselves as they fought for their lives and initially suffered defeat after defeat. However, they survived, and by doing so they brought the next fatal step upon the Jews: Hitler's decision to deny the British – whose war he had considered a "Jewish war" from the outset, even though the British did their best to evade this imagery by ignoring the Jews – a possibly ally and to make his dreams in Eastern Europe come true. He pounced on the Soviet Union, hoping to smash it "within three months." There he immediately began annihilating the Jews and the "commissars," whose lives he deemed fair game ab initio for ideological and security reasons. Indeed, he viewed the entire population of this territory as subhuman and the territory itself as a Pale of Settlement for Nazi colonial exploitation.

Next, after his Japanese allies attacked the United States, Hitler declared war on the latter, which had been extending aid, albeit limited, to the besieged British in what he considered yet another form of "Jewish war" against the Third Reich. Never mind that President Roosevelt did not allow Jewish interests to play any role in his considerations and took great care not to identify with them publicly at this critical phase. Thus, the war expanded to global dimensions, and the conditions for the obliteration of "the Jewish race" in Europe, as Hitler had predicted them, ripened. For the previous two years, the Jews of Poland had been languishing in ghettos under ghastly conditions or had been carrying on in their longtime countries of residence without realizing the horrific nature of the evil that was crouching at their doorstep. Once President Roosevelt began to help the British to the best of his ability, the Jews became valueless as hostages for America's "good behavior." Hitler declared this global war a "Jewish war" and the Nazi propaganda machine proclaimed the corollary: The West's soldiers were being, and would continue to be, sacrificed "for the sake of the Jews."

Various kinds of fears and motives figured in the discussions among the Western powers, including the West's refusal to receive millions of aliens just because Hitler did not want them – aliens whom the West considered a cause of ferment and disruption of consensus and, therefore, tools in Hitler's hands; the concern that the absorption of the newcomers would require massive maritime resources before the "battle for the Atlantic" had been won; the old fear that the refugees would be swarming with enemy agents; and concern that the Nazis would flood Palestine with Jews and complicate Western relations with the Arabs and the Muslim world.[72] Later on, the Zionists would be suspected on this account of having a nearness of interests with the Third Reich, even though the proximity of Palestine to Europe did make it a realistic emergency destination for large numbers of Jewish emigrants, if only such escape were possible. Thus, ostensibly, the Jews were trapped between the Nazi hammer and the Allies' anvil.

From their position outside this constellation, the Zionists and Jewish leaders were many times worse off than we can appreciate today due to the paradox of the establishment of the State of Israel and Jewish support for it in the wake of the Holocaust. Many Western elites, including half-Jews and assimilated Jews, did not distinguish between the Holocaust and the fate that Hitler intended for other subjugated peoples. To the members of these elites, including prominent leftists and especially neo-Marxists, the annihilation of the Jews seemed like an introduction, a dry run, a spearhead meant to get the Germans emotionally prepared for a general policy of genocide against other nations.[73] For them, the Holocaust was not a matter of central, principal, and material importance, but rather a phase in the lethal Nazi imperialism that was to follow. To begin with, there was the success of the Nazis' antisemitic propaganda, but there was also an assumption here that antisemitism – and hence the Holocaust – were more than a matter of propaganda: They were successful tools to unite the otherwise diverse and divided German society. If so, there was no point, in the propaganda and political senses, in emphasizing the Holocaust and threatening to punish the German people on its account.[74]

The Western leadership was afraid that any special Western connection with the Jews and their tragedy would confirm their murderers' claim about the "Jewishness" of the war. This fear was mirrored in the response of Nazi Minister of Propaganda Joseph Goebbels to a statement by the British Foreign Secretary, Anthony Eden, in Parliament in December 1942 – the only statement of its kind – that the extermination of European Jewry was indeed raging ahead and that the perpetrators of these crimes would be punished. Goebbels immediately construed this statement as part of the Allies' surrender to the supposed Jewish scheme and further evidence that the war was a Jewish war. Officials at the British Foreign Office regarded Eden's statement as ill-advised.

For his part, Ben-Gurion was not content with mere oratory, that is, demonstrations, pleas for help, and protests in the face of Allied inaction. He preferred real action, if possible – from the establishment of a Jewish army within the Allies' own armed forces to the mobilization of Jews for the rescue of fellow Jews and the prompt establishment of a Jewish state. In my opinion, too, Ben-Gurion was well aware that despite the rhetoric and demands that various Yishuv players were addressing to the Allied powers in early 1943 – as the Holocaust pierced their consciousness – the Yishuv stood alone and could rely only on itself. It could only hope to mobilize others on its behalf, especially American Jewry – a mobilization that could not be divorced from the West's war against Nazi Germany. As long as the war continued, it was necessary to preserve what had already been attained in Palestine and to advance the Yishuv's interests to the greatest possible extent, even if these interests and those of the Jews were the least of the Allies' considerations. One could attempt to change this state of affairs, but the objective global and regional situation left the Zionists with little latitude.

In a speech before the Asefat ha-Nivharim (Assembly of Electees) in March 1943, following the Yishuv's acts of protest against the ongoing slaughter in Europe, and in two sessions of the Assembly about the plight of European Jewry, Ben-Gurion's state of mind at the time is aptly reflected. He mentioned the protest events, which were aimed "outwardly to express the Yishuv's horror and dread upon the slaughter of European Jewry. This time," however, he added, "I believe it necessary to speak to ourselves." He mentioned, as Tuvia Friling relates, the three blows absorbed by the Yishuv, "one greater than the other: the White Paper, the war, the slaughter." Yet Ben-Gurion carefully refrained from simplifying what he would soon call "an incomparably complex situation." Thus, he understood that the Nazis held the key and that they were "beasts in human form" from whom nothing should be expected unless the underlying characteristics of the war, such as the West's demand for Germany's unconditional surrender, were to change. He acknowledged the considerations and internal relations of the powers that made up the grand alliance. Just the same, he did not see this as a reason to accept immobility:

The Yishuv can neither wait nor settle for victory over the Nazis, because there is a dual menace: while waiting in such a way the [Jewish] people will be lost and . . . the homeland will be lost. Hitler exists, the White Paper also exists, and political arrangements, perhaps irreversible, are being determined in the course of the war.[75]

One may interpret these remarks as a typical manifestation of Ben-Gurion's disregard of the top priority that should be given to rescue. However, one cannot blame the Western leaders for this; after all, the Jews' fate was not in their hands and their assistance was now needed both for reasons related to Zionist politics and for rescue. But how was rescue to be pursued?

When the Holocaust began, Western leaders did not concern themselves with the Jews' fate because it was happening in places well beyond their reach and did not seem to raise real concern on their part anyway. In 1942, as the extermination campaign expanded to all parts of Europe, these leaders were overextended in managing the war and mobilizing their nations to prosecute it; indeed, they spent most of that year suffering defeats. These circumstances undoubtedly influenced their considerations in regard to the Jews. At the next stage, the Western leaders considered the Jews' fate dependent on them only if they were to deal with Hitler directly, thereby compromising their war goals or indirectly playing into his hands by making the Jewish case their own publicly. Since their first duty was to their own peoples, whom they served within the framework of democratic rule, ultimately they believed that they had no choice but to behave as they did.

There is no telling when this realization dawned on Ben-Gurion and strongly affected his actions during and after Israel's War of Independence. It echoed in his remarks before the war and would echo afterwards in statements in defense of Churchill[76] and on behalf of General Charles de Gaulle after the latter had severed defense relations with Israel in 1968, that is, in remarks about de Gaulle's duty to serve his country's interests first. This exculpatory rhetoric may teach us something about Ben-Gurion in the grave context of the Holocaust and elsewhere as well: his realization that the democratic leadership of a democratic people is by definition obliged to look out for its people – especially in extreme situations of war or national disaster such as those that Churchill and de Gaulle faced – and that the sovereign Jewish state must behave as they did when the time came. The issue here is not one of lack of ethics but rather an ineluctable dictate of political ethics. Those who fail to respect this dictate will lose their people's trust and, in all probability, will be unable to assist a helpless third party whose fate emphatically lies in the hands of a common enemy. Hence, in Ben-Gurion's eyes, the rescue of European Jewry could not be leveraged significantly by public pressure on the Allies from some outside player, that is, one other than a citizen or a domestic political pressure group.

Ben-Gurion understood this as soon as he realized that it was the Germans, by having resolved to obliterate every last Jew, who were thwarting the Jews' departure from the areas under their control. Furthermore, from the moment the Allies publicly proclaimed the goal of seeking Nazi Germany's unconditional surrender, there was definitely no point in expecting the Allies to discuss anything with the Germans. The path to rescue, insofar as the Nazi extermination machine was penetrable at all, depended on secret activity backed by unyielding political pressure. An attempt – without excessive noise – would have to be made from neutral countries, such as Turkey, Portugal, and Switzerland, to reach countries that were German allies but not German-occupied, such as Romania, Hungary, and Slovakia, and thence, perhaps, to the ghettos in Poland. It would entail not only the rescue and removal to Palestine of Jews but also underground activity in occupied Europe, which depended on cooperation that the Jewish Agency had been trying to establish with Allied intelligence agencies since the beginning of the war. Such cooperation, itself an issue replete with difficulties and obstacles, would have to be developed to the greatest possible extent. Concurrently, political action would be pursued among American Jewry for the purpose of uniting this community behind the Zionists as an American group that had political rights within the United States. Its goal would be the establishment of a Jewish homeland in Palestine in the very midst of the war, a Zionist homeland freed of Britain's shackles. Ben-Gurion had established much of this infrastructure in 1942, and American Jewry did display growing unity behind the Zionist cause in the aftermath of the Holocaust. Even this, however, coupled with the War Refugee Board (established by Roosevelt in January 1944 for the rescue of Jews), and the operations of the Zionist rescue missions and non-Zionist Jewish entities in neutral countries, were able to rescue only a smattering of European Jewry.

Therefore, when we distinguish between the Zionists' actions and the likelihood of their success, we must keep in mind the trap that, in my opinion, Ben-Gurion fully understood in 1943. This is not to say that he and others in the Yishuv leadership fell into this trap. Tuvia Friling produced a highly detailed account of what they did to rescue whomever they could. We, too, will revisit several principal rescue issues in order to ask whether there was any reality to them. One of these issues has long since evolved into the famous and widely expressed claim, if not common coin, that the Allies could at least have bombarded the railroad tracks to Auschwitz, the bridges that carried them, and the gas chambers, and that the Yishuv leadership failed in its duty because it did not pressure them properly to do this, if not more. According to Albert Speer, Hitler's minister of munitions, however, whose task was to nullify the results of Allied bombing, which he was able to pursue quite successfully, the bombing of railroad tracks – en route to Auschwitz or to any other destination – was a waste of combat effort, a purposeless gesture, since railroad tracks were much easier to repair than to bomb. He also considered the bombing of remote railroad bridges that were heavily defended by anti-aircraft guns a very costly operation that stood scant likelihood of success. And bombing Auschwitz itself – the existence of which the British had known about almost from the time it was established – was deemed impractical because the Germans could always find other ways to exterminate defenseless civilians (mass shooting, to name only one). The Western Allies could calculate how the possibility of inflicting casualties on camp prisoners might also cause political complications.[77]

It is worth mentioning a letter from American Assistant Secretary of War John McCloy on August 14, 1944, in response to a request by Dr. Leon Kubowitzki (Aryeh Kubovy) of the World Jewish Congress to bomb Auschwitz and the railroad tracks leading to it. This was McCloy's second letter on the topic. In the first, McCloy had cited the standard operational arguments of the heads of the Western air forces, who believed that they could win the war by themselves if they had the requisite resources. At least, they concluded, these resources must not be diverted from the main goal, winning the war. The British had additional considerations of their own: At first they refused to bombard "civilian targets" at the behest of diverse players, such as the Polish government-in-exile. They rejected such demands due to concern that they would disrupt the concentrated nature of the bombing effort and reveal the fact that they were bombing nonmilitary targets – as they were, notwithstanding their public denials. Later on, they diverted their concerted bombing effort from Germany somewhat and rushed to the aid of the Poles, who were rising in Warsaw – but did not bomb the gas chambers in Auschwitz, even though they could have. To explain this inaction, they may have believed that if a great power is determined to murder defenseless civilians who are totally under its thumb, it cannot be stopped by damaging any specific facility used for this purpose so long as it can resort to other means, such as mass shooting.[78]

McCloy's second letter to prominent Jews who contacted the Roosevelt administration and requesting that Auschwitz be bombed cites a political rationale. There is a view that must be taken into account, McCloy wrote, that such a bombing attempt might "provoke even more vindictive action by the Germans." There is no way of our knowing who held such a view. It may have been expressed by OSS experts such as Franz Neumann or other experts on Germany who, aided by psychologists like Erik Erikson, had studied Hitler and forwarded their assessments of the man and his motives to the then-CIA. They said, for example, that Hitler's actions were often driven by vindictive impulse and that the man made special efforts to carry out what he had promised and "predicted" before.

My interview with Albert Speer, the Nazi minister of munitions, emphatically confirms McCloy's premise that had Auschwitz been bombed, Hitler would have ordered the annihilation of the Jews even faster by reverting to mass shooting. In the interview, Speer said that he did not understand why those on the outside were blaming themselves about the possibility of saving the Jews on the inside. Hitler, he said, would have flown into a rage and ordered the extermination of any survivors. Besides, only Hungarian Jews were at issue by that time, and they could have been shot closer to home.

According to an examination of the resources available to Hitler in areas where Jews were still surviving at the time of McCloy's letter to Dr. Kubowitzki, the Nazis probably could have exterminated these defenseless women, children, and men with the assistance of Hungarian gendarmerie and other auxiliaries. Indeed, this is what they did in the death marches that they instigated after the Soviets occupied Auschwitz. Even before Auschwitz, they had killed by gunfire most Soviet Jews who fell into their clutches and murdered masses of Polish Jews in improvised extermination facilities – such as Belzec, Sobibór, and Majdanek – that were beyond the Allied bombers' range.

Those who expressed heated displeasure with the Allies for not having bombed Auschwitz have found it to be a two-edged sword – an instrument that continues to wound those involved in the Holocaust and its horrors in our own time. In other words, even then, the demand to bomb Auschwitz and the rejection of this demand caused guilt to be equally apportioned, as it were, among the murderers, the West, and the Yishuv leadership, and that guilt continues to be debated.

Indeed, documentation uncovered in recent years shows that the Western Allies' main fear at this stage of the war was that the Nazis might be handed an opportunity to use the murdered Jews as a bargaining chip for the very reason of the immensity of the crime. Anything that might halt so enormous an atrocity, the argument went, was justified, including dialogue with the murderers. At this point, the Western perception won the day: Negotiating with the Third Reich over Jewish affairs would pollute the goals of the war, "Judaize" the war, and entangle the Allies in demands from occupied peoples and governments-in-exile that represented many clashing interests. The centrality of the Holocaust in the Nazi policy – a matter that remains disputed in left-leaning circles and among personalities who seek a "universalistic" explanation for it – was dulled and blurred by the suffering of other peoples who, while not having been exterminated outright, had been occupied, tortured, and abused.

Concurrently, the West became increasingly concerned that the Nazis would demand unacceptable changes in return for stopping the Holocaust. For example, they might inundate the West with masses of Jews, with whom no one would know what to do. Alternatively, they might exploit some Jews – wealthy and dubious types – for their needs. Such actions would impair the pursuit of the West's war goals and the economic, political, and ideological blockade that the West had imposed on Germany this time around, in response, among other things, to the kid-gloves treatment (as the West viewed it) that Germany had enjoyed at the end of World War I.[79]

At the peak of the Holocaust in Hungary, the West was about to land on the European continent. This would be its greatest military gamble during the war, an act liable to claim a ghastly price in blood in an American election year. Thus, the Western powers flinched from any act that might constitute a concession to, or a compromise with, Nazi Germany, the enemy power against whom their soldiers were about to face the supreme test of combat, one that might end in a horrific failure that would make a repeat round necessary. In the event of such a concession or compromise, the Western soldiers, most of whom were Americans boys in uniform, might feel that they were being sacrificed to obliterate the Nazi regime at one level while their leaders were dialoguing with it at another level. By implication, the argument that the war centered on the Jews' interests had staying power and they, the Allied soldiers, were being offered on the Jews' altar. Therefore, the West's refusal to concede to Nazi Germany on any point, to compromise with it on any issue, and to dialogue with it on any topic included the idea of stopping the Holocaust, about which a public proclamation had been made at the Bermuda Refugee Conference of 1943. It was a principled refusal, for many reasons that were anchored in the very nature of the systems of governance and the relations between elites and the public within them. Ben-Gurion, for one, was able to gauge these reasons and respond to them in a manner other than passive acquiescence and acceptance.

One of the reasons for the Allies' refusal was the immense importance that the West attributed to propaganda, a term coined in the mass era that began at the outset of the century and was an especially powerful device in World War I. The destruction of Germany's international status at that time, particularly in the neutral United States, was traced largely to British propaganda that was mostly inflated, if not false.[80] Thus, the Western Allies knew that propaganda about alleged German atrocities at the beginning of that war, even if incorrect and unjust, had indeed caused Germany immeasurable harm. Therefore, though assailed by guilt feelings about the overstatements that had been made during the war and revealed after it, they were mindful of the power of such propaganda. Consequently, the Allied propaganda agencies in World War II felt obliged to avoid complicity in sensitive matters, such as the attribution of atrocities to the Germans and against hated or controversial groups, such as the Jews. The greater the number of atrocities, the thinking went, the more people presumably would not believe them. Furthermore, Nazi propaganda was portraying reportage about Nazi crimes, among other things, as Western "atrocity propaganda."

Concern about foreign propaganda ruses took on several forms and occupied the Western elites at several levels after World War I. One level was the success of Soviet propaganda; another was the success, in Western leaders' eyes, of the Nazis' propaganda – especially in the Middle East, where it was aided by the Mufti of Jerusalem.[81] Indeed, a similar logic dictated the Allies' impression regarding the very effective German propaganda among Arabs. In a typical Nazi broadcast to the region in April 1943, taken seriously by U.S. Army Intelligence (G-2), the Germans claimed that "wicked American intentions toward the Arabs are now clear.... [T]hey are endeavoring to establish a Jewish empire in the Arab world. More than 400,000,000 oppose this criminal American (just 140,000,000) movement. Arabs!... Kill the Jews wherever you find them." This appeal, made by the former Mufti of Jerusalem, Hajj Amin el Husseini, triggered the following statement by American intelligence:

The Arab propagandists in charge of Berlin propaganda have staged the present show with great cunning. The anti-Jewish theme has in the past constituted a good half of the German propaganda directed to the Near East. Constant vilification of Jews in terms calculated to make them repugnant to the Arab mind have included alleged attempts by the Jews on the life of Mohammed and their imputed domination of the Allied policies in the Near East ("Allied Jewish nations") reached new peaks calling for violence in Palestine.[82]

Even the internal rot that led to the defeat of France could be traced to a combination of effective propaganda and an internal "fifth column" that employed mass media with huge success. This was a simplistic view; today we know much more about the internal developments in France that brought down the country and allowed the Vichy regime to succeed at first, and also about the limitations of the mass media that create and modify political attitudes. After the atrocities of World War I and the changes that it brought about, however, the Western elites in the first half of the twentieth century were afraid of their own masses. Their fear escalated in particular after they had observed what they considered a takeover by a vulgar mob – or, to be more exact, by people who emerged from the midst of the mob and demonstrated its baser characteristics, as Churchill put it – of a great country like Germany. This attitude toward the Nazi phenomenon did not negate Western values of freedom, religion, and tradition that the leadership had encapsulated in a few simple and pithy slogans that anyone could understand – slogans accompanied by powerful mobilization propaganda that said not a single word about Jews.

The notion of directing a well-oiled advertising mechanism at the urges, instincts, and lowest common denominators of its consumers required a measure of control over these advertising media. Western politicians such as Roosevelt and Churchill were quite familiar with this notion and used mass media for their needs at every stage of their political careers. The Nazi enemy took its propaganda to a higher level, they believed: It behaved without the restraint warranted in this field and therefore seemed to be very, very effective. Consequently, similar countermeasures or a gag on "sensitive" issues, such as the Jewish one, had to be used. Accordingly, the West did its utmost to control public opinion during the war and stanch the spread of enemy propaganda not only to its own peoples but also to vital parts of the globe. In one such region, the Middle East, Italian-German propaganda made extensive use of antisemitic anti-Western arguments among Arabs and non-Arab Muslims, with the assistance of the Mufti of Jerusalem.[83]

Two previously mentioned points deserve restatement here as well: the lessons of the November 1918 armistice, which prevented the essential reconstitution of Germany and paved the way to the endless troubles that followed, and the goal of destroying the Nazi regime by totally defeating it on the battlefield. All Allied leaders subscribed to this goal and viewed any deviation from it as an injury to the West. Thus, it was a source of perpetual concern in regard to Stalin, lest he be untrustworthy if provoked. This outlook was amenable to President Roosevelt and his senior aides, who in any case were overextended in running the war. It was according to this outlook that the West established its priorities, in which the interests of the Jews, let alone the Zionists, were deliberately marginalized. Eventually, the president did turn his attention to the question of rescue and established, in early 1944, the War Refugee Board under pressure from officials in his Department of the Treasury and Zionist-Revisionist circles in the United States. Even then, however, he remained mindful of the possible outcome of this demarche, that is, how the Nazis might try to meet their needs by using the Jews as hostages. (We will have more to say about this in our discussion of the Joel Brand affair.) The president did try to influence Germany's allies, including the Hungarian dictator Miklós

Horthy, to intervene in an effort to save their domestic Jewish communities. However, Horthy's influence was limited, as we will demonstrate.

Ultimately, the Zionist issue remained largely in British hands, at least until the end of the war.[84] The British picture began to change in late 1943; we shall glance at it later.

Rescue Efforts and Relations with the West

From 1943 on, as they realized how grievous the Holocaust was and as minimum conditions for their operations in the West matured, the Yishuv leaders took all possible action to induce the Allies to effect the rescue of the Jews.[85] They established a rescue mission in Istanbul, something that could not have been done without tacit British consent, and used it to maintain relations with Rezsö Kasztner and Joel Brand's Zionist "Rescue Committee" in Budapest and with the Zionist youth movements in Hungary, Romania, and Bulgaria. By means of these agencies, they even penetrated several ghettos in Poland and delivered funds from Palestine and resources that had been raised for the Yishuv in the United States, even though such transfers violated of the rules of the war.[86]

Relations among members of the rescue mission in Istanbul and the Zionist Rescue Committee in Budapest reflected the multipartisan, multi-institutional, and voluntary nature of the Yishuv.[87] At first, the party emissaries' loyalties went to their own institutions, the Histadrut, and the Jewish Agency, the supreme Zionist political entity, in that order. Later, they learned how to cooperate, to some extent.[88]

Even though Ben-Gurion held key positions in the Jewish Agency and his own party, which ostensibly controlled the Histadrut, the edifice at issue was but a shaky federation of entities headed by key personalities who lacked the practical and official power to manage Zionist affairs properly, be it in Palestine or in relations with communities abroad. Mapai was definitely a political instrumentality that could have surmounted this chaos, but its attempts to establish itself as a linchpin in Zionist politics provoked counterresponses from the other bodies and charges of "dictatorship" against Ben-Gurion and his associates in the high councils of the party. When the latter attempted to transform the Hagana into an effective political tool for pressure on the Mandate authorities, people speaking on behalf of Mapai's own left wing called Ben-Gurion and his comrades, Eliyahu Golomb and David Remez, "dictators."[89] Even within the Hagana, clashes and fissures came into the open in the aftermath of reports about the Holocaust as various officials in the organization pressed for action against the Mandatory regime. The Yishuv leadership regarded these pressures as threats to its status in the United States and Britain that contributed nothing at all to the likelihood of rescuing Jews. In the eyes of the British and their American counterparts, however, this leadership was – or was reputed to be – a monolithic, if not dictatorial, body that disserved Western interests and subjected the Arabs to intolerable harassment.

The head of the Jewish Agency Political Department, Moshe Shertok (Sharett), sometimes conducted talks with Arab leaders and hostile British and American officials who used his remarks for their own purposes.[90] A typical and telling example is a meeting in Cairo on February 6, 1944, between Shertok and Brigadier Cyril D. Quilliam, chief of PICME (British Political Intelligence Middle East), and an American colleague, Stephen Penrose, or his deputy, Lewis Leary. The American immediately reported Shertok's remarks to Washington, either in direct quotation or in indirect speech, whence they reverberated in the diary of the American secretary of war, Henry Stimson, on February 14, 1944. The Jews, Shertok allegedly said, wish to capture Palestine and expel the Arabs.[91] His interlocutors asked him straightforwardly about Zionist propaganda efforts in the United States, aimed at Congress, which they considered political intervention in American internal affairs. Specifically, he was asked about the enlistment of personalities and political parties on the eve of the elections in order to bring about the immediate establishment of a Jewish state, thereby relieving the Zionists of their total dependency on the British in rescue affairs and in every other respect. Shertok responded that the Jewish Agency was helpless in a country that put such stock in the freedom of the press that any attempts to curtail the expression of opinions were useless.

"Frankly," the senior American intelligence officer responded in his report to Washington, "I think he is telling a deliberate lie. I cannot believe that the Jewish Agency would be unable to stop the activities of its American Associates.... Shertok is a very charming and a very plausible talker but quite frankly he impressed me as a rogue and a liar."

Shertok then spoke "with surprising frankness" about the Zionists' aspirations. He was quoted as having said that "the Zionists laid claim to all lands occupied at any time by the twelve tribes of Israel." Accordingly, "such claims embraced Lebanese territory, including the area around Tyre and Sidon."

It is self-evident that Quilliam and his American counterpart (Lewis Leary or Stephen Penrose, heads of the OSS intelligence-gathering apparatus in Cairo and known "Arabists") placed in Shertok's mouth the phrasings that sounded scandalous and menacing to vital Allied interests when contemplated by non-experts, such as their superior, General George C. Marshall (U.S. Army Chief of Staff), and Secretary of War Henry Stimson. From then on, Shertok would be quoted as having said that the Jews had decided to settle in most parts of Arab Palestine, where they would have to be armed against Arab attacks, and to penetrate the territory's most important Arab districts.

Such "activism" was not totally unheard of among Zionists at the time. However, an effort has to be made to separate truth from anti-Zionist propaganda that was insinuated into Shertok's remarks. The empirical facts, after all, are plain: At that time, the Zionists' settlement efforts would be focused on the unpopulated Negev – especially the northern Negev – and not the West Bank. The issue of "transfer," today the focus of heated debate between "post-Zionist" historians (and others) and ostensibly "Zionist" historians, is also anything but simple: Its main test is whether at that time the Zionists believed that the Arabs of Palestine could be removed forcibly or wished to persuade the powers to favor the establishment of a Jewish state in Palestine, in the course of which they would attempt in an organized way to entice the Arabs of Palestine to move to Iraq. It is an empirical fact that Ben-Gurion himself regarded "transfer" as an impracticality that should be expunged from the agenda, even when the British Labour Party embraced it publicly at its 1944 convention. This view led Ben-Gurion inexorably to the solution of partitioning western Palestine without "transfer."

Farther along, Quilliam engaged Shertok in an interesting debate about the coexistence of Jews and Arabs in a sovereign Jewish state. Quilliam reflected British doubts already expressed years before, since the very inception of Zionism, about whether the Jews would be capable of respectfully treating others as sovereign rulers of their own independent state. Shertok replied, "The Jews would be only too willing and glad to have a certain percentage of the Arab population remain in Palestine." The PICME chief responded, "[Transforming the Arabs into a minority in their own country] is out of the question and entirely impracticable."

Quilliam then charged Shertok with two motives underlying his desire to maintain an Arab minority in a Jewish state. The first, Quilliam said, was the necessity of proving to the world how well the Jews could treat a minority within their own lands. Shertok "admitted" as much. Quilliam "doubted whether this good treatment would last for more than five or six years at the maximum. . . . Shertok denied this vehemently but neither Quilliam nor I [Penrose or Leary] were convinced. Quilliam accused Shertok quite openly (I believe absolutely correctly) [parentheses in original report] of hoping to maintain an Arab minority in Palestine to be used as slave labour in the development of Jewish industry and agriculture. . . . Shertok naturally denied this, but neither Quilliam nor I [again, Penrose or Leary] were impressed."

A second conversation, in the same file, between the American party to the previous conversation and Shertok took place in London on February 19, 1944, exactly a month before the Nazis occupied Hungary. Quilliam was not directly involved this time, but the record was typed on the same typewriter in British (not American) English. The purpose was to use Shertok's own words against him:

[Shertok] denied ever having suggested to me in Cairo that the Zionists had any interest in [Lebanese] territory. This was truly a startling revelation. . . . I believe he told the truth by mistake in Cairo and was lying to me this evening. . . . [I said that] the industrial development of Palestine would lead to bitter commercial rivalry between a Zionist state and England for Middle East markets.

Shertok replied that appropriate trade and economic treaties could avert such a danger. His American interlocutor demurred, noting that global trade is customarily governed by free-competition rules, whereas Shertok had in mind the regulation of clashing economic interests of relevant nations by means of appropriate treaties.

The American author of the report then changed the subject and took up the problem of water and the agricultural development of Palestine. The limits of the country's water reserves were known, he said, even after the Jordan River would be dammed and the Sea of Galilee used as a reservoir for Jewish agriculture. Shertok did mention the Litani River as a possible solution, prompting the eager question of whether the Zionists wanted to settle there, too, as proof of their lust to expand beyond Palestine itself. Shertok denied this and said that an agreement on this issue could be concluded with Lebanon as a result of "pressure" on the Arabs to cooperate with the Jews. "What pressure?" the American asked. "Military pressure?" (i.e., use of Western bayonets to promote the Zionist cause). No, Shertok replied; what he had in mind was "moral and practical" pressure. The exchange continued:

[Shertok] proclaimed a passionate faith in the ability of the Jew to live alongside of the Arab in peace and friendship. . . . I observed a missionary tone in [Shertok's] voice which suggested that he would like me to think that the Jews would do so much for the Arabs living in the areas adjoining the Palestinian frontiers, that in the end current hatred would be transformed into permanent affection and lasting cooperation. His arguments . . . were slick and plausible. He spoke with great fire, grace and conviction. Nevertheless, I cannot help but fear that his hopes and this burning faith of his were ill-founded and I got a definite impression that he himself knew that this was so.

On February 23, 1944, armed with these and other arguments that military intelligence had provided him, General Marshall was willing to testify to committees of Congress that any current action on motions that the Zionists and their supporters were seeking in regard to Palestine would be detrimental to the war effort.

I quoted this document at length to show how current it remains more than sixty years later, and also to illustrate the main difference between Ben-Gurion and Shertok (Sharett). Ben-Gurion had long since realized that Sharett's rhetoric alone would do no good and would be used against the Zionists. Actions were needed as well, including threats to employ the force of the Hagana (without sliding into anti-British terror à la IZL and Lehi) and effective use of the power of American Jewry.[92]

In the midst of these efforts, at the very peak of the Holocaust, the Yishuv leadership was stricken with fragmentation and internal disputes. To reunify the party and reestablish its legitimacy, Ben-Gurion called general elections for the summer of 1944. It was not "politics" that concerned him as the Holocaust roared to its climax but, rather, the reality in the Yishuv, which was seesawing between hope and utter despair.[93] A motley assortment of entities had sunk roots there, including Aliyah Hadasha (the German immigrants' party) and a group of veteran Yishuv intellectuals, who joined up with Jews of German and American origin to establish Brit Shalom, now a political entity called Ihud (Union).[94] The task facing Mapai was to sustain the existing loose coalition in the Yishuv and the Zionist Movement institutions, establish a strong party machine that would win the upcoming elections, and cement its standing at the ballot box.

It was this leadership that ultimately approved every request and idea related to rescue, inducing dubious notions such as bribing and negotiating with SS officers when they seemed to have realized that Germany was losing the war. Such ideas stood no chance from the Germans' standpoint, whereas in the Allied camp, they could – and did – reinforce the suspicion that the Zionists were collaborating with the enemy and sabotaging the war effort. The best known of these ideas was the "Europa Plan" of Rabbi Michael Weissmandel and his Zionist associate, Gisi Fleischmann of Bratislava, which the Zionist Executive adopted after much vacillation. This affair is too complicated to explain in detail here, but the captured German documents in the U.S. National Archives demonstrate that the Germans were wholly unwilling to participate in a rescue deal of any such kind.[95] According to the source quoted here, Dieter Wisliceny, Eichmann's agent in Bratislava, did his utmost to continue deporting Slovak Jews to extermination camps under the conditions that the Slovak authorities laid down, which limited and ultimately terminated his ability to act. The document at issue shows that Wisliceny was not the only Nazi official involved in the annihilation of Slovakian Jewry and not even the highest ranking. However, the rescue operatives on site had the impression that he had stopped the extermination transports by virtue of the bribe that they had paid him and that, given Germany's dire situation in the war, the rescue activities could now be expanded with the consent of his superiors, Eichmann and SS chief Heinrich Himmler himself, and applied to Jews elsewhere in Europe. It was this speculation that gave rise to the Europa Plan.[96]

The Yishuv leadership approved ransom payments to Wisliceny and also trained parachutists for underground activity in the Germans' rear lines, as well as offered and gave the Allies intelligence and mine-laying assistance as a partner in their war against the Nazis, while constantly asserting its right to establish a Jewish army within their ranks. In a sense, these actions were mutually exclusive. One of their goals, without doubt, was to prove to the Yishuv population and to posterity that something was being done. We do not know what Ben-Gurion felt about their purpose. However, his remarks about the Nazi "human beasts" and the Allies' demand for the Third Reich's unconditional surrender indicate his realization that the Jews were trapped in a dead-end snare between the Nazi rock and the Allies' and the Arabs' hard place, since the Allies were unable to take the actions needed to force the murderers to release their prey.[97]

Ben-Gurion took the greatest care not to display this awareness publicly. The free world that had abandoned the Jews had become a source of moral leverage for the unification of Jewry and the demand, backed by evidence of the crumbling of Nazi Germany, to rescue the Jews of Europe and move them quickly to Palestine or any other destination. Furthermore, if he were to present these matters in their full severity at the very height of the Holocaust, Ben-Gurion might generate political leverage for an eruption of despair in the

Yishuv concerning the inactions of the West. By acknowledging the devastating logic of the trap, the Yishuv might overlook the minuscule possibilities of rescue that were offered by the cooperative relations that it had developed with the Allies' secret services. Admittedly, it was not Ben-Gurion's job to tell the nation that it was stuck in an almost inescapable trap, but in the past, too, he had often expressed his belief that national salvation would never be effected by Gentiles but only by the Jews themselves – if they would unite and take correct political action within the democratic systems that might respond under the evolving circumstances of the war. Acknowledgment of the trap might tumble the Yishuv into a mind-set of despair, revolt against the British in the middle of a world war in which they were fighting the Nazis, as the Stern Gang and Begin's IZL were doing against the elected majority's will, and rage that would seek dangerous political release and impair the rescue efforts – if they stood any chance of success – during the war and ahead of Nazi Germany's demise.

After all, the Jewish island in the Middle Eastern sea depended on the West in all matters, from access routes in and out to rescue stations in neutral countries, several of which had been established by the American Joint Distribution Committee (JDC) and the World Jewish Congress, and from relations with these stations to the raising of financial support. If these rescue efforts were to go ahead, the Jewish rescue missions in the neutral countries needed Western support. Special permission was needed to forward rescue funds, train parachutists, and send them into occupied Europe. It would take a blend of measures to induce the West to help, even against its will, and two measures were to be avoided: an uprising against the British fueled by blind rage and a sense of despair, such as "Ya'ir" Stern's followers. Even the Holocaust should not be allowed to drive the Zionists away from their renaissance-like activism and optimism. Menachem Begin's quest for paths to the heart of the United States by means of a revolt against Britain, which would show Washington that the Jews were no less able than the Arabs to cause trouble, was another manifestation of the primitive daydreaming that typified Zionism's right wing.[98]

The tragic climax of the trap was manifested in the "Brand mission," the proposal – attributed to none other than Eichmann – to swap Hungarian Jewry for 10,000 trucks that the West would provide Germany for its war against the USSR. The offer turns out to have originated with the Budapest Zionists themselves; Eichmann latched onto it for his own needs.[99]

What were these "needs"? Seemingly, Eichmann had neither an interest nor authorization from his superiors to do anything other than the swift implementation of the Final Solution in Hungary. Given the lessons of the Warsaw ghetto uprising in the spring of 1943, it was his intention to prevent a Jewish uprising in Hungary. Thus, he had to mobilize the most activistic element among the Jews, the Zionists, in pursuit of rescue deals that they themselves had initiated. He was fully versed in their previous rescue activities because he had been receiving their letters through the offices of double agents.[100] Eichmann may have intended to fill these Zionists' heads with grand ideas of rescue that stood absolutely no chance of success from the standpoint of both his superiors and the Allies. Furthermore, so long as the Zionists were dabbling in these ideas, they were distracted from the main thing, that is, they did not sabotage the Final Solution. To keep the distraction going, Eichmann was even willing to release several hundred Jews who held Palestine immigration visas; ultimately, they became the 1,684 passengers who rode the "Kasztner train" to survival. This may indeed have been Eichmann's intention, and to carry it out he availed himself of a Jewish traitor, an Abwehr and Gestapo man named Fritz Laufer, who had penetrated the OSS intelligence agency and whom the Americans considered a reliable agent, code-named Iris. At issue was an American intelligence network that a Czech-Jewish engineer named Alfred Schwarz, and code-named Dogwood, had established from his base in Istanbul.[101] By 1943, "Iris" had already been meeting with the Jewish rescue activists in Istanbul and Budapest, and they presented them with the Jews-for-trucks idea. Thus, this notion predated the Brand mission of May 1944.

To understand the Zionists' rescue efforts, however, one must appreciate how deeply trapped the Jews were. To gain this understanding, one has to realize that from Hitler's point of view – and, therefore, from that of Eichmann's ultimate superior, SS chief Himmler – the Holocaust, once decided upon, was to be both a goal in itself and an outcome of the world war that the West had ostensibly imposed on the Third Reich. Thus, any action the West might take that would change this fact at this stage of the war, even indirectly – by providing trucks, for example – might prompt the Germans to extort the West for no gain whatsoever. Alternatively, the alleged deal might be understood as leading to negotiations about expelling the Jews from Europe without killing them, for which the West would have to deliver a political-strategic qui pro quo. This is exactly what the West, let alone Stalin, was unwilling and unable to do.

It stands to reason that Western officials continually anticipated a Nazi initiative of this kind and the possibility of Jewish support for it. The Brand mission provided telling proof of the correctness of this concern, especially when Brand showed up with another "courier," Bandi Grosz. Grosz was not an agent of Eichmann's and did not meddle in truck deals; instead, he represented Gerhard Clages, an official of the SD, that is, the Sicherheits Dienst of the SS, or Himmler's Intelligence Service, in occupied Budapest, and was delivering a direct offer to negotiate a separate peace between the West and Nazi Germany. The British apprehended this "courier" and interrogated him, just as they had separately with Joel Brand. The Allied intelligence agencies drew a connection between the "Brand-Grosz mission" and the liberation of several members of the Weiss family of Hungary, the condition for whose release was that the family sell its property to the SS through the mediation of Himmler's purchasing agent in Hungary, Kurt Andreas Becher. The release of this Jewish family by a regime that had vowed to kill Jews evoked suspicions of collaboration between the latter and the Jews, who had been pardoned in return for their property, against Allied interests.

A cable from OSS headquarters in Washington on July 4, 1944 – almost six weeks after Brand and Grosz reached Istanbul and following their separate interrogations by the British – deserves being quoted in full so that we contemporaneous readers may understand how encompassing the trap was:

1. [W]ith the complete assistance of the German government, the Weiss group mentioned in your [cable] #57377 (#178 to Madrid) reached Lisbon [further details in previous cables between OSS stations Bern and Washington] and also to Saint [OSS–X-2 or counterintelligence] about report that the signing of a 20-year lease of the Weiss works [by the SS] was forced as a bargain by the Germans.
2. There are additional indications that this may be a portion of a plant by 2 German double agents who reached Istanbul on the 5th of last month [meant are Brand and Grosz, who had reached Istanbul on May 19] with the outlandish proposition that in exchange for a supply of U.S. trucks and other staples they would deliver a group of Hungarian Jews. *The political move motivating this plant is the implication that American [sic] placed more worth on saving Hungarian Jews than on the war effort* [italics added].[102]

Another cable from OSS counterintelligence in Washington, dated July 7, 1944, demanded an American interrogation of the two emissaries, Brand and Grosz. Grosz was a double agent who also served the "Schwarz Dogwood network" under the code name Trillium and was known to the Americans as Andor Gyorgy:[103]

Please question Brand and Georgy about the "Brand plan" as it is called, losing no time in so doing. The German government has assisted about 30 refugees in flying by Lufthansa plane from Berlin to Lisbon. This group is now in Lisbon and consists of half a dozen prominent Hungarian Jews and their families [several among them were left behind in Vienna to guarantee the "good behavior" abroad of those who left, but they remained unmentioned here]. The Germans desire U.S. trucks and other material in exchange for these refugees [the trucks belonged to the separate "Brand mission"]. We believe that Brand and Georgy are aware of this incredible Nazi black maneuver. . . . *Obviously, the project is meant to cause the Allies embarrassment. Roosevelt is the chief target, for the Nazis claim that he is impeding the war effort by his attempt to rescue Jews* [italics added].

Western counterintelligence, already rather suspicious about anyone who emerged from occupied Budapest and already having uncovered Laufer's true nature, interrogated Brand and Grosz separately and soon began to suspect the matter as a desperate Jewish idea that Gestapo operatives had adopted for their own needs. To wit: They had made Brand and Grosz into the playthings of Eichmann, Laufer, and their accomplices, for the extortion of political and strategic concessions from the West. The trucks were meant for combat against the Soviets – or for the reaping of a propaganda coup: irrefutable proof, on the eve of the Allied landing at Normandy, that it was a "Jew's war" after all.

The result was an enormous entanglement at the political and security levels. The traitor, Laufer, was exposed as the concoctor of "separate peace" talks that were meant to rupture the anti-Hitler grand alliance, and he was using Jewish blood as a tool for this purpose on the eve of the enormous bloodshed that the West was facing in its imminent invasion of France. The Zionists – who had been in contact with Brand for two years and were trying to promote his mission – were also in contact with Laufer without knowing who he was, and were using the services of the entire American network that Laufer had penetrated, that is, the Schwarz Dogwood network, to transfer rescue money to ghettos and camps. Thus, the "Brand-Grosz mission" unleashed a torrent of internal American investigations that sought to flush out traitors in addition to Laufer himself. By the time it was all over, the Americans had dismissed no less than the head of the Schwarz network, Lanning Macfarland, the head of their intelligence station in Istanbul, and all of Macfarland's Jewish aides who had employed Laufer and fed from his trough. Simultaneously, a conspiracy – a lethal one from the standpoint of the Western intelligence officials – had jelled between the Jewish Agency emissaries in Istanbul, Teddy Kollek and Georg Überall (Ehud Avriel), who had trusted Laufer and Grosz both as Allied agents and as their own couriers to occupied Europe, and their American operators and recruiters – some of whom were also Jews, with Dogwood Schwarz at their head – at the OSS Istanbul station. The conspiracy seemed all the more lethal because the traitor Laufer – a half-Jew – had denounced to the Gestapo an Austrian anti-Nazi underground network, and because as an American agent who was considered reliable he had directed American bombers to empty their bomb bays onto open fields near Wiener Neustadt, the most important industrial city in Austria.[104]

The outcome of the Brand-Grosz mission – masterminded by Laufer, as the British interrogation of its principals revealed – was a wave of investigations about events at the OSS station in Istanbul,[105] the dismissal of the station chief and all of the station's Jewish staff members, and suspicions that a Zionist–Gestapo commonality of interest in removing Jews from occupied Europe was meant to help destroy the anti-Hitler grand alliance.

In this matter it is worth quoting a warning from a Major Barry, chief of the Counter Intelligence Corps (CIC) at American General Headquarters (GHQ) Middle East (this agency, part of the U.S. Army Forces in the Middle East, abbreviated USAFIME, was the U.S. Army counterintelligence organization, not to be confused with the Central Intelligence Agency/OSS) after, and as one of the lessons of, the collapse of the Grosz-Brand mission:[106]

a. There is proof that some representatives of the Jewish Agency *have been used by the German Intelligence Service* [italics added].
b. The greatest mistake made by Allied intelligence and security officials is the presumption that a Jew, any Jew, is perforce Anti-Nazi....
c. There is proof that their representatives, to serve the Jewish Agency, and to help Jews in Europe, will and do deal with Nazi party officials and

the German Intelligence Service, *sometimes "selling out" Allied contacts, agencies and operations* [italics added].

d. ...

e. There is a reasonable proof that [the Zionists'] representatives buy Nazi support with their own funds and the funds of Allied intelligence agencies if and when they get their hands on any of the latter.

After the fact, the CIC people were unable to totally demolish the Zionists' relations with American intelligence. For one thing, reports about the horrors of the Holocaust were roiling the waters; finally they penetrated the most hostile of CIC chiefs in Cairo and marked a turning point in American public opinion, which awakened in view of the devastation in Hungary. The dreadfulness of the Hungarian Holocaust, widely known almost from the moment it began, greatly amplified the enlightenment of public opinion to the Jews' catastrophe. Now the political leadership could afford to abandon its previous calculus in regard to the Jews, if only partly, especially since the invasion in Normandy was assuring victory. However, the Zionists never did find a way to induce the Roosevelt administration to support their cause in any real way.

The Yishuv leadership clung to the Brand-Grosz "mission" in order to buy time and persuade the Western Allies to open at least some form of negotiations with Germany.[107] The Zionists' main negotiator with the Allies was Moshe Shertok, who had also presented the British with Brand's proposal in Eichmann's name. American intelligence depicted Brand as "an important Hungarian Jew." In reality, he was a businessman and playboy who had joined the Zionist Rescue Committee in Hungary before the Nazis occupied that country. He could not have been an "important Hungarian Jew" because Hungarian Jewry's traditional leadership distrusted Zionists and held them all – an insignificant minority in the country to begin with – in severe contempt. Brand, the American report continues, had gone to Istanbul with another Jew named "Bondi" as emissaries from Hungary. Bondi, the report said, was an out-and-out crook who claimed to represent the Gestapo in Hungary. The two wished to meet with Shertok, but the latter could not obtain a Turkish visa. The Turks ordered both of them to leave the country and move back to Hungary or some other destination. According to the Zionist source of the report, the Turks acted in this fashion due to British prodding.

Be that as it may, Brand and Bondi decided to go to Palestine but were arrested by the British in Aleppo, Syria. There, Shertok had an opportunity to converse with Brand. He understood from him that the Gestapo had indeed sent them to contact the Jewish Agency and the Allies and offer them a deal: thousands of trucks and large quantities of supplies or a sum of money ($2,000 per Jew, deposited with a Swiss bank), in return for the departure of a large number of Jews from occupied Europe via Turkey or Spain. Brand believed that the proposal was serious and that the Gestapo had reason to think that its terms would be accepted. Furthermore, he said, the Gestapo would liberate several thousand Jews from concentration camps to demonstrate its bona fides.[108]

To appreciate the depth of the trap, one should note that when they interrogated Grosz and Brand, the British inferred from both men that the idea of swapping Jews for materièl had come up in talks between them and the Gestapo agent and traitor Fritz Laufer, and it was they who had "sold" it to Eichmann and his people. It was Brand who had expressed an ab initio commitment on the part of the Zionists, and therefore also on the part of the Allies, to shepherd the trucks deal to a successful conclusion, it being stipulated that the trucks would be used only for war against the Red Army. The information provided by the aforementioned Zionist source omits this detail: It was Grosz who had proposed negotiations between Nazi Germany and the West for a separate peace – against the USSR – because he did not consider credible the trucks deal and the notion of depositing money in Switzerland. Pursuant to this offer, he was sent with Brand on this mission and thus saved his neck. The British shipped the two emissaries to their Cairo headquarters and continued to interrogate them.

Then the affair became more complicated: Brand felt – as the aforementioned document went on to advise the OSS – that the great acceleration in the extermination of Hungarian Jewry was partly the result of his internment in Cairo. Absent an appropriate reply from the Allies, Brand claimed, the Nazis had decided to speed up the Holocaust in Hungary in order to press them to agree to the deal. What he did not realize, however, was that the Wehrmacht was demanding – as expressed in documents of its high command – the evacuation of Jews from the Hungarian countryside, considering them a security risk in view of the Soviets' progress toward the Carpathian Mountains. Hitler himself considered Hungary an inseparable part of the German empire and believed, even at this stage, that it would remain in his possession; he had long since sought the annihilation of its Jews. Nevertheless, Shertok attempted to cling to the deal and its offer. Since the Zionist organizations and their "underground" (youth movements) in Europe knew and trusted Brand – as the OSS report stated – Shertok took the offer very seriously. He (and Ben-Gurion, although the report did not note this) presented the issue to the high commissioner in Palestine, who deemed it too important for him to rule on. Thus, Shertok flew to London, where he met with British officials, who finally said something like this: *"But what will we do with a million Jews?"* They also spoke of the need to consult with the United States and the USSR. What he meant was that the British had no right to resolve the issue by themselves, but not only due to the principled injunction against negotiating with the enemy behind the backs of their allies.

Both Grosz and Shertok, however, encouraged the impression that the Nazis were using Jewish blood in order to attain larger strategic goals, that is, to extricate themselves from the tightening Western vise by allowing Jews to live. Theoretically, after all, Hitler could consider returning to the deportation policy that he had invoked against the Jews before the globalization of the war.

After analyzing the foregoing information, the American agencies concluded that the affair might be an attempt by the Gestapo to use Jews for their own purposes. On top of that, if Moscow were not consulted, the USSR might suspect the Americans and the British of dealing behind its back; thus, a wedge could be driven among the Allies. Alternatively, the purported offer might be an attempt to call the bluff of the British and Americans about the rescue of Jewish refugees, a policy that seemed to have been adopted by the Roosevelt administration, given Roosevelt's decision in January 1944 to create a special agency – the War Refugee Board (WRB) – for this purpose. If they took the bait, they would have to agree to absorb the refugees in the middle of the war, thus making Jewish refugees a matter of highest priority, something the United States never intended to do despite the creation of the WRB. Thus, friction would be sown between FDR and his own mobilized masses on the eve of the supreme military test in Normandy, and among the Allies. If they turned the offer down, the Germans could claim that the United States and Britain had allowed millions of Jews to die and were therefore culpable of it, and this would impel the Jews in the Western Allied countries to pressure these countries to do more for their rescue, thus playing into German hands by demonstrating that the war had become "Jewish" after all.

Paradoxically, this is what happened to some extent, since even today the trap seems to persist. The murder of Hungarian Jewry, after the Nazis occupied that country in March 1944, was an inseparable part of the Final Solution, which was continuing everywhere else at the time. Furthermore, it peaked quickly for the additional reason of the Wehrmacht's demand that the Hungarian countryside be rid of its Jews. The murder spree began about two and a half months after Roosevelt established the War Refugee Board in order to aid the Jews of Europe. The very formation of the WRB was a seeming provocation of Hitler: If the president truly wished to save Jews, the Nazi dictator "said," he should do it on my terms, that is, he should oblige me to release only a few Jews and should pay for them in the coin of antisemitic reactions at home and harm to his war goals. Alternatively, he should prove publicly that he is merely talking, not doing; this would subject him to even greater pressure and force him to continue entangling himself in Jewish affairs. And so on.

Eventually, Roosevelt and Churchill – as well as Ben-Gurion and Shertok – would be accused of fumbling their rescue attempts, especially in regard to this affair. After the fact, Eichmann and Brand themselves contributed to the besmirching of those involved in the Brand mission by arguing – each for his own reasons – that the mission had been for real but the Zionists did not know how to pursue it properly. The continuation of the report that we have been discussing, however, does not share this portrayal of what happened. Shertok, it says, doubted the Allies' willingness to respond. However, any postponement of the extermination campaign was crucial. Brand, Shertok thought, should return to Hungary and the matter should be left in abeyance as long as possible, absent a negative reply. Indeed, Shertok tried to attain such a postponement in their talks in London. They pleaded with the British to at least open indirect but official negotiations with the Nazis. "What does 'official' mean?" their British interlocutors asked them. And how do "indirect negotiations" square with "official" ones? In the meantime, the Western forces had landed in Normandy shortly after Brand and Grosz arrived. Only in August would they be able to break out from this bridgehead at a heavy price. The British did not tell the Zionists that they had figured out the treachery of Fritz Laufer, Brand and Grosz's main advocate in Budapest, the man with whom their mission had matured, since both emissaries had offered their mission to Laufer and his superiors. Be that as it may, in July the British leaked the story of the mission to the BBC after their interrogation was completed, thereby killing it publicly.

Once done questioning Brand in Cairo, the British released him and allowed him to return to Hungary empty-handed. However, he preferred to return to Palestine, where he became a Mapai functionary and subsequently asked the Yishuv leadership to send him on various missions for the rescue of Holocaust survivors, in view of his status as an expert on the topic. When the leadership demurred, he switched to the radical-rightist Stern Gang and subsequently recounted that it had been the British minister of state, Lord Moyne, who had allegedly interrogated him in Cairo. When Brand apprised Moyne of his mission, it was supposedly the latter who asked, in so many words, *"And what will I do with a million Jews* [from Hungary]*?"* Ever since, this question has been one of the key utterances of the Holocaust. It captures every possible connotation: the heinousness of the world, the powerlessness of the Yishuv leadership at the time, and the leadership's unwillingness or inability to rise up and exert proper influence on the West for the rescue of Jews.

The document cited here, however, shows that this sentence was a Zionist rendering of the tenor of remarks that British officials had made to Shertok in London, along with other things that they had said, but not to him. Shertok himself summarized their arguments in this manner, and after returning to Palestine he reported it to a Mapai gathering that Joel Brand attended. By the time they parted ways and Brand joined the organization that assassinated Moyne, the British were allowing Jews to enter Palestine (within the quota established by the White Paper, which sufficed because the Germans were blocking their departure) and Moyne himself was involved in discussions over the establishment of a Jewish state in part of Palestine within the framework of a comprehensive British settlement in the Middle East. It was then that Brand cited this question, which had not been put to him, as retroactive justification for the Sternists' assassination of Lord Moyne. Yet pursuant to the findings of Brand's own interrogation, Western governments could claim that the Jews, who were in the midst of being murdered, had become Nazi bargaining chips for the extortion of Western political concessions and goods and the destruction of the Western–Soviet coalition. Indeed, the various Western security services came around to this general conclusion. What is more, from the standpoint of key Western security officials, the Jews had been a problem from the outset and the Zionists a potentially lethal hindrance. The political leaders acted in view of these conclusions, and the British, as stated, leaked word of the deal to the press and, by so doing, terminated the debate over it.

Given the grievousness of the Holocaust, however, the Americans – though not before the landing in Normandy had succeeded – attempted in Switzerland to negotiate secretly, with Kasztner's help, with the aforementioned SS officer, Kurt Andreas Becher, to stop the Holocaust for no real gain in return.[109] The Kasztner–Becher negotiations were mediated by the WRB representative in Switzerland, Roswell McClelland; in their course, McClelland, with Becher's assistance, maintained direct contact with Kasztner in Budapest and other cities where he was staying. This affair, addressed in various published testimonies and studies, is too intricate for us to delve into here, but the Yishuv leadership noticed that the British subsequently allowed any Jew who managed to leave Europe to enter Palestine, even though they did not make this widely known at first, due to concern about Arab and Muslim umbrage. By noting this, I do not suggest that the British had repealed the White Paper policy; nor did they make things easy for the escapees. However, the Yishuv leadership applied maximum self-restraint not to cry to the heavens over what was taking place in the arena of slaughter. It did not gag itself totally, as evidenced by Ben-Gurion's direct appeal to Roosevelt, quoted by Friling, to make the most of Brand's mission. By implication, the leadership would have been willing by then to negotiate with the Nazis themselves if such talks stood any chance of success. After all, the Jews' fate hinged not on God but on the Germans. The continuing pressure on the Allies, which would have had better effect had it emanated from their citizens and not only from the Zionists, had a limit that Hitler, and not Churchill and Roosevelt, had drawn.

After protests and the American bombings of Budapest had prompted the Hungarian dictator, Horthy, to halt the deportation of Jews from the Hungarian capital to Auschwitz, the Nazis went ahead with the deportation on their own. The Hungarian Nazis deposed Horthy after a summer respite during which the West had hoped to finally defeat the Third Reich but had encountered stiff resistance that prolonged the war until 1945. With Horthy out of the way, the Holocaust in Hungary resumed among such Jews as remained, as happened at Theresienstadt.[110] Survivors were deported for slave labor, with the exception of the Jews in Budapest proper, which the Red Army liberated in February 1945. The war was resolved neither in the summer of 1944 nor in the autumn of that year but in May 1945, and the murder of the last flickering embers of European Jewry became not only Hitler's sole "victory" but also the core of his posthumous political testament. In this matter, he was both unwilling and unable to undermine his own policies by halting the exterminations unless it would help his regime to survive, an outcome to which the Allies could not accede. During most of this time, the Auschwitz death mill continued to claim victims in the thousands and tens of thousands.

As far as ransom deals were concerned, the Allies refused to pay the Nazis for Jews. They abided by this refusal until the end of the war, not only for reasons of high policy but also for fear that ransom money would be used by neo-Nazis to revive their activities after the war. Under these conditions, the Zionists, with great self-discipline, tried to salvage, in any way possible, whatever the Kasztner–Becher talks had to offer. They might hope, for example, that the extermination apparatus and the high leadership of the Third Reich would begin to fall apart. Alternatively, they might latch onto some undertaking by non-Zionist Jewish entities in order to save whoever could be saved. Battering the Allies with accusations was not only useless but also unjust; after all, the Allies had not been murdering Jews and could not be forced to make concessions to the Jews' murderers in order to save them or to give the murderers an antisemitic weapon while saving no one. Furthermore, if the Zionist leadership publicized the full reality of the trap and, by so doing, foisted extra responsibility on the West and not on the murderers themselves, it might also lead to waves of despair in the Yishuv, again without rescuing even one Jew. Directing the Yishuv's fury toward the British police and soldiers who remained in Palestine following the departure of most Allied forces there to fight in Europe would have frightened Western commanders in the theater and played into the hands of those among them who wished to torpedo the secret rescue efforts, close the gates of Palestine to larger-scale rescue, and deprive the Jewish Agency of its autonomous status, as Yoav Gelber has shown.[111]

Indeed, the "revolt" that Menachem Begin declared against the British in January 1944, precisely as they were allowing every survivor to enter Palestine after the fact, and the assassination of the British minister of state in Cairo, Lord Moyne, by the Sternists in November 1944, might have established in Western thinking a de facto common cause between the Zionists and the West's enemies to stab the West in the back as it bled in the war against the Nazis. What the Yishuv leadership finally did in response to Begin's revolt and the Moyne assassination was the so-called *Season*, when the Hagana turned over many members of Begin's group and the Sternists to the British authorities, who exiled them to British-held territories in Africa. By so doing. the Yishuv's elected leadership under Ben-Gurion also dissociated itself from the machinations of renegade minorities who acted against its will and espoused what they considered Zionist Fascism. By taking this road, the leadership convinced more and more Westerners that the Yishuv was justly demanding on behalf of the Jewish people a mere corner of its own in its historical homeland, thus assuring itself the tools with which to establish such a corner.

Although for the time being the British deliberations had not yet yielded a decision on the Palestine question – Churchill had deferred any such decision until after the war – his government sent to Europe a Zionist Brigade Group that had finally been created in the British Army, the establishment of which had been approved before the assassination of Moyne. The British government also approved Ben-Gurion's trip to the Balkan countries in late 1944 in order to mobilize the surviving Bulgarian and Romanian Jews for immigration to Palestine. All of this happened after the 1944 elections cemented Mapai's centrality in the Yishuv political picture.[112] Yet only a few years after Israel's birth, the extradition of the right-wing terrorist groups to British-controlled territories in Africa was declared by their leaders an act of high treason that Ben-Gurion had committed as a collaborator with the "Nazo-British." Rescue operations, such as ransom deals negotiated by Mapai's Kasztner, were said to have been acts of collaboration with the Gestapo. To this we shall return.

As the postwar world was taking shape, the problem of the Jews made its way to the "front of the line." The "miracle" of the Jewish revival, however, was more than an outcome of the Holocaust, since even at the end of the war the same antisemitic charges remained audible: that the Jews by nature and conduct had helped the Nazis rise to power, that the Nazis' preachings were not all that different from those of the Jews. There were even many in the West, especially in high British circles, who counted on most Jews, including non-Zionist Holocaust refugees, wishing to return to their countries of origin. This attitude was accepted by Foreign Secretary Eden himself and the high commissioner for Palestine, Sir Harold MacMichael, who had been replaced in late 1944; it was also reflected in the reports of the OSS representative in Palestine, the aforementioned Harold Glidden. Some of the Roosevelt administration's allegations against the Zionists concerned the fragmented stance of American Jewry on the Zionist question; this explained Ben-Gurion's need for the 1942 Biltmore Program, to which he continued to cling in order to meld the Jewish fragments into an outwardly monolithic front, even though future discords and controversies among them were inevitable.[113] Others in the West argued *against* allowing the Jews to return to their countries of origin in Europe. Those Jews would surely demand their high-ranking jobs back and would quickly become enemies of the West as they had been before Hitler's rise to power.[114]

Many others, however, realized that the Yishuv was a fact that could not be disregarded. Under these conditions and given the infrastructure that had been established there before and during the Holocaust, the Zionist solution began to jell as the only realistic one. Thus, the Holocaust survivors began to mobilize – of their own free will – for emigration to a country of their own, and nowhere else. The political facet of this "miracle" was the result of a pragmatic and sophisticated strategy that the Yishuv leadership had adopted to drive a wedge between the British and the Americans. It concentrated first on a demand to bring the Holocaust survivors to Palestine, coupled with dramatic success in reinforcing this demand by calling on an instrumentality available to it at the time, the homogeneous and efficient Mossad le-Aliyah Bet. This was the organization in charge of "illegal" immigration to Mandatory Palestine – a product of the lessons of the Holocaust and the solidification of Mapai's status in the Yishuv generally and in immigration specifically. Afterwards, the Yishuv agreed to solve the Palestine problem realistically by partitioning the country.[115]

The miracle could also be considered an outcome of the conceit and grassroots feelings commonly held among Palestinian groups and in Arab politics. Indeed, the Mufti's Palestinian leadership – the Mufti himself resided in Berlin

until the downfall of the Third Reich – still regarded Jews as "sons of death,"
even as the Nazis were careening toward utter defeat and the Jewish Brigade
Group was up and running. In response to the latter development, the Mufti
established Bosnian Muslim units in the SS ranks, and in early 1945 encouraged Arab terrorists to parachute into Jericho in order to enflame the Arabs of
Palestine against the British and the Jews. This affair, buried deep in the Mufti's
diaries in the Hagana Archives, shows how adroit this Palestinian leader was
in reading the global and regional map. Presumably, however, his broadcasts
inciting the Arabs concerning their numerical superiority and unchallengeable
supremacy were connected with the Holocaust. After all, the Palestinian Arabs
and their supporters could entertain the belief that Hitler had rid them of most
of the Jews who had threatened to settle in their country. Now, however, a
Zionist threat loomed, one that brooked no compromise and had to be defeated
by the power of the Palestinian Arabs, with assistance from the Arab states.

This message forced the Zionist side to perform a cruel analysis of the
regional reality and its dynamic (at least in terms of Ben-Gurion's lessons and
actions at the time). It was obvious that the Arab states would attack the
Jewish state the moment sovereignty was proclaimed and that preparations for
such an offensive had to be made insofar as this was possible under British
rule, which had taken a hostile turn after Churchill's electoral defeat and the
inauguration of Labour rule. The ensuing miracle was accomplished by the
natural "Zionization" of many survivors, including those who had been raised
on a meta-historical religious tradition that had little to do with Zionism's
attempt to return the Jewish people to their place in history.[116]

Today, the "new historians" have turned them all into mere foam atop
the turgid waters of a Jewish nationalism that ever since the 1930s has been
plotting to dispossess the Arabs of their country and made cynical use of the
Holocaust and its survivors to promote its nationalistic goals. Such arguments,
some expressed in neo-Marxist turns of phrase and others articulated in universalistic, neo-Kantian, and old-style Marxist locutions that were common
among German Jews, have burst to life today in the mouths of the grandchil-
dren and successors of British intellectuals and laypersons in "post-Zionist"
Israel. Therefore, we shall have to delve deeply, in bold and steady strokes,
into the discussion proposed here and retrace our steps to the early 1930s if
not earlier, so as to revisit the lessons of those days of the inception of Jewish
statehood.

3

Ben-Gurion between Right and Left

Ben-Gurion and the Zionist Right

Mapai was established in the early 1930s by the merger of two Labor parties, largely at Ben-Gurion's initiative. The idea behind it was to create a political instrument that would organize, represent, and dominate the other Yishuv entities and the entire Zionist Labor Movement, from the General Federation of Labor (the Histadrut) and the National Committee (the elected representative body of the Yishuv) to the various organs of the World Zionist Organization. The union came about roughly a year after the 1929 Arab violence, the gravest crisis that Zionism had experienced to that point. The outcome elevated Ben-Gurion to the Jewish Agency Executive a year after Hitler's rise to power and to the chair of the Executive in 1935. Therefore, his actions in this position of leadership should be viewed within the much broader context of the global and regional events of the time. One such event was the ascendancy of Hajj Amin el Husseini, the Mufti of Jerusalem, to a key position – although not an exclusive one for the time being – in local Arab public circles.[1]

These and other factors led to the eruption of the 1936–1939 "Arab uprising," which contributed mightily to the establishment of fighting organizations and the development of a security consciousness in the Yishuv. The "uprising" was not solely the Mufti's handiwork. In this early stage, his power focused on Jerusalem and the vicinity; what is more, the violence ebbed and flowed as a result of internal power struggles among the Palestinians, the Mufti's response to expectations of "the street" (radicals among his followers) facing new waves of Jewish refugees from Nazi Germany, the British authorities' stance and actions, and the terror and reprisal operations of IZL (Jabotinsky's National Military Organization) against the Arabs in response to Arab violence. By implication, the uprising presented the Yishuv leadership and specifically Ben-Gurion with lessons both external and internal.

The leadership's operating conditions began to change with dizzying speed at this time, thereby explaining Ben-Gurion's varied and ostensibly

contradictory moves. Ben-Gurion gained his appointment to the Zionist Executive, and later his elevation to the chair of this body, as the outcome of an
election campaign for the Zionist institutions after the successful merger of the
Labor parties, which had been mostly in the opposition until then. However,
the body that headed the movement, the Jewish Agency Executive, was a heterogeneous forum that included diverse Zionist and non-Zionist parties and
strained to maintain internal consensus. The Labor Parties themselves were
mixed creatures that had sponsored a number of pilot ventures, some of which
had initially failed, such as the development and construction cooperative Solel
Boneh in the 1920s, and others that had gained traction by virtue of outside partners and sponsors of ideas, such as agrarian cooperatives of diverse
kinds. The Histadrut had slowly evolved into an umbrella organization for the
efforts of the Labor Movement – a unique amalgam of rural-settlement groups,
employers, a federation of trade unions, and a provider of diverse services using
the money of its members and outside benefactors. In addition, however, it had
metamorphosed into the bastion of a minority faction on Mapai's left flank
that would eventually be known as Faction B. As such, it embraced the combination of a pioneering elitist ideology and an urban opposition to the Mapai
functionaries, some of whom had come from the Soviet Union. Several of these
Mapai stalwarts were unbending, rough-and-tough operators who established
power bases for their party in the labor councils (local union representatives)
and other public entities. Faction B, to which many kibbutz leaders belonged,
held these characters in contempt and eventually seceded from Mapai and
merged with other left-wing factions.

On the Right, as it is termed today, a new challenge to all Zionist parties came into being: Jabotinsky's Revisionist Party, which since 1925 had
been jelling as an alternative to the Socialist Zionist parties and challenged the
moderate leadership of the president of the Zionist Organization, Chaim Weizmann. Weizmann, for his part, cooperated with the Labor parties in the rural-
settlement enterprise, even though his non-Socialist views coexisted uneasily
with theirs.

At the dawn of the Mandate and with greater intensity after the spates of
violence in 1921 and 1929, the "Arab problem" became a steadily worsening
security issue and a political quandary of the highest order. It had great implications for the behavior of the British authorities for many reasons, including
antisemitic and anti-Zionist arguments that were striking a chord among the
British elites and imperial considerations, such as the problem of the Muslims
in India.[2] The disharmony that had begun to take shape between the Labor
Movement, with its various constituents, and Jabotinsky concerned a number
of issues. First, how should the Yishuv relate to the Arabs? Was dialogue with
them possible or not? Alternatively, should the Zionists persuade the British to
recognize the Jews and the area on both sides of the Jordan as Jewish sovereign
territory, open to mass Jewish immigration that would render the Arabs a
minority? Should the focus be on a Jabotinskyan grand political demarche that

would first attain its goal and then build the country on that basis, or should the country be built inch by inch, absent the fulfillment of a grand scheme of this kind? Finally, what sort of sociopolitical regime should the Zionist entity have – a liberal capitalist one, with fascist elements in the field of labor relations, such as Jabotinsky had adopted, or a social-democratic one?

According to the thinking behind Jabotinsky's "iron wall" metaphor, the Arabs would never accept Zionism willingly; therefore, there was, and would be, no choice but to impose the Zionists' will on them with British support that would be attained due to shared British–Zionist interest. Only when the Arabs acknowledged the Zionists' power would peaceful coexistence be possible between the Jewish majority on both sides of the Jordan and the Arab minority, once it became a minority. The attitude toward this future "minority" fluctuated among several permutations that Jabotinsky embraced between his iron-wall moment in the early 1920s and his death in 1940. Some of these approaches were liberal; others were semiracist, viewing "race" as patterned after the white man's supremacy over South African tribes that supposedly acknowledged this supremacy and, from the white man's standpoint, accepted it willingly.[3]

Jabotinsky adopted Herzl's traditional aspiration of first creating a "grand" political framework, based on a settlement with the Great Powers that would open wide the country's gates. Absent an appropriate arrangement with the British Mandatory power, Zionism would be reduced to one-by-one "infiltration" of the country, as had been the case in the First and Second Aliyot (waves of immigration). Ben-Gurion and his comrades took action without such an arrangement, seeking to establish a toehold of Jewish settlement by means of the few who would transform Zionist theory into practice, but without abandoning the quest for an appropriate political breakthrough at the propitious time. The Balfour Declaration of November 1917 was supposed to open Palestine's gates to large-scale Jewish immigration, a matter to which Weizmann had made an important contribution. However, the Jewish immigration that the Zionists had expected did not ensue, initially because the Zionists themselves were not ready to receive a large wave of impassioned immigrants who might land spontaneously in a poor country that was unprepared to support them. Later the expected immigration did not materialize because European Jewry was embroiled in the mammoth changes that World War I had brought about and because much of this collective had abruptly disappeared behind what would be termed, decades later, the Soviet Iron Curtain. Absent an infrastructure in Palestine worthy of the name, Weizmann and the Zionist Labor Movement continued to settle the country's hinterland inch by inch in their different ways, which, for the time being, overlapped. This method ran into hurdles created by the British administration and the Arab resistance that began with the 1920–1921 Arab violence.

At this time, Jabotinsky, by then the organizer of Jewish self-defense in Jerusalem, was arrested by the British, who accused him of taking the law into his own hands. His ensuing talk about the need for an iron wall to force the Arabs to submit to (the almost nonexistent) Jewish power in the early 1920s, and his otherwise radical rhetoric, spurred moderate Zionists such as Dr. Weizmann to try patiently to surmount the British administration's hurdles in Mandatory Palestine so as not to menace the continuation of support by the government in London. They realized that Jabotinsky was trying to impose a pretentious platform that the British would never accept and that would play into the Arabs' hands. Even before the 1929 "events" – an Arab tour de force that forced the British government to revise its Palestine policy – Jabotinsky had turned in an even more radical direction and sought to announce Zionism's ultimate goal publicly: the summary proclamation of statehood on both sides of the Jordan River. The vague wording of the Balfour Declaration about a Jewish "national home" in Palestine, he argued, had allowed the British to maneuver among the clashing promises that they had given the country's Jewish and Arab inhabitants. Indeed, they had negotiated this minefield in a way that left the tiny Yishuv enough leeway to develop and amass internal strength under a British patronage that, while problematic, could be modified by means of Zionist influence. Henceforth, it would be Jabotinsky's goal to persuade the British to accept the Jews as a party with whom it was worth concluding a strategic alliance – and granting, immediately, control of Palestine on both sides of the Jordan.

Both Weizmann and Ben-Gurion regarded Jabotinsky's ideas as vacuous bombast that proposed to abandon the slowly changing reality in Palestine in favor of bloated rhetoric backed by nothing. This rhetoric, they thought, might suggest to tomorrow's masses of Jewish immigrants that they should wait for the establishment of some "grand" political framework that would grant them, ab initio, a leg up on the country's Arab majority. Worse still, as Yosef Gorny says,[4] Jabotinsky did not understand that had the leadership of the Zionist Movement adopted his views back then, in the late 1920s, just as the British had begun to entertain doubts about the Balfour Declaration, this posture would have made it even easier for the British to abandon their commitment to the Zionist Movement – a commitment that originated in this declaration.

In 1928, Jabotinsky and his associates presented the British government with two demands: the creation of administrative, judicial, and agrarian conditions that would result in the formation of "a Jewish majority in Palestine on both sides of the Jordan," and the appointment of pro-Zionist British officials who would work for the fulfillment of this policy. Finally, they threatened to secede from the Zionist Organization unless the latter adopted their maximalist program. "Their political obtuseness," Gorny wrote, "reached its pinnacle" in the 1929 crisis. It was then that the British realized what trouble the Arabs would make for them if they persisted with their pro-Zionist policy. Concurrently, the standing of the Zionist Movement plummeted for reasons stemming from the influence of antisemitic and anti-Zionist players, who found common cause in liberal and radical circles in Britain that had access to government ears. Of all times, that was when Jabotinsky came out with his demand to announce

Zionism's ultimate goal, a Jewish state on both banks of the Jordan. The Zionist Movement mainstream eschewed sweeping political demands, preferring instead a vigorous response of its own to the Arabs' violent actions, which had been instigated in part by a Revisionist-related provocation at the Western Wall.[5] Weizmann and his Labor Movement colleagues mobilized certain British circles against the White Paper that Colonial Secretary Lord Passfield and his close associate, John Hope-Simpson, had drawn up; ultimately, by dint of their efforts, this document was converted into a much more sympathetic policy that granted immigration visas to specific categories of prospective Jewish immigrants – those who had money and young people who had skilled trades to offer – who became the infrastructure of the mass immigration of the 1930s.

Ben-Gurion's Second Aliyah, which reached Ottoman Palestine early in the twentieth century, took a complex approach toward the Arabs and the question of borders. This was an outcome of the movement's dual nationalist and Socialist complexion. As Socialists, the Labor Movement people could not embrace hyper-nationalism, and, if you wish, nationhood, in its simplistic form. Later, having mated Socialism with Jewish humanism and having construed the writings of the Hebrew prophets in this spirit, they had to tackle the question of how to treat the Arabs by fitting the conflict with class aspects, so as to resolve it by means of anticapitalist proletarian cooperation among the various Zionist Socialist parties or in cantonic, federative, or multinational ways. Eventually, the Palestinian Arab leadership resolved these vacillations under the tutelage of the Mufti and others of his ilk by adopting a totally negative policy toward a Jewish presence in Mandatory Palestine after the Balfour Declaration of November 1917. In the meantime, Jabotinsky inveighed against this two-sided flag under the slogan of "One Flag" or *had-ness* in Hebrew. It was this term that he chose for his national outlook, which had the appearance of striving toward a clear political and historical strategic goal that he, above all others, had defined properly.[6]

Jabotinsky was not only the co-patriarch (along with Joseph Trumpeldor) of the idea of the Jewish battalions in the Allied forces during World War I; he also sired the notion of an independent Jewish army and active self-defense against the Arab challenge in Palestine, as well as the idea of an independent Jewish state at a very early phase, dreams that leading Zionist establishmentarians, like Chaim Weizmann and Labor Movement stalwarts like Ben-Gurion perceived as unwise to proclaim before some kind of a state-in-being had been created on the ground. While the mainstream pursued the concept of settling the country inch by inch, "goat by goat," Jabotinsky's movement preached summary statehood and the immediate boatlifting of a million Jews from Poland – during ten years beginning in 1935 two years after Hitler's rise to power. By speaking this way at that time, Jabotinsky would be dubbed by his supporters the Prophet of the Holocaust. By implication, had he not been brought down by the narrow-mindedness of the Zionist leadership and, especially, by their fear that he would wrest power from them, many Jews would have been spared the horrors of the Holocaust.[7] These arguments amount to a mixing of the Holocaust in Zionist politics even before it began, which Jabotinsky never envisioned, as well as what one may term the "politicization" of the Holocaust, a practice that would eventually become a powerful asset in the political rhetoric of the Zionist Right.

In 1942, Ben-Gurion publicly embraced the demand for summary Jewish statehood in all of Mandatory Palestine west of the Jordan (also known as Cisjordan) in the so-called Biltmore Program, which the Zionist Left, including Mapai's left flank, denounced as a hopeless mistake because too few Jews lived there, which would necessitate the country's eventual division between the Arabs and the Jews – the partitioning of the country that indeed was finally adopted by Ben-Gurion before independence. Those on the Right termed it a belated adoption of their original idea, even as they continued to seek an undivided Palestine on both sides of the Jordan River. Ben-Gurion's demand for the immediate relocation of a million Jews to Palestine at this time does sound like a later adoption of an idea that was no less original when Jabotinsky broached it. Ben-Gurion's own argument in favor of having a "central guiding idea"[8] in various phases of his policy was considered the adoption of Jabotinsky's "monism" – the One Flag doctrine – by a leader who had seemingly freed himself of his Socialism. Ben-Gurion, however, maneuvered and operated within the framework of the voluntary Yishuv as a Socialist Zionist politician who wished to establish a Zionist state that would reflect his own tenets. He pursued this goal to the best of his ability in view of the internal, Palestinian, regional, and global realities and in accordance with priorities that dictated "central ideas" for the short, medium, and long terms – as opposed to the nationalistic One Flag idea. A brief examination of these maneuverings will enrich our discussion of his political behavior during the Yishuv period, his moves after statehood was achieved, and the reputation given him by his adversaries at the time, that of a "politician" whose main concern was sheer power, as opposed to that of a "statesman."

One of Ben-Gurion's typical characteristics in the early 1930s was his steadily growing awareness of the potential of Jewish nationalism and the need to defend against it and to mobilize it on behalf of his Socialist and national ethos. This ethos demanded change in the Jews' behavior and the overhauling of inter-Jewish relations. Thus, he disdained the rightist propensity to depict the Jewish people as a nation of *hadar* ("grandeur" or "class"), a nation of Jewish royal rule in Eretz Israel to which the people were entitled by historical circumstances and values that had to be adopted now by demonstrating grand political aspirations, military organization, and paramilitary education – what Gorny calls the Revisionist posture and the British imperial interest.

The rhetorical Jewish nationalism that drew on modern poetry and literature à la Gabriele D'Annunzio was embodied in the persona of the young Jabotinsky himself. This gifted poet and writer was the product of a largely assimilated generation in the colorful city of Odessa. He returned to Judaism and became an active politician who adopted various stances of the nationalism of the European periphery, that is, of Italy. Jabotinsky studied in Italy and was strongly influenced by the spirit that embued that country's Romantic-nationalist circles. At that early phase, however, he was partial to a Socialism akin to that of the young Mussolini himself, who was an estimable Socialist theoretician. Eventually, however, Jabotinsky disengaged from socialism and veered toward pure nationalism.[9] As a case in point, he observed partitioned Poland, which was striving for national rebirth. His attention was drawn to other national circles that trailed behind the developed European "center" and compensated for their subordination to Britain, France, and Germany (before and immediately after World War I) by means of excess nationalism. Independent Poland embraced this kind of quasi-Fascist nationalism during Marshal Pilsudski's tenure, and many of Jabotinsky's supporters either lived or came from there. Indeed, in the 1920s and 1930s, all of Central Europe evinced Fascist tendencies for reasons that varied from country to country. Quasi-Fascist thinkers who had despaired of Socialism or combined it with fiercely nationalistic teachings, along with ideologies of racial or cultural "spaces" that purported to organize the world on a new and "natural" basis, influenced young people who originated in Germany, Poland, and Russia and found a political home in Jabotinsky's movement, forcing him to take them into account.[10]

The Zionist Socialism of the Mapai mainstream, stewarded by Katznelson and Ben-Gurion, was a more complex and contemporary version of the nationalist phenomenon in terms of its values and concepts. Furthermore, neither of these men was the kind of leader who consulted public opinion in their actions; instead, they sought to bend the movement to their views. Socialist Zionist theory was a class theory that strove to return the Jew to productive life and create conditions of social equality and cooperation in view of actualities in the immediate surroundings, the region, and the world. It was a progressive-humanist ideology that flowed from an interpretation of Judaism by Katznelson, Ben-Gurion, and their predecessors, which nevertheless recognized nationalism and considered it an important and legitimate framework for the development of Jewish values.[11] This theory had no particular value that trumped all other values, although these leaders entertained tactical differences on this issue. Instead, it was the source of the multivalent approach that Jabotinsky fought by means of his One Flag idea. This multivalence inevitably influenced the attitude toward the Arabs in a way that seems today to be naive, hypocritical, and, worse still, a craftily planned and calculated "politics" that aimed to dispossess them of their land, by force if necessary.[12]

After the fact, what we are contemplating are diverse vacillations from the onset of the Second Aliyah in the 1920s and 1930s. Ben-Gurion had been involved in them from the Turkish era to the Arab riots of 1929, as evidenced in his very early acknowledgment of the fact that the country "is not empty" and his ideas about a Jewish-Arab federation of cantons.[13] The continuity in his thinking, as Ben-Gurion interpreted it at a closed meeting with the IDF high command in the early statehood period (January 14, 1951), is noteworthy.[14]

It concerned an Israeli "uniqueness" relative to other states and peoples, this being an outgrowth of Jewish history, Israeli and Middle Eastern geography, and regional demography. In this context, Ben-Gurion praised remarks by Chief of General Staff Yigael Yadin about

the importance of the Bible, not only in itself as the greatest spiritual creation of the Jewish people, but also for its current military importance because it was written in and about Eretz Israel. In other words, the geographic territory is a constant, static factor in defense affairs, but there is a dynamic factor that is no less important and perhaps more important than the static factors. The dynamic factor is history.

Here, Ben-Gurion asserted once again, "There is hardly any historical situation that resembles another." However important the Bible is, one should not learn from it what one cannot learn: "Just as we must study previous periods and our history in this country, the military history and the Jewish wars, we should also, if we want to be prepared for what is coming, observe and study the uniqueness of our times and not mistakenly follow historical examples that never recur." In other words, the sense of continuity between our time and Joshua's conquests, the wars of Gideon, and those who lapped the waters of the River Kishon, revived by such personalities as the British founder of the offensive wing of the embryonic self-defense units of the Hagana, Orde Wingate, and his disciples Moshe Dayan and Yigal Allon, is potentially dangerous. Thus, the artificial continuity, attributed to Ben-Gurion by his critics then and now, between the Bible and Joshua and the War of Independence and its aftermath was something that he regarded as an asset that could become a liability. After all, "a Jewish state existed here more than two thousand years ago, but this state [of Israel] is new and historically unique in the way it was established." In other words, the establishment of Israel does not resemble that of other states: ancient entities that rose atop the ruins of mighty empires and of colonial settlements in North and South America and gradually acquired a vitality of their own until they freed themselves of dependency on their mother countries.

Israel belongs to neither of these forms, Ben-Gurion continued at the same January 1951 meeting. The ancient Jewish state

has vanished, it was wiped off the map. [Even though] after the destruction it was poorly and sparsely settled, [Eretz Israel] was always occupied, always settled. And [Israel] did not come into being as did Canada, the United States of America, New Zealand, Australia, and so on. The birth of the State of Israel is historically unique. [Israel] arose by the return of a people of antiquity to a land of antiquity; . . . nothing in history compares to it.

He elaborated on this exceptional phenomenon,

not only because of its historical and conceptual uniqueness . . . but also due to its adverse and grave ramifications in terms of the security problem, because this country was occupied and this land was settled not only for hundreds of years but for nearly fifteen hundred years . . . by a people that had settled the entire surroundings, not only this land.

Thus, Ben-Gurion not only viewed the Arab claim to the country as self-evident but also acknowledged the connection between its exiled inhabitants and their surroundings in view of the Jewish people's own experience with exile. We learn two seemingly contradictory lessons from the exile: that the Jews maintained a "historically unparalleled" connection with their land *while* in exile. Although some non-Jews acknowledged this connection due to the Bible, they were not obliged to do so: "This thing was not something real that existed outside the minds of the Jews and a few Gentiles who were perceptibly influenced by that book." The Arabs have a similar connection with this country, and it should properly be recognized and considered a problem that must be tackled. He continued:

We will be making a mistake, first of all in terms of security, if we do not view the Arabs' connection with this country primarily through their eyes. . . . They do not have to acquiesce in the new facts, they have no reason to acquiesce in them, it's incomprehensible to them. . . . We should ponder the syllogism. If we did not acquiesce in being disconnected [from this country] after two thousand years, . . . it is preposterous to think that the Arabs, who were disconnected from this country three years ago, will overlook it and accept the new reality as an unchallenged fact.

Here, then, we have the dialectic, contradictory complexion of the Israeli–Arab conflict in Ben-Gurion's historical calculus. What practical conclusions should Ben-Gurion have drawn from this? (He drew several conclusions; we will discuss one that pertained to the longer term, the establishment of an Israeli nuclear deterrent, in its proper place.) Our discussion will be informed by the geographic and demographic argumentation that Ben-Gurion expressed in this speech, held behind closed doors, argumentation that corresponds to the way he developed the historical context. That is, he related his argument to the ascent of the forgotten and fractious Arab tribes to the stage of world history by virtue of a prophet who arose among them and united them under the banner of a new religion that not only imposed its authority on large parts of the known world but also imparted its language to the inhabitants. On the map that Ben-Gurion hung in his Jerusalem office, Israel was but a speck in this ocean. As he recalled: "Once, when the cabinet ministers came into my room, they told me, 'Take down that map. If a goy comes in here, he'll tell you that this people doesn't stand a chance. Our country is a tiny blue-and-white territory within a huge Arab territory.'"

The issue here, however, concerned not only the external threat but also the difficulties and fragility of Israeli society:

The main thing about our defense problem [is] that we are not yet a stabilized state. We are just a state in formation, and in the initial stages of formation. We are not a state that has settled down within its borders, and not only because these borders are not recognized in terms of international law. . . . It is true that there are no stable borders in history. There is no absolute stability.... Nothing is absolute in history. There is relative stability; it may persist for centuries or for decades. One cannot say that these borders are stable even in the relative sense of the term... and from the standpoint of those on the eastern... northern, and southern sides of this border. The thing that is unstable and strange in our eyes is also strange in others' eyes. And when we speak about defense affairs and matters of state, we must always look at this through the other's eyes as well.

Borders were not the only issue at hand; at the meeting, Ben-Gurion went on to discuss other key variables that were important in themselves and related in some way to the defense problem. However, the border question was very important; he immediately reverted to it:

We are at a formative stage in matters that may count for more than borders. For example, the economy.... This economy should not be viewed as an economy; it is just the beginning of the formation of an economy.... The same with culture. This is a state that has no culture. Culture is above all language.... With all the languages that are spoken in our country, people consider them figments of the past. Even though they cannot rid themselves of them for the time being, they do not want and do not hope to put up with them.

Thus, in Ben-Gurion's estimation, Israelis did not wish to retain their foreign mother tongues, although they would need them until they attained proper fluency in Hebrew. However, many Israelis had not attained this fluency and, accordingly, were living in two worlds:

A culture is coming into being. But culture is not just language and culture is not just knowledge and schooling. It is a lifestyle. We do not have a lifestyle that unites dust-people into a whole.... We do not yet have the lifestyle of a cultural historical whole.... It has only begun to form, and this has many implications for defense and for the other values of our lives.

The curious reader will find in these remarks an explanation not only of the values that Ben-Gurion wished to instill in the army but also of his subsequent behavior in the Lavon Affair. It does not stand to reason that a man who habitually related to "culture" as "lifestyle" and connected both with the proper conduct of defense affairs would subsequently accept the retroactive exoneration of a defense minister by executive authority, as Mr. Lavon demanded by applying various means of pressure, including "a trial by press" in his favor. We shall return to this battle, which Ben-Gurion would lose. At that early phase, however, as he skipped from one topic to another – in a manner atypical of his grand programmatic speeches – Ben-Gurion returned to the border problem and the special sensitivity of the borders of Eretz Israel in the eyes of "much of humanity." This issue would undoubtedly whet, and then amplify, his interest in the vast and unpopulated Negev desert, most of which was less sensitive politically than other parts of the Holy Land; events there did not raise international concern as did those in Jerusalem and the Armistice demarcation lines of the West Bank and the Galilee:

This country occupies a big place in the consciousness and minds of much of humanity. . . . In this part of the world, the Christian and Muslim world, . . . in this world our country occupies an important place. There's a connection, there are desires, there are interests, and there are relations. Just now it was reflected in the Jerusalem problem [the government's decision to establish the capital of Israel on the western side of the city, an act that most countries still reject de jure]. . . . Things that happen in this country reverberate as they don't in any other country of such size or of ten times its size.

Ben-Gurion then mentioned the riot that Menachem Begin's Herut movement had organized a week earlier in the vicinity of the Knesset against the reparations agreement with West Germany, and added:

This thing made a bigger echo than a coup in an entire Indian province could make. They might devote a few lines to that, but it wouldn't command main headlines in the press of the whole world. . . . The name "Jerusalem" says a great deal, the name Zion also says a great deal, and this country's past says a great deal to much of humanity. It is a factor; under particular conditions it may become a decisive factor [against us], just as it has become a decisive factor among ourselves.

Now Ben-Gurion went back to the border problem and said that every state had a neighbor that coveted its territory. This, in my opinion, was an oblique reference to both Herut and the left-wing parties, the heads of which were bemoaning the War of Independence armistice lines and their drawbacks:

There are always theories about how you need natural borders for self-defense. You need a mountain, [then another] mountain, and after you climb the mountain you see that to keep the mountain safe you need the valley and to keep the river safe you need its other bank, and it never ends. The first aspect of the defense problem is to keep the borders safe [and not necessarily to expand them – emphasis added]. The second aspect of the defense problem is maintaining independence.

What he meant here was the ability to avoid having to accept outsiders' dictates in crucial affairs, including Israel's armistice lines, which highly influential parties in the West wanted Israel to cede to Egypt in the southern Negev in order to curry Cairo's favor at that stage of the Cold War.

Ben-Gurion seemed finally to have adopted some version of Jabotinsky's "iron wall" – a nuclear iron wall, no less – in order to surmount the Arabs' incorrigible enmity. This, I claim, is the outcome of developments that had begun in the early 1930s and reached their tragic climax in the Holocaust, which, again, Jabotinsky had not foreseen. Even afterwards, too, there was no need to totally abandon hope for the "Jewish–Arab alliance" that Ben-Gurion had been positing as his final goal since the early 1930s. Indeed, his priorities were "defense, Jewish statehood, and a Jewish–Arab alliance," in that order, and he made this into a crucial value that should be instilled and offered to the Arabs despite their enmity.

Speaking of the 1930s, the necessity at the time was not about an iron wall but about emigration to Palestine and continuing, for as long as possible, to expand the toehold there for the increasingly beleaguered Jews. The sense of urgency in this matter was actually typical of Ben-Gurion; it prompted him to undertake various maneuvers that we will describe in general contours. From the early 1930s on, however, he had to wrestle not only with issues related to Arab enmity and the political activities of the Arab elites in Palestine and abroad, while striving to find common cause with Arab leaders, but also with matters relating to the internal challenge, that is, that within Jewish society.

It was not Jabotinsky's grand "political" solutions that Ben-Gurion viewed as preconditions for the success of the Zionist enterprise, but rather a territorially solid socioeconomic infrastructure. Only on such a basis was "politics" possible; everything else was so much hot air. Furthermore, within the framework of this politics, there was no need to define the Arabs as enemies as though by divine dictate; instead, repeated attempts should be made to dialogue with their leaders and hope that the very act of dialogue would demonstrate the Jewish side's goodwill without forfeiting its right to Eretz Israel – its historical land, the one-and-only land of a one-and-only people. Some historians regard this call for dialogue as a mere tactic; others do not know how to interpret his claims in the 1920s and 1930s that the Arabs, too, should be pleased by the Jews' return to their homeland.[15]

In my opinion, the answer should be sought in the unique complexion of the Ben-Gurionic Zionist renaissance, which believed in mixing and merging things that had defied integration theretofore. From the standpoint of some of his contemporaries, nothing was impossible. If only they opened their eyes, they would see the goodness that the intrinsic changes of history-in-formation would bestow on them. These changes were neither necessary nor given, but they were possible if people would only bring them about. This famous "vision," however, was firmly anchored in a reality that slowly dictated, among other things due to the mischief of Jabotinsky's people and their military "grandeur," the necessity of disengaging from the Arabs when the time for this would be ripe.

Ben-Gurion's awareness that the Arabs would not accept the Zionists' demands originated not in doctrinaire belief in the need for an iron wall but in conditions that necessitated mass immigration after the Nazis rose to power and the pro-Arab constellation that had jelled at this time in Palestine, the region, and the world – that would eventually play into the hands of the radical leaders among the Palestinians. The actions of Jabotinsky's people augmented these circumstances by influencing the Arabs' state of mind and the British responses. In Ben-Gurion's view, the conditions that had evolved since the mid-1930s dictated two courses of action: a heightened rural-settlement effort that would create a genuine countrywide infrastructure and immigration on the largest scale possible in view of the distress of European Jewry. But this reality also required a sincere and serious effort to confer with the Arab leaders and offer them a settlement that they might find amenable. At this stage, the envisioned settlement was a Jewish-Arab federation that would grant the Jews territory of their own and concurrently further the Arabs' development. However, in view of the looming alternative that Jabotinsky was offering to both Socialist

Zionism and Chaim Weizmann's moderate and long-range views, various internal political steps had to be taken.[16] This alternative had its own radical wing, which harbored blatant Fascist indicators and would eventually give rise to the Stern Gang.[17]

Unlike Weizmann, whose Zionist activity took place largely abroad and vis-à-vis the central authorities in Britain,[18] Ben-Gurion derived his power from his uninterrupted and ongoing practical activities in Palestine in the rural-settlement and sociopolitical fields. He considered himself a mobilized statesman as opposed to a "handy functionary," as he sometimes called Weizmann. He built a base, a bridgehead for the Jewish masses in the Diaspora, and engaged in mobilizing these masses for immigration and for support of the Zionist enterprise. This, to his own mind, entitled him to speak on their behalf vis-à-vis the British, the Arabs, and anyone else. To do this, however, he had to bring to his struggle for the image and policies of the Yishuv an awareness of the forces at work in the Yishuv itself and among Zionists in the Diaspora, so as to unite them as fully as possible for joint action against the emergency occasioned by Hitler's rise to power.

In this matter, Ben-Gurion resorted to several seemingly clashing moves that taught him various lessons. The first was a pitched battle against Jabotinsky and his supporters after the assassination of Chaim Arlosoroff, head of the Jewish Agency's Political Department. Arlosoroff had negotiated an interim agreement with the German government that allowed Jewish refugees from Nazi Germany to leave for Palestine with at least some of their property, a British-imposed precondition for their entry. Far-right Zionists, including Jabotinsky's semi-Fascist supporters, denounced the agreement as a pact with the devil and called for Arlosoroff's assassination. This took place amidst an election campaign for the Zionist institutions. Although the campaign was resolved in Poland in favor of the Zionist Labor parties,[19] it gave these parties primacy but not a conclusive victory and, for this reason, expanded their maneuvering room considerably but not adequately.

Ben-Gurion's second move was the accord that he and Jabotinsky concluded in London in order to prevent the secession of Jabotinsky and his supporters from the World Zionist Organization after the latter's electoral defeat. The defeat of the accord in a Histadrut plebiscite taught Ben-Gurion something about the strength of the left-wing Mapai and Histadrut factions that opposed it, and about the nature of direct democracy.[20] Furthermore, the absence of an agreement with Jabotinsky and his ultimate secession from the World Zionist organization in 1935 amplified the danger emanating from the radical wing of Jabotinsky's movement, in which Avraham "Ya'ir" Stern had begun to surface in opposition to the leader himself.[21] Although Jabotinsky defended this group – which had incited public opinion against Arlosoroff – from external criticism, he did not agree with the course of action that it had chosen. Thus, it found a way to influence his public stance.

In the next stage, Ben-Gurion accepted Lord Peel's partition plan of 1937 in common cause with Jabotinsky's archrival, Weizmann. Although the plan left the Zionists with only a small portion of Palestine west of the Jordan, at least it granted the Jews sovereignty and its concomitant freedom of action.[22] In fact, Ben-Gurion embraced the goal of Jewish sovereignty in Palestine – in addition to the vague but, at this stage, effective idea of a Jewish "national home" – because Hitler's rise to power convinced him that it was a practical course of action and a way out for German Jews. Instead, he wished to maximize immigration – to make it as close to unlimited as possible, with no selection among candidates and groups, unlike the selectivist leanings of the left-wing Zionist parties.[23]

Here is why: Even though Judaism and Zionism were facing a rising tide of criticism in Britain during the 1930s, the British governments did not abandon their commitment to the Zionists. Credit for this belongs to the British Zionists, foremost Weizmann, who had managed to marshal support for the Zionists in moderate left-wing circles and among Conservatives such as Winston Churchill and Leo Amery, as well as from American Jewish organizations, in which Ben-Gurion invested much energy in the early 1930s. So long as the Mandatory authorities allowed appreciable immigration, gave the fledgling Yishuv their patronage despite repeated hardships, and ultimately embarked on a protracted struggle against the Arab uprising of 1936–1939, there was no need to abandon this framework unless the British abandoned it themselves.

Lord Peel's partition plan, bruited in 1937, proposed their continued presence in an important fraction of the country as buffers and agents of moderation. The principles enumerated in the plan included the transfer of Arabs from the territory of the Jewish state. The Zionists themselves had indulged in this notion in their contacts with the British; when asked about the disposition of the Arab population in the Jewish state, they formulated this idea in terms of "voluntary emigration" until Ben-Gurion and his comrades dropped it officially. It had never been more than a Zionist stance on this topic that was expressed in response to British approaches about it then and later. The thing that Ben-Gurion and his colleagues desired above all was unrestricted immigration of millions of Jews to Palestine so that a canton-based federative settlement with the Arabs could be pursued. In this settlement, the Jews, of course, would be the majority that would recognize the status of the Arab minority in Palestine. If the Arab minority wished to dwell in Arab surroundings and avoid close (and, from its standpoint, untenable) proximity to a sovereign Jewish government, theoretically it could emigrate to some Arab country.

As stated, in my opinion, the matter at issue was a "stance" or argument that the Zionist leadership invoked in response to British queries and not a scheme for the forcible expulsion of Arabs. Either way, the Arab uprising and its expansion in the 1930s in view of the looming world war, coupled with the Arabs' influence on the stance of the world powers amid the global crisis and the Holocaust, which decimated European Jewry, as well as the lessons of that calamity, caused Arab–Jewish relations to deteriorate perceptibly and fomented the feeling that the two peoples truly could not live together.

For the time being, the partition plan ignited an acute internal controversy within the Labor Movement itself and the Mapai leadership, between its proponents and Jabotinskyites who waved the slogan, "The Jordan River has two banks," in its face.[24] It also became the topic of principled and political disputation in the various forums of the Zionist Executive. The disharmony that surfaced in the "partition polemic" of the 1930s[25] would necessitate a double measure of caution in addressing this issue from then on, so long as the collective was run by the voluntary organizations of a scattered and fractious "non-people people" and not by a state in the deep sense of the term, a sovereign setting that has appropriate institutions, practices rules of the game, and facilitates and demands statecraft.

Jabotinsky himself put forward his "million-man program," the idea of moving a million Jews from Poland to Palestine within ten years. His plan for staggered emigration from Poland, however, was proposed pursuant to the death of Marshal Pilsudski in 1935, because this event was expected to aggravate Polish Jewry's plight severely. Therefore, one cannot say that Jabotinsky hatched the idea as a consequence of the Nazis' rise to power two years previously and that he had "foreseen" the Holocaust.[26] His proposed population transfer was to be completed by 1945, at the end of World War II, which he had ostensibly foreseen.

By studying the practical political nature of Nazi antisemitism, however, Ben-Gurion had come around to the belief that Hitler meant to put his ideas into practice and that he was bound to entangle himself in a two-front war against forces that he would regard as incorrigible enemies: the West and the USSR. Once this expected development came to pass, the Jews would be teetering on the brink of an abyss.[27]

Ben-Gurion's close associates, including Katznelson, thought that he was overstating the case and had been swept up – as was sometimes his habit, they thought – in a hysteria of "vision," in this case a catastrophic vision that should best be soft-pedaled. As it turned out, however, Ben-Gurion read the situation better than they did. This was one of the sources of his growing confidence in his ability to understand "historical forces" and his conviction that a statesman is duty-bound to study them, trace their progress to the best of his ability, and avoid being captive to "historical inertia." But what kind of abyss did he envision? Was it the industrial-scale extermination of every Jew on earth? I do not think anyone imagined such a possibility until it actual began to happen nine years later, in the vise that Hitler was tightening as part of a global war. The imagery was one of a massive calamity: destruction of communities on an immense scale; economic, cultural, and psychological devastation; and ghastly mass abuse of Jews – a picture so dire that the Zionist escape route could now be offered more forcefully than before. Indeed, from now on, in Ben-Gurion's mind, Zionism was an urgent and immediate option.

Admittedly, most Jews could not have emigrated to Palestine immediately after the Balfour Declaration because Palestine lacked an infrastructure worthy of the name. Since then, however, an infrastructure had come into being in Palestine; now it had to be expanded and consolidated in the economic and social senses, and immigration on the largest possible scale should be made the object of struggle and given the highest priority. Ben-Gurion's forté was his ability to contemplate political forces and their origins, as opposed to sundry ideas that lacked real potential, and to fight for rejected ideas that took on real structure and strength.

When Ben-Gurion realized how the world had changed shortly after the Nazis' rise to power, he and several other optimistic Socialist comrades – people graced with long-range, long-term vision and belief in progress, who nevertheless sought some form of compromise between their dreams and the Middle East reality – became genuine statesmen of Realpolitik. Their attitude was strongly influenced by what was happening in Europe at the time: the supine collapse of German social democracy and the obliteration of all its endeavors, its many historical achievements, and its organizations and supporters at the hands of the Far Right. Since this Right had begun to take root in the Yishuv as well (mutatis mutandis), it was necessary to try to dialogue with its leader, Jabotinsky, in order to stanch its slide toward Fascism.

The attempt fared poorly for various reasons. For one, the Zionist Labor Movement itself was not cut of one cloth, and its flanks did not accept the stance of Ben-Gurion, who at the time was only one of several party leaders, on this issue among others. Thus, it was necessary to reinforce the movement's unity and leadership so that it could become a real political instrument in a political world that required politics next to, and sometimes on top of, social change and nation-building. In the next phase, once it became clear that Jabotinsky himself was following the lead of quasi-Fascist ideas that originated in Pilsudski's Poland or, to be more precise, among his supporters in Poland who had adopted these ideas, the Yishuv politics of the Labor Movement – notwithstanding the nuances among its constituents – embarked on a struggle against the Revisionist Right in Palestine and in the Diaspora.[28]

The Zionist Socialists adopted a policy of forbearance vis-à-vis the Arab uprising of 1936–1939, also for various reasons. One was to allow the British to quell the uprising with Jewish assistance and not to add the Yishuv to the roster of combatants against the British. Ultimately, they were stunned by the British capitulation as a result of the political challenges of this uprising, which bred the May 1939 White Paper on Palestine. Just the same, the Zionist Social Democrats aligned themselves with the camp that fought Fascism first. Furthermore, they had multiple aims: to fight the Nazis, to challenge the new British policy in Palestine, and to force the British – against their interests – to help European Jewry emigrate to Palestine. Eventually they would realize that it was not these interests that sealed the fate of European Jewry but rather the Nazis' actions. The "nationalists," those of the Second Aliyah, had always sought to align themselves with the Western progressive humanistic and universalistic tradition and even claimed naively that that it was Judaism that had helped to establish the infrastructure of this tradition. In contrast, British Liberals and Conservatives professed to see no difference between Zionist Socialist nationalism and Nazism; under their influence, some key American officials also found this argument compelling. The British high commissioner for Palestine, Sir Harold MacMichael, argued this way (as we have seen already) and Ze'ev Sternhell repeats this notion like a faint echo in our times.

It was this elaborate historical reality, replete with serpentine turns and impossible compromises, that sired the forbearance policy and gave rise during World War II – when the Stern Gang proved that Zionist Fascism did exist – to the "Small Season" against it and the "Grand Season" against IZL, sometime after the latter organization's new commander, Menachem Begin, proclaimed an uprising against the British while the latter were combating the Nazis. Begin did this even though the British, in cognizance of the Holocaust, were allowing Jews who found their own way out of Nazi-sealed Europe to enter Palestine. This complicated reality, with the Holocaust as the overarching feature, helped greatly to "Zionize" the survivors. It ultimately helped the Zionists to drive a moral and political wedge between the United States and Labour-governed Britain, deprived the Palestinian Arabs of their principal leader – the Grand Mufti of Jerusalem – because he had collaborated with Hitler, and abetted the disintegration of the array of forces that had failed to accommodate the meaning of the Holocaust and its impact on the Zionists specifically and the Jews generally.

The Yishuv's policy toward the hostile Mandatory government, too, was inseparable from the global drama, with Western Jewry playing an integral role in the West's war against the Nazi-Fascist Axis. As Ben-Gurion said in July 1943:

I cannot fight a war against the White Paper without, at the very least, moral support from world Jewry. Neither can I fight a war without the moral support of the forces of good in the world, our friends in England, our friends in America, because we by our own forces cannot attain everything.... A war of humankind is under way and I am part of it; I do not want it to be thought that I am not part of it.... After the war, there will be only a Jewish war, and then the well-being of the Jewish people will be the sole consideration, and then – a maximum of force [will be used] to fulfill and defend our right.[29]

This position, of course, also hinged on world public opinion and the moral image of the Yishuv.

Therefore, on the domestic (Yishuv) front, it was necessary to fight Fascist ideas and anything that appeared to establish a Zionist–Nazi nexus. One should bear in mind, however, that Ben-Gurion was active in many stages of the Nazi policy, which until 1941, when the "Final Solution" decision was made, concerned itself with deporting the Jews to the four corners of the earth.

This explains Ben-Gurion's willingness to accept the partition plan, which was bruited while Hitler was expelling Jews and before he began to murder them. In this context, the question of borders was secondary to the Jews' needs and their appalling distress, which carried some moral weight in the West. In other words, under certain conditions, morality equals power and distress could be translated into practical ability that would be facilitated by as much immigration as possible.[30]

After Jabotinsky's accord with Ben-Gurion fell through and the former seceded from the Zionist Organization, Jabotinsky turned in several directions of his own. On the one hand, he continued trying to impose himself on the British, whom he considered a partner in the region even though they had barred him from the country in 1934. On the other hand, he opposed the partitioning of Palestine that the British offered in 1937.

During the 1930s, he made public statements about Poland's alleged military power and its ability to withstand Hitler, the ostensibly rhetorical nature of Nazi antisemitism, and a possible commonality of interests between Fascist Italy and the Zionists. He also forged plans to establish a Jewish army in Poland in conjunction with the antisemitic government while adopting the formal command of the IZL, which had been established largely by Jabotinsky's supporters outside the Hagana.[31]

IZL operations against the Arabs during the 1936–1939 Arab uprising, which ended with the hanging of the organization's first martyr, Shlomo Ben-Yosef, threatened the Yishuv's relations with both the British authorities and aggravated the Arabs. When World War II broke out, however, Jabotinsky, speaking from his American exile, instructed his followers to support the British in their war against the Nazis. By so doing, he brought about the irreversible schism between IZL – his movement's militia – and Abraham Stern's Lehi. The split presented the Yishuv leadership with a new internal problem that forced it to take various moves that would metamorphose in the consciousness and historiography of that generation.

Where Ben-Gurion's consciousness is concerned, the actions of IZL and Lehi – which originated in their worldview and their unrealistic view of global, regional, and Palestinian events – were more than a topic that needed to be banned from public debate and "education" in the Yishuv. Those actions would eventually require a forceful reaction (i.e., the Grand Season) – if no other way were possible – in order to neutralize the influence of minorities (IZL and Lehi) that wished to impose their will on the majority. Indeed, it would take much toil to fashion and sustain this majority under the peculiar conditions of a world war.

The Road to Biltmore

Apart from numerous Zionist sources that deal with the period following the proclamation of the White Paper in May 1939, today one has to study British intelligence reports – and American ones, which at this time were largely based on British reports – about Palestine and the Zionists, most of which have been made available for research. Thus, in their preparations for war, the British established several new intelligence facilities in Cairo that were occupied intensively with the Zionists, Jewish immigration to Palestine, political intelligence, and counterespionage. One example is the MEIC (Middle East

Intelligence Center), under Brigadier Iltid Clayton, which metamorphosed into PICME (Political Intelligence in the Middle East), headed by the aforementioned Brigadier Quilliam, which played an important role – along with MI6 in London – in torpedoing the Brand-Grosz mission. The Biltmore conference was of much concern to these services; it even caused the OSS American agent in Palestine, Prof. Nelson Glueck – a leading personality in the anti-Zionist American Reform Movement – to ask his superiors to send him back to the United States so that he could fight this "fascist idea." His request was honored.[32]

By unveiling the White Paper in May 1939, Britain effectively rescinded the Balfour Declaration and renounced its undertaking to side with the Jews in the Palestine conflict. Ben-Gurion's hopes about the moral power of the Jews' distress – which the British government had not overlooked in ordinary times – was shattered in the face of the emergency of the eve of world war, the second such conflict within one generation. This war dwarfed the Jews' woes in comparison with the aforementioned considerations of the British defense and political establishments, considerations that meshed with the antisemitic views of key people in these establishments in Palestine and London.

The abandonment of the Jews at the onset of this drama impelled Ben-Gurion to take an "activist" stance toward the British. By so doing, he actually walked a tightrope between merely threatening their standing in Palestine and countenancing an outright uprising during the "phony war" of 1939–1940. To his mind, the Yishuv should pressure the British by using all conceivable political and moral means, including the hint that it might use its armed force, the Hagana against them. By accepting this approach, the Mapai leadership adopted a seemingly extreme stance that resembled the spirit of Jabotinsky's own views.

All his life, Jabotinsky was torn between his hope of obtaining the whole of mandatory Palestine on both sides of the Jordan River, specifically from the British, despite their interest in other and, from their standpoint, legitimate deals, and the objects of his main concern, the Jews of Poland, who had not yet moved to Palestine and had developed a hard core of support for his party. He believed that Poland would put up a good fight against the Wehrmacht and even toyed with the possibility of seeking a Zionist common cause with Fascist Italy, as described earlier. When that fallacy was exposed, he headed for America and instructed his followers in Palestine to enlist in the war against the Nazis and to cooperate with the British in prosecuting it. Shortly afterwards, he passed away, leaving the IZL minions perplexed about which direction to take, until they did side with the British and actively fought the Sternists, who tried to forge an anti-British alliance with Italy and even Nazi Germany.

Concurrently, the Jewish Agency Executive continued to conduct "illegal" immigration operations on the largest possible scale in 1939, after the Nazis had begun to deport Austrian Jewry en masse, and subsequently, when they expanded this policy to Czechoslovakia and Germany proper. After the fact, however, the "activists," such as Ben-Gurion and his colleagues Yitzhak Tabenkin and Berl Katznelson, sought to pressure, not to overthrow, the

Mandatory government. It was their hope that public opinion, Parliament, and the pro-Zionists in Britain itself would overturn the position of Chamberlain's government, which was now fighting the very man, Hitler, whom it had formerly tried to appease.

This neither-here-nor-there period was typified by vain hopes of all kinds. The British believed that by means of a naval and aerial blockade they could defeat Germany without resorting to an overland offensive. After all, they reasoned, Germany seemed to have reached the limit of its forces' capacity and had exhausted the rearmament effort in which it had invested for years. Therefore, they also took care to prop up their status in the oil-rich Arab Middle East and to prevent a repeated Arab uprising in this vital region by applying the White Paper policy. Subsequently, they developed the theory that Britain could mobilize the peoples of the continent, who by 1940 were suffering from the Nazis' tightening yoke, for a general uprising and guerrilla war that would burn the soil under the Germans' feet – an idea that ultimately proved very problematic but was taken as conventional wisdom at the time. In other words, His Majesty's government wished to avoid a situation in which, on the one hand, would foment a guerrilla war in Europe and, on the other hand, would risk exactly this kind of a war against itself in the Middle East by taking actions that favored the Jews, who were being deported from Europe, and infuriated the Arabs.

Eventually, the Yishuv leadership embraced the guerrilla-warfare myth by seeking to enlist parachutists who would train European Jews for an uprising of their own. Early on, the Yishuv leaders began to establish a so-called "secret relationship" with the British intelligence and guerrilla-warfare agencies, in the belief that they could avail themselves of them and help them by means of the Zionist organizations and youth movements in occupied Europe.[33]

In the meantime, however, France fell and Britain remained alone. Winston Churchill – almost the only member of his party's high leadership who continued to entertain pro-Zionist sympathies – became prime minister and minister of defense. Once in office, Churchill suspended the political clause of the White Paper, which proposed to cede political control of Palestine to the Arabs within five years. He even favored the militarization of the Yishuv in order to free British military forces in Palestine for war duties. The senior British bureaucracy and the military commanders in the Middle East, however, defeated this initiative.[34]

The whole region was under martial law, and London could not ignore the views of the British regional bureaucracy. The state of emergency was such that censorship of mail and telegraphy in Palestine was introduced. Although today the censor's findings are a gold mine that reveals the state of mind in the Yishuv, back then the censor severely crimped the leadership's ability to communicate freely with Jewish centers abroad.[35]

Three British security services – the Mandatory Police Department of Investigation and two branches of Military Intelligence, headquartered in Cairo – spied on the Yishuv and its leaders from the summer of 1939 onward. They enjoyed great success due to information provided by a well-developed network of agents and by data from other intelligence services about goings-on in all quarters of the Yishuv. The Mandatory government used this information to stir conflict among Yishuv entities and to burden the Yishuv leadership in Palestine, in London, and in the Americans' eyes as much as possible. It enforced the land provisions of the White Paper, which forbade the sale to Jews of land in most parts of the country. It deported Jewish immigrants who ignored the small quota that the White Paper had established, and within the Yishuv it created a sense of siege, to which Ben-Gurion initially responded by invoking his "activist" combination of moral-political pressure and threats against the Palestine government. Later on, contemplating developments outside the region, he realized that the enormous war presently under way would engender a basic change in the global and regional balance of power. One could expect a historical shift, a change in attitudes, and a revisiting of views due to the key position that the United States – neutral for the time being – would occupy in the global constellation. Since American Jewry could play a key role, a supreme effort to find a way to propel the cogs of world history should be made at this definitive moment. Ben-Gurion, however, could not foresee Hitler's response to the Americans' moves, the sealing of European Jewry's fate in the aftermath of these moves, and how impressed the British would be with the extent of American Jewish influence on the Roosevelt's demarches.[36]

As the Yishuv suffocated under the Mandatory government's yoke, Chaim Weizmann, seated in London, was trying to marshal opposition to the Mandatory administration in Western capitals in his old aristocratic way. In the United States, too, he was able to open doors by applying his discreet and, at times, dangerous working methods.[37]

Ben-Gurion had firmly made up his mind to influence the course of events in Western capitals by applying his analytic ability, his principles, and, if possible, a direct connection with the American Jewish masses. Among the leaders of these masses he discerned slackness, powerlessness, and typical fears in response to the grimly antisemitic climate around them. Thus, he left Palestine for lengthy periods in 1940 and again in late 1941 – before the war expanded to global dimensions, before Hitler decided on the Final Solution, and before Ben-Gurion and Western Jewish leaders realized the full severity of the goals and magnitudes of the disaster. Although this activity began with a series of failures and disappointments, as Friling describes, it ultimately led to the adoption of the Biltmore Program, which in essence demanded the establishment of a Jewish state in all of Palesine west of the Jordan River and the immediate repeal of all restrictions on Jewish immigration. Thus, the Jewish-Arab federation scheme was replaced by a Jewish demand for full sovereignty throughout the West Bank. This shift of goals seemed puzzling in view of the federative ideas that had dominated the debate in the past and Ben-Gurion's consent to the partitioning of the country five years earlier. However, he wished to make a public presentation of goals that were phrased with maximum clarity, that would undermine the Right, and that seemed to be justified in view of

Zionism's practical achievements and the global political drama. Ben-Gurion's goal was to unite most of Jewry that remained accessible, that is, that of America, behind the Zionists.

American Jewry at the time – as Dinnerstein and others have described it[38] – was in a precarious state. The antisemitism of the 1930s had metamorphosed in the 1940s into an outright plague that the ordinary observer today cannot imagine as having taken place during World War II. Jews were being accused of having dragged the United States into war by various means, including their control of the film industry – a charge that the Senate actually began to investigate. Jews were accused of profiteering from the war and refusing to serve in the combat units in favor of their own interests. Catholic and Protestant propagandists who wielded great media influence spread traditional antisemitic charges. As the antisemitic propaganda continued during the war, its seeds and fruits had been scattered in all directions and had been insinuated into the political domain in view of the mobilization of millions for the bloody war. According to Dinnerstein, the general antisemitic climate had caused most American Jews to despair of the result. Furthermore, there is no doubt – as we have argued – that Roosevelt was aware of this climate and the political risk that it carried for the prosecution and winning of the war.

American Jews, suspicious of their harsh and threatening environment, led a voluntarily segregated way of life on the East Coast and in the Northeast in general. Many young Jews were not familiar with America at all. Having emerged from their ghettos, they reghettoized themselves in their businesses and, in the 1930s, some walled themselves off in debate clubs at such universities as were willing to enroll them, where many of the most talented Jews became Marxists. These people, including some who would veer far to the right later in adulthood, did not really know America until it became a belligerent in the way against Fascism and did not identify with it until World War II was over. Under these conditions, the Zionist solution seemed reasonable. It gained acceptance during the Holocaust and evolved into a unifying principle for American Jewry, which until then had been fragmented and scattered in its views. In other words, the Biltmore Program became a de facto foundation stone for this Jewish collectivity, even though, as stated, it had been conceived before the full gravity of the Holocaust was known.

From Biltmore to the "Grand Season"

On the surface, Biltmore unified all Zionist entities – including the very cautious and essentially pro-British leadership headed by Weizmann, president of the World Zionist Organization – behind a formula that was consensual, simple, and sufficiently intriguing for the American imagination. It persisted even though Weizmann, the "dovish" wing of Mapai, and the factions to Mapai's left entertained severe doubts and reservations about its wisdom until after World War II. This largely expunged the partition debate from the public agenda in Palestine and among Zionist entities there and elsewhere by the time he returned to Palestine after this demarche; however, Ben-Gurion and everyone in the Yishuv leadership were aware of the magnitude of the Holocaust. The details were not fully known, for example, the centrality of Auschwitz relative to other death factories such as Majdanek, Sobibór, and Treblinka, which were better known but too far away to permit outside intervention. The leadership's main attention focused on the exiles in Transnistria, that is, Romanian Jews deported to an occupied area across the Dniester River, who at first were put to death by the Romanian occupiers in cooperation with the SS. But once Romanian dictator Antonescu realized that Hitler had been stopped at the gates of Moscow, the Romanian Jews – including the deportees and the Romanian Jews in general – were left alive until further clarification of the general war picture. Next to its desperate efforts to at least create contacts with, and send money to, the Polish ghettos, the leadership also focused on the possibility of a bribery deal to rescue Slovak Jews (which might expand to the rescue of all Jews in the Nazi satellites and the survivors in Poland), the emigration of Jewish children to Palestine in order to allay British concerns about Jewish spies and hostages in Nazi hands, the possible use by the Allies of German civilians in their hands in order to stop the extermination, and threats that would be publicly voiced for this purpose.[39]

Again, however, Ben-Gurion learned little by little that Allied opinion would accept no moves of this nature due to the logic of the trap and the global tragedy that was battering large nations and obfuscating the disaster that had befallen the Jews. The Soviet Union was reeling under the Germans' attacks; its survival was anyone's guess. If the USSR were to collapse, the main burden would be the West's to carry. The West was willing to assume this burden provided its peoples were willing to bear up to it. The suffering of the Soviet peoples, as manifested in the atrocity of the siege of Leningrad, was on everyone's lips. Their fate was ghastly indeed, and although it had been brought on to a great extent by the blunders of the Soviet leadership, no one observed or even knew about Stalin's blunders at the time.

By the same token, it became increasingly clear that the key to rescuing the Jews was held not by the West – even though one could easily hold the West accountable – but by the Nazis, who in the territories under their control were thwarting rescue in every possible way. Rescue might be possible in states allied with Germany, such as Romania, Bulgaria, and Hungary, where Zionist rescue organizations could be set up and an attempt made via them to reach the killing fields in Poland. These rescue attempts seemed to have been possible in Romania, and even there large-scale emigration to Palestine stood no chance due to the Germans' opposition. However, the Allied authorities in London and in the Middle East were worried about the rescue attempts and did their best to frustrate them due to concern about an Arab response in their rear, while calculating a Zionist uprising in Palestine in order to force the gates of the country open to Jewish immigration in the midst of a world war.[40]

The process of setting up the Yishuv's rescue mission in Istanbul, smoothing relations among its members, and enabling the Zionist emissaries in neutral Switzerland to function in terms of efficiency, as well as their ability to get along with one another, clashed diametrically with the image that these players wished to create in regard to aid from the Yishuv to the Diaspora.[41] The reality among the Yishuv rescue organizations in neutral countries was much different. Given the image sketched here, we pause for a moment to describe the reality in some detail – one of disunity and fragmentation at a time of supreme emergency, unauthorized autonomous moves by rescue emissaries, and competition for resources and control of them and of the rescue offices themselves. It was all part and parcel of the situation in Palestine. The Yishuv leadership had inflated the Hagana, the instrument that was supposed to pressure the hostile Mandatory government by its very existence, beyond its real dimensions, in order to instill among the British not only an awareness of the Jews' power but also the belief that the Hagana was backed by the might of the entire Yishuv, a full-fledged "state in the making." The leadership of this organization, however, was flaccid and vague. The Hagana had no clear defense conception for Palestine or for the region at either the defensive or the offensive levels. It had no unified command, reflecting the coalition nature of the Yishuv leadership and its own wish to maintain internal consensus.[42]

The Labor parties' relations with the "Civilian Bloc," headed by general Zionists such as Tel Aviv Mayor Yisrael Rokach, were marked by mutual suspicion. The Labor parties regarded the "civilians" as a bourgeoisie that had replicated its "exilic" (mainly Polish) way of life in Palestine and failed to mobilize to properly serve the needs of the day, that is, rural settlement and the adoption of the elite's Socialist credo in general. In this state of affairs, it was very hard to establish a unified staff whose high command could be controlled when, in his way, one of the standout Hagana commanders, Yitzhak Sadeh, subsequently commander of the Palmach (the Hagana's commando units), was noted for his doctrinaire leftist and anti-British activist approach, drawn on the Soviet ethos, in which he educated his minions.[43]

Under these conditions, many players contributed to the jelling of the Mapai apparatus as the instrument that would prepare the Yishuv for statehood. Several Mapai leaders came from the rural-settlement enterprise even though they operated in the urban sector. Some remained in Labor Movement settlements and provided Mapai with genuine pioneering content and flavor. Others came from Soviet Russia and possessed aggressive and finely honed tools that they had acquired there, such as pressuring members of the Histadrut at their places of work to enlist in the British Army after the Yishuv leadership decided that the conditions warranted this step. At large workplaces such as the Palestine Electricity Company, functionaries who controlled local Labor councils carved out power bases that generated economic benefits for their associates. Some of them amassed strength by manipulating these entities in ways that verged on corruption. The leadership swept these shenanigans under the rug or, at the very least, failed to investigate them properly.[44]

Shabtai Teveth's presentation of the concept is on target:[45] the people at issue, the thinking went, were "all we have" and had to be "lived with" if the short-term goals were to be attained. After all, such people were not tempted to adopt the vain positions of the leftist currents and accepted the leadership's authority in political affairs. Ostensibly, Ben-Gurion made a point of standing above the fracas and was fully aware of the parochial way in which the party apparatuses in Tel Aviv and Haifa had come together. In Haifa, a large minority of immigrants from Germany had organized under the banner of their own party, which sought to extend the British Mandate and conclude some kind of settlement with the Arabs. In the outlook of this party, the Jews' disaster took a back seat to the global anti-Fascist drama. It also viewed the Eastern European leadership, busy as it seemed to them to have been with its petty affairs, with growing revulsion – a revulsion that the party associated with the disaster that had befallen much of Jewry, in the sense that the young, idealistic pioneers who were supposed to have emigrated to Palestine and added a decisive new element to a society controlled by the old-guard Socialists were dead. The daily newspaper *Ha'aretz*, privately owned and closely associated with German Zionist doubts and despair of these kinds, echoed them every now and again, and its criticism of Ben-Gurion's behavior at the time would continue to be quoted by *Ha'aretz* columnists, such as Amos Elon and Tom Segev, today.

It was only natural that Ben-Gurion would learn his lessons from this situation, for which he was officially responsible even though he had no practical ability to change it in any real way for the time being. Thus, he prepared for a fight with the Left and Right in general elections for the Histadrut leadership when such would come about and for a majority in the Yishuv's Assembly of Representatives. Ben-Gurion used every public body available to explain the moves of the leadership – those that he could trust to adopt and disseminate them. A mass media organ was properly used: the newspaper *Davar*, which amassed much influence in the public domain. Instead of a united youth movement, however, several movements came into being, most influenced by the Left. Against Ben-Gurion's counsel, education was not standardized; instead, it took place in three "streams" – general, Labor, and religious – and the Labor system taught only a minority of the young.

When it came to rescuing Jews, things were not much different. The emissaries from the diverse and politically fragmented Yishuv complained bitterly about the lack of funds and, sometimes, the lack of attentiveness on the part of the Yishuv leadership to the requirements for rescue. Vis-à-vis the Jews themselves, in the Diaspora and in Palestine, however, the emissaries carefully projected the image of being sources of strength, encouragement, and real action.[46] After the fact, the emissaries accomplished little, and reasons and arguments in justification of their failure accumulated. Ben-Gurion was personally involved in every decision that pertained to them, even as they received a steadily expanding flow of financial resources from the Yishuv exchequer and its fund-raising mechanisms in Palestine and abroad.[47]

Ben-Gurion was also involved in dispatching Yishuv emissaries to Germany's allies for subversive actions and did whatever he could in those locations for the cause of Jewish emigration in the middle of the war. He preached activism and nonacquiescence but did not allow events in the Yishuv to spiral out of control. Thus, the small Yishuv became an increasingly central player in the rescue efforts even though the affected Jewish communities had not authorized it to play this role. Naturally, then, it attracted accusations of not having done enough. The leadership must have been aware of these charges – which were already cropping up then – but preferred to disregard them. It may not have thought it possible to contest them in view of the gravity of the disaster and the disputatious ways and traditional political behavior of the Jews. Given the severity of the catastrophe, any proposed rescue action demanded a response, and such responses were forthcoming after much vacillation and debate, even as Zionists abroad were trying to entangle the Yishuv leadership and the West in autonomous initiatives that played into the Gestapo's hands.

The aforementioned "Brand mission" is a case in point. Both Shertok and Ben-Gurion agreed that this desperate initiative had to be tried. However, they had to endure its outcome – the Allies' well-placed suspicion that the Nazis were toying with Brand and Grosz for their own purposes – and its failure, for which Brand would subsequently hold the Yishuv leaders responsible. Indeed, after Brand seceded to the Sternists, he continued to level false and grave charges against the Yishuv leadership for personal tactical reasons of his own, that is, so that he not be asked about his failure to return to Budapest after the British allowed him to, even if empty-handed, in order to share the fate of Kasztner and the others. After the fact, he justified Lehi's assassination of Lord Moyne on the false grounds that Moyne himself had defeated Brand's mission. Various voices on the Right would accuse the Yishuv leadership of having "collaborated" with the British; after all, it had not risen up against them as Lehi had, and as IZL eventually would, and had allegedly turned Brand over to them on his way from Istanbul to Palestine. This and the other allegations were sheer lies. Eventually, writers such as the aforementioned Elon and Segev would dip their pens into Brand's conflicting testimonies and invoke them – and the Holocaust – for their post-Zionist needs. By so doing, they would enlarge the trap and extend its effect from the Holocaust era to our own times. In this respect, they are much like the anti-Zionist Orthodox and erstwhile members of IZL and Lehi who continue, for reasons of their own, to cling to the emotions of vengeance and rage that consumed some among the Holocaust survivors.[48]

The autonomous activities of the radical organizations in the Yishuv constitute a story in itself. In late 1943, it seemed as if the Zionist Executive would soon witness a breakthrough in London: With victory on the horizon, Churchill established a ministerial committee for Palestine and tasked it with finding a solution that all sides could accept, including a Jewish state in part of Palestine as part of a British-sponsored comprehensive settlement for the Middle East.[49]

Accordingly, Lord Moyne, British minister of state for the Middle East, took up a new partition plan for discussion (the main points of the plan are not covered here) while survivors who left the territories of the Third Reich and its accomplices, be it with Zionist assistance or on their own, were being allowed to enter Palestine even though the White Paper had not been repealed. In the meantime, the Yishuv leadership was in turmoil amid clashing reports about what was happening in London or Washington, where Dr. Weizmann was maintaining the principal contacts in a problematic partnership with the rest of the Zionist Executive, with which he declined to consult. The turmoil peaked in February 1944 when British intelligence and its American associates used Shertok to engineer his own failure, as the previous quotations illustrated.[50] Other British officials who had a hand in the matter viewed Sharett differently: as the potential successor of Ben-Gurion, the zealous, nationalist, and extremist man of Biltmore. Sharett, they figured, would carry on in Weizmann's moderate and, from their perspective, amenable ways. They were wrong about both Sharett and Ben-Gurion; the latter would eventually consent to the partitioning of Palestine and abandon the Biltmore Program in view of the postwar realities.

By now, Churchill himself had acknowledged the Jews' entitlement to at least part of Palestine and, as a result, was increasingly inclined to make an immediate attempt to solve both problems, of the Jews and of Palestine, at the same time. This, however, subjected him to the bitter opposition of British officialdom in the region and of Anthony Eden's Foreign Office. Churchill believed that he could reopen the discussion of this dual issue with the assistance of a much more sympathetic public opinion toward the Jews in view of their disaster and of the Arabs' conduct during the war (i.e., their support for the Axis and their failure to aid the Allies in their war effort). Finally, Churchill used the Moyne assassination at the hands of Lehi in December 1944 to defer the decision about the future of Palestine until after the war, when general elections in Great Britain would be held. Churchill advised Roosevelt of his intentions. As early as October 1943, however, he had promised Weizmann that until then he would safeguard the Jews' rights vigilantly. So he did, symbolically and practically, by establishing the Jewish Brigade Group within the British Army in early 1944, in counsel with Roosevelt.

Thus, the "revolt" that Menachem Begin had proclaimed against the British in January 1944 did not reflect an understanding of the Zionists' situation at the time. Instead, it reflected a basic misunderstanding on Begin's part, stemming from the belief that an insurrection against the British would influence the Americans, of all people, and show them that the Jews were no less powerful than the Arabs. However, real action by the Yishuv mainstream against this minority – which Begin headed in his function as Jabotinsky's self-appointed successor – waited until after the 1944 Yishuv elections. In these elections, Mapai attained dominance in the Yishuv institutions at the expense of the Left. The result was the creation of an instrument – albeit a temporary one – of domestic governance: the party and the principal entity of the Labor Movement, the Histadrut.

In the meantime, Weizmann remained in London, his strength dwindling steadily as he failed to obtain a final decision on the Palestine question. Indeed, the British Foreign Office and its Middle East bureaucrats frustrated any such decision until after the war, if not later. The supremacy that Weizmann lost was gained by Ben-Gurion's "activist" stance, which had become the position of the Yishuv mainstream and had the mass support of American Jewry. It also invested Ben-Gurion with the political and moral power to stamp out Begin's revolt after the assassination of Moyne in November 1944, because this revolt endangered the Jewish Brigade Group that the British had begun to set up, the immigration efforts of those few who were leaving Europe, Ben-Gurion's initiative to visit Europe and mobilize the survivors for immigration, and majority rule. Now that Berl Katznelson had passed way and Yitzhak Tabenkin, head of Mapai's Faction B, had been defeated in the 1944 elections, Ben-Gurion rose to a position of definitive primacy in the Yishuv – from which he could, in various incarnations, have a conclusive impact on the doings of the Zionist Movement.

Further Remarks about the "Calculating Machine"

During the period just described, Ben-Gurion sought to neutralize Weizmann's influence, which he considered harmful at many junctures, by repeatedly threatening to resign all of his positions, including those at the Jewish Agency. Occasionally he actually did resign some post; once he kept up his resignation for quite a while.[51]

His outbursts of fury at the British (a prime reason for his resignations during, before, and after the "phony war"), Weizmann, and at times Shertok seemed to clash frontally with his aforementioned remark about behaving like a "calculating machine" in his political activities. Anything but. In the estimation of the British, as noted, and as portrayed in the contemporaneous American reports quoted earlier, Ben-Gurion was an "ultra-nationalist," a political radical, and an impulsive type who could hardly restrain his eruptions. His combustible style, however, was an expression of the behavior of "Renaissance man," or rather a democratic Machiavelli, a sort of a popular "Prince" who fully believed in what he thought was absolutely required and brooked no compromise, having created the democratic power base that he needed in order to make decisions pursuant to his analysis of the external forces at work. It was an extraordinary time, and people who were thrust into it, such as Ben-Gurion, refused to accept the ordinary (or "inertia," as he called it). Such acceptance on his part would have forced him to waive his beliefs and estimations of the necessities in order to achieve "domestic tranquility" for its own sake. Admittedly, such a man could acquiesce in domestic tranquility of that kind, and Ben-Gurion honored it strictly when political realities forced him to do so, for example, during most of the period at issue, as the foregoing quotations demonstrate. However, when reality dictated the surrendering of domestic tranquility, that is, at least a serious attempt to break out of it and move ahead, he was left with no choice but to embark on acrid disputation and polemics. Such were needed, he believed, in order to express views clearly, to sharpen contrasts, and to explain to the public what was at stake. Therefore, his disputatiousness was not an expression of impulsive anger, small-mindedness, and character deficiency, but they were, mostly, political tools.

Most of his eruptions were aimed at Dr. Weizmann. Ben-Gurion could – and did – collaborate with him as long as the Zionist endeavor was discussed between Weizmann and a few high British officials in the 1920s and the 1930s. But now he doubted Weizmann's modus operandi within the American demo-cractic system, where Weizmann hoped to deal directly with FDR while still maintaining his British orientation. Ben-Gurion distrusted his secret entrees with world luminaries that ultimately yielded little, and considered him con-descending and disloyal to his comrades in the Zionist Executive. Weizmann did find it very difficult to cooperate with others and treat them as equals. Fur-thermore, Ben-Gurion believed that he was better able to speak for the Jewish masses and understand the demarches and considerations of world leaders in order to make clear decisions on desired moves at specific moments and to implement such decisions by means of steady action in Palestine and abroad. One may, of course, construe Ben-Gurion's perception of his political advan-tage over Weizmann as a gratuitous lust for power. At issue, however, was his awareness that nothing would be accomplished without power and, as far as possible, institutionalized power. Such thinking was foreign to Weizmann, who throughout his career preferred to act alone and along diplomatic chan-nels. Ben-Gurion's advantage was his awareness that contrasts, difficulties, and internal contradictions could be resolved by attaining the supremacy that is needed at crucial moments – an awareness that dawns due to accurate under-standing of the forces at work in a variety of arenas. Concurrently, Ben-Gurion had the ability to change his mind about a political rival if he decided that the rival had changed his own views, and that he should be mobilized for common cause or put to use, if only for lack of choice. In other words, his attitude toward others was not "personal" but, rather, political in the most profound sense of the term; it corresponded perfectly to his distinction between politics and "statecraft," which he applied even at this early phase in his charges against Weizmann.[52]

For Ben-Gurion, "politics" as an epithet denoted amateurism and the advancement of personal and group interests irrespective, or even against, the main goals of the time. "Statecraft" meant the opposite. Therefore, to his mind, a statesman must seize the helm at decisive moments in Zionist history in which either/or decisions must be made. I will not delve into all the ups and downs of this history; Ben-Gurion's biographers have done this in great detail. Of concern here is the general picture and a somewhat detailed expan-sion on specific episodes, including the lessons of the Holocaust and changes that it wrought, which we defined as supremely important at the outset of our discussion.

We admit that personal "charisma" may matter at key moments; this became clear in the debate over the declaration of independence in view of the Arabs' war threats – a debate that Ben-Gurion resolved when the moment came. This charisma, however, had to be institutionalized. Until statehood, it had rested on persuasion campaigns, interminable debates in the Mapai institutions, and the public bodies that were under Mapai's influence (the Histadrut and the organs of the Jewish Agency), as well as on miscellaneous improvisations. Once statehood was achieved, it would be possible to shift from the improvisation stage to a regime worthy of a sovereign state, in which statespeople who were overly endowed with charisma and originally worthy but now outdated mechanisms would play a diminished role.

Jabotinsky, Ben-Gurion thought, had placed the cart before the horse by speaking about statehood on both sides of the Jordan River absent even the minimal infrastructure for such a demand in the territory west of the Jordan, an infrastructure that had to be created by individual toil and concerted group efforts. This was one of the definitive differences between the two personalities. To establish an infrastructure that would suffice for the state-in-the-making, the Zionists had to mobilize even as they discussed the matter with the Great Powers and not with the Arabs, who to no one's surprise did everything possible to thwart Jewish sovereignty in Palestine. The Arab political logic – unshakable for the time being but possibly shakable in due course – stiffened even more in view of the grave precedent of the Holocaust.[53] It was clear that unless the Zionists could persuade Churchill and a majority of his colleagues in the War Cabinet to accept the formation of a Jewish state during or at the end of World War II, even if success in this mission seemed to be at hand, they would have to mobilize American Jewry for coordinated action with the Yishuv and its actions. For this to happen, the Yishuv needed a leadership capable of deciding on and directly influencing developments in Palestine. After all, it was in Palestine, not in London or in the UN institutions, that matters would eventually be decided. The political decision about the departure of the British would be made abroad due to political and moral considerations that denied the Zionists the right to use terrorism or seek to overthrow the British, who, with the Americans, were fighting the Nazis.

On the ground, however, the matter would be resolved by force, as warranted by the Arabs' positions and the dynamics of relations among them and between them and the British. Weizmann lacked the competence to operate in all of these fields concurrently and detested the use of force. Political decisions ahead of the struggle would be made in view of the realities (for which reason Ben-Gurion eventually returned to the partition plan) and would entail a measure of flexibility that the Right lacked and, it was feared, might also be lacking on the Left, which by then had begun to display dangerous sympathies with Stalin's Soviet Union. It was the status of the mainstream leader that would decide the matter, and therefore the struggle for the power base concerned neither honor nor gratuitous power and status for status's sake. Ben-Gurion, however, saw clearly that his location in the middle of the road was a function of right-versus-left tussling that was not guaranteed to continue. Mapai stood at the center, between its erstwhile Faction B, which had seceded and become

Achdut ha-Avoda–Po'alei Zion, and Ha-Shomer ha-Tsa'ir, today's Mapam, both of which spoke about extending the Mandate in all of western Palestine, handing it to the United States and the USSR, or establishing a binational Arab-Jewish state in the entire country.[54]

To Ben-Gurion's mind, both positions of the left-wing parties were chimeras. Nevertheless, impassioned youth and important intellectuals, among others, subscribed to them. In the early statehood years, these two left-wing currents would merge into Mapam. Their journals and intelligentsia would nibble at Mapai's ideological and media core, the newspaper *Davar*, and would become an increasingly effective opposition on Mapai's left. The historiography and the contemporaneous image of the Yishuv were sometimes fashioned from the point of view, and using the tools of, this opposition, possibly because it appealed to the emotions of young people at the time. In any case, it contributed to the confusion that has typified its description ever since. However, Mapam and its young members were among the finest fighters in the War of Independence, and by virtue of this they sought to leave their imprint on the Israel Defense Forces and on Israeli society at large. This Ben-Gurion could not accept in any way. A truism at the time played into his hands: Mapam could not cooperate with the Zionist Right, which was composed of Jabotinsky's heirs. Mapai derived its power not only from the strength of its apparatus – after all, it was and remained a minority party, albeit the largest minority party – but also from its centrist positioning between the hawks on the Right and on the Left, who had no common language.

Thanks to Ben-Gurion's key position within Mapai, the durability of this situation ensured that the requisite decisions would be accepted until statehood. However, it was liable to cause many troubles during the War of Independence. Therefore, Ben-Gurion cemented his position as prime minister and defense minister only after surmounting the problems and learning the appropriate lessons by making several moves, including partial retreats. Similarly, his various demarches on the eve of statehood, based on his estimates about the forces in the local and global arenas and the need for an appropriate deployment that was not universally accepted, proved to be justified.[55] In his thinking, it was the less-than-complete mobilization of the Arab side for the struggle – a mobilization that peaked only in stages and helped the Yishuv to mobilize in a phased manner as well – that would allow him to cope with the Arabs' uncoordinated challenge and to defeat them one after another at the end of the War of Independence. Subsequently, Ben-Gurion was badly perturbed about what Israel would face once the Arabs learned their lesson.[56]

It was at this time, however, that Ben-Gurion amassed most of his prestige, the kind of prestige that only one person per generation can enjoy, and it seemed as though he would have it to use afterwards as well. Nevertheless, it was his estimation of the disposition of the forces, originating in his study of the lessons of the Holocaust and observation of developments in the West and the East, which was in the thrall of Soviet influence, that convinced him that no one would fight for the Jews. The Yishuv could mobilize moral political support in the West and accept Soviet aid gratefully, even if it were given for anti-British reasons. It could secure the political infrastructure that existed at the end of the British Mandate but not at the onset of statehood. Once the state came into being, by its own forces and with the assistance of world Jewry, it would remain on its own for quite a while and would have only a brief window of opportunity to consolidate until the Arabs recovered, learned their lessons, and took another run at wiping the Jewish state off the map. There were two reasons for this: the uniqueness of the Zionist phenomenon, in ordinary terms of the birth and consolidation of nations, and the international constellation, in which the Arabs possessed much clout. In other words, the establishment of the state would not in itself ensure the existence of the state, while the state was not the goal but rather an instrumentality for the rebirth and reform of what remained of the Jewish people.

The reform of the state's internal regime – when such would come into being – was a crucial matter that demanded a response, both intrinsically and because defending the country and applying a consensual foreign policy required a different kind of mechanism. That regime was one that could no longer depend on personal charisma, the entities that had come into being during the Yishuv period, and the Arabs' mistakes and weaknesses, as manifested in the War of Independence.

The War of Independence and the Protracted State of Emergency

This is not the place to discuss the array of institutions that were set up before independence to ensure necessary consensus in the Yishuv and the requisite effort to prepare it for war – the preparations that Ben-Gurion had been making since 1946 while shifting the main decision-making arena from the world Zionist Movement to the Yishuv institutions. The various moves that were needed in this respect, described in detail and depth in published sources (foremost *Pa'amei medina* [Steps toward statehood] and *Yoman ha-milhama* [War diary]) seem to be riddled with contradictions. The Hagana, which was not yet ready for battle, was beset in no small measure by internal sclerosis; Ben-Gurion regularly criticized this propensity in biting terms.[57] At an early stage, he had given orders to make procurement efforts abroad; it was these that won the day when the British left. He attempted to integrate former Jewish Brigade Group officers into the Hagana apparatus in anticipation of the day when the organization would become a regular military force.[58] These steps were accompanied, directly and indirectly, by protracted inquiries and investigations of the political background of the high command so that as many of "our people" as possible would be placed in various units, including the Palmach; this made Ben-Gurion suspect that the Palmach would be an autonomous formation within the IDF, answering to the Mapam Party.[59] This danger had to be averted, in due course.

Were this array of activities not enough, Ben-Gurion occupied himself incessantly with thousands of organizational, technical, and operational details ahead of the war and with determining its objectives, which changed commensurate with Arab and British moves in the field – those taking place then and those expected during and after the war. The objectives included "destroying the Arab pockets in the Jewish areas of Ramle, Haifa, Lod, and Beit Shean, seeds that pose a special menace in an invasion [by the Arab states, which came indeed the day after the declaration of Israeli independence, on May 15, 1948] and may pin down [our] forces."[60] Simultaneously, he tested the ability of Yishuv society to withstand the unavoidable challenge. The likelihood of success was reasonable due to a characteristic that Ben-Gurion would subsequently call *hosen pnimi* (internal strength, or resilience). We must bear in mind, however, that this critical scion of the Second Aliyah, who had transformed himself into the overtly self-confident representative of the state-in-the-making, had ongoing doubts about this "internal resilience" and the Jews' ability to attain internal consensus and rid themselves of the conventions (e.g., the Marxist leanings that were common among the Left) of a past that had become meaningless:

Although there is no collectivity more revolutionary than ours, equally there is no collectivity more devout and conservative: It does not easily abandon an idea that it had once held but that has become obsolete, and it does not relinquish an outer shell that has been sanctified even if its inner contents are gone. For the past two years . . . I have been trying to teach our public to view the defense problem in its new light and have been demanding a new approach toward the self-defense task, and I have hardly found an attentive ear. But I am confident that our public will not let us down as soon as it appreciates by itself the gravity of the danger and the immensity of the task.[61]

He harbored constant doubts, however, about the Jews' long-term consensus on issues that seemed to have been agreed upon, such as the slogans of "unrestricted immigration" and "Jewish state" that had become common coin on the eve of independence. We will briefly revisit the "unrestricted immigration" theme later because even this slogan was not universally self-evident and accepted, for example, concerning the mass immigration of the early 1950s. And what was a "Jewish state"? Among other things, it is an entity that has "coercive power," a concept that we encounter regularly in Ben-Gurion's remarks on the eve of statehood and that has important advantages. Even though a state cannot be run by coercion alone, it should not be discounted and at times – the right times – it should be wielded indelicately; in dismantling the Palmach command; responding to the general staff's "insurrection" against the minister of defense during the war, which required a temporary compromise;[62] and dismantling IZL and Lehi after the *Altalena* affair, during which Begin tried to keep his renegade organization intact at least in Jerusalem; and the assassination of Count Bernadotte, the UN envoy who tried to negotiate major Israeli territorial concessions as a key for future acceptance by the Arabs, at the hands of the Sternists.[63]

Ben-Gurion presupposed the limits of coercion because he knew his people. Jews could not be forced to do anything they did not want to do. They could be persuaded, mobilized, and coerced for a certain time, during which most forces would join in order to attain a desired outcome. Thus, he believed it possible to mobilize the public at the end of the War of Independence for a heroic effort in all fields in view of the "messianic era," as he put it, that would be under way, but he quickly backtracked in the realization that the resulting surge could not persist. In a totally different field, Ben-Gurion retreated from the austerity regime, a typical regimen of economic coercion that had been introduced in Britain years before it reached Israel and persevered in Britain long after Israel gave it up. He invoked all available tactics of jawboning and arm twisting in order to impose austerity but acknowledged the inability of these measures to surmount market and, especially, black-market forces. He also backed away from his intention to install an Israeli constitution after realizing that such a charter would mark the last word in highly sensitive fields such as religion–state relations. Majority public opinion would never accept a last word of this kind, especially since it would change in view of the expected mass immigration, and important minorities would not endorse it at any point. Therefore, constitutional provisions such as these would be "dead letters," and divisive ones at that. Thus, Ben-Gurion reasoned, sovereignty must flow from the legislature and not from a written constitution that unelected judges would interpret. This is why the First Knesset was not a constitutional assembly as had been intended. The Yishuv's elected institutions were adequate for the transition to this sovereign parliament, which functioned for the time being within the framework of a "compromise regime that [the prime minister] and minister of defense commands on a series of issues that are not ripe for final resolution."[64]

It was necessary, however, to give thought to the fragmented structure of the Knesset, which the new legislature had inherited from the Yishuv method; to examine the functioning of the parties; and to properly estimate their ability to cooperate and do what was needed to withstand the outcomes of the War of Independence, learn its lessons, and confront the challenges of the period to follow. Ultimately, Ben-Gurion came around to the conviction that this fragmented and fractious parliament and the government that grew out of it, one based on a minority party against which the majority had not yet learned how to unite, had to be reformed from top to bottom.

Ben-Gurion considered the domain of defense a *sine qua non* for everything else. After all, "the dead won't sing *hallelujah*," as Ben-Gurion was wont to repeat, adopting an expression from Psalms. With respect to defense, a broad consensus seemed to form slowly as the War of Independence ramped up. Thus, the Yishuv, though not properly prepared for the supreme test, ultimately mobilized and passed the test. Mobilization and willingness to sacrifice were very much the spirit of the day, not to mention the literal mobilization for military service of most adult males. Witnessing this kind of wide-scale mobilization, Ben-Gurion's imagination raced to the idea of sustaining it and making it a lever for the mobilization of all of society for the country's postwar needs in other respects, that is, rural settlement, building the economy, and social consolidation. After all, the country was about two-thirds empty (if we consider the Negev alone), its frontiers were porous, its money had run out, and its losses in lives were immense. It had to duplicate or triplicate itself as quickly as possible and amid unrelenting improvisation. Ben-Gurion included the party as a trusty source of leverage if it could function in all arenas as an active agent for the immense changes that were now needed, and if it could attain "majority status in another three-four years.... To do this, of course, the party will need a highly ramified apparatus."[65]

In the judgment of Anita Shapira, a historian who plainly tilts in the direction of Achdut ha-Avoda and its leaders, such as Yisrael Galili,[66] Ben-Gurion intended at the time that Mapai should have "rules similar to those of a Communist Party in a people's democracy." Shapira admits (p. 63) that he "did not swerve from formal democratic views.... On the contrary; he was incomparably loyal to the framework of parliamentarism, elections, and majority rule." Despite knowing nothing about the nature of British democracy and the historical British parties, however, Shapira distinguishes between "the formal-legalistic side of democracy" and Soviet-style, Nasserist, or Indonesian "'guided democracy' states of mind," which "Ben-Gurion had loyally represented" since the 1920s. Shapira cannot begin to grasp that the "formal-legalistic side" of democracy lies at the very core of the democratic rules of the game. What is more, she has no insight whatsoever about the highly variegated, apparatus-intensive, and organizational nature of the historical British parties, with which Ben-Gurion was fully acquainted. Ben-Gurion was also well aware of the power of the British state – an immense strength even in peacetime and a fortiori in emergencies, when it surpassed even that of the American administration.

Indeed, at this stage of his life, Ben-Gurion easily saw Galili and those of his like for what they were: meretricious but provincial people, ignorant and dangerous precisely due to their cunning and the social networks that they, or preachers like Yitzhak Tabenkin, the guru of the nationalist Left and the romantic dreamer of the kibbutz as the only worthy way of life in an unpartitioned western Palestine, had fashioned. And even if Galili himself dissociated visibly from Tabenkin's daily influence, he remained committed, ever since the Faction B controversy, to three things: opposing the partitioning of Palestine; a Soviet orientation, albeit moderate in keeping with his temperament; and an alliance with an even more pro-Soviet political entity, Po'alei Zion-Left, which excelled in tough talk and class radicalism. Therefore, Ben-Gurion felt it his duty to rebuild the army without their influence.

He quickly discovered that Israel could not sustain the world's largest army relative to population size and that the revolution that seemed essential and almost attainable could not be carried out by means of a climate of mobilization. It had to be radically downscaled and reorganized.

The "party" was also very badly needed for its future contribution to the transition from "state-in-the-making" institutions to parliamentary institutions that would have sufficient control, given the ongoing polarization of Left and Right and the expected return to an era of trivialities that might jeopardize everything attained.[67] However, the party itself was not immune to an "era of trivialities." Basically, it was just an instrument, albeit an important instrument in its time, for the attainment of the classical Zionist goal: gathering a non-people people in Eretz Israel so that it would become a sovereign nation under a Socialist social regime. In Ben-Gurion's thinking, the two were one and the same. "Socialism" meant social solidarity nourished by a political regime that grants it due legitimacy, as opposed to a dubious legitimacy engendered by miscellaneous coalitions and his own power, which was in any case limited and temporary. Socialism meant a high level of equality that was not absolute and utopian, on the grounds that equality and freedom do not necessarily contradict each other.[68] It also meant regulating the economy in the pursuit of these goals, national planning to settle the country without allowing profit considerations to rule, and mobilization of the individual in service of the public at his or her own volition – the thing known as "pioneerism."

Translating "contemporary Socialism" into the language of action, however, proved very problematic when it came to economic affairs. The process had to be modified in order to lay foundations for a multibranched and advanced welfare state in Israel's fledgling days, on the basis of the Labor Movement's achievements to that time. This contemporary Socialism revealed discrepancies between the elitist trends in the Labor Movement and the pressing needs of immigration and immigrant absorption. At the time, Ben-Gurion regarded the kibbutz movements, bastions of the Left, as important players in the pioneering effort, but condescending ones that were not doing enough for the nation at large. The old dispute about the movements' Soviet influence flared more furiously than ever due to their elitist social orientation, which tied into their criticism of developments in the army since their leaders had demobilized voluntarily or for lack of choice.

Thus, the army became the most important instrument that Ben-Gurion could shape directly and, for the time being, with hardly any outside interference. He was able to pull this off with the help of the continuing state of emergency. Indeed, the armistice accords did not serve their intended goal of auguring peace treaties. Peace, to Ben-Gurion, was not a value that stood alone; it had to reflect Arab willingness to accept the Jewish state and view it as a fait accompli and not a temporary reality that, having been imposed by armed force, could be undone by the armed force of a regional and international constellation that would act to the Arabs' benefit.[69]

Ben-Gurion wanted peace to rest on solid strategic conditions, not on "documents and decisions." He thought it unlikely that these conditions existed in the aftermath of the War of Independence. It might be possible to conclude a short-term agreement with one Arab ruler or another. A deal might be worked out with King Abdullah of Jordan, at a considerable price that might, in part, be worth paying due to Abdullah's control of a crucial area close to Israel's heartland and the countries' common interest against the Mufti of Jerusalem and his successors. Abdullah, however, was too weak to conclude an overt peace of this kind at a price that Israel might accept, and he was assassinated shortly after Ben-Gurion made his remarks. The international constellation was bogged down in the Cold War; this might amplify the Arabs' bargaining power due to their control of oil resources and their strategic positions. The Arabs, however, were still mired in the shock of their defeat and their internecine squabbles; Israel would have to exploit the respite to consolidate itself in the region before they managed to unite well enough to wipe it out. Such an act on their part would leverage their unification, their modernization, and the advancement of their values, all of which with the help of the Cold War.

In this matter, the lessons of the Holocaust paralleled those of the War of Independence. What were these lessons? Specifically, given the Zionists' operating conditions in so sensitive a part of the world, they could not expect outside assistance due to the singular complexion of this movement, the aftermath concerning the remnants of the Jewish people, and the changes and upheavals that the Arab world was about to undergo following World War II. However, the rules that applied to the peoples of Europe – within the special constellation in which they, and the superpowers on their periphery that would henceforth determine their fate, were organized – did not apply in the same way to developments in the Middle East.

In Central and Eastern Europe, boundaries were carved and millions became refugees (and were ultimately absorbed in their new environments) because of Hitler's war and the final defeat of Germany. The new European reality was very much the result of Soviet power, which later became nuclear. Any effort to change the status quo in Europe or allow the German refugees to return to the Central and Eastern European countries from which they were deported would have triggered World War III.

Thus, it was especially necessary to contemplate in the Middle East the Arab refugee problem, that is, the problem of those who had left the territory of the Jewish state and the area that it occupied during the War of Independence, or who had been driven out of it and had gathered along its frontiers in anticipation of the next round, thus creating a threatening belt of poverty, humiliation, and repression with the encouragement of their Arab brethren who intended to send them back to Palestine. In Europe, deliberate mass deportations had taken place: The Soviets, the Polish authorities that had gained vast German territories at the expense of those awarded to the Soviet Union, and the Czechs had expelled Germans from their soil. These mammoth demographic changes were outcomes of the war and of Moscow's clout and standing in this matter; usually the West treated them with tacit consent. By the time the dust settled, the refugees had been accommodated in West Germany. The "Palestinian refugee problem," in contrast, remained unsolved due to the stance of the Arab governments under whose control the refugees sought temporary or permanent havens as a result of the war that their leaders, with their support, had waged against the very birth of the Jewish state. The West, too, saw no similarity between it and the problem of the German refugees, instead supporting a UN General Assembly resolution urging Israel either to readmit the Palestinian refugees or to compensate those who did not wish to return.[70]

This was one of the main security issues that had begun to command Ben-Gurion's attention after the War of Independence was won. It proved to him that Israel's status was unique relative to that of states that were well established, concentrated in blocs, and woven into the pacts or alliances that were steadily being formed in Europe and elsewhere at the time. Due to the uniqueness of Israel's condition, this problem would be the cause of the next conflict. It was essential to draw inferences from the War of Independence and acknowledge why Israel had won it: the Arabs' coefficient of weakness and disunity, from which the IDF's coefficient of success was derived.

In an internal discussion about the outcome of the war, the defense minister said: "Let's admit the truth.... Seven hundred thousand [Jews] beat thirty million [Arabs]...not because our army did wonders but because the Arab army was rotten.[71] Thus, Ben-Gurion revealed his bivalent attitude toward the IDF. On the one hand, he extolled the army publicly, calling it an army of the few that had vanquished the many, that is, the enemy's abundant jackboots. In internal discussions, however, he claimed that even though by the end of the war the IDF had attained numerical parity with all the Arab armies and "controlled the skies," important war goals on the southern front had not been achieved or had been achieved with much difficulty.[72]

This bivalence was not a novelty in Ben-Gurion's policy; it should be viewed as a key to his political behavior at large. Outwardly, he presented a confident, proud, passionate, and triumphant posture in order to bolster morale, mobilize it to the utmost, and instill confidence and pride so that the public would internalize these values and integrate them into its behavior. This, however, is but one aspect of the leader's role. A statesman must also "admit the truth" and follow its dictates. In this respect, the diverse roles that Ben-Gurion intended for the IDF in the early statehood years arose from his concept of what one might expect of the country's population as it was, not as it was publicly portrayed. This population still carried many vestiges of the voluntary prewar Yishuv, and there was some doubt about whether its constituents could really be expected to meet the challenges of mass immigration. After all, they had not even passed the test of the austerity program with flying colors. After the great feat of winning the War of Independence, one might expect the members of the erstwhile "Civilian Bloc" and others to seek individualistic "normalcy" à la America. Indeed, such a mind-set could already be found in the pages of the "glitzy newspaper" (as Ben-Gurion called the daily *Ha'aretz*). Such people would regard mass immigration as an illness and an economic absurdity. Such tendencies might be expected in Gershom Gustav Schocken's daily, which preached that if it were to occur, "Israel won't even last as long as Canaanite Carthage."[73]

This mind-set had also made inroads in important Mapai circles and would have to be defeated by status and prestige of this "unique man of his generation."[74] The "party" continued to be a sine qua non for the formation of any government coalition that the country's proportional electoral system would warrant; it was also a foundation without which this coalition could not be controlled, provided that Mapai itself maintained the relative cohesion that had been attained among its leadership in the aftermath of its dispute with the Left and with Right. Indeed, the dispute had ended with the formation of a leadership that seemed to be cohesive in various moves that peaked in the 1944 elections, as we argued earlier. We do not know, however, how confident Ben-Gurion was of this internal cohesion. After all, the individuals at issue were people from diverse backgrounds, people with well-developed egos who operated in a political culture where, as his late comrade Berl Katznelson had complained, "They don't know what a party is." Now, a party is a collegial entity that accepts its leaders' authority and past entitlements so long as they maintain their beliefs, capacities, and willingness to heed their comrades without necessarily accepting their views. This elite is forged by formidable external and internal pressures. One must ask how it will comport itself when these pressures ease slightly or vanish, especially when people who are not endowed with political sagacity and the talent for shoving things under a rug search for cracks in which to hide. Mapai, however, was at least "the devil we know" – the kernel from which Ben-Gurion drew his people, his source of assistance in mobilizing public support – with a charisma to parallel his own exceptional popularity following his decisive role on the way to independence and after a victorious war. The party found its own ways to deal with the immigrants, ways that could be accepted for the time being, while Gadna, the paramilitary youth organization, and the IDF were charged with the care of adolescents and young adults. The question was what would happen to Israeli society in the longer term, by which time it would have changed irrecognizably.

Occasionally, Ben-Gurion realized that in some respects, the party apparatus possessed institutionalized power that surpassed that of its leader's personal charisma.[75] The concern was the extent to which party apparatchiks could be trusted to sustain an enterprise that was fundamentally creative and nonroutine. Might the apparatus distance itself from the people whom it had mobilized by using its methods and grown accustomed to controlling from on high? In the meantime, the left-wing parties and their literary journals and intellectuals were making inroads in the ideological "center," and the left-wing youth movements were rising to primacy among young people. How could this erosion be stanched? These problems, which surfaced around the time of Ben-Gurion's first retirement to Sede Boqer in 1953, were severe in terms of content but also concerned the need for fundamental change in the system of governance. This is why Ben-Gurion had to distance himself, for the time being, from government and from the "system" of which he was considered the founder. The governmental reform he had in mind was intended to culminate in the adoption of much of the British method.

Ben-Gurion wished to import to Israel a two-party system that hands one of the parties a mandate in general elections, allows the winning party to centralize the management of its affairs by means of its parliamentary faction, and provides for a cabinet that the prime minister manages, within limits, by applying consensual authority – but in the specific persona and special stature of a given political circumstance in which such personae operate. At this stage, however, we need to refocus the discussion on the Holocaust and its outcomes, because these would lead to Ben-Gurion's own downfall in due course.

One of the reasons for Ben-Gurion's hostility toward Mapam and toward Palmach and IDF personalities and officers who identified with that party was Mapam's attempt to speak on behalf of the Holocaust survivors, ghetto fighters, and partisans who had emigrated to Israel. Most of the Jewish people did not belong to these minorities, whose war against the Nazis had salvaged Jewish dignity but had not saved Jews. The IDF was supposed to fight in order to win, within the framework of a reality that had to be understood, and within which weaknesses, advantages, and drawbacks had to be found. Partisan rhetoric that originated in Nazi-occupied Europe had not saved anyone. Nevertheless, Mapam, established in January 1948 amid the emotional encounter with survivors,[76] had proclaimed itself "the main power among the survivors and the central player among the force that did the fighting, carried out the clandestine immigration, and settled the country."[77]

Mapam's self-proclaimed monopolization of the Holocaust survivors, apart from being bizarre and factually incorrect, was an attempt to politicize that tragedy for the benefit of a pro-Soviet party. Ben-Gurion must have sensed the need to predicate the IDF on the British apolitical tradition and opposed Mapam's attempt to embrace the survivors as its own. His retirement – or even his downfall – in 1963, however, would be associated with the Holocaust, or with what I call the "aftershock of the Holocaust." However, it would also be connected with his failure to align Israel's system of government with the British formula. For this reason, he had to confront the combination of the Left and Right against his stance and policy on the German issue, which he could foresee. This policy meshed with the main lesson that he had drawn from the Holocaust and the War of Independence alike: to work toward a nuclear option as a basic solution to Israel's security problem.

4

Ben-Gurion and the Israel Defense Forces – From Formation to the Suez-Sinai Campaign of 1956

The British Army as a Model

If Ben-Gurion enjoyed a close acquaintance with any army, as he was wont to say, it was the British Army. He himself was an "alumnus" of this army, having served in the Jewish Legion that had seen combat in World War I. Afterwards, he had many years' acquaintance with the British Army in Palestine and observed it while in England during the Blitz. His political sense and his experience taught him something about the connection between an army and a society at the end of a total war, such as World War I, in which an entire nation had been mobilized. In 1950, as defense minister of the State of Israel, Ben-Gurion stated in the Knesset:

I know of no greater privilege for a Jew in our times than that enjoyed by those who served in the Israel Defense Forces during that amazing year.... It seemed to them, however, that military life became pointless once the battles wound down. They were wrong: There was much point to it – but the point did not appeal to them.... In the months that followed the end of the fighting, we were not sure that the armistice negotiations would succeed; adequate military forces had to be maintained ... even though there was enormous pressure ... to disarm rapidly and almost totally.... For the army, this may have been the hardest period, harder than that of the battles.... It was also the general feeling in the Yishuv [this term remained in use even after independence as a synonym for the Israeli community at large], which continued to influence the army.... I was not privileged to be a soldier ... in this war, but I was a soldier in the Jewish Legion in the First World War. And I remember the sense of unburdening among the soldiers, both Jewish and British, when the war was over. Everyone wanted to go home. It was politically necessary to maintain the army – but the soldiers saw no point in their staying there, and discipline in the British Army slackened. The Israel Defense Forces did not even have the tradition of discipline and order and thrift that the British Army has. At this point of transition, the army went through a serious organizational and moral crisis.... Not all the rumors [about corruption, embezzlement, and waste in the IDF] were groundless, although the situation in the civilian Yishuv was no better.[1]

Here, we will not delve into the thicket of Israel's first postwar year. Ben-Gurion set up a four-person investigative committee – three members of the Knesset and, as chair, the Supreme Court Justice Yitzhak Olshan – to probe the rumors, which he assumed to be at least partly true. He consoled himself by noting that even General Washington's army, that of the American patriarch, "[was] established by a plantation owner in Virginia on a historical occasion slightly similar to ours . . . and I may say that our army, even in its most flawed manifestations, has nothing to be ashamed of in comparison with . . . Washington's army." True enough: Washington's forces suffered more defeats than victories and survived their gravest crises due to the greatness of their general – all of which until the French absolutist monarchy came to the nascent American republic's aid and tipped the scales in its favor, at an immense price that would eventually help to foment the French Revolution.

The right comparison to make, I would say, is not between the IDF, established on the eve of the War of Independence, and the American Army in the Revolution but between the IDF and the army of the North in the American Civil War, almost a century later. Such a comparison was recently made by the Israeli military historian Colonel (Res.) Professor Yehuda Wallach,[2] who availed himself, on the one hand, of Zahava Ostfeld's important study *Tsava nolad*[3] and studies by his Israeli pupils Elhanan Oren and Meir Pa'il, and, on the other hand, of a varied corpus of recent critical literature about the American Civil War. Systematically comparing all aspects of the almost ex nihilo establishment of an army in the midst of a lengthy and blood-soaked war in the United States with the establishment of the Israel Defense Forces, Wallach explicitly shows the superiority of the Israeli Army in many respects, from total mobilization – which did not work properly in the American North until the end of the war – to the training of commanders during the Hagana era, procurements, communications, tactics, and strategic conduct of the war, which in both countries was entrusted to the head of the political echelon. The secessionist Confederate states were ready to fight a life-or-death war – as they construed it – and viewed the conflict accordingly as a war of the many (the industrialized North) against the few (the agrarian South). The results of the war hinged largely on the involvement or assistance of foreign powers (Britain and France), which, the Confederacy hoped, might deem the independent South to be a fait accompli after observing developments on the ground and for economic and political reasons of their own. In other words, the correct comparison is with the South – which Wallach overlooked – and not with the wealthy, righteous, flabby, and rather corrupt industrial North, which was headed by an outstanding statesman. The correct comparison is with the intrepid but wrong South, fighting for its very existence as it perceived it under its talented commanders, Robert E. Lee, "Stonewall" Jackson, and Nathan Bedford Forrest, the likes of whom the victorious North did not have until the emergence of Ulysses S. Grant, William T. Sherman, George Henry Thomas, and Philip Sheridan. The North also triumphed because the southern political echelon fell immeasurably short of Lincoln's stature and made too many strategic mistakes.

The winning side in Israel's War of Independence, while being the weaker and poorer, was the one that had technological, tactical, and strategic advantages and enjoyed outside assistance that was withheld from the Arabs during the war. Due to the Arabs' dependence on Western arms supplies at the time, the West's embargo stymied both sides, while Israel was able to secure Soviet-authorized supplies because of Stalin's interest in weakening Western influence in the region. The question that arises here is this: From whom should we learn the lessons of the victory in the 1948 war, a victory attained at steep cost and under special conditions that could not persist for long, even in the realm of hope? The IDF and its commanders had to be taught not to rest on their laurels. The American Civil War had a "final" outcome: Once the South's ability to secede had been broken, the United States of America would remain one political entity. In contrast, it was not at all clear to Ben-Gurion that the War of Independence had attained a similar finality, given the geopolitical and strategic realities at the regional and global levels.

We will return to these realities presently; for the time being, we should mention foreseeable changes in the Arab world and in the quantitative balance of forces that would steadily turn in the Arabs' favor.[4] In his aforementioned speech in the Knesset, in June 1950, the minister of defense had the following to say:

I'm afraid that anyone who talks about power – cheap, easy, and convenient security – is oblivious to the security problem of this country and its population. We are one against forty. This balance of forces will not change even if immigration continues steadily.... We may be the only "non-conformist" people on earth. We are exceptional in the world of today, as we have been throughout our millennia of existence. We do not fit the general model of humankind. Some say it's because we are defective. I would say that it's because the general *model* [italics in the original transcript] is defective and we neither acquiesce in nor adjust to it.... One of the most pointed manifestations of our "non-conformism" is reflected in the Jerusalem issue [i.e., the recognition of West Jerusalem as Israel's capital by foreign powers, which has remained moot to this day]. There's a contrast and there's a difference. We are different from all the surroundings that envelop us – a cultural and social and economic difference, and this difference will steadily widen.[5]

All of this was said at a time when mass immigration would change the makeup and quality of Israel's population.

Ben-Gurion's solution to this dilemma in the conventional realm, as I understand it, was to turn around and establish a regular professional army along lines approximating the British model to the extent necessary. There would have to be differences, of course. For one thing, the Israeli Army would also be "a place where national unity will be created."[6] However, two issues troubled Ben-Gurion greatly. One was the typical Israeli way of shirking problems and responsibilities by mouthing clichés, such as "Trust me" and "It'll be OK." Ben-Gurion was well acquainted with this manner of conduct; he had encountered it in various types of Eastern European Jews, the so-called *luftmentshen* – a Yiddish term denoting people unhinged from reality – who in their years of exile had grown accustomed to passivity and unending improvisation. He also knew their opposites, people graced with keen tactical intelligence and much cunning, who busied themselves at "Jewish wars" in order to promote their sundry beliefs and attain prestige and power in a hostile world – for all the good this did them at times of crisis, such as the Holocaust. This "trust me" climate, coupled with the typical Jewish mind-set of "It won't happen to me" and "I'll surely survive," originated in the general nature of humankind whenever disaster loomed. It was also, however, one of the explanations for the shortsightedness that these Jews displayed on the eve of, and during, the Holocaust. Its origins should be sought in the exilic Jewish education and the sense of supremacy that it seemed to have given its victims. Now, this feeling needed an injection of new traits, related to the Jews' return to their place in history as it really was. Indeed, acceptance of the burden of sovereignty signifies not a gratuitous enslavement to a "state" and an "army" but, rather, a return to history and to an awareness of reality – and the abandonment of belief in miracles that would never come to pass.

An example of belief in miracles was the view– widely held in the Yishuv shortly before the War of Independence – that the Arab states would not intervene in the war, or that some would not intervene, or that faraway Iraq surely would not intervene. Thus, as the belief had it, the impending war might be a mere reprise of the 1936–1939 Palestinian guerrilla war; if so, why bother trying to obtain heavy weaponry abroad? Yes, individuals displayed immense heroism in the War of Independence, but such heroism often originated in improvisation born of necessity. While one should not condemn necessity, one also should not make it into a guideline for the next round of "Trust me" and "It'll be OK." Israel, in Ben-Gurion's thinking, dared not make the spirit of improvisation, the product of a combination of sophomoric "grassrootsism" and sectarian-group ideology, into the guiding philosophy of the army of a nation that had chosen to return to history and probably failed to appreciate how profound a decision this was.

The second issue that troubled Ben-Gurion concerned another unhealthy attitude flowing from the typical Israeli-Jewish method of improvisation: groups that waved this method aloft like a banner, took pride in it, and fought under its umbrella for their status and dignity with characteristic fanaticism that originated in group/personal interests, as was the case with the leftist Palmach commando. As soon as Ben-Gurion took up the defense portfolio, and afterwards as well, he studied the Hagana, roughly thirty years old, and found manifestations of group loyalties there, too: keeping information within the group instead of passing it along to others, bureaucratic muck, and "Jewish wars" that had been typical since time immemorial. These were problems of a nation unaccustomed to self-rule; by implication, Zionism had not yet adequately solved them despite its pretensions.

In terms of content, there were Palmach people who viewed Soviet-style *partisanka* as an original Israeli contribution to war theory, so to speak. Ben-Gurion suspected them not of sublime originality but of its absence. It was true:

The spirit of the "Men of Panfilov" (an account that described the heroism of the Soviet soldiers who defended Moscow in World War II) and Soviet guerrilla units that operated deep behind enemy lines pulsed through the veins of the disciples of Yitzhak Sadeh, the pre-state commander of the Palmach. Their passion for such stories, however, overlooked the fact that these partisans were but the irksome agents of a mighty regular army. Sadeh himself preached the image of a muscular, manly, Greek-like "fighting Jew," redolent with immaturity and wont to form insular groups under the leadership of a quasi-guru.

Sadeh eventually became one of the commanders of the first armored divisions in the Israel Defense Forces. Even then, however, he did not mask his admiration for Stalin's Soviet Union, and Ben-Gurion never gave him the trust that was needed to allow him to shape the IDF after the war. Several of Sadeh's former disciples, foremost Yigal Allon and Yitzhak Rabin, acknowledged the importance of large regular forces and contributed immensely to the forming and shaping of them. Allon, however, was a political creature and a member of a political party that was pro-Soviet during Stalin's lifetime. While serving as an active general in the IDF and afterwards, he had views of his own – about the desired expansion of Israel's frontiers on the West Bank and the imposition of peace on Egypt by occupying territories in Sinai – and he tried to persuade the general staff that he was right in these matters, without authorization from the minister of defense.

In this respect, Ben-Gurion faced a Gordian knot that had to be forcibly untied. Here was a political party – a coalition of two leftist groups under the leadership of Yitzhak Tabenkin and his Palmach disciples – that aspired to control and oversee the army or parts of it by keeping the Palmach's separate staff active alongside the IDF general staff after the war. This could not be allowed, especially in view of the party's Soviet orientation. Equally, Menachem Begin's IZL could not be allowed to maintain its own army, distinct from the IDF. Therefore, force had to be applied when this organization attempted to import weapons for the IDF and for its own separate units in Jerusalem, in an operation known as the "Altalena Affair." As an outgrowth of the lesson learned from these affairs, Ben-Gurion continued to hold up the British Army as a dual model: not only of a professional fighting force but also of a military entity subordinate to the elected political authority. If a "British-style" army was the desired model, we should first clarify what this means.

Before anything else, let us note that Britain itself went through a period of severe internal ideological fragmentation and polarization that not only resulted in religious wars and split the army into royalist forces and a militia that, in the course of a civil war, evolved into the so-called New Model Army, that is, that of a fundamentalist religious sect, but also carried this sectarian force – led by Oliver Cromwell ("Old Ironsides") and throbbing with Puritan religious passion – to victory. Cromwell, one of history's greatest generalissimos, ultimately became a military dictator who defeated the Scots and quelled the Catholic uprising in Ireland in an orgy of blood and fire that verged on genocide, leaving wounds that still remain unhealed fully today. During Cromwell's tenure as Lord Protector of England, Scotland, and Ireland, Britain was divided into regional military commands, each ruled by an officer at the grade of major-general, corresponding to the grade of *aluf* in the IDF. The British, however, overthrew this regime of generals and suffocating religious Puritan rule after Cromwell's death, setting out on a path that led to a constitutional monarchy governed by Parliament.

One of the fundamental aims of this method of governance, now entrenched as a tradition, would be to prevent the recurrence of military rule in Britain at all costs, that is, to keep the army out of politics and generals out of civilian affairs. In other words, the British system offered no passage from the military echelon to the political as a matter of course. Admittedly, for quite some time, senior officers were involved with various courtiers. However, Britain did not breed military nobility that wielded political influence and allowed no passage from the senior military echelon to the political one in modern times, except in anomalous cases such as that of Lord Kitchener, but junior officers, such as Churchill in his earlier incarnation, and middle-grade reserve officers, such as Clement Attlee, could engage in politics after having shed their uniforms.

Traditionally, membership in the officer corps often required family and personal wealth due to expenses related to military and social status. However, officers received their professional training in suitable military schools. Thus, most of them – by and large – were good professionals who received promotions by the seniority method that Ben-Gurion never dreamed of adopting. You could count on certain things about these officers: their allegiance to the political echelon no matter what, their discipline, their courage, their willingness to pay the supreme price required of their profession, and a consciousness of service instilled in them by their special education. Some became world renowned; others fit the "Colonel Blimp" description, that is, stupid, obtuse, unimaginative, arrogant officers who could not cope intellectually and socially – in their relations with commoner enlisted men – with the true challenges of modern war. The Colonel Blimp syndrome was even more complicated than that because this human type carried typical traits of the entire British heritage in the historical phase of decline and degeneration that marked the British upper classes after World War I. Chief among these traits were an empiricism that breached all limits of common sense, a short-term utilitarian way of looking at things, and refusal to take a long-term view of anything. "Don't rock the boat" was their adage, along with other clichés that might work in ordinary times but not at times of upheaval, ongoing pressure and conflict, war, and global transformations.[7] Indeed, this syndrome accounts for Britain's "appeasement policy" toward Nazi Germany and several of its worst defeats during the war.

Ben-Gurion himself, however, had nothing to do with such a syndrome; all his life he took the long-range view. Furthermore, in his eyes these indolent Britons, who seemed in the throes of decline and degeneration, were able, when confronted with a supreme crisis, to abandon their lassitude and prejudices in matters essential to victory, to overcome their exaggerated empiricism, and to set aside the vacillations about Hitler that typified the appeasement era, view him as a no-holds-barred enemy, and mobilize their nation for a war that would end with Hitler's defeat and the salvation of humankind.

Therefore, Ben-Gurion adopted the British model in several specific respects, especially the subordination of the army to the political echelon – the one that directed a political system that enabled a quiet transition from the appeasement policy to the Churchill-Attlee-Bevin fighting coalition – as well as the military professionalism and discipline that distinguish a regular army from volunteer militias, such as the half-trained British Territorials. The challenge was to maximize the advantages of this system and to avoid its disadvantages under Israel's radically different conditions.

It was true that Great Britain had gone through most of its imperial era without a conscript army; it had only a permanent army of long-term volunteers. The Royal Navy, which had been professionalized since the eighteenth century, inured the British Isles to foreign invasion. Over time, a second factor may have joined the first: awareness that dependency on the public at large – that is, the conscripts – in matters of war and peace would severely restrict the political echelon's latitude, exactly what happened when Britain instituted general mobilization during and at the end of World War I, as Ben-Gurion noted in his diary at the time it occurred. One of the manifestations of this phenomenon was the British government's refusal to counter Hitler with force until the nation formed a consensus on the topic, which it did only after the Nazis had built up so much strength as to become a grave threat that would have been less grave had the British stopped them in time. The British had left the Nazis unchecked for two reasons: because the military people who dealt with this problem were ridiculously empirical, as described – they initially disregarded the Nazi threat and understated it immeasurably at the time – and because the nation had not given its government an explicit mandate to go to war, a war that would entail another general mobilization. The price of stopping Hitler after the formation of consensus was much greater than the price that the British would have paid had they not waited for it. The problem of general mobilization of the people in a democracy, then, was a political one, and Israel, too, would have to cope with it.

The basic, underlying premise of the parliamentary majority, as formed over the generations, was that uncontrolled power corrupts and complete power corrupts completely, to paraphrase Lord Acton in the nineteenth century. Although every citizen in today's Western democracies accepts this fundamental truth, it did not lead in the British case to a U.S.-style institutional separation of powers or judicial review of the legislative authority's actions. The judicial branch did review government actions, but only within the framework of various articles of customary law – as interpreted by the judiciary itself – that Parliament was allowed to change at any time. The British, back then, did not consider American-style separation of powers worthy of emulation because it caused such fragmentation of power among the players that it could lead to their immobilization. This, Ben-Gurion noted, is exactly what a hostile Congress did to Franklin Roosevelt, largely tying his hands in foreign and defense affairs until the Japanese attacked Pearl Harbor. The British forged an alternative political culture, one of governance by "rules of the game," that guided Parliament and the government in order to tend to the general welfare or to "the common good" on the basis of a specific mandate received in elections. From the moment it received its mandate, the government was empowered to take concerted, forceful action and to rely on the legislature to give the executive branch the latitude that it needed. Members of the government owe the legislature "ministerial accountability," an agent's responsibility for the actions of the lowliest of his or her subordinates, whether such actions were taken with full knowledge or not. The judiciary protects personal rights within the framework of laws that Parliament may amend without the courts' intervention.

Today, an attempt has been made to transplant to Israel the U.S. system of separation of powers and, by force of a basic law to this effect, to situate the Supreme Court as the reviewer and interpreter of legislation. The argument behind this initiative is that all matters, including questions of war and peace, are "justiciable." Obviously, this attempt is incompatible with the British constitutional tradition, which postulates that power without parliamentary review corrupts. To be precise, parliamentary control is exercised by elected officials who may be included among members of investigative committees that wield judicial power if the executive authority so requests, for example, the Olshan Commission, or when public necessity arises. Judges serve on such committees, for the most part, but the judiciary per se does not function as the reviewer of other branches in political, strategic, and similar affairs, which by implication belongs to the legislature. Concurrently, British customary law allows every citizen to sue a government official – and his or her superordinates – for wrongdoing in view of the existing law and its amendments.

In the British method, members of the civil service class were raised at home, and in a special network of civilian and military schools, to respect the rules of the game and to serve the public. The importance of sports, especially team sports, in the upbringing of these public servants, and the influence of the Protestant value system of the middle and the upper-middle classes, often conflated to create a unique syndrome of behavior that other cultures did not offer and could not duplicate because they lacked a similar institutional-education infrastructure. As the previously quoted Joel Krieger says, however, the British bureaucracy wielded (and still wields) enormous power that eventually overshadowed the authority of Parliament, for reasons that include its everlasting permanence – after all, governments come and go in elections – and similarities in the education, experience and knowledge, and the cooperative tradition of its people. Two large ruling parties succeed each other due to rivalry, one party usually receiving an absolute majority that members are unwilling to violate lest they precipitate early elections.[8]

After the fact, the government did become increasingly involved in many areas of British life. This was an outcome of the Industrial Revolution and the urban revolution, which spawned intolerable social disparities and manifesta-tions of exploitation, severe poverty, and pockets of crime and protest on the British Isles that the traditional social system – the apparatus of the traditional courts and the law-enforcement authorities – were unable to surmount in tradi-tional ways. Therefore, the two large parties of the late nineteenth century, the Liberals – whose tradition eschewed government involvement in economic and social affairs – and the Conservatives, agreed to pass more and more welfare and social-service laws and to apply them by means of a modern bureaucracy that branched out over time. The government was definitely mindful of the lower classes' needs. And even if the traditional parties took a patronizing and often condescending attitude toward these classes, it was nevertheless very sensitive to the social dynamite inherent in the disparities between the lower classes and the elites and to the need for action to narrow the gaps, if not to eliminate them totally. Indeed, instead of the basic French Revolution concept of *égalité*, which clashed with the ways in which they expressed personal free-dom, the British adopted, practically if not necessarily theoretically, other and less pregnant tenets. One of them, which ultimately became prominent, was the aforementioned concept of fairness, which for its fulfillment required appro-priate rules of the game. The practical use of this concept did narrow the gaps among the British classes and did so without as much friction as égalité, which seemed inconsistent with the concept of freedom, would have engendered.

Thus, the ascendancy of the Labour Party, the Liberals' twentieth-century successor, created parliamentary tools for the participation of the working class in government; afterwards, the working class rose to parliamentary power in general elections. The process was neither simple nor easy: In the 1920s, ten-sion between Labour and the Conservatives was so strong and extreme that the British elites dispelled it in the 1930s only by acknowledging the social gaps and the need to find a common language with the working class and its party. The latter two accepted the principle of a market economy and refrained from risking revolution and the destruction of the existing economic order at times of global crisis, instead wishing to help to rehabilitate the system. The elites, in turn, made strenuous efforts to solve problems of housing, edu-cation, and employment due to concern for the lower classes and, as stated, acknowledgment of the potential for havoc that these classes represented.[9] In the mid-1940s, Labour came to power and set out to implement far-reaching programs in order to advance toward genuine equality in the British welfare state. Parliament passed any number of statutes and regulations for this pur-pose, with no power in the system to stop it. The rules of the game allowed this, just as they would allow a different elected Parliament to repeal several of these laws later on.

The "art of politics" – by which the British elites judged themselves as being more expert than others – was the art of leading and navigating a fractured, unequal class society. Such leadership prevented social meltdown and made it possible to correct injustices and improve the masses' ways of life by applying sensitivity and attentiveness to events among them, while neither despairing of the stability of the system nor losing control of it. Under such leadership, talented people from all classes could advance by means of the education system – including Oxford and Cambridge – to participation in the elite ranks irrespective of their origins. Members of the middle classes could be trained for public service at private schools and at the two elite universities, provided they could afford the privilege. However, the belief in "social engineering" per se – that is, gradual change and, at times, sweeping reform by means of parliamentary legislation that the civil service would apply – became increasingly the province of the elites in the twentieth century. Many of Ben-Gurion's demands and pretensions, as we shall see, cannot be understood unless one acknowledges this perspective of government and sound administration as factors that could transform the structure and contents of a society. Here our Renaissance model must be abandoned for a while.

The British Parliament and the government (the executive branch) that emerged from its midst, answered to it, and functioned as its executive arm wielded enormous power. One might say that so long as the government commanded a majority in Parliament – as it generally did because the constituency-majority electoral method, the product of history and tradition, usually gave one party an absolute majority – it was supposed to govern, that is, to carry out a policy in view of a mandate that the nation gave it in general elections, to be mindful of the nation's express desires even afterwards, and to make decisions on their merits. Thus, the British governing entities that were entrusted with defense, including the army, the navy, and the security services, historically displayed prodigious ability to execute within the framework of the British "rule of law" wherever matters of war, peace, and internal security were concerned.

The rule of law at times of crisis and emergency meant, for example, parliamentary legislation that outlawed Sir Oswald Mosley's Fascist Party and landed its members in detention camps by means of administrative orders. Theoretically, Parliament could have outlawed Nazi criminals as well – note the precision: Parliament and only Parliament could have done this – and let them be rushed to the gallows.[10] The British did try to accomplish this at the end of World War II, arguing that the Germans would construe the war crimes trials as persecution of the losers by the victors, thereby defeating the purpose of the tribunal by furnishing Nazi criminals with an undeserved defense. In other words, in British eyes, the problem of Nazism, and especially concern about its revival, related not only to punishing the criminals and how to go about this – after all, such criminals numbered in the tens if not the hundreds of thousands – but rather, and also, to offering a functional and efficient democratic alternative to the Nazi ideology and praxis.

From the traditional British perspective, the judicial system is limited in its ability to act for society's betterment because the main responsibility in this respect belongs to the political system. Obviously, interpreters of the American Constitution in the 1940s could not accept this. They subscribed to something like today's Israeli "everything is judiciable" outlook; that is, they saw everything as subject to judicial review. However, the application of conventional Western judicial norms – which the British themselves had fashioned into fundamentals of their "state of law" – to the external and internal enemies of the kingdom without political latitude was thought to clash with common sense. Common sense means that if one treats an enemy as an enemy at a time of war or emergency, afterwards the political echelon need not tie itself in knots of denial about having given orders to commit various acts of violence against him or her. A maximum of secrecy has to be maintained in this regard; otherwise, the political echelon would be held to political account for acts of violence that it had ordered or that its subordinates committed without its knowledge, in the event that some stupid or unreasonable action failed the test of topical review of its severity and damage. Once such review were to be pursued in Parliament and by the media, it would be a public issue from that moment on. It is in this manner that one may understand Pinchas Lavon's argument, expressed after he had been unseated as Israel's minister of defense, that he had been made into the victim by his subordinates' actions. So, too, may one construe his demand, years after the fact, for political exculpation and dismissal of responsibility for actions carried out within the framework of the ministry that he had headed as minister. If "everything is political" and judicial authority seems limited, then Lavon could demand political, and not judicial, exoneration. Here, however, Lavon made a gross error in regard to the British system itself.

The British rules of the game do not allow a serving government to absolve a minister in a previous government of ministerial responsibility or to investigate the actions of the previous government, except in pronouncedly criminal matters that are discovered after the fact. This is exactly the argument that Lavon employed, demanding that Ben-Gurion not investigate the actions of an executive who had served in the Sharett government, in which he himself had been a member and from which he had been ousted. Instead, he handed down his own verdict of innocence in view of new findings that had come to his knowledge and demanded total rehabilitation from a serving government that had not been involved in his ouster.

This business of rules becomes truly profound in the transition from an ideological society to an institutional one. The "culture of governance" – what is and is not done – is a cumulative collection of rules of behavior, of procedures, and of methods of reporting, verifying, and disseminating information, which everyone accepts as binding: members of the parliament, the members of the government in their relations with counterparts in the opposition, the prime minister, his or her ministers, and their subordinates who command the armed forces. The instilling of these rules among parliamentarians and the members of the government that emerges from the parliament is not just a matter of a tradition and the practices that it spawns and passes on intergenerationally in a traditional society, that is, one that values tradition and traditional values per se. It concerns a specific political method that rests on a two-party system and the entrenched factional discipline that Lavon would eventually shatter in all directions in his campaign to cleanse himself.

At this stage, as the method was taking shape, Ben-Gurion was hoping to instill parliamentary rules of the game and collective government discipline by exploiting his party's pivotal position in the coalition that he had put together after the 1949 elections. Eventually, however, he came to the conclusion that there really was no choice but to change the whole system and predicate it on the British electoral method and two-party paradigm.

How were worthy rules of the game instilled among members of the British Army? By means of education at home and via the military education system, from the moment the young cadet entered the Royal Military Academy in Sandhurst and continuing up to the Imperial War College. Afterwards, he strove for the summit of his military career, aiming for a position that would entail daily contact with the political echelon, which he would advise in matters of war and peace as one who knew the system and its constraints and vacillations. Such people know that most members of their caste will never cross into the political echelon and may even fall victim to their own blunders and those of democratic governments that do not prepare properly for war. They find their compensation in the typical coin of social prestige: the award of low and high degrees of nobility, various external manifestations of high class, and profound self-satisfaction with their devoted service to their homeland.

The assumption was that it would always be possible to recruit enough people, including the junior and senior noncommissioned officers around whom traditional regiments are permanently built, men who would treat the army not only as a profession but also as a lifelong mission, and who would regard war – if there were no choice but to prosecute one – as their occupation and the arena of their future success and advancement. Indeed, for many centuries, until our era, the atomic age, when wholesale conventional warfare became impossible – all the way to the profound changes in their social structures today and the emergence of multiculturalism – the peoples of Europe did produce such men, people who regarded combat as an occupation worthy of them and pledged their lives to its preparation and implementation. When there was no choice but general mobilization, it was they, these professional soldiers, who became the spine of the conscript British Army, and it was they who instilled discipline, pride, and esprit de corps in the army despite its many defeats in the two world wars, thanks to the traditional sense of citizenship and rules of the game that the British people found acceptable, and to its education system. In the following section, we observe the elements that Ben-Gurion wished to adopt from this army, true to his times, despite the many differences between the two peoples at issue, of which he was aware before he undertook this task.

The Creation of the IDF and the Decision to Disband the Separate Staff of the Palmach

Let us investigate the points discussed as reflected in the IDF's formative period.

The first point is the establishment of an apolitical army. At first glance, the IDF did not seem to be one. Ben-Gurion banished putative rivals from the embryonic Ministry of Defense and the IDF for illegitimate political activities or for politically inspired demands by untrustworthy people who represented vested interests. Examples were Yisrael Galili, whom he dislodged from his position as chief of the IDF national staff, and Yigal Allon, whose continued service as officer commanding (OC) the Southern Command he thwarted by replacing him with a trusted officer, later with General Moshe Dayan. What is more, he allowed uniformed associates – foremost Dayan – to engage in overt political activity such as rallies during the First Knesset election campaign, held in January 1949. He explained the dismissal of Galili and, indirectly, of Allon – insofar as they managed to understand it – by claiming that they had been "undermining the foundations of the army." If so, we should analyze these matters on their own merits and not only as Ben-Gurion explained them then and thereafter.

Dayan's case seems much more serious than the others, for here a high-ranking army officer was allowed to cross from the military echelon into the political domain almost directly – after a cooling-off period – and join the government. From then on, Dayan would put his military prestige as former chief of the general staff (COGS) to effective use until it elevated him to the post of minister of defense in the National Unity Government of 1967, the government headed by Levi Eshkol, the formation of which Ben-Gurion opposed.

Nevertheless, it is hard to view the personalities at issue as "professional military men" of the British stripe. Truth to tell, there were few of that kind. Among the few were former members of the Jewish Brigade Group, which served in the British Army during World War II, and the standing echelon of the Hagana, composed of the likes of Efraim Ben-Artzi, Fritz Eshet, Yochanan Ratner, and Ya'akov Dori, whom Ben-Gurion wished to integrate into the IDF high command when the army was very much in its infancy. Dori was indeed given his appointment but did not serve as active COGS during most of the war because of ill health. Others encountered resistance on the grounds that they were outsiders who had been "parachuted" into their posts; they served in various staff capacities even though Ben-Gurion regarded such former members of the British Army, or those who had previous European military experience, as "real soldiers." Although he placed some of them in high command positions, he was unable to foist them on the general staff that he had inherited from the Hagana period. In the middle of the war, he even had to contend with a mutiny in the general staff when he tried to dominate it as the authorized representative of the political echelon and when he dismissed Galili from his post as chief of the national staff while trying to appoint as many "soldiers" as possible to key functions in the IDF. The insurrection led to a debate in the provisional government, which even tried to set up a five-member committee among its members to teach the minister of defense how to behave in the future. The mutiny ended in response to the danger of resumed fighting in the summer of 1948; after this menace blew over, Ben-Gurion's definitive authority was accepted.[11]

Dayan had been a farmer and quasi-soldier since adolescence. Like his colleague and rival Yigal Allon, he was a protégé of the pro-Zionist British intelligence officer Orde Wingate, from whom he had learned irregular methods of combat. After having been wounded during the British invasion of Syria in World War II, he assumed political duties on the Hagana staff, such as maintaining limited contact with Menachem Begin's IZL and assessing Begin's intentions, in this capacity demonstrating good political judgment. Allon was later named commander of the Palmach and then became a full-fledged political person who followed the path of Mapai's pro-Soviet Faction B and the nationalist leftist Achdut ha-Avoda Party, which ceded from Mapai in 1944. Clearly, then, it was Dayan who, in Ben-Gurion's eyes, should be appreciated. He belonged to the right camp, the one from which the future IDF high command team would be formed, the one that loyally accepted the ruling majority's authority and the legal power therefrom. What is more, Dayan had acquired practical political experience when he negotiated with Menachem Begin before independence and, later, with officers of the Arab Legion as commander of the Jerusalem District following the 1948 war. Thus, it was hard to say ab initio whether Dayan was a soldier or a politician or both. He was of a generation in which the two intermingled.

The separation of these fields, however, was at least a principle – to which, as usual, there were exceptions – that Ben-Gurion adopted in the "British" style as one that should be imposed in all domains of the system of governance. Absent such a system, he preferred to subject at least the army to gradual apoliticization. After securing for himself a definitive position of power – as a minister of defense who represented the majority party in parliament, which had been granted constitutional legitimacy as a result of the First Knesset elections, held in January 1949 – he refused to share this power with anyone whom he suspected of sectarianism and lack of a state-service consciousness. He also refused to share it with members of a party that had previously demonstrated total blindness in regard to the continuation of the Mandate for Palestine, that wished to keep the country undivided under Soviet-American patronage, and that followed Yitzhak Tabenkin – a leader who, though not a member of the Knesset, instructed his people how to behave there. In Anita Shapira's opinion, at issue were several cunning demarches that caused injustice to selected individuals whom she considered defense experts, such as Yisrael Galili, who was neutralized during the War of Independence and wrongfully unseated from his post as chief of the defense staff because he had reported to his mentor and faction leader, Yitzhak Tabenkin, about what was going on in the army-in-formation. This disingenuousness introduced vagueness about Tabenkin's extraparliamentary status, since although he did not sit in the legislature and was not answerable to it, he received reports about matters that belonged to its sovereign purview and influenced them in his own way. However, it also blurred the principled and dire significance of the mutiny that members of the general staff had launched against the defense minister during the war.[12]

Given these special conditions of running the country at the helm of an unelected provisional government, Ben-Gurion had to force a decision by threatening to resign, which he did several times. As time passed, he crafted the IDF by pushing through numerous laws and government resolutions that, in total, established the nature of the army as an institution that serves the public and is totally subordinate to the political echelon. The provisional government and its successor, elected in January 1949, held extensive and recurrent debates about this matter and other security-related affairs, the army and its structure, and the civil service that would be established – following the British model to the greatest possible extent – during the essential phases of transition from Yishuv to state. However, these were not the top-down decrees of a dictator who treated the government of Israel as his personal fiefdom.[13] On the contrary: Since the elected government was – and remains – a coalition based on a proportional balloting system, Ben-Gurion was never free to ignore his coalition partners, and except for the defense portfolio, he did not succeed in introducing a civil service in all ministries that functioned under representatives of other political parties.

As for the structure of the IDF, at the end of the fighting, the minister of defense wished to establish a cadre of professional officers that would no longer be "subordinate to itself," as the Hagana had been. Thus, Ben-Gurion said on July 21, 1949, in a candid exchange with former Palmach members and others:

For all practical purposes, the Hagana was subordinate to itself. The [IDF] is not subordinate to itself and will not be subordinate to itself. It is subordinate to the state and to it alone. No officer, no staff, and no chief of staff will control the army, only civilians who will be appointed for this purpose by the state. The constitution and modus operandi of the army will emanate not from the army but from representatives of the state. This is not to say that the agents of the state are impervious to error or nonsense – [civilians and] soldiers can make mistakes, too – but these will originate in the authorized agents and institutions of the state. They alone will determine how the army goes about its affairs.

I totally agree with what Lieutenant Colonel Tabenkin [Yosef Tabenkin, a Palmach commander and son of the former head of Faction B and, afterwards, leader of the Achdut ha-Avoda–Po'alei Zion Party] said. His opinion is as meritorious as mine. His opinion may be more important than mine; I never had the privilege of being a lieutenant colonel. I was briefly a corporal [in the Jewish Legion of the British Army during World War I], and they took that away from me, too. On pioneering and kibbutz settlement, too, his views are definitely more important than mine because, after all, I'm considered the "destroyer of pioneering values." He can say whatever he wants. But there's one difference: A person who's an emissary of the state speaks with the authority of the state, and this gives his view a different status than that of Lieutenant Colonel Tabenkin. Tabenkin's . . . opinion is an opinion; it should be heard and he can express it anywhere and persuade the public. But one who speaks on behalf of the state has already persuaded the public to accept his opinion; it is not necessary for the entire nation to be convinced and to accept his opinion. And if the majority so determines, then it is law, and if the state's representative . . . has the authority, then his opinion is not merely someone's personal one. . . . If an authorized person or institution comes along and says, against . . . Tabenkin's view that he cannot engage in politics in the army and elsewhere [because he is in uniform], his view settles the matter because the army is subordinate to the state constitution. . . . One cannot be sure in regard to any law that it will not be violated. There's a law that says "Thou shalt not murder" and it gets violated, too.[14]

Ben-Gurion's claim that the "majority's decision" is "law" may sound odd in our times. Today, everyone talks about upholding minority rights and thwarting "dictatorship by the majority" by installing a constitution that supersedes ordinary legislation. We shall rediscuss the constitution issue separately, but we should state at this juncture that American concepts such as upholding majority rule had not been accepted in the United States in Lincoln's time, when a large and aggressive minority refused to accept the majority's decision on an issue for which the U.S. Constitution could be interpreted either way. In the British Parliament, too, a majority of members of the House of Commons could amend any statute – apart from laws of ancient provenance that lent themselves not to amendments but to endless refinements, for example, the traditional laws of justice. The only exception arose in emergencies that entailed action against minorities that threatened majority rule.

Sticking to his guns, Ben-Gurion continued his July 21 remarks:

I ask my comrades in one matter not to use . . . threats in the debate. . . . Therefore, I do not accept the threat that [Avraham Yoffe, formerly of the Palmach] expressed to keep me from running. I ran in the Knesset elections and I will run. Many people have also run and are running. So it will continue to be . . . because I believe in democracy and free [electoral] competition. The majority has to be persuaded, not physically forced. However, there must be no politicking in the army and no politicking among segments of the army and among the standing army and among serving reservists. The concept of overt "politicking" is something you have to forget about in any matter related to exploring military affairs. You can explore [ideas] in the army, you can have discussion, short or long, good or bad, and after the explorations there will be a consensual decision, not by the army but by the state, and that will put an end to it.

Here, we are alerted to the special meaning that Ben-Gurion invested in the concept of "state," a usage that evoked much antipathy and protestation against him then and today in its metamorphosis as *mamlakhtiyut*, a version of "étatism." The concept of "state" denotes "rule of law" within constitutional constructs that are governed by immutable rules of the game that apply to everyone. Even if someone violates said norm, it remains correct and valid. Members of the erstwhile voluntary Yishuv had to be educated in basic citizenship of this kind, and a fortiori those who are to serve in its army in the future. From this standpoint, Ben-Gurion considered it his personal duty to debate with former senior commanders of the Palmach who at the time were members of leftist parties, in an effort to educate them in his way. His attempt to rebuild the army after its postvictory slump, however, was pursued in accordance with "British" traits, foremost acceptance of the burden of discipline, order, and public service, coupled with the shaping of an ideal commander image, to which we will return. For the time being, he sparred with Shimon Avidan of Ha-Shomer ha-Tsa'ir, the Marxist kibbutz movement that merged with Tabenkin's Achdut ha-Avoda in January 1948 to form the united Mapam

Party. Avidan argued that the IDF command should not be staffed with Ben-Gurion's Mapai members but the other way around. After all, most of the command staff, including reservists, actually traced their origins to Mapam, an opposition minority party.[15]

Ben-Gurion quoted Avidan as having said, "When I am in the army, I am unwilling to relinquish my civilian rights," because he knew very well that a man in uniform is subject to a different regime: "The soldier's regime is unlike the whole civilian regime. It is the negation of rights, although not of all rights, of course." After all, he continued, "You don't ask [a soldier] whether he wants to do something or not, whether he is willing to do it or not." Then, although insisting that his audience would neither believe him nor heed him, Ben-Gurion declared, "Here the state and the army have no right to examine the views of people who serve in the army. The army can have people who belong to different parties, from the Communists to [Menachem] Begin or such other woes as we may have. These people will have full rights and their views will be equal to those of others" – provided, of course, that they, like all the others, accept the rule of the political echelon by virtue of its constitutional status, that is, the rule of law. "The state cannot examine the views of those in the army," he continued. "It must not examine their views; that's none of its business," unless their actions put the state at stake, that is, if they committed the sin of treason.

This issue certainly became more acute in view of Mapam's admiration of Stalin's Soviet Union as a "second homeland" and Mapam's blunt opposition to the pro-Western orientation that Ben-Gurion felt necessary to adopt from the early 1950s onward for reasons that came within the purview of the elected political echelon only.

At this stage in his remarks, the defense minister addressed, not for the first time, the charges about the loss of "vision, spirit, and pioneerism" that had come about, according to former Palmach and Mapam people, by Ben-Gurion's dismantling of the Palmach and "nationalization" of the IDF:

It has nothing to do with [matters of pioneerism, rural settlement, and their spirit]. It has to do with political activity within the army and by members of the army [which should be firmly thwarted].... From Tabenkin's words I get the impression that he said the following: "There's one group in the army and in Israel that holds title to the assets of pioneering, and this group in Israel and the army has the ability to fight." ... I don't think any group in Israel has a monopoly on pioneering, not even the pioneering groups. I admit that I was never a pioneer.... When I came to this country some time ago, they didn't know that word yet.... We – and I am speaking about those of my generation – began to work in this country forty-five years ago. We didn't start our careers in [Palestine] in the army, nor even in the Hagana, but with a simple and elementary thing – working, practicing a vocation. We looked at it as a mission.... The separation of mission from vocation is false, groundless, adopted from a foreign world.... Not everyone can and should make the army his vocation.... Anything that's needed for our defense and anything that's needed for immigration and immigrant absorption and rural settlement, that's a vocation and not just a mission. But the elite among our youth – and when I say elite, I don't mean only intellectual ability but also moral, intellectual, and physical ability – should be in the army. That's because everything depends on the security of the state and because the military is the most difficult and complex vocation. It demands constant training and total knowledge, the focusing of all strengths. Whatever one learns, it's not enough, one has to go on learning. And these fine people have to practice their vocation with the thought that it's a mission and should not be embarrassed to be practicing a vocation among us.

This jumble of assertions, expressed in a vein both sarcastic and conciliatory, reproachful and preaching, shows us that Ben-Gurion regarded the IDF – or, to be more precise, the segment of it known as the "standing army" – as a long-term vocation, as Anita Shapira claims disapprovingly,[16] a profession combined with the unique sense of mission that one hopes to find among the elite of the youth, since Israel lacked the aforementioned training mechanisms of the British officer corps and had no tradition of a proper political culture. In this matter, Ben-Gurion elaborated:

Today I heard a voice that joins this chorus. They wanted the Israel Defense Forces to have two kinds of people: one of inferior rank, the soldiers, and the other kind, the heroes. This is a disservice to historical truth and it's dangerous for the army, dangerous to educate the army that way, to have a privileged *Guardia* and a rabble.... Of course, once we had no army; all we had were people who performed feats of heroism [a reference to the Palmach, the only mobilized force on which the Yishuv leadership could call at first]. There is no monopoly on heroism, no monopoly on *esprit*, no monopoly on vision, and no monopoly on pioneering. I think – maybe wrongly – that my party is no less pioneering than other parties in this country, but I know people in it who are not pioneers. None of these matters has anything in common with party activity that endangers the army and has begun to erect barriers between those who are loyal and those who aren't.

Changing the subject to the disbanding of the Palmach, Ben-Gurion said that he appreciated the restraint ("repressing of the urge") that the participants in the debate displayed when they related to this topic. However, he added, "*It was done by the authority of the nation. The nation wanted a united army*" [emphasis added]. In other words, the issue was the democratic parliamentary legitimacy of the decisions of the political echelon, as in the classical British style, according to which this echelon may – and should – apply discretion of its own, especially in defense affairs due to their sensitivity and essential secrecy. Ben-Gurion's claim of representing "the state" at this stage was anchored in the relative majority that his Mapai Party had won in the January 1949 Knesset elections and in Mapai's pivotal standing between the Left and Right, which prevented any possible coalition-building without its consent and control of vital ministries, such as defense under the prime minister. At the same time, Ben-Gurion's public standing was at its highest due to his role as the architect of independence and of the victory in the ensuing war.

Israel's multiparty reality, however, was "first of all the erection of barriers between those who are loyal and those who aren't in the eyes of Mapam."

The work about Mapam's arguments should take place in the civilian public domain and be kept out of the army. The Hagana had left Israel a good legacy that should be maintained. The Hagana "also had parties and they made efforts to maintain internal integrity." Along with his criticism, one occasionally sees in Ben-Gurion's remarks this deliberate idealization of the past. However, as he explained to his listeners patiently, his point was that "this danger exists not only in the army; it also exists if soldiers take part in political activity outside the army. One cannot be an active participant in impugning the state and large population groups, something that's allowed under all laws, and afterwards to approach that portion of the public that one has impugned at rallies and issue them orders [in the army]."

Clearly, then, Ben-Gurion viewed military service as having the additional function of easing political controversy and friction in society at large. After all, those who serve in a people's army, especially in command positions – referring mainly to reservists – would find it hard to command subordinates who come from a "camp" other than their own, especially if they belong to a militant political minority in their civilian lives. This is the army's contribution to easing tension in Israel's schismatic and fractious society, in which the benefit of the British rules of the game is absent:

I'll give you an example, not because I want to dwell on this incident; any one of us can make such a mistake. There was a conference of soldiers, and at this conference the slogan, "The nigger has done his job – the nigger can go" appeared on a banner hoisted in the hall.... It exists in every army in the world: After the soldier does his job he is discharged. But there [at the conference of former Palmach people] that wasn't the intention, as I understand it. Instead, they meant it as a slur, and its purpose was to defame those who are running the country. That kind of thing can be done by any civilian, he's allowed to do it, any newspaper can do it.... A certain newspaper wrote that the prime minister sent only a certain kind of soldier to be killed, as David did to Uriah the Hittite. According to the law, that's a crime. But the minister of defense did not want to prosecute this newspaper on that charge [due to the principle of freedom of speech]. But if a soldier [makes similar remarks], he cannot do his duty as a partner in the fighting fraternity of which Tabenkin spoke. A great deal of fraternity is truly needed here, a great deal of partnership, because an army derives its effectiveness not from the effectiveness of an individual soldier or officer but from that of the public in which the officer and the soldier act together. There are some who can do this; they can stay in the army. Those who cannot wean themselves of it for more than two years should not be there.

Obviously, Ben-Gurion was not speaking only of conscripts, who served for two years, but also of those in the standing forces upon whom the duty of adjusting to the rules of the game resides: "You cannot reconcile this with the workings of an army.... It ruins the security of the state; it ruins the security of democracy." However, the vocational or professional complexion of the standing forces occupied Ben-Gurion again and again as the debate continued:

I heard ... from one of the officers, and it's a minority opinion, ... that we have nothing more to learn from others, we fought, we won, and we know no less than others.... We have a great deal to learn. And if the state and the army won't give officers and soldiers an opportunity to enhance their schooling and advance themselves, we will fail to attain the main goal, which is making the army more effective and capable. These opportunities to progress and take advanced training should be given in two ways. One is by setting up a series of courses here in Israel, each one at a higher level, until we get to the highest level, . . . and every officer, battalion commanders, and brigade commanders would also have to take these courses, and the other is by sending some officers abroad, if it becomes possible, to supplement their studies.

Basically, this was the format that evolved in the IDF from then on, in the absence of a British-, German-, or American-style military academy that graduates senior command (those fit to advance beyond the grade of major) after lengthy training and draws a clear distinction between commanders and staff officers. This distinction is also reflected in the formal relationship between the commander and his chief of staff. The latter is expected to excel in the ability to think and plan; the commander's traits belong to the area of command per se. Presumably, Ben-Gurion had not delved into this issue at that point in time; after all, there were no resources for such a program, and the defense minister did not wish to emulate others' practices at the micro level in any case, instead wishing to cull from them the essence that Israel needed under its special conditions. His purpose was to stress repeatedly to his audiences that "[i]n military affairs it is not the army that will make the decisions; it is the hallmark of a democracy that the army is subordinate to the civilian regime," which, whatever its decisions may be, has the full sovereign right to make mistakes and learn from them.

The formative "standing army," in Ben-Gurion's thinking, should be a core around which general mobilizations would take place when such could not be avoided. Here is the origin of the difference, warranted by Israel's basic traits – "a resource-starved, poor country immersed in distress, whose army is not an 'English, American, or Russian army'" – between Israel and others. However, it became Ben-Gurion's strict practice to send senior IDF officers to advanced training at British, specifically British staff, colleges (the practice of sending IDF officers to American academies began after his tenure), without belittling Israel's unique circumstances relative to those of the British Isles:

It's not right [to say] that my conclusion was that the army should rely only on the standing forces in the future. During the transition period, there will be intensive training so that we will have reserves that are ready for combat as soon as they are mobilized and can be mobilized quickly. We will have mobilized units [i.e., on active duty], admittedly just a few, but strike forces. We assume that all of our young people will receive training in rural settlement and also military service, so that when trouble strikes we can mobilize the entire nation. And to achieve this, we will train a command staff during these months and in the years to come.

From that point on, then, the nature of the IDF was set forth as follows: a relatively small regular army composed of a small professional officer corps and the rest made up of conscripts. It would carry out three duties: maintaining security in times of calm, training young people in rural settlement (this task was assigned to a separate unit, Nahal – acronym of *No'ar Halutsi Lohem* – pioneering fighting youth), and serving, alongside the senior reserve command and the entire reserve system, as an instrument for general mobilization if trouble strikes. This deployment rested on several basic strategic premises, discussed later in the chapter, that were deliberated by the Planning Division of the Operations Branch at IDF General Headquarters (GHQ) under Yitzhak Rabin.

The Givens, Aspirations, and Strategic Realities of Israeli Society

Ben-Gurion preceded this open debate with IDF commanders by giving a lecture, quoted in the previous chapter, about Israel's future security problems in their domestic social context. "We have to prepare for the future," he said in this programmatic address on January 14, 1951, "in ways that are suited to it and not those suited to the past":

Our victory in this war [of Independence] – although it was not total and not as we desired, we won on all fronts – left the security problem as grave and urgent as ever. And security, now and also in the near future, and in any event until circumstances change all over the world and war becomes altogether impossible in the world, will remain our premier concern. There are basic facts, geopolitical and historical facts, and nothing good that has happened to us in the meantime has changed them.

This premise led to action in several directions. One of them, already mentioned, was the continuation of the state of emergency, as implied by the absence of peace and the possibility of war sooner or later. Legal continuity in this matter was afforded by the emergency regime that the British had introduced in 1945 on the basis of procedures that were accepted not only in the British Empire but also in emergencies on the British Isles themselves, as noted previously. However, even before the War of Independence was over, Ben-Gurion had begun to seek unusual ways of addressing the overwhelming imbalance of forces between Israel and the Arab peoples, which had not yet mobilized in any real way to obliterate the disgrace of their defeat in their "first war" against Lilliputian Israel. The quest for long-term solutions to this problem included the nuclear option, whose origins should be traced to the War of Independence period; indeed, action in this field began immediately after the war. For the time being, however, the solution was not the atom but the conventional Israel Defense Forces.

Ben-Gurion reserved his sober view of the War of Independence for internal discussions; outwardly, he trumpeted the IDF's praises and proclaimed the outcome a triumph of the few over the many, thereby likening it to the Maccabeans' overthrow of the Hellenistic occupier of Eretz Israel. His purpose in doing this was to create an ethos that would become reality once the many and, in particular, the young believed in and internalized it. In contrast to the public talk of triumph, he repeatedly argued in internal discussions that the army had performed poorly in the War of Independence due to the midwar conditions of its birth and development. So he told the chief of the general staff, Moshe Dayan, in a pointed conversation in July 1956:

In the War of Independence we had as much manpower as the Arabs had and we barely held on [italics added]. I am not talking about the first month. In the first month, we were not armed so you cannot use that as evidence. Afterwards, we were armed: artillery, tanks, too. We even controlled the air space, but we could not take the [Gaza] Strip. . . . We were their equals in manpower and we did not take Falluja![17]

Indeed, the Egyptian force that the IDF had surrounded in the "Falluja pocket" was not defeated and ultimately was allowed to leave the area intact and without surrendering.

At that stage, concerned about eventual improvement of the enemy's capabilities relative to its historical condition at the time, Ben-Gurion categorically refused to launch a preventive war against Egypt despite the latter's provocations and the worsening state of emergency brought on by the operations of the Gaza Strip *fedayoun* (Palestinian guerillas operating inside Israel from Gaza, with Egyptian blessing and support given to them in due course):

Unless we boost our army's capabilities to the highest level now, we may find ourselves badly off in the worst way. *Our whole catastrophe is that we must never sustain a defeat, because then it's all over for us*; we must never sustain a defeat. They can sustain a defeat once and twice. We can knock Egypt down ten times – that's nothing. If they knock us down once – it's all over [emphasis added].[18]

Israel's basic strategic problem, then, originated in its inability to inflict on its counterpart the war damage or final outcome that the Arab side can inflict upon Israel. Furthermore, absent such a capability on the Israeli side, Israel must prepare for a war initiated by the Arab side – and must therefore "boost [its] army's capabilities to the highest level." The dangerous development that could be foreseen is that the Arab side would launch many recurrent rounds of war. Even if it would probably lose these rounds, the cumulative value of its defeats would doom Israel due to the price the latter would have to pay even if its army were duly fit. Such an outlook – a Yom Kippur War recurring once every ten years, if not more frequently – seems to have haunted Ben-Gurion until the 1973 war itself. Thus, he differentiated between a war at Israel's initiative and a state of nonwar that Israel must not violate and initiate in the absence of extraordinary justification for so doing. Therefore, we will eventually have to explain how he changed his mind about the 1956 war several months after he unburdened himself to Dayan in these matters and concluded his arguments by asserting firmly that Israel would respond to the Egyptians' actions not by instigating a war but by mounting "small but numerous sustainable attacks," that is, the continued but rather limited acts of retaliation following enemy attacks from Gaza and Jordan. Soon enough, Ben-Gurion consented to the preventive war against Egypt that he had a short time earlier opposed. This will occupy us in the rest of the chapter.

Ben-Gurion revealed some of his views about "boost[ing the] army's capabilities to the highest level" in his previously cited speech to the IDF high command on July 21, 1949:

When we were attacked, we faced a war of life or death. We could entertain no consideration – the economy, the finances, rural settlement, anything else – save one: full, total mobilization for the cause of victory.... That was our policy and I am sure it was wise and it saved us. However, such a thing is inconceivable now. We cannot call up everyone and shut down the farms...and sabotage industry.... The main goal of this country, of the war, of the losses, and of the effort is aliyah. And aliyah will demand exertions of us that lie beyond our abilities, because no such thing has ever been attempted: a small and impoverished country having to bring in so many new people, more numerous than its existing community, in a short period of time. When it comes to organizing our army, economic and financial considerations are crucial now. They did not exist a year ago; now they are crucial.... We must be a working, creative, and immigrant-absorbing country. And we must reduce to a minimum the amount of manpower that is mobilized in the army. For these two reasons – the deep-seated flaws in the structure of our army, its training, and its discipline, which we now have to disclose heartlessly, and the economic and financial changes ... – mean that we have to reorganize our army from the ground up... because we are facing an enormous contradiction. Our immigration and settlement needs mean that we must cut defense expenditure to a minimum.... It has already led to inflation and a cost of living that is throttling our development...and obstructs the inflow of foreign capital. By our strength alone we will not carry out the mission of ingathering the exiles.... By the same token, a minimum force is needed that will serve as a core for a fighting nation, if we are again attacked from without.

This gives us several insights onto Ben-Gurion's modus operandi during and after the War of Independence. His principal act was to establish an order of priorities that was necessitated by longer-term goals and external conditions, that facilitated change and use of the narrow window of opportunity so that Israel could quickly become sustainable – not only for its own sake but also so that it could serve as an instrumentality for the fulfillment of Zionism by building a socially and morally outstanding society. During the war, full mobilization was needed irrespective of its price. After it, the immigration and absorption needs clashed with the defense needs and their price. Furthermore, even though he sometimes assumed the posture of one who "doesn't understand economics" and does not dabble in this science at all, Ben-Gurion received thorough instruction, from David Horowitz – the future governor of the Bank of Israel – and others, about the meaning of inflation and the threat that it posed to the entire economy, including the capital inflow without which immigrant absorption could not be achieved. Therefore, Israel had to act on two levels: It had to establish a regular army to serve as "a core for a fighting nation," that is, for general mobilization when such would be necessary, and this "minimum force" would also serve as an instrument for "the absorption of [young] soldiers...those born in Israel and...immigrants," but mainly immigrants.

Continuing, Ben-Gurion admitted that he was not sure this was the ideal instrument, but its formation was the result of "months" of discussions and vacillations at the general staff and in the government, and not an ill-considered caprice or improvisation.

The New IDF and a New Strategic Doctrine Based on the Holocaust and Lessons of the War of Independence

In the July 1949 speech, Ben-Gurion also explained the principles of the embryonic strategic doctrine that was conceived after the War of Independence by or in consultation with the general staff. First, as stated, there would be a small, regular army ("a mobilized strike force") that would restrain an enemy offensive so that the reserves and, if necessary, "the entire nation," could be called up. No longer, however, would such a call-up be a general mobilization of civilians who would be sent into the battlefield with hardly any training, as had happened in the first months of the 1948 war. Instead, there would be regular and reserve brigades equipped with the service and support systems that an "independent military unit" needs. Thus, these brigades would not have to depend on the countrywide services that would be subordinated to the high command, which in the past had been torn between the two types of requirements. The IDF would be organized along the lines of autonomous brigades that could be activated without supplemental training, rearmament, and auxiliary services. In the British Army, too, the basic operational unit was the brigade, usually composed of traditional regiments and commanded by a senior officer at the grade of a one-star general. The Ben-Gurion model for the nature, training, and duration of service of active senior IDF officers was explicitly one of a British-style apolitical professional officer corps that pledges its entire active life to this profession, that is, whose active service does not end in midlife so that the officer can switch to an alternative civilian career.[19]

There is no doubt that Ben-Gurion projected onto the officers what he learned from his study of writings on military affairs and from the Yishuv's preparedness during his "defense seminar" period, from 1946 on, when he assumed responsibility as the supreme political decision maker in charge of the forthcoming inevitable war with the Arabs, and was convinced by this endeavor that he was reasonably knowledgeable in this field relative to others. However, he had great respect for those who possessed real professional authority and noted that the Hagana and Palmach amateurs had rejected most of them. He linked this amateurism to the conceit of "victory" following the 1948 War as two sides of one coin and clearly felt that this state of affairs must not be allowed to continue:

Our situation is such that in defense – and, in my opinion, in other fields – we shall have to attain the utmost capability, again because we are small in quantity.... I know of no vocation, be it economic, scientific, or artistic, that is as complicated, complex, and demanding of knowledge as the military. One who does not devote his whole life, time, and thinking to unrelenting training in this vocation cannot assume supreme responsibility for the security of the state and the responsibility that is even greater than this, because the security of the state is all-encompassing.... It will be necessary for those who are good, those who are talented, those who are pioneers, those who are gifted with the greatest moral and intellectual qualities, to devote their entire lives to the security of the state.

By implication, even if Israel were to have a professional standing army, its paradigm would not be that of the traditional British Army, which did not always attract the most morally and intellectually gifted Britons on earth. Given Israel's uniqueness and existential problems, it would have to mobilize the very best.

Ben-Gurion believed that overhauling and improving the fighting militias that had won the War of Independence would depend definitively on the quality of command:

Hundreds and thousands will have to volunteer for three to five years' permanent service. This is because enhancing the quality of administration – and maybe 80 percent of the army is administration – and of training, discipline, combat fitness, and intellectual endeavor are necessities for a small army. We will achieve discipline if it is based on the example that the commander sets: if his soldiers think of their commander as a paragon, if he inspires trust, respect, and love in his soldiers, trust in his knowledge, his loyalty, his pioneering qualities, his talent, his personality. Only an exemplary commander will inspire love and devotion, only one who truly devotes his life to the security of the state and loves his soldiers as though they were his sons.

Ben-Gurion's paragon commander seems to have been an adult, as opposed to a twenty-five-year-old company commander or battalion commander or even a thirty-year-old brigade commander who nowadays spends a short time with his unit and then races on to his next post at an early age and without lengthy intellectual and practical training. After all,

[t]he state presents the soldier with the ultimate demand: to kill and be killed. It presents the commander with even greater demands. The state has the right to present such demands. The nation [here Ben-Gurion explicitly corrected himself about the word *medina*, state, and replaced it with *uma*, nation] has the right to present such demands, because it is by virtue of the nation and on its behalf that we exist. However, every right carries an obligation.

Today, this view of the individual who exists by force of the nation may be considered antiquated, nationalistic, and unacceptable to a public whose prime concern is individual rights, from which norms that are supposed to survive in a democratic and egalitarian society are derived. Ben-Gurion, however, belonged to a generation that aspired to establish, as if it were something to take for granted, a "nation-state" of the British, French, Swedish, or Danish class and not a mere setting where people live.

Obviously, such a state serves the needs of the nation. Thus, according to Max Weber's definition, as quoted by Ernest Gellner for his own purposes,[20] the "state" is the segment of a society that has a monopoly on the use of force. The "nation," in contrast (*uma* or *le'om*), according to Gellner, is a circumstance-bound concept; so are nationhoods and states, but not in the same manner. The reasoning behind nationalism is that the two are destined for each other: Each is incomplete without the other. Before this happens, however, each must take form and each does so in a circumstantial and mutually independent way. So it was in Israel's case: The uma preceded the medina, that is, the state, the difficulties and metamorphoses of which we described earlier in the theory and practices of Zionism. However, when the time for statehood came, a new whole came into being, as it were, and Ben-Gurion labored to deepen and strengthen it from then on. The staying power of this state was not as simple a proposition as it seemed to be amid the tempest of the War of Independence. As he explained, "We have to present the able among us – and the war revealed immense ability among our young – with Jewish history's demand that the state be made secure." In other words, Jewish history does not generate Jewish war heroes by itself and cannot be trusted deterministically and simplistically to do so by itself. One must "respond to the demand of history": to act, to initiate, and to mobilize young people of valuable potential.

Indeed, Ben-Gurion recognized the image of the fighting *sabra*, the Israel-born soldier who is ostensibly identified with the fate of the collective – the conventional stereotype[21] – and viewed him as no more than raw material for an army that inhabited the sort of reality that concerned him: a real one, not a mythical one. After all, in contrast to this image of the sabra – the product of a youth movement, the Palmach, the kibbutz, as reflected in the verses of the poet Chaim Gouri – Ben-Gurion and, preceding him, Berl Katznelson definitely acknowledged the difficulties that beset the education provided by the youth movements. They resisted such movements as severely doctrinaire and cultivated one that was more pluralistic. The outer markings of sabra behavior were shared by the sabras of the time, but even members of left-wing youth movements were exposed to many diverse influences. They could not create an adult human type who entertained a profound cultural ideal that was connected to the educational doctrine on which they had been raised, a type free of serious conflicts that were resolved as they matured.[22]

Ha-Shomer ha-Tsa'ir people were exposed together to an experimental form of collective education that probably subjected many of them to hidden difficulties as they grew up. They were also exposed to a radical universalistic Marxist ideology that they had to reconcile with their Zionism, that is, to a no less extreme form of national indoctrination. They were exposed to authors, poets, and thinkers who were Marxists of various kinds, from Lenin himself to Plekhanov. Plekhanov's tract on "The Personality in History," which was reprinted in a gaudy modern version, had taught its readers at the pinnacle of the Stalin era that the personality is valueless when pitted against objective social forces, while his Israeli readers were educated to perceive in Stalin the "Sun of the Nations." Readers of the journals *Orlogin* (Timepiece) and *Massa* (The essay) were automatically exposed to poets like Pablo Neruda and artists like Pablo Picasso, who were frequently featured in Mapam's modernistic journals next to Israeli painters who strove to adopt "socialist realism," and to the literary supplements of newspapers, such as *Al ha-Mishmar* (On the guard), to which *La-Merhav* (To the expanses), organ of the nationalist-leftist Achdut ha-Avoda branch of the mainstream Labor Movement, also genuflected. Subsequently, these readers regarded Bertolt Brecht, the sometimes cynical, derisive, sarcastic, didactic modernistic German poet who often wrote in a vulgar Marxist vein, as something of a hero. Brecht himself and those of similar bent ignored Zionism in the best case and reviled it in the worst. They filled their disciples' hearts with hatred of the bourgeois and semibourgeois establishment, the sort that also existed in various incarnations in Tel Aviv and Haifa.

Young people raised on this ideological brew read the finest of world literature, translated by the successor generation to the creators of the Hebrew culture, and acquainted themselves secondhand with the "Shmuel" Pickwick, Oliver Twist, and David Copperfield of a Charles Dickens who had gazed upon the England of his time with conceit and hope as they saw it. However, they were also partners of Tom Sawyer boating down the Mississippi River and of Henry Morton Stanley in his forays into Africa, while transforming Winnie the Pooh into their childhood friend.

Of these young people, the city kids, and members of other youth movements, whose views were sometimes so divergent as to amount to mutual loathing, one could fashion an army at this time of supreme emergency that emanated from the preceding years of struggle. Henceforth, however, it would be necessary to extract from these masses not the "silver platter" that had made the victory in 1948 possible, a process that was being carried out rather spontaneously and efficiently at the time, but the best and the brightest, and to train them properly:

They have no moral right – although they do have the legal right – to take up any labor other than the security services. See, security demands the best and the most talented.... Recently I've had to touch upon a matter ... that is not easy to talk about. But I have to speak about it as plainly as I can speak about other things. I'm referring to politics and the army.... You know that the person who's speaking to you is a party man ... disputatious and contentious; so he used to be and so he will remain, because he believes in certain truths and rejects certain views. Every individual is entitled to do this and so is every group of individuals. The state and the army cannot read the minds of its soldiers and commanders. But there's one thing it must do ... and will do, although it hasn't done it thus far ... because it was concentrating on one thing only – winning the war.

The duty and obligation of a person in the army ... is to the army; this obligation nullifies and supersedes any other obligation. The soldier's connection to the army takes precedence over any other connection and nullifies it if they clash. Anyone who cannot withstand this connection cannot be in the army.... It won't prevent him from taking part in an election when elections are held and he has the right to vote. But he cannot be active, cannot be part of a struggle, a campaign, propaganda for any party. But it's not only in the political field. In other fields as well, his every endeavor will be defined and chosen by the army. Those who serve three years must abstain from political activism during those three years. They . . . do not have to renounce their views, they may proclaim them loudly, but they must not be political operatives. That's out of the question even in healthy nations. There is one nation [*uma*] with which we have relations in many fields. . . . I am referring to England. England has internal democracy with respect to personal freedoms, and to the best of my knowledge England does not fall short of other peoples in this regard. *But a soldier in England may not engage in any public activity, be it partisan or nonpartisan, be he a private or a field marshal, except where his superiors so instruct. We are not like the British or like other peoples that are healthier and more tranquil* [emphasis added]. Our ideological contrasts are not only conceptual but also psychological. We invest passion not only in good things but also in bad things. We are fanatics, we boil, we know no limits.

In other words, the Jews were not accustomed to Ralf Dahrendorf's "public virtues"; nor should one have expected them to be – at least not at this stage of their return to sovereignty. However, the army at least should be spared from the Jews' habitual "private virtues":

If we don't leave partisanship and political activism on the other side of the camp fence and instead let them into the army, we will have destroyed the army and we will have destroyed the security of the state. . . . That's what the majority thinks, and that's what will be. An army by "streams" [divided into various political groupings] is inconceivable. It is out of the question for a soldier's connection with anything, especially a political body, to take precedence over his connection with the army and the state.

Here, Ben-Gurion lashed out at members of the Knesset Foreign Affairs and Defense Committee, who made political use of information that they had received from military authorities – a mode of conduct that explains why Ben-Gurion found it objectively difficult to release information to them. The reverse of this argument, that is, the claim that the difficulty in keeping the committee fully informed originated in the "tyranny" of the chief of Mapai – was one of the most tragic ironies in Israeli politics from then until Pinchas Lavon's use of the committee.

Continuing, Ben-Gurion returned to "the nature of our people." "Some of them," he charged, relating to the public at large and especially the young, "are very set in their views." These views, however, were numerous and diverse, and if they were to collide in the army, civil war might erupt. After all, no member of these disputatious groups held a monopoly on violence and possession of arms, and Israel lacked the tradition of subservience that had allowed the German people, with its Socialist and Communist factions, to cringe before Hitler. Given its own lack of consensus and single-group monopoly, Israel had no choice but to honor the rules of the game of an electoral majority and the parliamentary governance from which this majority derived its legitimacy: "In this country, one may submit only to the state and to the verdict of democracy." For the time being, he was able to impose the view that since the army was enjoined against meddling in internal political affairs, "[n]o political activity within the army shall be allowed and military personnel may not engage in political activity even outside the army."

It will be for future research to determine whether Israel's typical military thinking and preparations for future wars were influenced by political outlooks and ideological attitudes that preceded the results of the War of Independence. Indeed, by the early 1950s, a group of senior officers on the general staff, including Yitzhak Rabin (commander of the Planning Division), Meir Pa'il, and Yuval Ne'eman were planning Israel's possible actions in the most crucial part of the country, the Jerusalem–Netanya narrow "waist." The actions at issue, designed to head off a future Arab invasion, included establishing a line along the Jordan Valley in order to stop the enemy and appropriate mobilization on the basis of early warning; they were a manifestation of caution given the lack of strategic depth in Israel's most vital territory. Menachem Begin's Herut movement, the political party that followed the disbanded IZL, however, scorned the 1949 armistice lines ab initio as an expression of the concession of Israeli rights. The left-wing parties, too, which listed Rabin and Pa'il among their supporters, regarded the partitioning of the country as problematic and disadvantageous, even if one of the parties that felt this way took a very "dovish" and pro-Soviet stance on the matter and the other adopted a combined approach of "activism," Greater Israel affinities, a pro-agrarian outlook, and a Soviet orientation of its own.

Yigal Allon, by now a political cogitator, regarded the country's partitioning as a reflection of the incompetence of the Israeli political echelon and the success of Western intrigues and Arab schemes. In his opinion, the IDF could have occupied the entire country "at least within its Mandatory frontiers" in the War of Independence: "[It] was definitely something that the IDF could have done during the War of Independence and that would have been tolerable in international political terms. It would have changed the Israeli defense system – not to mention other advantages – from one end to the other. Unfortunately, however, due to Western diplomacy, Arab cunning, and Jewish psychological weakness, the country remained split. This mishap is like a malignant lesion in [Israel's] body . . . and is immensely dangerous."[23] Allon's support for such a conquest, which would have delivered into the hands of the tiny Israel of 1949 the same West Bank Arab population that it found so hard to digest – nay, that it was unable to digest – twenty and forty years later, was very probably one of the reasons for Ben-Gurion's refusal to appoint Allon and others of like mind to key positions in the post-1948 Israel Defense Forces.

At that stage, it was difficult – but possible – to set up an army that would accept the authority of the political echelon in all respects, skirting all political-military polemics about Israel's security needs. Ultimately, one of the reasons for the ebbing of such polemics, the dissipation of Mapam underground activity in the army and elsewhere ahead of "World War III" (i.e., the prevailing view among Mapam's leaders that East and West would soon be at war with each other and that the Soviet Union would be the justified winner), and the thwarting of an alliance between Ben-Gurion and the Americans in the service of "Western imperialism" was rooted in the actions of Stalin himself. By adopting a tougher and tougher antisemitic and anti-Zionist line, the Soviet dictator left Mapam, which had always been a Zionist party and so remained, with few alternatives. In view of the persecution of Jews in the Soviet Union, the show trials against prominent Jews in the Eastern bloc on trumped-up charges of "Zionist" treachery, and the murder of writers and hounding of Jewish doctors at Stalin's instigation, the Mapam people had had their fill, sobered up more quickly than they might have otherwise, and fully submitted to the authority of the army and the state.[24]

The matter of concern to us at this stage of the discussion is the set of special solutions that were applied to the problems Israel faced at the end of the War of Independence, including the construction of "a chain of frontier defense settlements."[25] The use of this expression shows that the security doctrine of the time regarded rural settlement as a way to arrest the enemy's initial thrust. Therefore, rural settlement had not only a social and pioneering goal but also a defense one. Over the years, then, rural settlement became a Zionist catchword that persisted even after Ben-Gurion himself developed an unconventional security doctrine that elevated the nuclear option to primacy. In the country's first years, however, the integration of defense and rural settlement was an authentic plank in Israel's security doctrine and a prime mission for the IDF, by means of Nahal, even after it became clear that Ben-Gurion's plan to train every soldier for agricultural settlement during his first year of service was inconsistent with the other pressing needs of a small army.

Another mission that demanded an investment of thought in this context was education. Here, too, Ben-Gurion created a synthesis, integrating a sociocultural mission (so controversial today) that he considered essential, the "melting pot," with defense needs that seemed crucial to him at the time and that could be anchored in a broad public consensus. In the Yishuv, education had been divided into separate "streams" of conflicting ideological schools and political youth movements. It is true that in Israel's first years, the leadership of the main school systems (the State and the State-Religious) abolished the "stream" paradigm. However, it did not do away with the terrible political-party fragmentation that existed among the youth movements – prime purveyors of education at the time – of which the most left-leaning crowned themselves as seers and prophets. I personally remember the enmity that young people such as these – members of the Marxist Ha-Shomer ha-Tsa'ir [Young Guard] and the national-leftist Mahanot ha-Olim [Advancing Echelons] movements – fomented among sabras and recent immigrants who did not belong to their camp.[26] Ben-Gurion himself had his doubts about Holocaust survivors and immigrants from the desert caves of Libya, but also proposed a remedy:

If the army fails to educate the immigrants, it will have squandered its main role. This is because ingathering of the exiles is the foundation on which our strength will be built, our state will be based, and our independence will be sustained. First you have to lay the foundation, a foundation not of stones nor of wood nor of steel but of people. Now, the people who are coming to us are dust-people from the most shunned the most impoverished, the most downtrodden, and the lowliest countries. We shall receive the Jews who are returning to us with open arms, no matter what country expelled them, the most wretched of the wretched, the lowliest of the lowly. All Jews are sons of royalty, the offspring of Abraham, Isaac, and Jacob. We shall receive them lovingly; we shall extend them a loyal hand and brotherly aid so that they may sink roots in the homeland, in our culture, in our language, in our lives, and be a blessing to the Israel Defense Forces as well.[27]

Fragments of this argumentation, which recurred commonly in Ben-Gurion's rhetoric at the time, are cited today as "proof" of Ashkenazi elitism, the elite's condescension toward the *Mizrahim* (the contemporary term for Jews of non-European origin), and appalling contempt for their culture, identity, and historical achievements. Accordingly, we need to seek the source of Ben-Gurion's self-assumed authority to refer to the products of certain countries as "dust-people." The countries at issue, however, were not only Libya, Yemen, and the like but also countries in Central and Eastern Europe. Holocaust survivors from these countries had been interned in so-called DP camps in Germany. Ben-Gurion had visited these camps in 1946 and come away with the impression that many of the survivors were broken men and women, some engaging in black market and smuggling activities; he envisaged their rehabilitation as a major challenge for the Zionists. One of the sources of this authority, it seems to me – apart from the achievements of the Yishuv, which had created the infrastructure for this immigration – was a cultural renaissance syndrome of the sort described previously. In this syndrome, the Yishuv viewed its own culture as superior to others.

To Ben-Gurion and his contemporaries, the various Arab cultures were primitive ones, tainted with polygamy, paternalism, misogyny, and surrender to the dominance of strongmen and sorcerers. They did recognize, however, the dominance of the Bible over the Jewish offspring of these cultures. The Bible, they posited, should be shared by immigrants and nonimmigrants alike; after all, all were "offspring of Abraham, Isaac, and Jacob." The Bible carried the ethical principles and behavioral values from which the "People of the Book" could learn and according to which they should behave – even if it was not yet a people and did not follow the dictates of these principles and values, as combined with the ethos of democratic socialism.

A rabble cannot fight and endure difficult ordeals. And educating the immigrants and blending them into a national cultural bloc is one of the main tasks assigned to the Israel Defense Forces. Our army is not an English, American, or Russian army. It is the army of a poor, hardscrabble country . . . that is nevertheless a great nation (one of the greatest in the world, I believe) in spirit. . . . Some things are not yet in good order: We are not yet a people, and unless the immigrants achieve spiritual integration and are educated to be Jews, citizens, builders, and warriors, our army is unlikely to solidify and our security will not be consolidated.[28]

The story of education in the IDF deserves more than the terse summary that we can offer here. Indeed, the former Chief Education Officer Mordechai Bar-On – subsequently a researcher of that era – and others, such as Meir Pa'il, devoted themselves to writing its chapters. They regarded the IDF's educational mission as a necessity and calling of the highest order that was imposed on the command echelon. So, too, did they view the mobilization of the finest youth for Gadna (*Gedudei No'ar*, "youth battalions," a paramilitary program) in the mid-1950s specifically for duty as counselors for immigrant youth; this author was one such recruit. The public norms that Ben-Gurion established in this matter – the aspiration to appoint a "Yemenite chief of the general staff" soon, unrelenting emphasis on the imperative of "ingathering the exiles," and the posting of troops to auxiliary duties in the transit camps during the harsh winters of the early 1950s, to name only a few – was accompanied by biblical language and biblical references on the part of the Jewish prime minister of a Jewish state who was also a dominant and powerful figure, inducing profound identification with him on the part of very many of the people known today as Mizrahim.

As for the doings of the army's education system, we have written documents that shed light on the persona of the first chief education officer, Aharon Ze'ev, as well as Ben-Gurion's lectures to the IDF high command on this topic in the early and later 1950s, as we quote in the following. They do not tell the whole story, of course. They speak of principles and action plans, whereas the conflicted reality of Israel's first years makes itself evident in the jumble of idealism and a more power-focused, favor-seeking, and corrupt reality.[29]

What were these principles? A collection called *Education and Morale in the IDF*, published by the chief education officer in the 1950s, quoted excerpts of Ben-Gurion's lecture to the High Command on April 6, 1950:

The schools [i.e., the leadership of the state education system after the elimination of the "streams"] are educating our children. I am sure that in another generation the Yemenite, the Moroccan, the black marketer from Germany, and the Bulgarian Jew will no longer be recognized. They will be sabras, the sort of people in whom we take such pride, for good reason – due to their physical size, heroism, labor, and the boldness [that they displayed] in this war.... A commander in the Israel Defense Forces who is versed in all the regulations [à la those of the British army] in the world, the whole science of strategy and ruses, the conduct of war and a military economy, equipment and armaments, and everything related to the soldier's craft.

However, all the skills that Ben-Gurion himself considered so important in his foregoing remarks were not enough.

If he thinks that he can settle for that, he will not get by in the Israel Defense Forces. A commander in [our] army ... who does not keep in mind the ingathering of the exiles, the values of ingathering the exiles, the difficulties of ingathering the exiles, who will not educate himself, before anything else, in integrating the nation and who fails, before he makes [his recruit] a mortar operator or a gunner or a shooter or a pilot, to make him into a Jewish man and a son of Israel, a citizen of the state and a citizen of the homeland and a comrade, and [who fails] to uproot his German-ness or Moroccan-ness or Yemenite-ness and to instill in him the values of the Jewish national heritage and the new values that we are creating – he will not succeed in his craft, even if he is the best soldier and the most devoted commander.

If so, the point behind these "new values" that "we are creating" was, as stated, to upgrade the "black marketer from Germany" (immigrants who had spent time in DP camps in that country) and to uproot "German-ness," that is, to set an equal standard for immigrants from Europe and from the Arab countries. There had to be no discrimination among immigrant groups. Each group could be mocked equally, but this must be avoided and all groups should be accepted as equal. Ben-Gurion once commented on the topic of derision about the recent immigrants from Muslim countries by mentioning his own experience: He himself had come from Poland and "they said the Poles were thieves." As for the aforementioned new values, the reference is to an integration of diverse values: labor, return to nature, social solidarity, and equality in Jewish values, selectively aided by the values of the Bible. The point emphasized was the revival of the old and the integration into it of the new, and not about the new alone, as we argued in Chapter 1.

Further Development of Ben-Gurion's Strategic Thinking

In his lecture to the IDF high command on January 14, 1951, quoted previously,[30] the minister of defense mentioned the Bible as one axis of his strategic thinking and juxtaposed it with the second axis, "history." It was quite unlike the incisive, definitive, and sharply worded lectures that Ben Gurion gave at other opportunities, and it may have bored short-tempered listeners, such as Moshe Dayan, half to death. This may be what Dayan had in mind when he told this author, "Ben-Gurion was an old Diaspora Jew with fixations." We will dwell on the relationship between these two later on, but here it should be noted that even though Ben-Gurion promoted, appreciated, and even loved Dayan, he attempted in the course of events to use other people to keep his equilibrium.[31]

Dayan was the epitome of Israeli rootedness, of living the dream of returning to the soil and the Bible in one shot, as reflected in a book that he wrote toward the end of his life, *Living with the Bible*. Just the same, this first sabra was a short-tempered, condescending, and aggressive man. Ben-Gurion recognized this side of Dayan's original and colorful personality and leadership style but sought just the same to counterbalance him adequately. Thus, on the eve of the Six Day War, when he offered Dayan his services as an adviser – Dayan had just taken over the defense portfolio under pressure from public opinion – he thought that Dayan would at least heed his counsel. Dayan, however, in his own words, had learned to fly with his own wings by then and wanted nothing to do with advisers. Therefore, the "fixations" of the "old Diaspora Jew" deserve mention as he unfurled them before the IDF high command in January 1951 and afterwards. They were always predicated on the perspective of Israeli "uniqueness" among states and peoples, originating in Jewish history, Israeli and Middle East geography, or, rather, geostrategy, regional demography, and his use of the Jewish-Israeli "destiny" that stems from historical necessity and the culture of the people at issue. His interpretation of them in political-strategy terms might be defensive, cautious, and risk averse when it had to be, but it could also soar skyward under the power of schemes that Ben-Gurion himself termed "fantastic."

One such scheme was Israel's nuclear program, which came to fruition after much hardship and struggle. Other plans spoke of geostrategic changes in Lebanon of the sort captured in the expression "peripheral alliance," that is, between Israel and Ethiopia, Iran, and Turkey. Each of these schemes was anchored in that early analysis before the IDF high command in January 1951:

[The Arab states at the time] span an area of 2,700,000 square miles, almost as large as the United States of America. They've got a population of roughly 48 million.... Their population is forty-seven times larger [than Israel's population in 1948].

But that's not all. You also have to consider the Arab countries that will eventually become independent – from Libya to Algeria, Morocco, and Tunisia. Their area will add 1,700,000 square miles and tens of millions to the Arabs' ranks. Since they are members of a culture and language that used to be connected within one empire, one should expect them to wish to reunify that empire and, in any event, to wish to collaborate against Israel. In other words, the security problem has two aspects: very grave balances of forces and some form of Arab unity that will stabilize against the tiny and foreign Jewish player that has invaded its domain. But even this isn't enough. See, we're at the crossroads... of three continents. This is the main cause of the wars that have gone on.... And you can't assume that global conquerors... their armies won't try to cross this country. The armies of Hitler, one of those who tried to be a global conqueror, were only about one step away from this land.

One needs to examine the fears that existed in the late 1940s and early 1950s about a march by Soviet forces through the Middle East en route to Egypt, which, apart from Great Britain, was considered a suitable base for American nuclear bombers.[32] At the operating echelon, the West seemed seriously willing to include Israel in its Middle East defense organization for the time being. However, Britain's strength was flagging and the Arabs' might eventually attain a level that no Western player could disregard. Thus, the defense minister had good reason to speak about the historical changes that Israel would have to acknowledge and cope with. One of these changes was the decline of Europe, the former world-straddling power that now ranked second or third after the superpowers and the ascendancy of Asia. Here, Ben-Gurion clashed verbal swords with the Greeks, the Romans, and the Jews for their hauteur in anointing themselves civilization's chosen peoples in disregard of the great historical civilizations of Asia, foremost China and India. The last mentioned, Ben-Gurion cautioned, were reappearing on the global stage, this time as independent players. The Jews, of all peoples, he continued:

whose every political innovation and renewed independence, for the third time, are merely the results of its amazing ability to maintain the heritage of those of antiquity and see things that physically do not exist, that exist only in its mind, by the capacity of which the State of Israel came into being... absolutely must not dismiss in contempt the cultural antiquity of these two great peoples, not to mention the definitive fact of their hundreds of millions of people.

Seemingly, then, Ben-Gurion had begun to envision a way to eliminate Israel's dependency on the West, its disputes with the Communist bloc, and both blocs' powerful interests in the Arabs and other Muslim peoples in parts of the globe that knew and cared nothing about the history of Palestine and its contestants. The escape that he sought was always associated, in his mind, with culture, history, and defense. Then, in the manner of a gratuitous commentator on Jewish culture, Ben-Gurion added:

As for ourselves, for centuries we were mainly a European people that absorbed all the positive baggage that the concept of European-ness captures, but we've also brought a legacy of our own with us, one that European civilization has not assimilated despite Christianity [and its ostensible proximity to Judaism]. It is the product of this country [i.e., the Bible and its ethics], the westernmost part of Asia. We are returning to this little corner of the great continent as a hybrid people, heirs to the European culture and bearers of the ancient culture from four thousand years ago that was created in this East.

As we have noted, the very ability to "hybridize" in this manner was typical of the renaissance generation. However, the Jewish uniqueness, which while not totally European had adopted a full dose of "European-ness," seems to have been compatible with the images of the various schools of Zionists at the time, in the sense that they had rid themselves of all sorts of customs that had been common among Eastern European Jews in the "old days" and had become common again in Israel. Examples were the premature marriages of boys and girls or the marrying off of young girls to older, if not elderly, men among the Jews of Yemen; adherence to pagan religious customs as observed among Hasidic sects and, in our own times, the followers of Rabbi Yitzhak Kadouri, an ostensible kabbalistic miracle worker of the most primitive kind; the hygienic habits of destitute families from the Atlas Mountains; traditional attitudes toward work; and crafts such as silversmithing, trading in rugs, and other kinds of commerce – all the baggage that the members of the Second Aliyah and their followers had seemingly jettisoned. Those of the Second Aliyah purported at least to have done this under the inspiration of the "religion of labor" that they had adopted in the wake of Rousseau, Tolstoy, and American worshipers of nature and communal work, which had created the "working Palestine" ethos that the "Oriental" Jews were supposed to assimilate.

Ben-Gurion, however must have been referring to other "European" influences as well, such as the influence of Western science with its Greek origins, which combined mathematics and its tools with experimental observation and systematic scientific investigation of nature. Jews in Europe had been excelling in science since the middle of the nineteenth century; American Jews had enlisted in this trend somewhat later. In contrast, the Orthodox Jews of Eastern Europe – especially the Hasidim – lived as stagnantly as medieval Jews had, having added their own competing traditions and loyalties to their ruling rabbis and their courts. The rabbinical Jews opposed their modernistic counterparts as near-infidels, and the lives of the Oriental Jews gave evidence in these respects of the protracted lag of the Muslim world generally, and the Arab world particularly, behind the West. Some Jews had become "Levantine" in the sense of mingling the European languages and customs that they had adopted with typical, traditional, bourgeois behavior. Ben-Gurion's criticism of these co-nationals would likely anger those whom we call today "Mizrahim" if one quotes excerpts of his remarks that concern Mizrahim and not others.[33]

Ben-Gurion was much occupied with Eastern culture, however. Viewing it as not "European," he believed that its offspring had to be "kneaded" in order to accept the contents of the "Judeo-European" culture. This culture, however, was largely in its infancy, as Ben-Gurion himself noted, and one of its problems in the 1950s would be the challenge of investing it with greater depth and predicating it on Jewish and Western principles that Ben-Gurion would select, for which he was later criticized in typical ways, as we shall see.

On top of this Ben-Gurion feared, as already noted, that Arab culture and Arab-Islamic history would be unable to accept Israel and readmit the Jews to their homeland, and he was concerned about the mammoth global changes that were liberating the Arabs from Europe's yoke and were expected to integrate them into the universe of the Cold War. There, they would command maximum attention and steadily rising influence due to their vast numbers, abundance of territory, and oil reserves. Indeed, he continued in January 1951: "[T]his competition for global hegemony between the two most aggressive peoples economically and militarily ... is more than a great if not decisive political fact; it also affects our security problem considerably if not decisively." Indeed, the ostensibly uncompromising Arab stance that had overshadowed moderate Arabs since the 1930s gained strength many times over in the aftermath of the Israeli War of Independence and the outflux of most Arabs who had inhabited the territory that had become Israel's. The severity of the Arab challenge, however, was a function of the balance of forces between them and Israel, the Arabs' internal relations, and the nexus of the region, with its various components, as well as the global struggle currently under way.

Israel's security depended not only on these factors – and here again, we notice a material difference between Ben-Gurion's views and those of Ze'ev Jabotinsky and the latter's self-appointed spiritual and political successor, the head of the pre-state Irgun and now of the Herut movement, Menachem Begin – but on another factor as well: Israeli society's internal weakness and the absence of a deeply rooted common substance that would hold its diverse elements together. As quoted earlier:

A culture is coming into being. But culture is not just language and culture is not just knowledge and schooling. It is a lifestyle. We do not have a lifestyle that unites dust-people into a whole. . . . We do not yet have the lifestyle of a cultural historical whole. . . . It has only begun to form, and this has many implications for defense and for the other values of our lives.

Here, the curious reader will find an explanation not only for the values that Ben-Gurion wished to instill in the army but also for his eventual behavior in the Lavon Affair, which will preoccupy us presently:

But there's an even worse problem, and we are the only ones who have it: the problem of physical existence. After all, those nearby who are plotting against our existence are not plotting for borders. Their intention isn't just to expand their borders. Neither do they want to do away with our independence. To rid themselves of our independence, they have to rid themselves of us. We mustn't take our minds off this terrifying truth – the most terrifying truth in our defense problem – for even a moment. This is what makes our defense problem special.

This awareness explains Ben-Gurion's defense postulate for the future: The annihilation of Israel, the physical elimination of its inhabitants, is the key to the eradication of its independence and the settlement of the border problem. This "terrifying truth" slowly drove a wedge between him and his successor, Moshe Sharett. Sharett took over the premiership when Ben-Gurion retired to Sede Boqer in 1953 due to his realization that without effecting fundamental regime change, he would be unable to ensure the country's security and discharge the duties of the premiership and the defense portfolio that he believed essential. In my estimation, Ben-Gurion's resignation was brought on by a combination of cumulative fatigue – indeed, this is how he explained it to President Yitzhak Ben-Zvi[34] –and his refusal to continue tolerating a multiparty regime that was mired in trivialities and was oblivious to the dangers on the horizon.[35] After his resignation, Ben-Gurion claimed that while global and regional factors did not depend on Israel, many other factors did. The first was "internal fortitude," or "internal strength," in three respects: changing the regime, which is

a disaster for the state and for the nation because the government in this country is a federation of parties that [place the pursuit of] their interests [over anything else] and its parties are not political parties but sects. . . . Second, settling the unpopulated areas over the next few years. Third . . . the thing that's called the ingathering of the exiles. . . . It may be possible to create a unified people [in Israel]. To bring this about, the state will have to make an enormous effort . . . but no effort that the state makes will be enough; it will require a mass effort by the citizenry. . . . If the war breaks out before that, heaven forbid, we're done for.

To wit, not only would exclusive *mamlakhtiyut* ("statism") fail to do the job; an almost desperate effort would have to be made to mobilize the citizenry on a volunteer basis to absorb the immigrants and settle the country. Ben-Gurion was considered the founder and the person most responsible for the actions of the regime that he sought to change, and the question was how to change it at a time when he had relinquished public ministerial responsibility for its doings. However, from the War of Independence onward, Ben-Gurion had been mulling the possibility of escaping the stranglehold that was steadily closing in on minuscule Israel, according to his analysis, by home-manufacturing an atomic bomb or procuring the infrastructure for producing such a weapon from foreign sources.³⁶ In other words:

Another thing to which the state will have to pledge more resources is the development of science. Indeed, our security may ultimately depend on it. But I won't talk about it. It may be our last resort.

The Constitutional Debate and Ben-Gurion's Criticism of Israel's Political System

We have seen enough preliminary information in previous chapters to under-stand Ben-Gurion's remarks in the Knesset against the adoption an American-style, rigid constitution in Israel and his comprehensive doctrine on the rule of law and the essence of democracy, that is, the problem of freedom and authority:

For the State of Israel, two things in the legal domain have to be assured first of all because I believe our country's existence and future depend on them: rule of law and democratic governance.
    Personal freedom and national freedom do not depend on a proclamation of free-doms or on a constitution but on one matter of principle: the rule of law. Only in a state where everyone – civilian, soldier, official, minister, legislator, judge, and policeman – is subject to the rule of law and acts in accordance with the law; only in a country where arbitrariness does not exist among ministers or governors, among the people's represen-tatives and officers of the state, or even among political personalities and leaders – only in such a country is freedom for the individual and the masses, for the person and for the nation, assured. In a country where the law is not supreme, there is no freedom even if its constitution includes the most vigorous and advanced bill of rights in the world.³⁷

This preamble to the programmatic speech that follows alluded, in a manner of speaking, to the Soviet Union (which several heads of Mapam, the second-largest party in the Knesset at the time, considered a "second homeland"), where Stalin used the 1936 Constitution as a tool to cover up his crimes, and to Weimar Germany, where the most democratic and progressive constitution in the world had been enacted, only to become an instrument in Hitler's accession to power because the Weimar democracy did not know how to defend itself.
    We have already noted how puzzling it is that Ben-Gurion advocated "rule of law" and inveighed against "arbitrariness" while making lone-wolf decisions that led to the dismissal of the chief of the national defense staff, Yisrael Galili, and repeatedly imposing his views on his colleagues in other respects.³⁸ This modus operandi during Israel's fledgling period has even prompted some to regard him as the mentor of a "guided democracy," such as Sukarno's in Indonesia and Kwame Nkrumah's in Ghana.³⁹
    Ben-Gurion, however, took these actions concerning Galili and other mat-ters in the midst of a changeover from Yishuv to statehood and in a state of war. Elections could not be held at that time, and so he acted on the basis of the majority that his party had captured in the Yishuv institutions in the

1944 elections. He secured a majority for his positions only by defeating internal opponents in the provisional government and by threatening to resign. Afterwards, in the aftermath of the January 1949 elections, a complex process of changeover from Yishuv institutions and the Zionist Movement to elected institutions did begin. Although Mapai failed to earn an absolute majority in these elections, it became a linchpin without which no coalition could be established. This key position served as leverage for governance that was both stable and flexible enough to cope with the tasks facing the country. This position, however, was a political one, not anchored in institutions, the British election method, and agreed-upon rules of the game. For example, the first coalition government, established by Ben-Gurion in 1949, agreed to depoliticize the public services via give-and-take among the members of the coalition; the country had no civil service law until 1959. Thus, even though the principle of an apolitical civil service was accepted, ministers in the coalition could still pack their offices with "their" people. Naturally, then, Mapai staffed "its" ministries with its own people and professionals who shared its leanings and admired its leader.

In principle, even though the state of emergency persisted in varying degrees, Ben-Gurion wished to behave according to the British model as well as he could, including the tenets of the rule of law, to be specified. The state of emergency made it necessary to distinguish between foreign affairs and defense – in which the fledgling country had to apply controlled force, express its positions, and maneuver among its enemies and its few friends – and domestic affairs. The latter entailed a changeover from the habits of Yishuv society, the customs of its elites, and its power centers to the practices of a soundly functioning state. Since the process of the changeover was anchored in multipartisan coalition governments burdened by interest groups that were accustomed to "dividing the spoils" among them and were tainted with traditional corruption, a disparity took shape – and steadily widened – between Ben-Gurion's pretensions about rule of law and reality. The existing "system" had allowed Israel to win the War of Independence, absorb huge masses of immigrants up to that year and thereafter, and surmount the enormous initial difficulties of a Yishuv society that had become a sovereign one. However, this transition to a sovereign society had not been completed institutionally and in terms of worthy, adopted "public virtues." Additionally, the era of tumult that had begun in 1944, with its mammoth changes, began to sink into routine and into troubling internal changes, with no extreme external menace in sight for the time being.

The result was Ben-Gurion's first retirement to Sede Boqer in 1953, which turned into a campaign for a British-style transformation of the entire regime but ended with his return to the Ministry of Defense in the aftermath of the 1954 Lavon Affair. The Affair would metamorphose into a reprise of Ben-Gurion's struggle for the principles of the rule of law in 1960. After all, Lavon had demanded – and ultimately received, due to the pressure of several mass-media entities and much of the Israeli intelligentsia – exoneration by a majority of ministers in a government headed by Ben-Gurion and was publicly absolved of his responsibility for actions taken in Egypt six years earlier. The exoneration was awarded without the prime minister's knowledge and behind his back.

When the Affair first erupted, Lavon, as minister of defense, was forced to accept responsibility for the relevant actions undertaken in Egypt in 1954 by the army's intelligence and, accordingly, to resign from Moshe Sharett's government. The key issue, however, was not whether Lavon had actually given the orders behind the relevant actions but his demand that the executive branch clear him of responsibility for them, even though the executive authority in a British-style state of law does not, and is not authorized to, make such a deal. It is true that the British version does not prescribe an American-style separation of powers, but it assigns responsibility for legal investigations and the handing down of verdicts in the "state of law" to judges or other judicial instances. Furthermore, the British rules of the game usually forbid investigation by an incoming government of acts committed by an outgoing one, because the latter would then seek to avenge itself politically against its erstwhile rival and so on in a never-ending loop. Indeed, Moshe Sharett – the premier who initially induced Lavon to resign and then backed him in his struggle for absolution from responsibility for the "Affair," seized this opportunity to avenge himself against Ben-Gurion, who had unseated him from his perch at the Ministry of Foreign Affairs.

At first glance, the reader would say, Ben-Gurion could have avoided the tribulations of the Affair had he made sure to instill basic rules of separation of powers at the very onset of statehood. Even then, however, he did not disregard the independence of the judicial branch. In the Knesset debate of February 20, 1950, quoted previously, he defined the status of the judiciary – and of the legislative branch – as follows:

We need an elections law, a Knesset law, a law for the president and his powers and responsibilities, a law on how the government is elected and how it resigns, a law of the press and of assemblies, [etc.]. These laws define the rights and obligations of citizens, elected officials, civil servants, judges, and the police.... No constitution can play this role. Only within the framework of laws – that should be changed and amended occasionally in response to necessities of life that do not stand still. As long as they exist, they apply to all citizens of the state without exception, including the president of the state, members of the government and the Knesset, and also "simple" citizens – and only within this legislative framework can true civil and national freedom be assured and each and every individual's rights be preserved.

I deliberately steer clear of the internal debates that preceded this debate in the Knesset, one that sealed the fate of a written constitution in Israel and the draft constitutions that had been drawn up for the First Knesset, which convened under its original mandate as a constitutional assembly. Plainly, however, one of Ben-Gurion's rationales in thwarting the adoption of a written, rigid constitution was his fear that such a document would be compelled to establish "final" truths about the nature of the Jewish people and a formal definition of democracy. Democratic rule, he knew, has many facets and no agreed image. Different democratic systems trace their origins to the different histories, geostrategies, and cultures of the countries in which they grow. Indeed, the "mother of democracies" – Great Britain – never defined its democracy in a formal way that could be invested with legal interpretations external to its elected institutions. Ben-Gurion was obviously sensitive to matters of law and justice because he had studied law as a young man and because he feared hairsplitting and ambiguous legal texts. One cannot know whether he was also influenced by his rejection of the built-in pro-and-con legal debate culminating in the kind of sterile hairsplitting that he had found in the Talmud. Furthermore, he was afraid that formal definitions of the nature of the state would cement religion–state relations in ways that would be instantly rejected by various sectors in Israel's rapidly changing society. Alternately, they would hand decisions on fundamental issues to appointed judges who would lay down the law in a manner that would also be unacceptable to many. This, in turn, would defile the status of the court itself, as we will demonstrate[40] and as it did happen in today's Israel.

In the "constitution debate," Ben-Gurion continued – slipping into the acrid polemical tenor that he typically adopted when addressing political or ideological rivals, a tone of voice that he intended to restrain this time in order to set the dispute at the level of principle that it deserved:

Two champions of civil "liberties" stood out: Member of Knesset Begin [head of the Herut – "liberty" – movement] and Member of Knesset Ya'ari [a leader of Mapam]. But regrettably they didn't define what a liberty is. Does liberty mean everyone doing what he pleases? In my opinion, that isn't liberty; it's anarchy. In a true regime of liberty, you have to respect the rights, dignity, life, interests, and needs of the other, and you have to respect rights at large, the rights of the nation and the state, its security, its regime, its status, its needs. Only the law can draw a limit between freedom – not the freedom that a certain group monopolizes for itself, but the freedom of every citizen – and the rights of the other. Where there is no rule of law, there is no freedom.

The law has to apply to everyone without exception. The president of the state, the prime minister, and any other minister may do as part of his job only what the law allows him to do. In contrast, every citizen may do anything apart from things that the law prohibits him from doing. If someone thinks the law is bad, he has to obey it anyway. He can propose to amend it, but as long as it is in effect, it's binding. Because there's no assurance of freedom and rights other than the rule of law.

This argument, I would say, is consistent and pertinent due to Ben-Gurion's concerns – that he would take up again later in his speech – about the characteristic internal fragmentation of Israeli society and his own experience with attempts by minority groups in his party to impose their view on the Histadrut during the Yishuv era and on the Israel Defense Forces when this institution was in its infancy. These groups had acted in this manner for the sake of ideas in which they believed and others did not. The struggle among the "private virtues" of various groups, such as those associated with the Stern Gang in previous times, was also manifested in Begin's "revolt" in the middle of World

War II, the *Altalena* affair, during which Begin had tried to import weapons for his separate outfit in Jerusalem, and attempts by several leaders of united Mapam to stamp their imprint on the IDF even if this led to underground organizing by Mapam agents within the army. Ben-Gurion viewed his struggle against them not as the mere practice of politics, a power struggle for power's sake, but rather a struggle for the power to impose a "public virtue," that is, the rule of law. Put differently, he meant majority decision making that would be reflected in acts of parliament. Only this kind of a decision-making modality would preclude anarchy and unbridled struggle among extremists and minorities who were now demanding a formal, rigid written constitution, a document that might secure their interests and outlooks or shift the decision-making prerogative in their cause from a majority, which could be mobilized, persuaded, and won over, to a cadre of appointed judges.

"In a country dominated by law," he continued, "the people give the law and the judge supervises and upholds it. The people must not be limited in their lawgiving. Of course, the people can also make a mistake, but a free, unfettered people will correct the mistake." "Unfettered" people are those who are "unfettered by a [rigid] constitution" that thwarts the acute changes sometimes demanded by the changing times. The example given was the nationalization that the Labour government in Britain legislated after World War II, which Conservative Parliaments eventually repealed in equal measure, on top of the parliamentary revolt against Neville Chamberlain in 1940, based on public demand, which brought about his downfall and replacement by Churchill's national coalition.[41] In contrast:

[U]pholding the law, interpreting the law, [and] testing the incidence of the law in a specific situation in life, rest in the hands of the judge, who is independent of any individual and government [and answers] only to his conscience and understanding. The judge neither makes laws nor repeals them because even the judge, like any citizen of the country, is subject to the law. The judge merely interprets the law and applies it to specific cases presented to him for his adjudication. Reality is complex and intricate, and the legislator cannot foresee every case that may come about. The judge has to find the meaning and intent of the general law under the special circumstances of the specific case presented to him. *In a state where the rule of law prevails, the legislator's authority, entrusted to the elected representative body of the people, is totally separate from the power to exercise judgment, which is entrusted to a panel of judges who are appointed, but once appointed are independent of the executive authority* – a panel of judges who are versed in the law and loyal to it [emphasis added].

It follows that if the "elected representative body of the people" is too fragmented and disharmonious to deserve this title, if it "clings to trivialities," if it shows excessive concern for personal and group interests, and if it views life through the prism of the short term only, as Ben-Gurion said of the Knesset and its constituent parties around the time of his first retirement to Sede Boqer, then he cannot regard such a house as a "British Parliament" and as fit to be called an "elected representative body of the people." Hence, the investigation of acts of commission or omission of a minister, such as Lavon during his tenure as minister of defense, or of a minister's subordinates, that have the smell of criminality is no task for an "elected representative body of the people," that is, the government. Instead, it should be undertaken by the judiciary or in a judicial procedure within the framework of existing laws.

At this stage of the constitution debate, Ben-Gurion still believed that he could convince his listeners and trust his party to behave in accordance with the following principles:

Rule of law without rule of democracy is unthinkable. The people respect the laws and accepts their burden lovingly. After all, the laws are crafted in concurrence with its views, flow from its needs, and are harnessed to its will. A country where the people are not free to make their laws by means of representatives whom they elect as the outcome of freedom of choice does not have rule of law; instead, it has a regime of tyrants and arbitrariness. If the ruler who makes the laws is independent of the people, then the law is not the creation of free people, and wherever there is no freedom there is no rule of law.... There has never been a dictatorship in history that did not purport to rule in order to enhance the public welfare. Indeed, quite a few dictatorships came into being solely as the outcome of public rationales of national or social ideals. However, governance has an internal nature that is inescapable. When a governing authority is not subordinate to the people and is not chosen by the people in free elections, then governance becomes an end in itself, even if initially it is a means to an end, even a lofty end.... The State of Israel will not endure without rule of law and without the rule of democracy. The two are intertwined. This, not the constitution problem, is the country's basic legal problem....

Any totalitarian regime spells death for Jews and the Jewish people, be it physically or spiritually. These regimes doom Jews or Judaism or both to nonexistence. The State of Israel, too, cannot exist, however precariously, under such a regime because it severs the connection between the state and Diaspora Jewry. Jews as Jews can exist only in a country that has freedom of the minority, freedom of elections, freedom of thought, freedom of movement, freedom to oppose the government within the bounds of the law – in other words, democracy.... The fate of the Jewish people is bound to the fate of democracy.

Presumably, it was for this reason that Ben-Gurion felt it immensely important to grant political rights to the Arab minority, even as he hobbled this minority by placing it under military administration, viewing it as a hostile element in itself or as a potential partner in interests – legitimate interests – of its hostile siblings beyond Israel's frontiers. Furthermore, one of the reasons for his efforts to reform Israel's multiparty regime and introduce a "British" electoral system was his conviction at a very early stage of the game, given the fractiousness and fragmentation among the multiparty parliament's Jewish factions, that the Arab minority would eventually call the shots in the affairs of the Jewish majority. In fact, this forecast came to pass under the second Rabin-Peres government and helped to place the Oslo peace accords, concluded between Yitzhak Rabin and Yasser Arafat in 1993, under a cloud of illegitimacy.

At the time of concern here, however, Ben-Gurion developed his definition of democracy in the following way:

Under democratic rule, the majority holds sway and the majority's wish is the state's law and is binding on the minority. However, the minority retains its right to express its view, think as it wishes, and vote for whomever it pleases. Under democratic rule, the majority does not hold sway in matters of faith, thought, the arts, and science. In democracy, the individual's thoughts are not subordinate to law and government. Even if the entire nation subscribes to a certain accepted view, the individual may think differently and fight for his view.... Under democratic rule, there is no prohibition of criticism and debate; every citizen is fully free to elect his representatives as he wishes. The citizen is not asked to approve an exclusive list of candidates that the rulers present [as is done in "people's democracies"]; instead, he chooses his representatives himself and, for this reason, the representatives submit to the people's will and not the other way around.

Obviously, the practice of allowing political parties, including Mapai itself, to choose electoral candidates by means of "appointment committees" or "coordinating committees" was different from the single-party appointment of candidates as practiced by the Communist bloc. However, it had a bad taste to it, and Ben-Gurion would ponder this in his efforts to reform the entire Israeli political system in the aforementioned British spirit, especially since he hoped in this manner to strengthen elected officials' relations with their district electorates.

Ben-Gurion's statement that "[t]he majority's wish is the state's law and is binding on the minority" seems problematic when it comes to defending minorities' rights and, in particular, preventing a random majority from making decisions on basic issues that are protected by a written constitution, such as that of the United States. Again, however, even in the United States the terrible struggle that ensued during Lincoln's presidency was couched in terms of an uprising by minorities against a potential majority decision. Only at a late stage in the Civil War did the president dare to place the crux of the controversy – the slavery problem – on the public agenda and emancipate the slaves in the American South. Even in this act, he applied strategically and tactically judicious timing that flowed from internal and external considerations in the midst of a national emergency. As Ben-Gurion explained it:

Democracy is not a system of laissez-faire. The majority's decision is binding. The majority decides what action will be taken and what action won't. This decision becomes national law, binding on the entire public. And so long as the majority does not change its mind, either because the majority has not changed or because the same majority has not changed its mind, the law exists and is binding on every citizen in the country.

This interpretation of "action" and "law" reflects the Zeitgeist. Back in the Yishuv period, Ben-Gurion had pronounced "unlawful" such "actions" as had been taken against the British government by minorities, such as the Sternists and Begin's IZL that sabotaged the Yishuv's interests in contravention of the majority view. The decision in favor of the Palestine partition plan was an "action" that Ben-Gurion and his comrades had steered to fruition thanks to a majority that they considered "legal." So, too, they had deemed the majority that had seen to the dismantling of the Palmach. Some of these decisions, as well as others, were the topics of public debate at all levels of the Yishuv, and Ben-Gurion invested prodigious efforts in debating them. He had made several of these decisions in the middle and at the end of the War of Independence without addressing the public directly. Just the same, they were anchored in the majority that his party had secured in the 1949 elections, which was strengthened by its partners in the coalition that would eventually take shape.

The emphasis in his remarks was on the ability to act in the British manner and not the vitiation and neutralization of this ability by means of the American formula, which sometimes forces the head of the executive branch to do dubious things in order to gain maneuvering room vis-à-vis the other branches, as occurred under "imperial presidents" from Andrew Jackson all the way to Franklin D. Roosevelt. Furthermore – as I have demonstrated – American democracy has the special property of being anchored in a two-party system that, though established in a hit-or-miss fashion, assures its immunity from internal enemies (by practically ignoring radical minorities at the polls), if not its freedom of action against external enemies. According to Ben-Gurion:

Democracy will not exist if we render it powerless, inert, deficient in executive strength, and devoid of efficient self-defense mechanisms. . . . If democracy in Israel wishes to exist and endure, it should be armed with self-defense mechanisms and instrumentalities of action and execution that will prevent minorities – not only non-Jewish but also Jewish – from hijacking it from within or without, and one can hardly be so disingenuous as not to see that such minorities exist among us, even if some do not reveal their intentions and aspirations in this matter.

At the time, democracy's right to defend itself against enemies that seek to use its principles in order to destroy it was one of the most prominent lessons that the West had learned from the collapse of the Weimar Republic. In the wake of these lessons, the constitution of the newly created West Germany introduced a very high blocking percentage, meant to reduce Weimar-type political parties to a few large blocs, as well as a "chancellor democracy." This infrastructure precluded internal fragmentation and disunity and artificially reduced the chances of extreme parties gaining representation and exploiting a multiparty parliament for their purposes. The Zionist Yishuv also had extreme factions, including Stern's Lehi, which in the early 1940s considered taking over the elected leadership of the Yishuv in order to carry out a policy of collaboration with the Fascist Axis, and Menachem Begin's IZL, which rejected the Yishuv institutions' authority in other basic matters. At the very time of Ben-Gurion's remarks, the Israel Communist Party (Maki) was serving as a tool of Stalin's Kremlin, and Mapam was indulging in a complex flirt with the Soviet Union, having, on its left flank, introduced a regime of "ideological collectivism," that is, the enforced adoption by the rank and file of policies declared by the party's leadership. Just the same, Ben-Gurion's rivals to his right and left, and even his coalition partners, considered his actions and arguments affronts and usurpations of democracy and hurriedly engaged the Knesset mechanism in frustrating them as much as possible, that is, by passing immunity laws for members of the house that are unparalleled in any other parliament. They did this over the prime minister's vigorous opposition, shortly after he had made his aforementioned remarks from the podium of the house.

For the time being, however, Ben-Gurion had more to say:

The totalitarian regime has one "advantage": The ruling party enjoys 99 percent support. We have to obviate this "advantage" by all means that democracy possesses. One may express an antidemocratic view in a democracy, but democracy will commit suicide, sentence itself to helplessness, and leave itself without means of self-defense if it allows . . . its negators to take action. It is permissible in the State of Israel to be a non-Zionist; indeed, we have a non-Zionist faction in the Knesset [Maki], but its people must not be allowed to take us over by undemocratic means due to the liberal generosity of Member of Knesset Ya'ari [of Mapam].

Here, Ben-Gurion reverted to the polemic and provocative style that had helped to alienate his political rivals, raise the tension between him and them to a boiling point, and, in all probability, exacerbate the contrast between him and them. However, when he expressed clear and unequivocal stances that were rooted in that generation's political experience in Israel and in the West, he brought the ranks of his faction and most of public opinion under his umbrella.

Continuing, Ben-Gurion argued that the Declaration of Independence was Israeli democracy's charter document and that an additional Bill of Rights, as favored by advocates of a written constitution, was altogether unnecessary. However, he added the following:

The existence of the State of Israel [and this is the definitive difference between it and powerful and stable countries such as the United States and France] depends first and foremost on security, immigration, and rural settlement. Only if we perform these three tasks successfully and enhance defense, immigration, and rural settlement by applying our full abilities will the State of Israel hold firm. However, these three things require laws – a basic law and ordinary ones. The question is whether the rule of law and democracy, which Israel needs, would best be assured by an overarching constitution of special status or by a set of basic laws that would be no different in status from other laws.

Ben-Gurion evidently did not distinguish between "basic laws" – the passage of which seemed then, and would seem later, like a way of establishing a basis for the cumulative construction of a national constitution – and "ordinary laws." After all, even basic laws could be amended by an ordinary majority in the Knesset. However, as he perceived the matter, a problematic or erroneous basic law, such as the Basic Law years later that introduced the direct election of the prime minister but proved to be faulty and even impractical, would quickly show where it had to be amended and might then be amended by an ordinary majority.

Then Ben-Gurion turned to the crux of the debate:

The circumstances that necessitated and justified an overarching constitution of special status in America or even in France do not exist in Israel. On the contrary: If we want to teach the nation to respect the law, let us teach it to respect the law [at large] and not only a special-status law that's called a constitution. After all, it is the ordinary laws, and not a constitution, that determine the thousands and thousands of details that make up the citizen's daily life. If we wish to stamp out the contempt for law that was implanted in us by life in exile, on foreign soil, and in dependency, we have to rule out the bizarre idea that constitution aficionados such as Member of Knesset Begin preach: the idea that a "law on human rights" that has no special status [and the lack of] a previous constitution for every other law [makes such a law] a worthless piece of paper.

If a law made by the nation's emissaries is just a worthless piece of paper, what's the value of a constitution made by the selfsame emissaries?

This very Knesset, after all, was supposed to have been a formative assembly that would draft a formal constitution on the basis of the results of the January 1949 elections. If Members of Knesset Begin and Ya'ari ruled out a posteriori "control by a mechanistic majority," as Begin put it, or by a "'random, conjectural majority,'" to use Ya'ari's expression, how valid and valuable would a constitution crafted by this "mechanistic" and "random" majority be? Restraining his polemical skills, Ben-Gurion then reverted to his principled argument: "The existence of a constitution with 'special status' will not enhance [citizens'] respect for and connection with the law; on the contrary, it will bring the law into even greater contempt. Anyone who wants to flout the law will find a new argument: The law is unconstitutional." And since the constitution – any constitution – must rest on general and abstract principles, "[i]f any hairsplitter can find a hundred grounds to declare something that isn't kosher kosher, it's certainly possible to find a thousand grounds to delegitimize any law."

This argument was based, as we said at the outset of our remarks, on a critical fundamental principle in Ben-Gurion's Zionist outlook. According to this principle, Israelis

share the general characteristics of the Hebrew people, which have always been deficient in statecraft. This people, which in the first eight hundred years of its history gave rise to giants of humanity in the moral and social field, has hardly produced one statesman of major stature.... No sooner had this people achieved national unification under Saul and David than it split immediately, and in the Second Temple era, too, it displayed statecraft only for a short time under the early Hasmonaeans. Two thousands years of exile, migrations, and, of course, dependency did not engender qualities of statecraft among the Jews.... *There was nothing that the Jewish people coveted more intensively for centuries than a Jewish state. There was nothing that the Jewish people were less talented to administer than a Jewish state* [emphasis added].[42]

By implication, life in a worthy and proper Jewish state has the intrinsic goal of leading the Jews to self-correction as citizens who are capable of governing themselves: "It is not out of the question that the Jewish people will adopt the qualities of statehood that are needed for the conduct of a sound and sustainable state. Our people lacked the qualities of scientific thinking that the Greeks bequeathed to the peoples of Europe, but at long last we have acquired them. There is no essential reason that we cannot adopt the ability of statehood as well." The Israelis, however, are still "far from this":

Excessive party fragmentation despite unanimity of views on basic issues. Schisms within the Labor Movement despite common origins. . . . Inability to prefer the general interest over the sectarian interest, to prefer what matters more over what matters less. . . . The tendency to scan the world without looking at our situation, needs, and peculiar conditions, and its contrast: a provincial attitude of national egocentrism that ignores the wide world and its needs. . . . While in exile, the Jews did not see that they were exceptional among all the nations and did not understand why the world refused to adjust to the odd situation of the dispersed, disembodied Jews. It didn't occur to them that the blame resides not with the nefarious goyim but with their abnormal situation, and that ultimately they must either adjust to the nations among which they dwell or become an independent people in their own land. . . . Even today [after the Holocaust], we think that if the world does its own reckoning and if this reckoning does not identify with our own feelings, then the whole world is evil and should be given the boot. Our devotion to forms, mores, and habits – of thought and action – that took shape before there was a State of Israel, even though they are ill-suited to a life of statehood, is [another] manifestation [of these qualities].

Therefore, a form of rule that would allow these traditional Jewish qualities to paralyze governance, make public life an act of litigation, and place the decision-making prerogative in the hands of appointed judges would ultimately lead to protracted disorder and even threaten the status of the court, as in the case of Israel at the present writing (2008). Ben-Gurion, continuing the constitution debate in the Knesset of February 20, 1950, then took up the contrast between the British model and the American model once again:

The Americans are very willing – but not always, for all that – to accept it when the Supreme Court strikes down a law on the grounds of unconstitutionality. Would our public accept such a thing easily? Wouldn't such a thing subject the judges to grave dishonor? Both of these are equally dangerous to the state: disrespect for the law and distrust of the judge.

Lurking behind this argument, among other things, was Ben-Gurion's concern that the religious public would accept neither the constitution nor the decisions of a court that was based on its interpretation if these offended their beliefs and interests. However, any contemporary reader who studies former Chief Justice Aharon Barak's reasoning about the merits of the "reasonability test" as the instrument of choice in resolving basic issues, as well as Barak's claim that from then on such issues would be decided by the Supreme Court under the Basic Law: Human Freedom and Dignity – a statute that in fact was passed by a small majority in a hardly attentive Knesset without serious debate – will understand how problematic Barak's rationales are and how they may be used to cut in either direction. Where issues of religion and state are concerned, the question of reality persists in Israel to this day and has actually ballooned into a threat to the court's status due to its own judicial activism. Since the religious parties in Ben-Gurion's day were moderate on foreign and defense issues, and since the National Religious Party (NRP), the only one with a Zionist orientation, felt it its duty to perform "outreach" for Zionism and the State of Israel (indeed, all the religious parties established a "united religious front" in the First Knesset elections), it was proper to try to dialogue with all of them in the manner of parliamentary compromise. This compromise, Ben-Gurion thought, should be anchored in historical reality, that is, the pre-independence status quo in religious matters, and in the need to integrate the religious public into Israel's secular reality instead of crowding them out. The compromise to be pursued would give rise to consensual legislation, as opposed to rigid court verdicts reflecting general and abstract principles that could be established only in a rigid constitution:

> Democracy in Britain is strong not because the country has or hasn't a [written] constitution but because the British people respect the law and trust their judges. They respect the law because they elected the lawmaker. They trust their judges because the judges themselves are loyal and subordinate to the law and do not station themselves over it. In Britain, the king is no less subordinate to the law than a chimneysweep, and the prime minister no less than a shoeshine boy.

This use of the British model is, of course, simplistic and avoids the real character of British partisan politics in terms of rigid control by party whips over members of Parliament, especially in the case of the Conservatives. In Ben-Gurion's eyes, however, such discipline, when it proved historically necessary in Great Britain, the "mother of democracies," might as well be adopted – following the introduction of a British majority-constituency ballot – by two large political blocs in Israel that would be elected, as in Britain, by virtue of their various platforms.

At the same time, the British people "respected the law" not only because they elected the lawmaker but by dint of history and tradition. Here, Ben-Gurion, however, was relating in his own way to the British rules of the game – the basic sense of fairness that the British public employs publicly and privately – in his conviction that Britons at large treat each other fairly and strictly uphold the public virtues that underlie the British method.

Ben-Gurion's subsequent relations with the religious parties and the various currents in world Jewry, which prompted him to approach rabbinical leaders (among other personalities) in order to determine "Who is a Jew," exceed the bounds of our inquiry here. Although those relations did not proceed placidly, during his career they did not escalate into an irreparable explosion or a schism that was hard to bridge. One reason was the lack of a written constitution. For the purpose of our discussion, however, Ben-Gurion's objections to such a constitution originated not only in these factors but also in a concern about judicial intervention – as happens habitually in the American system when interested parties hitch the constitution to their wagon – in issues of national security, which even in the United States have no life-or-death importance for the population at large. It was Great Britain, of all countries, that deliberately granted the executive authority sweeping powers in matters of emergency and related national security. Britain maintained – and still maintains – strict censorship in these matters and is exceedingly tough about keeping official secrets secret even after the emergency blows over. Britain goes so far as to withhold immunity from members of Parliament whose activities endanger public security. An example is Sir Oswald Mosley's group, the British Union of Fascists, which, during World War II, was outlawed and its members interned in detention camps.

Concerning issues of security, Ben-Gurion continued (February 20, 1950):

An individual who menaces [the rule of law and democracy] must be denied his freedom under certain conditions in order to assure the rule of law and democracy. The British do not even flinch from revoking the "freedom" of a member of Parliament... by means of an emergency law for the sake of national security. Such a law poses no danger to the nation's freedom if it is established by force of the nation and its elected representatives in free elections.... In the eighteenth century, in which despotic rule was the defining characteristic, a bill of human rights was needed.... In the free countries, the democracies where the nation rules, it is a bill of obligations that is needed. In our quarters, this means obligations to homeland, nation, immigration, ingathering of exiles, building of the country, security, the other, the weak. We need a bill of obligations more than any other free democracy that basically assures human rights ab initio.... When the state was established, we stopped being demanders and became demandees.... We can no longer demand of others – we must demand of ourselves, first of all of ourselves.... There is a principled and vast difference between the revolution that we experienced and the revolution in America, France, ... Russia, and other countries. In all these countries, there was an uprising against a regime, and when the regime was changed the people got their wish. The Jewish national revolution was not an uprising against a regime.... The Jewish people rose up against a historical fate, the fate of an exile-nation, a dispersed nation that lacked a homeland, language, culture, and independence.

Ultimately, American democracy culled a great deal from the principles of the British "state of law and justice" and adapted the British values and institutions to its special needs. Concurrently, the American Founding Fathers – though without forethought – introduced a regional-majority electoral system that implicitly created a two-party system. This system, in turn, created two large parties that, as a result, aimed their appeals at the center. After all, any radical party expressed interests and outlooks that others did not share and, therefore, stood no chance of becoming a national party and rising to power. On the basis of this form of governance, the Supreme Court arrogated to itself the power to interpret the Constitution and, eventually, showered U.S. citizens with an abundance of rights – by implication, the right of the American Nazi Party to exist and express itself in the public domain, even though its electoral prospects were worse than nil. Thus, this singular and special governmental mechanism was partly the outcome of historical chance. Although reflecting an existing and stable tradition, it ordained structural tension among its components, which were relentlessly reselected as entities that represented diverse interests in ways that were disproportionate and, often, mutually hostile. Israel had no need whatsoever for a complex structure such as that of the American federation; it did need, however, a governing ethos of the type that Britain's American offspring inherited from it and considered self-evident.

To address this need, in the next phase – following the debate – Ben-Gurion sought to adapt elements from Judaism to principles of systematic thinking, rule, and democracy that he had found among the Greeks and in British democracy. When he returned from Sede Boqer in 1955, occupied above all with the British-style constitutional reform that he wished to introduce, Ben-Gurion invested much thought in, and spoke out on, his conviction that Judaism is basically a "religion of justice."

Ben-Gurion's exertions at this time – which were entangled with the Sinai-Suez War of 1956 and its outcome – to mobilize Jewish principles as the bases of Israel's regime, with a mixture of British-style institutions, as well as with Greek thinking, religion, and traditions that were recruited selectively for the necessities of a secular "state of law," even inspired him to look into the messianic idea. This idea imparted psychocultural content to personal lives in a society that lacked genuine religious content, as many Israelis no longer professed and practiced the faith. It offered people a way to escape the loss of traditional faith, as matters seemed in those days, while remaining bound to Jewish civilization as a set of norms. I refrain from taking up this intricate and serious issue until the next chapter. I will note here, however, that it sparked a wave of resentful counterreactions among Israeli intellectuals, of all people, who viewed secular "messianism" as a root cause of tyranny in its modern manifestations – Fascism and Communism – against which Ben-Gurion had fought all his life. Ben-Gurion sought in Judaism worthy principles on which one might base the rule of law in a secular Jewish state, a form of governance anchored in a worthy party system and the worthy elected parliament that this system would sire.

Thus, he could not but intervene in the Lavon Affair – a public campaign by Pinchas Lavon, a deposed former minister of defense who aspired to a renewed position of political power by trying to force the system to exonerate him politically for actions that he had taken while serving as minister – even though ostensibly it did not relate to Ben-Gurion personally (did not take place during his premiership) because it involved the blatant injustice of a trial by the political echelon and the media. If Jews employed their brilliance to find a hundred ways to render "kosher" an exceedingly grave issue of national security, such as the botched operation in Egypt which took place in 1954 under Lavon as defense minister, then they did not understand that their return to a place in history meant the assumption of sovereign responsibility, a matter that carries not only rights but also obligations. In this regard, Ben-Gurion came out against a "majority decision" – the decision of the majority in his government to

exonerate Lavon without a trial – on behalf of the principle of judicial investigation of the Affair. Ineluctably, he then had to take three actions: resign,
dissolve the Government that had exonerated Lavon unlawfully without even
saying who was guilty if Lavon were innocent, and turn directly to the people
so that it would render its verdict.

This matter of approaching "the people" is consistent not only with Ben-
Gurion's principles as described here but also with his reading of the nature
of the nation and its political behavior under a regime that he wished and
failed to reform. Ultimately, Lavon broke the rules of the game and violated
the collectivist spirit that had typified the Mapai high leadership until then by
rousing the media, orchestrating leaks from closed Knesset committee meetings, and mobilizing Mapai's historical enemies for his exoneration without a
judicial inquiry. By implication, Ben-Gurion wanted more than a proper legal
investigation of the 1954 Affair; he also wanted to fight a new round in his
old war for the maximal adoption of British rules of the game. These rules
could not take hold in the multiparty system that had come about in the latter
stages of his tenure, given the country's external pressures, the unification of
Far Left and Far Right against Ben-Gurion's policy on the German issue (to
be discussed), and the internal and external difficulties that cropped up at the
time of the construction of a nuclear reactor in Dimona.

In my opinion, however, the debate over the Affair reflected something
deeper: all the old fears that had attached themselves to the "mass democracy debate" from the French Revolution onward. Edmund Burke (quite a
few American Founding Fathers had their own conflicting ideas about these
issues) had proposed certain remedies against demagoguery, the manipulation
of the masses by interested parties, the "rule of mediocrity" (as reflected in the
influence of the mass media on this issue and others), and the perpetration of
injustice on behalf of justice. From that time on, those elements began to adhere
to the national fabric with growing tenacity until Ben-Gurion himself became
their victim – given Israel's half-baked regime and its inability and unwillingness
to adopt either the governmental tradition of Great Britain or the serendipi-
tous randomness of American history. Due to this randomness, the United
States had acquired a system of governance based not only on separation of
powers but also on a regional-majority electoral method and a two-party system
that ensured the stability and functioning of the entire body politic, including
the judicial system.

The Birth of the Nuclear Option

As noted, Ben-Gurion viewed the IDF as more than an instrument of defense; he
also expected his IDF to play a social role, integrating the exiles and ultimately
constituting a "people's army," that is, an army of general mobilization at
times of supreme emergency. He based this outlook on a highly pessimistic and
critical attitude toward what was accepted in Israeli society of the time.[43]

We need to reemphasize this view and its centrality in Ben-Gurion's thinking
and actions for the additional reason that he himself seems to have masked or

blurred it when he spoke in public about the Zionist enterprise. On those occasions, he cited the positive aspects of the enterprise, as though it had already succeeded, and of the Jewish resurrection:

We need to rip out and obliterate a false premise that we inherited from lowly and backward countries: that an army is a maddening, humiliating, and degenerate thing ipso facto. Now, there are such armies in the world, but they are the products of regimes that set up lowly armies because they themselves are backward and lowly. An army in a soundly functioning country can be, and our army . . . must be, an agent of elevation and healing. . . . Let us not forget that even here in this country, forces of separation and disintegration are still at work. Our partisan and ideological fragmentation in no way falls short of that of the lowliest and dysfunctional peoples. The superheated atmosphere of strife among parties and factions is useless in the rapid healing of the tatters of the exile. Apart from the school, which, too, is not totally free of this fragmentation, only the army can and should serve as a unifying and elevating player in shaping the new image of the nation and integrating it reliably into the new culture and society that are being created in the State of Israel.[44]

The IDF actually played this role in the early years of statehood. It was, in a sense, a great immigrant-absorption agency in terms of imparting language skills, commanders' treatment of soldiers and their families, and assistance in transit camps and frontier localities.

In 1953, however, when he decided to resign his dual portfolios (prime minister and defense) and head out to the nonpartisan kibbutz Sede Boqer, Ben-Gurion seems to have been convinced that he had failed to bring on the requisite changes in the lives of Jews in the Zionist state, be it with respect to the self-rule that the Jews had to internalize as a principle of their return to history as a sovereign nation and concerning the challenges of absorbing the immigrants and settling the empty Negev and the Galilee. The young had been drawn into the wake of the parties and youth movements of the Left, and the Mapai-affiliated movements responded to this criticism by going on the intellectual defensive. When he reached Sede Boqer, Ben-Gurion was occupied more by the question of youth than anything else. Shortly afterwards, however, he was "reoccupied" by something that had troubled him from the outset of statehood: regime change of the sort that would help the Jews become a sovereign nation that could take charge of its fate. Addressing the Second Knesset on June 8, 1953, he heatedly accused the political parties of "not being parties but rather sects" that looked out for their short-term interests and not for the public welfare. To place his remarks in clearer focus, he hurled at his listeners a scathing quotation from Bialik's poem, "I Have Seen You Again in Your Ineptitude." The changes he had in mind, insofar as they depended on him and the political system, had to involve the regime and its institutional infrastructure. Indeed, shortly after his resignation, Ben-Gurion launched his public campaign for fundamental regime change, that is, the introduction of a regional-majority electoral method and a two-party parliamentary system that, as noted, he considered prerequisites for the creation of a "sound regime."

Thus far, Ben-Gurion had created the infrastructure of the defense system, paying strict attention to the separation of the army, which concerned itself mainly with preparing for and engaging in combat but actually functioned as an immigration-absorption agency, and the Ministry of Defense (MOD), which dealt with sensitive political and financial matters related to defense procurement, including abroad. The MOD was also charged with the other interfaces of the army and civilian society, including the draft, paramilitary training of youth, and the mobilization of soldiers for work in rural and border settlements. The practical performance of the army in those early years, when it was an immigrant-absorption agency, was unsatisfactory. The second chief of the general staff, Lieutenant General Yigael Yadin, resigned or, truth to tell, was dismissed by Ben-Gurion when he objected to the slashing of his budget and its subordination to Israeli society's higher priorities in those times of mass immigration. The third COGS, Mordechai Makleff, a British Army veteran, was swiftly replaced by Moshe Dayan. Dayan himself had certainly been angling for this post and did not make Makleff's life easy. His appointment, however, seemed to strike the right blend of originality and due caution with the yoke of the political echelon and the display of initiative, the restoration of the IDF's fighting spirit from the War of Independence, and the engagement of young people's imagination so that they would regard the army as an enterprise worthy of its name.

When he headed off to Sede Boqer, Ben-Gurion could assume that the army was in good hands. At the MOD, too, the swift replacement of Ze'ev Schind with Shimon Peres as director general made it seem as if stability and proper subordination of the IDF to the political echelon had been achieved. It was the appointment of Pinchas Lavon to the defense portfolio that destabilized the defense system so badly – a point to which we will again return.

In the meantime, Arab leaders were steadily immersing themselves in a policy that put pressure on Israel (economic boycott, isolation from key countries in the Third World, guerilla operations inside Israel, blocking the Suez Canal and later the Tiran Straits to Israeli shipping) and gave the Israeli public a sense of siege and strangulation. Some were busy in domestic upheavals, but Ben-Gurion assumed that they might unite against Israel sooner or later due to the logic of modern Pan-Arabism and the enormous potential advantages in manpower, resources, and strategic positions from east to west vis-à-vis the tiny "illegal" Jewish island in the Arab ocean.

All these circumstances, which Ben-Gurion viewed as givens, plus the lessons of the Holocaust – that is, the "trap" situation in which the Jewish people found themselves during World War II – justified an effort to attain an "ultimate" weapon that would nip the conflict in the bud even if recognition of the legitimacy of this weapon would have to be struggled for, a struggle that lies beyond the concern of this chapter. What remains within the field of our concern is the historical reality, which largely ignored the fate of the Jews while favoring Arab interests and claims during the Holocaust. By the same token, the reality that immediately followed World War II requires our attention. The lessons of that war were as acute and permanent in people's minds as other values are today. Therefore, members of that generation thought in terms of total war and its prevention by any means, including means that would have stopped Hitler himself had they been taken in time. Specifically, had the West armed itself properly before allowing Nazi Germany to abrogate the prohibitions of the Versailles Treaty, and had Hitler been shown clearly that he had no chance of attaining his goals by force, World War II might have been precluded, as Churchill repeatedly claimed in the highly influential memoirs that he published in the early 1950s.

In the Israeli case, the Arabs had proclaimed publicly their wish and duty to annihilate an existing state born in the tumult of a war that they had instigated. By implication, they would attempt to destroy it by any means, be it the might of their armies or unconventional ways – if Israel allowed them to attain these ways before it did. How the Arabs would destroy Israel was immaterial to Israel. However, if Israel beat the Arabs in the race for nuclear capability, it could counter their existential threats by posing its own existential threat to them and their regimes. This capability would give the Arabs the option – which did not exist in the conventional era – of recognizing Israel's existence and suspending, if not terminating, the conflict. And even if the Arabs eventually obtained nuclear weapons and used them against Israel, they would incur a penalty so ghastly as to render Israel's destruction not worth their while. In this respect, the issue of World War II refugees – the millions of Germans who were uprooted as a result of Nazi aggression and crimes, and the many Japanese who were forced to leave Korea, Manchuria, and other territories – seemed to have justified the departure or forced exile of Palestinians following their war against the Jews in 1936–1939, the role of Palestinian leaders in preventing the rescue of Jews during the Holocaust, and the war waged by them against the UN Partition Resolution of 1947.

At this time, the United States leadership had not yet settled into the role of a power willing to risk itself in a nuclear war on behalf of its allies; consensual behavioral norms in this respect had not yet been determined and imposed. The very meaning of nuclear arms – were they instruments of combat or of its prevention? – had been debated in the United States since the days of Hiroshima. Amazingly, it took America until the late 1950s to develop a systematic theory of nuclear deterrence. From the outset, of course, there were important theoreticians in this field, including some who believed that nuclear weapons had ended an era in human history and would henceforth prevent the resolution of conflict by war. The U.S. Air Force, contrarily, regarded nuclear weaponry as perfect instruments of victory so long as the American nuclear monopoly held up. After the monopoly was breached, a debate erupted over maintaining the American quantitative and qualitative edge by shifting from atom bombs to hydrogen bombs, the power of which was theoretically unlimited. The possession of this power generated horrific fear in various American circles, prompting some to embrace the "better Red than dead" outlook, take their country's military-industrial complex to be a pack of irresponsible risk takers, and treat those abroad who wished to follow their lead – even if only for defensive purposes – with a mixture of fear and loathing. Others could see the case of Israel – in the aftermath of the Holocaust and given the Arabs' threats of annihilation – as an outlier that justified nuclear deterrence. This, at least, was the conviction of the French officials who wished to help Israel – and France – in this respect.

Very early in this era and even before they had their own A-bomb, the British chiefs of staff developed an explicit defense concept. From their standpoint, a Soviet threat to the homeland islands (or any other threat to the British Isles, given Germany's recent past) would result in a British atomic threat against the Soviet Union (or against Germany). Eventually, the hydrogen bomb prompted the British to rethink the maintenance of foreign bases that could be obliterated with one bomb, such as those in the Suez Canal area.

As these debates ebbed and flowed in the West, Israel was busy being born and hunting for uranium in the Negev by means of Hemed C, a special division of the Science Corps commanded by Efraim Katzir, the Hagana's chief scientist, with his deputy Shlomo Gur (Grazofsky). While on a mission to the United States, Gur made the acquaintance of Jewish scientists who were working on the atomic bomb. Evidently, Professor Ernst David Bergmann (Ben-Gurion's scientific advisor and, at an earlier time, founder of the Israel Biological Institute within the defense administration) and Gur were the fathers of an idea that Ben-Gurion had adopted even before the war was over. In his *War Diary: The War of Independence 1948–1949*, Ben-Gurion made the following entry on December 25, 1948, entitled "Hanukkah reflections":

We are facing the greatest upheaval in human life – *the discovery of atomic energy* – and its exploitation in the global economy. Our participation in readying this revolution and using its fruits is the scientific role of our generation. The adoption of science for the betterment of security and production . . . [emphasis added].

Ben-Gurion penned these reflections after his meetings with Professors Bergmann and Joel (Giulio) Rakach, a major nuclear physicist and later the rector of Hebrew University of Jerusalem, who alerted him to the seriousness and significance of the atomic revolution during the War of Independence and even put him in touch with Jewish nuclear experts abroad at that time.[45]

Bergmann – an organic chemist by training – had relations with French nuclear chemists, some of them Jewish, who had worked on the Manhattan Project in Canada. He himself had worked in France after its liberation. These French scientists – like Bergmann when he approached Ben-Gurion – had called General de Gaulle's attention to the atomic bomb and helped de Gaulle establish the French Atomic Energy Commission during the latter's tenure as prime minister of liberated France. The FAEC was a typical product of traditional French bureaucracy, pioneering creativity, and learning from the past, and Bergmann was associated with prominent individuals in its administration from its inception.

In the middle of 1952, about a year after delivering the programmatic speeches of January and April 1951, Defense Minister Ben-Gurion established the Israel Atomic Energy Commission – the "Umbrella Division," as one of its members, Professor Israel Dostrovsky, called it[46] – and appointed Bergmann to be its chair. The IAEC was formed after Hemed's probes in the Negev turned up phosphate deposits that contained small amounts of uranium. In 1950–1951, the Science Corps was civilianized, and efforts were begun to develop patents for the extraction of uranium from phosphates and the manufacture of the heavy water needed by nuclear reactors. Both patents were sold to France and Britain several years later.

When it came to implementing the idea, however, the debates that erupted hearkened back to the use of the term "wars of the Jews," which members of the Israeli elite were fighting behind closed doors at the time. One possibility was for Israel to build a nuclear reactor on its own, thanks to the aforementioned developments and Jewish genius abroad and in Israel itself and to the establishment of a steelmaking infrastructure in Acre using German reparation funds, not to mention the hopes that Ben-Gurion and Bergmann evidently pinned on the Jewish and Israeli scientific community. Indeed, talented physicists who had been sent abroad to study nuclear physics at the end of the War of Independence began to return to Israel at this time. They of all people, however, along with the heads of the Israeli scientific community, opposed the home-manufacture project for various reasons. One was their concern that the vast endeavor would consume all of Israel's scientific potential and capital in the absence of the industrial infrastructure that the implementation of such a venture required. Furthermore, moral considerations were already being expressed at this time – and would be voiced with greater intensity in the next phase – as the bombing of Hiroshima and the fear of interbloc nuclear war plunged the Western scientific world into horror and remorse. In 1958, responding to principled problems concerning scientists' retention of control over their handiwork, Ernst Bergmann's working methods, and the zeal of Director General of the Ministry of Defense Shimon Peres to put the idea into practice at almost any price, the entire commission resigned with the sole exception of its chair, Bergmann.[47]

Absent any chance of American or British assistance in this sensitive matter, and so long as the French nuclear infrastructure had not yet come together, the implementation of the idea had to take a time-out. The idea itself, however, remained alive and continued to occupy Ben-Gurion even after he had resigned his portfolios and relocated to Sede Boqer. His successor at the MOD, Pinchas Lavon, displayed no interest in the nuclear topic, as one may gather from Bergmann's direct contact with Prime Minister Sharett on this issue.[48] Sharett, considering Bergmann overly ardent, sought conventional solutions to the conventional problems that concerned him, for example, solving the water problem in northern Israel and exploring the possibility of a settlement with Egypt via American mediation. He thought it might be possible to solve the water problem by buying an American nuclear reactor for desalination. Be this as it may, Sharett thought it ill-advised to enrage Washington and, perhaps, elicit an undesired Egyptian response by developing Israel's own reactor. After all, President Gamal Abd el Nasser had become a personality of international importance during Sharett's tenure. In 1955, the Bandung conference of "non-aligned" states – which challenged the leadership of the nuclear superpowers – catapulted Nasser to the center of the global stage and transformed him into the leader of modern pan-Arabism. Concurrently, Nasser ordered from the USSR, and received, a small research reactor. Prime Minister Sharett and Defense Minister Lavon seemed unimpressed by this, each in his own way.

By then, Lavon had ensnared himself in disputes both with the COGS, Dayan, for various reasons including extreme reprisals that Lavon had initiated and Dayan ruled out, and with MOD Director General Peres, by attempting to crimp the latter's steps in regard to procurements of conventional weapons in France, viewing them as circumventions of his authority. We do not know whether at this stage Lavon actively opposed the nuclear option as well or, perhaps, thought of it as a pie in the sky. At this time, Bergmann visited Ben-Gurion in Sede Boqer and spoke with him about the nuclear option. Ben-Gurion described it as a goal toward which no effort should be spared and expressed confidence that "we shall have the bomb within ten years." Some time later, Defense Minister Lavon was forced to resign from Sharett's government due to a futile attempt to thwart the British departure from the Suez Canal area, that is, the "1954 Affair." Lavon would try to reopen the case in 1960 (described later as the "1960 Affair"). His resignation, however, brought Ben-Gurion back to the MOD as Lavon's successor and, after the 1955 elections, back to the Office of the Prime Minister as well.

In the meantime, the French nuclear infrastructure was nearly complete and the political echelons in Paris had to decide what to do with it: Should it be used to generate electricity for peaceful purposes or to make bombs for strategic and political necessities? Prime Minister Pierre Mendès-France had already made an initial decision in favor of the military-political calculus (the idea being to maintain a decisive French edge over West Germany) in his decision to extract France from Indo-China. No one at the time was able to make a similar decision on the Algerian question, where an armed uprising against France's grip on this "district" of the homeland was swiftly developing with Nasser's assistance and indirect Soviet support. This paved the way for Israeli–French cooperation against a common foe, Nasser, which in turn engendered nuclear collaboration as well. Such a partnership solved the problem of home manufacture of an Israeli atomic infrastructure and could justify conventional military collaboration for the dual purpose of occupying the Suez Canal zone and toppling Nasser.

The Road to the 1956 War

The image of the IDF, that of a well-trained and efficient army of a new sort that had taken shape in the War of Independence, was reinforced in foreign eyes by the reprisal operations of 1955–1956. Ben-Gurion's return to the playing ground in February 1955 piqued the imagination of the French defense minister,

Pierre Koenig, the hero of Bir Hakeim. Koenig and the chair of the French Atomic Energy Commission, Pierre Guillaumat, concluded an agreement on the issue of military credit to the latter's commission. By making this move, the French political echelon took another step toward the development of a nuclear bomb, a decision that was controversial among the commission members and throughout the French political system, which was badly fragmented to begin with. One of the sides in this controversy was the Socialist Party, which found itself running the country in the aftermath of the Fourth Republic turmoil in 1955. In the past, the Socialists had opposed the development of a French bomb. However, their ascent under Guy Mollet brought about the gestation of Operation Kadesh (the autumn 1956 Sinai War) and France's ultimate decision to follow its own nuclear path pursuant to the failure of the combined operation against Egypt, in cooperation with West Germany (a cooperation that also gave birth to the European Common Market).

In the aftermath of these demarches, Israel intensified its efforts to strengthen its ties with Bonn, a gambit that would make things very difficult for Ben-Gurion domestically and would intersect with a public campaign against his nuclear endeavor. Indeed, after the failure of the 1956 war, the French government decided to give Israel what Mollet called a "royal gift," that is, the Dimona reactor, the construction of which was given final approval by Mollet's successor, Maurice Bourgès-Maunoury, in October 1957.

To reduce this story to its phases, we must retrace our steps to Pierre Koenig. During Sharett's premiership and with his approval, the Israeli COGS, Moshe Dayan, approached Koenig and asked him to give his country some military assistance.[49] Matti Golan's biography of Shimon Peres[50] describes the web of relations that took shape between the man who had been named director general of Lavon's MOD and the French defense minister, a web predicated on "Koenig's admiration for Israel generally and the IDF particularly" – thanks to Ben-Gurion's return to the MOD in February 1955. Pierre Pean, an authoritative French source on whom I will rely as I continue, says that Israel was interested not only in the conventional French aid that it had begun to receive at this time but also in something more as well:[51]

Upon his return from Sede Boqer, the "old lion" wished to secure Israel's existence once and for all. And to do this, he wished to strengthen the scientific effort. . . . [He] reached the conclusion . . . that only France could help Israel to procure [a nuclear infrastructure]. . . . He approached Pierre Koenig, his French counterpart . . . and decided to adopt a nuclear option in order to deter the Arab aggression.

Ben-Gurion had already had this option in mind, as we have seen. In the meantime, however, he had learned from Bergmann and other Israeli envoys in France that it was the French option, now fully ripened, that could grant Israel a similar or identical infrastructure if convenient conditions for it were to come about – and these conditions came about on the way to and pursuant to the 1956 war. It is possible that Lavon's downfall – which left a vacuum at the MOD and was associated with the minister's struggles with the COGS and the director general – was connected with the possibilities that had opened up in France, of which Lavon may or may not have been aware, and greased Ben-Gurion's way back to the MOD. One of the reasons for Ben-Gurion's resignation in 1953, after all, had been the combination of immense fatigue and his realization that Israel needed a far-reaching constitutional reform and, in particular, the adoption of a regional-majority electoral system. His decision to return to the MOD without this reform may have been strongly influenced by the deterioration of relations with Egypt during Sharett's tenure and the sense of urgency in responding by way of the nuclear option.

Ben-Gurion expressed this thinking in a speech during his retirement, quoted previously, noting the importance of dispersing the concentrated population in Greater Tel Aviv "in view of the fatal factor of time [that must be exploited without delay]... because one bomb can destroy the whole country if it is concentrated around Tel Aviv."[52] Afterwards, he added, "Another thing on which we'll have to pledge more resources...is the development of science. It may even be that our security will ultimately depend on it. But I won't speak about it. *Perhaps it'll be the ultimate device that will save us*" [emphasis added].

Once Ben-Gurion returned from Sede Boqer, the foundations of Operation Kadesh (the Sinai War) were slowly laid. At long last the prime minister and defense minister agreed to go ahead with Kadesh despite his skepticism and doubts about a preventive war, as expressed in talks with his COGS, Dayan. The latter sought a conventional preventive war with Egypt in view of the failure of the reprisal actions that followed Egyptian-sponsored acts of terror inside Israel. The operation would aim to preempt the Egyptian army's rearmament with Soviet weapons and create an Israeli bridgehead at Sharm el-Sheikh, which would control the Straits of Tiran and the eastern access to the Suez Canal, blocked by Egypt to Israeli shipping. Several months before the operation, the defense minister responded with the following argument:

Unless we upgrade our army's capability to the ultimate level now, we may end up in the worst position. Our whole disaster is we must not sustain a defeat, for then we are done for; *we must not sustain a defeat. They can sustain a defeat. We can defeat Egypt once, twice, ten times – it's nothing. If they defeat us once – it's all over* [emphasis added].[53]

In other words, as stated, Israel's basic strategic problem stemmed from its inability to inflict on the opponent the same ultimate outcome of war that the Arab side could inflict on Israel. What the American colonists could do to the king of England and that Lincoln could do to the southern states – after failures that nearly allowed the enemy to win – resembles what the Arabs could do to Israel and that Israel could not do to them. Given this asymmetry, the thinking went, Israel must at least enhance its army's capabilities to the utmost. Even a perceptible improvement in the IDF's conventional ability, however, would not resolve the fundamental security inequality in the long run.

In the meantime, having returned to the MOD, Ben-Gurion authorized an extensive reprisal action in Gaza (February 28, 1955) that inflicted heavy losses on the Egyptians. Nasser seized on this operation to justify the large arms transaction that he had planned with Czechoslovakia. The deal prompted COGS Dayan, after having convinced himself that nothing was being gained by the reprisal policy as practiced thus far, to favor preventive war before the Egyptians could equip themselves with modern weapons. Prime Minister Sharett himself preferred to desist from reprisals and seek a political solution with Egypt, with American assistance. However, the Egyptian anti-Israeli demarches, the Lavon Affair (the failed operation in Egypt in 1954), and domestic public opinion, which he had to take into account in view of the guerrilla raids from the Gaza Strip, all converged to defeat Sharett's policy.

In March 1955, Defense Minister Ben-Gurion was quoted in Dayan's memoirs as having said, "There will be no choice but to occupy the Gaza Strip" in order to stop the attacks from this location once and for all.[54] Dayan added, in this same source, that the defense minister had asked him to provide him with data about the army's preparedness for war against Egypt and all the Arab countries. Continuing, Dayan claimed, "In Ben-Gurion's opinion, 'We can drive [Nasser out of the Gaza Strip] overnight without a peep in the international arena.'"[55] Dayan's purpose in saying this was to clash verbal swords with Prime Minister Sharett, who was chary of belligerent entanglement in this arena and others. Now, Israel also faced an Egyptian naval blockade of the southern port town of Eilat, and according to Dayan, the defense minister presented the government, "after preparations at the general staff, with a plan to break through the blockade." According to Dayan, the plan was defeated by a majority of members of the government "with Sharett at their lead." Even though the defense minister adopted Dayan's proposals to occupy Rafah in order to drive a wedge between Egypt and the Gaza Strip[56] and to occupy the Straits of Tiran, a majority of government ministers had the feeling that the army was itching for war and drawing the defense minister in this direction.

Here, however, we must distinguish between the limited goals of a limited and, under certain circumstances, legitimate war as Ben-Gurion saw it, about which he wrestled a great deal, and an all-out preventive war, toward which Dayan indeed seemed to be striving because of the Czechoslovakian deal and what he considered the failure of the reprisal operations. In other words, Ben-Gurion did not accept a defense concept that viewed the destruction of the Egyptian army, at Israel's sole initiative and instigation, and the takeover of the Straits of Tiran, which would give Israel indirect control of the approach to the Suez Canal, as a genuine solution to Israel's problems. Occupying the Strip or cutting it off from Egypt seemed legitimate to Ben-Gurion because the Strip was not Egyptian. It was Egypt's control of Gaza, part of Mandatory Palestine after all, that had drawn Egypt into active involvement in the Palestinian problem and had made Cairo a captive to its commitment to the Palestinians whom it controlled. He viewed the forcible opening of the Straits of Tiran as a legitimate thing to do because the Straits were an international waterway that had been open until Egypt had unilaterally closed them. Such an act – a violent breach of status quo and convention – justified a limited corrective response, such as the one that Ben-Gurion bruited at the peak of the May 1967 crisis, but no more.[57]

A total preventive war to destroy the Egyptian army, obliterate Nasser's regime, and redraw Israel's frontiers in Sinai and the Straits of Tiran – three distinctly different aims – by Israel's force alone or with the help of a medium-strength power that had its own calculus, such as France, and as the outgrowth of cooperation with such a power, was a complicated and dubious proposition. On December 16, 1955, Ben-Gurion spoke pointedly to the COGS against a preventive war conducted by Israel alone – remarks that he kept in mind until the crisis that led to the eruption of the Six Day War of 1967:

There is one basic premise, not only about the question that came up now [Egypt's blockade of the Straits of Tiran] and the menace that gathered strength after the inflow of Soviet weapons to Egypt. The premise is that there's one historical difference between us and the Arabs: they cannot be obliterated.... The situation from our neighbors' perspective is the opposite. They can assume that a last battle is possible, that they can deal Israel such a blow as to eliminate this whole problem and there will be no Israel–Arab question. *Therefore, after every future war and every war that we win, we will face the problem that we face [today] all over again. If war breaks out tomorrow and we win, we will face the fear of a third round, a fourth, and a fifth, endlessly* [emphasis added].[58]

In other words, victory in one conventional war – as in the Six Day War – would carry the seeds of the next war, the Yom Kippur War, and so on to our very day.

The defense minister then listed several rationales against a preventive war that, he said, were amenable to "the whole government" and "much of the nation." They included "the very destruction that any war causes," the setback of "five–seven years" in Israel's development, and the fear of hostile intervention by a third party. Britain was cited in the last-mentioned context. London was Jordan's patron power at the time; moreover, it still had entrée to Iraq. The aspiration that Ben-Gurion attributed to Britain was to divide the southern Negev between Egypt and Jordan. These remarks echoed, in a manner of speaking, Egypt's claims that Israeli possession of this area had driven a foreign wedge between the segments of the Arab world and the British–American Alpha and Omega plans of Eisenhower's first term, which envisaged Israel's ceding of parts of the Negev. There is no doubt, however, that Ben-Gurion was also concerned about the Soviet nuclear superpower, with which Nasser was gradually becoming a regional ally. Ultimately, he spoke in terms similar to those that he used in his January 1951 speech about the political aspects of a unilaterally instigated war, including the immense moral and practical damage that Israel would sustain if the world were to perceive her as an "aggressor nation."

On December 19, 1955, the defense minister spoke with the COGS about the Anglo-American Alpha plan, which had come to his knowledge, including its call for Israeli territorial concessions in the Negev.[59] He was afraid that in this matter, the powers would lean toward Nasser, who wanted an overland bridge from Egypt to Jordan and Saudi Arabia, and that the 1949 armistice demarcation line in Israel's South would be modified by a new UN resolution that the Egyptian army would be "sent" to carry out. In other words, Israel now had to give thought to war, but the IDF was inferior to its enemies and its soft underbelly was its obsolete tank force. Accordingly, Ben-Gurion embarked on an immense effort to build up the Armored Corps by appointing Deputy COGS Chaim Laskov to deal with the matter. For the time being, however, nothing more was done. Even the blockade of the Straits of Tiran, a possible casus belli for its victim, was holding firm.

Let us then reverse course and ask what it was that brought on the change in Ben-Gurion's consistent stance against war with Egypt at Israel's initiative. After all, back in July 1956, he had turned down Dayan's proposals of preventive war, mentioning the blunders of the War of Independence, as noted previously. One explanation should be sought in Nasser's move in late July to nationalize the Suez Canal, thereby throwing the British into the arms of the French. The French defense establishment had long wanted to give Nasser a pounding due to his role in the Algerian uprising. Now, the nationalization of the canal prompted the French and British political echelons to seek common counsel about how to reclaim the canal and give the Egyptian dictator his just desserts. Ben-Gurion was not delinquent in noticing this change, which could add the patron power of Jordan and Iraq, the power that had once wished to appease the Egyptian president at Israel's expense, to the list of Nasser's enemies. If the British could be induced to participate in a French–Israeli military action, they could neutralize Jordan and Iraq and allow the initiated war to proceed on the main front without threats from the eastern flank. Furthermore, the British were considered close allies of the United States, which was immersed in an election year, and were the world's only nuclear power other than the superpowers. If Ben-Gurion was afraid of the Soviets – Nasser's patrons – then the entry of the British into the game could allay this fear somewhat. The problem was how to induce them to cooperate with Israel, and not only with France, in a real way.

Another change that began to form at this stage concerned procurements from France. In particular, the state of the Armored Corps, previously of much concern to Ben-Gurion, had been improved, and the Air Force had begun to receive advanced Dassault aircraft, thanks to a previously concluded arms deal with France.[60] All of these were important elements in the package of the war, but were not the package itself.

The 1956 War: Reality and Perceptions

According to Peres's biographer, who quoted from his diaries and published a version that was amenable to him,[61] "the seed from which Operation Kadesh grew" was a cable that the director general of the MOD sent from Paris on

July 27, 1956. In the cable, according to this source, Peres reported about his meeting with the heads of the French defense establishment. They had asked Israel to furnish intelligence about the Egyptian order of forces and deployment ahead of their meeting with the British. The French, Peres went on to report, also "commented with a smile that Israel would surely be willing to do its share, if asked." For the time being, however, the British opposed any Israeli involvement. The next day, Peres was summoned to the French minister of defense, Maurice Bourgès-Maunoury himself. Bourgès-Maunoury, a leader of the Radical Party, simply asked Peres whether Israel would join France when it set out for war against Egypt. Peres answered in the affirmative at once, without authorization – according to his biographer – but explained his decision by saying "We can always retract" if his government were to disapprove.

Peres viewed the matter as an opportunity that would never recur because of what Israel might obtain for its assent: "conventional arms [and also] a nuclear reactor." He reached the conclusion that in this matter, the French would manage to surmount their inhibitions only if Israel offered something of equal or similar value in return, such as practical military cooperation: *"From then on, the nuclear reactor ... became an inseparable part, if not the catalyst, of the process that led to Operation Kadesh* [emphasis added]." For if it were a matter of getting Israel an atomic reactor, one might under certain conditions obtain Ben-Gurion's consent to a preventive war fought not by Israel alone, as Dayan had proposed in December 1955. Golan's account sheds clear light on Peres's original idea: that Israel should "replace Britain in a military partnership at a time of convenience to France" in return for the reactor and more.

The British preferred to wait "another two months or so" and plan the operation with proper thoroughness from their bases in Cyprus, whereas the French wanted to strike at once due to the U.S. elections and the anti-Soviet uprising in Hungary.[62] Since no one in the French political echelon was willing to act without the British, however, Peres's idea was a nonstarter. The difficulty was how to convince Anthony Eden's government to join promptly – no later than October 1956 – and to recognize Israel's partnership in the operation, if only surreptitiously. The delivery of the reactor, too, was not irrevocably assured even if France seemed willing to go ahead with it. Ultimately, it took until October 1957 to conclude the final delivery agreement, which General de Gaulle's France reneged on later.

Although this affair exceeds the bounds of our concern in this chapter, it may explain various moves that Ben-Gurion himself employed in the secret talks that preceded the operation, the conditions that he presented the French and the British, and his uncertainty about the sincerity of those two cunning and egotistic European powers when their national interests were at stake. Therefore, since Peres is the main source of the above-quoted Israeli publications on this issue, we must again consult Pierre Pean – our authoritative French source – to cross-reference the remarks. In the background, we have German studies about the French nuclear program and German publications about assistance from the Bonn government for Israel's atomic research after Operation Kadesh, which could have been its outcome.[63]

According to Pean, the *responsables* of the French defense establishment had long been striving for nuclear arms of their own – after having surmounted conventional inertia and interests within the army – and for a special alliance with Israel. Since the French military considered the two aims mutually "consistent," the French officials also saw room for Israeli–French cooperation in the nuclear domain. In the meantime, Israelis of consequence such as Ernst Bergmann had been involved in the French nuclear program from its outset, if only by having worked with some of its leaders. Bergmann, in particular, had been monitoring its progress closely. "France is isolated between the two superpowers," Pean quotes these security officials as saying, and is but a "middling" power – that is, it lacks the status of a "real" power but has scientific and industrial abilities that small countries lack. The Anglo-Americans had "embarrassed" Paris in the Middle East and in Vietnam; that is, the British had driven the French out of Syria and Lebanon without giving them a foothold in oil-rich Iraq like Britain's, and the Americans had become the rulers of the Saudi Arabian roost with its oil treasures – as seemed to be the case – and had not helped France properly in the national disaster of its war in Vietnam. (France had sought nuclear assistance to break the siege on Dien Bien Phu, a request that President Eisenhower rejected categorically.) "And now it is being attacked 'from inside' by the Algerian Arabs, who are being supported by Nasser," Pean writes.

At this time, "from inside" meant that France considered Algeria an integral part of itself and a testing ground for the nuclear bomb and missiles that it had not yet developed. Pean continues: "The bomb makes it possible to lift one's head. Israel is a dot of light in the Middle East and an ally ... against common foes." Although this outlook had taken root in the soil of the French defense establishment, it was not necessarily shared by the social-radical parties in Guy Mollet's coalition or by the French Socialist Party itself. The left flank of this party was headed by Jewish factotums such as Daniel Mayer, who opposed a French bomb vituperatively. The director general of the French Atomic Energy Commission, Jean-Francis Perrin, shared their feelings. Pean recalls that in his swearing-in speech for the premiership, Mollet proclaimed himself a sworn opponent of a French "national bomb" and spoke in favor of a "joint European nuclear enterprise," presumably for peaceful use. Even though there was talk of a national bomb, French Socialists were aghast about the possibility of seeing this weapon in the hands of France's traditional military officials, whom they suspected of harboring ultranationalist and right-wing sentiments to begin with. What is more, Mollet relied on the large Communist faction in the National Assembly at the outset of his term; in this respect, this faction served the Soviet interest of keeping the bomb out of the hands of any country not under the Kremlin's heel. Powerful players, however, including Defense Minister Bourges' Radical Party; the Gaullists – for whom a French national bomb was the apple of their eye – and various defense establishment officials forced the bomb down Mollet's throat.

The latter officials had convinced themselves that cooperation with Israel, a Socialist pioneering country persecuted by a quasi-Fascist tyrant – an imitation of Mussolini, so to speak, as they pictured Nasser at the time – would silence critical voices on the French Left and would help to legitimize the French bomb in the international scientific and political community. Therefore, giving Israel a reactor within a framework of mutual cooperation in nuclear matters was something that they needed for domestic and international reasons, and the Suez War created the practical strategic-political framework that would make it possible.

Therefore, Guy Mollet followed in Mendès-France's footsteps toward establishing an independent French deterrent, enlisting the Gaullist faction in parliament to absolve him of his dependency on the Communists. His main concern, however, was the uprising in Algeria. And this uprising – abetted by a common foe, President Nasser of Egypt – induced him to reach out to Israel so wholeheartedly that he promised it a nuclear reactor. It is not clear enough whether he intended to keep his promise and what exactly the French gained from Israel's information and services for the promotion of their own nuclear program, that is, that the reactor was not a "royal gift." Pean tells us that the Weizmann Institute calculated the parameters of the French bomb by means of American equipment that Washington refused to give France. The reactor in Dimona cost a great deal of money that was paid on time; obviously it helped to promote the French nuclear program.

These factors aside, however, according to Pean's account, it was actually the Soviets' threats to use nuclear missiles against Britain and France and to menace Israel's existence during the 1956 war, coupled with the subsequent failure of the entire French–British operation, that evidently convinced Mollet's government and that of his successor, Bourgès-Maunoury, to honor the initial undertaking and give Israel a nuclear-deterrence infrastructure of its own. That is, the severity of France's isolation and Israel's, the prestigious victory attained by Nasser due to the pressure of the two nuclear superpowers, and the Soviets' use of their nuclear missiles to rescue Nasserite Egypt converged to influence far-reaching decisions by Mollet's government in many fields. France finally assented to the establishment of a European Common Market, an idea that it had rebuffed until then due to its fear of Germany's economic superiority, and finally endorsed a military nuclear option and European cooperation in atomic energy for peaceful use. The possibility of collaborating with Germany and Italy in military nuclear matters was discussed afterwards as an alternative to the American nuclear umbrella, which had proved so disappointing in the Suez War. Shimon Peres, at least, pinned much hope on this European alternative to Washington.[64]

Pean then describes the road to Suez and back, a road that led Israel from occupied Sharm el-Sheikh to Dimona – a desert town in the Negev, near which construction of the French-supplied reactor began in 1958. According to this

French source, Guy Mollet was in the thrall of a "Munich reflex," that is, refusal to submit again and again to a Fascist dictator, as he considered Nasser to be. At issue here, according to Pean, are historical analogies to the 1930s that were typical of the lengthy period when Israel was considered a Socialist republic whose woes resembled those of the Spanish Republic in the 1930s. France had remained aloof during Spain's agonies, not helping the Republicans even during the premiership of the Socialist Léon Blum and not aiding Spain in its struggle against Franco's Fascists when the latter received assistance from Hitler and Mussolini. France had not impeded Hitler himself at the beginning of his career as dictator of Germany and had done nothing to stop Mussolini's aggression in northern Africa and Ethiopia for reasons that included its inability to secure British support and to overcome the isolationism of the United States. "In 1936 we didn't do a thing, but in 1956 I saved Israel," Mollet is quoted as having said. This touching historical argument, however, omits France's ongoing rule in Algeria.

One of the lessons of the past that Mollet, his colleagues, and Ben-Gurion kept in mind and treated as a matter of principle and geostrategic calculus in determining the fate of the war was the necessity of partnership with Britain. Ben-Gurion was reluctant to embark on a preventive war in conjunction with France unless basic conditions were investigated and satisfied. One of these conditions was the active involvement of Britain. If Britain were aboard, Jordan and Iraq would be neutralized, Britain's plans to detach chunks of the southern Negev from Israel would be mothballed, and French combat air squadrons would be stationed in Israel to defend its cities – all apart from Britain's nuclear capability, which was supposed to restrain the Soviets even though it was limited at this point, and from the equipping of Israel with a nuclear option, which was one of the clauses in Israel's accord with France.

The French battleship *Jean Barre* helped the Israeli forces to advance in Rafah by opening fire, and Dayan prepared a cover story for the launching of the hostilities. The parachuting of IDF forces into the Mitla Pass, close to the Suez Canal, was dressed up as a reprisal action so that it could be terminated if Britain and France were to abandon their intended role of separating the warring sides and fail to take action for the capture of the canal area. The outright eradication of Nasser's regime seemed to be a realistic goal in view of the success of the tripartite operation; some even believed it would be possible to enter Cairo and oust the Egyptian president by force.[65] Be that as it may, the IDF did its part from October 29, 1956, onward, and its allies adhered to their part of the agreement, "separating the rivals" and, in fact, taking over the canal zone. The British, however, went about this in a very desultory way. In the meantime, the Soviets quashed the uprising against their rule in Hungary and their prime minister, Marshal Nikolai Bulganin, sent messages to London, Paris, and Jerusalem containing an overt threat to use nuclear missiles against the capitals of France and Britain and to menace Israel's very existence. The United States, washing its hands of the war that its NATO allies and Israel had instigated behind its back, threatened Britain with economic damage. Eden's government sized up the threats and capitulated to the powers' demand at once. The opposition – the Labour Party and various Liberal and radical circles – made the campaign into a "tripartite conspiracy" against a third-world country that was reasserting its rights to property that the colonial powers had stolen from it in the previous century.

In Israel, Moshe Sharett, who before the operation had been dispossessed of the foreign affairs portfolio that he had held in Ben-Gurion's government, responded to them by echoing their allegations. Fringe radicals, such as Professor Yeshayahu Leibowitz, seconded this view, arguing that what had happened was a "conspiracy" between Israel and two tarnished colonial powers. They were wrong: Britain and France were, in fact, rising nuclear powers. France in particular, after many metamorphoses that are not of concern to us here, would follow the Suez operation and its failure with the gift to Israel of the basis for its future security and the peace process of the 1970s onward.

Even though the Soviet threat of nuclear missiles was evidently a bluff – one doubts that it was practicable in terms of available Soviet intermediate-range missiles – Britain's pullback under concerted Soviet–American pressure isolated France politically and dismantled a military partnership that had a nuclear dimension, however limited. Another outcome of the Soviet threat – as one may conjecture according to foreign publications – was the development of an appropriate response, French and Israeli alike, to the Kremlin's nuclear missiles. The hardware that would eventually be called the Israeli Jericho II nuclear missile was also born of the failure of 1956.

The British capitulation, according to Pean, did touch off a bitter and piercing debate in the French cabinet. Little had been accomplished around the canal to this point, and surrender now would consign the operation to total political and military failure. It would also mean leaving Israel to its own devices, with the Sinai (and the Gaza Strip) in its clutches, notwithstanding explicit promises to Jerusalem to the contrary. Mollet's government, however, rejected motions to continue fighting without the British and succumbed to the demands of the superpowers and the UN for a cease-fire and an unconditional pullback from Egypt. Israel immediately came under heavy international pressure to evacuate the territories that it had occupied – pressure that would eventually lead to its protracted refusal to vacate territories occupied in 1967. The logic behind this is the impression that Israel had retreated from Sinai and Gaza for nothing and that the IDF's glorious victory in Operation Kadesh had been squandered. Truth to tell, however, several things were obtained in return.

At first glance, Ben-Gurion had forfeited the territorial achievements of the Sinai War for the stationing of a UN force, as had been worked out in protracted negotiations with the Americans and UN Secretary-General Dag Hammarskjöld, both up and down the Gaza Strip and at the Straits of Tiran. For the next eleven years, UN soldiers would serve as an efficient buffer between Egypt and the Palestinians in the Strip and guarantee the nonrecurrence of the naval blockade on Eilat. Israel even received assurances about freedom of shipping to and from Eilat, since the presence of UN soldiers depended on

Egypt's goodwill. Indeed, it was over the UN force and the resumption of the naval blockade on Eilat that the 1967 crisis ostensibly erupted.

In retrospect, Nasser could have put these two factors to use if he had been dragged into doing so, or if he had wished to provoke Israel so that the latter would go to war on its own initiative, inasmuch as the reactor in Dimona and everything related to it were about to become an operational threat and turn the Middle East strategic equation upside-down so that Israel's existence could no longer be threatened.

According to Pierre Pean, Israel's foreign minister, Golda Meir, and the director general of the MOD, Shimon Peres, set out for Paris in order to probe the French intentions on the very day that Guy Mollet's government decided to accept a cease-fire in the Suez: "Ben-Gurion, upset about the threat of Soviet intervention in the Middle East, wanted to understand France's intentions before making a decision about the Sinai." The two Israelis met with French Foreign Minister Christian Pineau, Defense Minister Bourgès-Maunoury, and the latter's director general, Abel Thomás.

Pean quotes Thomás as saying that it was Peres who had directly brought up the matter of Israel's nuclear "deterrent force" on November 7, the day before Ben-Gurion's announcement about withdrawing from the Sinai. Peres's reason for doing this, says Pean, was that he "[did] not believe in others' guarantees [of the UN and President Eisenhower in regard to freedom of shipping to and from Eilat and the UN force in the Gaza Strip].... What would be your attitude if we were to establish our own [nuclear] deterrent?"[66] Pean says that the transition from buying a reactor to the object itself, that is, a nuclear infrastructure with everything it implies – including a facility for separation of plutonium for military purposes – was immediately answered in the affirmative insofar as Bourgès and Thomás were concerned. Even the director general of the French Atomic Energy Commission, Francis Perrin, who had withheld his support from the manufacture of a French national bomb, dropped his opposition in the aftermath of the Suez failure and added, following the lead of Prime Minister Guy Mollet himself, that France "has everything to gain from cooperating... in regard to Israel's 'deterrent force.'" Pean describes the prime minister as having been "obsessed" about giving Israel the bomb as a French moral and practical debt to the Jewish state, in view of the failure of the Suez war and the risks that Nasser's prestigious and Soviet-assisted victory had placed at Israel's door: "Egypt has to be avenged... and the party that would do the avenging is an Israel that has the atom bomb."

This version of events portrays Mollet as a wobbly personality who initially opposed even a French bomb and then, having gone ahead and developed it, handed it – in an unprecedented act – to a foreign country while trying unsuccessfully to quash a guerrilla war that an Arab majority was waging against a French minority in Algeria. A Gaullist aroma of erstwhile criticism about the lack of focus and strategic goals and a properly phrased policy, to which the French leftist camp had to adhere unswervingly, wafts from this source. Indeed, General de Gaulle, acceding to power in 1958, would impair the Israeli nuclear program that his predecessors had approved, although he could not stop it at the advanced stage that it had attained when he made his decision in this matter. It was 1960–1962, and de Gaulle had his hands full with the forthcoming pullout from Algeria and the disengagement of his security establishment from Israel in the nuclear context. Now, the struggle for the completion of the mission would shift to two other arenas: those of the superpowers and of the inter-Arab scene.

Back in Israel, the debate about the very construction of the reactor had been resolved. The debate over the contribution that Israeli scientists would make to its construction was over, too: Since there would be no need for an Israeli reactor, Israeli scientists would not be needed either. A French reactor would be imported in turnkey fashion and French technicians would build it secretly. For a construction project, most of the requisite professionals were no longer scientists but engineers. From then on, the "wars of the Jews" in this matter would become a tussle over sustaining the nuclear option against steadily tightening American pressure and the possible expression of Soviet displeasure. These struggles would insinuate themselves into the early 1960s crises that erupted with respect to relations with West Germany and the Lavon Affair. The story of the construction of Israel's nuclear infrastructure only began with the Sinai War; as it neared completion, this option would become an element in the next round of the domestic wars of the Jews and Israel's difficulties abroad. That is, it would play a role in the crisis that would end with the Six Day War.

5

From the 1956 War to the "Lavon Affair"

The Controversy over Ben-Gurion's Interest in the Jewish Messianic Vision

Although it had ended with an Israeli retreat and no palpable results from the standpoint of most of the public, the 1956 war and its aftermath catapulted Ben-Gurion to one of his highest levels of public esteem. Also, however, it helped to widen dangerous fissures in his relations with important elites.

When this period got under way, Ben-Gurion was exuding a conceited if not a condescending mind-set. It went beyond his conviction that his standing allowed, if not required, him to behave in this manner, as though he were an Israeli George Washington who also possessed the intellectual depth that the other Founding Fathers supplied in the American case, making him a cardinal figure in the country's birth and a paragon for posterity. It also seemed to him – for the time being – that Israel was truly a success story despite its horrific difficulties and bumps along the way. The country's population, originally tiny, had doubled and tripled without grave mishaps, at least thus far. Most of the Holocaust survivors had acculturated themselves by their own efforts – more because of their vitality and willingness to immerse themselves in Israeli society than due to society's willingness and practical ability to absorb them – and at the outset of our discussion, we showed that this matter was of paramount concern to Ben-Gurion.[1] However, as he had planned, the IDF had become one of the principal agencies for their absorption, just as the other state services – some directly controlled by Mapai and others controlled by other political parties – busied themselves integrating a motley collective of immigrants from Romania, Poland, and various Muslim countries – successfully to that point.

The embryonic economy, which had absorbed severe blows during the War of Independence and the lengthy foreign-currency crisis that followed, was beginning to grow with amazing vigor. Much progress was being achieved in agriculture and other areas of science – the latter given top priority by the prime minister, who, among other things, imposed upon reluctant and individualistic professors the creation of the Israel Academy of Sciences. The country's youth seemed to have extricated itself from the vise of Mapam, which had split in the mid-1950s and joined Ben-Gurion's coalition in its new two-flank form. Stalin and his Soviet ethos were dead and gone. After the fact, Ben-Gurion was enjoying a respite from his immediate concerns and, ostensibly, even from his long-term concerns about Israel's security. Nasser's army had been bludgeoned and needed a time-out for repair and rearmament. The 1949 armistice lines, though not "ideal" – as Ben-Gurion had noted in the past – could be lived with. This depended on the future of Jordan, whose king perched uncertainly on his throne, and on the political sensitivity of the West Bank, the inherent explosiveness of Jewish control of its Palestinian inhabitants, and Israeli control of East Jerusalem, which would have to be addressed in due course. The Algerian model – an uprising by an Arab majority against the French minority – had the potential of helping Israel in its relations with France in the short term.

In his meeting with de Gaulle in June 1960, however (discussed in the next chapter), Ben-Gurion suggested to the French president that he mimic Ben-Gurion's own priorities of settling the empty Negev Desert and not controlling Arab-populated territories such as the West Bank, that is, that the French should settle parts of the Sahara and eschew any attempt to retain Algeria's mixed towns:

I explained [to de Gaulle] the danger of adding a million Arabs [to the Jewish state].... An Algeria would rise up in our midst and might undermine the whole country.... Our urgent problem is the lack of Jews, not the lack of territory [emphasis added].[2]

Concurrently, the IDF's prestige was skyrocketing, the army commanding political value as a deterrent force and domestic value as an agency of social consolidation. Much of this was due to the minister of defense's own rhetoric after the Sinai War, which elicited responses of disapproval and protest in intellectual circles. The perpetual concern about the lack of foreign sources of arms had been abated by what appeared to be an effective military alliance with France, which was busy fighting in Algeria. Down in Dimona, as the nuclear reactor supplied by France was beginning to take shape in total secrecy at the end of the decade, the foundations for Israel's long-term defense infrastructure were being laid. At first, de Gaulle's accession in 1958 caused no delays in construction, even though the general had not been a party to the October 1957 agreement with respect to the reactor. For one thing, de Gaulle was busy overhauling the French domestic regime, a necessary pursuit that must have piqued Ben-Gurion's interest in him. Mainly, however, de Gaulle seemed to be interested in a close partnership with West Germany within the framework of an advanced European union that would eventually cooperate in economic and security affairs in addition to, and perhaps instead of, the continental states' dependency on the United States.

Israel had not received the kind of American defense commitment that Western Europe enjoyed under the NATO umbrella, even though the Soviet Union had threatened Israel's existence with nuclear missiles during the Sinai War. However, what appeared to be an important and promising European response to Washington's treatment of its French ally during the Suez campaign also entailed an Israeli rapprochement with West Germany. Here, the prime minister found himself at the threshold of a domestic political imbroglio that would worsen steadily and tie into the criticism of the nuclear option as the key to Israel's security, as opposed to conventional options that included the occupation of territories in order to create strategic depth.

At the end of the immediate aftermath of the Sinai War, Yigal Allon, now a leading personality in the Achdut ha-Avoda–Po'alei Zion Party – even though he had not joined the government on its behalf, for the time being – published a book called *Masakh shel hol* [Sandscreen] (1959). In this volume, Allon proposed an alternative strategy to Ben-Gurion's, largely entailing a "preemptive counterstrike," given the existence of any number of justifications for war that he listed at the outset of his tome. Eventually, Allon and his comrades would also subject Ben-Gurion's German policy to a crescendo of criticism and would find sympathetic ears in this and other respects within Mapai itself, at the expense of Ben-Gurion and his aides, who were dealing with the Dimona and Germany issues. In other words, it seemed as though at the end of this period, the prime minister was beginning to lose his grip on his party for several reasons that call for close investigation, foremost the 1960 Lavon Affair. This affair, however, was preceded and nourished by criticism emanating from a variety of intellectuals. The matter had first come up for debate shortly after and in the aftermath of the Sinai War, when a rather lengthy period of quiescence along the borders ensued. The outcome was an essential awakening of contrasts, doubts, and challenges to Ben-Gurion's leadership, which churned under the surface and gained further turbulence due to his meddling in matters of culture, ideological content, language, and literature.

At this time, Ben-Gurion was occupied not only in defining the nature of Zionism as a political movement that rested, among other things, on messianic yearnings for the Holy Land and a life of special value there, but also in repeatedly preaching to the public that it must be "a people of virtue and a light unto the nations." At this stage, Ben-Gurion did begin to attribute special value to the "state" – the state that he had initially viewed as "no more than an instrument" – and invested its current history with "messianic" and "visionary" importance that could not but outrage intellectuals of various stripes. However, as we argued in Chapter 1, this was not merely an effort on the part of a practical man to be a guiding light in matters of the intellect, since Ben-Gurion had always valued these matters, but also an outlook that he had developed over time: the State of Israel as a unique phase in the achievements of the Jewish people. This is not to say that he glorified the state. Instead, he argued that "[t]he state is also an idea . . . because it is a reality different from that inhabited by Jews anywhere [else] on earth." It is so," he said, "because it fulfills "ideas of revolution" amid unending revolution. These ideas of revolution were the settling of the Negev, the ruralization of an urban population, and the transformation of members of the middle class (recent immigrants, for the most part) into a productive Israeli working class.

This doctrine, however, also left room for an attempt to acknowledge the difficulties of this revolution and the expected disadvantages of Israeli society in the conceptual field proper, since Ben-Gurion found it necessary to engage in these matters because of the rapidly changing nature of this society. He had to offer his society worthy secular elements, given his realization that society was steadily divesting itself of values, that his generation had taken for granted. His involvement in these issues, however, was a response to reflections on matters of state and statism and the sense of emptiness and manifestations of the "angst" of the world that were emanating from the intellectual community itself. Israelis who felt this way seemed to have returned to the world of Diasporic *luftmentschen* even though they were supposed to have become "new Jews." And if a new Jew were at issue at all, on what cultural substances and beliefs could this Jew base his or her life if typical Diasporic doubts and vacillations had begun, termite-like, to reinfest the foundations of the Israeli intelligentsia?[3]

In Professor Michael Keren's opinion (*Ben-Gurion and the Intellectuals*), Ben-Gurion was behaving like a "philosopher-king" – mimicking the Platonic ideal of a leader who wishes to integrate rulership might with moral-political power and, by dint of both, to station himself above his nation and its elites as an omniscient guide. In my opinion, however, Keren makes rash and nonhistorical use of this concept of the philosopher-king, a Greek concept more than two millennia old. In fact, Ben-Gurion went about his Renaissance man performance within a democratic sociopolitical framework that he considered a given and desired state of affairs, which nevertheless needed fundamental structural reform. For the time being, he conceded, the existing political setup could be tolerated. Indeed, he tolerated it by finding a way to recruit ministers from the Achdut ha-Avoda Party in support of the Sinai War, thereby driving a wedge in this respect among them and between them and their former partner, the leftist Mapam. In the resulting state of affairs, Ben-Gurion could enjoy – for the time being – an unchallenged position at the center of the political map. One could only ask, however, how long this situation would last, and for this reason, he was already making an immense and strenuous effort to convince at least the members of his own party of the necessity of his "British" reform, even as he continued to involve himself in affairs of intellect and content.

Keren even enumerates, without the proper intellectual reflection, the contents of this philosopher-king's policies. Ben-Gurion, he says, put "political messianism" to use in the promotion of political causes, and since he was a "monist" – a man with a one-track mind – he tried to rewrite the Bible and biblical research for this purpose, to enlist authors in the service of the state, and to rub noses with philosophers without being able to understand their vacillations in matters of knowledge, its limits, and its criticism.[4]

Keren's book expresses perceptible sympathy toward Ben-Gurion as an individual but does not explore very deeply his relationship with Plato and the challenge that Greek philosophy presented to this scion of Judaism – a challenge that we must take up at this stage of our discussion. Its seeming crux, from Ben-Gurion's point of view, was his awareness that Greek science strove to understand the world as it was but invested this awareness with a secular moral and aesthetic quality. It is thanks to Greece that the negation of hubris – the individual's unlimited ambition in society and state – became a value. The vengeful hand of "nemesis" became an inviolable value in Western civilization, coupled with the positive virtues of "self-restraint" and the other cardinal virtues that Plato lauded. Judaism sought to shape the world as it wanted the world to be by the strength of a religious faith that seemed to have lost its hold on most of its offspring. Admittedly, it was Spinoza who liberated Western man of his dependency on the belief that man and the world were designed ab initio along lines imprinted in them by God, embedded with the sorts of codes that dictate their conduct. Plato's attempt to attract man to the ideals of good, morality, and behavior was a nonreligious attempt to make him better and more moral or, at least, to encourage the few spiritually superior individuals to reach out to these ideals and allow them to dominate their minds and political actions. It was an interesting attempt and an intellectual challenge, but plainly it could not respond to the requirements and challenges of ancient Greece itself. Furthermore, the thinking of Western man had come a long way since then, with the help and under the influence of Judaism and the Jews. Under Spinoza's influence, an immensely powerful intellectual tool was developed that obviated secular theories of human nature and humankind's debts to nature, and its embedded codes.

For Ben-Gurion, however, there remained a philosophical problem: how to integrate the world "as it is" into the world "as it should be" without religious faith. The philosophical solution, he said, lies in the Greek belief that there is truth in the very act of seeking the truth and that this truth is not amoral. The Jewish statesman hoped, despite his keen political acumen, that one could ask people – and certainly the intellectually capable among them – to seek the truth because there is truth in history. There is truth in people's doings and the investigation of people's doings, and one may connect this with the demand of people that they undertake to behave morally. One may do this because Judaism demands that we do it – even if one of the bases of Judaism's argument is religious and, as such, incongruent with "truth." Just the same, the truth exists and it is this: Judaism seeks justice for itself and others just as it abounds with messianic yearnings for change in its state and for Jewish redemption in the Jewish homeland. This, to Ben-Gurion, is a historical, not just a religious, truth, and therefore, from his standpoint, it should be recognized and nurtured without religious faith.

Western science, born in Greece and rediscovered thanks to the Arabs, who had preserved and developed it all the way to the Middle Ages, states that there is truth in nature, society, and history. There is mathematical truth, a physical truth that can be observed, expressed, and calculated in mathematical ways. And there is biological truth, which concerns itself with the functioning of cells in their simplest and most complex forms; its discovery may cure people of illness and make their lives much easier. This truth may take on the complexion of natural law. History and society are different in terms of deterministic regularity. However, there is historical truth, there are truths that explain societies and how they behave, and there are tools of analysis and judgment with which one may isolate them. The problem begins with the facts, those things that lie at the core of research and the judicial system, and the need to interpret them makes matters very complicated. It is a fact that every society has various elites, groups, and minorities. Each can be investigated, and one can, in one's investigation, reach out to the singular truth of each as a part or a minority that has its own different awareness in a national society or an American-style pluralistic one. The postmodern argument – that each of these players has a "truth" of its own, that all have intermingling truths or logics, and that there is no scientific way to prefer one truth over another – has made social and historical research of these phenomena impossible and deciding among them impractical. "Deciding" means determining what the historical facts are, where injustice was committed, and why, whether it was intentional, as in the acts of the Nazis, or the outcome of other processes, with neither criminal nor conscious intent or a corresponding ideology.

Obviously, the historian, the sociologist, and the judge must apply the severe humility and discipline that his or her profession entails when attempting to elucidate even phenomena less grave than the Nazis. Often the researcher will peer into an abyss of insufficient sources, secondary and clashing sources, and mist and noise emanating from the nature of his or her research. Scholars must, however, report accurately to their readers about these difficulties, the limits of their investigations, and the impermanent nature of their findings. The statesperson is absolved of the researcher's obligations, but not totally. A statesman-intellectual does try to seek the truth, and in Ben-Gurion's case, this meant not only collecting history and philosophy books that seemed to be relevant in his view but also reading them. In other words, Ben-Gurion was, in a sense, a statesman-scholar; for this reason, the rules that are binding on professional researchers, judges of various kinds, and anyone whose profession is the investigation of truth applied to him, albeit not as strictly. His interpretation of the Bible and Jewish history definitely embodied not only a quest for truth but also an attempt to use these "materials" to build a nation out of various fragments and to invest the resulting product with living spirit. Intellectuals of whatever kind who were – or became – Ben-Gurion's disputants in the 1960s preached the limits of human knowledge and the inability of truth-seeking persons to attain the truth. Some of them even had "truths" of their own, challenging Ben-Gurion's truths by citing the ostensible inability to attain the quest for truth or the existence of such ability.

Here, I will not delve into Professor Yeshayahu Leibowitz's moral and political arguments against Ben-Gurion in regard to the Qibya incident – an Israeli reprisal operation that Ben-Gurion publicly termed an unauthorized rogue action – and his futile attempt to deny IDF responsibility for the many civilian casualties that the village had suffered on its account. After all, the alternative ethical system proposed by Leibowitz – an observant Jew who could not explain why the Commandments should be observed and who totally separated his obligations as a Commandment-observant person from the state and its actions – left no room for debate.[5] Leibowitz aspired not only to moral public influence but also to political power. He established his own party, Hamishtar he-Hadash (The New Regime) along with Shmuel Tamir, a Ben-Gurion nemesis of a different type, a former far-right stalwart who had a score to settle with Ben-Gurion since the latter had wiped out his IZL in the 1944 purge known as "the Season." Tamir, no less ambitious a political creature than Leibowitz, actually managed, through the good offices of Uri Avneri's weekly magazine *Haolam Hazeh* (This world), to cook the question of Mapai's behavior during the Holocaust into a political scandal. When their party failed at the polls, Leibowitz eventually settled for public influence by running an anti-nuclear club, and finally became a religious moralistic anarchist. Furthermore, he behaved like those pronounced "humanists" who fought one another to the death during the sunset of the Renaissance and did not flinch from any rhetorical tool that they could acquire, as Burckhardt is quoted in Chapter 1. Indeed, that is how he treated Ben-Gurion in every respect – the construction of the reactor in Dimona is only one example – and belabored him to the best of his ability even after Ben-Gurion's death in 1973.[6]

From the early 1950s onward, however, Leibowitz's arguments about the place of the IDF in Ben-Gurion's thinking fell into alignment with a growing discomfort among other intellectuals, represented by Professors Nathan Rotenstreich and Martin Buber, concerning the role of messianism in Ben-Gurion's doctrine after the Sinai War – according to which the IDF had been "blessed with a messianic mission."[7] This military messianic mission, Keren argues, caused "the distinction between ideals and power" to blur, as one might expect when a flesh-and-blood army becomes something loftier than the nation behind it and the servant of values that surpass human limits and controls. The Lavon Affair was, as it seemed, a practical manifestation of this blurring of domains, whether its heroes indeed behaved as they did for "messianic" reasons or for totally different ones. Indeed, the quest for truth in the Affair and in various tangential matters, for example, Israeli–German relations and the construction of the nuclear reactor, became a condition for systematic discussion of Ben-Gurion's thinking and actions. However, as stated in Chapter 1, such a systematic discussion was difficult – if not impossible – to undertake in the political reality of Israel. Many participants in the discussion took no real interest in it. They had political goals, were convinced up front that the army had become messianic and had jettisoned all burdens of control, or thought that the Ben-Gurionesque "state" had become an authoritarian or semitotalitarian creature relative to their expectations and, above all, to their habits from the Yishuv or Diaspora period. All of this happened because their concepts of the state were weak, foggy, and therefore not based on adequate knowledge.

The inherent historical irony of their struggle against Ben-Gurion and their contribution to the destruction of his status are issues that will continue to occupy us, especially when we compare his quest for a reasonable degree of control by Israel over its future as defined in late 1954 to the criticism leveled against him after the Sinai War. Thanks to the Sinai campaign, which led to French and German aid, Israel was released from its almost complete isolation and enjoyed a reasonable degree of strength and inner and foreign support. In a speech at Ohalo, December 16, 1954, Ben-Gurion called for just such inner strength:

> There are things that we can't change, and these are the stances of the Great Powers, and those of the Arabs as well. The Jews are accustomed to being egocentric, and they judge America on the basis of the interests of the Jewish people, not on the basis of American interests. The Jewish people do not determine American interest . . . and clearly enough . . . the United States perceives itself, rightly, as the leader of the Free World, and perceives Russia as the main danger – and which watches a large space inhabited by Arabs, and acknowledges their importance. . . . [But] the danger [to Israel] from this is exaggerated, in my opinion . . . because much depends on us, in the forthcoming years, whether we shall be strong or not.[8]

Back to Michael Keren's arguments: One of his "truths," which he reiterated as if it were self-evident, was that Ben-Gurion aspired to "political messianism" and that this explains, as something that hardly needs proof, his striving for "state control of society."[9] "[Ben-Gurion treated] the state as a goal unto itself because [he allegedly saw] historical if not meta-historical significance in its very existence," states Keren, parroting arguments raised by Buber, Rotenstreich, and others before and during the Affair. If, however, we contemplate France from Stanley Hoffman's perspective as quoted in Chapter 1, then the French state would surely fail Buber's test. After all, the French obviously invest the existence of their state with historical "if not meta-historical" significance. Obviously, this significance should dominate French society, if only because French society has been badly fragmented and schismatic since the French Revolution and because the revolution created a strong state ethos that circumscribes French society's centrifugal forces and attempts – in keeping with its changing dominant states of mind – to tend to the "public good," safeguard historical and human values, and translate these values into the language of action.

Now, Buber and others were evidently speaking about Britain and its "civil society," and the historian Professor Ya'akov L. Talmon joined them with arguments that exuded a British "civil" redolence, as opposed to the aroma of revolutionary France that wafted from Buber's anger over Ben-Gurion's behavior in regard to the Affair. As we have said, however – and we will need to develop this point in the context of the debate over the Affair – where foreign and defense affairs and social and economic reform were at issue, Britain's civil society was loathe to deprive the state of the vast power that had been ceded to it. This society even regarded the defense agencies and civil administration as guarantors of its very existence and of respect for its traditions, including the civil society tradition itself. Therefore, there was no absolute contradiction between the immense power of the British state and its social and economic needs in the eyes of Britons generally and the British elites particularly. The person who subjected this to revolutionary change was Margaret Thatcher, who began to detach the state from the economy from a neoconservative perspective with which Buber, Rotenstreich, and their intellectual successors in our vicinity probably would not want to live.

Keren's argument about the Ben-Gurionesque "state" as busily training individuals to fulfill their "utopian role," as well as similar remarks along the lines of philosopher Rotenstreich's allegations as expressed in his correspondence with Ben-Gurion on the eve of the Affair, were incomprehensible to Ben-Gurion, and for good reason.[10] Ben-Gurion, the Renaissance man, saw nothing "utopian" about bringing forth the individual's "latent strengths" and hoisting society to a higher rung. He lived in a world where the individual could live a better, more beautiful, fuller, and more spiritual life than previous generations in exile had experienced if they so desired; therefore, to his mind, they should be helped in doing so. Thus, he wrote in some amazement to the author S. Yizhar and others who saw something Kafkaesque, desperate, and vacuous about the state of contemporaneous man. We should not find surprising this influence of the ostensibly Kafkaesque image on the world of 1950s Israel, since Kafka – and, in his own way, Max Weber – construed the anonymous bureaucratic state, a rational state in its own way that tramples on the individual and sterilizes his soul, as the ultimate expression of modernity. Israeli intellectual readers were influenced by Kafka, Weber, and changes that they discerned in Israeli society that were not to their liking. One of these changes, undoubtedly, was the challenge that Ben-Gurion's "youngsters" – Moshe Dayan and Shimon Peres – posed to the veteran Mapai leadership and the trepidation that they inspired because they represented military bureaucracies (which did what they did as necessities in the best case) or drew sustenance from their strength and prestige.

Let us now examine in greater depth Martin Buber's arguments against Ben-Gurion in view of the criticism of Buber's dialogic philosophy, which had gained much traction in the West. From Buber's standpoint, modern society generally, and Israeli society particularly, had undergone a process of "politicization" and "bureaucratization." "Politicization," to Buber, "dictates from on high as to how to behave, how to act, and how to think."[11] We discussed this concept in Chapter 1 of this book and maintained that for Ben-Gurion, politicization denotes nothing but the individual's acceptance of his or her obligations to the collective, as represented by an elected democratic government. Buber, however, seems to have sought his own form of utopia in the service of his opposition to politicization, an opposition that he deemed of such supreme political significance that it took on a politicization of its own. Indeed, "Society has assimilated into the state," Buber argued,

[as] modern industrial development and its regulated chaos that intrinsically involve dog-eat-dog struggle for access to raw materials and a larger share of the global market have succeeded the old struggles among states and entire societies. The individual society, which feels threatened not only by its neighbors' lust for aggression but also by the general state of things, knows no path to deliverance other than total capitulation to the principle of central power, and in the democratic forms of society no less than in its totalitarian forms it became a guiding principle.[12]

Thus, Buber found no satisfaction in the British model either, even though Britain was a strong country that looked out for its interests and its citizens' welfare and had fought to secure its markets as well as possible until it willfully dismantled and relinquished its empire. The American "individual-state," unlike the British one, had traditionally left its indigent citizens to their own devices until President Roosevelt forced it to acquire more strength and centralization than it had ever known – resulting in a state so strong, in fact, that it overcame the Nazi, Japanese, and Soviet aggression. Buber's refusal to distinguish between democracies and totalitarian regimes, and his grave ignorance of matters related to state aggression, its reasons, and the methods adopted, to the world's good fortune, to circumscribe it, are of pronounced political significance because it was Buber who wished to subject these domains to his autonomous discretion. In any event, he exercised this discretion from a posture that, while critical of Ben-Gurion, was also divorced from reality.[13] The Ben-Gurionesque "utopia" differed greatly from Buber's utopia and from Buber's understanding of reality; at this stage of his public life, it evoked Proverbs 29:18 ("Where there is no vision, the people perish"). This vision, in turn, evoked messianic yearnings for Eretz Israel that really did prompt people to action. According to this doctrine, the role of these yearnings in striving for historical truth must be acknowledged; nevertheless, the yearnings had to be cast in a moral, secular, progressive light that, while influencing the political behavior of a sovereign nation that was returning to its place in history, could never be allowed to become a blueprint for an actual political decision.[14]

The maligning of Ben-Gurion by Buber and his associates during the Affair contributed to his downfall. That is to say, it had important political significance at a time when Ben-Gurion was attempting to induce them to behave like "political" creatures as he perceived the concept: responsible people who accept the burden and rules of the game of self-sovereignty and do not spout moralistic platitudes in matters with which they are not acquainted, such as the botched operation in Egypt and Lavon's involvement in it.

It is not my wish here to delve into the principles of Buber's dialogic philosophy, ostensibly a modern moral tool for dialogue among individuals and between them and God, an instrument that seemed to offer solace to the contemporary individual's agonized soul. Society, according to the dialogic view, should become a collection of individuals who occupy themselves in dialogue and outpourings of the hearts with each other and with God – a society that provides a psychological balm for those who know no other way of action. In retrospect, however, it took much pretense to believe that such a dialogue would transform individual, social, and national life in a reality that was populated by good guys and bad guys, the deaf and the blind, mortal enemies, clashing values, and lusts and cravings – including Buber's own lusts, cravings, and pursuit of honor and power. It is not for nothing that Walter Kaufmann – one of the greatest scholars of Nietzsche, who was quite able to discern the difference between his subject and Buber – thought, in respect to Buber's dialogic philosophy, that the relative popularity of *I and Thou* (Buber's basic philosophical work) did not necessarily reflect well on its author. It is a faulty work, Kaufmann said, that owes its success largely to the deficiencies of the era during which it was published. The most salient of its defects, he continued, was its style, which seemed too artificial or imitative to be fair without concessions.[15]

Indeed, one of the characteristics that Ben-Gurion found in Diaspora Jews of the Buberian type was mimicry: the lack of thinking that could support itself without a Nietzsche here, a Max Weber there, and a Karl Marx next to both of them; the kind of thinking that repeats itself like a continual echo after it poses next to its patrons; and even truths that such people bruited without independent critical thinking. Yes, one may learn from Spinoza, Nietzsche, and Weber, but one must not imitate them without critical discernment, like a still pond that reflects the moon. Buber's *I and Thou*, Kaufmann charges, was influenced by the pose of Nietzsche's *Zarathustra* without even approaching his intellectual assets and irony. Authenticity is not everything, Kaufmann admits. The category of authenticity is itself simplistic; Nietzsche, for example, used veils and knowledge and said so. However, "the lack of authenticity in Buber's *I and Thou* is a grave flaw that makes the book itself simplistic. Its readers encounter a witless pose, lacking in irony, and a tone that verges on the voice of the false prophets."

Keren quotes Buber's remarks on government and state, for example – which Buber had expressed in direct criticism of Ben-Gurion – as though they were unchallenged pearls of truth. The reader, however, cannot but notice the vacuous, witless, and shallow nature of some of them:

Politicians believe that all they need to do is labor over what they take to be the benefit of the state at the moment. They have no specific intention of rebelling against morality. On the contrary: If somebody were to approach them and say that their behavior is immoral, they would silence him and reply that precisely their ambition and behavior are a moral imperative because they serve the life of the nation, as though the selfishness of the collective is more moral than the selfishness of the individual. People of principle take the opposite side. They address the matter in the name of general premises that define what is just and what is not, premises from which they adduce about the state of affairs at the moment. They do not reexamine each and every day what one may fulfill under that day's conditions without harming national life. To perform such an examination, two factors must be co-opted: a conscience that cannot be fooled and a reliable view of reality.[16]

This sentence abounds with convolutions and contradictions, just like the problems that Kaufmann finds in Buber's *I and Thou*. What, exactly, is "the selfishness of the collective"? The basic Western concept of "public good" (of which we spoke in Chapter 1), after all, is meant to circumscribe the selfishness of the individual and award the collective – the majority – the right to decide in public affairs, that is, the political power to look out for the weak, the minority, and those who cannot fend for themselves without the majority's support. Exactly what are those "general premises" of "people of principle"? Keren's exegetical voice falls mute. What we get instead is a dry, prickly, witless, and nonironic "pose" that, while absolving its adherents of a daily examination of what they may fulfill without harming national life, nevertheless requires them to behave as though they have "a conscience that cannot be fooled and a reliable view of reality." How, then, should a "person of principle" view things "reliably"? No answer is offered.

Kaufmann then addresses himself to the Buberian style itself. Buber himself, he says, viewed language not as a secondary and external matter but as something of supreme importance. It follows that the tenor of untruth in *I and Thou* demands attention as a warning signal. Indeed, Buber's criticism of Ben-Gurion in a number of specific respects sounded conspicuous alarms from Ben-Gurion's point of view, even though he strove prodigiously to prevent strife and excessive disputation with the esteemed philosopher until the Affair. Once the Affair had erupted, Buber and others dabbled in matters that entailed not only specific knowledge but also a recognition of the rules of the game that had been established not by themselves in a language of misty euphemisms – a language that allows no practical discussion of acts of governance and state – but by the most civilized states on earth, which had adopted them as their standard.

The Nuclear Project and the Affair

The Lavon Affair burst onto the scene in close proximity to two additional "affairs" – that of Israeli–German relations, which had taken on the properties of a public scandal, and the controversy over the construction of the reactor in Dimona – nicknamed among the few knowledgeable at the time as the "Wars of the Jews," which in this case took place largely behind the scenes.

This coincidence of affairs spilled into intellectual and moral issues that prompted Ben-Gurion himself to make repeated attempts to dialogue with the self-styled moralists, including Buber. Indeed, according to Keren – who bases his arguments on Buber as though the latter were his moral compass – the opaque excerpt quoted in the previous section is indicative of a "typology" that one may use to "explain the main moral conflict of the Ben-Gurion era: the problem of relations with Germany." Now, Israeli–German relations definitely were one of the basic problems of Ben-Gurion's time; ultimately, this issue even helped to bring him down. To seek the truth, however, one must first determine what was at issue here, an "ethical conflict" or the politicization of the Holocaust, as we noted briefly in Chapter 1. From a very early phase, Buber established relations of his own with German institutions that sought him out; therefore, he cannot serve us here as a "person of principle." After the capture of Adolf Eichmann, the Gestapo official in charge of the deportation of the Jews during the Holocaust, however, Buber chose to apply his own principles and proposed that the Nazi chieftain be brought to trial before an international tribunal, as opposed to an Israeli one, and took exception to the death sentence that the latter meted out to Eichmann.

The very prosecution of Eichmann, however, seemed to clash with Ben-Gurion's German policy by setting off what I call the *belated impact of the Holocaust*. Thorough examination of this issue is needed, of course. Nevertheless, in my opinion – I was, after all, a contemporary of the events – the outcome of the lengthy trial, reported to the masses on the air and in print and replete with the testimonies of people who had survived every act of the Holocaust death-drama, was that anyone who had managed to repress the Holocaust to that point, and or was simply loath to connect it with day-to-day realities and Israeli politics, began to create such a connection from then on. Indeed, the Holocaust penetrated the daily reality like a thunderbolt and became part of it. By implication, Ben-Gurion's vehement rhetoric before and during the trial about the existence of "another [meaning a better, new] Germany," his meeting in New York with West German Chancellor Konrad Adenauer shortly before the trial, and the tense relationship that did take shape between the Jewish state and West Germany – known best for Israeli sales of weapons and uniforms *to* the new West German army and not known for concurrent large-scale deliveries of weapons and materiel *from* West Germany to Israel and assistance in nuclear research – seemed to many people as something that posed a moral quandary of the highest order.

Michael Keren sees things the same way today because the majority believed them to be such back then, even though a scholar can examine matters on their merits from the superior perspective of adequate available knowledge. At issue, then, is Keren's methodology, derived from well-known American sociologists such as Edward Shills and his colleagues.[17] In the light of this methodology, an intellectual "expresses ideas based on knowledge," a definition "which implies that any individual is not only intimately familiar with the world of the book but also has some degree of social acceptability." According to this opaque definition – whose two portions have no logical connection – an intellectual may be a mouthpiece for social trends of thought even if they are not based on "true" knowledge. Indeed, Keren continues, the "new sociology" treats the "acceptability of ideas as a variable and not necessarily as a constant."[18] Pursuant to this definition, "The conditions under which ideas are communicated and disseminated are considered major factors in determining the intellectual's social role."

What is the practical upshot of this argument in regard to Israel–German relations and the Lavon Affair? Is it that if an intellectual feels that most of the public construed Ben-Gurion's Germany policy as a sacrilege and a pact with the devil, he should propagate this view and phrase the titles of his publications accordingly, or feel that the media fanned the flames of the matter so vigorously that he, too, must excoriate this policy? And if it is the Affair that concerns us here, should an intellectual intervene in a composite historical-political-legal issue because both knowledge of the matter and the media's stance oblige him or her to wage overtly a struggle for Lavon and against Ben-Gurion? Obviously, moralists (or self-styled "people of the spirit," to use the Hebrew term) argued this way in the Lavon Affair and became, collectively, protagonists in it. Keren, in turn, provides them with a theoretical infrastructure that the philosopher Allan Bloom calls "the relativity of values," that is, the notion that ideas are a variable in social life – and not a constant – that justifies people's actions. Under no circumstances could Ben-Gurion accept such definitions of knowledge and of the status of the intellectual, as flowing from Bloom's philosophy and that of his mentor, Leo Strauss – which, in turn, would place Ben-Gurion himself among today's right-wing intellectuals, even though he never read either Bloom or Strauss.

Israel–German relations had to be based on knowledge above all. This clashed head-on with the "acceptability of ideas" that viewed West Germany as a direct descendant of the Third Reich and considered defense relations with it as a pact with the devil. Furthermore, basic values are neither changeable nor relative; instead, they are imparted, acquired, and integrated into the under-lying "human conscience" by virtue of the "great books" – the Bible, Plato, Spinoza – even if experts debate their philosophical underpinnings. Justice is justice; morality is morality. One whose practice is immoral must know what he has brought about; many practitioners of immorality may know it but deny it for political reasons. In certain cases, they must be condemned and fought. The extent of "acceptability" of moral principles is a problem of education, politics, and media, and one must act to instill them as they deserve or to counter ideas that clash with them.

Ben-Gurion had been doing this all his life, and at this stage of his public career – after proving in full view of the public that his way was correct and after having endured the risks faced by a mobilizing leader of his type with faith mixed with great apprehension – evidently he had had his fill of the essential compromises that came with the birth and initial growth of the Jewish sovereign society. Obviously, he had no choice but to make coalition compromises that would subsequently weigh on him and impede the fulfillment of his German and nuclear policies; from then on in other accepted ways, he acted to lighten this weight by fighting for his British-style reform. It would appear, however, that in all three matters – the electoral reform, justifying relations with Germany, and, especially, the debate over the Affair – Ben-Gurion behaved like someone who had taken off the gloves and set out on an uncompromising struggle. After all, a sovereign state must learn to live uncompromisingly with its basic interests. Still, Israel had to remain cognizant of its own significance as the moral incarnation of the Zionist renaissance and of the fact that West Germany was not an offspring of Hitler's Third Reich but an important democracy with all its faults, and Ben-Gurion – at this late phase of his life – had either to guide it in so doing or to resign for both principled and practical reasons related to foreign and defense policies and domestic reform.

Leaders of this kind cannot function if they believe that they have been right thus far and that they have proved it, analyzed the events around them, and proposed the "right" policy. Absent a political structure that would allow this policy to be implemented, and as public opinion steadily falls captive to the "acceptability" of mistaken, false, and politically warped ideas, a leader like de Gaulle, Adenauer, or Ben-Gurion, or for that matter George Washington, cannot function as an executive at the top of the policy pyramid because he would perceive himself a titular ruler only.

For reasons of their own – which we shall examine presently – most of the "intellectuals" who had leaped into action in the Lavon Affair did not get involved in the debate over Israeli–German relations, which had actually begun in 1957 and resulted in Ben-Gurion's resignation, followed by the formation of an old-new government under his leadership.[19] However, they may have noticed that at the time of the public debate over this issue – and especially during the Eichmann trial in the early 1960s, and given the contradiction that surfaced between the public's feelings about Germany and Ben-Gurion's hard-fought "other Germany" policy – the prime minister's public standing did indeed take a beating.

Thus, two debates began at roughly this time: the overt debate over the Lavon Affair and the largely covert debate about the Dimona reactor, in which "intellectuals" such as Yeshayahu Leibowitz also had their say, and loudly.

Germany and the Affair

The relative disinterest of "intellectuals" like the philosopher Nathan Rotenstreich and those of like mind in the Israeli–German relations affair, even though they expressed doubts in matters of Ben-Gurionesque "messianism" and foreign and defense matters pursuant to the Sinai War, is explained systematically in a brilliant and uncompromising article by Michal Ben-Naftali Berkowitz.[20] (At the time, Rotenstreich had gone so far as to criticize overtly the slogan coined by the commander of the Israel Air Force (IAF), General Ezer Weizman – "The best become pilots" – and proposed a counterslogan: "The best become good; flyers become pilots.") The article provocatively accused the Israeli philosophers of living in two worlds – a Kantian, rational ideal world and a world of reality that blemishes the ideal world – that cannot be mingled and do not share consequences.

In Ben-Naftali Berkowitz's opinion, these intellectuals castrated themselves for reasons of philosophical methodology originating in the era and values of the Enlightenment. Since the Holocaust had disrupted the proper flow of this methodology as they imagined it, they did not attempt to cope with it and its philosophical and practical implications. Ben-Naftali Berkowitz accuses Roten-streich and his associates of professional conservatism and of seeking shelter from real reality in an imaginary reality. While she does this with immense talent, her argument has nothing to do with historical reality directly. Roten-streich was a highly political man who tended all his life to be as politically active as possible. His attempts in this direction, however, achieved no more than the considerable influence that he acquired during the brief time of the Lavon Affair and shortly thereafter, perhaps because Ben-Gurion suspected him of being a wolf in sheep's clothing, that is, a philosopher who wanted real power and used his profession to promote himself, his beliefs, and his views – none of which was more valuable than those of others.

Ben-Naftali Berkowitz observes adroitly that the aforementioned intellec-tuals were indeed embroiled at the time in "a debate over the ills of modern society," but that the ills they alleged seemed to have been culled from an inventory list originating with Max Weber

and sometimes... from the neo-Marxist oeuvre.... Passivity, pervasive consumerism, ennui, alienation, affluence,... atomization – these and other expressions [coined by Kafka and those of like mind, along with Weber] surfaced in the debates [among the Israeli intellectuals at the time] without confronting Nazi barbarism and being reeval-uated. Does bureaucratization really suffice to explain the phenomenon of Adolf Eich-mann and its ineluctable product?...] Is... the Holocaust really but a phase, perhaps a climax and an encapsulation, of structural processes in Western society?[21]

Here, in my opinion, the author erred, since the act of contending with these questions – at least the symbolic and practical contention with several of them, that was also, in my opinion, a consequence of the German relations affair and the Eichmann trial, as well as a consequence of a power struggle – took place precisely over the Lavon Affair. In fact, during the public debate over the rights and wrongs of what had happened in Egypt in 1954, the behavior of the IDF under General Dayan, supported by his civilian colleague Shimon Peres, was accused by Lavon of being the immoral conduct of a military-controlled society; Defense Minister Lavon, in turn, had supposedly tried to restrain the army but had been dismissed as a result of his alleged efforts in this regard. The entire line of reasoning assumed a sort of historical parallel to European forms of despotism, if not totalitarianism. Professor Ya'akov Talmon, an important modern historian and a leading voice in this regard, went so far as to liken Ben-Gurion to Maximilian Robespierre when the prime minister intervened in the public debate over Lavon's claims. Ben-Naftali Berkowitz dismisses the Affair as a "complication" of the nearly ideal logical picture of her argument.[22]

Here, indeed, an abyss opened up between Ben-Gurion and his intellectual critics because, among other reasons, Ben-Gurion's interpretation of Nazism and especially of its success could not possibly be viewed as detached from the politics of the Weimar Republic and the disarray among Hitler's opponents, some operating under Stalin's instructions, while he recognized very early the nature of Nazism as operational racism, which seemed to his peers to be rather exaggerated. Ultimately, to Ben-Gurion, Nazism was a political movement, and the definitive explanation of its success was political. Western civilization and Judaism's contribution to it – as well as that of the Enlightenment – were conjoined against Nazism and ultimately marshaled enough power to confront and defeat it. Finally, the Wehrmacht was defeated not only by moralists and ethicists or by politicians or statesmen such as Churchill, but also by armies, mobilized nations, and bureaucrats who toiled day and night. The only victims of Nazism whose losses could not be recovered were the Jews. This, too, happened for political-historical reasons that obliged Zionism to prevent another Holocaust against the Jews in their own homeland.

"The dead cannot praise God," Ben-Gurion was wont to repeat (quoting Psalms) in the debate over relations with West Germany, which had become leverage for the enhancement of Israel's security, as it did its best to disavow its Nazi past and offer a successful politico-economic alternative to it, thanks to Bonn's adoption of the 1949 Federal Constitution and its institutions. At the same time, he suspected Israeli intellectuals and left-wing politicians of adopting anti–West German slogans of Soviet origin (and real accusations against Bonn's mild treatment of former Nazis) and of organizing a politically aimed campaign against Adenauer's Germany in order to legitimize Communist East Germany, undermine NATO, and sustain Moscow's power in the heart of Europe.

Ben-Gurion's critics in the Affair did talk about military and defense mechanisms that, to their minds, had lost their luster – naturally enough – and about what they considered his futile effort to deny it and defend their past and present principals, including Ben-Gurion himself.

The Affair concerned a botched operation by IDF Military Intelligence (MI) in Egypt in 1954, during Lavon's tenure as minister of defense. MI was headed at the time by Colonel Binyamin Gibli. The COGS was Moshe Dayan, chosen by Ben-Gurion before his first retirement to Sede Boqer, and a personal enemy of the Palmach officers who had resigned from the IDF after the War of Independence, foremost Yigal Allon, due to their affiliation with the left-wing Soviet-oriented Mapam Party. Shimon Peres had been named director general of the MOD sometime after Ben-Gurion's resignation; he, too, was considered one of Ben-Gurion's premier protégés among the Mapai younger generation.

The prime minister was Moshe Sharett, who, though unaware of the operation before it was carried out, had to cope with its outcomes: the capture by the Egyptians of the MI cell that had carried out the operation (apart from its handler) and the vengeance wreaked by the Egyptians on its members – most of whom were Egyptian Jews – sentencing some to death, executing a few, and dooming others to lengthy prison terms. A secret investigation of the Affair failed to determine who had given the order to proceed with the operation, which had comprised a series of attacks against Western targets in Egypt in order to thwart the British departure from the Suez Canal zone by subjecting the Egyptian regime to calumny for its ostensible anti-Western nature. At the time of the inquest, however, the minister in charge – Lavon – attempted to point the debate in the direction of Peres and Dayan, arguing that they had undermined and ignored him during his term in office. Sharett deemed this an attempt to blur Lavon's own responsibility for giving the order, and after a lengthy and exhausting process of secret inquiries by a committee comprised of a former COGS and a Supreme Court judge, the 1954 Affair ended with Lavon's resignation from the government and Ben-Gurion's return – first to the MOD and subsequently to the premiership. Sharett went back to the Foreign Ministry, and eventually was dismissed – shortly before the Sinai War, which the foreign minister opposed among other demarches of the prime minister. With that, Ben-Gurion fired Sharett, having promoted Lavon's appointment as secretary-general of the Histadrut (the General Federation of Labor), a post that carried political, economic, and moral power.

In advance of the 1959 elections, Dayan became a politician who aspired to a seat at the cabinet table. Dayan, Peres, and representatives of the Mapai younger guard came out against the Histadrut establishment and in favor of reform of the party and its institutions. Dayan had been amassing prestige since the Sinai War; Peres was a nonelected official who wielded political but not public power. Clearly, however, their actions flowed not only from their personal prestige but rather, and also, from being considered Ben-Gurion's protégés – even though Dayan had opposed the withdrawal from the Sinai after the Sinai War. Peres's relations with Lavon had been sour to begin with – in fact, Lavon had excluded him from the loop as much as possible during Peres's tenure as his subordinate (director general) at the MOD. (Another issue worthy of investigation is whether this had something to do with Lavon's long-standing opposition to anything redolent of the acquisition of a nuclear option.)[23] Afterwards, Lavon tried to drag Peres and Dayan into the internal investigations that led to his ouster in the aftermath of the Affair.

On the eve of the 1959 elections, the two of them challenged Lavon's Histadrut and aimed their barbs directly at the "Fifth Floor," a euphemism for the secretary-general's office. This is the most important factor to keep in mind in understanding the political background of the Affair that would surely erupt. After all, Lavon had allies in the government, foremost the minister of trade and industry, Pinchas Sapir, one of the most aggressive Mapai bosses and the person who, along with the finance minister, Levi Eshkol, held the keys to the economy and its development. Both men believed it essential to keep the Histadrut under Mapai's authority and to cooperate with it lest the economy spin out of control. By attacking the Histadrut on the eve of the 1959 elections, Sapir and Eshkol believed, those "youngsters" were threatening the Mapai mechanism that controlled both the economy and the Histadrut. They also took the new gambit as a menace to the entire veteran leadership of Mapai, sensing that Dayan and Peres, supported by the party's younger echelon, aimed to leapfrog this leadership and claim Ben-Gurion's legacy, support, and – who knows? – encouragement.

Ben-Gurion's ongoing concerns about the essence and nature of Israeli youth – a matter that much preoccupied him at the outset of his first retirement to Sede Boqer, as already described – prompted him, typically, to praise these youths occasionally and express his admiration for their contributions to the IDF and the cooperative and collective settlements during the period at issue. Therefore, he did seem intent on "crowning" the representatives of the younger group in due course and skipping over the veterans. Were this to happen, the powerful foreign minister, Golda Meir, and her generational colleagues in the veteran leadership would throw their support behind Lavon and treat him as a political ally. The "kids" themselves, in turn – foremost Dayan and Peres – were not a monolithic, cohesive group, and not all trusted their ability to defeat the veteran leadership. The way to assure victory, it seemed to them, was to co-opt Ben-Gurion himself as their declared patron so as to calm the doubting Thomases among them and to appear in public as his prized children in order to drag the "vets" into a struggle not only against them but against him as well.

Intrigues of this kind sometimes constitute "politics" in the classical, narrow sense of the term, but here they were taking place at a historical crossroads that, for many different reasons, undermined Ben-Gurion's own status and also, at first, accomplished little as far as the younger group was concerned. Indeed, Meir and Ben-Gurion's self-pronounced successor, Eshkol, were very serious rivals who had allies other than Lavon. Golda Meir developed a profound, lifelong, personal antipathy toward Shimon Peres, who intruded in her domain by forging special relations with West German politicians, such as Defense Minister Franz Josef Strauss, and by his (in her view) amateurish if not dangerous view of a world that was much more complicated than his ability to comprehend it. As such, he could (to her mind), in collaboration with Dayan, have gone so far as to mastermind the 1954 Affair in Egypt and to hold Lavon responsible for it.

The deposed foreign minister, Moshe Sharett, also waited gloomily in the wings of the political scene to avenge his unseating and repay the debt that he felt he owed the political COGS, Dayan, whom the outgoing Ben-Gurion had forced on him during Sharett's term as prime minister.

The 1959 elections were a great victory for Mapai and its leader. Mapai won more mandates than ever before, at the expense of its rival to the left, Tabenkin-Galili and Allon's Achdut ha-Avoda, and at the expense of the moderate right-wing parties. One of the campaign slogans concerned Ben-Gurion's British-style reform, which Mapai had officially adopted, but again the electoral system denied Mapai an absolute majority. These factors led to some mayhem, the seeds of which would sprout upon the eruption of the Affair, irrespective of the debate that broke out during it; indeed, this was one of the reasons for Ben-Gurion's stance on the Affair.

The seeds were the following: To begin with, Achdut ha-Avoda despaired of becoming an alternative to Mapai and began to search for allies within the latter, a large pluralistic party, in order to influence it from within without losing its own identity. Dialectically, Mapai's triumph over its veteran rival since the 1940s created an opening – which Ben-Gurion felt very acutely – for an attempt by Achdut ha-Avoda to penetrate his party and forge new relations with potential allies within it precisely because of Achdut ha-Avoda's poor performance at the polls. In the Histadrut domain, at least, the Achdut ha-Avoda people and Mapam, the left-wing, Marxist-oriented party, could anticipate a dialogue with Sapir and Eshkol because the left-wing parties, for the most part, were taking a militant stance on wages, thereby encumbering economic growth. An alliance between Mapai and these parties would facilitate growth and silence or isolate the militant voices of the Left. A formal parliamentary alliance with Achdut ha-Avoda, however, might encumber Ben-Gurion's foreign and defense policies, especially relations with West Germany and the development of the nuclear option – an issue on which Yigal Allon had voiced public criticism ahead of the 1959 elections, as we saw. Hence, my assertion about the seeds of mayhem that were sown in the coalition that Ben-Gurion had to establish with Achdut ha-Avoda after these elections specifically. Ben-Gurion preferred to coalesce with the moderate-right General Zionist Party for this reason and for another: his concern that the General Zionists' electoral decline would throw this party into the arms of Menachem Begin's nationalist Right, thereby creating a right-wing combination or "alignment" that would counterbalance Mapai's rapprochement with the left-wing nationalist party, Achdut ha-Avoda.

The second seed of mayhem was the threat that Ben-Gurion's proposed British reform, which the "youngsters" had adopted with great enthusiasm, posed to the Mapai apparatus and to its traditional control of voters, which had been gained as a result of the immigrant-absorption services, jobs, and identity provided by the Histadrut, the government ministries controlled by Mapai and its associates, and its separate machines in various parts of the country, such as Tel Aviv and Haifa (run by local bosses but largely under the control of Sapir and Eshkol). If the country were partitioned into direct-majority electoral precincts, as Ben-Gurion proposed – following the British and American practice – a new situation, unfathomable to the veteran Mapai bosses, would take shape: From then on, voters could directly affect the election of candidates in their territorial constituencies. The party strongmen did not see how a Knesset elected under the existing method could marshal a majority in favor of this idea. Ben-Gurion's attempt to circumvent the ancien régime by appealing directly to public opinion in the 1959 elections did not deliver the definitive electoral results that would make such a comprehensive reform possible. Therefore, he had to fashion a coalition in the accepted way – with Achdut ha-Avoda, of all parties – in order to promote economic growth and silence left-wing militancy in economic and wage affairs, which were the principal bailiwick of Sapir and Eshkol. Sapir, however, was an unmitigated political dove in foreign and defense affairs and had his own doubts about Moshe Dayan, the politically cunning, erstwhile hawkish, military man, and Shimon Peres, who had seemingly established a fiefdom of his own at the MOD that controlled lots of money, lots of people, and secrets like the construction of the reactor in Dimona, which were beyond Sapir's control.

These reservations planted further seeds of mayhem – one immediate, one for the longer term – that influenced the Affair. Sapir noted that the 1959 elections had prompted Ben-Gurion to promote Dayan to the ranks of the government, albeit as minister of agriculture, a minor portfolio that offered no clout in political and defense affairs. Sapir also noticed that pursuant to these elections, Peres was elevated from the bureaucratic echelons to the posts of deputy minister of defense and member of the Knesset. I do not know whether Sapir realized at the time that the two newcomers were counterbalanced by pronouncedly dovish ministers – Abba Eban, who joined the government after concluding his tenure as ambassador to Washington, and Giora Yoseftal. Sapir may not have even known that Ben-Gurion wanted to bring the retired COGS, Yigael Yadin – who had become an archeologist – back to political life as a counterweight to Dayan.[24] Yadin refused, but these and other demarches – including Ben-Gurion's disapproval of the younger group's attack on the Histadrut – show us that the prime minister did not name successors but, in fact, supported Eshkol if he – or anybody else – could make it on his or her own. They also show that the path of Dayan and Peres to the top of the heap would be strewn with obstacles that, from their ostensible patron's standpoint, they would have to surmount on their own. It seems, however, that Sapir could not restrain himself, and in 1960, when the opportunity arose, he pitted Histadrut Secretary-General Lavon against the defense establishment from which Dayan and Peres derived their prestige, probably hoping that the information in Lavon's possession would harm the past and present paragons and leaders of this establishment.

I do not wish here to plunge into the ins and outs of the 1960 Affair, the outgrowth of the Lavon Affair that erupted almost immediately after Sapir gave Lavon new information about what had happened in 1954. In a nutshell, it amounts to this: Avri Elad, chief of MI in Egypt at the time of the Affair, was prosecuted in Israel in a secret trial in 1960 and found guilty of conspiracy with the enemy after the capture of the cell that he had commanded in Egypt in 1954. (By implication, he had escaped from the Egyptians – with their assistance – in the course of the anti-Western sabotage affairs.) When he testified, Elad incriminated his superiors at MI and accused them of forging documents and, thereby, prejudicing the quest for truth about the operation in Egypt. His allegations seemed to imply that the IDF – MI – was corrupt and mendacious and that its personnel or their superordinates had operated in Egypt without permission from Defense Minister Lavon. Armed with this information, Histadrut Secretary-General Lavon approached Prime Minister and Defense Minister Ben-Gurion and demanded that the latter rehabilitate him, that is, absolve him of responsibility for the 1954 Affair.

Ben-Gurion's response – given in 1960 (in 1954, he was in retirement) – was that the exoneration of Lavon was a topic for a judicial inquiry and not a political question that a minister or a government should answer. Lavon, then, threatened to seek justice elsewhere – with the Knesset Foreign Affairs and Defense Committee – and promptly turned to the media and the "intel-lectuals" as well. This marked the beginning of Lavon's campaign to destroy the political system of Israel. After all, the Affair had broken out at a historical crossroads: The construction of this system had not been properly completed; all the country had was a mishmash that was increasingly uncontrollable for historical, political, and personal reasons. Ben-Gurion's role in the system was to hold the disparate pieces together. No one knew better than he did that such a mechanism could not last forever and that action had to be taken – by him – to replace it by means of appropriate institutionalization. His struggle in the Affair, then, was one facet of a broader attempt to institutionalize political life in Israel, as a civilized country deserved.

6

From the "Lavon Affair" to the Six Day War

The 1960 Affair and the 1961 General Elections

Just as Lavon was reviving the Affair in May 1960, another grave crisis broke out and eclipsed the foreign and defense policies – which were doing well until then – of Ben-Gurion and his aide, Shimon Peres: French President Charles de Gaulle secretly advised Israel that he had decided to abrogate the 1957 accord relating to the construction of the reactor in Dimona. Thus, as the clouds of the Affair were threatening them domestically, Ben-Gurion and Peres (the latter being Lavon's main target) were preoccupied with the other crisis, which was concealed from the public eye and became widely known only years later.[1]

The only public expression of internal controversy over Dimona was sounded by the so-called Public Committee for Nuclear Disarmament in the Middle East, headed by Professor Yeshayahu Leibowitz and Eliezer Livne. The latter had been an important activist in Mapai in the 1930s and 1940s but had been ousted from the party before the crisis due to allegations of lifestyle improprieties. The real problem, however, seemed to be his close proximity to the American Embassy in Tel Aviv; since his ouster, he had been busying himself with apocalyptic public lamentation over the demise of Israel's pioneering and egalitarian spirit as a result of the German reparations. Another source of incessant personal incitement against Ben-Gurion was Uri Avnery's *Haolam Hazeh*. This weekly magazine, considered a reliable source of information among members of the erstwhile left-wing youth movements, had been hounding Ben-Gurion from the War of Independence onward. *Haolam Hazeh* disclosed the gist of the Affair obliquely and connected this matter with its previous campaigns against the Mapai regime generally and Ben-Gurion specifically. Now, Livne and Leibowitz were terming the nuclear option "an act of lunacy" on the regime's part – "to keep it in power forever, they're engaging in nuclear deterrence."[2] At that precise moment, the international constellation had become much more sensitive to nuclear affairs due to the escalation of the Cold War, the launching of the USSR's Sputnik 1, and the advent of Soviet intercontinental missiles – all of which plunged the United States into spas-modic dread, even though it continued to outperform the USSR in all nuclear respects. By campaigning as they did, Leibowitz and Livne sent Israelis a signal: Ben-Gurion and his associates were dooming Israel to immense trouble vis-à-vis the United States, allegedly its main patron, if not to a possible entanglement in Israeli–Soviet relations.

In fact, this is what happened in 1967 during the crisis that culminated in the Six Day War, but the nuclear project – Ben-Gurion's main target as far as Israel's long-range survival was concerned – survived and later became a major source of security and peace negotiations with Egypt and other Arab states that go beyond the scope of this book. Few Israelis, however, gave a thought to such a secret and serpentine issue.[3] In fact, as we shall see, American intervention and Soviet input regarding Dimona would play a role in Israel's road to the Six Day War of 1967, with some ironic, if not tragic, results.

In political high places, however, the construction and operation of the reactor in Dimona did generate controversy from the very beginning all the way to the early 1960s. After all, the British Labour Party – several of whose leaders consorted intimately with left-leaning personalities in Israel, especially Yigal Allon – had their own doubts regarding an independent British nuclear deterrent. It was in view of this stance that they judged Israel's nuclear option and fiercely condemned Shimon Peres behind the scenes.[4] Simcha Flapan of Mapam, editor of the journal *New Outlook*, even accused Peres of having gone astray after the French chimera of independent deterrence, which had no future in a world dominated by the superpowers.

If it was Lavon's intention to suggest to prospective supporters of his remarks that Peres had always been a questionable character and that he, Lavon, had attempted unsuccessfully to restrain him back in 1954 while serving as minister of defense, the resurfacing of the Affair in 1960 served his cause.

Ben-Gurion did not stop Lavon from pursuing this course. However, he conducted his own internal investigation of the 1954 Affair by means of his military secretary and, later, by means of the former attorney general, Justice Chaim Cohen – an act that Lavon found unacceptable since both investigators were free to judge for themselves. In neither case was it possible to determine once and for all who had given the order to instigate the 1954 Affair, although the inquests made it clear that middle-grade officers had forged documents. Then came another unanswered question: Had these officers covered up for themselves, as "big wheels" had sometimes done in such matters since Hagana times, or had their superiors put them up to it? The main player here was – and remains to this day – the head of MI in 1954, Colonel Binyamin Gibli. Gibli may have given the order for the operation in Egypt without the knowledge of the minister in charge, Lavon, or may have inferred from Lavon that the latter was interested in having the operation take place but could not prove it, or had received an explicit order from Lavon to do it. Gibli elected to maintain silence, and so he did to his dying day in August 2008, except for one interview in which he explicitly blamed Lavon for issuing the order to carry out the operation, albeit verbally. Be that as it may, Ben-Gurion held back Gibli's promotion when Lavon reignited the Affair in 1960 in view of the forging of documents that followed the operation in Egypt. Gibli was transferred to another post, his military career at the high echelons of the IDF over. Ben-Gurion felt that this was a sufficient response; he may have believed innocuously that Lavon would not accomplish much by approaching the Knesset Foreign Affairs and Defense Committee (FADC) and would accept the verdict of the internal investigations. After all, Lavon was presumably busy at the Histadrut, and Ben-Gurion himself was occupied with the Dimona crisis. Thus, in June 1960, the latter prepared to set out for France in order to discuss the matter with General de Gaulle in a tête-à-tête.

Various biographers of Ben-Gurion have considered it an odd weakness on the part of the aged statesman – he of the erstwhile keen political instincts – to have failed to foresee the predictable public tumult. As they view it, he could have contained the crisis in one of two ways: by launching a better and more convincing investigation than the one that he ordered, or by refusing to take part in the investigation of an affair that occurred while he was in retirement at his Negev kibbutz and held no government office.[5] The aberrant and intrinsically unpredictable behavior, however, was Lavon's. After all, Lavon broke the rules of the game that had been accepted in Mapai at least since the key elections in 1944, of which we spoke in previous chapters. That is, from Ben-Gurion's standpoint, it was not only a matter of bringing the truth to light; Lavon was demanding political rehabilitation from the executive branch as though he held a monopoly on the historical truth, while Ben-Gurion believed that he had given the matter the investigation that it deserved for the time being;[6] beyond that, the matter belonged to a judicial inquiry. Lavon's demand that the cabinet – that is, the executive branch – exonerate him of responsibility for the 1954 Affair was simply unconstitutional in the deepest sense of the term.

Slowly the public debate over the Affair escalated – under the instigation of Lavon and his supporters – into the grand menace that Ben-Gurion had always feared: the Jewish predisposition to power struggles on ostensibly moral grounds. Although he sometimes blamed this tendency on life in exile, he noticed it – and discerned the absence of the state-level thinking that is required to surmount it – in the independence era, too, with the nation implanted in the soil of its homeland. At issue here was the mobilization of justice for the perpetration of an injustice, that is, the rehabilitation of a man who demanded rehabilitation by means of political arm twisting and availed himself of a politically sensationalist media for this purpose. Lavon was now seen as being driven by urges and possessed by lust for power, very possibly hoping to taint Ben-Gurion's "kids" with responsibility for the 1954 Affair and, thus, blocking their path to his succession. He may have even hoped to taint Ben-Gurion himself as having ordered them in retirement to carry out the operation; thus he, Lavon, might become the successor. Either way, he was willing to trample on accepted procedures at the top of his party – which, having concluded its internal debates, accepted the authority of its elected chief and refrained from arming its political rivals in the Knesset Foreign Affairs and Defense Committee. Indeed, the delegates whom Mapai's rivals had posted to this committee thirsted for any incriminating information that originated with members of the Mapai leadership – be it wholly true, partly true, or untrue.

What we have, then, is the advancement of personal power interests, driven by lust, in the service of supposedly exalted beliefs and views, foremost the pursuit of justice. Now, all of these are "politics" in the accepted sense of the word, as we defined it at the outset of our discussion. Ben-Gurion, however, had never been fond of such politics, even though he used it himself on occasion. The question was whether it would become a definitive and accepted public norm. Admittedly, corruption exists in every administration and society. Who realized more than Ben-Gurion, who knew his people all too well, that many functionaries in the Mapai apparatus were not angels? The problem, however, involved not a quixotic attempt to banish corruption from the world – the forging of documents by MI wheelers and dealers had been known to occur before – but corruption at the highest levels of the state, that is, in Lavon's struggle to restore his reputation by means of pressure and extortion, which would translate into overt corruption on the grounds of the need to eradicate covert corruption. All of this was fueled by the mass media and with the support of powerful politicians whose sole interest had nothing to do with the injustice that had ostensibly been inflicted on Lavon.

It was this constellation of factors that steadily dawned on Ben-Gurion during the public debate over the Affair and made him a participant in it. He himself had to realize that Jewish political behavior – from the criticism of his "messianic vision" to the Israeli–German relations affair – is largely emotional, irrational, and contaminated with personal and power interests. However, the only way to extricate himself from this tangle, to his way of thinking, was to separate the various sides of the issue and stick to the historical truth. True, Jews are powered by messianic faith, but this faith is a historical truth. Furthermore, Jewish moral substance is associated with the doing of justice; apart from being fundamental to Judaism, it is an inseparable part of the "human conscience."[7] By implication, if Lavon were to be granted justice in the form of injustice, after having ignited a public scandal and mobilized growing support for his cause in the media and among sundry intellectuals, headed by Nathan Rotenstreich, his personal and political comrade, then Israel was facing more than a scandal. It was actually facing the corruption of "public virtues" on behalf of these very virtues and, worse still, the weakness of mass democracy, the sorts of ailment that had fettered democracy in the bleak days of the ascent of Fascism and had long rendered it helpless. This kind of democracy had been battered in France's Third Republic, Weimar, and Britain of the 1930s, until it regained its strength, at least in the case of the British. In such a predicament, it is the statesman's obligation to counter public opinion that has fallen prey to hidden manipulation and the manipulators themselves.

By then, however, the Affair was gathering momentum as the mass media – headed by the newspaper *Ma'ariv* and its editors, most of whom former

Jabotinsky supporters who, in their new role as journalists, were eager to cause dissention among the leaders of Mapai and build up circulation in so doing – fed itself on leaks from Lavon, his backers, and opposition and coalition members on the Foreign Affairs and Defense Committee. Even the rules of the game in security affairs themselves had begun to crumble, though the military censor obscured the names of the principals in the 1954 Affair and the details of the related document forgeries that had come to light in 1960. Indeed, in his appearances before the FADC, Lavon lodged sweeping accusations against the entire army and defense system, as he had attempted to do in the investigation of the Affair in 1954, at which time Peres and Dayan had been his main targets. Now, Lavon insinuated that the IDF, the apple of Ben-Gurion's eye, was a corrupt organization and that Peres – Ben-Gurion's deputy at the MOD – was capable of any action, no matter how underhanded, that might promote himself and his interests. This gambit placed at risk the enterprises for which Peres was responsible and had labored around the clock, such as the reactor in Dimona. Once again, historical truth took a beating for the sake of a unilateral "truth," to the real detriment of persons unrelated to the 1954 Affair. Behind the scenes, each side calculated the other's ability to deal the Histadrut a more-or-less severe blow and even made preparations for a struggle over Ben-Gurion's succession.

Given the coincidence of the Lavon Affair and the crisis with France over the reactor in Dimona, the stalwarts of the Public Committee for Nuclear Disarmament in the Middle East celebrated the failure of the "white elephant" that was under construction in the Negev and even tried – unsuccessfully – to make it public knowledge.[8] Several of them, however – such as Yeshayahu Leibowitz and the great Talmudic scholar Professor Efraim Elimelech Urbach – actually became involved as "intellectuals" who subjected the treatment of the 1960 Affair to a crescendo of protest. They and Lavon's comrade, Rotenstreich, set the bandwagon in motion and quickly were joined by Professor Ya'akov L. Talmon, the historian, the economist Professor Don Patinkin, and many other high-profile personages at the Hebrew University of Jerusalem. The grounds for their vocal mobilization was the ouster of Lavon as secretary-general of the Histadrut, which Ben-Gurion had ostensibly forced by saying, "Either me or him" – which they depicted as an act of tyranny and an almost Robespierrean beheading.[9]

Talmon's enlistment in this chorus and his criticism of Ben-Gurion, backed by his specialization in the history of the French Revolution and its degeneration into Robespierre's one-man dictatorship, is unsurprising per se. Talmon was no less a political creature than a historian; he even tried, to no avail, to be the mentor of a liberal-conservative center party that he had established at the time. In his best-known book, *The Origins of Totalitarian Democracy* (London: Sacker and Warburg, 1952), published and translated into Hebrew several years before the events described here – a work that gained him international fame – Talmon developed and perfected a critique that was well known at the time, dating from the French Revolution itself, against what he called "political messianism" – that is, the subordination of society to an abstract vision, an essentially religious aspiration for the redemption of man. As he saw it, this aspiration clashed irresolvably with the individual's aspiration to freedom. In this respect, Talmon was following the lead of the great Irish-British statesman and political philosopher Edmund Burke, who blamed the French revolutionaries' willingness to sacrifice the individual – the human being – in order to change the world. By so doing, Talmon aligned Rousseau or Burke to be more precise, with the terminology of his times and set him within the constellation of British and European conservatives, including members of the West German Christian Democratic Party vis-à-vis Soviet "People's Democracies."

Talmon's critics will find no small irony in his remarks, since systematic study of Burke's own teachings reveals quite a few commonalities between them and Ben-Gurion's statecraft, notwithstanding all the obvious differences between the great eighteenth-century Irish parliamentarian and the Israeli prime minister. Burke, though appreciative of religion and its institutions, was pronouncedly secular and espoused the most tolerant and pluralistic religious tradition imaginable where religious content was concerned. He was an empiricist who believed in the definitive importance of accumulated experience in policymaking, and in this sense Ben-Gurion was much closer to Burke than he could ever have been to the German-Buberian teachings quoted earlier. However, Burke was repulsed by the rampant wrongdoing and injustice in Britain's regime in India because, first of all, he regarded these as the corruption of British society proper. From this standpoint, his was far from Ben-Gurion's way of thinking because he sought not to destroy this regime but to enhance it, whereas Ben-Gurion objected to Jewish rule over an Arab population ab initio – and spared no effort to prevent it; yet he regarded military rule over an Arab minority that was detached from the enormous and threatening regional Arab majority – a sizable portion of which in Galilee and in central Israel had been unwillingly annexed to Israel following the 1948 war – as an inescapable necessity dictated by experience and circumstances and not a freedom-negating abstraction that Israel had adopted from the world of tyrants in thought and deed.

Burke reviled abstract thinking in matters of statecraft, and his attitude toward the intellectuals of his time was no more favorable than Ben-Gurion's, to put it mildly. He attributed vast importance to the cumulative human experience and to institutions that had earned their status due to its lessons. For this very reason, he fiercely opposed the French Revolution's attempt to destroy everything that had preceded it. Simultaneously, he opposed the absolute power that the French revolutionary state demanded and the destruction of the individual by this revolution if one were to obstruct it knowingly or otherwise. Thus, the French Revolution became the cradle of what Talmon called "totalitarian democracy" – the enslavement of the nation and its constituents in the name of "the people" by a small number of professional revolutionaries, as happened in the USSR. The French totalitarian democracy, however, was a phase that would lead this tortuous revolution to the guillotine, a phase that for some time obliterated the achievements of France per se. Ben-Gurion, unlike Talmon, acknowledged the achievements of the French Revolution and employed a perspective that transcended Burke's historical horizon. He believed that he, and those of like mind, gained from these achievements, that is, from the triumph of liberty and self-determination for the peoples of Europe – a triumph from which Zionism culled whatever it found suitable.

Talmon revived Burke's arguments against the dangerous intellectuals of the eighteenth century. Ben-Gurion himself would certainly have agreed with some of these arguments and rejected others due to their comprehensive and conservative nature. To Talmon, however, Ben-Gurion himself had become a tyrant of sorts who acted on the basis of abstract principles that clashed with freedom. But Ben-Gurion did not consider abstract "freedom" the first and last word, and he surely would have agreed with Burke that the individual has not only rights but also obligations to the collective – as he had been explaining all his life. Therefore, Talmon's liberal-conservative criticism of Ben-Gurion at this particular time was something of a riddle. Talmon, however, went about these exertions in the climate of the Eichmann trial. The Nazi chieftain had been captured and brought to Israel in May 1960, right at the eruption of the Affair, and the resulting atmosphere inspired soul-searching in regard to regimes that carried out similar atrocities, such as those of Stalin and Mao Zedong.

At the time of the Eichmann trial in Jerusalem, several giants of the generation were guests at Talmon's master's seminar; one of them was Hannah Arendt, who had been sent by *The New Yorker* magazine to cover the trial. These invitees, naturally enough, were occupied with the origins of totalitarian regimes and the contradiction between personal liberty and personal aspiration to redemption. Several of the guests – including their Israeli colleagues – were strongly influenced by the teachings of the philosopher Sir Karl Popper in regard to "the open society and its enemies," the seekers of various absolute truths since the time of Plato.[10] In this sense, the Affair was also an attempt by Israeli "intellectuals" to discuss the Holocaust, totalitarian regimes and their components, and the lessons of the Holocaust, and to replicate this debate, with some prudence, in the Israeli reality as they understood it. Several of these intellectuals mobilized the French Revolution model to criticize Ben-Gurion and his actions after the latter had aged, and his "children" seemed to be less interested, if at all, in Israel's socialist part, in the standing and achievements of major Mapai figures such as Levi Eshkol, Golda Meir, and Pinchas Lavon, but rather in military affairs, the nuclear project on top, on their way to succeeding Ben-Gurion.[11] Others mocked Ben-Gurion's aforementioned interest in Plato as evidence of his authoritarianism, allegedly grounded in Plato's teachings as interpreted by Popper, but in the best tradition of the rivaling *umanisti* of the Renaissance.

In Chapter 1, we argued that Ben-Gurion did not strive to redeem humankind by means of desecularization à la Marxism or Fascism. Accordingly, he could not fathom the criticism of him that tied into certain things that he and others had done during the Affair. According to these critics, he had proposed a messianic vision that contained a menace to freedom and that, on behalf of this "vision," subordinated society to the needs of a powerful, predatory, and unjust state that must, ostensibly, view its army as a supreme value and defend it. Ben-Gurion's motives were utterly different: using the IDF, as we have shown, as an absorption agency for people who had come to Israel from more than a hundred different countries by now. In anger, he had restricted its actual use to a small number of reprisal operations, all undertaken at night and excluding the use of armor, artillery, and aircraft, except for the special case of the 1956 Suez-Sinai War, which was a means for securing French cooperation in nuclear matters – the only long-range solution to Israel's strategic inferiority. He even found himself defending the achievements of the French Revolution, which he had previously considered a menace to Judaism due to its tidings of liberation and progress, which Jews of the time regarded as vehicles of short-lived deliverance for themselves.[12]

What follows is a brief review of the manifestations of "the Affair" that stoked the rage of the intellectuals – bearing in mind their proximity in time to the Dimona reactor crisis. First, as stated, Ben-Gurion did not accede to Lavon's demand for exoneration before flying to France for his tête-à-tête with General de Gaulle. According to the sources in our possession, the French president interrogated him thoroughly, the key question being "What do you want a nuclear option for?"[13] In response, Ben-Gurion insisted that Israel had no designs on territorial expansion, as quoted in the previous chapter. That is, it had no intention of rupturing the status quo in a sensitive region, in a world on the brink of a dangerous struggle between the nuclear superpowers, provided it had a nuclear option of its own. In fact, Ben-Gurion said, France should learn from Israel, which was developing its unpopulated Negev as far as possible, and could solve the Algeria problem by moving its settlers into the unpopulated Sahara. The Sahara also happened to be France's nuclear testing ground, which Israelis were allowed to visit. De Gaulle listened and smiled, but evidently – according to the sources in our possession – did not agree to unfreeze the construction of the reactor in Dimona for the time being. Such was his stance even though, or because, he had recently detonated the first French bomb, thanks (among other things) to American computer equipment that had been given to the Weizmann Institute in Israel, but not to France.[14]

De Gaulle had worked out his own way of solving the Algeria problem: the total, complete, and, in effect, unconditional evacuation of the country's French settlers. The main "condition" had to do with the desperate resistance that the settlers themselves and the French Army were expected to offer. The latter, fighting on behalf of the *pieds-noirs*, was actually convinced that it had found a way to quash the Arab uprising decisively, if not to do away with the political problem of a French minority ruling an Arab majority. Israel had maintained a great many connections with French Army officers in Algeria and in France proper since the time preceding the Sinai war and thereafter.

The IDF had been armed with French weapons – the United States, being careful not to kindle the Arabs' wrath, refrained from arming Israel directly – and de Gaulle had to keep this connection in mind. It is very likely that the crisis concerning the reactor in Dimona was meant to clarify to Israel that if it sabotaged France's exit from Algeria and offered any form of assistance to army commanders who wished to mutiny over this matter at some propitious time, it would end up with no nuclear reactor. The next stage of the crisis was about to erupt: American spy planes had discovered the construction of the reactor in Dimona and the Western media would surely report the fact at any moment.[15] Construction could not continue on the basis of the assumption that only those in on the secret knew about it. What is more, the French would need a public explanation about the construction of the reactor that could allow them to avert the nuclear superpowers' anger just as Paris was seeking to join the superpowers as an equal partner in the "nuclear club." The superpowers' opposition to nuclear proliferation was well known; it was for this reason that the United States had denied France equipment needed by the latter to complete its own atomic program. Now France had not only breached convention by joining the nuclear club unilaterally but had also handed over this weaponry to a small, controversial country. For the time being, de Gaulle instructed his people to desist from building the Israeli reactor.[16] Another French stratagem was to demand the French-supplied uranium rods once spent and partially transformed into plutonium, in order to deprive the Israelis of the most vital part of the project. If so, Israel would have to look elsewhere for the necessary isotope.

As Ben-Gurion and Peres were busy untangling this thicket, a way out seemed to be found in December 1960 when Ben-Gurion announced in the Knesset that an atomic reactor "for the purpose of developing the Negev" was being constructed in Dimona. A short time earlier, the government, with his consent, had set up a committee of seven ministers to discuss procedures for the investigation of the Lavon Affair. The day before Ben-Gurion made his announcement about Dimona in the Knesset, the ministerial committee overstepped its authority and granted Lavon the exoneration that he had demanded without identifying the true culprit in the 1954 Affair.

Readers who have come to know Ben-Gurion thus far in this book can imagine his reaction. The government, he said, had no authority to rule on any nonpolitical issue and members were not allowed to discuss such an issue merely because the media and Lavon himself, using resources that he had mobilized for this purpose, demanded exoneration. Lavon had leaked and lied about goings-on in the defense system to a Knesset panel in which members of the opposition put his "information" to use for political reasons. Now the government had exonerated Lavon behind the back of the man who headed it without advising him that the "Committee of Seven" had evolved from a procedural panel into something like a self-appointed tribunal. The individuals behind this demarche – Finance Minister Levi Eshkol and Justice Minister Pinchas Rosen, who aided him in so doing – were motivated by public pressure and by Lavon's threats to open a Pandora's box (on Mapai's dubious election funding). Tomorrow, Ben-Gurion added, such pressure would lead to similar and other errors and mendacities just because someone managed to line up the mass media behind his cause, or used other methods of blackmailing for his purposes. What is more, Lavon was not as pure as the driven snow. During his tenure as defense minister, he had ordered extreme and rash military reprisals that were ruled out by COGS Moshe Dayan, a pronounced hawk but a smart and prudent man.[17] Now, in his campaign to cleanse his name, Lavon was not only besmirching others unjustly but indeed threatening to air Mapai's dirty laundry. Therefore, the party's typical "bosses," such as Finance Minister Eshkol, had capitulated to him. Eshkol had great influence over the Mapai apparatus, the very apparatus that Ben-Gurion wished to repair and modify by means of his British-style reform, which would transfer some of the bosses' power straight to the voter.

As for Lavon, he was akin to the biblical Zimri who had committed wretched misdeeds and was being rewarded, not punished, by the biblical Pinchas. This being the case, Ben-Gurion's relations with this "Zimri" were irreparably tarnished. By Ben-Gurion's lights, no prime minister could possibly acquiesce in Lavon's exoneration. The government had perpetrated a breach of public virtues; such a government must be dissolved by the premier and replaced after setting a date for general elections. This is what happened. Until then – and this, in my opinion, was also related to the defusing of the Dimona reactor crisis – the government would serve in a transitional capacity and would be free of the ordinary parliamentary restraints. Since such a government could not be toppled, its dependency on the Achdut ha-Avoda ministers and others who might harm Israel–German relations and the resumption of the nuclear project was diminished for the time being. Finance Minister Eshkol then took a step that was meant to appease Ben-Gurion, since the latter's prestige among the public and, especially, the Mizrahi communities remained an asset that the party was loath to relinquish: Eshkol engineered Lavon's dismissal as secretary-general of the Histadrut. Concurrently, one of the most militant of Mapai's local "bosses," Yosef Almogi, launched a "wake-up campaign" to enhance public support for Ben-Gurion.

Both demarches – the ousting of Lavon from a post unrelated to the Affair on the grounds that he had caused grave damage to Mapai and the accepted rules of the game, and Almogi's wake-up campaign – enraged the intellectuals and forced the prime minister himself to intervene publicly in the Affair. He explained his stance on the Affair by corresponding directly with these individuals and by placing articles in the Histadrut newspaper *Davar*. Topical arguments, however, were of no use. Lavon's dismissal gravely damaged Ben-Gurion's status among the Israeli elites for reasons that entail investigation. One possible reason was that a public much broader than "the intellectuals" was pleased to witness the demise of Ben-Gurion's "bill of obligations" and to discover that Ben-Gurion himself was seemingly remiss in discharging the obligations of a prime minister and a party leader, that is, the obligation of properly treating Lavon and the government majority that had exonerated him of responsibility for what had happened in Egypt. Concurrently, Peres and Dayan – Lavon's targets – were talking to the media without consulting with Ben-Gurion, thereby strengthening the impression that Ben-Gurion's actions had been meant to defend their good name and the legacy that they were expected to receive from him.[18]

In the meantime, the Dimona crisis, too, had not blown over. It cast a shadow over Ben-Gurion's foreign and defense policies in a field that was literally and figuratively critical.

Indeed, in late 1960 the Dimona crisis took a turn for the worse and spilled into areas beyond Israeli–French relations. Now, it seemed as though the United States would intervene in the matter with such force as to threaten an incomparably grave crisis between Jerusalem and Washington, to the immense exultation of Leibowitz and Livne. In retrospect, however, things developed differently. The initial crisis with Washington, as it turned out, took place along the "seam" between the Eisenhower and Kennedy presidencies. This seems to have happened for good reason: The outgoing president, Dwight Eisenhower, chose in this transition to pressure Israel as much as he could on the topic of Dimona and managed to obtain from Ben-Gurion the Knesset declaration that transformed the project into one aimed at peaceful use. After the American elections, Ben-Gurion tested the new chief executive as to how he would behave on the Dimona issue. He quickly discovered that John Kennedy, though a Democrat whose election had been strongly supported by Jews, appeared determined to halt the construction of the reactor no matter what. The Knesset proclamation that Israel was indeed building a nuclear reactor in the Negev but that it was for "peaceful purposes" gave the French an out to continue building the reactor without supplying the uranium necessary to operate it.[19]

By making this announcement about the construction of the reactor "for peaceful purposes," Ben-Gurion bought Israel time that allowed the work to resume, but the disclosure created an obstacle of sorts in both the short and long terms because it allowed the Americans to obtain a change in the purpose of the reactor, at least publicly. From then on, Washington would try to make sure that the facility was not, in fact, being used for military purposes, on the basis of Israel's public word. Over time, this obfuscation of Dimona's objectives would inflict real damage on the veracity of Israel's defense doctrine, at least from the standpoint of domestic public opinion. After all, as opposed to providing "strategic territorial depth," the reactor in Dimona was intended to be decisive so far as Israel's very survival in the future was concerned, making its destruction impossible in terms of the price that the Arabs would have to pay for it. At this time, Ben-Gurion broached the idea of visiting the United States personally in order to meet with Kennedy and alert him to the dire state of Israel's security needs, and so he did in June 1961.

The encounter, which Ben-Gurion forced on Kennedy and that took place in New York because the president did not wish to host an Israeli premier on an official visit in Washington, shows us how badly off Israel was in those days in the eyes of the Kennedy administration – and not specifically in regard to the Dimona project. Today, we are accustomed to viewing the United States as almost an official ally of Israel; indeed, the matrix of relations that has developed between the countries over the years lends substance to this perception. Back then, however, Ben-Gurion did what he did in full awareness that Washington was reluctant to get too close to Israel and that the Kennedy administration would continue to strive to ingratiate itself with the Arabs, foremost Nasser, in view of the ongoing and escalating rivalry with the Soviet Union. He also knew that the administration's efforts would be mirrored in a series of actions vis-à-vis Israel. Research on Ben-Gurion's own maneuvers in both domestic and foreign and defense affairs in the early 1960s, including those related to the Affair, should be pursued within this inclusive context, one that is generally lacking in studies specifically addressed to the Affair and those relating separately to foreign and defense affairs, including Israeli–German relations.

In the meantime, the Germany issue had become many times stickier than it had been due to the sudden discovery of Egypt's program for missiles and unconventional weapons, which until then had been pursued surreptitiously by Austrian and German scientists in President Nasser's service. What the program meant, seemingly, was that Germans were involved once again in a looming new Holocaust against Israel with the blessings, if not the encouragement, of the Bonn government, which Ben-Gurion had publicly christened a "different Germany."

The affair of Egypt's German scientists did more than overshadow the rest of Ben-Gurion's tenure until his resignation in the summer of 1963. It also tied into the reverberations of the Eichmann trial and the actions of Isser Harel, who as head of Israel's security services had captured Eichmann in Argentina and delivered him to Israel. Harel had been a Ben-Gurion loyalist thus far.

Harel's involvement in Israeli–German relations touched off a crisis at the core of the defense establishment, in view of what he construed as the Bonn government's support of the German scientists' activities in Egypt or Bonn's criminal refusal to bring these activities to a halt, with the prestige of his bailiwick, the Mossad, at stake. (Two of his operatives had been captured in Switzerland while attempting to operate from that location against the family of one of the German scientists.) The crisis seemingly illuminated a grave contradiction in Ben-Gurion's domestic and foreign policies alike.

The foreign dimension of the matter seems clear. The most important Jewish leader of his time had proclaimed, not long after the Holocaust, that a "different" Germany had arisen. This Germany, however, was doing nothing to stop its scientists from helping Egypt to manufacture weapons of mass destruction that were being aimed at Israel.

Shortly before the elections called by Ben-Gurion in 1961 pursuant to the Lavon Affair, Israel launched a missile, called the Shavit II, into the atmosphere in order to preempt Egypt's doing the same. The launching was widely construed as a crude election stunt. Out of public earshot, the heads of Rafael, the government-owned defense manufacturer that had developed the Shavit, complained that Israel had no missile program of substance and that, this being the case, Shimon Peres had forced them to respond to the Egyptian missile challenge by sending a meaningless hunk of pipe into the void.[20] By this time, Isser Harel had become a sworn opponent of Peres and the latter's German ties. Subsequently, Harel would even allege that the launching of the Shavit II "justified" the Egyptian missile program because it made Israel appear to have instigated a missile race in the Middle East.[21] He added a warning about the seriousness of the Egyptian missile program in view of the German government's refusal to have its citizens recalled from that country.

Concurrently, Peres investigated the matter through the good offices of MI and concluded that the Egyptian missile program was so much hot air. The German and Austrian scientists, he found, had cheated the Egyptian government by building a true white elephant – a missile that lacked suitable means of guidance, in other words was militarily valueless. This set in motion a vicious rivalry between the Mossad and MI – between Harel and Peres – resulting in the consummation of an alliance between Harel and the foreign minister, Golda Meir, who viewed Peres as a brazen and dangerous contender for the crown. Meir had her reasons for feeling this way: She regarded Peres as a nimble, elbow-wielding, and enthusiastic provincial politician who too often sought to paint reality in colors that served his interests and those of his dreams, doing so by employing leaks to the media and other lowly public relations tricks.[22]

By this time, Peres had crowded the Foreign Ministry out of all areas in which he wanted freedom of action. Thus, inasmuch as his moves in foreign and defense affairs were linked to Lavon's campaign against the Affair, Golda Meir may have been willing to believe Lavon's version of it. Let us recall what Lavon's version was: Israel had the sort of defense system in which documents had been forged and innocents had been unjustly trampled; as for Peres, in his campaigns to promote the Dimona project, the man was capable of every form of nonsense and political error ever invented.[23]

Harel seems to have conveyed frightening information about a Soviet initiative in Washington in order to stop the construction of the reactor in Dimona.[24] Once these concerns dissipated, Foreign Minister Meir seemed to believe that Israel–U.S. relations ruled out the possibility of lying overtly about this massive project, that is, terming it a "reactor for peaceful purposes," or of asserting, as Peres did in an attempt to con President Kennedy, that "Israel will not be the first to introduce nuclear weapons to the Middle East."[25] Israel could not base its foreign policy on lies, especially since no one in Washington believed them. Instead, it should look the Americans in the face, tell the truth, and fight for the truth in the corridors of the U.S. governing apparatus, Congress on top, which Meir knew better than Peres and Ben-Gurion himself thanks to her American upbringings and close ties with leading members of the Jewish community.

This picture – an incomplete one, based not on full primary sources but on the principals' testimonies – shows how the British-style defense system constructed by Ben-Gurion had disintegrated into rival entities and personalities who, mired in internal politics, fought each other with no holds barred. However, the type of British reform long pursued by Ben-Gurion could not have prevented all of the struggles for power and prestige among defense agencies or even within the army and between it and the civilian defense system. Anyone who regularly delves into recent studies on World War I and World War II realizes that large bureaucracies of this nature and the leaders thereof are occupied with interlocking struggles over personal power, conceptions, budgets, and prestige, and that Great Britain itself was not exempt from such machinations, even at the peak of its valorous war against Nazi Germany.[26] The problem here, however, was twofold: At what point did these struggles spill into the mobilization of political support from appointed officials, such as Isser Harel, for mutual enemies – individuals and agencies – in the political echelon? And to what extent could the political echelon itself – after listening to the rival entities' competing conceptions and giving thought to various considerations of budget, prestige, and power – resolve these disputes one way or the other and put them to rest by making a firm decision at the right time?

The case of Isser Harel seemingly demonstrates the dangerous blurring of boundaries that occurred regularly during his tenure as czar of Israel's security services. He advised Ben-Gurion – head of Mapai and the minister in charge – on internal political matters and not only on foreign and defense affairs. Apart from being head of the Mossad, however, Harel also chaired the General Security Service, and his function there was to keep an eye on domestic political players who could damage Israel's stability and security.[27] He was a "Mapainik" who spoke openly with Ben-Gurion about "Mapai's enemies," as one may call them today. However, those enemies – extreme circles in Mapam, the Israel Communist Party, and the ultra-Orthodox community, as well as a few former members of ultraright groups such as the Stern Gang – were not only enemies of Mapai; in their different ways, they were also enemies of public order and of the state system of Israel. Eventually, Harel would become a real problem, of the kind that had brought down Admiral Lord John Fisher in the aftermath of the Gallipoli disaster, after having captured Eichmann and brought him to trial in Israel in his capacity as the legendary head of the Mossad.

The 1961 Elections and the German Complex

This development, however, would wait until the summer of 1963. In 1961, Ben-Gurion went to the polls and left Mapai with five fewer Knesset seats than the party had had before. The lesson – at least in the estimation of the party bosses – was that the public did not fully embrace Ben-Gurion's stance on the Affair and on the Germany issue, causing the party genuine harm at the ballot box. This conclusion only strengthened the bosses' tendency to cooperate with the nationalist-left Achdut ha-Avoda Party in the Histadrut, lest control of the Histadrut be lost, and toward formation of a governing coalition with it despite Ben-Gurion's wish to coalesce with the moderate Right, the General Zionist Party. His desideratum in this regard can be traced to his fear that the moderate Right would be pushed into Menachem Begin's far-right Herut (Liberty) Party, and that Achdut ha-Avoda might upset his German and nuclear policies. However, opposition to Ben-Gurion's style and to his German policy combined to unite all constituents of the Left and Right for the first time. He had foreseen this development, a wall-to-wall coalition of all parties other than Mapai in areas where Mapai had been the definitive player to date. Such an occurrence could not be staved off in the long term, unless the whole political system could be reformed and a two- or three-party regime installed after the British model. It did seem, however, that Ben-Gurion was rapidly losing control of his own party. His lengthy political career would conclude shortly; what mattered now was a struggle for the succession in a new reality. For the time being, Finance Minister and party boss Levi Eshkol was the one who hammered out a Mapai–Achdut ha-Avoda coalition for Ben-Gurion, who had no choice but to accept it in order to remain in power long enough to see the construction of the reactor finalized and in order to win as much military support from West Germany as possible.

Ben-Gurion still spoke uninterruptedly of the vision of settling the Negev, of a moral-messianic sense of duty and actual involvement, and of the obligation to read the European and global realities so as to understand the importance of relations with democratic West Germany. He still immersed himself in the Bible and its interpretation and still engaged the "intellectuals" in dispute. The image he conveyed, then, was that of a politician who entertained pretensions of omniscience and quasi-Stalinist omnipotence in making rules and ramming them down everyone's throat. Ben-Gurion, however, was not the sort of person who capitulated to such images; he knew full well that he was neither a Stalin nor a Robespierre, and he believed that the core of the struggle against him in the Affair, in regard to Germany, and on other issues concerned a problem of the Jews in terms of the Zionist revolution. Had the Jews learned, or would they learn, to debate matters on their merits and inhabit a realistic world, or would they dwell in a false world, an invented world, or a world that served their lusts?

In the midst of the Affair, as he stood on principle and insisted that the investigation and resolution of the issue be treated as a judicial matter and not as a political one (indeed, years after his resignation, the State Commissions of Investigation Act was passed into law as a result of this stance), the prime minister invited eleven senior academics to debate the tenets that were preoccupying him at the time: "Is it at all conceivable that we [Jews] will be a special people and a light unto the Gentiles? Can the redemption of the world and of the Jews really take place?"[28] It was an attempt to grab the bull by the horns, to exchange views with the intellectuals, that is, the various representatives of Israel's scientific community among his public opponents on these matters, with the clear intention of showing them that no nation, let alone the Jewish people, could manage without a vision, and that in this regard – the idealistic inspiration that Israeli society needed at this phase of its coalescence, an inspiration that should be provided by the statesperson, with the worthy assistance and initiative of intellectuals – the "intellectuals" offered no real alternative to this statesperson's vision.

The vision at issue was a matter of principle – "messianic faith" as he put it, or a creativity and passion that should be cultivated and not allowed to deteriorate into routine, as I define it. It also accommodated quite a few prosaic issues, such as security, settling the Negev, and using the Negev as a gateway to key countries in Asia and the Far East. In response, the invited intellectuals, each in his own way, challenged the use of "vision" as the sole guide for action, as Michael Keren defined it. After the fact, the encounter was a more acrid collision between the typical views of each of these personalities and the eclectic, Renaissance-like jumble of Ben-Gurion's vision. Professor E. E. Urbach, an acclaimed Talmudic scholar who had been campaigning against the construction of the nuclear reactor and was one of the main spokespersons on the Affair, chose to attack Ben-Gurion's use of the messianic-humanistic vision of the Jewish prophets for his purposes. The prophet Isaiah, Urbach claimed, had addressed only a few verses in his entire prophecy to messianism, devoting most of his message to criticism of the social and political realities in Judea of his time. By implication, the prophets' disciples had learned from their mentors that they should do more than offer a positive vision of redemption that could provide creative inspiration for the construction of a new Jewish commonwealth; they should also critique reality. Martin Buber also accepted this view of the role of the Jewish intellectual as a critic, and Ben-Gurion sought to contend with it as well as he could. "Criticism," after all, does not build a society; instead, perhaps, it shapes and is influenced by public opinion. Indeed, on behalf of principled "criticism," one could defend Lavon, condemn the construction of the nuclear reactor, and do as one pleases without knowing what is at stake or taking it into due consideration.

This brings us back to the problem of historical truth and the historical and philosophical sources of the arguments relating to it, given the contrasting argument that truths may not exist at all or may be relative, or that there may be moral truths that professional ethicists such as Martin Buber and Yeshayahu Leibowitz may determine.

Ben-Gurion found more in the Bible than social or political "criticalism." In his quest to invest the Book of Books with special importance in the public mind, he deviated from Joshua's conquest of the Land of Israel and the prophets' universal vision by attempting to make conscious use of this treasure trove – to lend content to the life of a society that was rapidly divesting itself of at least some the values that had motivated its founders. And as Allen Bloom put it many years later, the Bible has contents of substance, moral weight, and profundity that lead us closer to the truth. What Bloom meant, however, was not the shopworn argument that people's lives are fuller when they entertain myths on which they base their lives, but that a Bible-based life is closer to the truth than its counterfactual, and that the Bible supplies "material" for deeper investigation of, and more effective access to, the true nature of things. Several of Israel's founders had occupied themselves with this Jewish epos, regarding it as a positive, profound, and moral instrument for the construction of the most just society possible in Israel. Ben-Gurion augmented these interpretations with others of his own invention, concerning the abiding relationship between the land and the people of Israel. To his way of thinking, however, this "invention" was linked with facts, that is, with historical reality as he viewed it, as opposed to a reality that he consciously imagined. The declared purpose of this interpretation, strongly influenced by Yehezkel Kaufman's original biblical research, should instill consciousness of belonging to the Land of Israel in the mind of the public and of youth, who, he felt, did not "belong" to it adequately. He went about this as the intellectuals of the 1960s occupied themselves with modern bureaucracy and its ailments, by which they indirectly tackled the Holocaust.

To Ben-Gurion, however, the Holocaust meant something else. It was so ghastly a disaster, and its interpretation such an inescapable historical-political minefield for the victims within and their compatriots without, that he and those of similar mind spent many years avoiding public debate over the matter and refrained from peering into its depths, including the issue of rescue at that time until the public grew able to contemplate the contemporaneous state of the nation with its eyes wide open. The Holocaust was mentioned, among other things, in the Declaration of Independence of May 1948, as one among other justifications for Jewish independence, but Ben-Gurion, who authored the Declaration a priori avoided a deliberate policy of using the Holocaust as the foundation of the reconstituted social democratic society of the Jewish nation in the Land of Israel, whose secular religion was one of life and not of death. However, as Bloom remarks – seeking the roots of the matter in the penetration of German philosophy in the universities of the West – people (such as, I would say, some successors of the Israeli "intellectuals" of that time, led by several of today's "post-Zionists") cannot fathom the essence of evil and doubt that evil exists at all. To them, Bloom says, Hitler is an abstraction of sorts, a place filler in a null category stolen from Kant but conceived and born in the writings of Hannah Arendt, coiner of the cliché "the banality of evil," adopted by her from Karl Jaspers.[29]

In contrast to Urbach, the economist Professor Don Patinkin spoke about the gap between vision and efficiency. By adhering to a vision, he said, people allow themselves to disregard considerations of the cost of their "visionary" investments and the practical outcomes thereof. I do not know whether he was referring to the Dimona reactor and its price, the environmental effects of its construction, and similar issues. However, he was quoted as asking whether anyone had calculated how many schools would not be built due to the construction of the National Water Carrier, how many people should be settled in the Negev, how this would affect the economy and the quality of life in the other parts of the country, and so on. This area of inquiry is exactly what an economist would concern himself with, as opposed to the domain of vision, which seemed to have been phrased generally and, therefore, sweepingly and indefinitely.

Patinkin was undoubtedly right in most of his arguments, even though the scantiness of Israel's economic and social forces ruled out mass settlement of the Negev in any case. His remarks, however, mirrored the tendency – long evident notably among Zionistic intellectuals – to separate the ethos of nation-building, one of the major axes in Ben-Gurion's thinking and actions, from the prosaic doings of state and government. Ben-Gurion valued such things per se and regarded them and their improvement as the other side of the nation-building coin. He deemed it unacceptable to separate the two, least of all in regard to Patinkin's remarks about settling the Negev. Patinkin lacked the kind of broad "political vision" that would see how settling the Negev tied in with Israel's foreign and defense affairs. Ben-Gurion wondered whether the value of populating the Negev eluded Patinkin's line of vision in a definitive respect, since a populated Negev would be Israel's strategic depth – rather than the politically hazardous West Bank – and its gateway to the awakening Third World. From this standpoint, "vision" embodied the viewing of possibilities that, while not existent in the present, might exist in the future.

This line of thought did not seem totally senseless; Israel did manage to establish close relations with Burma, even though its attempts to form ties with the Peoples Republic of China (PRC) and neutral India were spurned angrily or coolly. Israel's outreach to Burma took place on a fanciful basis. While visiting the Asian country, Ben-Gurion spent several days in a Buddhist monastery, attempting to delve into the teachings of Buddha and to seek, by their means, a common language with the massive non-Western civilizations that adhered to them. This gambit transcended his Renaissance-like curiosity; as always, he had political and cultural interests in mind, wishing desperately to mitigate Israel's dependency on the Anglo-American West, during a period of time in which the West – under American influence – was itself entering the new era of the 1960s. He had deemed much of the West ignorant, if not hostile, and viewed its culture, as stated in the first chapters of this book, not only as a source of inspiration for historical Judaism but also as a cultural and political threat to it in the past, more so in the 1960s.

In my opinion, however, the definitive point in this matter lay elsewhere, and Patinkin did not give sufficient thought to it: By settling the Negev, Israel would shift its center of gravity from the coastal strip – vulnerable, narrow, and seemingly begging to expand into the Palestinian-inhabited and extremely polit-ically sensitive West Bank – to the vast, unpopulated, and politically unsensitive Negev. The failure to attain this goal would have an immediate implication – pursuant to the crumbling of Ben-Gurion's status and actions – concerning the prelude to and the aftermath of the Six Day War.

Ben-Gurion even went on to argue, in the spirit of the individual-will doc-trine that we addressed at length in Chapter 1, that experts of earlier times who had attempted to dissuade him from taking what they considered unintelligent actions (here, in my opinion, he was more than alluding to the stance of most of the Israeli scientific community on the nuclear project) had indeed discharged their professional duty. If one weighs all the scientific data, as Keren cites in his remarks, then the experts' stance was emphatically justified: "Science seldom oversteps its bounds, whereas the individual *qua* individual [who neither belongs to a scientific community nor accepts its conventions] can allow himself to do so. The individual can sense whatever he needs; this is vision." This "sense" of the "individual" is the Renaissance-like element in Ben-Gurion's customary thinking – an element that contained no small measure of brazenness and pretension in the eyes of contemporaneous scientists, such as Don Patinkin and those of like mind – even if they have had different senses or, rather, values and prejudices of their own. An example was Ben-Gurion's criticism of "professionals," even though he praised "professionalism" and himself as a professional when he spoke of the professional officer corps that the IDF should have. When it came to Israel's security, however, Ben-Gurion continued to regard himself and the competent IDF officers as professionals in a favorable sense, as he wrote to the intellectuals after the latter had signed a manifesto advocating the disbanding of a military government in Arab-populated parts of the country.[30]

In this debate with the intellectuals and scientists, Ben-Gurion based his remarks on "human intuition – a person's capacity to weigh things in their totality," even though previously, we quoted his criticism of the intuitive element in historical Judaism and his attempts to seek a firmer scientific basis for the moral pretensions of Greek culture. By now, however, he had tried everything in life and had reached some general conclusions. For Ben-Gurion at this stage, "professionalism" in the negative sense denoted scientific or technical knowledge in natural or social sciences that must not be allowed to defeat the human will and deeply seated human needs if mankind wishes to develop them in a worthy way. There is nothing at all bad about "human intuition." On the contrary, it facilitates the broadening of personal horizons and the opening of the individual's imagination to expanses that transcend the narrow confines of the modern natural and social sciences. And it allows the sciences to connect with Israel's concrete interests. In the meantime, Ben-Gurion had blocked the introduction of television to Israel, by arguing that "Jews should continue to read books."

The debate, however, was of little use, as in the course of the Affair, some of the intellectuals totally seceded from Mapai in protest over Lavon's ouster. They established a neo-Socialist journal called *Min ha-Yesod* (From the root), which eventually would have vehement things to say about Ben-Gurion: "One man in this country has a monopoly on everything: truth and honesty, justice and ethics, the dominion of the intellect and democracy." Indeed, the image of Ben-Gurion as a spin-off of Stalin took root among the readership of *Min ha-Yesod* due to domestic and foreign developments that had nothing whatsoever to do with the Lavon Affair.

Ben-Gurion's Resignation in 1963 and Prime Minister Levi Eshkol

The tempest that threatened to inundate Ben-Gurion, and that did seem to inundate him in the summer of 1963, broke out about a year earlier when, as stated, several agents in Isser Harel's Mossad were captured in Switzerland while trying to do whatever they could to drive the German scientists out of Egypt. Since "whatever they could" included threats against the scientists' family members in Germany, the Bonn government sought their extradition. Harel briefed Israeli press correspondents about the agents' detention and then flooded the press with a wave of hair-raising accounts of the potential dangers that the German scientists in Egypt represented. Thus, no sooner had the Eichmann trial ended (with the Nazi official's conviction and execution) than a second Holocaust began to loom on the horizon, at the instigation of Germans and Arabs acting in concert. There was talk, inspired by Harel, of toxic gas, radiation warheads, and bacteria that the Germans were developing for an Arab Hitler, a term that Ben-Gurion himself had once used to define Arab leaders such as Nasser.

Here, Ben-Gurion stumbled into a trap of his own making that ultimately left him beside himself with anger. The danger emanated from Nasser; the German scientists who operated in Egypt were individuals acting on their own counsel. However, Begin's Herut opposition and various media, foremost *Ma'ariv*, held the Bonn government responsible for the activities of the German citizens in Egypt; by so doing, they established a false continuity between Bonn and Nazi Germany. Meeting with newspaper editors on November 30, 1962, Ben-Gurion rejected the attempt to link the German scientists in Egypt with the German government and termed it "racist," even though at this very time his own chief of security services was doing his best to prove the opposite. Thus, Harel also cabled the Israel mission in Cologne about my arrival there as a correspondent for Israeli State Radio so that I might help him to advance this allegation (in fact, this position was rather precarious due to its political sensitivity, but it allowed me to pursue my studies on Nazi Germany later on).

At this time, the head of the mission – Ambassador Felix Shinar – was very much involved in a large conventional-weapons deal that Ben-Gurion had concluded after meeting with Chancellor Konrad Adenauer in New York, following Shimon Peres's entrées with the German defense establishment. Shinar was greatly concerned that the revelations would damage the secret transaction. Naturally enough, the deal, and the Bonn government's assistance in Israel's nuclear development at the time, were bathed in secrecy lest they harm Germany's relations with the Arabs, and Ben-Gurion could not defend his German policy fully and publicly. Concurrently, the West German government refused to establish diplomatic relations with Israel lest the Arabs respond by recognizing East Germany. Therefore, the public depiction of Bonn–Jerusalem relations was murky, even as massive quantities of German arms and matériel, mostly of American origin, were surreptitiously pouring into Israel at no charge. At his aforementioned meeting with the newspaper editors, Ben-Gurion said,

"[I] do not accept this fury about how there are Nazis in Egypt and the German people and the German state should be held responsible for it."[31] The outcome of the media tumult that Harel had touched off, however, was public hysteria and a demand by the opposition, joined by several Mapai politicians, to have the Knesset plenum debate the scientists affair.

Ben-Gurion himself, on vacation at this particular time, did not take part in the government session that discussed the tempest surrounding the scientists or the Knesset debate that followed it. He may have preferred to let other Mapai leaders – Finance Minister Eshkol and Foreign Minister Meir – find their way through the crisis since he was already mired in bitter controversy among Hebrew-newspaper readers and members of the coalition that Eshkol had so arduously cobbled together after the 1961 elections and the Affair. Seemingly, he could have trusted them to take the statesmanlike road; after all, they were as aware of the covert angles of the issue as the overt ones.

The prime minister, however, had approved ab initio the contents of the foreign minister's speech in the Knesset.[32] Before the debate, Meir handed an abstract of her speech to an ad hoc committee comprised of all factions save the Communists. Her purpose in doing so was to secure the broadest possible consensus in the plenum by explaining there that many details about the scientists had been disclosed to the various factions' delegates to the Foreign Affairs and Defense Committee and that it was impossible – for reasons of secrecy – to hand them to the plenum. However, if the foreign minister had counted on the FADC to debate the issue in a systematic way that would elicit a topical discussion in the plenum, she was mistaken. As noted earlier, this was one of the reasons for the tumbling status of the Knesset as a forum for pertinent debate on foreign and defense issues that Ben-Gurion himself considered sensitive. Suspecting that his polemical style might contribute to this outcome, Ben-Gurion had recused himself from the debate and allowed the foreign minister to conduct it without the strident tones of voice that his appearance would probably have generated. The FADC ostensibly adopted Mapai's stance, that is, that the factions should release statements only, avoiding a general debate in order to avert controversy, and that the committee should put together a summary announcement amenable to all factions save the Communists. The foreign minister spoke briefly about the "forbidden weaponry" that Egypt was developing "for the sole purpose of destroying the living," with the assistance of German scientists. Dismissing the Bonn government's claim that it had no legal way to stop citizens who wished to go abroad and work there, she demanded that it take legal and other steps to bring the scientists' activities to a halt.

It was not Ben-Gurion's view that this was a blow to Jerusalem–Bonn relations, since it was not he who had made this announcement about a country with which Israel's defense relations, in his judgment, were an asset of the highest order. However, after Meir finished reading the agreed-upon statement, the opposition broke its word. The head of Herut, Menachem Begin, attacked the government and Ben-Gurion personally, alleging that it was West Germany that was developing nonconventional weapons in Egypt in contravention of international treaties. In other words, the principal threat stemmed from concerted action by Germany and Egypt, and not by German scientists who were operating there on their own. Begin based his claim on the reasoning, backed by nothing but a gut feeling, that postwar Germany was no different from Germany following World War I, which in conjunction with the Soviet Union had developed weapons that the Versailles Treaty had forbidden it to develop. Now, Egypt had become the Germans' testing grounds, and the government of Israel – and here came the Herut leader's key piece of rhetoric – knew all about it and held its silence anyway. And why? Because Ben-Gurion's government had given Germany premature rehabilitation by concluding the reparations agreement of the early 1950s and fawning on Bonn thereafter. A pungent odor wafted from Begin's charges of collaboration between Mapai and the Nazi Satan and its successors, as well as Ben-Gurion's ostensible surrender to the "Nazo-British occupier" of the Mandate era.

The speakers from three other parties – the moderate Right (whose approach Ya'akov Talmon attempted to mold in a programmatic speech at the Mann Auditorium in Tel Aviv), Mapam, and the ultra-Orthodox Agudath Israel – displayed a better sense of proportion. However, the Communist delegate, Shmuel Mikunis, who was not bound by any prior agreement among the factions of the house, seized the opportunity to serve the Soviet interest by besmirching West Germany from the Knesset plenum to the limits of his ability. The Israeli government's German orientation, Mikunis claimed, was a chimera. Shimon Peres, in turn, had engineered Israel's arms deals with Bonn because of his view of relations with Germany as "shelter for a rainy day." Peres's policies, however, Mikunis declared, were bankrupt from both the German and the Israeli standpoints. Israel, he continued, should at its own initiative stop developing nuclear weapons in Israel *and in Germany*. Here he alluded overtly to Israeli–German collaboration in this field, which, as it were, explained Jerusalem's caution in relations with Bonn – a good explanation that he must have received from the Soviets. Israel ought to sever all contacts and relations with West Germany, he counseled. (The Soviets' involvement in the Dimona affair will be treated briefly in our discussion about the road to the Six Day War).

In his English-language memoirs, Peres recounts the serious run-in among himself, Golda Meir, and Isser Harel, which we addressed briefly.[33] He had been recalled to Israel from an important meeting in Africa, and once home he was informed rudely that the Soviet foreign minister, Andrei Gromyko, had gone to the United States to demand that the Americans bring the Dimona project to a halt. Peres – he says – claimed that the superpowers had no proof that the reactor was not intended for peaceful purposes. After all – as we construe Peres's writings – they did not know enough about the construction of the reactor's plutonium facility (which had been concealed under the reactor, according to the nuclear technician Mordechai Vanunu years later, and as shown in Vanunu's photographs of the underground story where the facility had been built). Thus, Peres managed to alleviate the grave concerns, shared by Ben-Gurion himself, about combined American–Soviet pressure in this matter.

It seems, however, that the Soviets had advised Mikunis that the construction of the reactor and its plutonium facility was indeed well along and that it was being aided by West Germany, Moscow's principal enemy in Europe and a power that was inclined at this time, in Moscow's judgment, to seek a way to procure a forbidden nuclear weapon for itself. We do not know how much aid Bonn was really providing, but there was some, at least in various scientific fields, as the Bonn government spokesman subsequently acknowledged.[34] Mikunis went on to claim – like his bitter rival on the Right, Menachem Begin – that Bonn was working actively on all fronts, including Egypt, where it had put its scientists to work, to produce nonconventional weapons in violation of its official obligations, and that by so doing it was directly endangering Israel (and might elicit a severe Soviet response). The chair of the Israel Communist Party then stated, however, that his faction would not submit a draft resolution and would abstain in the voting. Thus, Mikunis undermined the traditional cohesion of the Zionist factions against any Communist draft resolution.

The resolution adopted under these conditions established a quasi-consensus among all factions of the house, including Herut, and lifted the latter far-right faction from its isolation within the Knesset – all of which despite Begin's nonsensical charges against Mapai, especially in regard to the Versailles Treaty, and despite the damage that this resolution might inflict on Jerusalem–Bonn relations. The resolution augured the beginning of Begin's exodus from the political wilderness with the assistance of the left-wing factions and Mapai itself against the declared policy of Mapai's leader. This became possible, apparently, because the faction leaders were impressed by the public opinion tumult that had broken out in regard to West Germany, just as they had been impressed by the tumult that the Lavon Affair had set in motion. Ostensibly, they responded democratically; after all, their reaction corresponded to the public's sentiments. In reality, however, they dodged – once again – the necessity of leading the public and differentiating for the public's edification, as well as possible, between the truth and media-fanned emotion.

Golda Meir, for her part, was not shaken by the unity demonstrated by the Knesset on the Germany issue despite the agreement the ad hoc committee had worked out. On the contrary: She appeared to be impressed by it and refused to come out firmly against it. She did not protest against it in her summary remarks and did not defend the absent head of her faction against Begin's attacks. This left Ben-Gurion with no option but to launch his own one-man campaign, as he had done in the Affair. Meir did not even see fit to mention Ben-Gurion's main fear, the gravity of which the prime minister had repeatedly stressed in the past and the present: that the main danger facing Israel originated not in the weapons being developed by the German scientists but in the quantities and quality of the conventional weapons that the Soviet Union had resumed delivering to the Arab countries after the 1956 Sinai War. By now, this flow was figuring significantly in their calculations, which had it that they could vanquish Israel with the firepower in their possession and the rearmament of the Egyptian Air Force with medium-range bombers and advanced fighters. This genuine fear had prompted Ben-Gurion to ask for Hawk anti-aircraft missiles in his meeting with President Kennedy, and one may guess that his intention was to use them to protect the reactor in Dimona. When Kennedy linked the supply of this weaponry to American inspection of activities at the reactor, Ben-Gurion attempted, in a subsequent visit to Great Britain, to obtain Bloodhound missiles from the Macmillan government – and was turned down.[35] Thus, it transpires that Dimona – including its defense – was indeed the main axis of his policy at the time, as he repeatedly confirmed to Gideon Rafael, then a top official at the Foreign Ministry.[36] In this regard, one might have expected West Germany to help out, at least by providing anti-aircraft artillery, as eventually happened. This would provide final grounds for a breakdown in relations between Ben-Gurion and Meir on the eve of the former's resignation in the summer of 1963.

In retrospect, Meir acted in common cause, of sorts, with the leader of the nationalist opposition in the Knesset, who had spewed demagogic vanities at the plenum and by so doing harmed Israel's security. She must have had other considerations in mind, including the struggle for the legacy and weakening of Mapai's "young guard," the circle headed by Dayan and Peres. Concurrently, Achdut ha-Avoda, positioned to Mapai's left, had begun to tout itself not only as Mapai's political partner in the Histadrut and the Knesset but also as a political and defense alternative to Ben-Gurion and the Mapai "youngsters," in the embodiment of Israel Galili and Yigal Allon.

In the course of 1962, Ben-Gurion set up a debate on nuclear issues, chaired by himself, and in its course Galili and Allon confronted Dayan and Peres and expressed their own views on this cardinal issue. Thus far, Galili had not seemed to have a firm view on the nuclear issue and had not opposed Israel's nuclear activities openly or behind the scenes. Allon, however, had been arguing publicly against nuclear development since 1959. Now, it seemed, he took a deeper approach and corroborated his views with the assistance of British friends and theoretical literature.[37] Allon repeatedly stressed what he considered to be Israel's long-term conventional edge, which he connected with the strength of its society and its democratic and "progressive" regime. Ben-Gurion was not confident about the significance of such a connection in the context of historical wars and did not even consider it justified given the drawbacks of Israeli democracy. Later on, Allon would argue that if nuclear weapons were introduced into the region, the IDF would lose its conventional edge due to the loss of needed resources and the deterioration of its self-image.

In the 1962 encounter with Ben-Gurion, however, both Allon and Galili invoked a collection of rationales from the world of the U.S. academic deterrence theories to argue that were Israel to be the first in the region to go nuclear, the Arabs would surely follow and obtain a bomb of their own – perhaps with Soviet assistance, if Israel's West German connection persisted – and that Nasser would use this weapon to deal Israel a "first strike."[38] Then they contrasted this term, developed by American theoreticians, including Herman Kahn, Pinchas Sapir's cousin, to a "second-strike nuclear capacity" in response to the enemy's first strike. It was this second-strike capacity, the American theoreticians said, that would force the enemy to pay the price of its nuclear aggression. Some of them, however, thought that only the superpowers should have a well-developed second-strike capacity – even though arguments concerning this capacity originated in the wish to deny others the ability to follow the superpowers' lead and develop nuclear weapons of their own for a first strike. Their Israeli pupils may have believed that second-strike capacity of the sort that only the superpowers possessed required enormous production capacity, vast amounts of territory, and financial capabilities.

Here, however, Allon's and Galili's antinuclear argumentation tied in with their party's old tradition about the indivisibility of the Land of Israel. To wit, Ben-Gurion might suspect them of intending, in due course, to occupy the problematic West Bank and thereby create territorial "strategic depth." At any rate, as will be argued, the bomb could not serve Israel as a meaningful source of security due to the "irrational" behavior of its Arab enemies, according to Allon. Dayan and Peres, in contrast, were in favor of downsizing the conventional IDF and strengthening the nuclear option as the underpinning of Israel's security – both because they believed in this option and also, probably, because they wished to display loyalty to Ben-Gurion and forestall Achdut ha-Avoda's co-optation of the pluralistic Mapai as an equal partner.

Realizing that such a deployment was indeed a possibility, Ben-Gurion took action at several levels. In late March 1963, he accepted the results of a painstaking MI examination of the nature and dangers of Egypt's nonconventional weapons program, which were totally at odds with the estimation of Isser Harel's Mossad. The chief of MI, Major-General Meir Amit, reached the overall conclusion that the linchpin of the Egyptian program – short- and medium-range missiles – was absolutely meaningless absent appropriate navigation and guidance systems. Another idea that the Egyptians entertained, loading radioactive waste onto the warheads of their missiles in "response" to Dimona, was also a nonstarter. Thus, the menace of the Egyptian missiles existed only on the distant horizon, pending the development of navigation mechanisms. This menace would have to be countered by the swift completion of Israel's deterrent measures, including the development of an Israeli-made medium-range missile; such, at least, is my interpretation of the conclusions that Ben-Gurion drew from the MI assessment. Thus, the prime minister told Isser Harel, who had generated the public uproar concerning the German scientists, that he himself would present the FADC with reliable evidence that the danger flowing from Egypt's program had been immeasurably overestimated.[39] The czar of the security services construed this "reassessment" not only as a blow to his status and prestige but also as a scheme that General Amit had cooked up against him under the inspiration of the deputy minister of defense, Shimon Peres.

In principle, this represented nothing new in the "wars of the Jews," apart from the fact that the tempest roiled at the highest echelon of the defense establishment and carried implications for relations among the leaders of Mapai – a

phenomenon that thus far had occurred only in the Affair. Harel did not cross
swords with his superior in the FADC, as Lavon, the politician, had done to
Ben-Gurion in the same forum. Subsequently, however, he claimed that had
he been invited to appear before the committee, he would have disputed Ben-
Gurion's view ferociously. For one thing, he would have again accused the
Bonn government of great responsibility for the German scientists' activities
in Egypt for reason of its own interests, as he said in a conversation with me
many years later, since he was unwilling to repudiate his views and his conscience. However, he was unwilling to confront Ben-Gurion in the FADC and,
therefore, he resigned his positions. Truth to tell, Harel really had no choice as
an appointed official who disagreed with his elected superordinate minister on
a matter of principle. Still, in my opinion, his behavior can be traced not only
to his ego and to the interests of the Mossad, the agency that he headed, but to
his assessment of the political situation. To wit: His resignation would hasten
the end of the Ben-Gurion era and, accordingly, obstruct Peres and bring on
a changing of the guard. Then, one would naturally presume, his partner to
date in the struggle against Peres, Golda Meir, would take up the position in
the new arrangement with Levi Eshkol as Ben-Gurion's successor, and with
the anti-German Galili and Allon as Eshkol's close partners. Ben-Gurion had
not foreseen such wars of the Jews within the defense system. They must have
infuriated him since they were unfolding within an ostensibly "British" public
service in which such struggles were not supposed to take place and where, if
they did take place, the person at the top of the political echelon was supposed
to settle them topically one way or another.

Now, such phenomena were possible in Britain as well, notwithstanding
those "virtues" in which we have invested much ink in this study. One of
the best known was the dispute that erupted between the First Lord of the
Admiralty, Winston Churchill, and the First Sea Lord, Admiral Lord Fisher,
whose resignation after the Gallipoli disaster was followed by Churchill's own
unseating. There were many demands for Fisher's return, a matter of political
value to Prime Minister H. H. Asquith, but Fisher himself tried to dictate
preconditions to the prime minister. The very fact that they were expressed
by an appointed professional soldier, however prestigious, ruled out Fisher's
return and obliterated his status for good. Subsequently, in contrast, Churchill
as prime minister and minister of defense not only regularly sought advice
from his confidants, among whom were political personalities and experts
vested with enormous bureaucratic power, but also heard diverse views from all
corners of the defense system, some of which his close associates categorically
dismissed. In certain crucial cases, he came down in favor of the views opposed
by his associates, suspecting that the latter were tainted with prejudice and won
over by more solid evidence than their own.[40] Let us recall, however, that by
this time Churchill was a master executive – not only a great orator but also
a gifted administrator – and that in the 1940s, he operated under conditions
of war and had maximum powers, as had not been the case in a peacetime
Britain.

Ben-Gurion was convinced that Israel remained in a state of siege and emergency, but the climate in the early 1960s – for reasons that include the victory in the Sinai War – did not seem to justify extreme measures. Therefore, he did not force Harel to step down but began to treat him with the caution and suspicion that typified him whenever he encountered a political menace. He wrote to Harel that insofar as the government and the Knesset found his views amenable, "[t]hen you will be able to carry on with your work in the manner that you wish under a new prime minister." Harel, however, believed that Ben-Gurion would lose his battle with the Knesset and the government over the difficult (from the public standpoint) Germany issue and would then resign in any case. In his estimation, as he stated, if he (Harel) were to resign, the prime minister would also be forced to step down; Harel's resignation would be construed as the courageous act of a man of conscience who had surrendered his own status first.[41] So it was: The public greeted the resignation of the man who had captured Adolf Eichmann as further proof of Ben-Gurion's "Robespierrism" and his unethical insistence on following a dangerous course of action with Germany despite the protests of his pronounced loyalist, Isser Harel, whose conscience would not allow him to carry on in this deviant way.

Within the government, matters exceeded the bounds of the British rules of the game when the Achdut ha-Avoda ministers requested all original material in the prime minister's possession about the German scientists in Egypt so that they could work out their own views on the matter. Apart from expressing the coalition's flagrant nonconfidence in the head of the government in which they were serving as representatives of a party other than his own, the Achdut ha-Avoda demarche was, to some extent, a reprise of the proceedings used to investigate the Affair. It had been carried out behind the prime minister's back, and once it was over, several members of his government who were supposed to deal with proper procedure in regard to the inquiry into the 1954 Affair appointed themselves as judges behind the prime minister's back and without his permission. Now being adjudicated was a dispute between the prime minister and an appointed official, Harel, who had resigned – a step unimaginable according to the traditions of "public virtues," one of the main principles of which is teamwork among members of the government and acceptance of the prime minister's primacy. This principle had been dealt a blow within the Mapai team itself. Ben-Gurion refused to accept such a jurisdiction, of course, and when the matter of the appointed official's resignation was brought up for debate in the Knesset, he rose to his feet to defend his German policy and, in so doing, did offer a historical reckoning with Begin's Herut party and its stalwarts.

According to Yitzhak Ben-Aharon, a leading figure in Achdut ha-Avoda at the time, "Ben-Gurion went off the rails" in his attack on the Right generally and Menachem Begin in particular.[42] Even years later, when he attempted to repudiate the legitimacy of Begin's election to the premiership after the 1977 elections, Ben-Aharon failed to understand that he himself had legitimized Begin in the debate with Ben-Gurion over Germany in the early 1960s, and that Ben-Gurion had not gone "off the rails" but, instead, had responded in typical polemic language to Begin's vacuous allegations about collaboration with Nazis and with, to use the contemporary term, Bonn's "neo-Nazis." To use a tennis analogy, Ben-Gurion returned the historical serve to the court of Jabotinsky and his adherents, in spite of the differences between Jabotinsky and Menachem Begin, his self-appointed heir, stating that they and their successors in Herut were the ones who had taken Hitler for a paragon in the aftermath of his initial successes. (Those remarks were later expunged from the record by a decision of the House Committee, most of whose members belonged to the Left–Right coalition that had rebelled against Ben-Gurion in the aftermath of the Lavon Affair.)

Continuing, Ben-Gurion mentioned members of the Far Right in the 1930s, including Abba Achimeir, author of *Diary of a Fascist* (discussed at the beginning of this book), who had not disguised his pro-Fascist leanings. Ben-Gurion quoted articles by Achimeir that exuded this spirit; in them, indeed, the latter had spoken admiringly about Hitler, Atatürk, and Mussolini as the saviors of their nations. Then, to create a contrast, Ben-Gurion quoted his own remarks in 1935, when he had been elected chairman of the Jewish Agency Executive. Jabotinsky and his disciples at that time, he continued, had failed to foresee the Holocaust. In fact, one should add, they had bruited a mass but phased evacuation of Polish Jewry to Palestine because, among other reasons the Polish dictator, Józef Pilsudski, had died in 1935 and thus Polish Jewry lost his patronage. Two years previously, in contrast, Ben-Gurion had indeed recognized the mortal danger that Hitler's accession posed to the entire Jewish people, since Hitler regarded the Jews as carriers of the ideas of justice, peace, and freedom the world over. He also was the one who argued that the Nazi regime could not exist for long without a large-scale war that would evolve into a two-front conflict that would seal the Jewish people's fate. For this reason, Ben-Gurion had pursued the cause of mass Jewish immigration in every possible way. Yes, people had the idea that he and his associates were concerned back then with control of the Yishuv and were seeking to strengthen it by engineering the selective immigration of their own kind. This imagery was wrong and politically motivated.

Ben-Gurion's remarks on this occasion constituted a direct and indirect attack on all of the myths of Herut and the IZL from the British Mandate days to the early independence era. One of those myths was that Begin himself had been a survivor of the Holocaust and, therefore, qualified as the spokesman of the survivors at large. In fact, Begin had not been a Holocaust survivor because the Soviets had previously arrested him and exiled him to Siberia. His party was not active among Holocaust survivors, concentrating instead on the country's underprivileged "Sephardi" Jewish communities. In the Knesset, Begin had proclaimed himself the spokesman of people among whom Herut had not been active at all, for better or worse.

Summing up, Ben-Gurion said that just as he had been consistent in the early days in his opposition to "your movement's [ideology] on how to understand

Hitler's Germany," so today he opposed the Herut people due to their continuing political blindness, a blindness that could not distinguish between Konrad Adenauer and the contemporaneous German Social Democrats and the chieftains of the Third Reich.

Ben-Gurion waged this campaign alone; none of his colleagues took his side. *Davar*, the Mapai newspaper, even condemned his attack on Begin and defined the Knesset resolution of March 1963, to which Begin had been a party, as highly salutary. By implication, Ben-Gurion's standing in his party was badly undermined, and the question was whether he could rely on his ministers – including the foreign minister – in the next crisis, which would surely come.

The next crisis was not long in coming. In early 1963, President Kennedy issued NSAM (National Security Action Memorandum) 231, instructing the Department of State to work up a plan that would halt the development of advanced weaponry in the Middle East.[43] This activity prompted Moshe Dayan, now minister of agriculture, to come out against it in an article that he published in *Ma'ariv* in April 1963, by which time Peres had already made sure to hint to a foreign newspaper that Israel intended to develop only a very limited nuclear deterrent.[44] Naturally, since such a deterrent would be aimed solely at targets in Egypt (such as the Aswan Dam), claims concerning a "second-strike capability," the sort that the two superpowers needed, were groundless, and a nuclear deterrent against the USSR was not on the agenda.

At the time, however, Dayan and Peres were unfavorably regarded in the West; both were considered crude, elbow-wielding, and uninhibited men. Reports from Western embassies in Israel depicted Peres as having a corrupting influence on Ben-Gurion himself. By implication, if the Americans wished to stop the reactor project in Dimona, they had to try to approach Golda Meir (and Levi Eshkol, considered Ben-Gurion's successor-designate). To accomplish this successfully, they would have to show her some form of commitment to Israel's security and demonstrate achievements of some kind in Egypt. This they tried to do. Kennedy provided the foreign minister with a repetition of American promises – nonbinding promises long since issued – to defend Israel. Contrarily, however, the State Department was focusing its main efforts on Egypt at this stage.[45] The president also dispatched John J. McCloy, an important Democrat from the Roosevelt era who now specialized in nuclear disarmament (and Arab oil affairs), to the Middle East. McCloy offered a linkage – a deal – that Mordechai Gazit defined in the following way: "The U.S. will try to talk the Israelis into agreeing to international inspection of the Dimona reactor in return for Egyptian flexibility on [Nasser's] missile program."[46] In this way, the toothless Egyptian "white elephant" became an American bargaining card that could be played to sabotage the Dimona project, which was about to show its teeth right then. (According to a French source, the construction of the entire complex was to be completed by the end of 1963.)

Thus, according to one of his biographers, Ben-Gurion postponed his resignation – an inevitable denouement given the state of his party, the coalition, the Knesset, and most of public opinion – until the project was completed.[47] Foreign primary sources, however, paint a vastly different tableau that corroborates our conjecture that Ben-Gurion's resignation was related not only to the completion of the Dimona project but also to the expected clash with McCloy and his superordinates. The latter had more in mind than killing off the Dimona project. The Kennedy administration had from its first days been exploring various ways of solving the 1948 Arab refugee problem, and with the British – following a tradition dating to the Eisenhower administration – had been discussing Israeli territorial concessions in the Negev that the administration thought necessary. After all, one of Nasser's charges against Israel – apart from its very "illegality," to his mind – was that the country was a regional bone in the throat, a wedge between Egypt and its Arab sisters in the Arab Middle East to the north and east. By inference, if the West wished to find a common language with the most important Arab country and its charismatic leader – against the background of competition and escalating risk of confrontation with the Soviet Union – Israel had to make concessions to Egypt in the southern Negev in order to establish an overland bridge between Egypt and Jordan, Iraq, Syria, and Saudi Arabia.

Ben-Gurion attempted to repel the Kennedy administration's overall Middle East policy at several levels. First, he corresponded personally with Kennedy, de Gaulle, and other Western heads in order to show them that unless Israel were given a NATO-style guarantee or similar assurances from the two superpowers, the Jewish state would have no refuge from the inter-Arab dynamic of the 1960s.[48] This dynamic had led to the establishment of a new Arab union – an Egyptian–Syrian–Iraqi federation – sometime after the militant pan-Arab Ba'ath Party had seized the reins in Syria. Ben-Gurion heatedly warned his correspondents about this federation's public commitment to the annihilation of Israel. The U.S. administration tended to pooh-pooh the gravity of this attempt at Arab unity; after all, a full Syrian–Egyptian union had just fallen through. Worse still, Kennedy considered the Israeli premier's warnings and entreaties a smokescreen that was meant to conceal the Dimona project and vehemently demanded the right to inspect what was going on there.

As it turned out, no sooner had McCloy begun his fateful mission to the Middle East than Ben-Gurion resigned. The final pretext for his resignation was a severe clash between Ben-Gurion and Foreign Minister Meir over an Israeli military-training program in West Germany. Israeli soldiers had been sent there, uniforms and all, to master and operate the L-70 radar-guided anti-aircraft cannon that were needed, among other things, to defend Dimona against low-flying aircraft. Meir, construing the disclosure of the mission as yet another provocation against her and public opinion with respect to the charged German issue, demanded that all information about the mission be censored, and threatened to implement her own resignation. Ben-Gurion refused to order the military censor to blue-pencil the matter, deeming it totally legitimate, but could assume that the resignation of his foreign minister would bring his government down. Absent the support of this member of the government, who had been loyal to him in the past, Ben-Gurion evidently reached the overall conclusion that he could no longer function. Furthermore, even if he dissuaded Meir from resigning, he could not predict how she would receive the McCloy mission; she might show an untoward willingness to accommodate McCloy if he were to present her with an ostensible Egyptian concession on the missiles. Meir's American orientation – unlike Peres's emphasis on Paris and Bonn – was not new and eventually proved worthwhile, taking a serpentine course that originated at this time and continued until after the Six Day War. Israel's special relationship with the United States – which Golda Meir nurtured with all her strength – and Washington's willingness to be forthcoming with the foreign minister specifically among Israeli officials, might be put to a critical test if McCloy landed in Israel bearing offers that could not be refused in regard to Dimona once Meir listened to Allon and Galili regarding the dubious strategic value of the nuclear project and its price in terms of superpower opposition to it.

Therefore, one may say that Ben-Gurion was forced to step down and, no less, that he was ousted from his posts in the summer of 1963 by the combination of a revolt in his faction and among his senior appointed officials from within (if we mention the resignation of Isser Harel) and American pressure from without.

Ultimately, however, McCloy never made it to Israel. He first stopped in Egypt, knowing, as stated, that absent an Egyptian concession of some kind on the missiles, he would not be able to pressure Israel on Dimona. Nasser, however, refused to give him an explicit answer for several reasons, including his concern about the price he would have to pay in inter-Arab currency for a concession on this sensitive issue. As a result, McCloy headed for Athens to wait for Nasser's final response before proceeding to Jerusalem. As he waited, President Kennedy was assassinated; the entire American foreign and defense policy was then put on hold as Lyndon B. Johnson, Kennedy's successor, pursued his grand domestic priorities.[49]

Eshkol's Administration and Ben-Gurion's Criticism from Today's Perspective

Professor Yechiam Weitz tells us today that after Ben-Gurion's resignation – ostensibly brought on by the "end of his charisma" – he gradually became a grotesque, benighted, and vengeful figure, one who shattered his own historical monument, as the renowned cartoonist Dosh portrayed the matter in the daily *Ma'ariv*. As I have shown, however, Ben-Gurion's resignation was occasioned not by lack of charisma but by much more knotty processes, processes that he himself feared and had predicted due to the nature of the Israeli political system and the Jews' political habits. Seemingly, Ben-Gurion had transferred his offices to Levi Eshkol by handing his two government posts to this man with neither dislocations nor rancor, after which he settled in Sede Boqer for good. Soon, however, the external and internal circumstances that had led to his resignation changed. One of them was the assassination of Kennedy and the succession of Johnson; the other was a series of demarches that Eshkol slowly began to carry out on his own, such as an initial decision to scrap the Israeli-made medium-range missile and opt for a French one only. According to Yitzhak Greenberg, Eshkol's decision to stop the missile development program and continue the French project against Deputy Minister of Defense Peres's stance "displeased Ben-Gurion to the extent that he would blame Eshkol in due course for major security blunders without specifying details."[50]

In Weitz's opinion – which, in this matter, too, follows the lead of the journalist Amos Elon – Eshkol's succession marked the onset of a new era in Israel, one of domestic conciliation, as the high and mighty recognized the citizenry's maturity and democratic rights. This conciliation was reflected in several gestures. One was the fulfillment by government resolution of Jabotinsky's request, as expressed in his will, to have his remains exhumed from their place of burial in the United States and reinterred in Israel. The second was a move by Eshkol to readmit Lavon's secessionist group, which had assembled in Min Hayesod, to Mapai – a step that must have outraged Ben-Gurion and that ultimately sank into failure. A third measure illuminated the nature of the Eshkol administration; it concerned the transformation of the Voice of Israel, the public radio service, from a department of the Office of the Prime Minister into a public broadcasting authority. This action converted the direct political supervision of public radio that had been practiced until then (though largely formal except where Arabic programming was concerned) into an executive committee with a cumbersome plenum in which the governing coalition commanded a majority. The government appointed the chair and the director general of the authority and subordinated them directly and indirectly to its will. After the fact, Eshkol and his associates hoped to keep the authority tightly under their thumb, albeit in a roundabout way, but soon enough they lost control over the journalists, paving the way toward the introduction of television to Israel in a most haphazard and somewhat corrupt fashion under minister Galili. Finally, Eshkol did away with the military rule that had been imposed on the Arabs of Israel during the Ben-Gurion era and replaced it with indirect supervision by the security services.

The military government had been forced upon the heterogeneous Arab population in the Galilee and the "Little Triangle" – an Arab-inhabited region close to Tel Aviv that controlled strategic routes to Israel's settlements all the way to the north, most of which had been unwillingly handed over by Jordan to Israel after the War of Independence. The population at issue was also a national minority that belonged, in principle, to the enormous Arab majority in the region – a mass of humanity that, for the time being, rejected Israel and threatened to regroup and destroy it. Given the resulting state of protracted emergency, Israel's Arab minority was immeasurably better off than the American reservation Indians (until recently) and the Nisei in World War II. For one thing, Israeli Arabs enjoyed the franchise from the outset. The Nisei, in contrast, were doomed to their quarantine status until Japan surrendered unconditionally and accepted temporary American occupation. Ben-Gurion, however, had been concerned that the Jewish majority's internal fragmentation into camps and sects would invest the Arab minority with scale-tipping power vis-à-vis the majority. The maintenance of military rule was meant to allay these concerns somewhat without denying the Israeli Arabs political representation.

By abolishing this mechanism without continuing Ben-Gurion's campaign in favor of a British-style two-party regime, Eshkol gave Ben-Gurion an additional reason to be displeased with his successor. However, Eshkol's Israel put on a more democratic face than it had worn before, and the new premier and his associates conducted its affairs more gracefully and kindly. In one matter, however, Elon and Weitz were right: Under Eshkol, Ben-Gurion's "bill of obligations" expired. Although it did not happen in one stroke, Israelis of European descent, especially young ones during Eshkol's tenure, began to adopt the American-style liberal "bill of rights" approach, as they construed it. The Israelis of Mizrahi descent did not count much as active participants in the political process except as Mapai's instruments of power and policy agents. Most of them, living in the periphery or otherwise in development towns, were dependent as before on Histadrut's health services and jobs, and on government investments in old and new economic enterprises. Mizrahi enclaves of poverty, and growing criticism of this "system" on the periphery of the big cities such as Haifa and Jerusalem, produced violent protests, but the process of Mapai's decline started with the election results following two – very different – wars and a breakup of Mapai's base among members of the upper class.

Eventually, that outlook would find political expression within the framework of a parliamentary party – the Citizens Rights Movement, later, a new party called Change (Shinui in Hebrew) – that would catapult Menachem Begin to the Office of the Prime Minister. Thus, they played into the hands of the Right four years after Ben-Gurion's death. However, the path to that destination was serpentine and owes its immediate origins to the Six Day War and its ramifications. In the crisis that preceded this war, Eshkol lost control of the whole system and forfeited his standing even among loyal supporters in his inevitable struggle with Ben-Gurion. In other words, the "system," whose endless difficulties Ben-Gurion had recognized and within which Eshkol thought he could operate in order to undertake internal and external moves with considerable latitude, ultimately tripped him up with the help of Ben-Gurion himself – a helping hand that deserves a closer look. Furthermore, the thing that Weitz, parroting Elon, described as a surfeit of democracy in Israel created an opening for a new foreign and defense policy that minority factions were allowed to influence perceptibly. By then, in fact, Mapai had lost its definitive status in these fields as the central pillar of the political edifice.

It is but natural that Ben-Gurion would not merely contemplate the changes that Eshkol had begun to introduce in Israel's domestic affairs from the sidelines but would do his best to keep abreast of Eshkol's moves in foreign and defense affairs. For the time being, Shimon Peres remained in his post as deputy minister of defense, and Moshe Dayan continued in the cabinet as minister of agriculture. Therefore, one could assume a strong measure of continuity in Eshkol's policies, at least in regard to Dimona, if not on the issues of Germany and the missiles, to which we will return presently. Ben-Gurion, who was now free to investigate the 1954 Lavon Affair once and for all, hired the journalist Haggai Eshed to rake the muck. The conclusions of Eshed's inquiry led inexorably to a confrontation between Eshkol and Ben-Gurion, in which the former prevailed and, in effect, maneuvered the latter out of Mapai.

The dynamics in the Middle East arena, Europe, and the global theater, however, did not give the winner much of a respite. Furthermore, the appointment to the post of COGS of Yitzhak Rabin, a vastly experienced professional military man but nevertheless a protégé of Galili and Allon – Eshkol's senior partners in the coalition that he had reassembled after Ben-Gurion's resignation – had the effect of granting practical and political power to a man who would represent the army vis-à-vis a civilian minister who was inexperienced in this field. Indeed, Rabin would soon respond in his own way to changes in the Middle East arena that had begun to occur at a quickening pace until they peaked in May 1967. For the most part, too, he did this with prior or reluctant and ex post backing from the prime minister and defense minister, Eshkol. By the time Eshkol roused himself to stop the army and preclude the "preventive war" that all IDF leaders found inevitable, he had lost control of the entire political system, including the IDF. This loss contributed to the eruption of the war in the way that it did and as it spread to all theaters.

The regional and global changes that ultimately triggered the war were a mixture of the old and the new – a concurrence of long-existing problems and interests and dramatic changes in regional and global leadership:

a. Kennedy's assassination in 1963 and the accession of Lyndon Johnson to the American presidency turned the focus of interest at the White House toward sweeping domestic reforms. The foreign policy establishments, however, continued striving to check the Soviet Union and its allies everywhere. The change was particularly evident in Vietnam, in regard to which the president also had the domestic consideration of avoiding attacks on his home turf for being "soft" on the enemy. Concurrently, these establishments sought to work out an agreement with the Soviet Union on nuclear antiproliferation – a goal that took them until 1968 to attain. They also sought compromises in the Middle East that would tilt in the West's favor and looked for ways to stop Israel's nuclear program in return for some form of Egyptian consideration. When they failed at this, they acted to head off a war over this program, which developed steadily in the 1960s and became an official Egyptian casus belli by early 1965. At that stage, however, the Arabs were taking no direct action in this regard.

b. The downfall of Khrushchev in 1965 and the accession of Leonid Brezhnev and Alexei Kosygin created a new situation in superpower relations that initially centered on the Soviets' intentions, which appeared to be vague. However, two pending problems stood out in this "new" situation: Vietnam and the lessons of the Cuban missile crisis, which seemed to have ended with a victory for Kennedy and may even have contributed to the ousting of Nikita Khrushchev. But why had Khrushchev been deposed? Was it because he had "capitulated" to Kennedy and removed his missiles from Cuba, or because he had taken the grave risk of sparking a nuclear world war there? This must have been related to the abiding concern on the part of Kennedy himself, and on that of his successors in Johnson's foreign and defense establishments, of an even greater entanglement than the one that they had escaped by the skin of their teeth in respect to isolated Cuba. Cuba, where Khrushchev had been snared in a web of lies, was their backyard. In its surroundings, the Americans enjoyed total naval and air supremacy.

What would happen if the Soviets were tempted to respond, or felt that they must respond, to challenges in areas of vital concern to them – such as the Middle East – and would station missiles in Egypt or Syria? Israeli nuclear missiles, especially to ranges that would cover not only obvious targets in the Arab world, such as the Aswan Dam, but also targets in the Soviet Union itself, could be developed to cope with such a challenge. The Soviets, however, might neutralize the Israeli threat by equipping the Arabs with a response of their own or by furnishing them with a nuclear guarantee. In all, this was a threat that could thoroughly destabilize superpower relations and subordinate them to demarches among clients whose conflics had escalated and had an internal logic of their own.

An aggressive school of thought seemed to exist, at least in the Soviet defense establishment – surrounding the deputy defense minister, Andrei Grechko – which sought to aggrandize the Soviet Union's status and naval might in Middle Eastern countries, such as Egypt, Ba'athist Syria, civil-warring Yemen, and Aden, which the British were about to evacuate. These countries' receptiveness to Soviet military influence and presence was rising steadily. The USSR also wished to build up its strength in the Third World in response to the downfall of the pro-Soviet regimes of Muhammad Ben Bella in Algeria and Ahmed Sukarno in Indonesia. Indeed, winding up a visit to Egypt in late 1955, Marshal Grechko seemed to have given Egypt a prospective nuclear guarantee "if Israel attains nuclear weapons."[51] Concurrently, the Soviets directly approached Israeli delegates to talks in Geneva over the projected nuclear anti-proliferation treaty and warned them not to develop the bomb. "The moment you have the bomb, so will the Arabs," they argued, among other things.

This reasoning might put terror into various personages on the Israeli Left who continued to view the USSR with a mixture of affection and immense awe. Such a person was Transport Minister Yitzhak

Ben-Aharon.[52] From then on, Ben-Aharon's cohorts in the Achdut ha-Avoda faction – ministers Galili and Allon – could argue that such a guarantee severely weakened Israel's nuclear deterrent or, in any event, enjoined Israel against deploying medium-range missiles that might threaten the Soviet Union itself and sabotage superpower relations. It seemed that Eshkol's newly formed government would have to make decisions about missile development, it having become clear that the Shavit II had been nothing but a public relations gimmick and that Israel had no practical missile program of its own, unless Eshkol were ready to use the existing infrastructure and skilled manpower and spend enormous resources on it.

Eshkol decided to abandon the Israeli missile project and opted for France alone, whereas Ben-Gurion would have retained both options. The decision, as Professor Yuval Ne'eman wrote,[53] was to assign the development of two prototypes – a short-range missile called the MD 620 and a medium-range model termed the MD 660 (the initials relate to Generale Aeronautique Marcel Dassault, the vendor) – to France. The medium-range missile was due for delivery in 1967.[54] By implication, this issue – and this year – would present Arabs, the Soviets, and the Americans with a challenge of the highest order if they wished to eradicate Israel's nuclear option before it could pass the point of no return.

c. Events in the Arab world at this time assured inter-Arab rivalry but also guaranteed a measure of unity in regard to Israel and related specific issues, from the problem of the Jordan River after Israel began to pump water from the Sea of Galilee to the Negev, to the Dimona problem, and in between to an issue that was as unresolved as ever – the 1948 Palestinian refugees. The last-mentioned problem had itself taken on the typical complexion of inter-Arab rivalry. Since 1964, Syria's militant Ba'ath regime had been aiding Fatah in its guerrilla operations against Israel under the inspiration of the FLN's war against the French in Algeria and of North Vietnam's war against the Americans. In 1964, President Nasser had established a Palestinian organization of his own called the Palestine Liberation Organization and stationed Ahmed Shuqairy at its head. This entity was also supposed to undermine the status of King Hussein of Jordan and incite his numerous Palestinian subjects against him. For the time being, Nasser was not allowing the Palestine Liberation Organization (PLO) to operate directly against Israel from the Gaza Strip, which had been surrounded by UN peacekeeping forces since Israel evacuated it in 1957. His restraint in this matter, however, exposed him to accusations from his conservative and radical Arab enemies and rivals to the effect that instead of practicing what he preached – working toward the goal of annihilating Israel – he was hiding behind the skirts of the UN forces.

d. Nasser himself was embroiled in a great many struggles in various arenas during these years. In 1961, he had been forced to withdraw from his union with Syria. In 1963, he countered a militant and provocative pan-Arab Ba'ath regime in Damascus that had cast a shadow over his moral and political leadership throughout the Arab world. Concurrently, Egypt had intervened in the civil war in Yemen on the side of the anti-Imam forces and, as a result, found himself in an indirect struggle with Saudi Arabia, which favored the Imam, and with Jordan. These two countries diligently protected their monarchy regimes and their separate interests, and Saudi Arabia made sure to reserve its oil treasures for itself. Their opponent, the impoverished socialistic Egypt, depended on American aid (cheap grain shipments) to feed its citizens, who were multiplying at an unprecedented rate.

e. Just then, another acute change took place in Syria. In February 1966, an even more radical sect of the Ba'ath Party seized the helm. The new regime seemed willing to take escalating risks vis-à-vis Israel, either on its own or by means of Fatah, and to operate in areas that had been agreed upon at Arab summit conferences from 1964 onward. Said areas were two: an operation in conjunction with Jordan and Lebanon to divert water sources for the Sea of Galilee in response to Israel's use of them to irrigate the Negev, and operations that pertained specifically to Israeli–Syrian–Palestinian relations, including the shelling of localities in the Galilee in response to the use that Eshkol's Israel was making of the demilitarized zones in the north of the country for agricultural purposes. Yasser Arafat's Fatah organization was even allowed to operate from Syrian bases, provided that this was done under appropriate Syrian supervision and not directly but via Jordan. Damascus seemed keen on precipitating a general war with Israel and mobilizing Egypt for this cause. At least it was "doing something" and creating the challenge of a real struggle against the Zionist state, as opposed to Nasser's hot air, which, for the time being, was not being backed by action.

One issue, however, stood all by itself: how the Arabs should respond to the Dimona project. This matter, which had been the theme of at least one summit meeting in 1965, had led thus far to a public pronouncement by Nasser that if Israel crossed the nuclear threshold, the result would be war. The Ba'athists in Damascus and Arafat and his associates could argue that, from their standpoint, the Israeli nuclear option did not present a genuine challenge in this era of guerrilla warfare. Egypt, in contrast, could view Dimona as a challenge to itself, a very grave threat that must not be taken lightly by any means, on top of the threat that the bomb would indeed guarantee Israel's existence no matter what. Ahmed Shuqairy turned this delicate issue into a topic of shrill public alarm, suspecting that the Arab states would not fight for the Palestinians if they were to face the menace of an Israeli nuclear challenge. After all, the Arab states had not lost territory nor the homes of their citizens to Israel, as did the Palestinian refugees. The Israeli bomb could therefore drive a wedge between the Palestinian refugees and the Arab states, as it indeed has done until today. If so, the time to fight and destroy Israel was now – before Israel went fully nuclear.

There lay the origins of Israel's future security dilemmas and even the Americans' vigorous endeavors to "prevent war" from 1965 on. All those factors quickly jelled to bring on the preventive war of 1967. Although Israel had neither planned nor wanted that war, nevertheless it was occasioned by prior plans that became real under the pressure of events. From the standpoint of our discussion, however, the main issue concerns Ben-Gurion's role along the road to that war and what he did to head it off.

Ben-Gurion's "contribution" was manifested in several domains up to the 1965 elections. The first was the resurrection of the Affair and the heated struggle pertaining to it, due to which he finally resigned and subsequently was ousted from Mapai as a traitor. Second, after (or perhaps before) his resignation, Ben-Gurion decided to set up a party of his own for the 1965 elections. Admittedly, the new entity did not do well enough at the ballot box to acquire blocking power to influence the structure of the coalition that Eshkol reassembled after the elections. However, its stances during and after the election campaign marred Eshkol's credibility in foreign and defense affairs; these issues entail elucidation in view of the actions of Eshkol's coalition per se. The third question has not been clarified adequately to this day: where the security issue figured in Ben-Gurion's considerations in running for office in 1965 at the head of his own list, since conventional wisdom usually links his decision to domestic affairs, foremost the resurrection of the Affair.

Indeed, after receiving the findings of Haggai Eshed's investigation of the 1954 Affair in Egypt, which held Lavon responsible for having given the order to carry out a stupid and risky action in that Arab state, Ben-Gurion acted at several levels. Most importantly, he tried to have the decision of the ministerial committee that had exonerated Lavon annulled. In this matter, he was supported by Dov Joseph, Eshkol's minister of justice. The nullification of the decision – which Eshkol had sponsored at the time it was adopted – could have had several clashing outcomes. One of them, to which Ben-Gurion aspired, would not only establish that he had been right in his lengthy struggle on this principled issue but also place him in a new public light after having absorbed calumny from every direction since the beginning of the public debate of the Affair. Debunking the ministerial committee that had exonerated Lavon would set the tenets concerning "rule of law" and "public rules of the game" on firm ground. Lavon's exoneration after the government's improper investigation of his case had been akin to trampling the rules. After such a proceeding, Ben-Gurion's thinking presumably went, people viewing the matter after the fact would think that if he had personally lost such a game against Lavon and the media, why should they bother to fight a battle of principles, when even Ben-Gurion himself has not been able to win? Therefore, it was of supreme importance to restore the deserving rules to their proper place or to fight for their adoption.

Another possible outcome – that Eshkol had calculated and found useful to him and Mapai from his standpoint – was the prevention of the very demarche just described, for more than a few reasons. One of them, certainly, was Eshkol's sense that he himself would be wounded by the repeal of the government resolution that he himself had sponsored. Furthermore, his leadership and that of his party colleagues – Foreign Minister Golda Meir, Finance Minister Pinchas Sapir, and Education Minister Zalman Aranne – would be blemished, to the benefit of Ben-Gurion and his apparent young successors, Dayan and Peres. After all, the nullification of Lavon's exoneration would of necessity clear them of the suspicions and vicious charges leveled against them by Lavon in the course of the Affair. These suspicions and charges had clouded their reputations even though they had never been proven, and Eshkol could manage more easily to maneuver between them (Dayan and Peres) and their traditional foes (Allon and Galili), whose partnership he needed, at the very least, in order to establish internal harmony at the Histadrut.

Another motive was Eshkol's slightly cynical attitude toward the British-style rules of the game and state of the law. Eshkol was a man of compromise and a master of give-and-take who, at this stage of his public career, had become a professional politician eager to maintain both of his portfolios and his own record of achievements in them. Ben-Gurion's shadow weighed on him – whether Ben-Gurion was right or not – and at this stage he definitely did not want his predecessor to return to the arena as a moral victor of sorts, let alone a political one. He also understood rather well that most of Ben-Gurion's enemies in the Affair had taken no interest in the matter per se; instead, they had regarded it as an opportunity to get back at him in various personal and political disputes. Therefore, it puzzled them greatly to see Eshkol suddenly inspired to conduct a topical investigation of a matter about which the public had had its fill. Accordingly, he found it in no way problematic to refuse to reopen the debate over the Affair, knowing that those "enemies" probably wanted no part of an investigation with no axe to grind. Lying, legal-political injustice, and mendacious manipulation of the sort that Ben-Gurion attributed to Lavon were despicable acts per se, and their entrenchment as an accepted norm posed an immense danger for the future. Eshkol, however, placed his trust in the Israeli public's fatigue with the Affair.

Thus, after appearing to be willing to discuss the ministerial committee's decision to exonerate Lavon per the recommendation of the minister of justice, Eshkol recanted, resigned, dissolved the government, and put it back together again without subjecting the matter to any debate at all. When the Mapai Central Committee took a vote on the issue, Eshkol came away with a 60 percent victory. Moshe Sharett, verging on death, used this forum to deliver a prosecutorial and vengeful speech against Ben-Gurion, who had dismissed him from the Foreign Ministry way back then, and in defense of Lavon, whom he himself had once ousted from the Ministry of Defense in the sincere belief that Lavon had been responsible for the botched operation in Egypt. Ben-Gurion came away with 40 percent of the tally.

It was a smashing victory indeed. However, it throttled all further pertinent public discussion of the issue and cleared the way, in Ben-Gurion's opinion, for the continued deterioration of public life in Israel into a regime of deceit and mendacity that rewarded their practitioners.

The reader may of course ask: Hadn't this regime originated in the defense system, a closed, self-contained system that was exempt from real public supervision? The method, it appeared, had originated during Ben-Gurion's time, and Lavon had revealed its true face, whether he had been responsible for the Affair in Egypt or had resorted to the forging of documents that had indeed been committed in order to clear his name and expose the system's drawbacks publicly. Furthermore, whether Ben-Gurion had designated Dayan and Peres as his successors or not, after their maneuverings following the Affair they were perceived publicly as contenders for the throne; therefore, they posed a threat to Eshkol and his associates.

The prime minister and defense minister were not fond of the ambitious Moshe Dayan, the wily, rough-and-tumble minister of agriculture, who seemed to have plenty of media entrée and potential for public support. Eshkol, along with his cohorts Allon and Galili, seemed so willing to dump him or, at the least, to crimp his style, that Dayan would eventually claim – nothing less – that he felt as though he had stumbled into a concentration camp where the guards shoved him through the fence just so they could gun him down. Dayan promptly resigned from the Eshkol government, seemingly bringing his public career to an end.[55]

Shimon Peres, in contrast, attempted to survive in the government and in Mapai, knowing that he needed this large and powerful party as a platform for his advancement within its framework. Therefore, we do not know whether it was of his own volition and for reasons of loyalty to its former leader that he ultimately seceded from Mapai and joined the party that Ben-Gurion established in 1965, that is, whether he did it for pertinent reasons relating to disagreements with Eshkol about security matters or for lack of choice. In 1965 and immediately afterwards, pertinent disagreements about security issues might have concerned two issues: a new American move on the Dimona matter, which for the first time in Israel's history was now linked to direct American supply of offensive weapons, and a grave crisis in Israeli–French relations that had germinated in 1964 and ripened in 1965. The crisis prompted General de Gaulle to perform a comprehensive review of bilateral relations and seemed to threaten the delivery of the medium-range missile that France had promised Israel.

On the Dimona issue, the Americans had pinned hopes on Eshkol from the moment he took over the premiership and the defense portfolio, and they were willing to be more forthcoming with him than they had ever been with Ben-Gurion.[56] The first scholar to publicize an "American guarantee of the 1949 Armistice Demarcation Lines" that Eshkol had received as soon as he took office was Michael Brecher. In his public writings, Professor Brecher never elucidated the reason for this. In an oral communication with this author in 1976, he explained that it was, in fact, an American attempt to find a surrogate for Dimona. To my mind, however, the guarantee was problematic in many respects. First, it was secret, that is, valueless from the standpoint of the Israeli public. In fact, if it ever became clear that Washington was not coming to Israel's aid as expected, as seemingly happened in May–June 1967, those in the know would have asked what Eshkol had obtained from the Americans in return for what he had given, and the answer would have been basically nothing. Second, the right to conclude a secret guarantee such as this was one of the powers that the administration had arrogated to itself in foreign and defense affairs at the time; its value in American terms was dubious because the Senate had not approved it, meaning that it could not be deemed equal to an overt NATO-style military alliance. At the critical moment, the president himself might repudiate the guarantee, arguing – justifiably in itself, and therefore many times worse – that it lacked sufficient support in the Senate and in public opinion. This indeed seems to be what happened in the crisis that precipitated the Six Day War.

For the time being, however, Eshkol seemed, contrarily enough, to be following in Ben-Gurion's steps, at least on the Dimona issue. Ahead of his first visit to the United States in June 1964 – where he expected to face direct questioning about Israel's nuclear program – John Badeau, the American ambassador in Cairo, reported the following to Washington: The only circumstances that would prompt the Egyptians to even consider a surprise attack on Israel would be *their realization that the Israelis had obtained or would soon obtain nuclear weapons.* In such a case, Badeau continued, the Egyptians' goal would be to destroy the Israeli facilities with the greatest celerity and efficiency and then pull back behind its frontier, counting on international opinion and its pressure to prevent Israel from hitting back. In this case, however, the calculus behind the Egyptians' actions would be defensive, not offensive.[57]

By phrasing his last sentence as he did, Badeau indirectly justified an Egyptian demarche of this kind, that is, an overland march on Dimona. Even if the chiefs of the IDF were unaware of the cable, they certainly knew that the Egyptian Army could burst into the Negev if this overland front were unprotected and advance on Dimona and Beersheba. For that to happen, the Egyptians would have to man the trench lines that they had established in the northern Sinai after Israel's retreat from this area in 1957 and to amass serious armored forces along them. To forestall this possibility, Israel would have to seal the border, at the very least. This is how we will explain Israel's initial decision to mobilize reserves in the May 1967 crisis, following an Egyptian march into the Sinai and photo flight over the reactor.

As for the Egyptians' motives on the Dimona issue, we may glean some understanding from a document produced by the National Security Council (at the White House) or the Central Intelligence Agency in December 1964, that is, after Eshkol's visit to the United States. According to this paper, Israel's nuclear program seemed to be pledged to research since January 1964 but might correspond to a program for the manufacture of arms. Prime Minister Eshkol, the paper continued, had told the president that Israel's nuclear activity was meant for peaceful purposes. However, neither Eshkol nor his predecessor,

Ben-Gurion, had ever ruled out the development of nuclear weapons by Israel if the Middle East situation were to justify it.[58]

As for the question itself, the authors of the document, which was released for publication after censorship and extensive reediting, determined that Israel had the technological ability to develop a bomb. The United States, the authors continued, believed that Israel, without outside assistance, could detonate its first nuclear device two or three years after it decided to develop nuclear capability. The production of more advanced weapons would require another year or two. In the meantime, the United States had compelling evidence that a French company was developing for Israel a two-stage solid-fuel missile with a 450-kilometer range. A warhead with a 1,500–2,000-pound carrying capacity, usable for both high explosives and a nuclear payload, was being planned. Israel considered the existence of its own military deterrent crucial to its survival. *Given this approach*, the authors adduced, *the arms race in the Middle East had advanced to a dangerous level.* As the United Arab Republic (i.e., Egypt) progressed and Egypt's missile technology improved, Israel was acting to develop a counterdeterrent that would be as unique as it was frugal. It would probably lead to the development of nuclear warheads for missiles that Israel had ordered from France. Lower-level Israeli officials spoke openly about Israel's Egyptian strategy: *(a) surface-to-surface missiles aimed at the Nile Delta and (b) the ability to bomb the Aswan Dam and release its waters. To destroy the Aswan Dam, a nuclear warhead would be needed.*

As for Egypt itself, the report had the following to say: Among all countries in the Middle East, Egypt is the most vulnerable to a nuclear attack. A single nuclear device, properly aimed, would send a flood of water 400 feet high down the narrow Nile valley, where the entire Egyptian population was concentrated. Israel was also vulnerable, but due to the strangeness of its frontiers, a nuclear attack against it would harm the neighboring Arab countries almost as much as it would harm Israel. Therefore, *to assure its own survival, Egypt evidently believed it advantageous to thwart the use of nuclear weapons and, in turn, to thwart the introduction of such weapons in the Middle East.*

Thus, an official American document dating to this time established explicitly that if Egypt wished to head off the advent of "the bomb" in its region, it felt this way in order to "assure its own survival." And why was its survival at stake? Because Cairo wanted or had been obliged, or both, to annihilate Israel to begin with. The introduction of an Israeli bomb, therefore, gave Israel the only tool that could assure its own existence by threatening Egypt's. By seeing things this way, however, the Israelis clashed not only with Egyptian ideology, public commitments, and pan-Arab interests but also with U.S. priorities and global policy at the time.

Indeed, the White House national security team – a holdover from the Kennedy administration – not only viewed the Dimona project as a challenge per se but also seemed to expect the Soviets to respond by giving the Arabs at least the belief that they would come to their aid in this respect. Or they might do something much worse, that is, station nuclear missiles of their own in Egypt or in Syria, avenging Washington many times over for the Cuba incident. After all, Cuba was isolated in America's backyard and surrounded by American forces that had a decisive edge. These concerns must have surfaced – one may at least suppose as much – during Eshkol's visit to the United States on June 1–12, 1964. After the visit, the State Department circulated a cable that it had sent to the International Atomic Energy Agency in Vienna (in a circular to its ambassadors in all Arab capitals, Paris, and Rome). In the cable, the United States said that it had restated its position to assure the territorial integrity and the political independence of Israel and the other Middle Eastern states against aggression and the threat or use of force. The United States, the cable continued, had reported to the Israeli side its belief that Washington's commitment to resist aggression should make a major contribution toward alleviating Israel's security concerns. The United States expressed hope that its renewed assurances to Israel would allow progress to be made in the common cause of restraining the arms race.

Farther on in the document, the following was stated: "The Administration believes that Egypt's missile capability will remain essentially a psychological threat and Cairo will not develop nuclear capability. The U.S. is concerned about an escalation of the Middle East arms race and opposes the proliferation of missiles and nuclear weapons." Then, quoting Prime Minister and Defense Minister Eshkol, the author of the document said: "Israel appreciates the United States' support but is convinced that it must maintain its own deterrent in view of the possibility of an Arab offensive. The rank-and-file Israeli," the document continued, "regards the Egyptian missile threat as a real one. Just the same, *Israel will postpone the public display of missile capability for a year or two*" [italics added].[59]

Given the current state of the documentation, one cannot know whether Eshkol had conceded only "the public display of missile capability" for a year or two, during which time the French missiles would be in their development phase – therefore amounting to no real concession at all – or whether his American interlocutors noticed this and would eventually apply more adamant pressure in regard to the missiles. At least in regard to the necessity of an independent Israeli deterrent, Ben-Gurion's successor seems to have remained true to his precursor's policy.

In 1965, however, things began to move in all directions, domestic and external – including bygone parochial concerns, such as Ben-Gurion's resurrection of the Affair and Eshkol's gagging of the same – and became entangled even where no prior intent existed. In early March 1965, the U.S. Air Force attaché in Tel Aviv reported to his superiors (and thence immediately to the White House) that, according to an Israeli source who had just returned from abroad, the testing of a French surface-to-surface missile intended for Israel had begun in Île du Levant, and after several initial mishaps, the missile had evidently performed satisfactorily.[60] The "source" went on to state that Israel would evidently concentrate on setting up stationary launching bases because its size dictated this

326

course of action and because the enemy targets were known and immobile. When the American attaché responded by arguing that an Israeli surface-to-surface missile with a conventional warhead was valueless, the Israeli source retorted, "Don't worry, if we'll need the appropriate warhead, we'll get it, and after that there'll be no more troubles in this part of the world."

The Americans' harsh response probably took the loose-lipped "source" by surprise: In early January 1966, Washington "leaked" the existence of the medium-range missile under construction in France to the *New York Times* and the news department of the large television networks.[61] This made the Egyptians' political/strategic quandary many times worse than it had been: Should they remain idle until Israel took possession of the missile? And couldn't they exploit the mantle of illegitimacy that Washington itself had draped over Israel's nuclear program? This mantle created problems for all parties involved, since it was bound up with American inspection visits to the Dimona reactor, which Eshkol was forced, or preferred, to accept in 1965 and again in 1966 – visits that, on the one hand, Nasser did not find convincing and, on the other hand, got Eshkol into domestic hot water.

In the meantime – we are still in 1965, in several ways a key year en route to the Six Day War – Nasser decided to cancel his pretentious missile project, finally realizing that it was a costly failure. Under these conditions, he could promise Johnson that Egypt would not develop weapons of mass destruction.[62] This had been the goal of the mediator McCloy during that time, and for its sake Washington had pressed Israel to cancel its nuclear program. Now, Egypt had made a commitment in this respect for no prior consideration. Nasser, however, could entertain the expectation that, having dropped out of the race for the manufacture or acquisition of weapons of mass destruction, Israel would come under mounting superpower pressure. Late that year, the USSR gave him something resembling a nuclear guarantee, which was widely publicized after Deputy Defense Minister Marshall Grechko's visit to Egypt.[63]

Indeed, even before Grechko's visit to Egypt, an American mission headed by the roving ambassador Averill Harriman visited Israel on his way to India, where he would attempt to pressure that country, too, to refrain from developing an independent response to the just-tested Chinese bomb. With him was Robert Komer, a National Security Council official from the Kennedy days. Komer, who had already invested much effort in trying to cancel Israel's nuclear program, visited the country now as representative of McGeorge Bundy, chair of the council, and had some grave things to say not only about Dimona but also about the missiles.[64] We have quite a few sources about the Harriman-Komer visit,[65] foremost Yitzhak Rabin's memoir *Pinkas sherut* (Service diary).

According to Rabin, the Israeli COGS at the time, the two American officials wished to predicate the Israeli–American "strategic understanding" on three agreed principles: (1) Israel would not initiate a preventive war against the Arabs; (2) it would not take comprehensive military action against the Jordan River diversion programs that the Arabs had begun; and (3) it would not undertake to become a nuclear power *in possession of nuclear weapons* (indeed, such a distinction was made). If Israel agreed to these provisos, it could send a military mission to Washington to discuss the procurement of aircraft, tanks, and artillery. Here, Washington was dangling an enticing carrot along with the stick: an opportunity for Jerusalem to escape its absolute dependency on France and West Germany for the procurement of conventional weapons. The offer was made just as West Germany's secret arms deliveries to Israel became public knowledge, and the Bonn government had been forced to terminate them and replace them with the establishment of diplomatic relations and economic aid.[66] Furthermore, the expression "secret understanding" with the United States carried the important potential of a quasi-alliance with the Western superpower, something that Israel had coveted dearly since Ben-Gurion's tenure at the helm. Even though the price seemed unbearably high, Israel thought it unwise to flatly reject the outstretched hand. The proper thing was to try to grasp it as firmly as possible without paying the full price that it entailed.

Rabin states that he rejected the first two points and continued that Komer – and, to a slightly lesser extent, Harriman – took a very tough line on the nuclear-weapons issue. The visitors persisted, disallowing Rabin's claim that Prime Minister Eshkol had announced in his recent visit to the United States that Israel would not be the first to introduce nuclear weapons to the region. Shimon Peres had attributed this phrasing to himself, and the minister of defense seemed to have found it satisfactory even after the construction of the reactor was completed and the Arabs had information to the effect that it had already produced "eight kilograms of plutonium" in 1966.[67] Therefore, Komer requested a personal meeting with COGS Rabin and used "rough language" that contained a threat: If Israel followed this path, it was liable to bring on the gravest crisis experienced thus far in its relations with the United States. We do not know what the (Jewish) official was referring to, but he may have apprised Rabin of the danger posed by a Soviet Union that would respond to the arrival of medium-range missiles in Israel and the existence of armed nuclear warheads there, which Moscow might construe as a direct threat against it by an impudent American client. Therefore, the Soviets might hold Washington responsible for this threat and for the possible offshoot of an entanglement between its Arab clients and a nuclear Israel – and might respond accordingly. By implication, Israel's conduct posed a potential threat to the United States itself or, rather, endangered a forthcoming US–USSR agreement on a nonproliferation treaty. In response, Rabin told Komer that American emissaries had visited Dimona and knew "exactly" what was going on there.

Rabin was referring to a very recent American inspection visit to Dimona that had been kept under wraps. Shortly afterwards, another inspection visit took place and was leaked to the American press. We can assume, in terms of the available records, that these successive inspections (which continued until the Americans terminated them unilaterally in 1968) were the outcome of a deal that Harriman and Komer had concluded with Eshkol during their visit, but we do not know whether the deal was related only to the inspection visits or also to the nondeployment of the MD 660 missiles that had been ordered in France. According to primary sources at the Johnson Library, a deal for the supply of Skyhawk aircraft and Pershing tanks to Israel was signed in March 1966, sometime after the placement of Israel's order to France for the missiles had been leaked to the *New York Times*. The question is the price that Eshkol paid for the transaction: Was it only the acceptance of the inspection visits, or also his consent not to set up the missiles? Were the medium-range missiles ready, since we are told that they were due for delivery in 1967? Either way, when Eshkol asked Harriman who would defend Israel from the threats of the Arabs' patron power – the same Moscow that had brandished the bomb as a threat to Israel's very existence at the time of the Suez-Sinai War – the American replied that in one matter at least, the late President Kennedy had cured Soviet leader Nikita Khrushchev and his associates of their penchant for threatening nuclear war. Harriman's purpose in saying this was to assuage the Israelis' concerns about a 1956-style Soviet nuclear threat and, as it were, to obviate an Israeli medium-range missile. Komer augmented Harriman's diplomacy with a casuistic touch of his own, since Khrushchev had in the meantime been deposed; who knew how his successors would behave? Moreover, as stated, he explicitly threatened a grave crisis with the United States if the missile were deployed.[68]

Ultimately, Washington and Jerusalem did conclude the transaction and agreed on the purchase of Skyhawk aircraft (to be delivered several years later) and Patton tanks. The deal, however, was not perfect from the American point of view and, in their opinion, could not placate the Egyptians. After all, American inspection at Dimona was not necessarily an efficient way to deactivate the facility. Egypt could use this knowledge in order to accept Washington's reports that the reactor was not serving military purposes – if Cairo wished to accept it and avoid war. If Cairo wanted war, the very fact of the inspection and its concomitant, the continuing delegitimization of the Israeli nuclear program by both superpowers would provide it with a casus belli at the time and place of its choosing. Indeed, Nasser could argue that the Americans' inspection amounted to a cover-up of Israel's nuclear program, which Washington itself viewed as illegitimate ab initio. However, the matter of the delivery of medium-range missiles drew a red line in terms of time from the standpoint of Egypt and the Soviets, since so long as Israel lacked these missiles, it furnished Cairo with a good casus belli without a nuclear deterrent to speak of that would prevent it.

All these points are considerations that must have tormented Eshkol's government during the May–June 1967 crisis, but they have a factual basis in a cable from the State Department to the U.S. ambassador in Cairo immediately after Harriman and Komer concluded their visit to Israel. According to the cable, the Harriman-Komer talks had eased the situation "but the main problems remained unsolved and constituted a potential casus belli. The U.S. Government," the cable continued, "would continue to press Israel not to implement its nuclear program. Nasser must have been aware of the American inspection visit that the press had just reported." (The original cable boldfaced these contents.)[69]

This inspection visit (and its successors in 1966) got Eshkol into domestic hot water but did not placate Nasser at all. Thus, the U.S. administration was trapped between Cairo and Jerusalem, even though its power of influence was limited to one side only, if the other were to opt for war in the belief that the United States lacked the ability to restrain Israel in this respect. Such is implied by a cable from the U.S. embassy in Cairo to Washington in mid-April 1965 about a meeting with President Nasser conducted by the ambassador, Lucius Battle, and Assistant Secretary of State for Near Eastern Affairs Philips Talbot.[70] Talbot explained to the Egyptian president why the problem of American inspection at Dimona had come up, that is, why the United States had come onto the scene, and said that the Israeli side had refused to accept appropriate inspection by the International Atomic Energy Agency. The United States, Talbot added, would "also" be concerned if the Israeli reactor were to be put to use for military purposes; this, he said, would create an issue between the United States and Israel and not only between Egypt and Israel. Talbot had permission to tell Nasser, the cable continued, that the State Department had satisfied its curiosity in this matter. Nasser replied that while understanding Washington's concern, he must note that Egypt, unlike Israel, had no influence in the United States. In response, Talbot termed nuclear proliferation a global problem and urged Nasser to believe that from its perspective, Washington was dealing with it in the service of global interests (and not those of American domestic politics).

The whole thing did nothing to placate the pan-Arab leader and equally enraged Israel. Things reached such a point that the editor of the daily *Ma'ariv*, Aryeh Dissenchik, met in July 1965 with the director of the U.S. Arms Control and Disarmament Agency, William Foster, and gave himself the latitude to comment explicitly about Dimona.[71]

Dissenchik was as intimate with Moshe Dayan and Shimon Peres as with Levi Eshkol and Menachem Begin. There is no telling whether he was acting with authorization, but either way he told his stunned interlocutor – who hurriedly reported the Israeli newspaperman's remarks up the ladder – that given Nasser's incessant threats to destroy Israel, he "regretted" having leaked to American television what, he said, the United States knew about goings-on in Dimona. After all, this leak must have damaged the credibility of the Israeli deterrent and, at the very least, delegitimized it in American eyes. In the same breath, Dissenchik went on to say that Israel did not want war with the Arabs – even a victorious war – due to its cost in human life and property. What seemed important to him was that the other side knew that Israel had a four-to-five-year head start in the nuclear domain and could quickly put the finishing touches on a bomb. Under these conditions, he continued, the Arabs should think twice: Israel possessed a crucial deterrent. Foster sharply expressed his hope that Israel would go no farther in the military direction than it had already gone and explained Washington's concern about the threat that would ripple through the entire Middle East if Jerusalem were to persist. Dissenchik continued in his own vein. The main threat, he said, was the expected nuclear nonproliferation treaty, since presumably it would omit India – Egypt's close friend, which by then was well along in developing a bomb of its own.

It is hard to believe that the editor of *Ma'ariv* was pursuing a private initiative in this matter, but he fanned the flames. Shortly after his visit, the Soviet deputy defense minister came to Egypt and gave Cairo at least the appearance of a Soviet nuclear guarantee if and when Israel were to obtain the bomb. It was then, too, that the administration leaked to the *New York Times* the fact of Israel's order of medium-range missiles from France.

There is no documented way of knowing how the powers' maneuvers affected the Eshkol government. One may conjecture that the Achdut ha-Avoda ministers, Galili and Allon – who had long been apprehensive about a Soviet response to the missiles and belittled the nuclear deterrent at the end of the Ben-Gurion era – came to the general conclusion that Israel would do best not to deploy the missiles and, perhaps, should content itself with aircraft such as the American-offered Skyhawks, which theoretically could deliver nuclear payloads to short ranges in spite of American prohibition to use them for that purpose, or even to scrap the nuclear option itself. Building on the assumption that modern conventional warfare would always leave the Arabs behind the IDF, both ministers would opt for better boundaries as security zones – ideologically their parties' most important obligation since the pre-state days. Eshkol himself accepted the American inspection visits to Dimona and at roughly this time, and even decided to "civilianize" the Atomic Energy Commission and forgo the services of Professor Ernst David Bergmann, the commission's veteran chairman since Ben-Gurion's days. (In Washington's eyes, Bergmann had for years symbolized Israel's quest for the bomb.)

This clutch of measures did create the impression that Israel had down-scaled, if not scrapped, its nuclear program. Indeed, a historian close to Galili and Allon maintained years later that the Eshkol government "scaled down" the Dimona reactor itself.[72] One cannot know whether, at least in regard to the missiles, Israel's actions did much to relieve the Egyptians of their apprehensions about the bomb. They did believe that Israel possessed nothing but a few antiquated French subsonic bombers and, in all probability, had no aircraft advanced enough to threaten the Aswan Dam and the delta – and, by extension, Soviet targets – as seriously as a medium-range ballistic missile could. One doubts, however, that they believed that Israel had truly written off the missiles; therefore, the delivery date in 1967 became critical from their standpoint, and from a Soviet view, so far as Eshkol's government was concerned. Since the Egyptian archives are not accessible to scholars, we do not know what the Egyptians' considerations were. The government of Israel, however, could not afford a hiatus such as this, since in 1965 its crossing of the nuclear threshold became an official Egyptian casus belli, as Nasser said again in 1966 despite the American inspection visits to Dimona. At this time, the government hid this casus belli from the Israeli public by making extensive use of the military censor and the media, but Eshkol tried to inform the Soviets that no medium-range missiles were deployed, as I interpret a recent publication in this regard.[73] However, when the Egyptian army made its sudden thrust into the Sinai in May 1967, and when Egyptian photo reconnaissance flights over Dimona immediately followed, the government had to determine the reasons for these actions and to weigh countermeasures, all without the public correctly understanding – to this day – the true reasons for the government's concern and its protracted hesitancy.

Before we bid farewell to 1965, however, we should remember that this was the year when Fatah embarked on its Vietnam- and Algeria-style guerrilla operations from Syria via Jordan, which severely troubled the IDF high command. Under General Rabin, the IDF was preparing to meet conventional challenges, and some sort of a Vietnam-inspired guerrilla onslaught by Yasser Arafat's and other Palestinian organizations, based on and supported by the radical Syrian regime, were much more on his mind than a half-baked nuclear deterrent.

It was also in 1965 that Ben-Gurion returned to political life, established the Rafi (Israel Workers List) Party, brought Dayan back from the wilderness, and forced Shimon Peres to join him. Rafi emblazoned a large collection of slogans on its standard: It would restore public life to health in view of the handling of the Affair, instill proper *mamlakhtiyut* ("state-worthy" behavior) in the spirit of Ben-Gurion's government reform, and so on. Cognoscenti, however, called Rafi "the nuclear party."[74] In the 1965 elections, Rafi came away with ten Knesset seats – quite a failure relative to the pretensions of a party headed by David Ben-Gurion. Levi Eshkol reassembled a center-left coalition with Achdut ha-Avoda and Mapam, after the former faction had joined a parliamentary "alignment" with Mapai without risking its status at the ballot box and retaining the option of seceding from the alignment – to the immense rage of Ben-Gurion, who loathed such manipulations in the party constellation. Indeed, the alignment had reserved the small faction's seats in the Knesset without elections and allowed it to secede from Mapai, the larger party, at any time, or to threaten to do so in order to promote its own goals when such were incompatible with the views of the larger faction. On top of this, the alignment's power was based upon the General Federation of Labor, the Histadrut, which had become very much the guardian of the power and privileges of organized labor and the unions, which controlled most of the nation's key services and many industries. Dayan and Peres had criticized this state of affairs in public back in 1959, without Ben-Gurion's explicit support, but the limits of social democracy, based on a number of old-fashioned yet powerful bureaucracies supported by multiparty, partially corrupt, political alignments became a permanent feature of Israeli society and politics, and will remain so until the political system itself can be reformed.

Concurrently, the establishment of the center-left alignment brought an old fear of Ben-Gurion's to fruition: The relatively moderate Right, embodied in the Liberal Party as it was known back then, now established an alignment of its own with Menachem Begin's Herut movement (named Gahal, signifying Herut–Liberals); by implication, the spineless Liberals fell into the snare of the populist-nationalist Right. Indeed, the Liberals' action rescued Begin from the political wilderness into which Ben-Gurion had maneuvered him and created a parliamentary infrastructure for the changes that the Six Day War would create. The political instrument of Ben-Gurion's own creation, Rafi, would also slip from his control and become a factor of the highest order on the eve, and in the aftermath, of the 1967 war.

After Eshkol's electoral victory, however, 1965 saw the beginning of a move to restrain and stabilize the economy after the election year. The intolerable length of an Israeli election campaign, among other factors, had forced the incumbent government to loosen the economic reins and inundate the voters with goodies. When Eshkol now sought to bring the economy back under control, however, a severe recession ensued – the first of its kind in a society whose upper crust had become accustomed to a perpetually rising standard of living. Although one cannot say that this slice of society had attained genuine affluence, the unexpected recession took a toll on its morale. In the background, too, with clouds massing in the foreign affairs and defense arena, Eshkol's strength in the increasingly gloomy domain of defense had also become questionable due to repeated guerrilla operations by Palestinians based in Syria and to Syrian shelling of Israeli settlements when disputed border areas were cultivated by Israelis. As for the qualities of his leadership, the man was clever and humorous, but ideologically and culturally empty and hollow in comparison to Ben-Gurion; he had no real message to communicate comparable to Ben-Gurion's old "vision" and no alternative to offer. This is why many Israelis who had tired of Ben-Gurion's constant admonishments about diminishing spiritual commitments and moral demands, plus his warnings that the existing, multiparty system could make Israel ungovernable, took pleasure in Eshkol. Until then, the contextual void had been filled with Eshkol's immense personal grace, his cleverness, and the twinkle in his eye. Now his political and defense leadership would be put to steadily escalating tests.

1966 – From the "Big Blunder" to Operation Samu

Additional key milestones on the road to the Six Day War were crossed in 1966, amid a downslide in both domestic and foreign affairs. The "Ben Barka scandal" (collaboration between the Mossad and the Moroccan security services, in the course of which the former turned over to the latter a Moroccan opposition leader who had sought asylum in France) became publicly known. In the aftermath of the scandal, General de Gaulle instituted a comprehensive review of Israeli–French relations, including defense relations on the part of various entities in and out of his government. One cannot know for sure whether this review menaced the development of the medium-range missiles or their delivery to Israel, but the scandal, which Rafi voices termed a "big blunder" on the part of Eshkol's government (because it originated in ambiguous orders from the prime minister to the Mossad, which he was supposed to have controlled), joined the ranks of other government actions that the opposition spokesmen of Rafi, headed by Shimon Peres, censured heatedly. Ben-Gurion himself did not spare his successor from criticism, pronouncing him unfit for responsibility for Israel's defense affairs due to some big blunder of which no details were disclosed.[75] Ben-Gurion may have been referring specifically to the Ben Barka scandal; Peres and Dayan, in turn, spoke both on and off the record about the American inspection visits to Dimona.[76] It may even be that Eshkol's aforementioned decision to scrap the Israeli-made medium-range missile, plus his troubles with de Gaulle regarding the Ben Barka scandal, which may have endangered the delivery of the French MD 660 missile, outraged the leaders of Rafi. Or it may also have been the transfer of the Atomic Energy Commission from MOD to the Office of the Prime Minister, thereby "civilianizing" it and, by so doing, dispensing with the services of Ernst Bergmann, since they viewed this as Israel's contribution to the delegitimization of its own nuclear option and the devaluation of its strategic value to a "last resort," or something less than that without the French medium-range missile.

Now – in February 1966 – an extremist faction of the Ba'ath Party had risen to power in Syria and began straightaway to implement the Arab summit decisions about diverting the sources of the Jordan River that fed the Israeli Sea of Galilee, in order to prevent Israel from using it to irrigate the Negev Desert. Israel's response was initially proportionate and measured, that is, destruction of the Syrian diversion equipment by direct tank fire. The Syrians, however, merely moved the work deeper into their own territory. As the year progressed, border incidents with the Syrians escalated greatly and the latter responded by shelling Galilee localities from the Golan Heights, while Israel continued to cultivate areas in the demilitarized zone in the north that had not been farmed at all in Ben-Gurion's time. Contrarily, it was Levi Eshkol – a lifelong devotee of rural settlement – who approved this action; OC of the Northern Command David Elazar, itching for battle, backed his decision and named himself the spokesman of the Israeli localities on the Syrian border. The Syrians further provoked the Egyptians, as if to say that they were bearing the burden directly while Egypt, despite its pan-Arab pretensions and its public obligations to destroy Israel, was hiding behind the aprons of the UN peacekeeping force in the Gaza Strip. The Syrian foreign minister, Ibrahim Makhus, mocked and ridiculed Israel's nuclear option in public, alluded to Egypt's fears on this issue, and said that France and the United States, each of which had "tons of atomic bombs," had been expelled from Algeria and were being driven out of Vietnam, respectively. The IDF command, headed by a longtime intimate of Allon and Galili, faced a conventional challenge that, from its standpoint, demanded a conventional response.[77] After all, Syria's demarches dovetailed with Fatah's guerrilla operations, even though the latter were negligible compared with those that would follow the Six Day War. Israel responded by stepping up its military actions against Syria and Jordan alike.

Why Jordan? Two reasons: because it seemed that King Hussein might join, in a very concrete way, a common Arab military command and because the Fatah operatives crossed his territory on their way from Syria to Israel. Israel's operations against Syria expanded into massive use of its air force to destroy the diversion equipment, down Syrian aircraft, and ultimately chase the craft as far as Damascus. Against Jordan, a massive operation in broad daylight against the town of Samu, in the southern West Bank, was planned and carried out in November 1966. This action totally deviated from anything in the accepted category of reprisal actions during Ben-Gurion's time.[78] Against all of these – not to mention the strident propaganda of Ahmad Shuqairi's PLO, the Egyptian-sponsored Palestinian outfit that was supposed to counterbalance Yasser Arafat's Syrian-based Fatah, which called for immediate war on Israel before it could complete its nuclear program – Egyptian President Nasser stood empty-handed for the time being. His spokesman, Muhammad Hasanein Heikal, berated Syria's brand-new militant Ba'ath regime; Egypt, he said, would go to war when it was ready to do so. However, the same Heikal had much to say in his newspaper, *Al Ahram*, about Israel's nuclear option as an ostensible casus belli, and Nasser himself repeated this threat in early 1966 in an interview with a British newspaper. Israel's operations in Syria and Jordan may have been meant to demonstrate its conventional might and to draw a line in the sand as a deterrent to war. Their outcome, however, seems to have been the exact opposite – as Moshe Dayan protested to the head of the IDF Operations Division, Major General Ezer Weizman, and to coalition members of the Knesset Foreign Affairs and Defense Committee.[79]

We do not know what considerations dominated Nasser's thinking in 1966, as he refrained from coming to Syria's aid and sealed his ears to Shuqairi's outcries. Ultimately, the PLO, though a prized Egyptian protégé that had been set up as an alternative to the Syrian-sponsored Fatah and was supposed to incite the Palestinian population in Jordan against King Hussein, nevertheless served the Palestinian interest of destroying and supplanting Israel before it went fully nuclear. From the PLO's standpoint, Israel's nuclear option – once consummated – would pose a grave threat to the Arab states and Egypt above all. If those countries were menaced with nuclear disaster, they might abandon the Palestinians. Nasser, it seems, was unwilling to budge until he could assure himself a proper degree of Soviet support, which at that stage of events was not forthcoming. Now, it seemed as though Israel's actions vis-à-vis Syria were encouraging him to believe that he had obtained – or could obtain – enough Soviet assistance to take the risk of a limited demarche, which quickly spun out of his control, just as the Israelis' actions swiftly spun out of their control.

Thus, the snowball began to roll across the entire Middle East, to David Ben-Gurion's immense chagrin. His stance at the time of the June 1966 crisis is worthy of study, since had he been in charge, the war probably would not have erupted or would not have expanded as it did.

Ben-Gurion and the Six Day War

The Israel–Syria wrestling match continued into 1967. At the beginning of the year, COGS Rabin – to Prime Minister Eshkol's great displeasure – expressed public threats against the survival of entire Syrian regime.[80] In light of the current state of the sources, we cannot know what Rabin had in mind: to deter the Syrians once and for all or, perhaps, to take serious military action against Syria. In any case, ministers Galili and Allon backed him and even defended him against Eshkol's justified fury.[81] Such an operation – if it were indeed being weighed – was plausible if one could assume that Egypt would remain on the sidelines, as well it might because much of its army was immersed in the civil war in Yemen. Therefore, the Egyptian forces that poured into Sinai on May 15, 1967, appears to have been a threat of an initially vague nature.

Rabin's general staff soon became gravely concerned, however, as the Egyptians seemed to have carried out a photo overflight of Dimona on May 17.[82] (The pilots, as would be proved later, were Soviet.)[83] The Israeli leadership was mindful of Egypt's threats about Dimona as a casus belli and related Soviet warnings. At first, this photo overflight turned the attention of the entire government to the question of the reactor's anti-aircraft defenses. No one found convincing the COGS' testimony that Dimona was protected beyond a shred of doubt. Even Rabin himself sounded doubtful about it; furthermore, he was not convinced that the IAF's plan to preempt and attack the Egyptian air force on the ground – which had probably not been submitted to the government plenum – would solve the problem completely.

These issues still need to be researched if and when the archives are opened. Be that as it may, at least one of them requires no proof: In the aftermath of the photo mission, the minister of defense authorized a partial call-up of reserves in order to seal the porous Negev frontier. The reserve mobilization, however, had to be tied into the dimly illuminated doctrine of preventive war that had been accepted in the IDF since the 1950s, when Rabin himself had commanded the IDF Planning Division, and perhaps also to the "preemptive counterstrike " doctrine that, as stated, Yigal Allon had spelled out in his 1959 book *Sandscreen*. One may also trace the provenance of this preventive-war doctrine to the future general Avraham Tamir[84] during Rabin's term as COGS. The doctrine offered no details about the goals of such a preventive war, if one were necessary in response to a threat, in terms of border adjustments and political achievements. What is more, Eshkol's political echelon never adopted it *en bloc*. This echelon, however, included Ministers Allon and Galili – who had replaced Ben-Gurion, Dayan, and Peres – and Allon had an explicit outlook of his own on nullifying the partitioning of the country and drawing the new border at the Jordan River. For the purposes of his "preemptive counterstrike" – a concept that he had culled from nuclear-deterrence theory and had applied, contrarily enough, to a conventional context – he listed a series of justifications, or red lines, including the closure of the Straits of Tiran, the appearance of a foreign Arab army in Jordan, and "an attack on nuclear targets in Israel." Thus, Allon added Dimona to his basically conventional military thinking as a last resort, so to speak, that Israel must retain after exhausting its conventional options, or at least deter the Arabs from trying to destroy it, while its deterrent value remained negligible in his eyes, if not neutralized, by a Soviet nuclear guarantee to Egypt.

The Israeli cabinet must have feared a surprise attack on the reactor that would discharge a hazardous cloud of radioactivity; therefore, the reactor must have been shut down at the time of the partial mobilization of the reserves, called up to seal off the open Israeli-Egyptian frontier. The closure of the Tiran Straits, however, had been an official Israeli casus belli since the Sinai War and had been declared by Ben-Gurion as such. Until then, the status of the straits as an international waterway had been assured by the UN force at Sharm el-Sheikh and the ostensible guarantees that the UN had given Ben-Gurion, and should have prompted American intervention to reopen them. While Minister Galili (his partner Allon visited Moscow at the time but returned soon enough to advocate a similar move) and General Rabin were pursuing now an immediate Israeli military response to the closure of the straits, Prime Minister Eshkol was trying to mobilize Washington to do the job. In other words, if the real issue were Dimona, and if the Egyptians and Soviets were waiting to destroy it if Israel fired the first shot, why give them this opportunity?

Paradoxically, Brigadier-General Aryeh Brown, subsequently military secretary to Defense Minister Moshe Dayan,[85] argued later on that the appointment of Dayan to the MOD in early June 1967 triggered the radical change that was needed to go to war and, to a large extent, dictated the results of the war, including the occupation of the West Bank and Gaza, following the escalated crisis and King Hussein's decision to join his erstwhile enemy, President Nasser of Egypt, and to place his army under Egyptian command. General Dayan focused on Egypt itself, fearing that should Nasser be allowed to get away with his previous bellicose acts, the Egyptian leader would become pivotal in all further developments in the Middle East and gain an intolerable degree of strategic freedom vis-à-vis Israel, not to mention much maneuvering room vis-à-vis Washington, with Soviet backing. Focusing on Egypt, Eshkol and Dayan then allowed the Israel-initiated war against Egypt to escalate to the West Bank, following King Hussein's intervention in support of Egypt.

This action would not have been expected of Ben-Gurion, who always rejected the idea of Israeli rule over the large Palestinian population of the West Bank and feared that Ministers Galili and Allon might drag the weak Eshkol toward such a development. By implication, however, Ben-Gurion, by establishing the Rafi Party and bringing Dayan back to political life, had created, with his own hands, a personal and political instrument that swerved from his own views about this war. One may even argue that Dayan's public weight – irrespective of Rafi – grew steadily insofar as Eshkol's declined during the prewar crisis. Subsequently, Dayan went so far as to act in rivalry with Allon and Galili – within a national unity government whose members included Menachem Begin – and with Eshkol, who did not want Ben-Gurion as minister of defense. However, Rafi – and its helmsman, Ben-Gurion – had been making its own contribution to the criticism of Eshkol and the waning of his status from the time it was established. Nor does it matter for the moment whether

Rafi's principal critique was masked from public view because it concerned the American inspection visits to Dimona and the Ben-Barka scandal, as well as Dayan's vehement criticism of Rabin's escalations against Syria and Operation Samu'.

Nasser began an escalation of his own after marching his troops to the Sinai all the way to the Israeli frontier, banishing the UN force from the Gaza Strip and the Straits of Tiran, and closing the straits to Israeli shipping. We do not know what his initial intentions were. It was under pressure from his Arab rivals and competitors – who argued that Egypt was hiding behind the UN's aprons and had been sitting on its hands since Samu and amid the subsequent blows and counterblows between Israel and Syria – that Nasser instructed the UN peacekeeping force to evacuate the border area and confine itself to its camps. UN Secretary-General U Thant – taking his cue from his American deputy, Ralph Bunche – evidently assumed that Egypt was bluffing. Although the presence of the UN force did depend on Egypt's goodwill, Nasser was told that the force should protect the border as before or be evacuated from Egyptian territory altogether. Faced with this choice, the Egyptian president opted for the latter. At this early phase of the escalation, it is hard to know what he had in mind.

In my opinion, it is doubtful that Nasser himself had truly made up his mind about what to do once his army entered Sinai after the expulsion of the UN force. He may have been aiming for a controlled crisis, which would explain the supremely overt nature of his army's march across the Suez Canal. Most of the Egyptian armor, without which no offensive is possible, remained in the canal zone; therefore, the demarche amounted to manning the front lines in northern Sinai in a comprehensive deployment of a defensive nature. By engineering a controlled crisis such as this, Nasser would strengthen his hand in the Arab world and also in Washington, which did not take a kind view toward his cooperation with the Soviets and which several years earlier had suspended its assistance to Egypt in the form of grain shipments. However, Nasser had to keep the crisis under control and, at the very least, retain some worthy military options if he wanted his moves to lead to American appeasement in return for his demand that they deal properly with the Dimona reactor and the Palestinian cause. He may have been tripped up by Rabin's threats and actions vis-à-vis Syria, considering them sufficient provocation of the Soviet Union to give him enough room to maneuver between the superpowers – this had always been his heart's desire – without starting a shooting war on his side.

A darker assessment of Nasser's moves could be that he intended to draw Israel into starting a war and then to deliver a response that, while controlled, would deal Israel a destructive blow. That is, he would use as a springboard the common knowledge about the preventive war that Israel would start if Egypt were to disregard the red line drawn by Israel, without himself being the first actually to open fire. The very fact of Israel's launching a war – no matter how seriously provoked – would give Egypt several options: bombing the Dimona reactor (shut down in the meantime), while presenting Israel as the aggressor and earning Soviet support and the self-evident backing of the Third World in the UN Security Council; assuring Soviet assistance that would make up for Egypt's losses in matériel; and neutralizing possible U.S. involvement. Afterwards, with the IDF bumping up against the Egyptian defense lines in Sinai, Nasser could exploit the absence of an imminent resolution on this front, where most of Israel's forces would be concentrated, to occupy isolated Eilat. Indeed, as the crisis unfolded, a select Egyptian armored unit – known as the Shazli force, for its commander – stationed itself opposite Eilat, which, if occupied by Egypt, would allow the latter to establish a land bridge between it and Jordan. The very fact of eliminating the Israeli presence on the shores of the Red Sea would solve once and for all Jerusalem's previous role of using the Straits of Tiran and give Nasser an opportunity to directly influence events in Jordan. From this location, too, he could at some future time establish a direct connection with Syria and threaten Israel's heartland.

None of these conventional moves, however, solved the problem of the very existence of the Jewish state; if the Arabs wished to deal Israel a coup de grace at the end of this process, they would still have to bear its nuclear potential in mind. At first glance, the 1967 crisis could also solve this problem: If Israel launched a preventive war – that is, if it were the first to actually open fire – the Egyptians could use this to justify an attack on Israel's nuclear project. Of course, this would be an unprecedented feat, given the potential radioactive fallout released from such an attack; however, presumably the reactor would have been deactivated at the very beginning of the crisis.

Whatever Nasser's original intentions were – or, perhaps, as they had been improvised as matters progressed in view of the UN secretary-general's response, the absence of any substantive U.S. response to his demarches, and the extent of the encouragement that he imagined receiving from Moscow – their immediate outcome was a surge of fervor in the Arab world that restored Nasser's status as the only folk leader in that world. Thus, Nasser had to allow the Palestinian guerrillas to resume their operations from the Gaza Strip just as the UN force was being evicted from the Strip, and also to allow units of the Palestine Liberation Army within the ranks of the Egyptian forces that had been stationed there as the crisis developed to open fire across the Gaza frontier. Obviously, too, he would have to close the Straits of Tiran to Israeli shipping the moment the UN soldiers quit that location. The two necessities clashed to some extent, since the resumption of terror operations from the Gaza Strip was a form of warfare and the closure of the straits was an official Israeli casus belli and a breach of international norms. The Egyptian president's bombastic speeches during the crisis, in which he said that it had come time to obliterate Israel literally, had the same effect a fortiori.

By then, Levi Eshkol – according to his military secretary, Yisrael Lior[86] – was fearing the worst of all: that Egypt would indeed block the Straits of Tiran, bomb the reactor in Dimona, and then launch an all-out offensive against Israel. Yet Eshkol still hoped to narrow the issue to the reopening of the straits, thanks to American commitments and ensuing moves, and for the time being he agreed to a general mobilization of the IDF reserves.

Since Ben-Gurion did not share Eshkol's fears, his stance during the crisis preceding the Six Day War is a topic of much interest forty-two years after the war in view of his categorical opposition to an Israeli preventive war. In Ben-Gurion's opinion, this crisis had come about due to the nature and modus operandi of the Eshkol government, which he had long considered unfit to manage Israel's defense affairs. Furthermore, he considered the man who headed this government a moral and political mediocrity. It was Eshkol, after all, who had approved the massive reprisal operation at Samu, which had dealt a blow to Israel's de facto ally, King Hussein, and had caused heavy losses among his armed forces. Indeed, the Arab Legion had rushed to the aid of this town, which the IDF had attacked in broad daylight because Fatah terrorists had been crossing it on their way from Syria. Worse still, the Samu operation had given Nasser the appearance in the Arab world of a man who talked but did not act. In Jordan (i.e., the West Bank), in turn, the operation had ignited a Palestinian uprising that Hussein had to quash by force. The Jordanian armored forces that had entered the West Bank to quell the unrest were allowed to stay there as a threat to Israel, even though their American tanks had been delivered to Jordan on the condition that they never be taken there. There was no point in asking the Americans, who were furious about the Israeli operation, to have them removed.

Thus, Ben-Gurion's reasoning (as I interpret it) continued: Instead of addressing the root of the evil, Syria, in a measured fashion, Israel had launched a major attack on a de facto ally, King Hussein of Jordan, sending a message that encouraged the Syrians to continue their provocations. In the aftermath of the operation, Eshkol's government had been drawn into a protracted slugging match with Damascus that might rile the Soviets and, in turn, provoke Nasser to embark on a limited operation, that is, to introduce Egyptian forces into Sinai and close the Straits of Tiran. The question, however, is whether the Egyptian president intended to go further, that is, to bomb Dimona and to open a ground campaign. According to known sources that illuminate Ben-Gurion's stance (the sources are still incomplete for the time being, especially in regard to his full diary[87]), the former prime minister doubted that Nasser had truly made up his mind to go to war, and he expressed these doubts in a difficult meeting with COGS Rabin at the latter's request. At this meeting, Ben-Gurion seriously criticized the call-up of the entire reserve army following the closure of the straits and emphasized the defensive nature of the ground deployment of the Egyptian forces. He also claimed that the reserve mobilization had tied Israel's hands. It could not be sustained for long because, unlike the Egyptian army – a professional, not a conscript, force that Nasser could keep mobilized at any time – Israel's reserve divisions had to be sent home in order to spare the economy and society from general paralysis. Nor could one expect Nasser to demean himself by removing his forces from Egyptian sovereign territory in face of the Israeli deployment of its reserves along the frontier. By implication, the very act of mobilizing the reserves gave Israel a reason to use its armed forces by its decision to mobilize, the Egyptian provocation aside.

We do not know what Ben-Gurion said to Rabin about Dimona. However, had the Egyptians wished to bomb Dimona, they would already have done it in a surprise attack – and if they had not done so thus far, they were probably waiting for Israel to start a war in order to justify such a far-reaching demarche. This differentiation – between a state of conflict at the level of less-than-war and opening fire at Israel's initiative – was not new to Ben-Gurion; he had used it on the eve of the Suez-Sinai War. Now, in fact, he fell victim to the popular notion that in 1956 he himself had launched a preventive war in response to similar Egyptian provocations. As we have said, however, Cairo's provocations were not severe enough to send Israel on the warpath. It was Israel's alliance with France and Britain that had induced Ben-Gurion to take the risk of going to war in 1956 because of what Israel stood to gain from it: a French nuclear reactor, as well as external military and political assistance.

Now, too, Nasser could come away with several cards in hand, including the return to the 1956 status quo ante, a handsome achievement that would satisfy him for some time. Nasser and the other Arabs may even have expected Rabin to start a war so that they could seize the opportunity to wipe out Dimona and, once free of the nuclear threat, eradicate Israel, and Rabin himself had played into their hands by attacking Samu and then threatening Syria's pro-Soviet Ba'ath regime. Indeed, in his memoir *Pinkas sherut* and, in particular, his introduction to the 1968 album *Six Days* (in Hebrew *Shisha yamim*),[88] Rabin "sort of" admitted that his actions had contributed to the escalation and mentioned his talk with Ben-Gurion in this context. He considered this exchange clear and edifying, compared with his relations with Shimon Peres, who sought, for motives relating solely to his personal power struggle with the COGS (so he believed), to undermine him in order to oust him from his post. Rabin suffered a health crisis after his talk with Ben-Gurion. He conferred separately with Rafi leader Dayan and with Interior Minister Moshe Chaim Shapira, the moderate and very cautious leader of the National Religious Party. Shapira's colleague Yosef Burg told me in an interview on January 14, 1972, that these ministers' main concern was the possibility of a Soviet response if Israel started a war. The Dimona reckoning was not only between the Arabs and the Americans and Israel; the Soviets had a hand in it as well. And if Rabin, in his tussling with the Syrians, managed to frighten the Russian bear out of its slumber, what grounds would he have for bewilderment if Moscow were to intervene – in one way or another – if Israel attacked Egypt, and if it seized the opportunity to help the Arabs get rid of the reactor and everything related to it? The COGS definitely felt acute distress at this stage, since he was considered the man responsible for Israel's moves, and his moves, thus far limited to deterrence and alerts, had been counterproductive.

A crucial question asked at that point concerned the nature of the Americans' response to Nasser, who had breached the status quo. Eshkol had been flirting with the Americans on his own after having authorized the inspection visits to Dimona and the civilianization of the Atomic Energy Commission, while engrossed in trying to manage the issue of the French medium-range missile, in order to avoid trouble in this regard with the superpowers, while the Ben-Barka scandal may have deprived him of the missile anyway. But what good had this done him? Washington had not lifted a finger thus far, if only because it was pinned down in Vietnam.

In any case, after these talks Rabin fell ill and asked to have his duties handed over to his deputy, Ezer Weizman, coming back rested and with his composure regained. What matters to us, however, is Ben-Gurion's stance after his meeting with Rabin amid the moves that were taking place around him – because it suddenly seemed as though the "old man" was about to return to the MOD to command the IDF in an unavoidable war.

The paradox was obvious: The person who wanted to bring Ben-Gurion back to the MOD in order to win an unavoidable war had no idea how firmly he opposed the war. During my term as military correspondent for Israel State Radio, I personally heard Ben-Gurion say this while addressing a group of media representatives at Neot Midbar Hotel in Beersheba, where he had gone to live during the escalating crisis. Among those who spoke on Ben-Gurion's behalf at this hotel I found Major General (Res.) Yehoshafat Harkabi, a former chief of military intelligence who had been fired by Ben-Gurion but now joined him. Shimon Peres was also seen going in and out of this location in the service of the old man and his campaign to head off the war.

I do not remember the gist of Ben-Gurion's argument, but I may assume, in view of the publications cited here and Abba Eban's quotations of Ben-Gurion as saying in this matter, that he had termed the impending clash "the wrong war at the wrong time and against the wrong enemy." The argument may have concerned the timing and the objects of the war: Since the nuclear deterrent had not yet been completed and the medium-range missiles had not been deployed, and also because Eshkol had scrapped the development of Israeli missiles back in 1963, Israel should wait and not give the enemy carte blanche to destroy Dimona by initiating hostilities. Relations with de Gaulle's France – in serious trouble since the Ben-Barka scandal because of Eshkol's incompetence – should be safeguarded with maximum care in order to – possibly – save the missile deliveries in due course; Israel should not limit its efforts to the United States only. Finally, in Ben-Gurion's opinion, to repair relations with France Israel should – among other things – remove Eshkol, the man responsible for the scandal and whose government, to a large extent, was answerable for the current crisis, which, in turn, created a chance to bring about such a change in leadership, "as happened to [Neville] Chamberlain back then." As for the crisis with Egypt, Ben-Gurion seems to have preferred its risks – for example, the resumption of terror operations from Gaza and even the closing of the Straits of Tiran, which had remained closed for two years during his tenure without an Israeli response – to the risks of an Israeli preventive war without outside assistance. He cited an additional risk: the formidable influence of the

Allon-Galili faction in Eshkol's government (a detail that was expressed by allusion; I remember it specifically from this meeting with military correspondents in Beersheba) and its perennial aspiration to undo the partitioning of western Palestine. If Eshkol unleashed the IDF against all of Israel's enemies in the current crisis – "all" including Jordan and Iraq, both of which joined Egypt in this category – it would occupy the entire West Bank. This might bring a large Palestinian population under Israeli control, a situation that Ben-Gurion had spared no effort to avoid, including by refusing – sensibly – to readmit the 1948 refugees. While considering the terror emanating from Gaza and the West Bank a very bad piece of business, he thought it immeasurably less severe than the total occupation of the West Bank and the Gaza Strip, which could delegitimize Israel itself.

Now, the man who could accomplish all of this quickly would be Moshe Dayan, Ben-Gurion's protégé, with Eshkol's consent, although he would not do it intentionally and would have no direct control over developments in the West Bank, at least at the beginning of the war. Dayan shared Ben-Gurion's views about the mistakes of the Eshkol government from Operation Samu onward, and he even criticized in public the American inspection visits to Dimona. All of this, however, was so much water under the bridge; a new situation had come about, one that may have stoked his ambition and imagination and appealed to the military man inside him. Ever since his term as OC of the Southern Command, he had yearned to occupy Sinai – trapping the Egyptian forces that were stationed in the peninsula – and to capture Sharm el-Sheikh, especially given its control over the direct approach to Eilat and the indirect approach to the Suez Canal. The canal had been closed to Israeli shipping since the early 1950s. Wresting the strategic initiative in the region from Egypt – whose forces were on alert in Sinai and were running interference for the Palestinians and their army (the PLA) in Gaza – was, to Dayan, a fitting response to the intolerable change in the status quo brought about by Egypt. Therefore, once Eshkol had rejected Ben-Gurion's return as the MOD outright by arguing that "both horses could not pull the same cart, and besides, the Americans would not like it" (due to Ben-Gurion's role in creating Dimona), and once it became clear that Ben-Gurion would not return to fight a war that others (but not he) saw as no choice but to fight, while Eshkol would have preferred to continue waiting for President Johnson's help – which his own general staff perceived as illusory, especially when the State Department's spokesman declared the U.S. stance in the crisis as neutral in thought and deed – the result was that most of Eshkol's own coalition members, as well his own party colleagues, decided to force him out of the Ministry of Defense. A curious combination of public pressure, media outcries, and partisan interests converged to remove him, as he himself had removed Ben-Gurion.[89]

Eshkol had to accept Dayan as a consequence of the existing political system, which had supported him against Ben-Gurion during the crisis over the Lavon Affair. In other words, media and public pressure forced Eshkol to accommodate the appointment within the framework of a national unity government.

In due course, Dayan would pay an enormous price for accepting the appointment under these conditions as a result of the IDF's initial failures during the 1973 Yom Kippur War. However, the outcome of Dayan's willingness to join the Eshkol government – just as Ben-Gurion sought to unseat it – and his subsequent refusal to avail himself of Ben-Gurion as a political adviser was the full and final isolation of the founding father. When a disloyal Shimon Peres followed Dayan's lead, this isolation escalated into an act of abandonment, as it were, by his own "youngsters." Finally, Dayan would play an important role as Menachem Begin's foreign minister after the 1977 elections, which made Begin prime minister. He contributed much to the peace process with Egypt and to the peace treaty of 1979, thanks among other things to the Israeli nuclear option that had survived the Six Day War.

The remaining steps to the Six Day War should be recalled briefly here only as background matter that elucidates Ben-Gurion's stance against the war in view of its long-term outcomes, the effect of which are still perceptible and of which he had warned an otherwise euphoric Israel.

After the closure of the Straits of Tiran (until which Rabin himself had not come out clearly in favor of a preventive war), the COGS decided wholeheartedly to embark on such a war given the failure of the Israeli conventional deterrence, which had been meant to keep Egypt from crossing an explicit Israeli red line.[90] According to Brigadier General Brown – the author of the most up-to-date study in this field, informed by IDF studies that remain unpublished to this day – the COGS was willing to give the political echelon another forty-eight hours. The government used this time-out to send Foreign Minister Abba Eban to Washington and then to Paris on his way back, in order to solicit some straight talk from President Johnson about the American position. After all, Johnson's predecessor, Kennedy, had given Eshkol a secret guarantee of Israel's current frontiers in order "to influence what's going on in Dimona," and the Johnson administration had squeezed Eshkol to allow the inspection visits and defer the deployment of medium-range nuclear missiles, if at all available, as a result of the Ben Barka scandal. The Straits of Tiran, however, were not exactly Israel's "frontier," and President Eisenhower's assurances in this matter were buried in his archives. Eshkol himself had justified the Israeli "independent deterrent" in his 1964 visit to the United States, arguing that Washington might be "busy elsewhere" at the moment of crisis. Indeed, Washington was now busy in Vietnam. From the American vantage point, however, Israel's independent deterrent was illegitimate, even though at this stage it did not yet seem to be a real deterrent in the absence of medium-range missiles. Clearly, too, the United States would not intervene practically to head off an attack on the reactor or to punish Egypt in any significant way if the reactor were destroyed, since it agreed that this particular Israeli deterrent was patently illegal.

This may explain the acute sense of isolation that had begun to infect the Israeli leadership. Indeed, in a meeting with the cabinet on the night of May 28,

Rabin demanded immediate action against Egypt, if only because its forces seemed to be digging into northern Sinai. The longer it took to dislodge the Egyptian forces from that area, Rabin argued, the more costly the operation would be to Israel. At this stage, he was supported in the cabinet by Galili and, later on, by Allon, who had just returned from a visit to the Soviet Union. Most of the ministers, however, foremost those of the National Religious Party, opposed war – and some even threatened to resign from the coalition.[91] At this point the "system" stepped in: The views of a minority faction influenced the calculus of the majority, which did not want a coalition crisis just then. (In due course, the NRP ministers would play an important role on the path to the formation of a national unity government that would include Moshe Dayan and Menachem Begin, after the latter retracted his proposal to hand Ben-Gurion the defense portfolio in place of Eshkol.)

The foreign minister had just returned from his travels carrying a promise from the American president to open the Straits of Tiran with the assistance of other naval powers.[92] Eban read out loud to members of the government an American memorandum concerning the Soviets' efforts to talk the Arabs out of war and their appeal to Washington to intercede with the Israelis for the same purpose. If the Americans failed, the Soviet Union would offer the Arabs "far-reaching assistance." The government took this to mean that Johnson had not only warned Israel to refrain from unilateral action but had also promised to have the straits opened. Eban reported on his meeting with President de Gaulle, who had warned Israel not to "fire the first shot." His most important reason for taking this stance, I believe, was his concern that an eruption in the Middle East might set the nuclear superpowers against each other. The general expanded his advice by imposing an embargo on the export of Mirage aircraft to Israel, irrespective of the fact that Israel had already paid for them.

Faced with these developments, the government decided to wait for several weeks more, and Eshkol took to the airwaves to report the government's decision to the public. In the middle of his remarks, he tripped over his words due to an impromptu handwritten correction that his secretary had made in the text. For this reason, the address went down in Israeli history as the "stuttering speech" of a prime minister who was too befuddled and confused to act. At first, Eshkol did not realize how badly the incident had hurt his public standing, if only because he rushed off to a meeting with the general staff. At the meeting, however, a tumultuous debate broke out – an unimaginable thing in Ben-Gurion's time – during which the generals hurled barbed criticism at the political echelon and the prime minister responded with firm remarks.[93] As minister of defense, he rejected the involvement of army officers in political affairs, a response that though apt, came too late if we recall that at the beginning of the crisis Eshkol had acted on the basis of the COGS' recommendations. He had approved the Samu operation, repeatedly approved escalation actions against Syria, and, under pressure from Galili and Allon, left Rabin in place even though the latter had overstepped his authority, threatened the very survival of the Ba'ath regime in Damascus, and mobilized reserves per the recommendation of the military officials. The mobilization sent the economy and social life into a dire paralysis that had fanned war expectations among the public and fomented the disillusionment brought about by his stuttering speech. At his meeting with the general staff, however, Eshkol took a more Ben-Gurionesque line than even the "old man" had, stating that the Egyptian military concentrations in the Sinai were not threatening Israel. Nasser, the prime minister continued, was operating in Egyptian sovereign territory, making the massing of his forces in Sinai "legitimate" from this standpoint and inconsistent with Yigal Allon's reasons for a preemptive strike and the IDF high command's conventional wisdom at the time.

Allon took part in this meeting in his capacity as Eshkol's senior military aide but added nothing to the discussion, hoping that the prime minister would hand him the defense portfolio. The generals returned to their posts severely disappointed and even reported their verbal exchanges with the prime minister to the military correspondents who had been attached to their units.

On May 29, Nasser informed his people that the "results of the 1956 aggression" had been reversed and that it was now time to undo the "results of the 1947–1948 aggression." On May 30, King Hussein capitulated and concluded a defense treaty with Egypt, placing his army under Egyptian command, while Israel received word that an Iraqi expeditionary force had set out for Jordan. On June 2, Eshkol relinquished the defense portfolio to Moshe Dayan within the framework of a national unity government. Several days earlier, the chief of the Mossad, Major General Meir Amit, was dispatched to find out what the Americans were really willing to do. Abba Eban was found to have misled the government, knowingly or otherwise:[94] The United States would do nothing to open the straits but did give Israel a "yellow light" to act on its own, according to Amit, but nothing in the American war records substantiates this.

According to Brigadier Geneneral Brown, Eshkol was willing to continue waiting and hoped for American intervention just the same. However, Dayan's powerful position in the newly established emergency government, the acute sense of isolation that gripped Israel after Jordan and Iraq joined the Egyptian siege, the intense Holocaust memories brought back to the surface by the Arab threats, the steadily escalating hysteria that engulfed the Arab masses, and Washington's inaction came together to push the government plenum to war.[95]

Ben-Gurion's stance at this stage deserves mention because, as stated, both he and Peres had been acting to thwart the war until the emergency government was formed. Peres even seems to have suggested in his memoirs that he had proposed a nuclear test in the Negev to prevent the war, but added that his proposal was turned down.[96] There may be no better proof than this of my claim that the Six Day War revolved mainly around the Dimona issue – even though, due to the silence in high quarters on this sensitive issue, the Israeli public did not, and still does not, realize that such was the case, instead viewing the main issue as a conventional threat that had to be removed in conventional ways. If Peres had indeed floated such a proposal, he must have had two things in mind: to dispel any Arab doubts that this "ultimate weapon" had been fully developed and was in Israel's possession, and to take this opportunity to add Israel officially to the "nuclear club." Indeed, the nuclear antiproliferation treaty had reached its final negotiating stages and would define the members of this "club" – which henceforth would be exempt from the restrictions of the treaty – as those countries that had "conducted a nuclear test thus far."

We do not know whether the government plenum ever discussed the proposal but there was no shortage of reasons to reject it, including the provocation that it would be targeted at both the superpowers and the Arabs, who would consider an attack on the reactor more justified than ever. At this stage, however, Peres evidently remained loyal to Ben-Gurion's view of conventional war at Israel's sole initiative as the wrong way to proceed; afterwards, he changed his mind as a result of Dayan's moves. From the public standpoint, Peres's change of heart dovetailed with the widely held perception that the time for a preventive war had come, just as it had come before the Sinai War erupted – even though Peres and Dayan were fully aware of the conditions that, once satisfied, prompted Ben-Gurion to opt for war in 1956, and that were very different from the conditions in 1967.

The IDF's plans for a preventive war and Allon's doctrine on the same topic, however, seemed to be forced on a befuddled political echelon that suddenly realized that its public standing was steadily losing ground. Within Mapai itself, challengers to Eshkol as the minister in charge of Israel's defense took a stand, and the very monster that Eshkol himself had put to use during the Lavon Affair – a hysterical "public opinion" created by the media, and a Mapai Central Committee that not so long ago had come out against Ben-Gurion and in favor of Eshkol's position on the Affair – would henceforth determine his own fate. Although it did not come to a formal vote this time, Eshkol acknowledged the trends of thought among his supporters and realized that his standing in their eyes had slipped badly.

Ministers from other parties, too, mulled the possibility of replacing him and, as stated, their candidate as his successor at the MOD was at first none other than Ben-Gurion. The most conspicuously proactive player was Menachem Begin, who may have believed that the army should be led by a more warlike civilian leader, such as Ben-Gurion, in view of the impending struggle. Begin had no idea that Ben-Gurion opposed the war. Perhaps, too, Begin viewed his backing of Ben-Gurion as part and parcel of his own exodus from the political wilderness into which Ben-Gurion had maneuvered him decades earlier. After all, he may have thought, if a politician recommended that his most bitter rival reassume supreme responsibility in wartime, the public would consider him a person with only its welfare in mind and would deem him fit for membership in the national emergency government.

Whatever Begin's calculus may have been, Eshkol categorically ruled out the idea, pronouncing these "two horses" unfit to pull the same cart. When Ben-Gurion realized that the media had pronounced Dayan the fittest candidate to replace Eshkol as minister of defense, and that the pressure from his NRP partners to establish an emergency government with Rafi and Begin's Gahal bloc had gathered increased momentum, he did what he could to maneuver Rafi into a position to have Eshkol himself unseated in return for allowing Dayan and Rafi to join. Obviously, this would have amplified Ben-Gurion's own influence, since he was the familiar leader of the party that he had set up and, as such, might have provided Dayan with the greatest possible guidance if war were unavoidable. One may surmise that he would have tried to contain the action to opening the Straits of Tiran and would have done his best to limit its expansion to the entire West Bank.

Ben-Gurion's maneuver was doomed to failure because Dayan had firmly made up his mind to march with Eshkol and not against him, within a large national coalition government in which he, as defense minister, would have enough influence to steer it toward a war of annihilation against the Egyptian Army and the occupation of at least most of the Sinai, and because Peres marched with Dayan. In this manner, "Ben-Gurion's kids" left the "old man" all alone. Israel's founding father had become its King Lear, though with his eyesight intact.

Epilogue

The Renaissance That Waned and Its Leader

The time that lapsed until the Six Day War – the lengthy "waiting period" from the marching of the Egyptian Army into Sinai in mid-May until the outbreak of war on June 6, 1967 – dragged on and on. It helped the Israel Air Force in its successful attack on the Egyptian airfields and the ground forces in smashing through Nasser's positions in Sinai. Contrary to the fears of IDF generals, the protracted wait weakened the Egyptians' preparedness while the IDF's capabilities improved steadily, and the snowball effect in the Arab world ruled out any diplomatic settlement. When the time came, Ben-Gurion himself saw no choice but to attack Egypt – but probably would have limited the goals of the war. He offered Dayan his services as political adviser – and was turned down.

Thus, the Six Day War swiftly spread from the Egyptian front, where Defense Minister Dayan's attentions were focused, to Jerusalem and the entire West Bank. The decision to occupy East Jerusalem was adopted by the national emergency government under pressure from Ministers Allon and Begin. Prime Minister Eshkol and Defense Minister Dayan, after having been empowered for this purpose by the defense cabinet, gave prior approval for the occupation of the rest of the West Bank – from Jenin to Nablus and Sheikh Hussein Bridge, and from Shu'afat, east of Jerusalem, and Ramallah to Allenby Bridge (and initially beyond) on the Jordan River. Since Israel controlled the airspace over the West Bank, having destroyed the Jordanian Air Force and an Iraqi Expeditionary Force from the air, the occupation of the West Bank was not militarily necessary, and its return to King Hussein, under the new circumstances, could have been negotiated once the king released himself from Nasser's clutches. Instead, the euphoria that followed the victory, including over Hussein – Nassar's aggressive ally during the war – prevented any such thing.

Ben-Gurion had withdawn from occupied territories in 1949 and 1957 in spite of similar euphoria, when required. Dayan's memoir *Avnei derech* (*Story of My Life*) and other sources give us reason to doubt that the defense minister – Dayan, and Eshkol, the prime minister himself – had approved everything that the IDF did in these territories in terms of freedom of action on the ground, which drove the IDF all the way to the Suez Canal against Dayan's orders, to an early occupation of the Gaza Strip, also against his instructions, and to a complete takeover of the West Bank that seemed to be justified militarily but was not. The occupation of the Golan Heights was decided under pressure of the Israelis who had been exposed to Syrian bombardment for years, and immediately became a matter of national consensus and settlement endeavors. Yet the tradition of close political supervision over the army's doings, introduced by Ben-Gurion in the War of Independence and especially at its end, was violated once again. Concurrently, new facts were created on the ground within the ambit of the existing political "system." These facts are important per se: Israel acquired additional territories that could serve as bargaining chips to end the conflict and so improved its international standing unrecognizably. From then on, American Jews and many Soviet Jews would view it as a pride-inspiring success story. The Arabs had been trounced in a game that they thought they would ultimately win – conventional warfare – and henceforth the atomic bomb could stay in the basement because Israel no longer needed it for its security, except as a last resort.

Few in those days could recall Ben-Gurion's warnings, expressed again and again since the 1950s, that victory in an Israeli-initiated war would lead to another war, that Egypt could not be "toppled" because it would stand up again with Soviet assistance, that the Arabs would eventually improve and learn from their defeats, and that all they needed for this purpose was unity – or, we may add, a measure of unity. It is true that the Six Day War gave them a much more realistic goal than they had entertained to date: the liberation of occupied territories instead of Israel's destruction. It is also true that under the leadership of Nasser's Egypt, the Arabs were unwilling to offer anything real in terms of directly negotiated peace in return, even if Israel were to surrender all the occupied territories without war.

Ben-Gurion contemplated this thicket after the Six Day War and could not do a thing to untangle it. As he looked on, his "kids" again joined Eshkol's Mapai and with it (and Achdut ha-Avoda) established the Israel Labor Party in 1968. Thus, Mapai became, even more than in the past, a spineless center party that was susceptible to pressure from Allon and Galili from its left and Dayan and the Rafi faction, without Ben-Gurion, from its right. The historical Mapai had lost its definitive importance by then, but now it had to acknowledge Allon's pressure to settle in Hebron and Galili's pressure to settle in what would later be called the city of Yamit in northern Sinai. In view of this competition, Dayan ultimately preferred to join their bandwagon so as not to lose points in public opinion, which was important to him, and to maintain an unwritten alliance with Menachem Begin against the majority in Mapai, headed by Eshkol, which viewed Dayan as having stolen the glory of the Six Day War. The partitioning of western Palestine, which had become a reality in Ben-Gurion's time, and the absence of Jewish rule over the Palestinian population of the West Bank had meant that Israel would not be responsible for the

Palestinians' future and rights therein. Now all of this seemed to recede into the past.

Ben-Gurion himself knew that the circumstances had changed and that, for this reason, opportunities were opening up for peace negotiations in which occupied territories could be used as the aforementioned bargaining chips or could be negotiated. For him, as we have followed Ben-Gurion's strategic thinking from 1948 onward in this book, real peace could not be a matter of "papers" alone – peace pursued as an abstract, moral idea, as important as that is. Peace must be the result of at least a strategic balance, for example, based not on "strategic territorial depth" but on proper strategic deterrence, when cultural-historical common denominators are missing and economic common interests are not yet established. However, the settlement initiatives undertaken in the West Bank, approved or accepted by Eshkol's wall-to-wall coalition were quite a source of concern for him. No longer could he influence the steps that had to be taken for this purpose within the existing political system. The times had changed beyond recognition, some for the better and some for the worse. On the one hand, there was no belittling Israel's great victory in the Six Day War and its potential for generating new Jewish enthusiasm at home and abroad. On the other hand, the circumstances still included a flawed political method, a competitive and divided elite, a hardly controllable and dangerous electoral procedure, and young people who (in part) lacked a thorough understanding of historical and cultural substance and had not internalized it as the imperative of worthy Zionist aspirations. In other words, they did not understand that the crux of Zionism was the return of the Jews as a revived and reformed cultural-political entity within boundaries free of any rule over alien Arabs, that is, within the constraints, difficulties, and imperatives of history.

In a number of interviews given soon after the war was over, Ben-Gurion endorsed the unification of Jerusalem decided upon by Eshkol's grand coalition as a result of Begin's and Allon's initiative. This was a fait accompli that could not be reversed by dividing the city again and returning its eastern half to Arab rule, which had closed its Jewish shrines to Jewish worshipers since 1948. He further was quoted as having endorsed the Israeli occupation of the Golan Heights and even a Jewish presence in Hebron, no less important to Jews than Jerusalem's Wailing Wall, but I could not find any direct statement to this effect made by him.

Yet Ben-Gurion's main concern remained the populations of the occupied territories, most of which could in theory be ceded in return for the end of the conflict, helped along by the nuclear option that was always in the background. Otherwise, continued Israeli rule over multitudes of Palestinians could bring about the delegitimation of Israel itself and reopen the Palestinian refugee issue in a different, much more serious, context, since this issue coupled the occupation of Arab land with the problem of the 1948 refugees. Ben-Gurion was quoted in the Israeli press as having contemplated a unilateral Israeli withdrawal from occupied territory, as was his old nemesis, Pinchas Lavon. I could not find a direct statement made by Ben-Gurion to this effect either;

such a far-reaching measure necessitated a governing system that could make decisions of this kind, but that system did not exist. Such a system dictated historical and cultural essentials that could be adopted by confused young people of European origin who were subject to different influences at home and abroad than those that Ben-Gurion had attempted to cope with in bygone years by invoking the slogan of "uniqueness and destiny."

The more traditional Israelis of Sephardic background were subjected to the old, secular melting-pot strategy carried out by the Founding Fathers, but now they would endorse a growing nationalistic-religious orientation based more and more on ties to the unpartitioned Palestine. This orientation could be mobilized by Begin's far-right party, now a legitimate member in Eshkol's grand coalition, combined with a growing sense of neglect and discrimination by Mapai's party machine.

The changes among the youth of European background had already occurred in the 1950s when the young people educated to join the kibbutzim left for institutions of higher learning and were exposed to different ways of life. Many among us literally grew up in movie theaters and internalized visions of America, and later the various messages of Italian and French cinema of the time. True, the Holocaust was an integral part of our identity, and would resurface not only as a matter of political controversy but also as a major unifying factor among Israelis during the crisis of May 1967. Yet Ben-Gurion's positive, ever-demanding and warning posture – that Israel must be "a light for the nations" – was abandoned during Eshkol's times in favor of an intellectual vacuum in most of the 1960s, known as the "Espresso Generation," that was replaced by a sense of intense danger and of enormous relief following the victories of 1967, in which the IDF did serve as an integrative factor for the rank and file. The inputs from the West during the upheavals of 1968, including the British-American music of the time, would play their role soon enough, during an ugly and costly "war of attrition" launched by Nasser along the Suez Canal. Now, however, Ben-Gurion's Renaissance-like terminology sounded obsolete and dusty, like his green "shack" at Kibbutz Sede Boqer, where he spent his last years sitting totally alone, having lost his beloved wife Paula a few years before his death in 1973, and attempting to write his memoirs in order to bequeath them to the younger generation.

The Zionist renaissance – that synthesis of primordial past, classical past, and rationale for the future – was attacked in the present in a way that hardly offered a return to it at the end for such a distinctively unique period in history. At the end of this renaissance, which, though areligious, maintained a selective connection with the cultural and moral components of a national religion, the Six Day War led to a renaissance of the religion itself: a combination (either highly complicated or highly simplistic) whereby the meaning of the Holocaust could be given a new interpretation from the standpoint of a religious person. The territories occupied in that war could be viewed in a mystical yet politically binding fashion by the so-called "Block of the Faith" – a militant settler movement active in the West Bank and the Gaza Strip – and even by its secular supporters as the old–new, legitimate Israeli possession, where the settlers would be crowned as the heirs of the old pioneers. Soon enough, the Holocaust would be interpreted by the Block leaders as a divine decision to destroy the Jewish people in exile in order to revive them in Israel, especially in the occupied territories, as a holy mission, reinforced by the emergence of a "Greater Israel" movement in Mapai itself and in the Allon-Galili group.

We do not know how much Ben-Gurion studied the teachings of Israeli thinkers who had stripped historical Judaism of the central concept of "religion of justice," the very concept that Ben-Gurion had labored to contextualize in the 1950s, and had argued that the very core of Judaism is faith. By extension, values such as "justice" cannot possibly exist and function in a Jewish state that lacks faith, the prime mover of Judaism since time immemorial. Several Zionist intellectuals of his generation had argued that the Jewish faith could not experience a renaissance in exile. Berl Katznelson repeatedly entertained similar thoughts in his final years, including personal transcendental insights or, as one may say, fleeting quasi-religious visions. Katznelson's attitude toward the traditional ritualistic side of the Jewish religion, of which many of his disciples know nothing – including observance of the Sabbath, the dietary laws (to whatever extent), and other religious commandments – has been illuminated by Avraham Tzivion, his best biographer.

Ben-Gurion, however, could not let himself be snared in the Jewish religion and faith, even though he treasured such thinkers and shared many of their interests, albeit in a different way. Ben-Gurion was a product of an era that could not revert to faith or attribute to faith a central role in a nation's life. One could not demand of Machiavelli that he become a believer, nor the products of the Jewish Enlightenment era, nor those who, like Ben-Gurion, had been influenced by Berdyczewski. One could expect this sober-minded statesman to offer others a transcendental-messianic-historical option without arranging its internal contents for them and without allowing it to serve as a political guide for Israel's internal and external life. After all, he did acknowledge the vacuum that existed in the psyches of modern secular Zionists, but his blend of social democracy, return to nature, and physical work; the connection between the Bible – its lessons as a permanent struggle between good and evil and its treatment of humans, endorsing justice in spite of their own faults – and the Land of Israel (or rather parts of it); his messianic vision as a hope and inspiration, rather than a political program; and the fight for a sovereign, just, moral, and governable Jewish state all seemed to be products of an age and its time.

How does one mold the Jews into a people capable of deriving from its religion enough components and tools of ethics and political conduct to usher it into a future existence that holds only the unknown in store? The (un)anticipated results of the June 1967 crisis would allow the revival of the old–new quest for Jewish return to and control of all of western Palestine, expressed immediately after the war by major Israeli writers and poets, many associated with Mapai, in terms of the forbidding of any Israeli withdrawal from the West Bank. The renewal of bonds to ancient holy places in the West Bank would soon enough produce a religious substitute for the old secular connection between Bible and Land, not just parts of it. Lessons of the Holocaust would be misused by right-wing and nationalistic-Orthodox politicians to oppose any pragmatic territorial concessions, as were typical of the historical Mapai, to Arabs. That Jews and Israel were a unique phenomenon that the world watched with awe, hatred, criticism, and great interest had been a given in Ben-Gurion's times, but it was not necessarily understood as a historical fact that required higher moral standards from the Jews in their independent state, now a strange empire in the postcolonial reality, shaped also by continued Arab enmity. By reviving the reality of the Bible, were the Jews following paths similar to those that had brought about the destruction of the First and Second Temples?

Ben-Gurion hoped that his memoirs and struggles, which he had seemingly set aside in order to become a fatherly, not a controversial, figure in his final years, would reverberate in the hearts of the masses or, failing this, in the hearts of the few. After all, he and his contemporaries had been such a few and had pulled off numerous feats, creating an infrastructure. What has grown atop this infrastructure, and what will yet grow? The last portrait of Ben-Gurion, his forehead creased and his eyes gazing into a future that defies all guesswork, teaches us only that the founding father ultimately laid down the tools of his trade. His time had expired. The ability to build and destroy, to add and subtract from the edifice whose foundations he had tried to shape to the best of his ability – for better or worse – would belong to future generations.

Archives

Ben-Gurion Archive, Ben-Gurion Institute, Ben Gurion University, Kiryat Sede Boqer

M.Y. Berdyczewski Archives, Holon, Israel

British National Archives, Kew, Surrey

Central Zionist Archives, Jerusalem

CID (Criminal Investigation Department, Palestine Police) Archives, British, kept with the Hagana Archive

Franklin Delano Roosevelt Presidential Archive, Hyde Park, New York

German Federal Archive, Berlin Lichterfelde

Hagana Archive, SHAI (Hagana Intelligence)

Israel Defense Forces (IDF) Archive, Tel Aviv

Israel State Archive, Jerusalem, and the related publications of the series pertaining to Prime Ministers David Ben-Gurion, Levi Eshkol, and Yitzhak Rabin

Jabotinsky Archive, Tel-Aviv

Lyndon Baines Johnson Presidential Archive, Austin, Texas

John F. Kennedy Presidential Archives, Boston, Massachusetts

Mapai Archive, Tel Aviv

United States Library of Congress, Stimson Papers, records pertaining to Israeli Nuclear Weapons

United States National Archives, College Park, Maryland, and the related volumes of the foreign relations of the United States, Arab–Israeli Dispute, abbreviated FRUS, especially vols. 19 and 20

Interviews

Most of the interviews listed here were conducted by the author in his role as printed press, radio, and TV person (and as Knesset candidate in Moshe Dayan's political party Telem in the 1981 elections) from the 1960s until the 1990s. Dates seemed not to be relevant because of ongoing contact with several interviewees, and if kept they were removed when the interviews were published in my *Conflict and Bargaining in the Middle East* (Baltimore: Johns Hopkins University Press, 1979) and my various "nuclear books" (see Published Sources).

Almogi, Yosef
Ben-Aharon, Yitzhak
Brecher, Michael
Burg, Yosef
Dayan, Moshe
Eshkol, Miriam
Evron, Efraim
Gazit, Mordechai
Hadari, Ze'ev "Venia"
Hashai, Yehuda
Harel, Isser
Ne'eman, Yuval
Rabin, Yitzhak
Rafael, Gideon
Rotenstreich, Nathan
Sheck, Ze'ev

Abbreviations

BGA	Ben-Gurion Archives
CIA	U.S. Central Intelligence Agency
CIC	Counter Intelligence Corps, United States Army
CID	Criminal Investigation Department, British police intelligence
COGS	chief of the general staff of the Israel Defense Forces
CZA	Central Zionist Archives, Jerusalem
DMI	director of military intelligence, London
DNI	director of naval intelligence, U.S.
DP	displaced person
FADC	Foreign Affairs and Defense Committee of the Israeli parliament
FAEC	French Atomic Energy Commission
GHQ	general headquarters
IAEC	Israel Atomic Energy Commission
IAF	Israel Air Force
IDF	Israel Defense Forces
IZL	Irgun Zva'i Le'ummi, "The Irgun" / National Military Organization
JDC	American Jewish Joint Distribution Committee
Lehi	Lohamei Herut Yisrael, Sternists / Jewish Freedom Fighters
MEIC	Middle East Intelligence Center
MI	Military Intelligence of the Israel Defense Forces
MID	Military Intelligence Division of the U.S. Department of War
MOD	Israel Ministry of Defense
NA	United States National Archives, College Park, Maryland
NRP	Israeli National Religious Party
OC	officer commanding
OSS	Office of Strategic Services, U.S. Army Intelligence agency and precursor of CIA
PICME	British Political Intelligence in the Middle East
PLA	Palestine Liberation Army
PLO	Palestine Liberation Organization
PRC	People's Republic of China
WRB	U.S. War Refugee Board

Notes

Preface and Acknowledgments

1. See his *Churchill: A Biography* (New York: Farrar, Straus and Giroux, 2001), p. 794. For a critical study of the British party system (Labour included), see Ross McKibbin, *Parties and People: England, 1914–1951* (New York: Oxford University Press, 2010).

Introduction

1. Ben-Gurion at the Labor Palestine Congress, September 27, 1930.
2. In this regard, see the most recently revised collection of Ya'akov Katz's studies: Jacob Katz, *Tradition and Crisis: Jewish Society at the End of the Middle Ages* (New York: New York University Press, 1993).
3. See Asher D. Biemann, *Inventing New Beginnings, On the Idea of Renaissance in Modern Judaism* (Stanford: Stanford University Press, 2009), Preamble.
4. The reader may find a diverse and novel discussion of Jewish nationalism and its origins in the collection *Leumiyut u-politiqa yehudit: Perspektivot hadashot* [Nationalism and Jewish politics: New perspectives], J. Reinharz, Y. Shalmon, and G. Shimoni, eds. (Jerusalem: Zalman Shazar Centre, 1997). This author shares the views of some of the contributors to this volume, Shalmon among them, that Jewish nationalism existed from earliest times and that, therefore, it cannot be linked specifically to modernization or other explanations for nationalism that have been bruited since the nineteenth century and are dealt with by other contributors, even though modernization processes did contribute to the birth of modern Jewish nationalism. It is also self-evident that secular Jewish nationalism originated in the crisis of traditional Jewish society, with which I deal later in my habitual way, i.e., by following a historical approach that cannot resort to theoretical models of nationalism originating in the social sciences. In this vein, see Hedva Ben-Yisrael, *Be-shem ha-uma* [In the name of the nation]; Y. Shalmon, "Dat u-leumiyut ba-tenuah ha-tsiyyonit me-reshita [Religion and nationalism from the outset of the Zionist movement]," in Reinharz, Shalmon, and Shimoni, *Leumiyut u-politiqa yehudit* [Nationalism and Jewish politics], pp. 115–140. See also Aviel Roshwald, *The Endurance of Nationalism* (New York: Cambridge University Press, 2006), pp. 8–22.

5. In the sea of research literature about Herzl, Yeshayahu Friedman recently stressed the anti-Socialist nature of Herzl's Zionism, which raised interest among his interlocutors in Imperial Germany. See: Y. Friedman, *Germania, Turkiya ve-ha-tsiyyonut* [Germany, Turkey and Zionism], *1897–1918* (Jerusalem and Beersheva: Bialik Institute, 1996), particularly pp. 56–57. Zionism as an alternative to Jewish support for Bolshevism and Communist Parties outside the Soviet Union played an important role in Winston Churchill's endorsement of the Zionist cause; see Martin Gilbert, *Churchill and the Jews: A Life-Long Friendship* (New York: Henry Holt, 2007), and Michael Makovsky, *Churchill's Promised Land, Zionism and Statecraft* (New Haven and London: Yale University Press, 2007).

6. D. Sadan, "Shilush u-moqdo: od al Berl Katznelson u-sevivo [A triumvirate and its focus: More about Berl Katznelson and his surroundings]," *'Iyunim bi-tequmat Yisrael* [Studies on the Jewish Rise] 6 (1996), pp. 1–15.

7. S. Tzemach, *Pinqasei reshimot 1962–1973* [Notebooks 1962–1973], foreword by Ada Tzemach, epilogue by Hanan Hever, ed. and annotation by Hanan Hever and Ada Tzemach (Tel Aviv: Am Oved, 1996).

8. It is appropriate to list the main biographies of Ben-Gurion in this Introduction for later reference. The principal work is the first volume of a multivolume biography by Shabtai Teveth, *Kinat David*. The first volume is *Hayei Ben-Gurion ha-tsa'ir* [David's Zeal: Life of the young Ben-Gurion] (Jerusalem and Tel Aviv: Schocken, 1976). The other volumes of this work are listed under Teveth in Published Sources. Another is M. Bar Zohar's three-volume biography, *Ben-Gurion* (Tel Aviv: Am Oved, 1975–1977). Researchers and critical readers would also do well to study Ben-Gurion's own scholarly publications and memoirs, as edited by Meir Avizohar and others. For our purposes, vol. 6 of his *Zikhronot min ha-izavon* [Memoirs from the estate] (Tel Aviv: Am Oved, 1987) is very important, as are the volumes *Zikhronot min ha-izavon: Likrat kets ha-mandat* [Memoirs from the estate: Toward the end of the Mandate] (Tel Aviv: Am Oved, 1993); *Zikhronot min ha-izavon: Pa'amei medina* [Memoirs from the estate: Steps toward statehood] (Tel Aviv: Am Oved, 1993); and the three volumes edited by G. Rivlin and E. Oren, *Yoman ha-milhama: Milhemet ha-'atsmaut* [War diary: The War of Independence] *1948–1949* (Tel Aviv: Ministry of Defense, 1982). A few of Ben-Gurion's published speeches and articles deserve mention here: *Medinat yisrael ha-mehudeshet* [The renewed Jewish state] (Tel Aviv, 1969); "Yihud ve-yi'ud [Uniqueness and destiny] (Tel Aviv, 1971); and *Kokhavim ve-afar: Ma'amarim mishenaton ha-memshala* [Stars and dust: Articles from the government yearbooks] (Ramat Gan: Israel Information Centre, 1976). These articles should be contrasted with Ben-Gurion's speeches in *Divrei ha-Knesset* [Knesset records] and the minutes of government meetings that the Israel State Archives recently released for publication; his speeches to the Israel Defense Forces high officer corps, recently released by the IDF Archives; and his stance on various issues as found in the files of his correspondence in the Ben-Gurion Archives (hereinafter: BGA). Likewise, our discussion will cite original documents of foreign organizations – British and American – about Ben-Gurion and other Zionist leaders.

9. "Ne'um Ben-Gurion lifnei no'ar ha-moshavim [Speech by Ben-Gurion to settlement youth], November 1, 1947," *Pa'amei medina*, pp. 454–455. The excerpts quoted were delivered after Ben-Gurion's visit to the displaced persons (DP) camps in Europe after the Holocaust.

10. Minister of Defense Ben-Gurion at meeting of IDF General Staff, April 23, 1953, Central Zionist Archives (hereinafter: CZA), Document 21.74/13.

11. Letter to Teachers' Union, January 15, 1952, BGA, Correspondence.
12. The worst controversy of all, without a doubt, was the so-called Lavon Affair. The "Affair," which ostensibly concerned a security mishap and the proper ways to investigate it, quickly took on an overlay of principled criticism on the part of various intellectuals concerning Ben-Gurion's views on the state and the army, dating back to the aftermath of the Sinai Campaign of 1956. The spirit of the intellectuals' arguments is explained in greater detail in a work that has scholarly pretensions: M. Keren, *Ben-Gurion ve-ha-intelektualim* [Ben-Gurion and the intellectuals] (Sede Boqer: Ben-Gurion University of the Negev, 1988). See also detailed discussion of Keren's book in Chapter 3 of this study.
13. On the cultural products that influenced Ben-Gurion as a young man, foremost were the Bible, Ahad Ha'am, Berdyczewski, and Bialik; he was also influenced by Spinoza, coping with him in his writings, and by Goethe, Shakespeare, and Tolstoy (see Teveth, note 8 in this chapter, pp. 28–76).
14. See "Yihuda ve-yi'uda shel medinat yisrael [The uniqueness and destiny of the State of Israel]," in *Medinat yisrael ha-mehudeshet*, pp. 1ff.
15. David Ben-Gurion, *Kokhavim ve-'afar* [Stars and dust], excerpted from a lecture on army and national education to the upper echelons of the IDF, in *Government Yearbook 1951* (in Hebrew), p. 6; on Ben-Gurion's use of Plato, see quotes in Keren (see note 12 in this chapter), pp. 23, 45, 67, 94, 127, 132, 145, 152–154, 158, 161, as well as correspondence with Yochanan Bader on "Aplaton, Shpinoza ve-ha-nesiga mi-Sinai [Plato, Spinoza and the retreat from Sinai]," *Ma'ariv*, January 4, 1957.
16. Speech at Mapai Central Committee, September 16, 1954, BGA.
17. Correspondence, August 15 and 16, 1954, BGA.
18. Ibid.
19. For details and critical discussion, see Yoel Krieger in M. Kesselman et al., *European Politics in Transition*, 3d ed. (Boston and New York: Houghton Mifflin, 1997), pp. 83ff.
20. See *Yoman ha-milhama*, vol. 3 entry of June 13, 1949: "At the party meeting I insisted [that] everything be discussed in the [Knesset] faction, and that the faction should give directions both to [the members of] the government and to the members of the [Mapai-led parliamentary] committees."
21. See Z. Zameret, *Alei gesher tsar: Ha-hinukh be-yisrael bi-shnot ha-medina ha-rishonot* [On a narrow bridge: Education in Israel in the first years of statehood] (Kiryat Sede Boqer, 1997).

1. The Intellectual Origins of Ben-Gurion's Zionism

1. See, in this regard, Charles G. Neuret, Jr., Introduction to *Humanism and the Culture of Renaissance Europe* (New York: Cambridge University Press, 1995), titled "The Attack on Burckhardt's Renaissance," pp. 1–7. For an introduction to and discussion of Renaissance philosophy by contemporary historians, see *The Cambridge History of Renaissance Philosophy* (Cambridge: Cambridge University Press, 1990).
2. See in this regard Brian Vickers, "The Idea of the Renaissance Revisited: 'Jacob Burckhardt's Idea of the Renaissance,'" in *SEDER: Yearbook of the Spanish and Portuguese Society for English Renaissance Studies*, 12 (2002), pp. 69–96.
3. In his dispute with Moshe Sharett over the Qibya affair (an Israeli reprisal against a Palestinian village that was used to launch terrorist attacks against Israel, in which

operation many civilians were killed – described by Ben-Gurion in public as if it had been carried out by Israelis acting on their own), Ben-Gurion did mention Jean Valjean, the protagonist in Hugo's *Les Miserables*, as a model for situations in which a person in the right should lie when the falsehood serves principled justice.

In respect to nineteenth-century European Heroism, see F. Ewen, *Heroic Imagination: Creative Genius of Europe from Waterloo (1815) to the Revolution of 1848* (Secaucus, NJ: Citadel, 1984).

4. One manifestation of the image of Ben-Gurion as a "small man" whose main aspiration, even during the Holocaust, was to fortify his and his party's political power in the little Yishuv instead of taking an interest in the Jewish people at large, who were being exterminated, appears in T. Segev, *The Seventh Million: Israelis and the Holocaust*, trans. Haim Watzman (New York: Hill and Wang, 1993), which was turned into a documentary film. The affairs involving projects to ransom Jews during the Holocaust, Segev says, were too grand for the leaders of the Yishuv, including Ben-Gurion, who had all been elected to their positions years before the Holocaust.

5. In this regard, see S. Baron's discussion in his article, "Leumiyut bi-mei ha-benaim ve-ha-shi'abud ha-yehudi [Nationalism in the Middle Ages and the subjection of the Jews]," which focuses on the rise of central monarchies in Spain, France, and England, as translated into Hebrew in a collection of his writings, *Meimadeha ha-olami'im shel ha-historia ha-yehudit* [The worldwide dimensions of Jewish history] (Jerusalem: Zalman Shazar Centre, 1996), pp. 119–139; and cf. his article on modern nationalism and the Jewish emancipation, "Gishot hadashot yoter la-imantsipatsia shel ha-yehudim [Newer approaches to the Jewish emancipation]," particularly pp. 175–182, ibid. I will not join the debate between the "Jerusalem school" of Yitzhak Baer, which stresses the uniqueness of the Jews throughout the generations, and Baron's attempts to set Jewish history within general history.

6. Hans Cohn, who began his career as an active Zionist and played key roles in this capacity at the Versailles peace conference and in Palestine in the 1920s, abandoned Zionism in the early 1930s and became a militant pacifist. He was a professor at several American universities until his death. An expression of his aforementioned outlook can be found under "Nationalism" in *Dictionary of the History of Ideas*, vol. 3 (New York: Charles Scribner's Sons, 1973, p. 324). There Cohn writes, among other things, that the idea of a nation chosen by God – with a specific territory promised by God, to which its native inhabitants have lost the right, or with a territory acquired with the assistance of a God who fights on the side of "His" people – is one of the most dangerous nationalistic ideas that originated in the biblical era and in the history of the Canaanite conquest. The question for research here, of course, is whether the Zionism of the era discussed in this study, which was of course a nationalist movement that made selective, secular use of various parts of the Bible as suited its needs, adopted this early biblical version of the conquest of Eretz Israel as religious extremists in today's Israel have adopted it. An even more important question, which Cohn did not consider, is that of "chosenness," which has been typical of various powerful cultures and traditions, e.g., the ideal in Chinese culture, which considered other cultures barbaric relative to itself without knowing the Bible at all.

7. Various articles in Reinharz, Shalmon, and Shimoni (Introduction, n. 4) deal with the question of whether Zionism was a "rebellion against the exile" or a typical nationalist "invention" of its time – an imitation of narrow, tribal European

nationalism that was atypical of the Jewish history that preceded it, as the Marxist British historian Eric Hobsbawm says. In a lecture in Budapest on the dangers of nationalism, Hobsbawm even claimed, following Segev's *The Seventh Million*, that Zionism used the Holocaust "for its own narrow nationalist purposes." See the discussion on this subject in my article, "'Al ha-post-tsiyyonut ve-ha-masoret ha-antishemit ba-ma'arav [On post-Zionism and the antisemitic tradition in the West]," in P. Ginosar and A. Bareli (eds.), *Iyyunim bi-tequmat yisrael – tsiyyonut: Pulmus ben-zemanenu* [Studies on the Jewish rebirth – Zionism: A contemporary polemic] (Qiryat Sede Boqer: Ben-Gurion Heritage Center, 1996), and my "The Post-Zionist Discourse and Critique of Israel: A Traditional Zionist Perspective," in *Israel Studies*, 8 (1) (Spring 2003), pp. 105–129.

8. Kalman Katznelson, letter to the editor, *Ha'aretz*, December 23, 1996.

9. For an interesting attempt to reconcile the "synthetic" character of Zionism with contemporary theories of nationalism, particularly the model of Anthony D. Smith, see G. Shimoni, *The Zionist Ideology* (Hanover and London: Brandeis University Press, 1995). This writer's purely historical approach rules out the use of theoretical models of nationalism due to the large extent of abstraction found in all such models, which threatens to divorce them from historical reality.

10. In this regard, see S. Collini, D. Winch, and J. Burrow, *That Noble Science of Politics: A Study in Nineteenth-Century Intellectual History* (Cambridge: Cambridge University Press, 1983).

11. There is no point, in this book, in listing any of the comprehensive studies written about Burke recently. I would do better by citing a critical review about Burke and his intellectual successors: R. Nisbet, *Conservatism: Dream and Reality* (Minneapolis: University of Minnesota Press, 1986).

12. Research on the intellectual history of modern nationalism that claims to trace itself to Rousseau, as appears in the writings of Herder, Fichte, Mazzini, and Ernst Renan – who coined the expression that every instance of nationalism has an element of both historical connection and freedom of choice – see Hedva Ben-Yisrael, *Be-shem ha-uma* [In the name of the nation] (Beersheva: Ben-Gurion University of the Negev, 2004).

13. Y. Kolatt, "Ha-im ha-yishuv ba-arets hu hagshamat ha-leumiut ha-yehudit? [Is the Yishuv in Palestine the fulfillment of Jewish nationhood?]," in Reinharz, Shalmon, and Shimoni, p. 177.

14. A scholar who contributed much to the reinforcement of this impression as an expert on the French Revolution and its ideological origins, via his lectures at the Hebrew University during the Lavon Affair, was the late Professor Ya'akov Talmon. Regarding Talmon's publications on this issue and other matters, see Keren, *Ben-Gurion ve-ha-intelktualim* [Ben-Gurion and the intellectuals], pp. 21, 11, 65, 73–74, 105, 113, 131, 162; and cf. Yisrael Kolatt's introduction in memory of Talmon in Z. Baras (ed.), *Meshihiut ve-eskhatologia* [Messianism and eschatology] (Jerusalem: Zalman Shazar Centre, 1984). Kolatt claimed an intellectual connection between Talmon and contemporary English liberal philosophers such as Isaiah Berlin. The problem with this, as Kolatt admitted, is that Talmon was actually an oracle for the British conservatives, and he established, from their perspective, a historical continuum between Edmund Burke's criticism of the French Revolution – plus a dose of Tocqueville – and their fears of Stalin and the Soviet Union. Talmon's criticism of Ben-Gurion in regard to "the Affair" only helped to defeat their shared goal of establishing stable governance in Israel following the British

model. Moreover, the destruction of Ben-Gurion's status, thanks partly to Talmon, created a void in the center of the Israeli political map, which his successors could not fill. They were dragged into the Six Day War, which Ben-Gurion opposed, as we shall see. Later on, as a result of the Yom Kippur War of 1973 and various sociopolitical processes that we discuss later, the void was filled by the Israeli Right.

15. For a recent, characteristic article, see I. Berlin, "On Political Judgment," *New York Review of Books*, October 6, 1996.

16. Ben-Gurion's rejectionism in this matter prompted his public denunciation of economics as a science, evoking resistance from the late Professor Don Patinkin among other "intellectuals" during "the Affair." This author also experienced Ben-Gurion's approach: When I invited him to lecture at the Political Science Department at the Hebrew University, he wrote back that he would come "if there is such a science." He wrote similarly to the head of the university's Political Science Department, the late Professor Binyamin Akzin.

17. For the development of German views of man and society as a subject for academic inquiry, see Ralf Dahrendorf, *Gesellschaft und Demokratie in Deutschland* (Munich: Piper Verlag, 1965) and his further contributions to the study of "public" and "private" virtues as keys to understanding the difference between British and German behavioral traditions.

18. See M. Keren, op. cit., pp. 132–134.

19. S. Hoffmann, "Look Back in Anger," in *New York Review of Books*, July 17, 1997.

20. Hoffmann notes that this approach is much closer to Rousseau than to the American Federalists. We develop this idea later.

21. It goes without saying that in Hoffmann's eyes, each of these elements is menaced within today due to the pitiful political state of the elites and the deterioration of the traditional means that once served to blend the various players of French society into a whole, such as the education system, military service, and the shared consciousness of the working class that maintained both internal solidarity and national pride. In foreign affairs, the loss of control over imports and the influx of foreign workers have contributed to the sense that France has been marginalized.

22. Cf. G. Shimoni, "Ha-leumiut ha-yehudit ke-leumiut etnit [Jewish nationalism as ethnic nationalism]," in *Jewish Nationalism and Politics: New Perspectives* (Introduction), n. 5, pp. 18–29.

23. Following the Dutch political scientist Arend Lijphart, quoting his articles entitled "Consociational Democracy," in *World Politics*, 21 (2) (January 1969), and "Comparative Politics," in *American Political Science Review*, 65 (3) (September 1971), D. Horowitz and M. Lissak termed the Yishuv government a "consensual democracy." See Horowitz and Lissak, *Mi-yishuv le-medina: Yehudei Eretz Yisrael bi-tequfat ha-mandat ha-briti ke-qehila politit* [From Yishuv to state: The Jews of Eretz Israel during the British Mandate as a political community] (Tel Aviv: Am Oved, 1977), p. 317ff. Lijphart, however, had in mind the Dutch approach, which attained a high degree of consensus despite the religious, regional, class, and local contrasts that characterized Dutch society. British politics, too – until Margaret Thatcher's time – showed a very high degree of consensus in economic and social affairs. Still, these examples are nothing compared to the degree of consensus – and lack of consensus – that might have prevailed in the Yishuv were it not dominated by a major party like Mapai, which was ruled by a man who refused to compromise at key times, e.g., the decision on whether or not to establish the state, or had

various forces and events not energized and mobilized the Yishuv for the common good, particularly to defend itself from destruction.

24. This conflation, typical of Berl Katznelson's thinking, is not well expressed in Anita Shapira's biography, *Berl*, vols. 1 and 2 (Tel Aviv: Sifriyat Ofakim/Am Oved, 1980). To explore it, consult the lesser-known study of A. Tzivyon, *Ha-morasha ha-yehudit be-itsuv olamo shel Berl Katznelson* [The Jewish heritage in the shaping of Berl Katznelson's world] (Jerusalem: Hebrew University of Jerusalem, 1982). A similar conflation, though much closer to the Hasidic source and – insofar as it carries markers of ostensibly primordial Christian symbolism – Tolstoy's teachings, appears in the writings of A. D. Gordon. Here consult A. Shapiro, *Or ha-hayyim be-"Yom Katnut": Mishnat A. D. Gordon u-meqoroteha ba-qabala u-va-hasidut* [The living light in *Yom Qatnut*: The teachings of A. D. Gordon and their sources in Kabbala and Hasidism] (Tel Aviv: Am Oved, 1996).

25. In this regard, see a typical Ben-Gurion speech: "*Ruheinu lo nafla, retsoneinu eitan, u-ve-ma'amats meshutaf nagshim et ha-matara* [Our spirit has not fallen, our will is firm, and by striving together we shall attain our goal]," Paris, published in *Davar*, July 19, 1946.

26. On Ratosh and his political philosophy, see Y. Porat, *Shelah ve'et be-yado: Sipur hayyav shel Yonatan Ratosh* [Fence with a pen in his hand: The biography of Yonatan Ratosh] (Tel Aviv: Mahbarot le-Sifrut, 1989).

27. On Nietzsche's attitude to Jews and Judaism, see Y. Yovel, *Hida afela: Hegel, Nietzsche ve-ha-yehudim* [Dark riddle: Hegel, Nietzsche and the Jews] (Jerusalem: Schocken, 1996) and Ya'akov Golomb's critique in the *Ha'aretz* book supplement, August 7, 1996.

28. On Martin Buber, see D. Sadan, *'Iyyunim bi-tequmat yisrael* [Studies in the Jewish rebirth], 6 (1996). Buber, though a leading exponent among the early German Zionists, did not "make aliyah" (emigrate to Eretz Israel) until the late 1930s. The attitude of German Zionists such as Buber toward aliyah, which they delayed repeatedly in favor of what they called "current work" in the Diaspora, is too complex to discuss in a footnote; therefore it is discussed in the text proper.

29. In this regard, see Mordechai Geldman, "*Nezirim budhisti'im be-glimot humot heviu imam dumiya gedola* [Brown-robed Buddhist monks brought with them a great silence]," *Ha'aretz* supplement, June 10, 1997, and Hagai Dagan's response in the same supplement two weeks later: "*'Al ha-ahava ve-ha-rahamim ba-yahadut* [On love and compassion in Judaism]."

30. Dagan, response.

31. See Keren (see n. 4 in this chapter), p. 27.

32. See Ben-Gurion, *Zikhronot min ha-izavon: Pa'amei medina* [Memoirs from the estate: Steps toward statehood], pp. 195–200, for one of many examples.

33. In Ben-Gurion's own words ("*Medinat yisrael ha-mehudeshet*" [The renewed Jewish state], p. 4), "This eruption of faith in Jewish power and will after centuries of exile and dwelling in foreign lands ... and in [the nation's] *creative and combative* [emphasis in original] ability drew on three sources: the renewed influence of the Bible, which came with the literature of the Haskala, the national and social revolutions in Europe ... and the productive contact with the soil of the homeland."

34. Ben-Gurion considered the disengagement from Soviet Jewry a "heavy blow" of a kind that had not befallen the Jewish people since the Bar Kochva–Hadrian strife (see ibid.).

35. See *Yoman ha-milhama* [War diary], vol. 2, p. 286, for abstract of lecture on September 9, 1948, after Ben-Gurion had become convinced of the scope of the victory in the War of Independence: "What were the 'goals' of the war? Our strength is not just physical; our advantage is spiritual. It is important to know what we are fighting for: ingathering the exiles, building souls, a workers' society. How shall we overcome the difficulties in accomplishing these three aims, the difficulties occasioned by the Arab surroundings, a faint, backward, feudal Nazi society with cheap labor and few needs? Compared with [the Arabs], we are few even if mass immigration ensues.... We are about to operate at a time of world contrasts. Our dispersion among the nations, and despite our independence here – the subjection of the Jewish masses to foreign will, to opposing desires. The difficulties that are occasioned by our country – small territory, lack of coal and metal, scanty rainfall and water, *internal difficulties – fragmentation, devotion to trivial causes, inability to compromise*" [emphasis added].

36. Cf. Ben-Gurion in January 1930: "[Weakness originating in] our sin – that we have been sinning for two thousand years now... the sin of our weakness. Woe to the weak! This is the philosophy of history, and grumbling will not help us.... The times are times of a policy of strength.... The ear is deaf... and can hear only the sound of the cannons. And Jews in the Diaspora have no cannons." S. Teveth, *Ben-Gurion ve-arviyei eretz yisrael* [Ben-Gurion and the Palestinian Arabs] (Jerusalem: Schocken, 1982), p. 304.

37. See "The Renaissance 1493–1520," *The New Cambridge Modern History*, vol. 1 (Cambridge: Cambridge University Press, 1957), pp. 273ff.

38. See *The renewed Jewish state*, p. 5: "The Jewish people rejected physical supremacy, the supremacy of physical strength. However, rejecting this supremacy does not mean repudiating physical strength. We would be repudiating Jewish history from the time of Joshua Bin-Nun – even from the time of Moses – up to and including the Israel Defense Forces – if we nullified the value of physical strength. The negation of physical strength is the negation of this world, of life. Such a negation has always been foreign to the Jewish spirit, and here lies one of the fundamental differences between Jewish doctrine and Christian doctrine." Ben-Gurion parsed his terminology carefully; here he speaks of "Christian doctrine" and not of the actions of Christian rulers and states. Later he expanded on the dualism of the physical and the spiritual, which originated with the Greeks and which, in his opinion, never took hold in Judaism. Michael Keren interprets this philosophical stance as a manifestation of Ben-Gurion's monism. "Monism," however, also means one-sidedness, a decided preference of one value over another, a characteristic that we find more particularly in *had-ness*, one goal alone – a notion coined by Jabotinsky of all people.

39. Amery is quoted in the classic (and outdated) book on the British governmental system: S. H. Beer and A. B. Ulam (eds.), *Patterns of Government: The Major Political Systems of Europe*, 3d ed. (New York: Random House, 1979), pp. 277–278.

40. Ben-Gurion constantly stressed this point from 1939 onward. See, for example, *The renewed Jewish state*, p. 234.

41. Cf. minutes of conference in Beersheva about the induction of youth, *BGA*, July 19, 1954, doc. 5712 001, in his remark about "the Jewish Carthage, which will not last even as long as the Canaanite Carthage." Also cf. speech at a Mapai convention at Ohalo, its intellectual center, December 16, 1954, in the presence of Prime

Minister and Foreign Minister Moshe Sharett, in which Ben-Gurion criticized the government for being nothing but "a federation of parties [that safeguard] their own interests above all, and parties that are not political parties but rather sects," a class in which he included Mapai, for failing to settle the "wildernesses" [i.e., the large Negev Desert] and failing to assure immigrant absorption worthy of the name. "I'll start from this: The fact is that we do not have a people, and this is the change that has occurred in our times, as of now, 1948 [in contrast with the indicators of unity in the Arab world].... It is possible for us to become one people. It will require an immense effort... by the state, but no effort by the state will suffice; it requires voluntary effort by the masses of citizens.... If war breaks out before [this happens], we're done for."

42. Ben-Gurion, *Zikhronot min ha-izavon* [Memoirs from the estate], vol. 6, p. 349.
43. Ibid. Ben-Gurion's closing words to the Mapai Council, April 16, 1939.
44. J. Burckhardt, *Tarbut ha-renaissance be-italia* [Renaissance culture in Italy] (scientific ed. H. Peri) (Jerusalem: Mosad Bialik, 1966), pp. 112–202.
45. On the secession of Yitzhak Tabenkin's Faction B from Mapai before these elections, and for a thorough account of the history of Mapai and Ben-Gurion's argument from 1936 onward that this party should be put to political use for the purpose of electoral victories geared to the establishment of a state that would "save the people," see M. Avizohar, *Be-re'i saduq: Idialim hevrati'im u-leumi'im ve-hishtaqfutam be-'olama shel Mapai* [In a cracked mirror: Social and national ideals and their reflection in the world of Mapai] (Tel Aviv: Am Oved, 1990). According to Anita Shapira (*Berl*, pp. 680–705), Katznelson and Ben-Gurion agreed that this minority faction's attempt to foist upon the majority its unrealistic views and its organization made the split inevitable, and the two leaders maneuvered the faction into leaving.
46. On the one hand, several Faction B leaders accused Ben-Gurion of acting like a "dictator" when he tried to use the potential power of the Hagana (the Yishuv's military underground) to pressure the Mandatory government; on the other hand, several leading personalities among the immigrants from Germany and Brit Shalom Ihud (a small club of pacifists led by Judah L. Magnes, the first chancellor of Hebrew University) accused the Mapai leadership of not doing enough to placate the Arabs. Both sets of accusations figured prominently in British and American intelligence reports from Palestine. These intelligence sources are of the greatest importance in understanding the difficulties experienced by the Yishuv leadership during the war, and we shall return to them and to the stance of Ha-Shomer ha-Tsa'ir at the time.
47. On Mapai's maneuverings among the German immigrants and for Ben-Gurion's sensitivity to them ahead of the 1944 elections, see Y. Rimmer, *Peretz Naphtali: Sotsialdemokrat bi-shnei olamot* [Peretz Naphtali: A social democrat in two worlds] (Jerusalem: World Zionist Organization/The Zionist Library, 1996), pp. 195–229.
48. See M. Avizohar, *"Sha'on hol* [Hourglass]," Introduction, *Pa'amei medina* [Steps toward statehood], pp. 52–91; and cf. Z. Tsahor, *Hazan – tenu'at hayyim: Ha-Shomer ha-Tsa'ir, ha-Kibbutz ha-Artsi, Mapam* [Hazan – a movement of life: Ha-Shomer ha-Tsa'ir, ha-Kibbutz ha-Artsi, Mapam] (Jerusalem: Yad Izhak Ben-Zvi, 1997), pp. 175–176.
49. See S. Tzemach, *"Kishlono shel mi?* [Whose failure?]," *Ha'aretz*, March 14, 1947. Tsemah claims that it was not the British government that failed in the Eretz Israel issue but rather the undisciplined, overstated, aggressive Zionist policy [in its

active opposition to the White Paper]. Tzemach repeated this position even more
forcefully in *Ha'aretz* on April 14, saying that the Zionists should appease the
British as much as possible: "to go to London and express complete regret for the
past and to ask [the British] to be the Jewish people's advocates in the international
arena" (quoted in *Steps toward statehood*, p. 80e).

50. See Anita Shapira, "Rekhivim shel ha-etos ha-leumi ba-ma'avar mi-yishuv le-
medina [Components of the national ethos in the transition from Yishuv to state],"
in *Leumiyyut u-politika yehudit* [Jewish nationalism and politics] (see Introduction,
n. 4, pp. 272–352). Shapira's article reflects the traditional opposition of members
of Mapai's Faction B to the transition from voluntary society to state.

51. See Shapira, *Berl*, vol. 2, p. 470n; Ben-Gurion, *Zikhronot* [Memoirs], vol. 6, p.
644. On Lavon's performance as head of the leftist-anarchist Gordonia movement
at the time and his relationship with Katznelson, see Shapira, ibid.

52. In this regard, see the development of Yitzhak Tabenkin's socioideological network
in the Po'alei Tsiyyon party in Poland, which combined Zionism and Marxism with
specific personal and social inputs, as illuminated brightly in M. Mintz, *Haver ve-
yariv: Yitzhak Tabenkin u-mifleget Po'alei Tsiyyon 1905–1912* [Friend and foe:
Yitzhak Tabenkin and the Po'alei Zion Party 1905–1912] (Tel Aviv: Hakibbutz
Hameuchad, 1986). Pay special attention to n. 16, p. 157, on the presocialist period
of another member of that party – Ben-Gurion – who, according to Tabenkin,
challenged his reasoning in those early days, saying that there was no need to
connect Marxism with the principle of aliyah and settlement in Eretz Israel. "We
simply love Eretz Israel," Ben-Gurion ruled. Tabenkin disputed this, as he said
years later: "But we couldn't help it. We were already disciples of Marxism and
we wanted to explain the power of Eretz Israel to ourselves [in Marxian terms]."
Cf. the route taken by another leftist Marxist leader from his mother's house to
Ha-Shomer ha-Tsa'ir: Tzahor, *Hazan – tenu'at hayyim* [Hazan – a movement of
life] (see n. 48 in this chapter), pp. 53–55.

53. See Achimeir, A., *Ketavim nivharim: Atlantida o ha-olam she-shaka* [Selected writings: Atlantis or the world that sank], vol. 5 (Tel Aviv: Ministry of Defense,
1996); see also Pinchas Ginosar's review in the culture and literature supplement
of *Ha'aretz*, November 15, 1995.

54. See E. E. Urbach, *Al tsiyyonut ve-yahadut: iyyunim u-masot* [On Zionism and
Judaism: Studies and essays] (Jerusalem: The Zionist Library, 1985), pp. 247–251.
In this collection, Urbach, a moderate religious philosopher, decries the breaking
of the chain of tradition, "the singularity of the Jewish people, which carries at
the forefront of its historical consciousness the act of the Giving of the Torah, the
covenant between itself and its God." This act of disengagement occurred, in his
opinion, as far back as 1906, at the Helsingfors Conference, where "Jewish law
stopped. [Since then], anyone who acknowledges Jewish nationhood, regardless
of faith and religion, is a member of the Jewish national camp; even a Christian
can be a Jewish national" (ibid., p. 248). Ben-Gurion did not take part in that
conference; instead he immigrated to Eretz Israel. Prominent future Zionist leaders
who attended were Z. Jabotinsky and I. Grünbaum. Further on (p. 249), Urbach
makes profound but critical remarks about Ben-Gurion, his demand of the Jewish
people that it be a "chosen nation," and, particularly, the Israel Defense Forces:
"The idea that underlies our existence is the idea of double chosenness. What
does it mean? . . . Who chose whom – the Jewish people its God or God the Jewish
people? . . . On the one hand, it is a choice compelled; on the other hand, it is a choice

freely made. As a person of deep intuition and a sense of Jewish history – a sense that has not always found its proper expression – Ben-Gurion of all people knows this secret, and for that reason he occasionally returns to the chosen-people issue. As I construe it in its latest incarnation, it says that this is the talent to absorb military training more quickly than other peoples." Cf. Yeshayahu Leibowitz's religious-radical-anarchist lecture, "The Art of Esau Cannot Be Turned into Education," published in his book *Torah u-mitsvot ba-zman ha-ze* [Torah and mitzvot in our times] (Jerusalem: Massada, 1954) and republished in *Ha'aretz*, September 27, 1996.

55. See Dr. Yosef Burg's attack on Ben-Gurion's studies of Plato, interview in *Ha'ir*, August 16, 1996, in which Burg, in a letter that he sent to the prime minister in 1953 while serving as minister of health argued, in the spirit of Karl Popper's then-popular theory, against "the sole sovereignty of the state" in the theory of Plato, whom Popper made out to be the father of modern totalitarianism. Burg aligned himself with the neo-Kantian school of Hermann Cohen and Franz Rosenzweig's studies of Judaism, with the modern interpretation of *Torah im Derech Eretz*, i.e., Jewish law plus civil duties and liberties that were particularly sensitive to the social problem – unlike Leibowitz's approach, which centered on unquestioning observance of Torah commandments. This did not prevent Leibowitz from cooperating with Ben-Gurion's Mapai for a while, until they parted ways and Leibowitz became a Lithuanian-style religious anarchist. As for Dr. Burg and his mentor, Hermann Cohen, Urbach tells us that Cohen said of Zionists, "Those fools want to be happy."

56. In reference to the challenge of the nineteenth century, Ben-Gurion quoted Simon Dubnow and carried on in the classic spirit of Zionism. See *Kokhavim ve-afar: Ma'amarim mi-shenaton ha-memshala* [Stars and dust: Articles from the *Government Yearbooks*], p. 11.

57. See updated summary of Don Yihye's important studies in this area: E. Don Yihye, *Ha-politiqa shel ha-hasdara: Yishuv sikhsuhim be-nosei dat u-medina* [Politics of arrangement: Resolution of conflicts in matters of religion and state] (Tel Aviv: The Open University of Israel, 1997).

58. Leibowitz's attacks on Ben-Gurion carried a strong bent of personal politics and were expressed in his involvement with Shmuel Tamir, who was at the center of the campaign to discredit Mapai in the Kasztner affair, to be described later, in which Mapai was accused by Tamir of collaboration with the "Nazo-British" and with the Gestapo itself – and later in the open struggle to prevent the adoption of a nuclear strategy for Israel. In this regard, see my books: *The Politics and Strategy of Nuclear Weapons in the Middle East* (Albany and London: State University of New York Press, 1992) and its extended translations (Jerusalem: Academon, 1994), pp. 13, 30, 204–268, and 2006 updated version.

59. In her book *The Origins of Totalitarianism*, Hannah Arendt spoke of Zionism as a product of the Dreyfus affair and in seemingly positive terms. See H. Arendt, *The Origins of Totalitarianism* (New York: Harcourt Brace, 1951; paperback edition, Cleveland: Meridian Books, 1963), p. 12. She said this within the framework of her accusations against the traditional Jewish elites, who, in her opinion, lacked political awareness and understanding of the world in which they lived. Arendt defined the Zionists as at least "political enough" in comparison with others. In a previous article, however, titled "Zionism Reconsidered," she argued that the Zionist Labor Movement "emancipated from Jewish orthodoxy was entirely

'unpolitical' and innocently oblivious of the 'very existence' of the Arabs in Palestine. They escaped to Palestine as one might wish to escape to the moon, to a
region beyond the wickedness of this world. True to their ideals, they established
themselves on the moon; and with the extraordinary strength of their faith they
were able to create small islands of perfection." Typically cruel and sharp, in the
best of the tradition of Heinrich Heine as she understood him, Arendt dealt here
with portions of the kibbutz movement, and some of her arguments have a basis in
Ben-Gurion's own criticism of *Hakibbutz Hameuchad*, the kibbutz movement affiliated with Mapai's Section B led by Tabenkin, described earlier. There, however,
Ben-Gurion referred not to the Arabs but to the supercilious attitude of Hakibbutz
Hameuchad toward other Jews who refused to adopt the idealistic kibbutz way of
life. However, Arendt's argument against the traditional Jewish elites in particular
and Jewish elites in general drew her to accuse the Yishuv leadership of collaborating with the Nazis after Hitler's accession to power. She based her opinion on
the leadership's actions in transferring Jewish property from Germany to Palestine
in order to further Zionist interests, even though Western Jewry was weighing
a boycott against Nazi Germany, and on the Zionist Labor Movement's interest
only in young immigrants and others fit for agricultural work in Palestine (an old
misunderstanding based on ignorance of the Mandate government's immigration
criteria, which forced the Yishuv to limit immigration to young people and those
fit for manual labor). She also accused the movement's leadership, under David
Ben-Gurion, of suffering from an irrational pursuit of the old, vain fantasy of a
sovereign Jewish nation-state at a time when the nation-state had gone bankrupt
in favor of the structures of the future – empires or federations. I suppose that by
empires she meant not only the British Empire but also the Soviet empire.

   In an earlier publication, Arendt discussed political Zionism as founded by
Theodore Herzl. Her argument against Herzl was that his Zionism was a product
of antisemitism – an old claim that German-Jewish intellectuals brought against
Herzlian Zionism – i.e., that it was an escape from reality rather than a confrontation with it. Herzlian Zionism sought to secure the escape route by concluding an
agreement with the Great Powers irrespective of the wishes of the Jewish masses,
upon whom Herzl sought to impose his solution by force – a claim that found
support in some of Herzl's own writings, which spoke of leading the masses to the
desired goal when they are unable to recognize it by themselves. This claim formed
a basis for anti-Zionist arguments in the West from the early 1920s on.

   Arendt drew up her final reckoning with Ben-Gurion's Israel in her book *Eichmann in Jerusalem: A Report on the Banality of Evil*, in which she inveighed
against the use that the Zionist state had made of Eichmann – a cog with no
apparent say in the totalitarian machine – "for its narrow nationalist purposes,"
while blurring the ostensible universal significance of the Holocaust, an issue that
we will take up again. On these issues, see H. Arendt, "Zionism Reconsidered,"
Menorah Journal (August 1945), pp. 162–196; "The Jewish State: 50 Years After.
Where Have Herzl's Politics Led?" *Commentary*, 1 (May 1946), pp. 1–8; *Eichmann in Jerusalem: A Report on the Banality of Evil* (New York: Penguin, 1965).
Given that Arendt's book abounds with historical and legal errors and false accusations against the Jewish leaders and their "contribution" to the Holocaust, it
should be read and compared with J. Robinson's corrections in his book *Ha-aqov
le-mishor* [And the crooked shall be made straight] (Jerusalem: Bialik Institute,
1965], Hebrew translation.

60. See B. Dinur, *Be-olam she-shaqa: Zikhronot ve-reshumot mi-derekh hayyim* [In a world that is no more: Memoirs and writings from a way of life] (Jerusalem: Bialik Institute, 1958).

61. For this insight I thank Professor Arnold Band of the University of California at Los Angeles. For a deeper discussion of this important figure and his influence on Berl Katznelson, see Tzivyon, *Ha-morasha ha-yehudit* [The Jewish heritage], and H. Goldberg, *Israel Salanter: Text, Structure, Idea* (New York: Ktav, 1982).

62. For emphasis on the Jewish-messianic foundation of the Haskala, i.e., the input of non-Jewish modern philosophy, science, literature, and poetry on the Jews in Russia, see Y. Frankel's review of research literature in this field in Eastern and Western Europe: "Hitbolelut ve-hisardut be-qerev yehudei eropa ba-me'a ha-tsha' 'esre [Assimilation and survival among European Jewry in the nineteenth century]," in *Jewish nationalism and politics: New perspectives* (see Introduction, n. 4), pp. 23–56. Cf. M. Mintz, "Leumiyut yehudit u-leumiyut shel mi'utim aherim be-medinot rabot-leumi'im [Jewish nationhood and nationhood of other minorities in multinational states]," ibid., pp. 201–204.

63. M. J. Berdyczewski, *Pirqei yoman: amal yom ve-haguto* [Diary chapters: A day's work and thought], Hebrew trans. Rachel Bin-Gurion (Holon: Moreshet Micha Yosef, 1975), pp. 106–107; Aliza Klausner-Eshkol, *Hashpa'at Nietzsche ve-Schopenhauer al M. J. Bin-Gurion (Berdyczewski)* [The influence of Nietzsche and Schopenhauer on M. J. Bin-Gurion (Berdyczewski)] (Tel Aviv: Dvir, 1964). This scholarly study compares texts and argues that Berdyczewski was incurably torn between Schopenhauer's pessimism and Nietzsche's intellectual activism; cf. E. Bin-Gurion's critique, *Qore ha-dorot* [Reader of the times] (Tel Aviv: Reshafim, 1981), p. 193.

64. On the periodization of M. J. Berdyczewski's life and oeuvre, see G. Shaked, *Ha-siporet ha-'ivrit 1880–1980* [Hebrew literature 1880–1980], vol. 1: *Ba-gola* [In the Diaspora] (Jerusalem: Keter and Hakibbutz Hameuchad, 1978), pp. 165*ff.* Shaked discusses the influence of Nietzsche and Schopenhauer on Berdyczewski and considers German "Neo-Romanticism" an important source of influence on Berdyczewski. However, he views Berdyczewski the storyteller – which is his main interest – as a Romantic.

65. In this regard, and concerning the surprising influence of Nietzsche in the United States, see A. Bloom, *The Closing of the American Mind* (New York: Simon & Schuster, 1987).

66. In the matter of "Diaspora collectivism," see: M. J. Berdyczewski, "Tahanot be-hashqafati al she'elat ha-yehudim ve-ha-yahadut [Stations in my thinking on the question of the Jews and Judaism]," *Pirqei yoman* [Diary chapters], pp. 105–106. The date is May 27, 1905. Berdyczewski presented some of these arguments in an article in German that was published that year under a title that was translated into the Hebrew as "Clarification of Matters"; see publisher's explanation, E. Bin-Gurion, *Be-reshut ha-yahid: Micha Yosef Berdyczewski be-esrim shnotav ha-ahronot* [In the private domain: Micha Josef Berdyczewski in his last twenty years] (Tel Aviv: Reshafim, 1980). On Katznelson and his attempt to induce and shape a new Jewish society in Eretz Israel from "Jewish traditional and cultural roots," and the special status that he granted himself, see Avizohar, *Be-re'i saduq* [In a cracked mirror], pp. 287*ff.*

67. See the following study, which has never received the public recognition it deserves: S. Dotan, *Adummim: Ha-miflaga ha-komunistit be-erets yisrael*

[Reds: The Communist Party in the land of Israel] (Kfar Sava: Shevna Hasofer, 1991), p. 26: "On one side stood... the members of the "national trend" headed by David Ben-Gurion, a former member of Po'alei Zion in Poland, a Zionist group that had adopted Marxism but preferred principled Palestinism, which was based on "love of the land" rather than elaborate theories that tried to combine Marxist theories with Zionism, as preached by others such as Yitzhak Tabenkin.

68. See Teveth, *Qinat David* [David's zeal], vol. 1, p. 47: "'I like to write only about what *I want* and about what *I desire* and not about what is *endorsed to the will of others*' [emphasis in the original]. To Ben-Gurion, willpower is man's greatest virtue. He noted the special qualities with which Herzl was blessed... the strength of the Maccabis, the cunning of David, the courage of Rabbi Akiva, the modesty of Hillel, the beauty of [the sage] R. Judah the Nasi, the passionate love of [the Medieval poet and philosopher] Yehuda Halevi. He failed to find a human parallel for only one of the virtues: he called Herzl 'possessed of the will of the gods.' Unwittingly, perhaps, he sketched the ideal leader: war hero, master strategist, courageous on the civil front, humble, handsome, abounding with love for his people, and, above all, 'possessing the will of the gods.' Willpower was required for two things: performing the task itself and instilling it in others, i.e., the imparting of will. 'The powerful craving for the work of revival, which the possessor of the will of the gods instilled in us, will churn inside us until we complete the great work for which the great leader sacrificed his exalted life.' This is neither Marxist language nor the philosophic language of Tolstoy in his conclusion to *War and Peace*, in which the individual – great as he may be, even Napoleon himself – is insignificant in the face of deterministic historic forces: the masses, the diverse, simple, uncorrupted masses, as represented by Platon Carataev. In this sense there was a difference between Ben-Gurion and Berl Katznelson, who was influenced by Tolstoy to an extreme: 'Katznelson believed that the Hebrew labor movement was driven by historic social forces that did not depend on individual fluctuations in individuals' consciousnesses.'" See Avizohar (op. cit.), p. 283. In this respect, Ben-Gurion was undoubtedly the greater skeptic; see more in the text proper.

69. Berdyczewski and Brenner, *Halifat igrot* [Correspondence] (Tel Aviv: Hakibbutz Hameuchad, 1962), p. 147. Berdyczewski's criticism and polemics presage his future literary oeuvre and what Professor Gedalia Elkoshi would call "his heroes, who generally excel at something strange and wonderful and who carry the legacy of their forebears in their blood." Berdyczewski subsequently attached to this "the fear of the chasms in the human soul and of the inescapable heavy hand of fate" – for it is this that determines will. See Berdyczewski, *Diary chapters*, p. 66: "Sorrow purifies the human soul and cleanses it of what the will has defiled in it" (June 9, 1906). This concept of the will harks back to Schopenhauer's. Cf. a fragment of an entry in the journal ten days previously: "The will is the voice of nature [in the wild, barbarian sense] in the heart of man." Berdyczewski prefaces this statement with writings in the spirit of the "Vitalist" philosophy that was popular in Germany at the beginning of the twentieth century, in a certain way, and in Henri Bergson's France as well: "All wisdom evaporates when confronted by the spirit of life."

Nietzsche's characteristic psychologism and his ardent interest in Dostoevsky (and decidedly not in Tolstoy), which we find in Berdyczewski as well, particularly during his later periods, and the return to Schopenhauerian pessimism in regard to the nature and limitations of the will, are not characteristic of all the Zionist leaders of concern to us here. Berl Katznelson was sensitive to nexuses such as these and even drew a connection between Berdyczewski and Kafka. See B. Katznelson, "Ish ha-razim [The man of secrets]," a letter to Rachel Katznelson-Shazar in early 1940 about Berdyczewski that was first published in Nurit Govrin, "Micha Josef Berdyczewski ve-erets yisrael [Micha Josef Berdyczewski and the Land of Israel]," *Alei siah* [Pages of discourse], 17–18 (1983) (in the appendix to the article). The later Berdyczewski, however, no longer persuaded people like David Ben-Gurion, whom he had influenced at the turn of the twentieth century and who had soon afterwards emigrated to Eretz Israel, flush with the wish to prove to Berdyczewski, whose pungent criticism of Zionists his students among the Second Aliyah had internalized in their way, that they were not among those who do nothing but talk. See Emmanuel Bin-Gurion, "M. Y. Berdyczewski ve-ha-aliyah ha-sheniya [M. Y. Berdyczewski and the second aliyah]," in *Qore ha-dorot* [Reader of the times], pp. 194–195; and E. Bin-Gurion's quotation of remarks by Katznelson: "If Berdyczewski knew, without an audience and without hope that anyone would listen to his words... how to expose the slackness of Zionism, the Second Aliyah came along and offered a solution to his dream."

70. See: Avizohar, op. cit., p. 287.

71. See Bin-Gurion, *Be-reshut ha-yahid*, pp. 160–161. This is a continuation of Berdyczewski's May 1905 work "Tahanot be-hashqefotai," in which he claims a "total change in the account of my philosophical world" after having met Nietzsche. Then, he says, "I began to appreciate the religious factor in human history for its worthiness" – but he did not change "one bit" his demand for a secular revival for Jews. "Concurrently I began to acknowledge the impossibility of bringing about the Jewish program [at this time, he wrote elsewhere that 'The world is divided among the nations' and that in this respect the Jews had missed the boat]. It is hopeless.... I turned my back on the Zionists' organization.... I began justly to cast doubt on the sincerity of their wish to leave the lands of the Diaspora and to devote themselves to their own lives."

72. The early Berdyczewski appealed to them at the beginning of his third period but not later, even though at later times, too, his views about the human will veered in various directions. In the introduction to Volume 4 of his diary, which he began to write in late 1905, he speaks of the will as follows: "I embrace the wide world and I am the master of the whole world, and even my death will not erase what my mind has devised, what has ventured from my mind into the world. One can live without God; one only needs a goal, and a goal can be found, although not easily." Elsewhere, Berdyczewski enlists Nietzschean terminology by arguing: "Any work within Judaism is a voice in the wilderness... but in this respect I must be an Übermensch.... Each person has the license to do that which nature has destined him to do; if he finds the path blocked, he should remove the obstacle and has the power to do so. Fate does not destroy a man's life; fate breaks down an open door. When destruction comes upon me, I myself have invited the destroyer" (first quote from *Pirqei yoman* [Diary chapters], p. 9; second quote: ibid., p. 78.)

73. In this matter, see S. H. Bergman, "*Yavne vi – yerushalayim (ha-be'aya ha-tsiyyonit al pi Berdyczewski)* [Yavne and Jerusalem (the Zionist problem according to Berdyczewski)]," in the M. J. Berdyczewski Bin-Gurion Archives, pp. 18–19.

74. See Teveth, *Qinat David: Hayei Ben-Gurion ha-tsa'ir* [David's zeal: Life of the young Ben-Gurion], vol. 1, p. 28: "It was as if Berdyczewski had read everything – research, notes, and books. His essays impressed David and his friends more than Ahad Ha'am's."

75. Pursuant to his debates in the Knesset and in his correspondence with Israeli reli-
    gious leaders over the "Who is a Jew" issue, Ben-Gurion wrote to Rabbi Dov Tzvi
    Rottstein on March 28, 1954 (*Correspondence*, BGA): "You think you have the
    authority to decide what is heresy and what is Judaism. I deny this authority of
    yours.... Permit me to tell you in all sincerity, and with all the respect that is due
    to any man, that in you and in those who think like you there is a bit of hubris. You
    have appropriated Judaism, the Torah, the Jewish people, and all past generations
    for yourselves, and each of you seemingly carries the entire people on his shoul-
    ders. But this is far from the case. You are just one part... of the Jewish people
    and of Judaism, and we are one part, and none of us needs license or consent
    for our belonging to the Jewish people and Judaism as we understand it.... You
    and your ilk are definitely trying to fulfill everything written in Karo's *Shulhan
    'aruch* [i.e., the Orthodox code of religious duties, assembled by Rabbi Yosef Karo
    (1488–1575)]. I am not sure if you are trying to fulfill the words of [the prophet]
    Micha of Moreshet: '*What does God demand of you? To do justice and love acts
    of kindness and to walk humbly with your God*' [emphasis in original]. Be a bit
    humble, esteemed Rabbi." This did not prevent the conclusion of a compromise
    along the lines of the religious status quo in regard to the "Who is a Jew" question.
    Later in the same letter, Ben-Gurion developed his argument in favor of includ-
    ing Spinoza in the confines of Jewish experience and history: Historical Judaism
    should recognize him as one of its own, just as religious Zionist leaders, of all peo-
    ple, annexed Albert Einstein – a heretic no less "dangerous" than Spinoza in certain
    respects – to Judaism, basking in his aura as they did in that of other famous Jews
    for some comment of Einstein's that they interpreted as recognition of religious
    faith.
76. In this regard, see A. Barzel, *Al mivne ha-yahadut* [On the structure of Judaism]
    (Tel Aviv: Sifriyat Poalim, 1994), pp. 284–289, and the author's debate with Y.
    Yovel, *Spinoza ve-kofrim aherim* [Spinoza and other heretics] (Tel Aviv: Sifriyat
    Poalim, 1988).
77. See *War diary*, vol. 3, p. 109: "The thing we must maintain is Hebrew independence,
    which is not only political but above all moral and intellectual, not to submit to
    the materialistic, ideological glitter of the giants of this world, but to continue to
    travel on our individual path – not out of detachment, estrangement, or distancing
    from the world but not with imitation and subservience either.... Freedom and
    independence begin in the heart.... The greatest thing in Jewish history [is that
    the people] never accepted the decree of outside coercion. Maintaining our moral
    and intellectual freedom is a prerequisite for everything.... Without this freedom,
    a state and all it contains will be useless."
78. Teveth, *Life of the young Ben-Gurion*, vol. 1, p. 74.
79. *Pirqei yoman* [Diary chapters], August 18, 1906, p. 58: "When you look at the
    world, you see all the aspirations drowning in the morass of democracies and all
    power squandered in social squabbling. People born as masters now have no time
    to grow up." Cf. the entry on January 26, 1906, p. 70: "The outcome of the rule
    of the masses is a return to nature, a return to barbarism."
80. See letter Sir Dudley Dunbee, Secretary of Lord Lloyd, British Secretary of the
    Colonies, to the author, Teveth, *The ground is burning*, p. 354. Dunbee had taught
    in Greece, and both men compared ancient Greek terms with modern ones when
    Ben-Gurion spent several months in London in 1940. Dunbee wrote that Ben-
    Gurion's learning at the time was not a form of entertainment on top of his

political dealings with the British: "He did have real interest in ancient Greece and wondered whether Greek ideals could become the ideals of the future [Jewish] state.... Judaism and Hellenism were combined in some strange fashion."

81. All references to Berdyczewski in this book were taken from his archive and published in Hebrew by Professor Avner Holzman under the Hebrew title *Ginzei Micha Yosef* (Tel Aviv: Reshefim) in various installments during the 1980s. Berdyczewski's transformation included pungent criticism of the Western powers and the German pacifists, among them Karl Liebknecht: "Liebknecht – he was either a villain or a fool" (p. 195) for ostensibly having sabotaged German national unity in wartime. Berdyczewski's son Emmanuel was raised as a patriot of imperial Germany.

82. In this regard, two of Heine's sayings are widely quoted: one from *Dat ve-filosofia be-germania* [Religion and philosophy in Germany], and the second from *Nashim ve-na'arot shel Shakespeare* [Shakespeare's women and girls]. I culled both from S. Perlman's translations of these works into the Hebrew (Tel Aviv: 1950, and Tel Aviv: 1954, respectively). The latter quotation seems to deal not with Germany but rather with the fate of the Jews: "If the day comes and victory is attained by the demon, the sinful pantheism from which all the saints of the Old and New Testaments and the Koran have protected us, then a storm of persecution will descend on the heads of the poor Jews, in comparison with which their erstwhile sufferings will be as nothing." The first quote, however, concerns the destruction of Christianity in Germany: "And when the restraining amulet, the cross... is broken, the savagery of the ancient martial Teutons will resurface and rampage.... The spectacle that will present itself in Germany will make the French Revolution seem like an innocent idyll."

83. See Heine, *On Religion and Philosophy in Germany*, trans. Ritchie Robertson, in *The Harz Journey and Selected Prose*, 1993.

84. See B. Cheyette, *Constructions of "The Jew" in English Literature and Society: Racial Representations, 1875–1945* (Cambridge: Cambridge University Press, 1993), pp. 13–21.

85. *Diary chapters*, March 15, 1906: "Let us not fool ourselves: Whatever the Jews created after the Bible dangles like a mass of lead; and not a single ray of light penetrates through it to the heart.... A nightmarish vision of primacy hovers before their eyes, but in truth it lost this claim long ago." Ibid., p. 47; cf. May 9, 1906: "Every time I read the Talmud, I feel again the narrowness of these people's thinking. How limited their view is regarding political matters! They have no sense for things that are the life of the nation. Rabbinic Judaism is like a bird that builds her nest atop an elephant and dares to scorn the elephant." Ibid., p. 15; also cf. Ben-Gurion's wording in a letter to Dr. Chaim Gvariahu, April 10, 1954, *Correspondence*, BGA: "I know the Bible is neither our people's only creation nor its last; our intellectual heritage contains many precious works from the distant and near past. But I do not know of any cultural or educational treasure in our literature or in the literature of any other people that can compare to the Bible. For various reasons, perhaps justified in their own time, the luster of the Bible was dimmed during our walk in exile and to some extent it became a peg on which our people's sages in later generations hung their opinions and demands. To some extent, the image of the Bible was bent so as to tailor it to the beliefs and needs of a time in which we had ceased to be a nation rooted in its homeland and standing on its own authority both politically and spiritually." Berdyczewski himself was inclined to revisit Zionism and view it as the only way to escape his critique of Judaism,

saying in his book *Reshut ha-yahid* [Private domain] (i.e., personal authority),
p. 161, that "If Zionism fails, then Diaspora Jewry will face total annihilation
because they will be left with no foundation, corporeal or intellectual, for spiritual
inquiry of their own."

86. Y. Lossin, *"Heinrich Heine: Yehudi min ha-sug ha-shelishi* [Heinrich Heine: A
Jew of the third kind]," *Ha'aretz* Culture Supplement, December 13, 1996.
87. See A. Shapiro on A. D. Gordon and cf. Avraham Tzivyon on Berl Katznelson,
both in Hebrew.
88. J. L. Sammons, *Heinrich Heine: A Modern Biography* (Princeton, NJ: Princeton
University Press, 1979).
89. *Medinat yisrael ha-mehudeshet* [The renewed Jewish state], vol. 1, pp. 14–15.
90. Keren, op. cit., pp. 65–95.
91. Keren, ibid. See throughout his book, particularly in his discussion of "the Affair."
92. H. Arendt, "Heinrich Heine: The Shlemihl and Lord of Dreams," *Jewish Social
Studies*, 6 (2) (February 1944), pp. 99–122, esp. pp. 100–101.
93. See a rather positive evaluation of Buber's person and motives in G. Scholem,
"Le-demuto shel Martin Buber, shiv'im ve-hamesh le-holadeto [On the figure of
Martin Buber, on the 75th anniversary of his birth]," in *Devarim bego* [Remarks
from within] (Tel Aviv: Am Oved/Ofakim, 1975), p. 46.
94. Ibid, p. 46.
95. Ibid. p. 455.
96. Ibid, p. 457.
97. Ibid, p. 458. Cf. Leo Strauss's letter to Gerhard Scholem dated December 15, 1963,
typed on University of Chicago letterhead (corrections on manuscript), Gershom
Scholem Archive no. 159991 at the National Library in Jerusalem, quoted by
Eugene R. Sheppard, *Leo Strauss and the Politics of Exile: The Making of a
Political Philosopher* (Waltham, MA: Brandeis University Press, 2006), p. 178, n.
22: "But let me say a few words about your *sitra achra*, your admiration for Buber.
I have not overlooked the qualifications but it is still too much for me. I always
loathed him and I still loathe him. I always sensed the absence of genuine.... The
utmost that I am willing to grant is that he is a first-rate perfumer [*sic*]. *His
absolute indifference to historical truth* is perhaps the clearest symptom of his lack
of intellectual honesty which shows itself in his uncontrollable drive for acclaim
and his showmanship [italics added]. If I am not altogether mistaken he is a good
example of what my teachers called 'priest craft' for they meant of course that this
kind of deceiver is also deceived." Continuing, Professor Sheppard added that *sitra
achra* is literally the other side, referring in kabbalistic texts to the devil. In fact,
Scholem had his own doubts about Buber's scholarship, and had him appointed
professor of social philosophy rather than professor of Judaic or religious studies
at Hebrew University, upon his arrival in Jerusalem in 1938.
98. Ibid., pp. 460–461.
99. See Keren for Ben-Gurion's correspondence with Buber and Buber's criticism of
Ben-Gurion on various issues, including bringing Eichmann to trial in Israel and
the Lavon Affair.
100. R. Daherndorf, *Gesellschaft und Demokratie in Deutschland*, as above.
101. Ben-Gurion's diary and speeches from the 1930s and 1940s abound with critical
comments about British colonial rule in India, where he stopped off on his way
back to Palestine after visiting Britain and the United States. Similarly, he criticized
the "high-handed British rulers" (McDonald and Chamberlain) at the Saint James

Conference, which preceded the publication of the White Paper in 1939, and he distinguished between the political and bureaucratic echelons in the Middle East and in London, but recognized the typical working of both as a matter of studying and, to an extent, imitating.

102. Yisrael Kolatt, "Zionism and Messianism," in *Meshihiut ve-eskhatologia* [Messianism and Eschatology], p. 427.

103. To explore this complex issue, which I have abbreviated to less than the requisite minimum, see: Y. Shalmon, *"Ha'imut bein haredim le-maskilim bi-t'nu'at hibat tsiyyon bi-sh'not ha-80* [The conflict between the ultra-Orthodox and the Maskilim in the Hibbat Tsiyyon movement in the 1880s]," *Ha-tsiyyonut*, 5 (1978), pp. 43–77.

104. Regarding the British prohibition of Jewish immigration in 1905 and the roots of his own "Zionist" credo based upon a distinction between "bad" Jews (later on: Bolsheviks) and "good" Jews (such as those who contributed to Britain's economy and imperial power, and later, the Zionists thanks to their nationalist alternative to Bolshevism), see Martin Gilbert, *Churchill and the Jews: A Life-Long Friendship* (mentioned earlier). Yet Churchill appreciated Jewish power inside Britain, as a young member of Parliament from Manchester and, subsequently, to a degree that sounds exaggerated. Later, he ascribed to Zionism a cultural superiority over the Arabs of Palestine, a major contribution to transform it to a modern, civilized country, and a common interest with British imperial ethos and goals in the region. See Michael Makovsky, *Churchill's Promised Land* (mentioned earlier).

105. M. Mintz, *"Leumiyut yehudit u-leumiyut shel mi'utim aherim* [Jewish nationhood and other minorities' nationhood]," (mentioned earlier).

106. The story of Jewish pioneers in the western United States was different, due to the specific conditions under which everyone had to live at first; see in this regard Harriet and Fred Rochlin, *Pioneer Jews, A New Life in the Far West* (New York and Boston: Mariner Books, 2000), and see further, Frances Dinkelspiel, *Towers of Gold: How One Jewish Immigrant Named Isias Hellman Created California* (New York: St. Martin's Press, 2007).

107. S. Esh, "Ha-tsiyyonut ke-teshuva la-be'ayat ha-yehudi ha-moderni – mishnato shel Kurt Blumenfeld [Zionism as an answer to the problem of the modern Jew – the teachings of Kurt Blumenfeld]," *Molad* [Birth] (1964), pp. 181–182.

108. See United States National Archives (NA) Joint Censorship Collection Agency, G-2 Palestine files, box 3027, envelope 3000–3020 Pal. submitted by R. Cutler, Assistant Reporting Officer, letter dated March 18, 1943, from Dr. G. Landauer, Central Bureau for the Settlement of German Jews, Jewish Agency, to Kurt Blumenfeld in New York. Landauer argues there against the Biltmore Plan, as if it had proposed the establishment of a "wretched" Jewish state instead of Herzl's grand vision that preceded the slaughter of the Jews in the Holocaust. He did not spare criticism, castigating the Mapai leadership and its partners for their patronizing behavior toward the German-Jewish immigrants (whom he also scorned). However, he also wished that they would act more forcefully toward the voluntary Yishuv in areas that mattered to him, including enlistment in the British Army and action against forms of corruption, such as war profiteering. These attitudes ultimately prompted Landauer, a member of the Jewish Agency Executive and one of the earliest German immigrants, to resign from political life in the Yishuv and to disappear from the landscape of the nascent State of Israel. See Rimmer, *Peretz Naftali*.

109. See Ben-Gurion, *Pa'amei medina* [Steps toward statehood], pp. 201–301, speech
     in Mapai Central Committee, April 26, 1947: "The 'sin' of bringing the extremes
     together in a coalition – I have been committing it for fourteen years; I don't know
     if I've ever done anything else. It's the only thing I do in the Executive – keeping
     it from falling apart. . . . I do it all the time, because by compromising the main
     thing can be maintained – and the main thing for me is the unity of the Zionist
     movement, the unity of the Zionist movement for a purpose. The purpose may
     change each time – this time it's a Jewish state. If it is impossible to maintain unity
     for the sake of a state, I'll quit the Executive." One may add that if it were not
     possible, in due course, to develop and perfect the system of government so that
     it would be worthy of a soundly functioning state, he would quit the government,
     as indeed he did.
110. See *Steps toward statehood*, Chap. 5: "Likhbosh ha-arets, kula o helqa [To con-
     quer the land, all or part]." The question of how deeply to enter the West Bank
     during the War of Independence, whether to occupy the entire area or part of the
     mountain range, including Nablus and Ramallah, in order to assure Israel's claims
     in Jerusalem, as expressed in *War diary* after the fact, is too serious and intricate
     an issue to be glossed over here; we return to it in the course of our discussion.
111. *Steps toward statehood*, speech to moshav members, November 1, 1947, p. 452.
112. See Ben-Gurion's farewell broadcast on December 7, 1953, the day he resigned
     and left for Sede Boqer: D. Ben-Gurion, *Devarim e-havayatam* (Things as they
     are) (Tel Aviv: Am Hasefer, 1965), p. 11: "We undertook a titanic three-level
     struggle: *a struggle with ourselves* [emphasis in original], with the Diaspora tem-
     perament, with unproductive habits, and with the defective structure of life of a
     people with no homeland, dispersed and dependent on the kindness of strangers;
     a struggle with the nature of the land [emphasis in original], its desolation, poverty,
     and destruction by man and heaven; *a struggle with the forces of evil and malice*
     [emphasis in original] in the wide world both near and far, which neither under-
     stands nor wishes to understand the wondrous uniqueness and destiny of our
     people from the time it first stepped onto the stage of history in ancient times to
     our very day."
113. This complex issue will occupy us later. In the meantime, see A. Bareli,
     "Mamlakhtiut u-t'nuat ha-avoda be-reishit shenot hahamishim: Hanahot mivniot
     [Statism and the labor movement in the early 1950s: Structural assumptions]," a
     manuscript accepted for a collection edited by Mordechai Bar-On on theory and
     practice in the early 1950s.
114. See Hanna Yablonka, *Ahim zarim: Qelitat nitsolei ha-sho'ah bi-medinat yisrael
     1948–1952* [Alien brethren: The absorption of Holocaust survivors in the State of
     Israel 1948–1952] (Jerusalem: Yad Izhak Ben-Zvi, 1994).
115. An echo of the comparison that stuck to Ben-Gurion as a mimic of Lenin or
     Hitler – a comparison that was rife among the British during World War II, as
     we will show – is audible in the writings of Paul Johnson, a British leftist who
     moved right and become a sworn Thatcherite (*Modern Times: The World From
     the Twenties to the Eighties* (New York: Harper & Row, 1983). Ben-Gurion,
     Johnson said, "expressed a deterministic view – unlike [Dr. Chaim] Weizmann,
     who recognized the choice between the injustice that would be done to the Arabs
     if a Jewish state arose in Palestine and the greater injustice that would occur
     should the country be denied to the Jews. History has decreed that we must return
     to our land and establish a Jewish state here," Johnson quotes Ben-Gurion as

stating. By so saying, according to Johnson, Ben-Gurion was speaking in Lenin's or Hitler's voice. There is no one called History, says Johnson; it is people who decide. Needless to say, Ben-Gurion was not at all sure that "history" itself would found a state for the Jews. Instead, he believed that Jewish history has a moral force and a collective memory according to which human beings called Jews are meant to be impelled by their force to establish a sovereign state in this historic land or part of it.

116. S. P. Huntington, "The West: Unique, Not Universal," *Foreign Affairs* (November–December 1996), pp. 28–46.

117. Consult the work of the neo-Marxist historian F. M. L. Thompson, particularly *The Rise of Respectable Society: A Social History of Britain, 1830–1900* (Cambridge, MA: Harvard University Press, 1988).

118. Conspicuous in this regard was the Socialist British writer and politician Beatrice Webb, a leader of the Fabian Society and, later in her life, wife of Sidney Webb, the future Lord Passfield. To this day, the Passfields – although both of them, particularly Beatrice Webb, supported Stalin's Soviet Union in their later years – are considered key figures in the Anglophone Left. They founded, among other things, the London School of Economics, where the historian Arnold Toynbee was active for many years and in the 1930s became, like them, a staunch opponent of Zionism. Lord Passfield, the colonial secretary in MacDonald's government in the early the 1930s, published the first anti-Zionist White Paper after Britain received its Mandate for Palestine. Lady Passfield was even more critical of Judaism and, in particular, of Zionism. See discussion based on her published writings and journal in Y. Gorny, "Yahadut ve-tziyyonut be-hashqafata shel Beatrice Webb [Judaism and Zionism in the thinking of Beatrice Webb]," *Zionism* 5 (1978), pp. 115–140. The late Professor Edmond Silberner ("Webb, Sidney James and Beatrice," *Hebrew Encyclopedia*, vol. 15, pp. 751–752) had the following to say about the Webbs: "In the autumn of 1887, Beatrice Webb investigated the conditions in the sweatshops in East London and, among other things, came to the conclusion that passion for profit was the strongest motive among the Jewish race. True . . . the Jewish immigrant was blessed with exalted virtues but lacks the greatest virtue of the human spirit, the social ethic. . . . Jewish workers are neither capable of nor interested in unionizing. . . . Jews [strive] for success only by means of competition, and their typical style of competition has neither inhibitions nor limits rooted in appreciation of the value of humankind, class loyalty, and professional integrity." In the first two editions of their book *History of Trade Unionism*, which became a basic text in this field in the late nineteenth and early twentieth centuries, the Webbs omitted all mention of Jewish trade unions and even ignored the many strikes that Jewish workers conducted in England. In their book *Industrial Democracy*, they expressed the opinion that Jewish immigrants to England from Eastern Europe were a permanent source of degenerate influence on the British public. However, antisemitism was a fixture not only among the liberal-left elite but also among the public at large. In this regard, see also Thompson, *The Rise of Respectable Society*.

119. See Ben-Gurion letter February 2, 1958, to Joshua, brother of the late Dr. Yisrael Kasztner, State Archives, Doc. 1366/5432/C. He explains in the letter that all public discussion of the Holocaust in Hungary at this time would fall prey to political motives and that, therefore, it was better to leave the final decision to historians who were free of such motives. See Y. Weitz, *Ha-ish she-nirtsah pa'amayim: Hayyav, mishpato ve-moto shel Dr. Yisrael Kasztner* [The man who was murdered

twice: The life, trial, and death of Dr. Yisrael Kasztner] (Jerusalem: Keter, 1995), p. 346 and note. Weitz belittles this assertion, which was the crux of Ben-Gurion's letter, and in fact hardly mentions it. Instead, he criticizes Ben-Gurion, who added in his letter that he himself had not been well versed in rescue matters at the time and that, for this reason, "I would not take upon myself to determine the facts."

120. As some did. Contributors to this interpretation, with various nuances, were Shmuel Tamir of Herut, who besmirched Mapai at the Kasztner trial and indirectly led to his assassination; Orthodox leaders who used the Slovakian Holocaust affair for this purpose; the Orthodox rescue activist Rabbi Michoel Ber Weissmandel in the writings that he left behind, published posthumously as *Min ha-metsar* [From the distress] (Bnei Brak: private publisher, 1955); and contemporaneous authors: Y. Elam, *Memalei ha-pequdot* [The fulfillers of orders] (Jerusalem: Keter, 1990); T. Segev, *The Seventh Million: The Israelis and the Holocaust*, trans. Haim Watzman (New York: Hill and Wang, 1993); and I. Zertal, *Zahavam shel ha-yehudim: Ha-hagira ha-yehudit ha-mahtartit le-erets yisrael 1945–1948* [The gold of the Jews: Underground Jewish immigration to the land of Israel, 1945–1948] (Tel Aviv: Am Oved, 1996) and *Ha-shoa veha-mavet* [The Holocaust and death: History, memory, politics] (Tel-Aviv: Dvir, 2003). And cf. critique by Elhanan Yakira, *Post tsiyyonut, post sho'ah* [Post Zionism, post Holocaust: Three chapters on denial, forgetting, and the negation of Israel] (Tel-Aviv: Am Oved, 2006), English translation published by Cambridge University Press, New York, 2009. On the self-serving use of the Holocaust by various post-Zionist authors, see my article, "Al ha-post-tsiyyonut ve-ha-masoret ha-antishemit ba-ma'arav [On post-Zionism and the antisemitic tradition in the West]," in *Iyunim bi-tequmat yisrael – tsiyyonut: Pulmos ben zemanenu* [Studies on the Jewish rebirth – Zionism: A contemporary polemic] (Beer-Sheva: Ben Gurion University, 1996). See also my article, "The Post Zionist Discourse and Critique of Israel: A Traditional Zionist Perspective," *Israel Studies*, 8 (1) (Spring 2003), pp. 105–129.

2. The Holocaust and Its Lessons

1. A part of the documentation underlying this chapter that deals with the Holocaust appears in greater detail in my book, *Hitler, the Allies, and the Jews* (New York: Cambridge University Press, 2006). However, that book dealt with the period of 1933–1945 only. Here and in the ensuing chapters the time frame has been broadened, with the relevant documentation, to the period between 1919 and the post-Holocaust reality of Israel.

2. In his book *She'at ha-efes* [Zero hour] (Jerusalem: Edanim, 1980), A. Elon attempted to draw a seemingly sophisticated distinction between Moshe Shertok (Sharett), who at least did everything he could for the rescue, and Ben-Gurion, who seemingly did nothing. T. Segev developed this claim into a general indictment of the entire Yishuv leadership, and of Ben-Gurion in particular, in his book *The Seventh Million*. For another expression of this sort of attack – unrelated to the Holocaust for the time being – see Z. Sternhell, *Nation-Building or a New Society? The Zionist Labor Movement (1904–1940) and the Origins of Israel* (Tel Aviv: Am Oved, 1995).

3. See Rimmer, *Peretz Naphtali*, pp. 207–208, regarding the Landauer-Mapai dispute in the autumn of 1940, specifically Shazar's reply to Landauer, "which [was] typical of the paternalistic approach of veteran Mapai leaders toward German

immigrants and their absorption in the Yishuv." The gist of the dispute is described later in the chapter.

4. See H. Yablonka's serial study, "The Commander of the 'Yizkor' Order: Herzl, Holocaust and Survivors," in N. Lucas and S. I. Troen (eds.), *Israel: The First Decade of Independence* (Albany: State University of New York Press, 1996), pp. 211*ff*.

5. See Rimmer, op. cit., pp. 199*ff*. The subject of the Association of German Immigrants and the establishment of the Aliyah Hadasha party is discussed later.

6. See Ben-Gurion, *Memoirs from the estate*, vol. 6, p. 270, Ben-Gurion's speech to the council of the World Association of Po'alei Zion, April 26, 1939: "This is how movements are, just as this is how people are: Their understanding always lags behind events. Thinking depends on inertia, routine, habit. . . . Thinking is always lazy and it assumes that whatever was will be, which is not the case with events. It is true that events also have inertia, but they also have dynamics, and life and nature are always full of clashes, struggles between forces; the world does not stand still, history does not stand still, nature and mankind do not stand still, but people's thinking generally lags, and when at a given time a given system starts to collapse, people's thinking still refuses to see it because that would obligate it to greater efforts to find new paths, and that is hard, since people have a limited amount of energy; they have to invest it in the struggle for existence and cannot turn their thoughts to see the changes in history." This criticism of the mental and behavioral inertia that afflicts most people, including his own colleagues and subordinates, remained fundamental in Ben-Gurion's thinking and behavior even after World War II and would be applied vis-à-vis the Hagana and in discussions with IDF officers, as we will show.

7. See M. Sharett, *Yoman medini* [Political diary] (Tel Aviv: Sifriyat Ma'ariv, 1968). In his remarks, Moshe Sharett, director of the Jewish Agency Political Department in 1936, reflects this Zionist perception of the British before Lord Peel's Royal Commission reached the country. For the subsequent period, see *Memoirs from the estate*, particularly vol. 6.

8. Ben-Gurion, "Ha-gola ve-ha-yishuv [The diaspora and the Yishuv]," *Ba-ma'arakha*, 3, February 26, 1941.

9. See "Metihut tsiyyonit, devarim be-mo'etset Mapai [Zionist tension, remarks before the Mapai council]," *Ba-ma'arakha*, 3, March 5–8, 1941.

10. Ibid., p. 58.

11. Regarding the severity of American antisemitism from the early 1920s, its religio-historical roots, and its attainment of plague-like magnitudes in the 1930s and 1940s, see L. Dinnerstein, *Antisemitism in America* (New York: Oxford University Press, 1994).

12. On liberal antisemitism and the uncertainty about the future of parliamentary democracy in view of the crises of the twentieth century, see B. Cheyette, *Construction of "The Jew" in English Society*.

13. In regard to Beaverbrook and his concern that the Jews were dragging Britain into their war against Nazi Germany, see T. Kushner, *The Persistence of Prejudice: Antisemitism in British Society during the Second World War* (Manchester and New York: Manchester University Press, 1989), p. 12. The dispute over the goals of the war as reflected in his concerns persisted afterwards as well. One of its manifestations may be found in the work of J. F. C. Fuller, a renowned British military personality and a forefather of modern armored warfare: J. F. C. Fuller,

A Military History of the Western World, vol. 3 (New York: Funk & Wagnalls, 1956), pp. 374–376. Fuller did not flinch from suggesting, even after the Holocaust, that the British government had been snared in a "Jewish crusade" against the Third Reich instead of allowing the two great totalitarian powers on the continent – Nazi Germany and Soviet Russia – to destroy each other and to step in at the end, at the appropriate time, for the sake of good old British interests, as had been Britain's practice throughout its history. Fuller was by no means an inconsequential figure; even though he had been considered a dangerous pro-German "appeaser" in his time, the British government could not ignore his allegations – which, in his aforementioned book, he based on antisemitic Polish and Nazi sources – and had to avoid providing him and his like with pro-Jewish ammunition during the war.

14. It is within this context that one must contemplate Chamberlain's appeasement policy, which was preceded by the pursuit of a vigorous internal reform policy by Prime Minister Stanley Baldwin. The reform greatly improved living conditions in Britain and, by so doing, surmounted the economic crisis of the early 1930s. See Johnson, *Modern Times* (Chap. 1, n. 109), pp. 309–312, 336. See also discussion of pacifist and radical influences on the fickle English public opinion of that time. As for British antisemitism and its severity in the 1930s, see Kushner, *Persistence of Prejudice*, pp. 78–105. Here a fatal nexus took shape between the Bolshevik Revolution in Russia, which in British circles was widely depicted as a "Jewish revolution," and the crisis of the Western elites at the end of World War I. The London *Times* exposé of the *Protocols of the Elders of Zion* as a forgery in 1921 did not reverse the association of Judaism with Bolshevism and, in turn, Judaism's threat to the existing social order – a connection that was widely held among the conservative elite of the time. Kushner (op. cit., pp. 93–94) notes that the ideas of H. G. Wells were often quoted in attacks on Jewish exclusivity. In Wells's universalistic world, says Kushner, any idea of a "chosen people" was anathema. Wells was not originally interested in Nazi antisemitism; afterwards, however, he saw it as a reaction to the Jewish pretension to be a "chosen people." While Wells's influence as a Socialist faded with the escalation of World War II, Kushner continues, his attitude toward the Jews seems to have gained popular support. Moreover, when Gen. Sikorski of Poland quoted Wells to the effect that the Jews must not be addressed as a nation, for by so doing the West would be playing the Nazis' game, the Foreign Office and Ministry of Information fully agreed. According to Kushner, other radical Socialists, such as George Bernard Shaw and George Orwell, completely agreed with Wells in his criticism of Jewish exclusivity. Shaw argued on several occasions during the war that Nazi antisemitism was a natural outgrowth of the Mosaic faith.

15. Such was the belief of the American ambassador in London, Joseph P. Kennedy, and Chamberlain himself. Arthur Schlesinger, the Kennedy family historian, quotes Chamberlain as saying that Ambassador Kennedy told former U.S. President Herbert Hoover, in the name of the British prime minister, that Chamberlain saw the issue of a British guarantee to Poland as giving satisfaction to the Jews, which might "seal the fate of civilization." See A. M. Schlesinger, Jr., *Robert Kennedy and His Times* (Boston: Houghton Mifflin, 1978), pp. 34–84; cf. W. W. Kaufman, "Two American Ambassadors: Bullitt and Kennedy," in G. Craig and F. Gilbert (eds.), *The Diplomats, 1919–1939*, (Princeton, NJ: Princeton University Press, 1953).

16. U.S. National Archives, abbreviated NG, RG 165, Records of the War Department, General and Special Staffs, Military Intelligence Division, Regional File, folder 3030–3040 Palestine, Prepared by MI2, Positive Branch, Military Intelligence Division, General Staff.
17. Cf. *The Protocols of the Wise Men of Zion* (New York: Beckwith, 1920) and, for systematic scholarly discussion of the *Protocols*, N. Cohn: *Warrant for Genocide: The Myth of the Jewish World Conspiracy and the Protocols of the Elders of Zion* (New York: Harper & Row, 1967).
18. The newspaper was the *Dearborn Independent* and the affair, the best known of its kind at the time, led to an American Jewish boycott of Ford products and eventually prompted Ford to apologize. See Cohn, op. cit., pp. 158–162, 164, and cf. L. Dinnerstein, *Antisemitism in America*, pp. xxvii, 80–83, 102, 111–112, 115, 136, 163, 226, 236. Not only did the inquirers denounce Trotsky, Zinoviev, Kamenev, Karl Radek, and Rosa Luxemburg for threatening to "take over the world," but they also made Theodor Herzl himself into an antidemocratic subversive and claimed that after comparing his writings with the *Protocols*, they could scent the spirit of the latter in the former – a charge that prompted the intelligence people to reopen their examination. We do not know what conclusions, if any, they drew. See Extracts from the Secret Zionist Protocols and Substantiations of these Extracts from Jewish and pro-Jewish Sources, NA, RG 165 as in n. 16 of this chapter, folder 3030–3040, 1920, p. xxvii.
19. See biography of Parvus: Z. A. B. Zeman and W. B. Sherlau, *The Merchant of Revolution* (London: W. & J. Mackay, 1965).
20. See biography of Trebitsch-Lincoln: B. Wasserstein, *The Secret Lives of Trebitsch Lincoln* (New Haven, CT: Yale University Press, 1988).
21. NA, RG 165, Entry 77, box 2726, Palestine, Doc. 3700.
22. Ibid., source titled "M.A." Switzerland, #2442-Dec. 6, 1920.
23. Report on "Jewry from psychologic, environmental, physical, and racial points of view." Ibid., source not cited in further detail.
24. T. B. Veblen, "The Intellectual Preeminence of Jews in Europe," *Political Science Quarterly*, 34 (1919): "Only by escaping from his cultural environment could the gifted Jew – a naturalized, though hyphenate, citizen in the Gentile republic of learning – come to his own as a creative leader. It is by loss of allegiance, or at the best by force of a divided allegiance to the people of his origin that he finds himself in the vanguard of modern inquiry." Veblen's claim may have fallen on the accepting ears of one of his most prominent admirers, the influential journalist Walter Lippmann, who as a young man had written slanderously about the economic behavior of Jews of East European origin in the United States. Afterwards, including at the peak of the Holocaust, he avoided all comment about the Jews' affairs. By then, of course, sundry antisemites were perceiving him as emblematic of Jewish influence in America. See R. Steel, *Walter Lippmann and the American Century* (New York: Vintage Books, 1981), especially pp. 186–196. According to Steel (p. 189), Lippmann, in an article that he published in the *New Republic*, took the view that the persecution of Jews had created the ghettos, Zionism, and also the Jew's bad economic habits and his exploitation of simple folk, which caused his victims to stress their nationality.
25. See T. Sjøberg, *The Powers and the Persecuted: The Refugee Problem and the Intergovernmental Committee on Refugees* (Lund: Lund University Press, 1991). Sjøberg's study, the last in a lengthy series of works that tackled this issue, sheds

powerful light on Roosevelt's political considerations in calling the Evian Conference in 1938. His main goal, according to Sjøberg, was to begin extricating
the United States from its isolationism and not to alleviate the plight of the Jewish refugees. Sjøberg also presents important data on congressional opposition to
Jewish immigration and the reasons for it, which traced in part to public opinion
polls.

26. See n. 23 in this chapter in respect to this paraphrase and all others that are credited
to the "authors of the American study."

27. Most of the information, twisted to fit the authors' purposes, was taken from
Maurice Fishberg's *Jews, Race, and Environment*, first published in 1911 (London:
Walter Scott). In fact, Fishberg argued against jumping to conclusions about "brain
research" of the kind adopted by the MID authors, and stressed the variety of
Jewish communities against the perception of common Jewish traits. His book was
republished in 2006 with a new introduction by William H. Helmreich (New York:
Transaction Books).

28. Here I first call the reader's attention to the reports of the American intelligence
agent Harold Glidden, alias Robert Laing, who served in Palestine during World
War II. I traced his name by studying NA, RG 226, Entry 108, Cairo boxes, Box
83, Index of OSS Code Names and Numbers. I also corresponded with Mr. Glidden
in the late 1980s and attempted to interview him. He refused, even though in a
telephone conversation he expressed an interest in Israel's troubles with the Palestinians at the time. Agent "Laing" wrote a thick report about the Palestine problem
and the Zionists in August 1943 and forwarded it to British political intelligence, as
quoted from an OSS summary report about developments in the Middle East at the
time (Report 185). Brigadier Iltid N. Clayton, chief of British political intelligence
in the Middle East (PICME) at the time, was eager to publish Laing's report in
the United States. See June 1943 Bulletin No. 2 from British Political Intelligence
Center, Cairo, Egypt: "Ben-Gurion remains fanatically nationalistic.... Further
confirmation has been received of the intention of Hagana to play a large part in
Palestine politics." August 12, 1943: "PICME fears armed outbreak in Palestine
if Britain and U.S. declare in favor of Jewish Political State. Danger of attacks
on Jewish property developing into Anti-Christian and Anti-foreign riots. Military
transients will require convoy under guard. Serious political and economic effects
inevitable." August 14, 1943: "Teheran states in event of armed conflict between
Arabs and Jews in Palestine, Moslems would stage Anti-Jewish riots and distur-
bances. Iraq government would assist Arabs"; cf. R&A Psychological Warfare
Roundup, Europe-Africa Division, Near East-African Section 1090.3, April 17,
1943 [authored by Glidden], p. 20: "Psychologically our position among Arabs
very poor.... We have to convince the Arabs that they'll get a fair deal vis-a-vis
Jews at peace table"; cf. No. 1090.11, June 1–7, 1943 [authored by Glidden]:
"Jews are not fighting for U.S. or Britain but for themselves"; cf. report 1090.16,
July 6–13, 1943 [undisclosed author]: "Shertok impressed with advice of British
friends not to confuse question of rescue of European Jews with Zionist demands,
as was attempted at time of Bermuda Conf."; cf. British High Commissioner for
Palestine Sir Harold MacMichael's "Note on Jewish Illegal Organizations, Their
Activities and Finances," FO 371/31375 E2026, and MacMichael's introductory
letter to the note, October 16, 1941, sent to Colonial Secretary Lord Moyne.

This summary is based on reports from British Intelligence in Palestine and sum-
maries from British MI agencies in the Middle East that were first presented to the

Mandatory government. Most of these intelligence reports are available today in Div. 47 of the Hagana Archives.

29. There is some truth to this image with respect to the behavior of various Mapai personalities in education and economic affairs during Israel's early years. However, it does not explain the reasons for their behavior and Ben-Gurion's own attitudes toward these issues. It is unfit for even metaphorical use in respect of the Yishuv period; instead, it had an effect not only in the minds of Mapai's political rivals at the time but also in the eyes of a broader public, including contemporaneous intellectuals who wish to reform Israel's political system, such as Professor Uriel Reichmann, progenitor of the (since repealed) Direct Election of the Prime Minister Law. See G. Bechor, *Huqa le-yisrael* [A constitution for Israel] (Tel Aviv: Ma'ariv, 1996), Introduction.

30. To gain an understanding of this "constructivism," the most important study to consult is Horowitz and Lissak, *Mi-yishuv le-medina* [From Yishuv to state]. With respect to the mainstream's uncertainties about how to relate to the Arabs, cf. Y. Gorny, *Ha-she'ela ha-aravit ve-ha-be'aya ha-yehudit: Zeramim medini'im-ideologi'im ba-tsiyyonut be-yahasam el ha-yeshut ha-aravit be-erets yisrael ba-shanim 1882–1948* [The Arab question and the Jewish problem: Political and ideological trends in Zionism in relating to the Arab entity in Palestine 1882–1948] (Tel Aviv: Am Oved, 1985).

31. See Z. Sternhell, *Founding Myths of Israel: Nationalism, Socialism, and the Making of the Jewish State* (Princeton, NJ: Princeton University Press, 1998) and cf. A. Shapira's critique, "Sternhell's Complaint," in *Studies on the Jewish rebirth*, vol. 6 (1996), pp. 553–567, cf. Sternhell interview in *Ha'aretz* weekly magazine, March 7, 2008.

32. "The corollary of this [a new one] was that the gentlemanly ethic need only apply among gentlemen; which acted as a release for the amoral energies that may have been particularly strong in the sort of men and women who undertook secret service work. They justified their amorality in two ways. The first was that national survival depended on it: During the First World War . . . because of the 'total' nature of it; and against the Red menace, which was also 'total,' although in a different [ideological] sense. The second was that the enemy was acting even more amorally, which made it necessary to respond in kind." B. Porter, *Plots and Paranoia: A History of Political Espionage in Britain 1790–1988* (London and New York: Routledge, 1992), p. 170.

33. An instructive example of this brand of German Zionism is captured in the persona of Peretz (Fritz) Naftali, as described in Yehuda Rimmer's biography. Naphtali's devotion to the tradition of his political cradle, the German Social-Democratic Party (SPD), in which he had been a leading exponent in economic and social affairs, prompted him to merge with Mapai and pledge allegiance to it and its leaders at this time, even though he had no profound connection to Eretz Israel and Zionism. In contrast to him was George Landauer, a German Zionist of great merit whose loyalties to Zionism, the Yishuv leadership, and Mapai slackened somewhat at the climax of the crisis of World War II, which he perceived as a greater drama than a solely Jewish issue could be. Ultimately, Landauer established a German immigrants' party that rivaled the principal Yishuv parties and reflected less intensive Zionist orientation. Naphtali fought Landauer with all his strength, for reasons including the tradition of the SPD and the lessons he had learned from its internal schisms, and not only his Zionist consciousness.

34. For a thorough and detailed discussion of this issue and other matters related to joining the British Army and its extensions, see Y. Gelber, *Toldot ha-hitnadvut* [History of volunteering], 4 vols. (Jerusalem: Yad Izhak Ben-Zvi, 1979–1985).

35. See A. Shapira (n. 31 in this chapter), in a recent article that analyzes Ze'ev Sternhell's allegation that the Mapai leadership abandoned social reform in favor of nation-building as soon as it ostensibly had the tools and the time to accomplish this.

36. On this complex topic, see Avizohar, *In a cracked mirror*, pp. 201–203, and A. Shapira, *Berl*, vol. 2, pp. 470*ff.*

37. See publications of Min ha-Yesod and cf. Keren, *Ben-Gurion and the Intellectuals*, pp. 94*ff.*

38. See Mintz, *Friend and foe: Yitzhak Tabenkin and the Po'alei Zion party*. The residues of the past are evident in the opinions of historians who were raised in Ha-Shomer ha-Tsa'ir, such as Idith Zertal, and in the political behavior of several leaders of Peace Now, whose origins trace to this movement or the "Hebrew Communists." An example is Asher Reshef, a well-to-do Jerusalem businessman who did a great deal of behind-the-scenes action in this and other fields and was among Ben-Gurion's opponents. After World War II began, Ha-Shomer ha-Tsa'ir and the other left-wing parties embraced a hostile attitude toward the West and, especially, the United States, for pro-Soviet and anti-imperialist ideological reasons. During the war, these parties defeated their members' wish to join the British Army and rejected Ben-Gurion's immediate quest for independence during and after the war. Ultimately, Ha-Shomer ha-Tsa'ir sided with Ben-Gurion due to its disagreements with Ben-Gurion's rival in the Zionist Movement at the time, Dr. Chaim Weizmann. See Tzahor, *Hazan – a movement of life*.

39. Interview by the author with Arthur Goldberg, former U.S. Supreme Court associate justice and ambassador to the United Nations, quoted in detail in my book *Hitler, the Allies, and the Jews*, 2004 edition, p. 123. Goldberg, who described his young years in Chicago of the 1930s in this fashion, became an attorney who specialized in trade union affairs. It was as such that he was recruited for the OSS in 1940 as liaison with Europe's Social Democratic Parties. He was involved in the Zionist attempts, engineered by Weizmann and Ben-Gurion, to establish contact with the OSS and place the Zionist networks in occupied Europe at its disposal – a wholly unrealistic idea, of course. Afterwards, he went over to the OSS branch in London as chargé of the desk responsible for labor movements in occupied Europe; in this capacity, he immersed himself totally in the "war on Fascism." For this reason, by his own account, he took no special interest in the Holocaust until the war was further along. In the summer of 1944, he resigned from the OSS and returned to Chicago for various reasons, including his feeling that the Allied breakthrough in Normandy spelled the end of the war. At that time, the German surrender was still some nine months away and the Holocaust was roaring ahead with hardly a lapse.

40. In this matter, see Y. Slutzky's multivolume study, *Toldot ha-hagana* [History of the Hagana], published in Tel Aviv in the 1950s and the 1960s. Note Slutzky's assertion that the "civilian" (not politically organized) city of Tel Aviv mobilized sluggishly for the Yishuv's defense effort, prompted by and in the aftermath of the "events," as the Arab violence was called; note the memoirs of Eliahu Sakharov, a key official in the Hagana and the signal and procurements system of the Hagana and its successor, the fledgling IDF, unpublished but made available to me:

"I think I wouldn't be disserving the truth if I were to define that era, the 1930s and 1940s, as a heroic time in the history of the Yishuv, a time that left a deep imprint on our personal development and shaped our world of values, a time typified by manifestations of willingness to sacrifice, pioneering, volunteering spirit, and passionate desire to serve the nation in disregard of materialism, economic enticements, careerism, and pursuit of an easy and hedonistic life." One can recognize in these remarks the dominant sense of superiority that this elite, specifically its younger members, entertained toward others, including Jews who had not immigrated to Palestine earlier and now were going like "lambs to the slaughter."

41. See memoirs of Y. Almogi, *Be-rosh muram: Hayalim erets-yisraeli'im ba-shvi ha-nazi* [With a raised head: Palestinian [Jewish] soldiers in Nazi captivity] (Tel Aviv: Ministry of Defense, 1989), p. 36: "The total count [of prisoners who fell into German hands in Greece] added up to around 1,500 people. Some 200 of them were 'Sokhnutniks,' i.e., Palestinian volunteers who had enlisted in response to the call of the Jewish Agency [Heb: *sokhnut*, 'agency']. Another group... of 200–300 men was made up of inductees who had reached the British Army from the fringes of society in Palestine – adventurers who hoped to find a release for their urges in the ranks of the army and scraping-by types who had no better way of making a living in the civilian market and were displeased with the organized Yishuv. All the others were recent immigrants who enlisted as soon as they reached Palestine"; and on p. 55: "Those of us who had retained their wits understood... that you had to behave responsibly and maintain your dignity not only toward the Germans but also internally, among the POWs. Also, however, we were not lacking for types who belittled the whole thing. There were Palestinians [Jews] who gravitated to the Sokhnutniks' side during the crisis of being taken prisoner.... It was obvious to them that we all had to behave with unity.... Now that we had seemed to arrive at a permanent place of respite [a regular POW camp, and when it was recognized that the Jewish prisoners' rights were equal to those of the British], the level of fear declined a little and the prisoners discovered that the POW camp was in some way part of the great world, that it even had opportunities for easy profiteering. Then they thought they could return to their vile ways. The conditions created a convenient background for dubious dealings and gave birth to a 'black market.' Commodities in demand that had run out were peddled at exorbitant prices.... There were the card games, too,... and the losers, who were sometimes stripped of their last cent... sometimes entangled themselves in crime.... Some told me, 'What's it to you? We have different pleasures in life from yours and the Sokhnutniks – you like books and we like cards. We're not trying to educate you, so don't try to educate us.'" The former group, led by Sgt. Almogi, displayed exemplary discipline and together withstood the hardships of captivity. The others did as they pleased, played cards, cheated one another, and tried to swindle the camp authorities. When Almogi moved on to another camp, the behavior of these Jewish prisoners destroyed discipline in the previous camp, and the camp commander threatened to restore it by executing a few of them. A German officer of the old school stepped in and had Almogi brought back to the camp in order to impose order there – a form of order that people today might call "Mapainik" or even "Bolshevik." Almogi would become Mapai's party "boss" in Haifa after the war, and its secretary general during the Lavon Affair.

42. See correspondence between the members of the Rescue Committee in Budapest, Samu (Samuel) Springman, Joel Brand, and Dr. Yisrael Kasztner, with the Zionist

Rescue Mission (Moladeti) in Istanbul, in Hagana Archives: Rescue Committee Documents, Files 1–10. Copies of the correspondence were sent from Istanbul to the Jewish Agency in Jerusalem, and since most were written in German they were first read by Teddy Kollek, who had been with the Jewish Agency Political Department since late 1943. Many of the documents also carried the signatures of Ben-Gurion and Eliahu Dobkin, head of the Agency's Immigration Department.

43. For a detailed description of the establishment of this mission, relations among its members, and its relations with the various entities that had sent it to Istanbul, based on unclassified Zionist archive sources, see Dina Porat, *The Blue and Yellow Stars of David: The Zionist Leadership in Palestine and the Holocaust 1939–45* (Cambridge, MA: Harvard University Press, 1990). A more up-to-date account of the vacillations of the leadership in Palestine, and especially of Ben-Gurion himself, based on his archives, is available in T. Friling, "David Ben-Gurion ve-sho'at yahadut europa" [David Ben-Gurion and the Holocaust of European Jewry] (Ph.D. diss., the Hebrew University of Jerusalem, 1990), and in his book, based on this dissertation and other sources: *Hetz ba-arafel* [Arrows in the dark: David Ben-Gurion, the Yishuv leadership, and rescue efforts during the Holocaust] (Beer Sheva and Sede Boqer: Ben-Gurion Heritage Center/Tel Aviv University/Ben Gurion University, 1998; English translation published by University of Wisconsin Press, 2005).

44. See D. Porat, *Hanhaga be-milkud: Ha-yishuv nochach ha-sho'ah 1942–1945* [A leadership trapped: The Yishuv facing the Holocaust 1942–1945] (Tel Aviv: Am Oved, 1986), p. 229. See also Porat's *The Blue and the Yellow Stars of David*.

45. Archive source: NG, G-2 Palestine box 2724, evaluated "A-2" (usually the highest evaluation).

46. See D. S. Wyman, *The Abandonment of the Jews: America and the Holocaust 1941–1945* (New York: Pantheon, 1984, Hebrew translation 1990), pp. 113–120 on the period between 1941 and the Bermuda Conference in April 1943.

47. On British stances, see B. Wasserstein, *Britain and the Jews of Europe 1939–1945* (Oxford: Oxford University Press, 1979), pp. 183–221.

48. For the British complex at the time, Wasserstein, op. cit., pp. 183-221.

49. Central Zionist Archive (CZA) – Jerusalem, file S25/7570), dated March 4, 1943.

50. See report by Reuven Zaslany-Shiloah about his actions, Jerusalem, November 27, 1944, Central Zionist Archives Division S25, Doc. 1205.

51. Cf. NG, RG 226, Entry 120, Box 31-7, File TC 319.1, Origin: Cairo, Subject: Jewish Fighting Force for Europe, date: September, 16, 1944, Sender: Captain Habeeb, Theater Censor, secret, contains list of cables from and to Shertok re "Jewish Partisan Groups for the Balkans," difficulties with the [British] authorities.

52. RG 226, Entry 88, Box 495, Wash-Commo-R+C-381–382, London-Bern-Ankara-Istanbul; the box also contains documents from OSS substations in Izmir, Sofia, Bucharest, and Jerusalem.

53. See discussion in Wyman, op. cit., Hebrew translation (*Netishat ha'yehudim*), pp. 212–228.

54. Richter's documents were ultimately entered into the records of the OSS (RG 226 DgesBukarest, under heading "Deutsche Gesandschaft Bukarest"), U.S. National Archives (NA). Other important documentation for discussion of what the Nazis knew about the Zionists' rescue plans and their seriousness is available in NA, Collection of Foreign Records Seized, 1941 (RG 242), Microfilm T-175.

55. See the aforementioned Div. 70 in the Hagana Archives: letter from Kasztner to Rescue Mission in Istanbul, June 18, 1944. Here I simplified the contents of the letter, which deserves separate study.

56. There is a ramified literature that speaks specifically about the Zionist youth movements' actions in Hungary, their relations with one another, and their rescue operations in Poland. These matters occasionally prompted Kasztner – a Mapai man who was older than the movement activists and who did everything he could to arrange cooperation among them – and Gisi Fleischmann, the Zionist rescue activist from Bratislava, to make despairing remarks in their letters to Istanbul; see the aforementioned correspondence. Asher Cohen summarizes the matter in his study, *Ha-mahteret ha-halutsit be-hungaria* [The pioneering underground in Hungary] (Tel Aviv: Hakibbutz Hameuchad, 1984).

57. See aforementioned letter from the high commissioner for Palestine, Sir Harold MacMichael, Note on "Jewish Illegal Organizations, Their Activities and Finances," FO 371/31375 E2026, to Colonial Secretary Lord Moyne. This summarizing document was based on reports from CID (the British Police Department of Investigation) in Palestine (cf. sources in Div. 47 of the Hagana Archives) and reports from MEIC, the British Middle East intelligence center. See also my book, *Hitler, the Allies, and the Jews*, pp. 79–101.

58. Source: G-2 Regional File 1933–1944, Palestine, NA, RG 165, Entry 77, Box 3027, Jan. 1, 1944: "Pinkerton agrees ... that the influence of Zionism in America [underlined in the original] is at present being highly exaggerated out here by British, Jews and Arabs alike, but at the same time he feels that the amount of pressure which the Roosevelt administration is prepared to bring upon Britain in favor of Zionism is unpredictable. As he tartly remarked, Felix Frankfurter [the Supreme Court associate justice, whose ties with Roosevelt had been considerably weakened since Pearl Harbor] may well catch the President off his guard at any moment – or some miserably rainy morning, for example, or when suffering from a passing spell of dyspepsia – and convince him. He [Pinkerton] agrees with me [his interlocutor, Major Snyder from the War Department] that such a Zionist state as that advocated by the Jewish Agency would be a festering sore on the face of world peace after the present war is ended and would merely establish that very ape of nationalism which we are presently striving to destroy."

59. See RG 165, Folder 3800, Palestine, Box 3029, dated September 1, 1943: "The Jewish problem is a difficult one. I can see no hope for it.... However bitter the experience, the Jews never learn. They are fearfully angry about the Allied powers not saving the Jews from Europe. I've told a lot of my friends that if they'd only suggest once that all [underlined in the original] the persecuted in Europe be saved, it would go over better, but they only want the Jews saved to bring them to Palestine, and the Arabs are going anti-American, because the Jews put so much in their papers about what America, including Wendell Willkie, are saying about the Jews and Palestine. This is a tragic, almost a cursed country." The author of these remarks was an American woman who was either serving in Palestine or was there for other reasons; the British censor distributed her letter among his British and American correspondents in locations ranging from London and Washington to India.

60. This claim was voiced by sources in the United States associated with the Zionist Revisionists. In this matter and in regard to the Kasztner affair in Hungary, see B. Hecht, *Kachash* [Perfidy] (Jerusalem: Milah, 1961); see also Rabbi M. D.

Weissmandel, *Min ha-metsar* [From the distress]. Weissmandel's book was published by anti-Zionist ultra-Orthodox sources in regard to the Europa Plan for the bribing of SS leaders, discussed later – a scheme that, in different variations, aforementioned post-Zionist writers endorsed.

61. See I. Zertal, *Zahavam shel ha-yehudim* [The gold of the Jews], pp. 105*ff*, and especially Zertal, *Ha-sho'ah veha-mavet* [The Holocaust and death], throughout the whole book.

62. I.e., Zertal's use of the poet Nathan Alterman for her purposes.

63. See my book, *Hitler, the Allies, and the Jews*, and its sources. For a typical vestige of this outlook in the postwar British intelligentsia, see C. Sykes, *Crossroads to Israel: Palestine from Balfour to Bevin* (Bloomington: Indiana University Press, 1973). Christopher Sykes, son of Sir Mark Sykes, served as a British intelligence officer in Cairo during World War II.

64. See Y. Bauer, *Diplomatia ve-mahteret ba-mediniut ha-tsiyyonit* [Diplomacy and underground in Zionist policy] (Tel Aviv: Sifriyat Poalim, 1966), p. 40; cf. discussion in Friling, *Hetz ba-arafel* [Arrows in the dark], vol. 1, pp. 45–52.

65. See Slutzky, "Mi-ma'avaq le-milhama" [From struggle to war], Introduction, *History of the Hagana*, vol. 3 (Tel Aviv: 1965). The editorial board of this "official history of the Hagana" was headed by Benzion Dinur, Israel's third minister of education and the most "mobilized" historian among the board members in Jerusalem. The other members included Shaul Avigur, who had been involved in many of the events that this official history recounts and who censored its final version. Thus, this detailed study should be viewed not only as a factual history but also as a mirror of its authors' views at the time they wrote it.

66. For Churchill's efforts on behalf of the Zionists later during the war, see Makovsky, *Churchill's Promised Land*, pp. 196–199.

67. The Jewish Agency should have been careful not to support the clandestine immigration policy overtly, but one of the considerations in favor of not supporting it was the concern, which proved well founded, that the illegal immigrants would be subtracted from the quota of legal immigrants that the British authorities approved from time to time until the White Paper policy was introduced. After the White Paper, the Jewish Agency favored clandestine 'aliyah both on its own merits and also as a way to fight the White Paper. Here I have severely condensed and simplified a complicated story that the reader should study by consulting Bauer, *Diplomatia ve-mahteret*, pp. 56*ff*. See also Slutzky, *History of the Hagana*, vol. 2, Part 2 (Tel Aviv: 1964), pp. 1033–1052; Dalia Ofer, *Derekh ba-yam: 'aliyah bet bi-tequfat hah-sho'ah* [By sea: Aliyah Bet during the Holocaust] (Jerusalem: Yad Izhak Ben-Zvi, 1988), pp. 11–38.

68. See summary of new documentation on Operation Barbarossa, by Hans-Erich Volkmann, director of research at the Bundswehr Institute of Military History, in the Hamburg weekly *Die Zeit*, June 13, 1997. The summary was published after the inspector-general of the Bundswehr, General Trattner, claimed that Hitler's invasion of the USSR had been a justified preventive one: Hans-Erich Volkmann, "Die Legende vom Praeventivkrieg."

69. See Kushner in regard to H. P. Downey, chief of the Middle East division of the British Colonial Office; cf. stance of Sir Alexander Cadogan, director general of the British Foreign Office, on British disclosure of the persecution of Jews and Downey's claim that the refugee vessel *Struma* was "a Gestapo spy ship," Kushner, *Persistence of Prejudice*, pp. 153–157.

70. Kushner, op. cit., as well as pp. 157–160; cf. Wasserstein, op. cit., who revealed the stances of the Colonial Office and Foreign Office officials before Kushner did but focused on the Palestine problem, whereas Kushner focused on the question of British antisemitism that originated in domestic calculus.

71. See Nuremberg document NG–2586b: "The Madagascar Plan, the Jewish Question in the Peace Treaties," signed by Franz Rademacher of the German Foreign Office, July 3, 1940. Note the following remark in particular: "This aside, the Jews remain in German hands as hostages for good future behavior on the part of those of their race in America."

72. Apart from the aforementioned basic works on this topic, see M. Gilbert, *Auschwitz and the Allies* (London: Michael Joseph, 1981), Hebrew translation, pp. 262–282.

73. See B. M. Katz, "The Criticism of Arms: The Frankfurt School Goes to War," *Journal of Modern History*, 59 (1987), pp. 439–478, esp. p. 472; cf. Petra Marquardt-Bigman, "Amerikanische Geheimdienstalasysen des nationalsozialistischen Deutschlands," *Tel-Aviver Jahrbuch für deutsche Geschichte*, 23 (1994), pp. 325–344. See further, Michael Salter, *US Intelligence, the Holocaust and the Nurenberg Trials: Seeking Accountability for Genocide and Cultural Plunder*, vols. 1 and 2 (Leiden and Boston: Martinus Nijhoff, 2009).

74. See NG, RG 59, R&A (Research and Analysis Branch, OSS) Report 1113.9, Central European Section May 18–24, 1943, Psychological Warfare, authored by Franz Neumann.

75. Friling, op. cit., vol. 1, pp. 150–154.

76. Ibid., pp. 154–156.

77. See my interview with Speer, quoted in *Hitler, the Allies, and the Jews*, Chap. 33.

78. In this matter, see Richard Breitman, *Official Secrets: What the Nazis Planned, What the British and the Americans Knew* (New York: Hill & Wang, 1998), p. 89 which quotes a key British official as saying that he sees no difference between using gas to kill Jews or machine guns.

79. For this complex and the ensuing discussion of Allied behavior, see the relevant chapters in my book, *Hitler, the Allies, and the Jews*, including related documentation.

80. An early analysis by Captain B. H. Liddell-Hart of the internal reasons for Germany's collapse in World War I acknowledges this indirectly. Liddell-Hart credits the British naval blockade as the main factor behind Germany's defeat but adds, "We should not discount unduly, the unwilling tribute paid by the Germans to the effectiveness of Allied, and especially British, propaganda. In the later stages of the war it was skillfully directed and intensively developed." B. H. Liddell-Hart, *The Real War 1914–1918* (Norwalk, CT: Little, Brown), 1994, p. 474.

81. See detailed study of the American side in World War II propaganda: C. D. Laurie, *The Propaganda Warriors: America's Crusade against Nazi Germany* (Lawrence: University Press of Kansas, 1996).

82. NA, Weekly Review of Foreign Broadcasts, FCC No. 118(2).

83. The Mufti began his activities vis-à-vis Berlin by trying to establish cooperative relations with the German consul general in Jerusalem immediately after Hitler's rise to power. To probe this matter, however, one must first analyze documents of British intelligence in Palestine, kept in the aforementioned Div. 47 of the Hagana Archives, most of which actually deal with Arab affairs.

84. By putting it this way, I have greatly simplified a more complex picture that revolves largely around Roosevelt's clashing and vague promises to the Zionists, his discussions with the British, the involvement of his emissaries and envoys in the region under British influence, combined with American strategic intersts, etc., as set forth in detail in Amitzur Ilan, *America, britania ve-erets-yisrael: Reshita ve-hitpat'huta shel me'oravut artsot ha-berit ba-mediniut ha-britit be-erets yisrael 1938–1947* [America, Britain, and Palestine: The origin and development of American involvement in British policy in Palestine 1938–1947] (Jerusalem: Yad Izhak Ben-Zvi, 1979), pp. 111–177.

85. The most detailed and up-to-date study in Hebrew in this field, without which this intricate issue cannot be understood, is Friling's aforementioned *Hetz ba-arafel*, translated as *Arrows in the dark*. Here I chose several relevant key issues. For an outdated summary dealing specifically with Ben-Gurion and the rescue efforts, see S. Teveth, *Ben-Gurion and the Holocaust* (New York: Harcourt Brace, 1966).

86. The British frowned on this activity; initially their stance related concretely to the belief that Jews could in fact be removed from Romania and children throughout occupied Europe saved if only the requisite funds were found. In this matter and the British–American dialogue about it, which ultimately led to the intervention of (non-Jewish) high officials at the U.S. Department of the Treasury against the negative British stance, see Wyman, *The Abandonment of the Jews*.

87. See letter by the Committee of Youth Movements in Budapest, signed by Dov Weiss, Yoshke Baumer, Eli Shiv, Meir Kahane, Yehuda V., and Dr. Yisrael Kasztner, to Rescue Mission in Istanbul, July 7, 1943, Div. 70, Hagana Archives.

88. See letter by Rescue Committee, April 21, 1943, Hagana Archives, Div. 70, unsigned but evidently written by the Mapai activist Samu Springmann, about difficulties with "Ya'ari" (the Ha-Shomer ha-Tsa'ir people) and "Mizrach" (those of the Mizrachi national religious movement), who had formed a coalition in view of the outcome of the Zionist institutions' elections before the war; cf. in this letter: "To this day the movements [in Poland] cannot come to terms. The others, apart from ourselves and Kolodny [the Ha-Oved ha-Tsiyyoni youth movement] are interested only in their share of the [Palestine immigration] certificates and this has been spoiling everything for years."

89. The reports of British intelligence in Palestine, forwarded to the OSS under the name of Aharon Zisling of "Faction B," are indicative of these agencies' keen interest in the Yishuv's internal rifts. The reports stress – disproportionately – the importance of the Ichud (Union) faction, the successor to Brit Shalom.

90. See RG 165, G-2 Regional File, Entry 77, Box 3029, Folder 3800, orig. Pal 5940–P, A 23310–P C 1975.

91. See Stimson diaries, microfilm U.S. Library of Congress, vols. 5–25, Film 8.

92. The Shertok–Quilliam conversation in February was preceded by lengthy correspondence between the latter and the director of military intelligence (DMI) in London, General Davidson, in which Quilliam warned the chiefs of staff that the situation in Palestine had escalated into a virtual insurrection and that the Zionists would oppose and attempt to thwart any action by the Mandatory government in accordance with the White Paper or any measure incongruous with the principles of the Zionists' Biltmore Program. This cable, or a report based on it, came into the possession of Hagana intelligence; a translation in Hebrew is found in CZA, S25/230; see Y. Gelber, "Ha-mediniut ha-Britit ve-ha-tsiyyonit 1942–1944 [The

British and Zionist policies 1942–1944]," in Y. Shavit (ed.), *Ma'avaq, mered, meri* [Struggle, uprising, revolt 1941–1948] (Jerusalem: Domino, 1987), p. 191e. See discussion that follows.

93. See, for example, the American censor's documents in 1943 in the aforementioned File PAL 3800: documents from the British-American censor at Bermuda, including personal correspondence with Yishuv officials. I photocopied these thousands of documents at the U.S. National Archives in Washington; they still await systematic scholarly publication.

94. See Report 3825, Jerusalem, July 25, 1943, to OSS in Washington. The source is "Poney" – evidently Harold Glidden – or his colleague Nelson Glueck, a leading personality in the American Reform movement, then in Palestine in the capacity of OSS Agent 203: *Latest Aspects of the Palestine-Arab Problem*, Chap. 4: "Current Attempts to Solve the Palestine Problem," pp. 6ff. The source is kept in the aforementioned file.

95. See NA, Microcopy T-175, Records of the Reich leader of the SS and chief of the German police, RG 242, Roll 584, SD-Leitabschnitt Wien, no frames, letter by SS-Untersurmführer Urbantzke to SD-LA Wien, Abteilung III B, z.Hd. SS-Hauptsturmführer Herrmann, den 22.8.1942, Betr. Judenaussiedlung.

96. For further information, see Y. Bauer, *Jews for Sale? Nazi-Jewish Negotiations 1933–1945* (New Haven, CT, and London, Yale University Press, 1984), pp. 74–81.

97. Friling, op. cit., vol. 2, pp. 939–952. Alongside occasional barbed comments at protest actions in which he participated in the early stages of the Holocaust, there were public eruptions of anguish during it and at its end, although they were few in number and restrained by the intertwining of rescue needs and Zionist interests.

98. Begin gave agents of the Hagana several different versions of the matter. One of them appears in the Hagana intelligence files that were released for research – Div. 112 ("Shai Secessionists"), Hagana Archives, File 117. The document is a report from an important Hagana activist about his meeting with Begin on October 1, 1944: "I asked [Begin] about what their goals were.... He spoke about the great utility that their action was bringing. The Gentiles begin to appreciate the strength of the Yishuv when they see what a tiny group of Jews there can do [operations related to IZL's "revolt" against the British that year].... He, Begin, knows that there is no real goal behind these operations. As long as the war is on, they will not be able to do much. The operations are for training. After the war, a general uprising will have to be organized: occupation of the cities and holding on there for several months. The British will be in trouble. There will be pressure from public opinion. The Americans have an interest in oil – they will apply pressure [on the British in favor of the rebelling Jews in order to secure their oil interests]. Obviously [the British] will be able to finish off the rebels quickly with the help of their tanks, but it will not be simple. In Warsaw, too, the Germans didn't wind it up quickly." One may imagine the dread that the Yishuv's elected leadership felt when it received this report, sometime before the decision to fight the IZL and the Stern Gang all the way through was taken. In fact, the Germans quashed the Warsaw Ghetto uprising at the pace of their own choosing, sustaining hardly any losses in doing so.

99. See R. Breitman and S. Aronson, "The End of the 'Final Solution'? Nazi Plans to Ransom Jews in 1944," in *Central European History*, 25 (222) (1993), pp. 177–293.

100. See documents from Eichmann's bureau in Bucharest (n. 95 in this chapter) and photocopies in OSS, RG 226, Entry 154, Box 26, Folder 374. One of those involved was a Swiss Gestapo agent named Karl Gyr, who met in April 1943 with the Hakibbutz Hameuchad emissary in Istanbul, Venia Pommeranz (Hadari), and the Jewish Agency's representative there, Chaim Barlas. Even at this early stage of the activities of the Yishuv's rescue mission in Turkey, Gyr presented Eichmann's agent in Bucharest, Gustav Richter, with an accurate report about his talks with the rescue agents and copies of their letters; so did other "couriers" who acted on behalf of the mission. The Bucharest Gestapo files, however, sketch a rather accurate picture of the various kinds of Zionist activity, the connections that the Zionist operatives had maintained with Jewish collectives in occupied Europe since 1941, and letters and money that the JDC agent in Switzerland, Saly Mayer, code-named Franz Keller, had forwarded to Romania and Hungary, which were intercepted by the Gestapo.

101. Several studies describe the activities of Dogwood's network, including B. Rubin, *Istanbul Intrigues: A True-Life Casablanca* (New York: McGraw-Hill, 1989); Y. Bauer, *Jews for Sale?* pp. 120–144. Friling, op. cit., adds important information about relations between the Yishuv leadership and Schwarz (whom they called Shahor, the Hebrew equivalent) and his agents. My contribution to the discussion of this intricate affair comes from my study of the OSS archives in Washington, including Schwarz's relations with Laufer, Bandi Grosz, Teddy Kollek, and other Zionists. See RG 226, Entry 134, Box 254.

102. Cable 53647 REGIS in Washington to USTRAVIC in London, copies to OSS chief, to OSS deputy chief for counterintelligence – X-2 – for Middle East and Europe war theaters, and to Madrid. Source: RG 226, Entry 134, Box 254, Folder 1499, WASH-SECT-R&C-75.

103. Cable 54234, SAINT, copies to London and Istanbul. Source: RG 226, Entry 134, Box 254.

104. A-2, 15th Air Force comment on Dogwood's reports on military targets in Austria and bombing results in that country, originating partly in Iris-Laufer and partly in bona fide agents whom he betrayed. RG 226, Entry 190, Box 74, AIRO-SI-OP 7–10.

105. See background investigation on the establishment and functioning of the Dogwood network: OSS internal inquiry memo signed by reports officer Harry H. Harper, Jr., undated. NA, RG 226, Entry 148, Box 34, Istanbul-OSS-OP-1+2 SI-AD-1.

106. Signed Major Barry AUS, RG 226, Entry 190 – Caserta-SI-OP-48–67, Box 172, Jewish Agency folder; see also organizational table, CIC Middle East, RG 338, AMET, misc. 095 (1945), according to which the chief of CIC was directly subordinate to the assistant chief of staff (ACS), G-2, USAFIME (United States Army Forces in the Middle East).

107. In regard to Ben-Gurion's stances during the "mission" period, see Friling, op. cit., vol. 2, p. 657. Although Friling's account suggests in-depth involvement in the affair from its outset, Ben-Gurion seems to have preceded Shertok in realizing that there was nothing real to it and may have been somewhat doubtful about it from the start, infuriating the rescue emissaries in Istanbul who were involved in it and its offshoots and who expressed this disappointment in their postwar memoirs.

108. RG 226, Entry 146, OSS R&A Report #85291, Aug. 5, 1944. Subject: Exchange of refugees. Country: Hungary. Date of information: 10 July 1944. Place of

origin: Cairo. Evaluation of items: B-2 1,4,7; B-1 3,5,6,8; B-4 2.9.10. Confidential. Dissemination included: MID [Military Intelligence Division, War Department], DNI [Director of Naval Intelligence]. The report was described as emanating from a well-qualified source (around July 5) who brought the information directly from Shertok. Obviously, its author stated, it represents the attitude of the Jewish Agency.

109. See also NA, RG 84, American Legation Bern, cable #5197, August 11, 1944, secret, from McClelland to WRB via State Department, decimal file 840.1, Box 31, 1944; and Bauer, *Diplomatia ve-mahteret* [Diplomacy and underground], pp. 152–196.

110. In regard to this grave episode – the extermination of most inmates in Theresienstadt in the last months of 1944 – see my article, "Theresienstadt im Spiegel amerikanischer Dokkumentation," in *Theresienstaedter Studien und Dokumente 1994, Edition Theresienstaedter Initiative Academia* (Prague: Miroslav Karny u.a. [Herausg.], 1994), pp. 11–15.

111. Gelber, "Ha-mediniut ha-Britit ve-ha-tsiyyonit [British and Zionist policies]", pp. 187–193.

112. This trip was assured, among other things, with the help of cable correspondence between Ben-Gurion and the rescue activists – cables that the OSS sent behind the backs of the British. This effectively proves that the Yishuv leadership and the OSS continued to cooperate – without many practical results. See Friling, op. cit., and also my book, *Hitler, the Allies, and the Jews*, pp. 301, 303.

113. For much detail, see A. Ilan, *America, britania ve-erets-yisrael* [America, Britain, and Eretz Israel].

114. See NA, RG 226, Entry 106, Box 4, Folder 34: "All of our Allies make no [illegible] about demanding American-born leaders whose ancestors came to America at least two generations ago. They do not trust naturalized nationals who have migrated to America as leaders to be trusted. They are also very much afraid that our representatives to these countries for post-war reconstruction will be appointed from the mass of Jewish refugees who came out of these European countries and will be looking for a job in the post-war world. They insist that if the American government does not insist on non-refugee personnel of two or three generations in America ... the great percentage of our advisors for post-war reconstruction will be the unwanted Jews. They realize that the American of several generations will be more certain to have the American idea of justice and fair play, but that on the other hand he will naturally desire to stay in his homeland and let Aaron or Isaac go over to Europe ... or influence things in the Middle East according to *Aaron's or Isaac's distorted sense of justice* [emphasis added].

Cf. rhymed verses of poetry by Dwight Chaplin, a bureaucrat at the enemy wing of the British Foreign Office, in response to an appeal by a Jewish refugee from Germany, a resident of Colombia who had been a metal manufacturer in his country of origin, who offered Churchill to help reconstruct the steel industry in the Rhineland:

> From Colomb's sun scorched strand,
> Urgent there streams an eager Hebrew band,
> Imbued with our desire to serve the aims
> of Allied justice, see them stake their claims
> to jobs in Germany. They know the ropes ...
> 'Till Hitler came and rudely thrust us forth
> We helped the men who laid the powder train. ...

In T. Bower, *Blind Eye to Murder: Britain, America and the Purging of Nazi Germany – a Pledge Betrayed* (London: Andre Deutsch, 1981), pp. 169–170.

115. For a description of the homogeneous and efficient activity of the Mossad le-Aliya Bet, see Idith Zertal, *The gold of the Jews*.

116. On the transformation of products of the non-Zionist Orthodox tradition into literally fighting Zionists, see the memoirs of N. Lau-Lavie, *Am ke-lavie* [A nation like a lion] (Tel Aviv: Sifriyat Ma'ariv, 1990), and cf. meta-historical attitudes among rabbinical ethicists in Palestine that largely remained intact despite the Holocaust and were adjusted to accommodate the lessons of the calamity as it was occurring and immediately thereafter: G. Greenberg, "Musar Response to the Holocaust: Yehezkel Sarna's *Le'teshuva ule-tekuma* of 4 December 1944," in *Journal of Jewish Thought and Philosophy*, 7 (1997), pp. 101–138. See further Dov Schwartz, *Ha-tsiyyonut ha-datit bein higayion li-mashichiut* [Religious Zionism between logic and messianism] (Tel Aviv: Am Oved, 1999), and cf. Schwartz, *Etgar u-mashber be-chug ha-rav Kook* [Challenge and crisis in Rabbi Kook's circle] (Tel Aviv: Am Oved, 2001).

3. Ben-Gurion between Right and Left

1. See Mufti communication to German Consul in Jerusalem after Hitler's rise to power for the purpose of establishing an Arab–Nazi alliance: B. Lewis, *Semites and Anti-Semites* (New York: W. W. Norton, 1986) and sources therein.

2. A wealth of research literature describes British attitudes at this time, paralleled by the memoirs of principals such as Sir Ronald Storrs, governor of Jerusalem. However, thoroughgoing investigation is needed to examine the change of heart that took place among neutral and even pro-Zionist officials under the influence of George Antonius, a "Palestinian-Arab Weizmann" from the late 1920s onward. Some say that it was he who caused Arnold Toynbee to change his mind about Zionism so drastically. Research has yet to determine when this change occurred, since Toynbee was not only a key figure at the London School of Economics, established by Sidney and Beatrice Webb – later Lord and Lady Passfield, whose antisemitic and anti-Zionist views were mentioned previously – but also an important personality among the British foreign and intelligence services until the 1940s.

3. See the discussion of Jabotinsky's concept of race in S. Avineri, *Ha-ra'ayon ha-tsiyyoni li-gvunav: Peraqim be-toldot ha-mahshava ha-leumit ha-yehudit* [Complexions of the Zionist idea: Chapters on the history of Jewish national thinking] (Tel Aviv: Am Oved, 1980), pp. 190–195.

4. *Ha'aretz*, October 6, 1996.

5. On the "Western Wall affair" and the crackling tension between the Revisionists and the Labor Movement people in the late 1920s, including quotations from Achimeir's column *Mi-pinqaso shel fashistan* (From a Fascist's notebook) and the response of Ben-Gurion and his colleagues, see S. Teveth, *Qinat David: Ben-Gurion: Ish midot* [David's zeal: Ben-Gurion: Man of virtues] (Jerusalem: Schocken, 1980), pp. 548–553.

6. On Jabotinsky's "humanism" and his social doctrine, see Avineri (n. 3 in this chapter), pp. 167–205.

7. See reverberations of this argument in a contemporaneous article: Esther Stein-Ashkenazi, "Tenu'at betar be-erets yisrael ve-ha-yedi'ot al ha-sho'ah" [The Betar movement in Palestine and reports about the Holocaust], *Kivvunim, Journal on Zionism and Judaism*, 10 (47) (December 1996), p. 68.

8. See remarks at Mapai Central Committee, *War diary*, vol. 2, pp. 619–620.

9. See Avineri, op. cit., pp. 196–197.

10. They were a motley group of people of various generations and backgrounds. We mentioned one of them, Abba Achimeir, in n. 5 in this chapter. In the early 1920s, Achimeir established in Palestine a quasi-Fascist circle called Brit ha-Biryonim (the Strongmen's Alliance) and had a newspaper column called *Mi-pinqaso shel fashistan* (From a Fascist's notebook). In this matter and for Ben-Gurion's response, see Y. Shavit, *Mi-ivri ad kena'ani, peraqim be-toldot ha-ideologia ve-ha-utopia shel "ha-tehiya ha-ivrit": Mi-tsiyyonut radiqalit le-anti-tsiyyonut* [From Hebrew to Canaanite, chapters in the history of the ideology and Utopia of the "Jewish renaissance": From radical Zionism to anti-Zionism] (Tel Aviv: Domino), 1984, pp. 12, 43–59, 84, 91, 146. The book deals, among other things, with a young Revisionist activist of German origin named Helmuth Ostermann, who was strongly influenced by Karl Haushofer's geopolitical ("spatial") theories and rendered them into a pronouncedly nationalist version for the Middle East. Eventually, Ostermann changed his name to Uri Avneri and engaged, among other things, in political punditry in a manner that was also originated in his country of birth. See also Z. Tsahor, *Ha-hazon ve-ha-heshbon: Ben-Gurion bein ideologia le-politiqa* [Vision and reckoning: Ben-Gurion between ideology and politics] (Tel Aviv: Sifriyat Poalim, 1994), pp. 87–122; Y. Heller, *Lehi 1940–1949*, vol. 1 (Jerusalem: Zalman Shazar Centre and Keter, 1989), pp. 19–28. See Y. Shavit, *Ha-mitologia shel ha-yamin* [The mythology of the right] (Tel Aviv: Beit Berl and Moshe Sharett Institute, 1986), from which we later quote the author's discussion of Jabotinsky's "evacuation plan"; see the aforementioned biography of Yonatan Ratosh, Y. Porat, *Sehlah ve'et be-yado: Sipur hayav shel Yonatan Ratosh* [Fence with a pen in his hand: The biography of Yonatan Ratosh].

11. See M. Keren's discussion of Ben-Gurion's relations with the author S. Yizhar and Ben-Gurion's response to the Kafkaesque, pessimistic, and dispirited states of mind that he encountered in the writer Yizhar Smilansky's work and in the expressions of philosopher Shmuel H. Bergman: Keren, *Ben-Gurion ve-ha-intelektualim* [Ben-Gurion and the intellectuals], pp. 126–129. Keren typically sides with Yizhar and Bergman in this debate; thus, he makes Ben-Gurion look like an authoritative tyrant insensitive to the afflicted soul of the modern individual.

12. One of the first to allege the existence of a scheme of this kind was Simcha Flapan of Ha-Shomer ha-Tsa'ir, editor of the journal *New Outlook* and an inveterate politician. Yoram Nimrod, an associate of the same circles, wrote a doctoral dissertation in this vein. In his wake came the self-declared "new historians" of our time, such as the Arabist Ilan Pappé and journalist Tom Segev, and their personal approaches.

13. In this matter, see Y. Gorny, *Ha-she'ela ha-aravit* [The Arab question] and its sources, and cf. D. Ben-Gurion, *Anahnu u-shekheneinu* [We and our neighbors] (Tel Aviv, Davar, 1931).

14. BGA, Document 88/1162/81, published here in English for the first time, to the best of my knowledge.

15. See comparison of Ben-Gurion's attitude toward this issue with that of Dr. Judah L. Magnes, whose views were closely aligned with those of Brit Shalom: G. Shimoni, *The Zionist Ideology*, pp. 180–181.

16. In regard to the syndicalist and quasi-Fascist dimension of Jabotinsky's teachings, his Betar organization, and the nature of Jabotinsky's struggle against Socialist Zionism in the 1930s, see Avineri, op. cit., pp. 201–206.

17. In this matter and in regard to the Russian ideological infrastructure of the future Stern Gang, abbreviated in Hebrew as Lehi, see Heller, *Lehi*, vol. 1, pp. 82–91.

18. On the cementing of Weizmann's status vis-à-vis the British elite up to the Balfour Declaration and in its aftermath, the granting of the Mandate to Britain, see J. Reinharz's ongoing study, *Chaim Weizmann: The Making of a Statesman* (Hanover, NH: Brandeis University Press/University Press of New England, 1985). In the early 1930s, these connections helped Weizmann to undermine the colonial secretary, Lord Passfield, also known as Sidney Webb – a move that widened the already-existing rift between the Passfields and the Jews, particularly the Zionists. As the Weizmann–Ben-Gurion relationship evolved from the Arab uprising of 1936 onward, Ben-Gurion was concerned that Weizmann was willing to halt immigration for some time if only to assuage the Arabs' concerns and, therefore, felt it his duty to "watch over him." See S. Teveth, *Qinat David: Ha-qarqa bo'er* [David's zeal: The ground is burning] (Jerusalem: Schocken, 1987), pp. 141*ff.*

19. In this context and on the development of relations within the Zionist Movement, see Teveth, *The ground is burning*, pp. 11–150.

20. See ibid., pp. 102–107.

21. See Heller, op. cit., pp. 41–82.

22. See Teveth, *The ground is burning*, pp. 168–215.

23. This marked a shift of emphasis in Ben-Gurion's thinking and actions; he expressed it publicly in his book *Mi-ma'amad le-am: Peraqim le-virur darka shel tenu'at ha-po'alim* [From class to nation: Chapters for clarification of the path of the labor movement] (Tel Aviv: Ayanot, 1955), first published 1933.

24. On Katznelson's opposition to the plan and the development of the internal controversy in Mapai on this issue, see Shapira, *Berl*, vol. 2, pp. 541*ff.*

25. For more on this issue, see S. Dotan, *Pulmus ha-haluqa bi-mei ha-mandat* [The partition controversy during the Mandate era] (Jerusalem: Yad Izhak Ben-Zvi, 1980).

26. On this issue, see also S. Dotan, *Pulmus ha-haluqa.*

27. See Teveth, *The ground is burning*, pp. 437–438.

28. This affair, mentioned earlier, was no simple proposition; it reflected disagreements between the radical Marxist wing of Mapai, headed by Yitzhak Tabenkin, who regarded the Revisionist Right as Fascist ab initio and categorically opposed any attempt to find common language with it, and Ben-Gurion, who hoped that by concluding the London accord with Jabotinsky, such a language could be devised. See Avizohar, *Be-re'i saduq* [In a cracked mirror], pp. 164–169.

29. Gelber, "Ha-mediniut ha-Britit ve-ha-tsiyyonit [British and Zionist policies]."

30. Teveth looked into this matter in depth and gave it this heading in his book *David's zeal: The ground is burning*, especially in Chap. 8, pp. 150*ff.*

31. Heller's study on Lehi, which explores these issues nicely on pp. 41–82, wishes to trace the schism in the IZL and the growth of Lehi as the outcome of Jabotinsky's orders to the IZL, when the war began, to join the British in their war against the Nazis and his sudden death afterwards. A primary source that was not fully available to Heller and to other IZL and Lehi scholars in regard to that period and up to the end of World War II is the Criminal Investigation Department (CID) – British police intelligence – Archives, most of which are kept today at the Hagana Archives (Div. 47), and the Hagana Intelligence Archives ("Secessionists," Div. 112). For a preliminary report on this documentation, see my article for the Yad Vashem and Leo Baeck Institute international conference in Jerusalem,

February 1997: "British Policy, Allied Intelligence and Zionist Dilemmas in Face of Hitler's Jewish Policies 1939–1941." For more comprehensive use of this and related sources in the Hagana Archives, see note on the sources in my book, *Hitler, the Allies, and the Jews*.

32. NA, RG 226, Entry 190, Box 76, Folder 70, OSS SI Cairo to Gordon Laud, SI. "Hicks [i.e., Glueck] is an executive of the Association of Washington Reformed Rabbis, in whose absence from the States a substitute was at work who drove those Rabbis toward the Zionists. Hicks' friends who were opposed to the Zionists put pressure to bear on him to return and alleviate the situation, and as a result he submitted his resignation [from the OSS]. OSS Cairo was very much in favor of accepting Hicks' [Glueck's] bid to return and fight the Zionists due to those reasons." One of the documents read by the British imperial censor was a letter from Glueck to his colleagues in the American Reform Movement at roughly this time, in which he termed the demand for the establishment of Jewish statehood in Palestine (i.e., the Biltmore Program) a "fascist solution." However, Glueck decried the White Paper policy and proposed – in the spirit of Brit Shalom viewpoints – that Jewish immigration be allowed until equilibrium between Jews and Arabs were attained. Such an equilibrium, he said, was a condition for the establishment of a Jewish canton within the framework of an Arab federation. In his letter, however, Glueck explained that the Reform Movement – of which he was a leading figure – should pursue its reinforcement in America as its main desideratum.

33. For an up-to-date list of studies about the "secret connection," see Friling, *Hetz ba-arafel* [Arrows in the dark], pp. 381–496. In addition to Friling's sources, it is worth adding that Ben-Gurion's attempts to establish relations with various American governing bodies and his appeals to Jewish organizations during his visits in and after 1941 were reported to an OSS office called FNB (Foreign Nationalities Branch), which forwarded the reports to the State Department intelligence agency. In my possession is testimony in this matter by Dr. Avraham Ducker, the official in charge of the agency's Polish desk. Obviously, scholarship has to investigate how the FBI may have treated Zionists, even though there seems to have been a division of labor between the entities.

34. There is copious research literature on Churchill and the Zionists; I cannot delve into it here. An important study in this respect, M. J. Cohen, *Churchill and the Jews, 1900–1948* (London: Frank Cass, 1985), claims that Churchill merely pretended to be a friend of the Jews and a Zionist. For a more complex account, see R. W. Zweig, *Britain and Palestine during the Second World War* (Woodbridge, Suffolk: The Boydell Press, 1986), and more recent works such as Makovsky's and Gilbert's.

35. In this regard, the history of the Hagana communications system needs to be examined. The system was established in the 1930s and had the capacity to cable London and Washington in Morse code. For the time being, however, I do not know whether it had the capacity of bidirectional communication in real time. As evidence that it did not, I note that the Yishuv leadership asked the OSS to help it send cables, and eventually the OSS agreed to do so.

36. During his visit to the United States in 1940, Ben-Gurion met with Col. William Donovan, who had just established the OSS under a different name. One doubts whether Ben-Gurion knew that Donovan had previously toured Europe and the Middle East at the initiative of the chief of MI6 in New York, the Canadian businessman William Stephenson, in order to report to Roosevelt about Britain's chances of surviving this phase of the war. Returning from his trip, Donovan

reported that the British would survive and would maintain their status in the Middle East. They had learned how to avoid fomenting enmity among the various Arab and Muslim players. In this matter, see B. F. Smith, *The Shadow Warriors: O.S.S. and the Origins of the C.I.A.* (New York: Basic Books, 1983), pp. 46–53.

37. See discussion of the 1936 Weizmann–Nuri Sa'id affair in S. Teveth, *Ha-shanim ha-ne'elamot ve-ha-hor ha-shahor* [The vanished years and the black hole] (Tel Aviv: Dvir, 1999), p. 281, and the Weizmann–Philby–Ibn Saud affair in Ilan, *America*, pp. 125–129. The two affairs were similar in the sense that Weizmann gave himself the latitude to operate intimately in his contacts with foreign players, e.g., with the Iraqi statesman Nuri Sa'id with respect to the immigration moratorium – an episode that touched off a direct collision between Ben-Gurion and Weizmann. The Philby–Ibn Saud affair was ostensibly many times more severe, since Weizmann, who seems to have claimed that the Saudi king could be bribed into accepting Zionist demands, presented this to the American administration as a fact and entangled it in a groundless scandal.

38. See Dinnerstein, *Antisemitism in America*, pp. 133–149, and cf. Wyman, *The Abandonment of the Jews*, p. 9.

39. For a wealth of detail about these hopes and moves of the Zionist Executive from autumn 1942, see Friling, op. cit., vol. 1, pp. 286*ff.*

40. See Y. Gelber, "Ha-mediniut ha-britit ve-ha-tsiyyonit [British and Zionist policies]," in Y. Shavit (ed.), *Struggle, uprising, revolt 1941–1948*, pp. 169–224.

41. The person most victimized by this image was the subsequent emissary of the Dror Zionist youth movement in neutral Switzerland, Nathan Schwalb. Schwalb and his associates at the rescue mission in Istanbul did attempt to bolster the morale of the Jewish collectives that stayed in touch with him by retelling events of the Yishuv in the most heroic terms possible, even as their relations with the Yishuv leadership were anything but simple due to what they considered a chronic lack of resources. Rabbi Weissmandel of Bratislava, however, accused Schwalb of having the resources that were needed for the success of the Europa Plan but being delinquent in forwarding them. Adding insult to injury, he also alleged that the blood being shed in the Diaspora would become grease for the wheels of Zionism. Eventually this charge was dramatized in the play *Perdition*, which debuted in London in the autumn of 1986. The playwright was an anti-Zionist; Schwalb sued him but later withdrew the suit. The "Weissmandel letter" affair became the topic of exchanges of allegations between Shabtai Teveth, Ben-Gurion's biographer, and Hava Eshkoli in *Ha'aretz* in September–October 1995.

    Ironically, the Nazis also monitored Schwalb's correspondence with the Jewish collectives in occupied Europe and exploited them for the imperative, from their standpoint, of thwarting rescue to the greatest extent possible. See photostated lists and intercepted letter to Dr. Silberschein in Geneva, Schwalb's colleague in this respect, concerning smuggling of Jews from Poland, mainly from Lwów (Lemberg) into Romania, RG 242/1010, NA Microcopy T-175, DGesBukarest XL 13172, Roll 660, frames 85–302. Schwalb's name was mentioned in a group of twenty-one files that cover the 1941–1944 period, along with the names of other Zionist rescue activists, including Samu Springman in Budapest. These files, as described in publications of the American National Archives, also contain information reports on the Jewish question by the combined Gestapo-SD central office in Berlin pertaining to international Jewish organizations and, in the main, to the Zionists. These reports originate in information that fell into the hands of Eichmann's agent in

Budapest, the aforementioned Gustav Dichter, and in letters from Schwalb himself and his colleagues on the mission in Istanbul, including a detailed report on the "Baltimore [*sic*] Program of the Emergency Committee for Zionist Affairs" in New York, headed by Weizmann, Wise, Ben-Gurion, and others. In this fashion the Gestapo came into possession of letters that Schwalb had sent to rescue activists in Romania in December 1943 and records of correspondence between Schwalb and "Menachem," i.e., Menachem Bader, a leading official at the Zionist rescue mission in Istanbul.

    The Gestapo knew not only about the activities of Schwalb and Bader but also of Saly Mayer, the JDC agent in Switzerland whom Eichmann and his people knew by his alias, "Franz Keller." The resources at issue were JDC funds that Mayer had forwarded to Bucharest and Budapest in 1941–1943. Subsequently, Mayer conducted the negotiations with Kurt Andreas Becher that Kasztner had begun in Budapest.

42. In 1946, when he assumed the Zionist Executive's defense portfolio, Ben-Gurion delved into the Hagana's affairs and received a close-up lesson about what the organization was up to. His remarks about what he found, interspersed throughout his book *Steps toward statehood*, combine with similar remarks in *War diary*, vol. 1, and his overt criticism of the Hagana, which the editors of volumes 1 and 2 of the diary discuss in detail.

43. Thus, it comes as no surprise that Ben-Gurion made efforts to minimize Sadeh's influence and, in particular, to prevent him from shaping the image of the IDF. We revisit this issue in our discussion of the phases in which the IDF was established along "British" military lines.

44. The problem of corruption in the Yishuv was one of the main motives behind the establishment of the Aliya Hadasha Party, as information that came into the possession of the British-American censor indicates. Some Mapai loyalists, such as Peretz Naphtali, were also well aware that their public activities required them to "dirty their hands" or do things that verged on turpitude, including sloppy and impromptu management habits, sweetheart deals, dubious ways of funding the party and its organs, and distribution of favors to close associates. See Rimmer, *Peretz Naftali*, pp. 237–238.

45. Teveth, *The ground is burning*, pp. 270–271: "As the dangers that he foresaw drew nearer and in fact were beginning to happen rapidly, Ben-Gurion urgently needed an instrument – a party – in as-is condition. As they say, when the house is burning it's not the time for maintenance."

46. For a broader context in this matter, see research literature in recent years: Y. Weitz, *Mapai le-nokhah ha-sho'a 1943–1945* [Mapai facing the Holocaust 1943–1945] (Jerusalem: Yad Izhak Ben-Zvi, 1994); Hava Eshkoli, *Elem: Mapai le-nokhah ha-sho'a 1939–1942* [The mute: Mapai facing the Holocaust 1939–1942] (Jerusalem: Yad Izhak Ben-Zvi, 1994). For the most recent research see Dina Porat and Aviva Halamish (eds.), *Shoa mi-merchak tavo: Ishim ba-yeshuv ha-eretz yisraeli vey-achasam la-nazism ve-la-shoa, 1933–1945* [When disaster comes from afar: Leading personalities in the Land of Israel confront Nazism and the Holocaust, 1933–1948 (Jerusalem, Yad Ben-Zvi, 2009), and Yosef Gorny, *Kria bein onim: Ha-itonut ha-yehudit be-eretz yisrael, be-britania, be-arzot ha-brit u-bivrit ha-moezot le-nochach ha-shoa, ba-shanim 1939–1945* [A cry in the wilderness: The Jewish press in the Land of Israel, in Britain, in the United States and in the Soviet Union confronting the Holocaust, 1939–1945] (Tel-Aviv, Hakibbitz Hameuchad, 2009).

47. See Friling, op. cit., vol. 3.
48. A case in point is the debate in the Haifa Municipal Council in winter 1996 over naming a city street for Kasztner. One of the councillors read out a letter from Lili Maor, a Holocaust survivor from Hungary, to the effect that "Kasztner and his people" had personally placed Jews from an outlying town near Budapest aboard a train that transported them to Auschwitz. Afterwards, she stated on local television that even if this (groundless) detail was incorrect, she could not forgive Kasztner for the fact that her parents had not been among the passengers on his survivors' train. The attorney Yosef Tamir, son of Shmuel Tamir (who as Malkiel Grünwald's attorney had turned Kasztner's libel suit against Grünwald into the "trial" of Kasztner himself), represented Mrs. Maor in this debate and petitioned the High Court of Justice to repeal the council's compromise decision to name a public park for Kasztner.
49. Consult the copious research literature on this topic, especially Gelber, Gorny, and Friling, and cf. Y. Bauer, *Diplomatia ve-mahteret* [Diplomacy and underground], and the corrected English edition thereof, *From Diplomacy to Resistance; A History of Jewish Palestine, 1930–1945* (New York: Random House, 1970). See also Gelber, op. cit., and Makovsky, *Churchill's Promised Land*, pp. 196–216.
50. See Gelber, op. cit., pp. 192–204.
51. One such resignation at the height of the Holocaust, in late 1943, may be considered an ugly and small-minded act of personal "politics." It aroused keen interest among the aforementioned British and American intelligence offices, which considered Ben-Gurion a "nationalist" and a "militant" relative to the moderate Weizmann. Ben-Gurion, however, quickly resumed his functions at the Jewish Agency in view of the grave challenges at hand and bided his time.
52. See Teveth, *The ground is burning*, p. 139: "Ben-Gurion tumbled into a frustrating trap that he had helped to create. Ben-Gurion, the quintessential builder of authority, was deprived of the possibility of building it in the Zionist Organization. Weizmann was not an appropriate base on which to build it; after all, he did not 'live' the movement, gave no thought to how it was organized, was not a statesman, and, generally speaking, acted only when the spirit moved him."
53. The matter of how the Holocaust affected the radicalization of thinking among the Arabs, who viewed it as a precedent in eradicating the Jewish problem by exterminating the Jews, recurs in Ben-Gurion's writings, in all volumes of his *War diary* and in his subsequent public depictions of the Jewish–Arab conflict.
54. See Ben-Gurion's reckoning with Ha-Shomer ha-Tsa'ir in *The renewed Jewish state* and the Knesset debate that it quotes.
55. Golda Meir is believed to have said – I did not find the source – that "Ben-Gurion turned out to be right in everything that we hadn't seen at first." It is also worth noting the various estimates, widely held on the eve of the War of Independence, that only the Palestinian Arabs would take part in the impending conflict and that Arab states, such as faraway Iraq, would not intervene. One of the exponents of this view was Eliezer Liebenstein (Livne), who would eventually join up with Yeshayahu Leibowitz and the erstwhile Faction B in opposing the Dimona reactor in the belief that Israel's conduct in this matter would antagonize both superpowers. See my book, *The Politics and Strategy of Nuclear Weapons in the Middle East: Opacity, Theory, and Reality, 1960–1991* (Albany: State University of New York Press, 1992), pp. 61–82.

56. On the phased mobilization of the Yishuv and the centrality of how little time Israel had in view of expected developments in the Arab world, see *War diary*, vol. 3, p. 964.

57. See, for example, Ben-Gurion's conversation with Yochanan Ratner and Fritz Eshet, two exponents of traditional military service, on December 19, 1947: "Ratner ... doesn't believe he can fix it. There's a corporative spirit in the 'organization' [the Hagana] that can't put up with any new force. Even Fritz doesn't believe that corrections can be made." As for Ben-Gurion's criticism of the Hagana, see the three volumes of *War diary*, pp. 52, 53, 160–161, 180, 195, 210, 228, 273–274, 275, 312, 354–355, 374, 512, 574, 686 (consecutive pagination); this is but a selection. Cf. Anita Shapira's criticism of the *Diary* as an inadequate source in her book *Mi-piturei ha-rama 'ad peruq ha-palmah: Sugiyot ba-ma'avaq 'al ha-hanhaga ha-bit'honit* [From the dismissal of the chief of national staff to the dissolving of the Palmach: Issues in the struggle over the defense leadership] (Tel Aviv: Hakibbutz Hameuchad, 1984), p. 23. We will revisit Shapira's book again in the following and in Chap. 4.

58. See *War diary*, vol. 1, p. 5.

59. Ibid., entry February 5, 1948, p. 208: "I told (COS IDF) Ya'akov [Dori] not to approve any additional person for the [Palmach] Brigade staff without my prior authorization. At the moment, there are three comrades: Yigal (Allon), Yitzhak Rabin, Eliezer Shoshani. They are about to appoint Shalom Havlin. They are also proposing Elchanan (Yishai)." "They" meant Ben-Gurion himself, since Yishai was a loyal member of Mapai. In this matter, see Shapira's claim that, absent a civil service tradition in the Yishuv, all of Ben-Gurion's considerations were "political" – Anita Shapira, *From the dismissal*, p. 20 – and cf. foregoing discussion of the definitions of "politics" and "statecraft."

60. See *War diary*, vol. 1, p. 410.

61. *Liqrat mifne*, Ben-Gurion remarks to defense committees, January 15, 1948, toward a turning point, *War diary*, vol. 1, pp. 154–155.

62. See research literature on this affair, e.g., Anita Shapira's aforementioned book, which we shall take up again. For the time being, I have greatly simplified and abbreviated the story of the affair as presented in *War diary*; see index of vol. 3: "Mapam – 'mered' arba'a havereha ba-matkal" [Mapam – the "insurrection" of its four members on the general staff], pp. 572–573; "Tsahal, mashber ha-piqud ha-'elyon" [IDF, high command crisis], pp. 511–559.

63. I treat this matter the same way. See the very detailed entries on Etzel, Begin's Irgun, *War diary*, vol. 3, p. 1087, and on Lehi, ibid., p. 1110.

64. Ben-Gurion speech at Session 233 of First Knesset, March 5, 1951, about the Security and Defense Service Law, 5711 (1951), copied from *Yihud ve-yi'ud* [Uniqueness and destiny] (Tel Aviv: Ministry of Defense, 1991), p. 136.

65. Ben-Gurion at meeting with a group of colleagues (at the Office of the Prime Minister), April 8, 1949, Mapai Secretariat Archives, 49/15.

66. A. Shapira, *From the dismissal*, p. 63.

67. After the 1949 elections, Ben-Gurion tried to sustain the climate of mobilization that the war had created and even invited the left-wing parties to merge with Mapai: "We are living in a messianic era. It is high time to carry out our Socialist Zionist vision, not in one stroke but in its entirety." *War diary*, vol. 3, p. 469. Given the outcome of the First Knesset elections, however, Meir Ya'ari and Ya'akov Hazan of Mapam did not accept the Mapai majority rule that underlay this arrangement.

Two of the Achdut ha-Avoda members who were invited to the meeting with Ben-Gurion on this topic, Yisrael Galili and Berl Repator, did not come, and Ben-Gurion did not see fit to write down the response, if any, of one of those who did come, Yitzhak Ben-Aharon.

68. *War diary*, vol. 3, pp. 901–902. The "Hanukka reflections" that Ben-Gurion recorded in his diary on December 25, 1948: "In the social and political regime, two principles must be imposed that people try to separate today: liberty and equality. The separation is artificial. The two principles are interlinked. There is no true freedom without equality, nor is there equality without freedom." After developing this argument to the limits of his ability, Ben-Gurion went on to claim that there were historical reasons for the development of labor movements in certain countries. The triumph of Bolshevism in Russia was a necessity in the history of the Russian people but was not in the logic of Socialism itself or a historical necessity that the labor movement carries wherever it goes. Ben-Gurion concluded the debate with Mapam by saying, "We can follow our path and not imitate others. . . . The worker as the subject of Socialism and not as its object. Not on behalf of the worker but rather by him, not on behalf of the people but rather by the people – that is democracy." These maxims reveal Ben-Gurion's aspiration to "educate" the public, at least in its proletarian segment, in order to generate grassroots legitimacy for the tasks at hand.

69. See Ben-Gurion's remarks in a meeting with front and divisional commanders in November, *War diary*, vol. 3, p. 803: "The end of the war – will there be an 'end' even if the war ends now? . . . And if peace is concluded – is there a war that was not preceded by peace? You have to look not at documents and decisions but at historical reality. What is our reality? Arab peoples have been pummeled by us. Will they forget this quickly? Seven hundred thousand defeated thirty million. Will they forget this insult? . . . We will try to make peace – but it takes two sides to make peace. . . . Let's admit the truth: We won not because our army did wonders but because the Arab army was rotten. Must this rot persist? Is it impossible for an Arab Mustafa Kemal to come forth? The global situation encourages revenge: There are two blocs, there is fear of a world war, and this encourages anyone who has a gripe." Taken by one of his outbursts of enthusiasm, Ben-Gurion talked about the conquest of the whole country and the IDF as "the best army in the region," but soon enough he retreated from occupying the Jordanian-controlled West Bank and even the sensitive East Jerusalem. His initiative to broaden the shoulders of the corridor leading to West Jerusalem was defeated by his own government.

70. See UN resolutions, the powers' attitudes toward the Palestine question, the armistice accords, and the collection of documents in J. N. Moore (ed.), *The Arab-Israeli Conflict*, vol. 3 (Princeton, NJ: Princeton University Press, 1974), pp. 259–313, 313–340, 380–407.

71. See n. 69 in this chapter.

72. See minister of defense discussions with chief of general staff in the autobiography of Dayan: M. Dayan, *Avnei derekh* [Story of my life] (Jerusalem: Idanim, 1980), pp. 212–213, 217.

73. Minutes of conference in Beersheba on the mobilization of youth, BGA, July 19, 1954, Doc. 001/2175, aforementioned.

74. One of the conspicuous opponents of mass immigration was David Horowitz, subsequently governor of the Bank of Israel, who believed that the fragile State of Israel was attempting to carry out different and clashing large-scale activities all

at once without real economic resources. Horowitz was right in principle, yet his own efforts as director general of the treasury coupled with a major cut in defense expenditures and the timely arrival of German reparations and American foreign aid, headed off economic disaster in Israel's early years. See the memoirs of D. Horowitz, *Hayyim ba-moqed* [Life at the focus] (Ramat Gan: Massada, 1975), pp. 11–14.

75. Apart from education in localities where immigrants had settled, mentioned previously, see Ben-Gurion–Almogi correspondence about the Ata strike, a "wild" strike, i.e., an uncontrolled act of breaking labor relations usually controlled by Mapai, in BGA.

76. A. Shapira, *From the dismissal*, p. 14.

77. Ibid., p. 26.

4. Ben-Gurion and the Israel Defense Forces – From Formation to the Suez-Sinai Campaign of 1956

1. Ben-Gurion speech in the Knesset on defense affairs, June 20, 1950. See *Yihud ve-yi'ud* [Uniqueness and destiny], pp. 136–137.

2. Y. Wallach, *El ha-degel: Haqamat tsava amami tokh kedei lehima* [To the flag: The establishment of a people's army in the midst of combat] (Tel Aviv: Ministry of Defense, 1997).

3. Zahava Ostfeld, *Tsava nolad* [An army is born], 2 vols. (Tel Aviv: Ministry of Defense, 1994).

4. See Ben-Gurion speech, January 14, 1951, to IDF high command, which we quote in detail further on.

5. See note 1 in this chapter.

6. *Uniqueness and destiny*, p. 251.

7. A. L. Rowse, *All Souls and Appeasement* (London: St. Martin's Press, 1961), p. 115; cf. W. K. Wark, *The Ultimate Enemy: British Intelligence and Nazi Germany* (Ithaca, NY, and London: Cornell University Press, 1996), p. 239.

8. M. Kesselman et al., *European Politics in Transition*, pp. 126–128.

9. In this matter, see J. A. Garraty's well-known study, *The Great Depression: Inquiry into the Causes, Course and Consequences of the Worldwide Depression as Seen by Contemporaries and in the Light of the Nineteen-Thirties* (New York: Harcourt, Brace Jovanovich, 1986); and cf. G. M. Luebbert, *Liberalism, Fascism, or Social Democracy: Social Classes and the Political Origins of Regimes in Interwar Europe* (New York and Oxford: Oxford University Press, 1981), esp. pp. 191–193, 234–236.

10. Such legislation, known as a bill of attainder, outlaws an especially dastardly criminal. As for the British stance ahead of the Nuremberg trials and the use they wished to make of a bill of attainder instead of an international tribunal, see G. L. Weinberg, *A World at Arms: A Global History of World War II* (New York: Cambridge University Press, 1996), p. 853.

11. The affair is described with restraint and precision by the late Netanel Lorch, the "official historian" of the War of Independence, in his book, *Qorot milhemet ha-atsma'ut* [History of the War of Independence], corrected ed. (Tel Aviv: Modan, 1989), pp. 380–387.

12. See A. Shapira, *From the dismissal of the chief of national staff to the dissolving of the Palmach*, esp. pp. 50–51.

13. In this matter, in addition to official publications, consult the following list of selected government meetings and brief summations of Ben-Gurion's remarks at them, prepared at my request by Mr. Razi Yahel of the Ben-Gurion Research Institute:

Date	Contents
May 19, 1948	Symbols and flag.
May 20, 1948	Flag.
May 23, 1948	Discussion of the Israel Defense Forces Ordinance.
May 26, 1948	Continued discussion and final wording of the IDF Ordinance.
May 30, 1948	Wording for the pledge of allegiance to the IDF and dismantling of the secessionist organizations, IZL and Lehi.
June 6, 1948	Report on the state of IDF manpower and stocks.
June 1948	Emblem and flag of the state; arrangements in occupied areas and for abandoned property.
June 20, 1948	Discussion of supplemental mobilization for military and labor service, the situation in Jerusalem, the *Altalena* affair.
July 25, 1947	Jerusalem, discussion of censorship, discussion of transferring education to the government.
Aug. 4, 1948	Israel Day (Independence Day) and IDF Day.
Sept. 5, 1948	Manpower report – the IDF had 35,000 combat soldiers at the time.
Sept. 18, 1948	Discussion of the Bernadotte assassination, the implications of Jewish terrorism, and the death penalty [Count Folke Bernadotte was a Swedish diplomat who served as UN emissary in Israel during the 1948 war and adopted a rather anti-Israel approach, whereupon he was assassinated by the Stern Gang's Lehi. Ben-Gurion reacts to this act of violence by disbanding Lehi and arresting its best-known activists].
Sept. 22, 1948	Press censorship and supervision; approval of antiterror regulations.
Sept. 26, 1948	In a debate about widening the flanks ("shoulders") of Jerusalem ("the everlasting lament"), Ben-Gurion asked whether the UN resolution should be accepted or whether the IDF should be put to use for further conquests. He remarked, among other things: "[If] we could attain the minimum by [concluding] an agreement with the Arabs – I would do it, because I am very fearful and anxious about the militarization of our country's youth. I already see it in the children's souls and I didn't dream about such a people and I don't want it. . . . But the Arabs don't want to agree to this and we have no choice . . . but we will be ready to fight."
Nov. 14, 1948	Mobilization and army manpower data.
Dec. 15, 1948	Constitution, regime, and conduct in the army. Nahal ("Pioneering Fighting Youth" – a formation of the IDF, created to replace the partisan Palmach) as a surrogate for the Palmach training facilities.
Dec. 19, 1948	Change in balance of forces and power between IDF and Arabs.
Dec. 29, 1948	Dismantling the Palmach staff.
March 3, 1949	The government after the First Knesset elections: basic guidelines – collective responsibility. Goals and principles: defense, a worthy foreign policy, freedom, and equality. A four-year development and immigrant-absorption plan. Public education. Rehabilitation of soldiers. Labor laws. Discussion of religion and state, relations between the political echelon and the army, and the functions and

Date	Contents
	powers of government ministers. Ben-Gurion brings up the problem of manpower in the public administration: "A huge issue . . . that I think is fundamental is the recruitment of people for public administration. It's not easy, and it's not easy to rip out the [existing] practice. I know of only one country where everything about this matter is fine: England, because there is a political genius that guides it. Civil service [employees] are hired after being tested. There's a committee and an official has to be tested by it. I don't think all bureaucrats should be hired that way. You can divide up [the public administration] into three categories: a) Confidential officials, meaning a person in whom a minister has personal trust. But the number of such people is very small. b) Ordinary workers – they should be hired by means of the [labor] bureau. . . . As for experts – a civil service law that includes a test of proficiency has to be put together. Until then, things should remain as they are: a ministerial committee for the apparatus [in order to maintain administrative continuity in the changeover from Yishuv to state]."
May 6, 1949	Structure of the army.
May 10, 1949	Continued discussion of structure of the army.
June 14, 1949	Military Jurisprudence Bill: Minister [of Justice–Liberal] Pinchas Rosenbluet reports about the presentation of the bill to the Knesset. The bill contains the abolition of the death penalty even for treason, except in times of emergency. Ben-Gurion favors the death penalty and gives examples. His view is that the threat of this penalty should be maintained but it should not be carried out in practice. Discussion of a compulsory education law. Ben-Gurion about the Negev: This is the most difficult "slice" [of the country] and the one with the most potential. The question of allowing certain [Arab] refugees to return.
June 12, 1949	One of the places that Ben-Gurion regrets that Israel did not occupy is Jerusalem. We have to hold Jerusalem as far as the Dead Sea. That is, the intention is to establish continuity between Jerusalem and the Jordan Valley without occupying the entire West Bank. Afterwards, pros and cons about the Gaza Strip.

14. BGA, Doc. 1162/59/42.
15. Continuation of minutes of minister of defense meeting with IDF commanders, July 21, 1949.
16. Shapira, *From the dismissal*, p. 50.
17. Moshe Dayan, *Avnei derekh* [Story of my life] (Jerusalem: Idanim, 1976), pp. 212–213.
18. Ibid.
19. Ben-Gurion speech to IDF commanders, July 21, 1949.
20. E. Gellner, *Nations and Nationalism: New Perspectives on the Past* (Ithaca, NY: Cornell University Press, 1983 [Hebrew translation: Leumim u-leumiyut (Tel Aviv; The Open University of Israel, 1994)].
21. The Haifa sociologist Oz Almog recently attempted to tackle this stereotype and describe it in its various facets. However, I do not share his methodology and many of the findings, as a historian rather than a social scientist.

22. I refer here to Erik H. Erikson's definition of the shaping of the adult "I"; see Ericson, *Childhood and Society* (New York: W. W. Norton, 1950) [Hebrew translation: Yaldut ve-hevra (Merhavia: Sifriyat Ha-Poalim, 1974)].

23. See Y. Allon, *Masakh shel hol* [Sandscreen] (Tel Aviv: Hakibbutz Hameuchad, 1968), p. 80.

24. In this matter, see Ze'ev Tsahor's aforementioned study about the Mapam leader Ya'akov Hazan: *Hazan – movement of life*. Natan Shaham, editor of Sifriyat Poalim, Mapam's publishing house, refused to publish the study under his imprint; ultimately it was published by Yad Izhak Ben-Zvi in Jerusalem. According to Yaron London in *Yediot Aharonot* (March 14, 1997), Tsahor listed the members of a Mapam "military committee" in which high-ranking reservists such as Yigal Allon, Yitzhak Sadeh, Moshe Carmel, and Shimon Avidan served. This was an official committee, which existed in various incarnations even after Mapam's schism in the mid-1950s; its documents are found in its participants' archives at kibbutz Efal. However, the party also had a parallel "secret committee," headed by Baruch Rabinov of kibbutz Beit Alfa. On the basis of Rabinov's documents, Tsahor reported that Yaakov Hazan accused Ben-Gurion of having entered into a conspiracy with the British even before the establishment of statehood, promising them bases and aspiring to make Israel a Western appendage in the Middle East. As one aspect of this ostensible conspiracy, Ben-Gurion had purportedly conceded the conquest of the entire country, from the Mediterranean to the Jordan River. This combination of conspiracy theory, pro-Soviet thinking, and fealty to the indivisibility of Eretz Israel was typical of all of Mapam. In 1950, Hazan charged Rabinov, a veteran of the Hagana, with establishing clandestine Mapam cells in the security services and, said Tsahor, "At least fifty kibbutzim had secret arms caches." The party's cells in the IDF were compartmentalized on the basis of the "finest of underground rules," and their members "discussed insinuating the spirit of mutiny into the tents of the army and the need to prepare for the day the order is given." Schemes were concocted to slip Mapam people into key positions in the army, apart from the many positions that were already in their hands, or so Rabinov bragged.

25. Continuation of the minister of defense's lecture on July 21, 1949.

26. I am referring to childhood experiences at New High School in Tel Aviv in the 1950s, particularly a public reenactment of the Prague trials that I initiated with the consent of the principal, the late Tony Halle. At the trial, the Ha-shomer ha-Tsa'ir representative, Chaim Ben-Shahar, defended the perpetrators of this show trial and won a majority vote. I was a member of the non-Marxist Scouts.

27. Prime minister's speech to IDF high command, Tel Hashomer, April 6, 1950, IDF Archive, Doc. 44/77.

28. Ibid., IDF Archive.

29. This idealism was epitomized by some amazing people, one of whom was an education officer named Barzilai, first name unfortunately unknown. He was active in the Hagana before the War of Independence and led a very austere life at the edge of our bourgeois neighborhood in central Tel Aviv. His wife, younger than he was, peddled flowers; therefore, we thought of her as something of a low-life. The neighborhood children bullied her son because of his inferior status and his guilelessness, a little like the way we bullied religious children because of their faith. After the war, the father came home in uniform wearing the bars of a major, a respectable grade in our eyes, but looking old and spent. So it went until we heard

him one day – when I was a young Gadna cadet – preaching to us passionately to treat the transit-camp children well because our security depended on them. His eyes glittered with fire; his age was no longer evident. I was gripped with immense regret over the things we had done to his son back then. The purpose of this vignette is to show how alienated urban teens were from the ostensible general mobilization for pioneering and egalitarian values during the Yishuv period.

As for the corruption that typified that era, again I testify from my innocent experience as a cadet in the Gadna command. An officer of Mizrahi origin became acquainted with this corruption in a very interesting way. He would roll around the Yiddish expression *gesheftn* – i.e., all kinds of corrupt deals and kickbacks with which he must have been confronted – on his tongue and add an animated bit of Arabic profanity, his flashing eyes revealing profound cunning. Eventually, this officer made himself a fine career in the IDF, evidently because he had learned from his teachers but also because the climate in the army at the time was convenient for the advancement of talented officers like him, for reasons including their origin.

30. See Ben-Gurion's speech of January 14, 1951, addressing the IDF's high command.
31. I refer to his appointment of Dayan after the 1959 elections as minister of agriculture – a portfolio devoid of political/security nature – as his colleague, Shimon Peres, was elevated from the executive echelon to the political one as deputy minister of defense. These appointments were counterbalanced by the appointment of Abba Eban – a pronounced "dove" who did not share Dayan's and Peres's military-based outlooks – to the posts of deputy prime minister and minister of education, and the appointment of Giora Josephtal – another centrist who held moderate security views – as minister in charge of welfare. Ben-Gurion even approached Yigael Yadin, a former COGS, at this time and asked him to plunge into political life after a lengthy period of research and teaching, to no avail.
32. See plans of the British and American chiefs of staff during this time, who sought Israel's active cooperation as a key or an alternative to Egypt, in M. J. Cohen, *Fighting World War Three from the Middle East: Allied Contingency Plans, 1945– 1954* (London and Portland, OR: Frank Cass, 1997), especially pp. 210–228, in regard to Gen. Sir Brian Robertson's visit to Israel in February 1951, about a month after Ben-Gurion spoke before the IDF high command.
33. Obviously, anyone who reads Ben-Gurion's comments about Jews who were originally from the Arab world may interpret them as an ostensibly racist indictment of the Mizrahim, akin to the leftist politician and agitator Yossi Sarid's manipulation in similar remarks that he made for his political needs. See interview by author with former Mapai Member of the Knesset Yehuda Hashai in March 1989.
34. For a full version, see A. Shealtiel (ed.), *David Ben-Gurion: Rosh ha-memshala ha-rishon* [David Ben-Gurion: The first prime minister] (Jerusalem: Israel State Archives, 1996), pp. 254–256.
35. Ben-Gurion speech at Ohalo, December 16, 1954, BGA.
36. See discussion of the acquisition of the Dimona nuclear reactor further in the text.
37. Remarks at the Knesset, February 20, 1950, *David Ben-Gurion: The first prime minister*, pp. 141–146. This is the source of all Ben-Gurion quotations that follow in this section, unless stated otherwise.
38. See Anita Shapira, *From the dismissal*.
39. Ibid., p. 36. We did note earlier that Shapira was oblivious to the British model that Ben-Gurion wished to adopt for Israel, *mutatis mutandis*.

40. Anyone who regrets the absence of a written constitution that would have solved the problem of religion and state might argue that the British solution has left Israel with a society "captive to politicians" instead of an American-style "civil society" based on a written constitution. In this matter, see Y. Shapira, *Hevra bi-shvi ha-politiqa'im* [Society in the thrall of politicians] (Tel Aviv: Sifriyat Poalim, 1996). The reader may guess that I do not share the attempt made by Shapira and his disciples in the leftist Meretz Party to criticize Ben-Gurion for being an "old tyrant" (as M. K. Yossi Sarid said in a radio broadcast in April 1997). I also do not share their attempt to distinguish between a civil society and an ostensible "regime of politicians," which, from their standpoint, is the direct outcome of the lack of a written constitution such as that of the United States, for the further reason that the U.S. Constitution was crafted and interpreted under unique conditions and circumstances. In this matter, consult a milder critic of the Yonatan Shapira school: E. Ben-Rafael, "'Society in the Thrall of Politicians' and the Onslaught of the New Radicalism," *Mifne: Bama le-inyanei hevra* [Turning point: Forum on social affairs], April 1997, pp. 54–60. "Another way of explaining the nonpassage of a constitution when Israel first came into being," Ben-Rafael says, "is the immanent difficulty of establishing 'final' truths about the problem of defining a collective in terms that are consistent with the requirements of a liberal democracy."

41. See Lynne Olson, *Troublesome Young Men: The Rebels Who Brought Churchill to Power and Helped Save England* (New York: Farrar, Straus and Giroux, 2007).

42. Letter to Zalman Aranne, January 6, 1951, in Shealtiel, *David Ben-Gurion: The first prime minister*, pp. 225–227.

43. See minister of defense's lectures at his meetings with the IDF high command and also prime minister's speech in the Knesset and his responses in the general debate over the Security Service Bill, August 15, 1949, in *Medinat yisrael ha-mehudeshet* [The renewed Jewish state], pp. 389–399.

44. Ibid., p. 391.

45. "Hanukkah reflections," *War diary*, pp. 902–903. On the meetings with Bergmann and Racah, see ibid, p. 827.

46. Remarks by Professor Yisrael Dostrovsky at a conference on "Ben-Gurion and Science," sponsored by the Israel Academy of the Sciences and Arts on April 23, 1987, to mark the centennial of Ben-Gurion's birth. Dostrovsky entitled his lecture "David Ben-Gurion and the Development of Science in Israel."

47. On the commission's resignation, see letter of resigning commission members, February 17, 1958, given to me courtesy of member Professor Shmuel Sambursky, the first director of the "science council" at the Office of the Prime Minister. According to the members who resigned, the commission had not been called into session since 1956, that is, since the opportunity to import a nuclear reactor from France had come about, eliminating the need for home-manufacture.

48. See M. Sharett, *Yomanei Sharett* [Sharett's diaries], vol. 5 (Tel Aviv: Sifriyat Ma'ariv, 1978). Sharett reported in this diary not only on his meetings with Bergmann but also with other scientists and with the director general of the Office of the Prime Minister, Teddy Kollek, ahead of the meetings with Eric Johnston, U.S. special representative for water issues, pp. 400, 483, 533–534, 565.

49. The authoritative French source in this matter is P. Pean, *Les deux bombes* (Paris: Fayard, 1984), pp. 38–39.

50. M. Golan, *Peres* (Tel Aviv: Schocken, 1982), p. 41.

51. Pean, *Les deux bombes*, pp. 38–39.

52. Minutes of conference in Beer Sheva on the mobilization of youth, BGA, Doc. 001/2175, July 19, 1954.
53. Dayan, *Story of my life*, p. 143.
54. Ibid.
55. Ibid., p. 208.
56. Ibid., p. 167.
57. Ibid., p. 174.
58. Ibid.
59. Ibid., p. 217.
60. For details on this transaction, see Peres's account in his English-language memoirs: S. Peres, *Battling for Peace: A Memoir*, ed. David Landau (London: Weidenfeld and Nicolson, 1995), pp. 120–121.
61. See Golan, *Peres*, pp. 54, 120–131. In his aforementioned memoirs, Peres offers a different version that is largely conventional in its reading of the goals and preliminaries of the war. On p. 130, however, Golan mentions the acquisition of the nuclear reactor in Dimona (and, in an evident compromise with the Israeli military censor, refers to it as a "small reactor") as an inseparable part of the protocols of the Israeli–French negotiations at Sèvres, which co-opted Israel into the war. See text that follows.
62. Golan, *Peres*; cf. Peres, *Battling for Peace*, p. 125.
63. In this matter, see H. P. Schwarz, "Adenauer und die Kernwaffen," *Vierteljahreshefte für Zeitgeschuchte*, 4 (1989), pp. 567–593, and cf. Aronson, *The Politics and Strategy of Nuclear Weapons in the Middle East*, vol. 1. Consult the chapter that discusses the press conference called in the autumn of 1964 by the Bonn government spokesman, Guenther von Hase, concerning nuclear cooperation between Israel and West Germany. In the aftermath of this cooperation – said the *Frankfurter Rundschau* the next day – Israel would soon have an atomic bomb and that German scientists had helped to develop it.
64. See J. Newhouse, *War and Peace in the Nuclear Age* (New York: Knopf, 1989), pp. 131–132; cf. C. McArdle Kelleher, *Germany and the Politics of Nuclear Weapons* (New York: Columbia University Press, 1975). In its dying days, according to Newhouse, the Fourth Republic concluded an agreement with the West German minister of defense, Franz Josef Strauss, concerning funding from the Bonn government for the French nuclear program. Kelleher claims that the French–German–Italian accord existed as an idea only (mentioned in Ben-Gurion's diaries at the time) and did not take form until de Gaulle came to power. Immediately after his return, the general terminated this cooperation, which clashed with his outlook on an exclusively French "national bomb." According to Matti Golan, Shimon Peres originally believed that de Gaulle would not stay in power for long and that Mollet would resume the reins "within a year and a half." See Golan, *Peres*, p. 81.
65. Golan, *Peres*, pp. 58–59.
66. Pean, *Les deux bombes*, p. 83.

5. From the 1956 War to the "Lavon Affair"

1. See Hanna Yablonka, *Ahim zarim* [Alien brethren]; and cf. her "Qelitat nitsolei ha-sho'ah bi-medinat yisrael – hebetim hadashim [Absorption of Holocaust survivors in the State of Israel – new aspects]," *Iyyunim bi-tqumat yisrael* [Studies in the Jewish rebirth], 7 (1997), pp. 285–289.

2. Quoted from his unpublished diary in Michael Bar-Zohar, *Ben-Gurion: Biographia politit* [Ben-Gurion: A political biography], vol. 3: *Yoman Ben-Gurion* [Diary of Ben Gurion] (Tel Aviv: Am-Oved, 1997), entry of August 19, 1958, p. 1343. At the time, Jordan was being menaced by Nasser and survived by means of direct British [and indirect Israeli] assistance, including aid for its grip on the West Bank. Ben-Gurion revealed his attitude toward this country in a remark a short time later at a meeting with his Defense Ministry aides (p. 1343): "For us, the best thing would be for the status quo to hold on. Then neither Egypt nor Syria nor Iraq [would take over Jordan]; instead, it would be a weak country that no one is afraid of."

3. See Keren's discussion of Ben-Gurion's debate with the author Chaim Hazaz in 1962, *Ben-Gurion ve-ha-intelektualim* [Ben-Gurion and the intellectuals], pp. 132–134. See also Ben-Gurion correspondence with the author S. Yizhar, who complained that "[o]ur generation is a generation of empty souls," and Ben-Gurion's response to the philosopher Shmuel Hugo Bergman's jeremiad about how "[m]an has been replaced by the Kafkaesque mannequin, a faceless and nameless mechanism, clerks and secretaries," ibid., pp. 127–129.

4. In this matter, see the fascinating debate between the physicist Amos de-Shalit and Ben-Gurion on the question of science and truth, quoted in Keren, ibid., pp. 40–50. In this debate, de-Shalit invoked quantum mechanics to argue the relativity of physical reality, and from said point of departure – Keren claims – stated that "[t]he mind is no longer a means of discovering the truth but rather a means of organizing constantly changing truths." Keren, of course, credits de-Shalit with the advantage of modern thinking as against the obsolete "Spinozian" thinking of Ben-Gurion, who believed that the human mind could fathom nature and discover unquestionable truths in it. We can argue that the physicists of the 1950s were far off in their quest for the meaning of the quantum revolution, which was limited to the world of subatomic particles.

5. In this matter, see Keren, ibid., pp. 82–84.

6. In conjunction with Eliezer Livne, Leibowitz established the Public Committee for Nuclear Disarmament in the Middle East and spared no effort to lambaste the nuclear project in Dimona as a failure, a threat to Israel's security, and "a tool for the attainment of political power for Ben-Gurion and his people" such as Shimon Peres, director of the nuclear project; see S. Aronson, with Oded Brosh, *Nesheq gar'ini ba-mizrah ha-tikhon* [Nuclear weapons in the Middle East], 2 vols. (Jerusalem: Academon, 1994 and 2004) with an update in 2006. Subsequently, Leibowitz and Livne parted ways and turned in different directions after finding convenient topics for their public activity: One became a Greater Israel enthusiast and the other a crusader against Israel's occupation of the West Bank in 1967.

7. Keren, *Ben-Gurion and the intellectuals*, p. 83.

8. Speech at Ohalo, December 16, 1954, BGA (no microfilm frames available).

9. Keren, op. cit., p. 84.

10. Ibid., p. 73.

11. Ibid., p. 85.

12. Ibid., p. 86, note.

13. Upon Hitler's ascendancy as chancellor of Germany, but representing the Nazi Party in a conservative coalition as a minority party, Buber wrote: "[T]he Hitler people will either remain in the government, regardless; then they'll be sent [by the conservative majority] into battle against the proletariat, which will split their party

and will render them harmless. Or they'll quit [the government]: then there will be presumably a state of emergency in which ... the technical superiority of the army vis-à-vis the [Nazis] will undoubtedly win the upper hand. As long as the present coalition prevails, any real prosecution of the Jews ... or anti-Jewish legislation is unthinkable." Source: Fred Weinstein, *The Dynamics of Nazism: Leadership, Ideology, and the Holocaust* (New York: Academic Press, 1980), p. 22.

14. Keren, op. cit., pp. 72, 73.
15. W. Kaufmann, "Buber's Failures and Triumph," in H. Gordon and J. Bloch (eds.), *Martin Buber: A Centenary Volume* (New York: Ktav, 1984), pp. 8*ff*. This collection is composed largely of discussions at a symposium on Buber's thinking at Ben-Gurion University of the Negev. The approach taken by its editors, who considered themselves Buber's truest disciples, had already changed after the Six Day War. The late Jochanan Bloch became an ultranationalist Greater Israel advocate and Chaim Gordon became no less extreme a critic – to the extent of hatred and public struggle over various matters in which he lacked expertise – of everything that happened in Israel after the Six Day War.
16. Keren, *Ben-Gurion and the intellectuals*, p. 86, note.
17. Ibid., pp. 14–15.
18. Ibid., p. 14, n. 12.
19. For details, see Aronson *Nuclear weapons in the Middle East*, vol. 1, pp. 267*ff*.
20. Michal Ben-Naftali Berkowitz, "Ha-philosophim ha-yisraelim ve-ha-shoah [The Israeli philosophers and the Holocaust]," *Teoria u-bikoret* [Theory and criticism], 4 (Autumn 1993), pp. 57–77.
21. Ibid., p. 65.
22. Ibid.
23. Professor Yuval Ne'eman told this author that Lavon had caused the development of the nuclear option to be set back "for years."
24. Bar-Zohar, *Ben-Gurion*, vol. 3, p. 1441, describes Ben-Gurion's attempts to place Yadin at the forefront of the "Young Turks" circle ahead of the 1959 elections.

6. From the "Lavon Affair" to the Six Day War

1. For details, see Aronson, *Nesheq gar'ini ba-mizrah ha-tikhon* [Nuclear weapons in the Middle East], rev. Hebrew version (1994), vol. 1, pp. 61–82.The original English version was translated into Hebrew and published by Academon Press, Jerusalem, in much larger and detailed versions – one in 1994–1995 in two volumes (with the assistance of Oded Brosh) and one updated volume in 2006. The notes in this book are taken mostly from the Hebrew versions; if not, they explicitly refer to the original English.
2. See testimony of Yehuda Ben-Moshe, a member the committee, to the weekly journal *Koteret Rashit*, November 26, 1986: "Esrim ve-chamesh shana lifnei Vanunu [Twenty-five years before [Mordechai] Vanunu]."
3. Ibid. This indifference persisted even though Leibowitz and Livne insinuated this issue and others into articles that they published in the *Encyclopedia Hebraica* [Hebrew Encyclopedia], which Leibowitz edited. For an example, s.v. "Ben-Gurion, David," pp. 666–677, written by Leibowitz.
4. Denis Healey, the British secretary of state for defense on behalf of Labour, took the rhetoric to the higher level of terming Peres a "fascist." Testimony of Israeli ambassador to London, Efraim Evron, to the author.

5. Here we find a perceptible overlap among Shabtai Teveth, who devoted to this allegation his book *Qalaban: al ma nafal David Ben-Gurion?* [The banana peel: What brought David Ben-Gurion down?] (Tel Aviv: Ish-Dor, 1992); Bar-Zohar, *Ben-Gurion*, vol. 3, pp. 1479–1484; and Golan, *Peres*, pp. 114–115.

6. In his book *Devarim ke-havayatam* [Things as they are], Ben-Gurion provides a detailed explanation that he wrote to Martin Buber about his investigations of the Affair.

7. Ben-Gurion to Yariv Ben-Aharon. See Keren, *Ben-Gurion ve-ha-intelektualim* [Ben-Gurion and the intellectuals], pp. 87–88.

8. The journalist Dan Margalit, who launched his career at this time as a junior correspondent for Uri Avnery's *Haolam Hazeh*, was summoned to a meeting with Leibowitz and Livne, who told him about the crisis with de Gaulle and described what they knew about the "failure" of the reactor construction project. The meeting took Margalit much by surprise; he kept its details to himself, as he told this author years later.

9. Even a contemporaneous historian such as Professor Yechiam Weitz regards the unseating of Lavon as an uninhibitedly dictatorial act and claims that in the early 1960s, and a fortiori later in that decade, Ben-Gurion deteriorated into a vengeful, tragic, and marginal personality after having exhausted his "charisma," the secret of his lengthy rule. Weitz's sources for this matter are Ya'akov Talmon, Ben-Gurion's longtime rival; Yitzhak Ben-Aharon, a leftist politician; the author Amos Oz – a young confidant of Lavon's; and the journalist Amos Elon, on whose criticism of Ben-Gurion Weitz bases his opinion; e.g., in Elon's *The Israelis: Founders and Sons* (1971). See Y. Weitz, "Qets ha-reshit: Le-berur ha-musag 'reshit ha-medina' [End of the beginning: Elucidating the concept of 'genesis of the state']," in Y. Weitz (ed.), *Bein hazon le-revizia: Me'a shenot historiografia tsiyyonit* [Between vision and revision: A century of Zionist historiography] (Jerusalem: Yad Izhak Ben-Zvi, 1997), pp. 244–247. Weitz used a rather polemical expression by quoting a remark about "Ben-Gurion's inexplicable rage over the conclusions of the 'internal committee of seven.'" In fact, Ben-Gurion's stance about a judicial – not a political – inquiry into the Affair, such as the one undertaken by the ministerial committee of the seven and similar complexes, had been accepted long ago, by means of the Commissions of Inquiries Act of 1968.

10. I can attest to this personally from my studies at the Departments of Political Science and General History at the Hebrew University at the time. Popper's influence was especially conspicuous at the former department. However, the scholars who were then considered the giants of their time in the West – such as the now-almost-forgotten American sociologist Talcott Parsons – were accepted as teachers of Israeli colleagues such as S. N. Eisenstadt, who started his career under Martin Buber.

11. There is no doubt that it was Lavon himself – thanks to his connections with Rotenstreich and others – who encouraged various intellectuals to behave this way, even though some of them, such as E. E. Urbach, had already enlisted in Leibowitz and Livne's Public Committee for Nuclear Disarmament in the Middle East.

12. See Ben-Gurion, *Things as they are*, p. 24, which quotes opinion pieces that he wrote during the 1960 Affair.

13. See Aronson, *Nuclear weapons in the Middle East* (1995), vol. 2, p. 69, and cf. Aronson, *Conflict and Bargaining in the Middle East: An Israeli Perspective* (Baltimore and London: Johns Hopkins University Press, 1978), pp. 41–42.

14. A principal source for France's views on this issue is the aforementioned Pierre Pean, *Les deux bombes* (1984 and new reprints).
15. Professor Ze'ev "Venia" Hadari – one of the scientists involved with the reactor – told the author that in response to the Americans' discovery of the construction of the reactor and the imminent publication of the discovery in American and British newspapers, Ben-Gurion gave orders to cover up the infrastructure that had already been installed. However, Hadari and his associates opposed this and threatened to "cover themselves up" in the soil along with the facility.
16. On Ben-Gurion's meetings with de Gaulle during this period, see Y. Bar-On, "Met-siyut ve-dimayaon: Mikhtavim u-mifgashim bein Ben-Gurion ve-de Gaulle [Reality and imagination: Letters and meetings between Ben-Gurion and De Gaulle]," *Medina, mimshal ve-yahasim benleumi'im* [State, government, and international relations], 38 (Spring–Summer 1993), pp. 77–95. Bar-On, who served at the office of Israel's military attaché in Paris, provides a general account of Israel–French relations at the time on the basis of his experience, his research, and attestations of the ambassador, Walter Eytan. According to Eytan, Peres's initiatives – including the leaking of remarks by de Gaulle during Ben-Gurion's visit to the effect that "Israel is our friend and ally" – had led to French anger and much exaggeration in Paris–Jerusalem relations.
17. See Ben-Gurion–Sharett correspondence in Bar-Zohar, *Ben-Gurion*, vol. 3, p. 1498: "Lavon . . . instructed Fati [Yehoshafat Harkabi, who had been named chief of MI after Gibli's resignation] to attack the British Consulate in Amman and a bridge in order to initiate a conflict between the U.K. and Jordan, and MD[ayan] cancelled the order." The envisaged operation resembled that in Egypt in 1954, which took place while COGS Dayan was visiting the United States.
18. Almogi published his version of the Affair and Ben-Gurion's downfall years later in his book, *Ha-ma'avaq al Ben-Gurion: Be-iqvot ha-parasha* [The struggle for Ben-Gurion: In the wake of the affair] (Jerusalem: Yedioth Ahronoth, 1988), arguing that the "Dayan-Peres group" had made unauthorized use of that public scandal to piggyback on Ben-Gurion's reputation and actions and pose publicly as his successors. Actually, Lavon himself had contributed to this because as the public debate over the Affair escalated, he insinuated that Ben-Gurion himself had given the order for the abortive operation in Egypt, routing the instruction to people whom he had left behind in the defense system, i.e., Gen. Dayan and Shimon Peres; thus, as it were, he had manipulated them from his seat in Sede Boqer.
19. In this matter, see Pean, *Les deux bombes*, pp. 104–107.
20. See I. Harel, *Mashber ha-mad'anim ha-germani'im be-mitsrayim, 1962–1963* [The crisis of the German scientists in Egypt, 1962–1963] (Tel Aviv: Ma'ariv, 1983), pp. 7–17. To prove his contention that the Shavit II was nothing but a "meaningless hunk of pipe," Harel cited M. Mardor, *Rafael* (Tel Aviv: Ministry of Defense Publishing House, 1981), p. 319.
21. Harel, *Mashber ha-mad'anim.*
22. In his book, *The struggle for Ben-Gurion*, Almogi claimed that Peres deliberately leaked home-brewed conjectures about Ben-Gurion's intention of passing over his veteran comrades in favor of Peres and his "young guard" colleagues. In a conversation with this author, he further alleged that Peres had even leaked information to the British *Observer* and *Middle East Review* about Foreign Minister Meir's severe illness, a deeply guarded secret between Ben-Gurion and the head of the opposition, Menachem Begin. In his book (pp. 318–319), Almogi quoted an entry from

Ben-Gurion's diary concerning Meir's "resentment" of Peres and Ben-Gurion's response that, indeed, "There's something to it."

23. For support of this argument, see Bar-On's article (n. 16 in this chapter) and Peres's estimation, cited by Golan, that de Gaulle's regime would soon fall and the helm of France would be reclaimed by Guy Mollet.

24. See Peres's version of the Affair in *Battling for Peace*, pp. 138–140.

25. Source: Golan, Kennedy–Peres meeting in April 1962, in *Peres*, pp. 123–124.

26. Even after the various British intelligence services worked out a high level of cooperation, the "chiefs of staff" forgot the existence of a senior scientific adviser to the commander in chief of the Royal Air Force and the chief of foreign intelligence in their investigation of the German missile threat against London, thereby creating unnecessary redundancy and causing waste of precious time in this crucial matter. The resulting Gordian knot was ultimately sliced by Churchill himself, if not completely. See N. Annan, *Changing Enemies: The Defeat and Regeneration of Germany* (New York: W. W. Norton, 1995), pp. 87–88. Lord Annan served in British Military Intelligence during World War II; his testimony is but one of many.

27. See Harel's own account in his book *Bitahon ve-demokratia* [Security and democracy] (Tel Aviv: Idanim, 1988).

28. For a detailed account and discussion, see Keren, *Ben-Gurion and the intellectuals*, pp. 90–92.

29. Allan Bloom, *The Closing of the American Mind*, p. 67. Concerning Karl Jaspers, see Elhanan Yakira, *Post Zionism, Post Holocaust* [Post-tsiyyonut, post-sho'ah]: *Three Essays on Denial, Forgetting, and the Delegitimation of Israel* (New York: Cambridge University Press, 2010), p. 275.

30. See quotation of his response in Keren, *Ben-Gurion and the intellectuals*, p. 93.

31. See Y. Gilad, "Da'at ha-qahal be-Yisrael al yahasei Yisrael ve-Germania ha-Ma'aravit ba-shanim 1949–1965 [Public opinion in Israel on Israel–West Germany relations in 1949–1965]," Ph.D. diss., Tel Aviv University.

32. Ibid., p. 295.

33. Peres, *Battling for Peace*, pp. 138–140.

34. The spokesman, Karl-Günther von Hase, called a press conference in October 1964 and reported on aid that the German government had provided in regard to Israeli nuclear research programs. His disclosure may have been prompted by a severe attack against his government by the Israeli minister without portfolio, Israel Galili, in regard to the scientists in Egypt: "Germany's scientific and technologic potential," Galili charged, "has converged with the Nasserite war machine." This groundless allegation was voiced just as Bonn was supplying vast quantities of conventional weapons to Israel. Galili also asserted his willingness to do without Germany's aid to Israel.

35. On Ben-Gurion's visit to Britain on his way back from his meeting with Kennedy, see Aronson, *Nuclear weapons in the Middle East* (1992), pp. 72–74.

36. Following a discussion on Israel Channel 1 television about the Six Day War, in which Shimon Peres furiously disputed my claim that Dimona had played a central role en route to the war, Gideon Raphael, by then a key official at Golda Meir's Foreign Ministry (among other things, he phrased Ben-Gurion's messages to President Kennedy concerning this issue), contacted me by telephone and said that I was undoubtedly right. "Dimona," he said, "was the linchpin of Israeli diplomacy in the early 1960s." Raphael even regarded Ben-Gurion's resignation in 1963 as

a "noble" act that averted an exceedingly grave crisis in Israel–U.S. relations in regard to the reactor problem.

37. Here see Y. Evron, *Ha-dilema ha-gar'init shel yisrael* [Israel's nuclear dilemma] (Tel Aviv: Hakibbutz Hameuhad, 1987), pp. 17–18.

38. In this matter, Galili's right-hand man – Arnan Azaryahu, better known by his nickname, "Sini" – gathered the requisite theoretical literature, including published opuses by Albert Wohlstetter and others. See Aronson, *Nuclear weapons in the Middle East*, p. 74.

39. In regard to this "reassessment," see ibid., p. 81, note.

40. The matter at hand concerned a dispute over the significance of the German missile program. Churchill's chief scientific adviser, Lord Cherwell, belittled the severity of the problem as against the views of a much younger and lower-ranking scientist, Dr. R. V. Jones, which the prime minister ultimately accepted after weighing and debating them at length. See n. 26 in this chapter.

41. See Aronson, *Nuclear weapons in the Middle East* (1995), vol. 2, pp. 317*ff*.

42. Ibid.

43. See Aronson, *Nuclear weapons in the Middle East* (1992), p. 26.

44. See editorial in the *Jewish Observer and Middle East Review*, December 28, 1962, headlined, "Independent Deterrent Force for Israel." This journal, which often solicited Peres's views, stated here that the Cuban missile crisis demonstrated overtly how hesitant the United States would be to embroil itself in a nuclear war on behalf of interests that were marginal from its standpoint, and that Israel understood this. Pursuant to this lesson and its precursor, the Holocaust, however, the Israelis realized that a much smaller and more sophisticated deterrent, one that was deliberately limited from the standpoint of potential aggressors, such as the Soviet Union, was crucial for their security and existence.

45. In regard to the State Department's actions, the president's directives, and Ben-Gurion's responses to them, and in regard to my sources – mostly from the Kennedy Archives in Boston and, in smaller part, of Israeli origin – see Aronson, *Nuclear weapons in the Middle East* (1994), vol. 1, pp. 296*ff*.

46. On McCloy's mission, see Aronson, *Nuclear Weapons in the Middle East* (1992), pp. 79–92, 317 note, 318 note, 320 note.

47. See Bar-Zohar, *Ben-Gurion*, vol. 3, pp. 1522–1526; cf. ibid., pp. 1554–1559.

48. On Ben-Gurion's correspondence with Kennedy and his concurrent appeals to the leaders of the other Western powers, see Bar Zohar, *Ben-Gurion*. Gideon Rafael, in an oral communication with this author, added that it was he who had phrased Ben-Gurion's messages. Their purpose, he said, was to justify the Dimona project, which was Ben-Gurion's principal concern at the time.

49. Notably, quite a few Arab newspapers alleged at the time that Israel had been behind the president's assassination.

50. See Yitzhak Greenberg, "Tashtit ha-mechkar ve-ha-pituach be-maarechet ha-bitachon: Aspectim shel mediniut ve-tikzuv [The foundations of Israel's security R&D: Aspects of policy and budgeting]," published in *Iyunim be-tkumat yisrael* [Studies in the Jewish Rebirth, Studies in Zionism, the Yishuv and the State of Israel: A Research Annual] (Sede Boqer: Ben-Gurion Research Center, Ben-Gurion University of the Negev Press, 1999), vol. 9, pp. 167–187. Quoted in my article "David Ben-Gurion, Levi Eshkol, and the Struggle Over Dimona: A Prologue to the Six Day War and Its (Un)Anticipated Results," published in *Israel Affairs*, 15 (April 2009), pp. 114–134.

51. Grechko visited Cairo in December 1965; a report that the USSR would guarantee Egypt's security if Israel were to develop or obtain nuclear arms appeared in the *New York Times* in early 1966.

52. Quondam minister Yitzhak Ben-Aharon to this author.

53. Yuval Ne'eman, "Lama hitpatarti mi-misrad ha-bitachon [Why I resigned from the MOD]," *Ha'aretz*, February 6, 1966.

54. Interview by the author with Ze'ev Sheck, Israel's envoy in Paris at the time. Sheck spoke explicitly about the "medium-range missile" and regarded its continued current development by France as a principal test of the soundness of relations between de Gaulle and Israel.

55. On Dayan and his published writings at the time, see Aronson, revised and updated Hebrew version of *Nuclear Weapons in the Middle East* [Nesheq gar'ini ba-mizrah ha-tikhon] (2006), vol. 2, p. 17.

56. In this matter, see M. Brecher, *Decisions in Israel's Foreign Policy* (New Haven, CT: Yale University Press, 1975), p. 332, and cf. M. Gazit's detailed and evenhanded study, partly based on primary sources from the John F. Kennedy Presidential Library and Museum in Boston: M. Gazit, *President Kennedy's Policy toward the Arab States and Israel: Analysis and Documents* (Tel Aviv: Shiloah Center for Middle Eastern and African Studies, 1983).

57. Department of State, Cable 737A, April 11, 1964, on U.S.–Egypt relations (Secret). Source: Lyndon Baines Johnson Presidential Library and Museum, Austin, Texas, NSF UAR – Container 158, Item 39. Badeau was a typical "Arabist" who had served as president of the American University in Cairo before entering the U.S. Foreign Service.

58. Limited circulation. Source: Johnson Library, NSF (National Security Files), Committee on Nuclear Proliferation, Container 1–2, Problem 2, Item 1.

59. Diplomatic Cable 2447, sent to Vienna on June 26, 1963, to International Atomic Energy Agency in a circular to all Arab capitals (classified Confidential). Source: UPA microfilms, Israel: National Security Files 1963–1969, K4–128b [Kathy], Library of Congress Microfilm Reading Room, 86–89264 (85–4561 MICRR).

60. Copies of this cable were sent to the chiefs of staff, the White House, Special Ambassador Averill Harriman, and other agencies of the administration. Source: Johnson Library, NSF Israel, vol. 4, Cables 2/65–11/65 (Secret).

61. According to the *New York Times* (January 7, 1966), the United States believed that Israel had ordered thirty medium-range missiles from France in an action that apparently signaled its intent to develop atomic weapons. According to the same source (March 7, 1966), influential newspaper editors in Israel were secretly demanding the termination of the governmental and self-imposed ban on discussion of the dissemination of nuclear weapons. The *Times* added (March 14, 1966) that, according to the Israeli "nuclear expert," Peres, Israel had not decided to convert an inspection accord relating to Dimona into U.S. financial aid and expected a big debate to ensue if Washington were to bruit such a demand. According to the *Times* of May 19, 1966, Prime Minister Eshkol repeated Israel's self-declared obligation not to be the first party to introduce nuclear weapons in the Middle East. On June 20, 1966, the same paper reported a third American inspection visit to Dimona.

62. Secretary of State Dean Rusk to President Johnson. Source: Johnson Library, Austin, Texas, UAR (Egypt), Containers 159–161, Cables, vol. 2, Item 99a.J.

63. The visit took place in late 1965, even though the wording of the nuclear "guarantee" that Moscow would give Egypt, if Israel were to "develop" or "obtain" nuclear arms, did not appear in the *New York Times* until early 1966.

64. Previously, Komer had been involved in simulation games that were set up by Thomas Schelling of the Rand Corporation, a renowned social scientist and activist against nuclear proliferation. In this matter and on the firm stance against nuclear proliferation of McGeorge Bundy, national security adviser to Presidents Kennedy and Johnson, see Aronson, *Nuclear weapons in the Middle East* (1994), vol. 1, p. 155 and its sources.

65. See Yitzhak Rabin, *Pinqas sherut* [Service diary], pp. 129–130.

66. On Israel–German relations at the time, see Aronson, op. cit. (1994), vol. 2, pp. 45–51.

67. See cable U.S. Embassy in Egypt (signed by the ambassador, Lucius Battle, no. 2379, sanitized wording (without names), Johnson Library, NSF, UAR File, Containers 159–161, Item 20.

68. Efraim Evron, subsequently deputy mission chief in Washington, to the author.

69. Johnson Library, NSF, UAR File, Containers 159–161, Item 6.

70. Ibid., Item 21a.

71. U.S. Arms Control and Disarmament Agency, memorandum about a talk on the prospects of a nonproliferation accord and related matters, July 13, 1965, for restricted circulation, UPA – Library of Congress, copies to White House and U.S. embassies in Moscow, Cairo, Paris, UN mission, and Special Ambassador Harriman.

72. See Uri Izhar, *Bein hazon le-shilton: Mifleget Achdut-ha-Avodah Po'alei Zion bi-tkufat ha-yeshuv ve-ha-medina* [Between vision and power: The history of Achdut ha-Avodah Poalei Zion Party] (Tel Aviv: Yad Tabenkin, 2005), p. 313.

73. See Isabella Ginor and Gideon Remez, *Foxbats Over Dimona: The Soviets' Nuclear Gamble in the Six-Day War* (New Haven, CT: Yale University Press, 2007).

74. See my "David Ben-Gurion, Levi Eshkol and the Struggle Over Dimona: A Prologue to the Six Day War."

75. See I. Harel, "An Incomparably Unsavory Business," in *Bitahon ve-demokratia* [Security and democracy], pp. 452–453. Harel, who had become Eshkol's security affairs adviser, resigned this post in the aftermath of the Ben Barka scandal. In his book, Harel claimed that Eshkol had brought on a disaster in Israeli–French relations due to some vague order that he had given the Mossad in regard to the scandal. According to Harel in a talk with this author, however, it was being whitewashed everywhere at the time, and the whitewashers included the Knesset Foreign Affairs and Defense Committee and the Committee of Newspaper Editors.

76. See Dayan, "Germania, Dimona ve-ha-Yarden [Germany, Dimona, and the Jordan]," *Ha'aretz*, March 26, 1965.

77. Y. Rosenthal (ed.), *Yitzhak Rabin, rosh mimshelet yisrael: 1974–1977|1992–1995* [Yitzhak Rabin, prime minister of Israel 1974–1977|1992–1995], vol. 1 [1922–1967] (Jerusalem: Israel State Archive, 2005), pp. 335–337.

78. In this matter, see S. Aronson and D. Horowitz, "Ha-istrategia shel tagmul mevukar: Ha-dugma ha-yisraelit [The strategy of controlled retaliation: The case of Israel]," *Medina u-mimshal*, 1 (1971), pp. 77–99 (in Hebrew).

79. On Dayan's criticism of the air force operation on April 7, 1967, in which some 140 Israeli aircraft downed six Syrian MiGs and pursued the others to the outskirts

of Damascus, see E. Weizman, *Lekha shamayim, lekha eretz* [Autobiography of Ezer Weizman] (Tel Aviv: Sifriat Ma'ariv, 1975), p. 207. According to this source, Dayan angrily told his brother-in-law, who as head of the Operations Division had initiated the operation, that he and his superiors had "lost their minds" and were "leading Israel to war."

80. See E. Haber (ed.), *Ha-yom tifrots milhama: Zikhronotav shel tat-aluf Yisrael Lior, shalisham ha-tsva'i shel rashei ha-memshala Levi Eshkol ve-Golda Meir* [Today war will break out: The memoirs of Brig. Gen. Yisrael Lior, military adjutant of Prime Ministers Levi Eshkol and Golda Meir] (Tel Aviv: Idanim, 1987), pp. 147–148. Lior attributed other motives to Eshkol in his relations with Rabin, foremost the enormous prestige that the COGS had amassed in his numerous media appearances, which allowed this military man to overshadow the civilian defense minister.

81. Remarks by Miriam Eshkol to the author, approximately 1970.

82. See Haber, *Today war will break out*, p. 161, and cf. interview with the IAF commander at the time, Mordechai Hod, to *Ha'aretz*, June 11, 1993: "The reactor in Dimona was the most sensitive place in Israel and was feared to be a target of the highest priority for the Egyptians."

83. See Ginor and Remez, *Foxbats Over Dimona*.

84. The so-called "Sons of Light" plan; see Aronson, *Nuclear weapons in the Middle East* (2006), vol. 2, pp. 16–17.

85. See A. Brown, *Moshe Dayan ve-milhemet sheshet ha-yamim* [Moshe Dayan and the Six Day War] (Tel Aviv: Yedioth Ahronoth, 1997), pp. 31–35. Since Brown based his research on IDF documents that have not yet been released for publication (among other sources), his book should be considered a contribution to broader knowledge about the Six Day War from the requisite critical perspective.

86. Haber, *Today war will break out*.

87. See Rabin, *Pinqas sherut* [Service diary], p. 150, who states that Ben-Gurion had serious doubt about Nasser's intent to attack, and cf. Bar-Zohar, *Ben-Gurion*, vol. 3, pp. 1588–1591.

88. M. Brown (ed.), *Shisha yamim* [Six days] (Tel Aviv: Ministry of Defense, 1968), p. 3.

89. For the American deliberations before the May crisis, revolving as before around Dimona and the French missiles, and during the crisis, see *Foreign Relations of the United States 1964–1968*, vol. 19: *Arab-Israeli Crisis and War, 1967* (Washington, DC: Government Printing Office, 2004). For Eshkol's confrontation with the generals before his forced resignation from the MOD, Haber, op. cit., pp. 194*ff*.

90. A. Brown, *Moshe Dayan*, pp. 20–21.

91. Ibid., p. 24.

92. Ibid.

93. Lior was the first to publish a report on this meeting; A. Brown (*Moshe Dayan*, pp. 25–26) seemingly expanded on and fleshed out Lior's account.

94. On the thirtieth anniversary of the Six Day War, a Jewish weekly in Washington ran several interviews with personalities who had been involved in the war. Walt W. Rostow, the national security adviser during the crisis, said that the president had indeed tried to "internationalize" the conflict and create a multinational expeditionary force that would breach the Egyptian blockade of the Straits of Tiran, it being the American intelligence assessment that Nasser was not of a mind to

attack Israel. As stated, Ben-Gurion shared this view. See *Washington Jewish Week*,
June 5, 1997.

95. See Bar-On, "Metsiyut ve-dimayaon [Reality and imagination]," pp. 34–35.

96. See Peres, *Battling for Peace*, pp. 103–107. His allusion to the matter provides no
details, of course; cf. D. Margalit, *Ra'iti otam* [I saw them] (Tel Aviv: Zmora Bitan,
1997), p. 60.

Published Sources

Books in Hebrew

Achimeir, Abba. *Ketavim nivharim: Atlantida o ha-olam she-shaka* [Selected writings: Atlantis or the world that sank]. Vol. 5. Tel Aviv: Ministry of Defense, 1996.

Allon, Y. *Masakh shel hol* [Sandscreen]. Tel Aviv: Hakibbutz Hameuchad, 1959, updated 1968.

Almogi, Y. *Be-rosh muram: Hayalim erets-yisraeli'im ba-shvi ha-nazi* [With a raised head: Palestinian [Jewish] soldiers in Nazi captivity]. Tel Aviv: Ministry of Defense, 1989.

Almogi, Y. *Ha-ma'avaq al Ben-Gurion: Be-iqvot ha-parasha* [The struggle for Ben-Gurion: In the wake of the affair]. Jerusalem: Yedioth Ahronoth, 1988.

Aronson, S., with the assistance of Oded Brosh. *Nesheq gar'ini ba-mizrah ha-tikhon* [Nuclear weapons in the Middle East]. 2 vols. Jerusalem: Academon, 1994 and 2004, rev. ed. of vol. 2, 2006. Original English version published in one volume in 1992 by State University of New York Press at Albany.

Avineri, S. *Ha-ra'ayon ha-tsiyyoni li-gvanav: Peraqim be-toldot ha-mahshava ha-leumit ha-yehudit* [Complexions of the Zionist idea: Chapters on the history of Jewish national thinking]. Tel Aviv: Am Oved, 1980.

Avizohar, M. *Be-re'i saduq: idealim hevrati'im u-leumi'im ve-hishtaqfutam be-olama shel Mapai* [In a cracked mirror: Social and national ideals and their reflection in the world of Mapai] (Tel Aviv: Am Oved, 1990).

Baras, Z. (ed). *Meshihiut ve-eskhatologia* [Messianism and eschatology]. Jerusalem: Zalman Shazar Centre, 1984.

Bareli, Avi. *Mapai be-reshit ha-atzmaut 1948–1953* [Mapai in Israel's early independence 1948–1953]. Jerusalem: Yad Ben-Zvi, 2007.

Baron, S. *Meimadeha ha-'olami'im shel ha-historia ha-yehudit* [The worldwide dimensions of Jewish history]. Jerusalem: Mosad Bialik, 1996.

Barzel, A. *'Al mivne ha-yahadut* [On the structure of Judaism]. Tel Aviv: Sifriyat Poalim, 1994.

Bar-Zohar, M. *Ben-Gurion: Biographia politit* [Ben-Gurion: A political biography]. 3 vols. Tel Aviv: Am Oved, 1975–1977.

Bauer, Y. *Diplomatia ve-mahteret ba-mediniut ha-tsiyyonit* [Diplomacy and underground in Zionist policy]. Jerusalem: Sifriyat Poalim, 1966.

Ben-Gurion, D. *Anahnu u-shekheneinu* [We and our neighbors]. Tel Aviv: Davar, 1931.

Ben-Gurion, D. *Devarim ke-havayatam* [Things as they are]. Tel Aviv: Am Hasefer, 1965.

Ben-Gurion, D. *Kokhavim ve-afar: Ma'amarim mi-shenaton ha-memshala* [Stars and dust: Articles from the *Government Yearbook 1951*]. Ramat Gan: Israel Information Centre, 1976.

Ben-Gurion, D. *Medinat yisrael ha-mehudeshet* [The renewed Jewish state]. Tel Aviv: Am Oved, 1969.

Ben-Gurion, D. *Mi-ma'amad le-am: Peraqim le-virur darka shel tenu'at ha-po'alim* [From class to nation: Chapters for clarification of the path of the labor movement – From a Class to a Nation]. Tel Aviv: Ayanot, 1955, first published 1933.

Ben-Gurion, D. *Yihud ve-yi'ud* [Uniqueness and destiny]. Tel Aviv: Ministry of Defense, 1991.

Ben-Gurion, D. *Yoman ha-milhama: Milhemet ha-atsmaut 5708–5709* [War diary: The War of Independence 1948–1949], G. Rivlin and A. Oren (eds.). Tel Aviv: Ministry of Defense, 1982.

Ben-Gurion, D. *Zikhronot min ha-izavon* [Memoirs from the estate], M. Avizohar (ed.). Tel Aviv: Am Oved, 1987.

Ben-Gurion, D. *Zikhronot min ha-izavon: Liqrat qets ha-mandat* [Memoirs from the estate: Toward the end of the Mandate], M. Avizohar (ed.). Tel Aviv: Am Oved, 1993.

Ben-Gurion, D. *Zikhronot min ha-izavon: Pa'amei medina* [Memoirs from the estate: Steps toward statehood], M. Avizohar (ed.). Tel Aviv: Am Oved, 1993.

Ben-Yisrael, H. *Be-shem ha-uma* [In the name of the nation]. Beersheva: Ben-Gurion University of the Negev, 2004.

Berdyczewski, M. Y. Ginzei Micha Yosef, the Archives of M. Y. Berdyczewski Bin-Gurion. Vols. 6 and 7. Tel Aviv: Reshafim, 1986 and 1987.

Berdyczewski, M. Y. *Pirqei yoman: amal yom ve-haguto* [Diary chapters: A day's work and thought]. Trans. Rachel Bin-Gurion. Holon: Moreshet Micha Yosef, 1975.

Berdyczewski, M. Y., and Y. H. Brenner. *Halifat igrot* [Correspondence]. Tel Aviv: Hakibbutz Hameuchad, 1962.

Bin-Gurion, E. *Be-reshut ha-yahid: Micha Yosef Berdyczewski be-esrim shnotav ha-ahronot* [In the private domain: Micha Yosef Berdyczewski in his last twenty years]. Tel Aviv: Reshafim, 1980.

Bin-Gurion, E. *Qore ha-dorot* [Reader of the times]. Tel Aviv: Reshafim, 1981.

Brown., A. *Moshe Dayan ve-milhemet sheshet ha-yamim* [Moshe Dayan and the Six-Day War]. Tel Aviv: Yedioth Ahronoth, 1997.

Brown, A. (ed.). *Shisha yamim* [Six days]. Tel Aviv: Ministry of Defense, 1968.

Burckhardt, J. *Tarbut ha-renaissance be-italia* [Renaissance culture in Italy]. Scientific ed. H. Peri. Jerusalem: Mosad Bialik, 1966.

Cohen, A. *Ha-mahteret ha-halutsit be-hungaria* [The pioneering underground in Hungary]. Tel Aviv: Hakibbutz Hameuchad, 1984.

Dayan, M. *Avnei derekh* [Milestones]. Jerusalem: Idanim, 1976. English title: *Story of My Life*.

Dinur, B. *Be-olam she-shaqa: Zikhronot ve-reshumot mi-derekh hayyim* [In a world that is no more: Memoirs and writings from a way of life]. Jerusalem: Bialik Institute, 1958.

Don Yihye, E. *Ha-politiqa shel ha-hasdara: Yishuv sikhsuhim be-nosei dat u-medina* [Politics of arrangement: Resolution of conflicts in matters of religion and state]. Tel Aviv: The Open University of Israel, 1997.

Dotan, S. *Adummim: ha-miflaga ha-komunistit be-erets yisrael* [Reds: The Communist Party in the land of Israel]. Kfar Sava: Shevna Hasofer, 1991.

Dotan, S. *Pulmus ha-haluqa bi-mei ha-mandat* [The partition controversy during the Mandate era]. Jerusalem: Yad Izhak Ben-Zvi, 1980.

Eshkoli, H. *Elem: Mapai le-nokhah ha-sho'a 1939–1942* [The mute: Mapai facing the Holocaust 1939–1942]. Jerusalem: Yad Izhak Ben-Zvi, 1994.

Evron, Y. *Ha-dilema ha-gar'init shel Yisrael* [Israel's nuclear dilemma]. Tel Aviv: Hakibbutz Hameuchad, 1987.

Eyal, Y. *Ha-intifada ha-rishona: Dikuy ha-mered ha-aravi al yedi ha-zava ha-briti be-eretz yisrael 1936–1939* [The first intifada: The oppression of the Arab revolt by the British Army 1936–1939]. Tel Aviv: Ma'arachot, 1998.

Friedman, Y. *Germania, turkiya ve-ha-tsiyyonut, 1897–1918* [Germany, Turkey and Zionism, 1987–1918]. Jerusalem and Beersheva: Bialik Institute, 1996.

Friling, T. *Hetz ba-arafel* [Arrows in the dark: Ben-Gurion, the Yishuv leadership, and rescue attempts during the Holocaust]. Beer Sheva and Sede Boqer: Ben-Gurion Heritage Center/Tel Aviv University/Ben-Gurion University, 1998. English translation published by University of Wisconsin Press, 2005.

Gelber, Y. *Toldot ha-hitnadvut* [History of volunteering]. 4 vols. Jerusalem: Yad Izhak Ben-Zvi, 1979–1985.

Gellner, E. *Leumim ve-leumiut* [Nations and nationalities]. Trans. M. Barkai. Tel Aviv: Open University, 1994.

Golan M. *Peres*. Tel Aviv: Schocken, 1982.

Gorny, Y. *Ha-she'ela ha-aravit ve-ha-be'aya ha-yehudit: Zeramim medini'im-ideologi'im ba-tsiyyonut be-yahasam el ha-yeshut ha-aravit be-erets yisraaael ba-shanim 1882–1948* [The Arab question and the Jewish problem: Political and ideological trends in Zionism in relating to the Arab entity in Palestine 1882–1948]. Tel Aviv: Am Oved, 1985.

Gorny, Y. *Kria bein onim: Ha-itonut ha-yehudit be-erets yisrael, be-britania, be-arzot ha-brit u-bivrit ha-moezot le-nochach ha-shoa, ba-shanim 1939–1945* [A cry in the wilderness: The Jewish press in the Land of Israel, in Britain, in the United States and in the Soviet Union confronting the Holocaust, 1939–1945]. Tel Aviv: Hakibbutz Hameuchad, 2009.

Haber, E. (ed.). *Ha-yom tifrots milhama: Zikhronotav shel tat-aluf Yisrael Lior, shal-isham ha-tsva'i shel rashei ha-memshala Levi Eshkol ve-Golda Meir* [Today war will break out: The memoirs of Brig.-Gen. Yisrael Lior, military adjutant of Prime Ministers Levi Eshkol and Golda Meir]. Tel Aviv: Idanim, 1987.

Harel, I. *Bitahon ve-demokratia* [Security and democracy]. Tel Aviv: Idanim, 1988.

Harel, I. *Mashber ha-mad'anim ha-germani'im be-mitsrayim, 1962–1963* [The crisis of the German scientists in Egypt, 1962–1963]. Tel Aviv: Ma'ariv, 1983.

Hecht, B. *Kachash* [Perfidy]. Jerusalem: Milah, 1961.

Heller, Y. *Lehi, 1940–1949*. Vols. 1 and 2. Jerusalem: Zalman Shazar Centre and Keter, 1989.

Horowitz, David. *Hayyim ba-moqed* [Life at the focus]. Ramat Gan: Massada, 1975.

Horowitz, Dan, and M. Lissak. *Mi-yishuv le-medina: Yehudei eretz yisrael bi-tequfat ha-mandat ha-briti: ke-qehila politit* [From Yishuv to state: The Jews of Eretz Israel during the British Mandate as a political community]. Tel Aviv: Am Oved, 1977.

Ilan, Amitzur. *America, britania ve-erets-yisrael: Reshita ve-hitpat'huta shel me'oravut artsot ha-berit ba-mediniut ha-britit be-erets yisrael 1938–1947* [America, Britain, and Palestine: The origin and development of American involvement in British policy in Palestine 1938–1947]. Jerusalem: Yad Izhak Ben-Zvi, 1979.

Izhar, U. *Bein hazon le-shilton: Mifleget ahdut-ha-Avodah-Poalei Tsiyyon bi-tkufat ha-yeshuv ve-ha-medina* [Between vision and power: The history of Achdut-ha-Avoda Poalei Zion Party]. Tel Aviv: Yad Tabenkin, 2005.

Kadish, A. (ed.). *Milchemet ha-atsmaut tachach–tashat* [Israel's War of Independence 1948–1949]. Tel Aviv: Ministry of Defense, 2004.

Keren, M. *Ben-Gurion ve-ha-intelektualim* [Ben-Gurion and the intellectuals]. Sede Boqer: Ben-Gurion University of the Negev, 1988.

Klausner-Eshkoli, A. *Hashpa'at Nietzsche ve-Schopenhauer 'al M. Y. Bin-Gurion (Berdyczewski)* [The influence of Nietzsche and Schopenhauer on M. Y. Bin-Gurion (Berdyczewski)]. Tel Aviv: Dvir, 1914.

Lau-Lavie, N. *Am ke-lavie* [A nation as a lion]. Tel Aviv: Sifriyat Ma'ariv, 1990.

Leibowitz, Y. *Torah u-mitsvot ba-zman ha-ze* [Torah and mitzvot in our times]. Jerusalem: Massaa, 1954.

Lorch, N. *Qorot milhemet ha-atsma'ut* [History of the War of Independence]. Corrected ed. Tel Aviv: Modan, 1989.

Mardor, M. *Rafael*. Tel Aviv: Ministry of Defense, 1981.

Margalit, D. *Ra'iti otam* [I saw them]. Tel Aviv: Zmora Bitan, 1997.

Mintz, M. *Haver ve-yariv: Yitzhak Tabenkin u-mifleget Po'alei Tsiyyon 1905–1912* [Friend and foe: Yitzhak Tabenkin and the Po'alei Zion Party 1905–1912]. (Tel Aviv: Hakibbutz Hameuchad, 1986.

Ofer, D. *Derekh ba-yam: aliya bet bi-tequfat hah-sho'ah* [By sea: Aliya Bet during the Holocaust]. Jerusalem: Yad Izhak Ben-Zvi, 1988.

Ostfeld, Z. *Tsava nolad* [An army is born]. 2 vols. Tel Aviv: Ministry of Defense, 1994.

Porat, D. *Hanhaga be-milkud: Ha-yishuv nochach ha-shoa 1942–1945* [A leadership trapped: The Yishuv facing the Holocaust 1942–1945]. Tel Aviv: Am Oved, 1986).

Porat, D., and A. Halamish (ed.). *Shoa mi-merchak tavo: Ishim ba-yeshuv ha-eretz yisraeli veyachasam la-nazism ve-la-shoa, 1933–1945* [When disaster comes from afar: Leading personalities in the Land of Israel confront Nazism and the Holocaust, 1933–1945]. Jerusalem: Yad Ben-Zvi, 2009.

Porat, Y. *Shelah ve'et be-yado: Sipur hayyav shel Yonatan Ratosh* [Fence with a pen in his hand: The biography of Yonatan Ratosh]. Tel Aviv: Mahbarot le-Sifrut, 1989.

Rabin, Y. *Pinqas sherut* [Service diary]. Tel Aviv: Sifriyat Ma'ariv, 1979.

Reinharz, J., Y. Shalmon, and G. Shimoni (eds.). *Leumiyut u-politiqa yehudit: Perspektivot hadashot* [Jewish nationalism and Jewish politics: New perspectives]. Jerusalem: Zalman Shazar Centre, 1997.

Rimmer, Y. *Peretz Naphtali: Sotsialdemokrat bi-shnei olamot* [Peretz Naphtali: A social democrat in two worlds]. Jerusalem: World Zionist Organization/The Zionist Library, 1996.

Robinson, J. *Ha-aqov le-mishor* [And the crooked shall be made straight]. Jerusalem: Bialik Institute, 1965.

Rosenthal, Y. (ed.). *Yitzhak Rabin, rosh mimshelet yisrael: 1974–1977|1992–1995* [Yitzhak Rabin, prime minister of Israel 1974–1977|1992–1995]. Vol. 1 [1922–1967]. Jerusalem: Israel State Archive, 2005.

Schwartz, D. *Etgar u-mashber be-chug ha-rav Kook* [Challenge and crisis in Rabbi Kook's circle]. Tel Aviv: Am Oved, 2001.

Schwartz, D. *Ha-tsiyyonut ha-datit bein higayion li-mashichiut* [Religious Zionism between logic and messianism]. Tel Aviv: Am Oved, 1999.

Shaked, G. *Ha-siporet ha-ivrit 1880–1980* [Hebrew literature 1880–1980]. Vol. 1: *Ba-gola* [In the Diaspora]. Jerusalem: Keter and Hakibbutz Hameuchad, 1978.

Shapira, A. *Berl.* 2 vols. Tel Aviv: Sifriyat Ofakim/Am Oved, 1980.

Shapira, A. *Mi-piturei ha-rama ad peruq ha-palmah: Sugiyot ba-ma'avaq al ha-hanhaga ha-bit'honit* [From the dismissal of the chief of national staff to the dissolving of the Palmach: Issues in the struggle over the defense leadership]. Tel Aviv: Hakibbutz Hameuchad, 1984.

Shapira, Y. *Hevra bi-shvi ha-politiqa'im* [Society in the thrall of politicians]. Tel Aviv: Sifriyat Poalim, 1996.

Shapiro, A. *Or ha-hayyim be-"Yom Qatnut": Mishnat A. D. Gordon u-meqoroteha ba-qabala u-va-hasidut* [The living light in "Yom Qatnut": The teachings of A. D. Gordon and their sources in Kabbala and Hasidism]. Tel Aviv: Am Oved, 1996.

Sharett, M. *Yoman medini* [Political diary]. Tel Aviv: Sifriyat Ma'ariv, 1968.

Sharett, M. *Yomanei Sharett* [Sharett's diaries]. Vol. 5. Tel Aviv: Sifriyat Ma'ariv, 1978.

Shavit, Y. *Ha-mitologia shel ha-yamin* [The mythology of the right]. Tel Aviv: Beit Berl and Moshe Sharett Institute, 1986.

Shavit, Y. *Mi-ivri ad kena'ani, peraqim be-toldot ha-ideologia ve-ha-utopia shel "ha-tehiya ha-ivrit": Mi-tsiyyonut radiqalit le-anti-tsiyyonut* [From Hebrew to Canaanite, chapters in the history of the ideology and utopia of the "Hebrew renaissance": From radical Zionism to anti-Zionism]. Tel Aviv: Domino, 1984.

Shealtiel, E. (ed.). *David Ben-Gurion: Rosh ha-memshala ha-rishon* [David Ben-Gurion: The first prime minister]. Jerusalem: Israel State Archives, 1996.

Slutzky, Y. *Toldot ha-hagana* [History of the Hagana]. 3 vols. Tel Aviv: 1954, 1956, and 1964.

Teveth, S. *Ben-Gurion ve-arviyei eretz yisrael* [Ben-Gurion and the Palestinian Arabs]. Jerusalem: Schocken, 1982.

Teveth, S. *Ha-shanim ha-ne'elamot ve-ha-hor ha-shahor* [The vanished years and the black hole]. Tel Aviv: Dvir, 1999.

Teveth, S. *Qalaban: al ma nafal David Ben-Gurion?* [The banana peel: What brought David Ben-Gurion down?]. Tel Aviv: Ish-Dor, 1992.

Teveth, S. *Qinat David: Ben-Gurion: Ish midot* [David's zeal: Ben-Gurion: Man of virtues]. Jerusalem: Schocken, 1980.

Teveth, S. *Qinat David: Ha-qarqa bo'er* [David's zeal: The ground is burning]. Jerusalem: Schocken, 1987.

Teveth, S. *Qinat David: Hayei Ben-Gurion ha-tsa'ir* [David's zeal: Life of the young Ben-Gurion]. Jerusalem: Schocken, 1976.

Tsahor, Z. *Ha-hazon ve-ha-heshbon: Ben-Gurion bein ideologia le-politiqa* [Vision and reckoning: Ben-Gurion between ideology and politics]. Tel Aviv: Sifriyat Poalim, 1994.

Tsahor, Z. *Hazan – tenu'at hayyim: Ha-Shomer ha-Tsa'ir, ha-Kibbutz ha-Artsi, Mapam* [Hazan – a movement of life: Ha-Shomer ha-Tsa'ir, ha-Kibbutz ha-Artsi, Mapam]. Jerusalem: Yad Izhak Ben-Zvi, 1997.

Tzemach, S. *Pinqasei reshimot 1962–1973* [Notebooks 1962–1973]. Tel Aviv: Am Oved, 1996.

Tzivyon, A. *Ha-morasha ha-yehudit be-itsuv olamo shel Berl Katznelson* [The Jewish heritage in the shaping of Berl Katznelson's world]. Jerusalem: Hebrew University of Jerusalem, 1982.

Urbach, E. E. *Al tsiyyonut ve-yahadut: iyyunim u-masot* [On Zionism and Judaism: Studies and essays]. Jerusalem: The Zionist Library, 1985.

Wallach, Y. *El ha-degel: Haqamat tsava amami tokh kedei lehima* [To the flag: The establishment of a people's army in the midst of combat]. Tel Aviv: Ministry of Defense, 1997.

Weissmandel, M. D. *Min ha-metsar* [From the distress]. Bnei Brak: Private publisher, 1954.

Weitz, Y. *Ha-ish she-nirtsah pa'amayim: Hayyav, mishpato ve-moto shel Dr. Yisrael Kasztner* [The man who was murdered twice: The life, trial, and death of Dr. Israel Kasztner]. Jerusalem: Keter, 1995.

Weitz, Y. *Mapai le-nokhah ha-sho'a 1943–1945* [Mapai facing the Holocaust 1943–1945]. Jerusalem: Yad Izhak Ben-Zvi, 1994.

Weizman, E. *Lekha shamayim, lekha eretz.* Tel Aviv: Sifriyat Ma'ariv, 1975. Wiezman's autobiography.

Yablonka, H. *Ahim zarim: Qelitat nitsolei ha-sho'ah bi-medinat yisrael 1948–1952* [Alien brethren: The absorption of Holocaust survivors in the State of Israel 1948–1952]. Jerusalem: Yad Izhak Ben-Zvi, 1994.

Yakira, E. *Post-tsiyonut, post-sho'ah* [Post Zionism, Post Holocaust: Three essays on denial, forgetting, and the delegitimation of Israel]. Tel Aviv: Am Oved, 2006. English translation: New York: Cambridge University Press, 2010. French translation in print.

Yovel, Y. *Spinoza ve-kofrim aherim* [Spinoza and other heretics]. Tel Aviv: Sifriyat Poalim, 1988.

Zameret, Z. *Alei gesher tsar: Ha-hinukh be-yisrael bi-shnot ha-medina ha-rishonot* [On a narrow bridge: Education in Israel in the first years of statehood]. Sede Boqer: Ben-Gurion Heritage Center, 1997.

Zertal, I. *Ha-sho'ah ve-ha-mavet* [The Holocaust and death]. Tel Aviv: Dvir, 2003.

Zertal, I. *Zahavam shel ha-yehudim: Ha-hagira ha-yehudit ha-mahtartit le-erets yisrael, 1945–1948* [The gold of the Jews: Underground Jewish immigration to Eretz Israel, 1945–1948]. Tel Aviv: Am Oved, 1996.

Articles in Hebrew

Aronson, S. "Al ha-post-tsiyyonut ve-ha-masoret ha-antishemit ba-ma'arav [On post-Zionism and the antisemitic tradition in the West]." In P. Ginosar and A. Bareli (eds.), *Iyyunim bi-tqumat yisrael – Tsiyyonut: Pulmus ben zemanenu* [Studies on the Jewish rebirth – Zionism: A contemporary polemic]. Qiryat Sede Boqer: Ben-Gurion Heritage Center, 1996.

Aronson, S., and D. Horowitz. "Ha-istrategia shel tagmul mevukar: Ha-dugma ha-yisraelit [The Strategy of controlled retaliation: The case of Israel]." *Medina u-Mimshal* [State and government], 1 (1971): 77–99.

Bareli, A. "Mamlakhtiut u-tnuat ha-avodah be-reishit shenot hahamishim: Hanahot mivniot [Statism and the labor movement in the early 1950s: Structural assumptions]." Manuscript accepted for a collection edited by Mordechai Bar-On on theory and practice in the early 1950s.

Bar-On, Y. "Metsiyut ve-dimayaon: Mikhtavim u-mifgashim bein Ben-Gurion ve-de Gaulle [Reality and imagination: Letters and meetings between Ben-Gurion and de Gaulle]." *Medina, mimshal ve-yahasim benleumi'im* [State, government, and international relations], 38 (Spring–Summer 1993): 77–95.

Ben-Moshe, Y. "Esrim ve-chamesh shana lifnei Vanunu [Twenty-five years before (Mordechai) Vanunu]." *Koteret Rashit* [Main headline], November 26, 1986.

Ben-Naftali Berkowitz, M. "Ha-philosophim ha-yisraelim ve-ha-shoah [The Israeli philosophers and the Holocaust]." *Teoria u-bikoret* [Theory and criticism], 4 (Autumn 1993): 57–77.

Ben-Rafael, E. "Hevra bi-shvi ha-politikaim ve-mitkefet ha-radikalism ha-chadash [Society in the thrall of politicians and the onslaught of the new radicalism]." *Mifne: Bama le-inyanei hevra* [Turning point: Forum on social affairs], (April 1997): 54–60.

Ben-Yisrael, H. "Mechkar ha-Leumiut ke-panorama historit [Study of nationalism as a historical panorama]." In J. Reinharz, Y. Shalmon, and G. Shimoni (eds.), *Leumiyut u-politiqa yehudit: Perspektivot hadashot* [Jewish nationalism and Jewish politics: New perspectives]. Jerusalem: Zalman Shazar Centre, 1997, pp. 57–80.

Berdyczewski, M.Y. "Hakirat ha-devarim [Exploration of matters]." In E. Bin-Gurion, *Be-reshut ha-yahid: Micha Yosef Berdyczewski be-esrim shnotav ha-ahronot* [In the private domain: Micha Josef Berdyczewski in his last twenty years]. Tel Aviv: Reshafim, 1980.

Dayan, M. "Germania, dimona ve-ha-yarden [Germany, Dimona, and the Jordan]." *Ha'aretz*, March 26, 1965.

Esh, S. "Ha-tsiyyonut ke-teshuva la-be'ayat ha-yehudi ha-moderni – Mishnato shel Kurt Blumenfeld [Zionism as a response to the problem of the modern Jew – The Teachings of Kurt Blumenfeld]." *Molad* [Birth] (1964): 181–182.

Frankel, Y. "Hitbolelut ve-hisardut be-qerev yehudei eropa ba-me'a ha-tsha'esre [Assimilation and survival among European Jewry in the nineteenth century]." In J. Reinharz, Y. Shalmon, and G. Shimoni (eds.), *Leumiyut u-politiqa yehudit: Perspektivot hadashot* [Jewish nationalism and Jewish politics: New perspectives]. Jerusalem: Zalman Shazar Centre, 1997, pp. 23–56.

Gelber, Y. "Ha-mediniut ha-britit ve-ha-tsiyyonit 1942–1944 [The British and Zionist policies in Palestine, 1942–1944]." In Y. Shavit (ed.), *Ma'avaq, mered, meri* [Struggle, uprising, revolt 1941–1948]. Jerusalem: Domino, 1987.

Gilad, Y. "Da'at ha-qahal be-yisrael al yahasei yisrael ve-germania ha-ma'aravit ba-shanim 1949–1965 [Public opinion in Israel on Israeli–West German relations in 1949–1965]." Ph.D. diss., Tel Aviv University.

Gorny, Y. "Yahadut ve-tziyyonut be-hashqafata shel Beatrice Webb [Judaism and Zionism in Thinking of Beatrice Webb]." *Zionism* 5 (1978): 115–140.

Govrin, N. "Micha Yosef Berdyczewski ve-erets yisrael [Micha Yosef Berdyczewski and the Land of Israel]." *Alei siah* [Pages of discourse], 17–18 (1983): Appendix.

Greenberg,Y. "Tashtit ha-mechkar ve-ha-pituach be-maarechet ha-bitachon: Aspectim shel mediniut ve-tikzuv [The foundations of Israel's security R&D: Aspects of policy and budgeting]." In *Iyyunim be-tkumat yisrael* [Studies in the Jewish rebirth, studies in Zionism, the Yishuv and the State of Israel: A research annual]. Sede Boqer: Ben-Gurion Research Center, Ben-Gurion University of the Negev Press, 1999, vol. 9, pp. 167–187.

Kolatt, Y. "Ha-im ha-yishuv ba-arets hu hagshamat ha-leumiut ha-yehudit? [Is the Yishuv in Palestine the fulfillment of Jewish nationhood?]" In J. Reinharz, Y. Shalmon, and G. Shimoni (eds.), *Leumiyut u-politiqa yehudit: Perspektivot hadashot* [Jewish nationalism and Jewish politics: New perspectives]. Jerusalem: Zalman Shazar Centre, 1997, pp. 225–252.

Kolatt, Y. "Tsionut ve-meshichiut [Zionism and Messianism]." In Z. Baras (ed.), *Meshihiut ve-eskhatologia* [Messianism and eschatology]. Jerusalem: Zalman Shazar Centre, 1984, pp. 419–431.

Leibowitz, Y. "Ben- Gurion, David." In *Encyclopedia Hebraica* [Hebrew Encyclopedia], Y. Leibowitz (ed.). Jerusalem, 1967, supp. vol., pp. 674–680.

Leibowitz, Y. "Umanut Esav eina nitenet le-hinuch [The art of Esau cannot be turned into education]." In *Torah u-mitsvot ba-zman ha-zeh* [Torah and mitzvot in our times]. Jerusalem: Massada, 1954. Republished in *Ha'aretz*, September 27, 1996.

Lossin, Y. "Heinrich Heine, yehudi min ha-sug ha-shelishi [Heinrich Heine, a Jew of the third kind]." *Ha'aretz*, Culture suppl., December 13, 1996.

Mintz, M. "Leumiyut yehudit u-leumiyut shel mi'utim aherim be-medinot rabot-leumi'im [Jewish nationhood and nationhood of other minorities in multinational states]." In J. Reinharz, Y. Shalmon, and G. Shimoni (eds.), *Leumiyut u-politiqa yehudit: Perspektivot hadashot* [Jewish nationalism and Jewish politics: New perspectives]. Jerusalem: Zalman Shazar Centre, 1997, pp. 201–204.

Ne'eman, Y. "Lama hitpatarti mi-misrad ha-bitachon [Why I resigned from the MOD]." *Ha'aretz*, February 6, 1966.

Sadan, D. "Shilush u-moqdo: od al Berl Katznelson u-sevivo [A triumvirate and its focus: More about Berl Katznelson and his surroundings]." *'Iyyunim bi-tqumat yisrael* [Studies in the Jewish rebirth], 6 (1996): 1–15.

Scholem, G. "Le-demuto shel Martin Buber, shiv'im ve-hamesh le-holadeto [On the figure of Martin Buber, on the 75th anniversary of his birth]." In *Devarim bego* [Remarks from within]. Tel Aviv: Am Oved/Ofakim, 1975, p. 46.

Shalmon, Y. "Dat u-leumiyut ba-tenuah ha-tsiyyonit me-reshita [Religion and nationalism from the outset of the Zionist movement]." In J. Reinharz, Y. Shalmon, and G. Shimoni (eds.), *Leumiyut u-politiqa yehudit: Perspektivot hadashot* [Nationalism and Jewish politics: New perspectives]. Jerusalem: Zalman Shazar Centre, 1997.

Shalmon, Y. "Ha'imut bein haredim le-maskilim bi-t'nu'at hibat tsiyyon bi-sh'not ha-80 [The conflict between the ultra-Orthodox and the Maskilim in the Hibbat Tsiyyon movement in the 1880s]." *Ha-tsiyyonut* [Zionism], 5 (1978): 43–77.

Shapira, A. "Rekhivim shel ha-etos ha-leumi ba-ma'avar mi-yishuv le-medina [Components of the national ethos in the transition from Yishuv to state]." In J. Reinharz, Y. Shalmon, and G. Shimoni (eds.), *Leumiyut u-politiqa yehudit: Perspektivot hadashot* [Jewish nationalism and Jewish politics: New perspectives]. Jerusalem: Zalman Shazar Centre, 1997, pp. 272–352.

Shapira, A. "Tlunato shel Sternhell [Sternhell's Complaint]." *'Iyyunim bi-tqumat yisrael* [Studies on the Jewish rebirth], 6 (1996): 553–567.

Shimoni, G. "Ha-leumiut ha-yehudit ke-leumiut etnit [Jewish nationalism as ethnic nationalism]." In J. Reinharz, Y. Shalmon, and G. Shimoni (eds.), *Leumiyut u-politiqa yehudit: Perspektivot hadashot* [Jewish nationalism and Jewish politics: New perspectives]. Jerusalem: Zalman Shazar Centre, 1997, pp. 18–29.

Silberner, E. "Webb, Sidney James and Beatrice." *Encyclopedia Hebraica* [Hebrew Encyclopedia], Y. Leibowitz (ed.). Jerusalem, 1952, vol. 15, pp. 751–752.

Stein-Ashkenazi, E. "Tenu'at betar be-erets yisrael ve-ha-yedi'ot al ha-sho'ah [The Betar movement in Palestine and reports about the Holocaust]." *Kivvunim* [Journal on Zionism and Judaism], 10 (December 1996).

Weitz, Y. "Qets ha-reshit: Le-berur ha-musag 'reshit ha-medina' [End of the beginning: Elucidating the concept of 'genesis of the state']." In Y. Weitz (ed.), *Bein hazon le-revizia: Me'a shenot historiografia tsiyyonit* [Between vision and revision: A century of Zionist historiography]. Jerusalem: Yad Izhak Ben-Zvi, 1997.

Yablonka, H. "Qelitat nitsolei ha-sho'a bi-medinat yisrael – hebetim hadashim [Absorption of Holocaust survivors in the State of Israel – new aspects]." *'Iyyunim bi-tqumat yisrael* [Studies in the Jewish rebirth], 7 (1997): 285–289.

Books in English, German, and French

Annan, N. *Changing Enemies: The Defeat and Regeneration of Germany*. New York: W. W. Norton, 1995.

Arad, Y., Y. Gutman, and A. Margaliot (eds.). *Documents on the Holocaust*. Jerusalem: Yad Vashem, 1999.

Arendt, H. *Eichmann in Jerusalem: A Report on the Banality of Evil*. New York: Penguin, 1965.

Arendt, H. *The Origins of Totalitarianism*. New York: Harcourt, Brace, 1951. Paperback ed., Cleveland: Meridian Books, 1963.

Aronson, S. *Conflict and Bargaining in the Middle East: An Israeli Perspective*. Baltimore and London: Johns Hopkins University Press, 1978.

Aronson, S. *Hitler, the Allies, and the Jews*. New York: Cambridge University Press, 2006. (Paperback ed.)

Aronson, S. *Israel's Nuclear Programme, the Six Day War and Its Ramifications*. London: King's College London Mediterranean Studies, 1999.

Aronson, S. *Nuclear Weapons in the Middle East*. Albany and London: State University of New York Press, 1992.

Bauer, Y. *Jews for Sale? Nazi–Jewish Negotiations, 1933–1945*. New Haven, CT, and London: Yale University Press, 1994.

Beer, S. H., and A. B. Ulam (eds.). *Patterns of Government: The Major Political Systems of Europe*. 3d ed. New York: Random House, 1979.

Biemann, Asher D. *Inventing New Beginnings: On the Idea of Renaissance in Modern Judaism*. Stanford, CA: Stanford University Press, 2009.

Bloom, A. *The Closing of the American Mind*. New York: Simon & Schuster, 1987.

Bower, T. *Blind Eye to Murder: Britain, America and the Purging of Nazi Germany – a Pledge Betrayed*. London: Andre Deutsch, 1981.

Brecher, M. *Decisions in Israel's Foreign Policy*. New Haven, CT: Yale University Press, 1975.

Breitman, R. *Official Secrets: What the Nazis Planned, What the British and Americans Knew*. New York: Hill & Wang, 1998.

Breitman, R., and A. M. Kraut. *American Refugee Policy and European Jewry 1933–1945*. Bloomington: Indiana University Press, 1987.

Burckhardt, J. *The Civilization of the Renaissance in Italy*. New York: Penguin Classics, 1990.

Cheyette, B. *Construction of "The Jew" in English Society: Racial Representations 1875–1945*. Cambridge: Cambridge University Press, 1993.

Churchill, W. S. *The Second World War*. Vol. 4: *The Hinge of Fate*. London: Cassell & Co., 1964.

Cohen, M. J. *Churchill and the Jews, 1900–1948*. London: Frank Cass, 1985.

Cohen, M. J. *Fighting World War Three from the Middle East: Allied Contingency Planning, 1945–1954*. London and Portland, OR: Frank Cass, 1997.

Cohn, N. *Warrant for Genocide: The Myth of the Jewish World Conspiracy and the Protocols of the Elders of Zion*. New York: Harper & Row, 1967.

Collini, S., D. Winch, and J. Burrow. *That Noble Science of Politics: A Study in Nineteenth Century Intellectual History*. New York: Cambridge University Press, 1983.

Dahrendorf, R. *Gesellschaft und Demokratie in Deutschland*. Munich: Piper Verlag, 1965.

Dinkelspiel, F. *Towers of Gold: How One Jewish Immigrant Named Isias Hellman Created California*. New York: St. Martin's Press, 2007.

Dinnerstein, L. *Antisemitism in America*. New York: Oxford University Press, 1994.

Ericson, Erik. H. *Childhood and Society*. New York: W. W. Norton, 1950. Hebrew translation: *Yaldut ve-hevra*. Merhavia: Sifriyat Ha-Poalim, 1974.

Ewen, F. *Heroic Imagination: The Creative Genius of Europe from Waterloo (1815) to the Revolution of 1848*. Secaucus, NJ: Citadel, 1984.

Feingold, H. L. *The Politics of Rescue: The Roosevelt Administration and the Holocaust, 1938–1945*. New Brunswick, NJ: Rutgers University Press, 1970.

Fishberg, Maurice. *Jews, Race, and Environment*. London: Walter Scott Publishing, 1911. Republished with a new introduction by W. H. Helmreich. New York: Transaction Books, 2006.

Fuller, J. F. C. *A Military History of the Western World*. Vol. 3. New York: Funk & Wagnalls, 1956.

Garraty, J. A. *The Great Depression: Inquiry into the Causes, Course and Consequences of the Worldwide Depression as Seen by Contemporaries and in the Light of the Nineteen-Thirties*. New York: Harcourt Brace Jovanovich, 1986.

Gazit, M. *President Kennedy's Policy toward the Arab States and Israel: Analysis and Documents*. Tel Aviv: Shiloah Center for Middle Eastern and African Studies, Tel Aviv University, 1983.

Gellner, E. *Nations and Nationalism: New Perspectives on the Past*. Ithaca, NY: Cornell University Press, 1983.

Gilbert, M. *Auschwitz and the Allies*. London: Michael Joseph, 1981.

Gilbert, M. *Churchill and the Jews: A Life-Long Friendship*. New York: Henry Holt, 2007.

Ginor, I., and Gideon Remez. *Foxbats Over Dimona: The Soviets' Nuclear Gamble in the Six-Day War*. New Haven, CT: Yale University Press, 2007.

Glantz, David M. *Red Storm over the Balkans: The Failed Soviet Invasion of Romania, Spring 1944*. Lawrence: University of Kansas Press, 2007.

Glantz, David M. *Zhukov's Greatest Defeat: The Red Army's Epic Disaster in Operation Mars, 1942*. Lawrence: University of Kansas Press, 1999.

Goldberg, H. *Israel Salanter: Text, Structure, Idea*. New York: Ktav, 1982.

Goody, Jack. *Renaissances: The One or the Many?* Cambridge: Cambridge University Press, 2010.

Harshav, B. *Language in Time of Revolution*. Berkeley and London: University of California Press, 1993.

Heine, H. *Zur Geschichte der Religion und Philosophie in Deutschland* [On the history of religion and philosophy in Germany]. Trans. John Snodgrass. Paul Lawrence Rose (ed.). Townsville, Qld., Australia: Dept. of History, James Cook University of North Queensland, [1834] 1982. See further *On Religion and Philosophy in Germany*, trans. Ritchie Robertson, in *The Harz Journey and Selected Prose*, 1993.

Jenkins, R. *Churchill, A Biography*. New York: Farrar, Straus and Giroux, 2001.

Johnson, P. *Modern Times: The World from the Twenties to the Eighties*. New York: Harper & Row, 1983.

Katz, I. *Tradition and Crisis: Jewish Society at the End of the Middle Ages*. New York: New York University Press, 1993.

Kesselman, M., et al. *European Politics in Transition*. 3d ed. Boston: Houghton Mifflin, 1997.

Kushner, T. *The Persistence of Prejudice: Antisemitism in British Society during the Second World War*. Manchester: Manchester University Press, 1989.

Laurie, C. D. *The Propaganda Warriors: America's Crusade against Nazi Germany*. Lawrence: University Press of Kansas, 1996.

Lewis, B. *Semites and Anti-Semites*. New York: W. W. Norton, 1986.

Liddell-Hart, B. H. *The Real War 1914–1918*. Norwalk, CT: Little, Brown, 1994.

Luebbert, G. M. *Liberalism, Fascism, or Social Democracy: Social Classes and the Political Origins of Regimes in Interwar Europe* Oxford: Oxford University Press, 1981.

Magee, B. *The Great Philosophers: An Introduction to Western Philosophy*. Oxford: Oxford University Press, 1988.

Makovsky, M. *Churchill's Promised Land, Zionism and Statecraft*. New Haven, CT: Yale University Press, 2007.

McArdle Kelleher, C. *Germany and the Politics of Nuclear Weapons*. New York: Columbia University Press, 1975.

Moore, J. N., ed. *The Arab–Israeli Conflict*. Vol 3. Princeton, NJ: Princeton University Press, 1974.

Neuret, C. G., Jr. *Introduction to Humanism and the Culture of Renaissance Europe*. New York: Cambridge University Press, 1995.

Newhouse, J. *War and Peace in the Nuclear Age*. New York: Knopf, 1989.

Nisbet, R. *Conservatism: Dream and Reality*. Minneapolis: University of Minnesota Press, 1986.

Olson, L. *Troublesome Young Men: The Rebels Who Brought Churchill to Power and Helped Save England*. New York: Farrar, Straus and Giroux, 2007.

Pean, P. *Les deux bombes*. Paris: Fayard, 1984.

Peres, S. *Battling for Peace: A Memoir*. David Landau (ed.). London: Weidenfeld and Nicolson, 1995.

Porat, D. *The Blue and Yellow Stars of David: The Zionist Leadership in Palestine and the Holocaust 1939–45*. Cambridge, MA: Harvard University Press, 1990.

Porter, B. *Plots and Paranoia: A History of Political Espionage in Britain 1790–1988*. London: Routledge, 1992.

Reinharz, J. *Chaim Weizmann: The Making of a Statesman*. Hanover, NH: Brandeis University Press/University Press of New England, 1985.

Rochlin, H. and F. *Pioneer Jews: A New Life in the Far West*. New York and Boston: Mariner Books, 2000.

Roshwald, A. *The Endurance of Nationalism*. New York: Cambridge University Press, 2006.

Rowse, A. L. *All Souls and Appeasement*. London: St. Martin's Press, 1961.

Rubin, B. *Istanbul Intrigues: A True-Life Casablanca*. New York: McGraw-Hill, 1989.

Salter, M. *US Intelligence, the Holocaust and the Nuremberg Trials: Seeking Accountability for Genocide and Cultural Plunder*. Vols. 1 and 2. Leiden and Boston: Martinus Nijhoff, 2009.

Sammons, J. L. *Heinrich Heine: A Modern Biography*. Princeton, NJ: Princeton University Press, 1979.

Schlesinger, A. M., Jr. *Robert Kennedy and His Times*. Boston: Houghton Mifflin, 1978.

Schmitt, Charles, Quentin Skinner, Eckhard Kessler, and Jill Knave (eds.). *Cambridge History of Renaissance Philosophy*. Cambridge: Cambridge University Press, 1990.

Sheppard, E. R. *Leo Strauss and the Politics of Exile: The Making of a Political Philosopher*. Waltham, MA: Brandeis University Press, 2006.

Shimoni, G. *The Zionist Ideology*. Hanover, NH: Brandeis University Press, 1995.

Sjøberg, T. *The Powers and the Persecuted: The Refugee Problem and the Intergovernmental Committee on Refugees*. Lund: Lund University Press, 1991.

Smith, B. F. *The Shadow Warriors: O.S.S. and the Origins of the C.I.A.* New York: Basic Books, 1983.

Steel, R. *Walter Lippmann and the American Century*. New York: Vintage Books, 1981.

Sykes, C. *Crossroads to Israel: Palestine from Balfour to Bevin*. Bloomington: Indiana University Press, 1973.

Teveth, S. *Ben-Gurion and the Holocaust*. New York: Harcourt Brace, 1996.

Thompson, F. M. L. *The Rise of Respectable Society: A Social History of Britain, 1830–1900*. Cambridge, MA: Harvard University Press, 1988.

Wark, W. K. *The Ultimate Enemy: British Intelligence and Nazi Germany*. Ithaca, NY: Cornell University Press, 1996.

Wasserstein, B. *Britain and the Jews of Europe*. Oxford: Oxford University Press, 1979.

Wasserstein, B. *The Secret Lives of Trebitsch Lincoln*. New Haven, CT: Yale University Press, 1988.

Weinberg, G. L. *A World at Arms: A Global History of World War II*. New York: Cambridge University Press, 1996 and new ed. 2005.

Wyman, D. S. *The Abandonment of the Jews: America and the Holocaust 1941–1945*. New York: Pantheon, 1984.

Young, Julian. *Friedrich Nietzsche: A Philosophical Biography*. Cambridge: Cambridge University Press, 2010.

Zeman, Z. A. B., and W. B. Sharlau. *Merchant of Revolution*. London: W. & J. Mackay, 1965.

Zweig, R. W. *Britain and Palestine during the Second World War*. Woodbridge, Suffolk: The Boydell Press, 1986.

Articles in English and German

Arendt, H. "Heinrich Heine: The Shlemihl and Lord of Dreams." *Jewish Social Studies*, 6 (February 1944): 99–122.

Arendt, H. "The Jewish State: 50 Years After. Where Have Herzl's Policies Led?" *Commentary*, 1 (May 1946): 1–8.

Arendt, H. "Zionism Reconsidered." *Menorah Journal* (August 1945): 162–196.

Aronson, S. "British Policy, Allied Intelligence and Zionist Dilemmas in Face of Hitler's Jewish Policies, 1939–1941." *Yad Vashem International Conference*, Jerusalem, February 1997.

Aronson, S. "David Ben-Gurion, Levi Eshkol and the Struggle over Dimona: A Prologue to the Six Day War and Its (Un)Anticipated Results." *Israel Affairs*, 15 (April 2009): 114–134.

Aronson, S. "The Post-Zionist Discourse and Critique of Israel: A Traditional Zionist Perspective." *Israel Studies*, 8 (Spring 2003): 105–129.

Aronson, S. "Theresienstadt im Spiegel amerikanischer Dokkumentation." In *Theresienstaedter Studien und Dokumente 1994, Edition Theresienstaedter Initiative Academia*. Prague: Miroslav Karny u.a. [Herausg.], 1994, pp. 11–35.

Berlin, I. "On Political Judgment." *New York Review of Books*, October 6, 1996.

Breitman, R., and S. Aronson. "The End of the 'Final Solution'? Nazi Plans to Ransom Jews in 1944." *Central European History*, 25 (2) (1993): 177–203.

Cohn, H. "Nationalism." In *Dictionary of the History of Ideas*. New York: Charles Scribner's Sons, 1973, vol. 3, p. 324.

Editorial. *Jewish Observer and Middle East Review*, December 28, 1962.

Greenberg, G. "Musar Response to the Holocaust: Yehezkel Sarna's *Le'teshuva Ule-tekuma* of 4 December 1944." *Journal of Jewish Thought and Philosophy*, 7 (1997).

Hoffman, S. "Look Back in Anger." *New York Review of Books*, July 17, 1997.

Huntington, S. P. "The West: Unique, Not Universal." *Foreign Affairs* (November–December 1996): 28–46.

Katz, B. M. "The Criticism of Arms: The Frankfurt School Goes to War." *Journal of Modern History*, 59 (1987): 439–478.

Kaufman, W. W. "Two American Ambassadors: Bullitt and Kennedy. In G. Craig and F. Gilbert (eds.), *The Diplomats, 1919–1939*. Princeton, NJ: Princeton University Press, 1953.

Marquardt-Bigman, P. "Amerikanische Geheimdienstanalysen des Nationalsozialistischen Deutschlands." *Tel-Aviver Jahrbuch für deutsche Geschichte*, 23 (1994): 325–344.

"The Renaissance 1493–1520." In *The New Cambridge Modern History*. Cambridge: Cambridge University Press, 1957, vol. 1, pp. 273*ff.*

Schwarz, H. P. "Adenauer und die Kernwaffen." *Vierteljahreshefte für Zeitgeschichte*, 4 (1989): 567–593.

Veblen, T. B. "The Intellectual Preeminence of Jews in Europe." *Political Science Quarterly*, 34 (1919).

Vickers B. "The Idea of the Renaissance Revisited: 'Jacob Burckhardt's Idea of the Renaissance.'" *SEDER: Yearbook of the Spanish and Portuguese Society for English Renaissance Studies*, 12 (2002): 69–96.

Yablonka, H. "The Commander of the 'Yizkor' Order: Herut, Holocaust, and Survivors." In N. Lukas and S. I. Troen (eds.), *Israel – The First Decade*. Albany: State University of New. York Press, 1996, pp. 211*ff.*

Name Index

Ben-Gurion Subject Index

Achdut ha-Avoda Party (formerly Mapai's
Section B), relations with, 205–206, 217,
263–264, 279–280, 292, 297, 306–307,
309, 318, 331, 350, 421n72
Altalena Affair, 183, 195, 232, 408n; *see also*
IZL
American Jews, mobilization by, 114, 149, 172
antisemitism, 122, 127; *see also* Holocaust
Arab Rebellion in Palestine, 1936–1939, 151,
164, 166
Arab refugees, *see* Palestinian refugees
Arab states' invasion 1948, postwar attitude
toward Israel adopted by, 183, 193–194,
203, 214, 217, 224, 246, 351
Arabs, Israeli, military government imposed on
by, xix, 288
dissolution of, 301, 314
Athenian democracy, Greece, xvii, 55, 67
Atomic Energy Commission, created by, 247,
330, 333, 341
Auschwitz, bombing of, 129, 131
austerity program, failure of, 184, 188
autonomy of thought pursued by, xv, 9

Bible, relevance and irrelevance to modern
Israel defined by, 9, 12–13, 29, 32, 54–55,
67–68, 88, 158–159, 221, 223, 225, 264,
266, 274, 297–299, 354
Biltmore Program, 1942, pursued by, 77, 149,
156, 169, 171–172, 177, 394n92
blockade of Tiran (Eilat) Straits, 251–253,
258–259, 422n94
boundaries, warned against unnecessary
expansion, 46, 161, 351

British Army, as model, and various
characteristics of adopted by, 16,
191–197
British government model, British-inspired
reform of Israeli government, British
Rules of the Game or Public Virtues,
pursued by, ix, 198–202, 206, 209, 218,
230, 239, 242, 253, 272, 285, 287; *see
also* Dahrendorf, Ralf (*in Name Index to
this book*)

Christianity and Judaism, compared by, 10,
13
citizenship, definition by, 6–7, 66–67, 202
civil service, birth of, 16, 200
constitutional debate, 38, 228–241
criticism of, as a "nationalist," socialist,
"Bolshvik," xix, 21, 26, 87, 112, 389n41
criticism of, as servant of British, Americans,
Nazis, *see* Lehi; IZL

decision making, 232
democracy and representation, 12–13, 15, 23,
25, 39, 51, 82, 163, 185, 206, 209, 228,
233–235
destiny and singularity of Israel, 10, 84, 87–93
Diaspora, imported to Israel, xiii, xvi, 4, 6–7,
27–29, 33, 43, 52, 76, 79, 94, 112, 120,
268, 271, 368n36, 380n112

economic theory, social sciences, criticism by,
25, 366n16
education, reform of, pursued by, 10–11, 17,
45, 175